SOCIETY
THE BASICS

SIXTH EDITION

John J. Macionis
Kenyon College

Upper Saddle River, New Jersey 07458

Library of Congress Cataloging-in-Publication Data

Macionis, John J.
    Society : the basics / John J. Macionis. — 6th ed.
      p. cm.
    Includes bibliographical references and index.
    ISBN 0-13-041048-9 (alk. paper)
    1. Sociology.   I. Title.
HM586.M1657 2001
301—dc21   00-053756

Senior Acquisitions Editor: Christopher DeJohn
AVP, Publisher: Nancy Roberts
VP, Editorial Director: Laura Pearson
Editor-in-Chief of Development: Susanna Lesan
VP, Director of Production and Manufacturing:
    Barbara Kittle
Production Editor: Barbara Reilly
Copy Editors: Amy Macionis, Mary Louise Byrd
Proofreaders: Karen Bosch, Marianne Peters Riordan
Editorial Assistant: Christina Scalia
Director of Marketing: Beth Gillett Mejia
Marketing Manager: Christopher Barker
Marketing Assistant: Judie Lamb
Prepress and Manufacturing Manager: Nick Sklitsis

Prepress and Manufacturing Buyer: Mary Ann Gloriande
Creative Design Director: Leslie Osher
Art Director: Anne Bonanno Nieglos
Cover and Interior Design: Laura Gardner
Line Art Manager: Guy Ruggiero
Line Art Illustrations: Lithokraft II
Maps: Carto-Graphics, Inc.
Director, Image Resource Center: Melinda Reo
Interior Image Specialist: Beth Boyd
Manager, Rights and Permissions: Kay Dellosa
Photo Researcher: Barbara Salz
Permissions Coordinator: Debra Hewitson
Cover Art: José Ortega/Stock Illustration Source

This book was set in 10/11 Janson by Lithokraft II
and was printed and bound by Webcrafters, Inc.
The cover was printed by The Lehigh Press, Inc.

For permission to use copyrighted material, grateful
acknowledgment is made to the copyright holders listed
on pages 491–92, which is considered an extension of this
copyright page.

Printed in the United States of America
10 9 8 7 6 5 4 3 2

ISBN 0-13-041048-9

Prentice-Hall International (UK) Limited, London
Prentice-Hall of Australia Pty. Limited, Sydney
Prentice-Hall Canada Inc., Toronto
Prentice-Hall Hispanoamericana, S.A., Mexico
Prentice-Hall of India Private Limited, New Delhi
Prentice-Hall of Japan, Inc., Tokyo
Pearson Education Asia Pte. Ltd., Singapore
Editora Prentice-Hall do Brasil, Ltda., Rio de Janeiro

Printed on Recycled Paper

BRIEF CONTENTS

CONTENTS

WELCOME TO THE INFORMATION REVOLUTION!   28

6 DEVIANCE   132

7 SEXUALITY   160

NEW INFORMATION
TECHNOLOGY AND
SOCIAL STRATIFICATION   298

12 ECONOMICS AND POLITICS   300

16 SOCIAL CHANGE: MODERN AND POSTMODERN SOCIETIES   434

MAPS

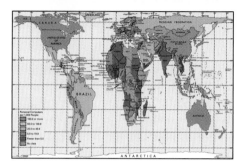
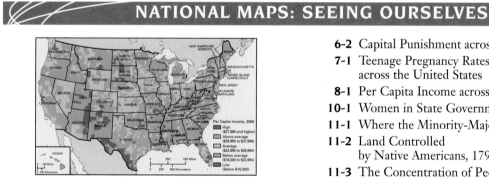

BOXES

CRITICAL THINKING

GLOBAL SOCIOLOGY

SOCIAL DIVERSITY

CONTROVERSY & DEBATE

FEATURE ESSAYS
NEW INFORMATION TECHNOLOGY AND SOCIETY

PREFACE

It was just five or six years ago that people were beginning to talk about the Internet and the Information Revolution. Today, computers and other new technology already play a part in how people entertain themselves, stay in touch with others, shop for everything from gadgets to groceries, teach classes, and study for exams. One can only imagine the extent of the transformation that will unfold over the course of this new century.

Yet there remains a contradiction in calling this the "information age." No one doubts that students have more information available to them than ever before. But who can deny that students (especially young people just out of high school) still know little about their own society and even less about the larger world? It is here that old-fashioned sociology has a crucial part to play. By developing students' sociological imagination, we help them see the shape of the society that guides their lives, as well as appreciate ever-present forces of change. This same imagination also lets them place this society in a global context, highlighting the worldwide structures and systems that affect us all.

The daily e-mail I receive from students across the United States and around the world is testimony to the power of sociology to transform people's way of seeing the world. All instructors know the deep satisfaction of making a difference in the lives of our students. Indeed, there is no greater reward for our work, and, in my case, there is no better reason for reaching ever further with each new edition of the text. In this spirit, I am delighted to offer this revision of *Society: The Basics*, the discipline's most popular text, and a book that never stands still.

The heart of this high-technology learning package is, of course, the book. As in the past, this sixth edition of *Society* is authoritative, comprehensive, stimulating, and—as student e-mail messages testify—plain fun to read. This major revision elevates sociology's most popular text to a still higher standard of excellence, and offers an unparalleled resource to today's students as they learn about both our diverse society and the changing world.

But the book is only one part of a complete learning package. Found in the back of every new copy of *Society: The Basics, Sixth Edition*, is a CD-ROM, included *at no additional cost to the student*. This CD-ROM is the best of its kind—not only does it contain a full study guide and approximately 80 percent of the textbook, but it also includes fully interactive study features such as author's tip videos, video applications, multimedia chapter introductions, interactive maps, a full glossary, and hundreds of links to Web sites around the world. Simply put, no other CD-ROM offers students a better opportunity for review, assessment, and feedback.

In addition, students using *Society: The Basics, Sixth Edition*, can log on to a full-featured Web site, **http://www.prenhall.com/macionis**, also at no cost to them, using the access code packaged with this new textbook. From the main page, simply click on the cover of this text to reach a learning site that includes chapter overviews and learning objectives, suggested essay questions and paper topics as well as multiple-choice and true-false questions that the server will grade, chapter-relevant Web destinations with learning questions, and a chat room where students can share experiences and opinions with others taking the course. Faculty will find a full complement of resources as well, including the syllabus manager system that allows posting a course syllabus to the Internet without having to learn hypertext markup language (HTML); the Prentice Hall server does the work for you. Prentice Hall and EBSCO, the world leader in online journal subscription management, have come together to develop an innovative new feature of our *Companion Website*™—ContentSelect. With database access to more than 100 academic journals and leading popular sources, ContentSelect provides a twenty-four-hour-a-day window into the most reputable content in the discipline of sociology.

Textbook, CD-ROM, and Web site: A three-part, multimedia package that is the foundation for sound learning in this new information age. We invite you to examine all three!

ORGANIZATION OF THIS TEXT

Society: The Basics carries students through sociology's basic ideas, research, and insights in sixteen logically organized chapters. Chapter 1 ("Sociology: Perspective, Theory, and Method") explains how the discipline's distinctive point of view illuminates the world in a new and exciting way. In addition, the first chapter introduces major theoretical approaches and explains the key methods sociologists use to test and refine their knowledge.

The next six chapters examine core sociological concepts. Chapter 2 ("Culture") explores the fascinating diversity of human living that marks our world. Chapter 3 ("Socialization: From Infancy to Old Age") investigates how people everywhere develop their humanity as they learn to participate in society. While highlighting the importance of the early years to the socialization process, this chapter describes significant transformations that occur over the entire life course, including old age. Chapter 4 ("Social Interaction in Everyday Life") takes a micro-level look at how people construct the daily realities that we often take for granted. Chapter 5 ("Groups and Organizations") focuses on social groups, within which we have many of our most meaningful experiences. It also highlights the expansion of formal organization and points up some of the problems of living in a bureaucratic age. Chapter 6 ("Deviance") analyzes how the routine operation of society promotes deviance as well as conformity. Chapter 7 ("Sexuality"), which is new to this edition, explains the social foundations of human sexuality. Based on recent research, this chapter surveys sexual patterns in the United States and also explores variations in sexual practices through history and around the world today.

The next four chapters provide more coverage of social inequality than is found in any other brief text. Chapter 8 ("Social Stratification") introduces basic concepts that describe social hierarchy throughout history and around the world. The chapter then highlights dimensions of social difference in the United States today. Chapter 9 ("Global Stratification") extends this text's commitment to global education by analyzing the social ranking of nations themselves. Why, in other words, do people in some societies have abundant wealth while, in others, people struggle every day just to survive? *Society: The Basics* also provides full-chapter coverage of two additional dimensions of social difference. Chapter 10 ("Gender Stratification") describes how gender is a central element of social stratification in the United States, as it is worldwide. Chapter 11 ("Race and Ethnicity") explores racial and ethnic diversity in the United States, explaining how societies use physical and cultural traits to construct and rank categories of people in a hierarchy.

Next are three chapters that survey social institutions. Chapter 12 ("Economics and Politics") looks at the economy of U.S. society, beginning with how the Industrial Revolution transformed the Western world. This chapter contrasts capitalist and socialist economic models, and investigates how economic systems are linked to a society's distribution of power. This chapter also contains coverage of the military and the important issues of war and peace. Chapter 13 ("Family and Religion") spotlights two institutions central to the symbolic organization of social life. The chapter begins by focusing on the diversity of families in the United States, making frequent comparisons to kinship systems in other parts of the world. Basic elements of religious life come next, with an overview of recent religious trends. Chapter 14 ("Education and Medicine") examines two institutions with special importance in the modern world. The chapter looks first at the historical expansion of schooling, noting many ways in which the scope and kind of education are linked to other social institutions. Next, we look at medicine, which also has become a central institution during the last century and a half. The chapter concludes by explaining the distinctive strategies various countries—including the United States—employ to promote public health.

The final two chapters of the text focus on dimensions of social change. Chapter 15 ("Population, Urbanization, and Environment") is a new synthesis that begins by spotlighting the growth of population in the world. Then, our attention turns to the rise of cities in the United States and to the urban explosion now taking place in poor nations of the world. Finally, the chapter explains how the state of the natural environment reflects social organization. Chapter 16 ("Social Change: Modern and Postmodern Societies") concludes the text with summaries of major theories of social change, a look at how people forge social movements to encourage or resist change, analysis of various benefits and liabilities of modern social patterns, and the emergence of a "postmodern" way of life.

CONTINUITY: ESTABLISHED FEATURES OF *SOCIETY: THE BASICS*

Society: The Basics is no standard textbook: In sociology, it represents *the* standard of excellence. How else can one explain the fact that this book is selected by far more faculty than any other? The extraordinary success of *Society: The Basics*, as well as *Sociology*—the market leader among comprehensive hardback texts—results from a combination of the following distinctive features.

The best writing style. Most important, this text offers a writing style widely praised by students and faculty alike as elegant and inviting. *Society* is an enjoyable text that encourages students to read—even beyond their assignments. No one says it better than the students themselves, whose recent e-mail includes testimonials such as these:

> I'm a college student in California and my sociology class used your book, *Sociology*, 8th edition. It was by far the best textbook I have ever used. I actually liked to read it for pleasure as well as to study. I just wanted to say it was great.

Thanks for writing such a brilliant book. It has sparked my sociological imagination. This was the first textbook that I have ever read completely and enjoyed. From the moment that I picked the book up I started reading nonstop.

I have read four chapters ahead; it's like a good novel I can't put down! I just wanted to say thank you.

Your book is extremely well written and very interesting. I find myself reading it for pleasure, something I have never done with college texts. It is going to be the only collegiate textbook that I ever keep simply to read on my own. I am also thinking of picking up sociology as my minor due to the fact that I have enjoyed the class as well as the text so much. Your writing has my highest praise and utmost appreciation.

I am taking a Sociology 101 class using your text, a book that I have told my professor is the best textbook that I have ever seen, bar none. I've told her as well that I will be more than happy to take more sociology classes as long as there is a Macionis text to go with them.

A global perspective. *Society* has taken a leading role in expanding the horizons of our discipline beyond the United States. *Society* was the first brief text to mainstream global content, introduce global maps, and offer comprehensive coverage of global topics like stratification and the environment. No wonder this text has been adapted and translated into half a dozen languages for use around the world. Each chapter explores the social diversity of the entire world as well as explains why social trends in the United States—from musical tastes, to the price of wheat, to the growing disparity of income—are influenced by what happens elsewhere. Just as important, students will learn ways in which social patterns and policies in the United States affect poor nations around the world.

A celebration of social diversity. *Society: The Basics* invites students from all social backgrounds to discover a fresh and exciting way to see themselves within the larger social world. Readers will discover in this text the diversity of U.S. society—people of African, Asian, European, and Latino ancestry, as well as women and men of various class positions and at all points in the life course. Just as important, without flinching from the problems that marginalized people confront, this text does not treat minorities as social problems but notes their achievements. A scholarly comparison of sociology texts published in the American Sociological Association's journal *Teaching Sociology* evaluated Macionis's *Society* (the hardback

edition of this text) as the best of all the leading texts in terms of integrating racial and ethnic material throughout (Stone, 1996).

Emphasis on critical thinking. Critical-thinking skills include the ability to challenge common assumptions by formulating questions, to identify and weigh appropriate evidence, and to reach reasoned conclusions. This text not only teaches but encourages students to discover on their own.

Engaging and instructive chapter openings. One of the most popular features of earlier editions of *Society* has been the engaging vignettes that begin each chapter. These openings—for instance, using the tragic sinking of the *Titanic* to illustrate the life and death consequences of social inequality, telling the story of Linda Brown to explore racial inequality in the United States, or describing textile sweatshops on U.S.-controlled Pacific islands to examine the extent of social inequality worldwide—spark the interest of readers as they introduce important themes. This revision retains five of the best chapter-opening vignettes found in earlier editions and offers eleven new ones as well.

Inclusive focus on women and men. Beyond devoting two full chapters to the important concepts of sex and gender, *Society* mainstreams gender into *every* chapter, showing how the topic at hand affects women and men differently, and explaining how gender operates as a basic dimension of social organization.

Theoretically clear and balanced. This text makes theory easy. The discipline's major theoretical approaches are introduced in Chapter 1 and are carried through later chapters. The text highlights the social-conflict, structural-functional, and symbolic-interaction paradigms, and also incorporates other theoretical approaches including social-exchange analysis, ethnomethodology, and sociobiology.

Focus on new information technology. One of the strengths of this text is the focus on computers and new information technology in every chapter. In addition, the text offers five cyber.scopes, a series of essays spread throughout the text. Cyber.scope essays start by explaining what the Information Revolution is all about and go on to show how computers and new information technology are changing the shape of people's lives here and around the world. The five cyber.scope essays are titled:

I: Welcome to the Information Revolution!
II: How New Technology Is Changing
   Our Way of Life

III: New Information Technology and Social
    Stratification
IV: New Information Technology and Social
    Institutions
V: New Information Technology and Social Change

These essays, illustrated with photos, figures, and maps, provide an opportunity for instructors to pause at several points during the course to consider new information technology or, alternatively, to assign the essays together as a "chapter" on new technology and society.

Recent research and the latest data. *Society: The Basics, Sixth Edition,* blends classic sociological statements with the latest research, as reported in the leading publications in the field. More than 1,000 research citations support this revision, and more than one-third of them were published since 1990. We have used the latest sources to ensure that—chapter to chapter—the text's content and statistical data are the most recent available.

Learning aids. This text has many features to help students learn. In each chapter, **Key Concepts** are identified by boldfaced type, and following each appears a *precise, italicized definition.* A listing of key concepts with their definitions appears at the end of each chapter, and a complete **Glossary** is found at the end of the book. Each chapter also contains a numbered **Summary** and four **Critical-Thinking Questions** that help students review material and assess their understanding. Following these are a number of **Applications and Exercises**, which provides students with activities to do on or near the campus. Finally, each chapter ends with an annotated listing of worthwhile **Sites to See** on the Internet.

Outstanding images: photography and fine art. *Society: The Basics, Sixth Edition,* offers the finest and most extensive program of photography and artwork available in any comparable book. The author searches extensively to obtain the finest images of the human condition and presents them with thoughtful captions, often in the form of questions.

Moreover, both photographs and artwork present people of various social backgrounds and historical periods. For example, alongside art by well-known Europeans such as Vincent Van Gogh and U.S. artists including George Tooker, this edition has paintings by celebrated African American artists Jacob Lawrence and Henry Ossawa Tanner, outstanding Latino artists Frank Romero and Diego Rivera, renowned folk artists including Anna Bell Lee Washington, and the engaging Australian painter and feminist Sally Swain.

Thought-provoking theme boxes. Although boxed material is common to introductory texts, *Society: The Basics, Sixth Edition,* provides a wealth of uncommonly good boxes. Each chapter typically contains three boxes, which fall into four types that amplify central themes of the text. **Global Sociology** boxes provoke readers to think about their own way of life by examining the fascinating social diversity that characterizes our world. **Social Diversity** boxes, which have been expanded for this revision, focus on multicultural issues and present the voices of women and people of color. **Critical Thinking** boxes teach students to ask sociological questions about their surroundings, and help them evaluate important, controversial issues. Each Critical-Thinking box is followed by three "What do you think?" questions. **Controversy & Debate** boxes present several points of view on hotly debated issues and conclude with "Continue the debate" questions to stimulate thought and generate spirited class discussion.

Society: The Basics, Sixth Edition, contains fifty-one boxes in all, including thirteen that are new to this edition. A complete listing of this text's boxes appears after the table of contents.

An unparalleled program of forty-six global and national maps. Another popular feature of *Society: The Basics* is the program of global and national maps. Window on the World global maps—twenty in all— are truly sociological maps offering a comparative look at income disparity, favored languages, the extent of prostitution, permitted marriage forms, the degree of political freedom, the incidence of HIV infection, and a host of other issues. The global maps use the non-Eurocentric projection devised by cartographer Arno Peters that accurately portrays the relative size of all the continents.

Seeing Ourselves national maps—twenty-six in all—help to illuminate the social diversity of the United States. Most of these maps offer a close-up look at all 3,014 U.S. counties, highlighting suicide rates, per capita income, college attendance, divorce rates, most widespread religious affiliation, the 2000 presidential election, and, as measures of popular culture, where baseball fans live and where households drink wine or beer. Each national map includes an explanatory caption that poses several questions to stimulate students' thinking about social forces. A complete listing of the Seeing Ourselves national maps as well as the Window on the World global maps follows the table of contents. All of the global and national maps are interactive on both the CD-ROM and the *Companion Website*™.

An annotated instructor's edition. This is the only brief text available in an instructor's edition with a full program of annotations—written by the author—on every page. These annotations provide additional data, notable quotations, suggestions for class discussions, and comments about maps and end-of-chapter study questions.

INNOVATION: CHANGES IN THE SIXTH EDITION

Each new edition of *Society: The Basics* and *Sociology* has broken new ground, one reason that almost 3 million students have learned from these sociological bestsellers. A revision raises high expectations, but, after two years of planning and hard work, we are pleased to offer a major revision that sets a new standard for brief texts. Here is an overview of the innovations that define *Society: The Basics, Sixth Edition*.

New technology that keeps getting better! Last time around, we offered the first complete high-tech learning package, combining a text, CD-ROM, and *Companion Website*™. Put the text, the CD-ROM, and the Web site together for more information *and more ways to learn* than ever before. When combined with our new online journal research database, *ContentSelect*, students have unparalleled resources to enhance their studies. For additional details on all our textbooks as well as quick links to dozens of sociology sites, visit the author's personal Web site: **http://www.the sociologypage.com** or **http://www.macionis.com**

A new chapter on sexuality. This revision offers a new chapter. Chapter 7 ("Sexuality") is a sociological look at a central dimension of human existence. The chapter begins by explaining the biological and cultural foundations of sexuality, surveys changing sexual attitudes in the United States, explores the myths and realities surrounding sexual orientation, and then provides balanced discussion of sexual controversies including teen pregnancy, pornography, prostitution, and sexual violence. The chapter concludes with various theoretical analyses of sexuality.

A new synthesis: population, urbanization, and the environment. This revision draws three closely related issues together into a new synthesis. Chapter 15 begins by outlining the study of population, moves to the steady rise in the share of humanity residing in cities, and then links both topics to the state of the physical environment.

A greater emphasis on social diversity. A long-time strength of this text is its emphasis on social diversity. In this revision, from chapter to chapter, race, class, and gender receive even more attention, with more discussions, more Diversity Snapshot figures, and more Social Diversity boxes.

Sites to See. Another new feature is a listing of worthwhile Internet sites. Placed at the end of each chapter along with explanatory annotations, these sites will introduce students to a wide range of organizations involved in relevant research or social action.

New chapter-opening vignettes. This revision keeps the best of the popular chapter-opening vignettes and adds eleven new ones. All vignettes add interest as students begin a chapter, and provide important lessons about the topic at hand.

The latest statistical data. Instructors count on this text for including the very latest statistical data. The sixth edition comes through again, making use of the latest data from the Internet as well as conventional bound publications of various government agencies and private organizations. The author guarantees that the newest available statistics are used throughout the text—in many cases for 1999 and even for 2000. In addition, the author regularly reviews more than one dozen journals as well as a wide range of media publications. The result: Readers will find several hundred new research citations as well as many familiar current events that elevate the interest of students.

New topics. The sixth edition of *Society: The Basics* is completely updated with new and expanded discussions in every chapter. Here is a partial listing, by chapter:

• **Chapter 1 Sociology: Perspective, Theory, and Method:** A new chapter opening contrasts the rich and poor in Boston, Massachusetts; there are updates of suicide patterns in the United States; the discussion of social change and the emergence of sociology has been reorganized; find an update on women in professional sports as well as a new Diversity Snapshot figure on race and football; the sociological methodology section has been heavily revised to contrast three approaches: scientific sociology, interpretive sociology, and critical sociology; the chapter ends with an updated and expanded list of Applications and Exercises as well as new Sites to See.

• **Chapter 2 Culture:** A new chapter opening traces the rise of hip-hop culture; two new national maps showing beer and wine consumption illustrate high and popular culture; many updated examples and illustrations are found throughout the chapter; the chapter ends with an expanded list of Applications and Exercises as well as new Sites to See.

• **Chapter 3 Socialization**: This chapter includes an update on U.S. television watching, a new national map on newspaper readership, and recent research on television and violence; a new figure highlights young people's trust in parents; expanded and updated Applications and Exercises are included as well as numerous new Sites to See.

• **Chapter 4 Social Interaction in Everyday Life**: This chapter now has more emphasis on applications throughout; an expanded Applications and Exercises section includes new on-campus activities; there are also several new Web destinations in the Sites to See.

• **Chapter 5 Groups and Organizations**: A major reorganization of this chapter adds discussion of early scientific management and traces the evolution of organization toward a flatter, flexible, "intelligent" form; the chapter also contrasts the rise of intelligent organizations doing highly skilled postindustrial work with the countertrend toward low-skill service work, often called "McJobs."

• **Chapter 6 Deviance**: A new chapter opening points out weaknesses in the criminal justice system; there are new sections on corporate crime and organized crime; all crime statistics are updated; a new Critical Thinking box explains the recent decline in violent crime; the chapter ends with new Applications and Exercises as well as new Sites to See.

• **Chapter 7 Sexuality**: This new chapter highlights the socially constructed character of human sexuality; the chapter takes a global view of sexuality, and also surveys a number of sexuality issues, from sexual orientation to sexual violence; there are several new boxes, a new national map on births to teenage women, and new Applications and Exercises as well as new Sites to See.

• **Chapter 8 Social Stratification**: This chapter has a reorganized discussion of caste and class; recent changes in the British aristocracy are noted; find updates on income and wealth disparity in the United States; there are new data tracking rising African American affluence; new Applications and Exercises and new Sites to See conclude the chapter.

• **Chapter 9 Global Stratification**: A new opening profiles wage slavery in the sweatshops of a Pacific territory controlled by the United States; a dramatic new Global Sociology box describes the culture of slavery in North Africa; the chapter includes updates on global wealth and well-being; several new Sites to See direct students to sources of global data and further study.

• **Chapter 10 Gender Stratification**: A new chapter opening highlights the 1848 Seneca Falls convention and the women's movement it began; the chapter includes statistical updates on women's pay, schooling, and jobs; a new Diversity Snapshot figure details who does the housework in the United States; many of the Applications and Exercises as well as Sites to See are new.

• **Chapter 11 Race and Ethnicity**: A new Social Diversity box highlights the role played by immigrants in the U.S. economy; the chapter adds a set of four national maps showing the diminishing lands controlled by American Indians; updated statistics reflect the social standings of all racial and ethnic categories in the United States; several new Applications and Exercises as well as new Sites to See end the chapter.

• **Chapter 12 Economics and Politics**: There is a new chapter opening on the trend toward using temporary workers; find updated statistics on the U.S. labor force—including unemployment rates and the gender, racial, and ethnic composition of the labor force; a new Controversy & Debate box highlights corporate welfare; we've added another national map showing where jobs will be a decade from now; the chapter includes an update on political freedoms around the world; a new national map shows the popular vote by county in the 2000 presidential election; there is an update on nuclear proliferation worldwide; several new Applications and Exercises as well as Sites to See complete the chapter.

• **Chapter 13 Family and Religion**: A new chapter opening presents the "family values" debate in terms of a new Vermont law establishing civil unions for same-sex couples; a research update reports on the causes and consequences of cohabiting; a new Critical Thinking box evaluates the covenant marriage law in Louisiana; the chapter notes the rising number of Muslims in the United States; a new Controvery & Debate box looks at the resurgence of prayer in school; find many statistical updates on various measures of religiosity; a new national map shows membership in religious organizations across the United States; there are statistical updates on all the trends regarding family and religious life, as well as new Exercises and Applications and Sites to See.

• **Chapter 14 Education and Medicine**: A new chapter opening looks at a controversial school-funding law in Vermont; a new national map shows life expectancy for women and men across the country; a new Global Sociology box describes the free-fall in life expectancy among men following the collapse of the former Soviet Union; statistical updates are included for all measures of educational achievement and health, and the chapter ends with a number of worthwhile Web sites on these important issues.

• **Chapter 15 Population, Urbanization, and Environment**: This chapter is a new combination of population, urbanization, and environment; a new chapter opening reports on the rapid urban development in Atlanta; find the latest global population figures as well as new demographic data for the United States; there is an update on the development of urban regions and sprawl; throughout the chapter the focus is on the interplay of population, urbanization, and the physical environment; many new Applications and Exercises as well as Sites to See complete the chapter.

• **Chapter 16 Social Change: Modern and Postmodern Societies**: A new chapter-opening vignette illustrates the extent of social change over the course of the twentieth century; expanded coverage of the theories of social movements includes a new discussion of culture theory; a new Critical Thinking box evaluates the changing quality of life in the United States; there are many Applications and Exercises as well as new Sites to See.

A WORD ABOUT LANGUAGE

This text's commitment to representing the social diversity of the United States and the world carries with it the responsibility to use language thoughtfully. In most cases, we prefer the terms *African American* and *person of color* to the word *black*. We use the terms *Hispanic* and *Latino* to refer to people of Spanish descent. Most tables and figures refer to "Hispanics" because this is the term the Census Bureau uses when collecting statistical data about our population.

Students should realize, however, that many individuals do not describe themselves using these terms. Although the term "Hispanic" is commonly used in the eastern part of the United States, and "Latino" and the feminine form "Latina" are widely heard in the West, across the United States people of Spanish descent identify with a particular ancestral nation, whether it be Argentina, Mexico, some other Latin American country, or Spain or Portugal in Europe.

The same holds for Asian Americans. Although this term is a useful shorthand in sociological analysis, most people of Asian descent think of themselves in terms of a specific country of origin (say, Japan, the Philippines, Taiwan, or Vietnam).

In this text, the term "Native American" refers to all the inhabitants of the Americas (including the Hawaiian Islands) whose ancestors lived here prior to the arrival of Europeans. Here again, however, most people in this broad category identify with their historical society (for example, Cherokee, Hopi, or Zuni). The term "American Indian" designates only those Native Americans who live in the continental United States, not including Native peoples living in Alaska or Hawaii.

Learning to think globally also leads us to use language carefully. This text avoids using the word "American"—which literally designates two continents—to refer to just the United States. For example, referring to this country, the term "U.S. economy" is more correct than the "American economy." This convention may seem a small point, but it implies the significant recognition that we in this country represent only one society (albeit a very important one) in the Americas.

A WORD ABOUT WEB SITES

Because of the increasing importance of the Internet, each chapter of this new edition of *Society: The Basics* ends with a listing of Sites to See. The goal is to provide sites that are current, informative, and, above all, relevant to the topic at hand.

However, students should be mindful of several potential problems. First, Web sites change all the time. Prior to publication, we make every effort to ensure that the sites listed meet our high standards. But readers may find that sites have changed substantially and some may have gone away entirely.

Second, sites have been selected in order to provide different perspectives on various issues. The listing of a site does not imply that the author or publisher agrees with everything—or even anything—on the site. Indeed, we urge students to examine all sites critically.

Third, many of the Web sites listed in this text are popular. Because many people visit them, the sites may be slow in responding. Please be patient or, if a site is too busy, simply move on.

SUPPLEMENTS

Society: The Basics, Sixth Edition, is the heart of an unprecedented multimedia learning package that includes a wide range of proven instructional aids as well as several new ones. As the author of the text, I maintain a keen interest in all the supplements to ensure their quality and integration with the text. The supplements for this revision have been thoroughly updated, improved, and expanded.

FOR THE INSTRUCTOR

Annotated Instructor's Edition. The AIE is a complete student text annotated by the author on every page. Annotations, which have been thoroughly revised for this edition, have won praise from instructors for enriching class presentations. Margin notes include summaries of research findings, statistics from the United States or other nations, insightful quotations, information highlighting patterns of social diversity in the United States, and high-quality survey data from the National Opinion Research Center's (NORC) *General Social Survey* and from the Inter-university Consortium for Political and Social Research (CPSR) *World Values Survey*.

Data File. This is the "instructor's manual" that is of interest even to those who have never used one before. The *Data File* provides far more than detailed chapter outlines and discussion questions; it contains statistical profiles of the

United States and other nations, summaries of important developments and significant research, and supplemental lecture material for every chapter. The *Data File* is available in Windows format as well as the traditional print version.

Test Item File. A revised test item file is available in both printed and computerized forms. The file contains 1600 items—100 per chapter—in multiple-choice, true-false, and essay formats. Questions are identified as simple "recall" items or more complex inferential issues, and the answers to all questions are page-referenced to the text. Prentice Hall Custom Test is a test generator designed to allow the creation of personalized exams. It is available in DOS, Windows, and Macintosh formats. Prentice Hall also provides a test preparation service to users of this text that is as easy as a call to our toll-free 800 number. Please contact your local Prentice Hall representative for this number.

Film/Video Guide: Prentice Hall Introductory Sociology, Sixth Edition. Keyed to the chapters of this text, this guide describes more than 300 films and videos appropriate for classroom viewing. It also provides summaries, discussion questions, and rental sources for each film and video.

ABCNEWS **ABC News/Prentice Hall Video Library for Sociology.** Few will dispute that video is the most dynamic supplement you can use to enhance a class. However, the quality of the video material and how well it relates to your course still make all the difference. Prentice Hall and ABC News are working together to bring you the best and most comprehensive video ancillaries available in the college market.

Through its wide variety of award-winning programs—*Nightline, Business World, On Business, This Week, World News Tonight, 20/20,* and *The Health Show*—ABC offers a resource for feature and documentary-style videos related to the chapters in *Society: The Basics, Sixth Edition.* The programs have high production quality, present substantial content, and are hosted by well-versed, well-known anchors.

The authors and editors of Prentice Hall have carefully selected videos on topics that complement *Society: The Basics, Sixth Edition,* and have included notes on how to use them in the classroom. An excellent video guide in the *Data File* carefully and completely integrates the videos into your lecture. The guide has a synopsis of each video, which shows its relation to the chapter and offers discussion questions to help students focus on how concepts and theories apply to real-life situations.

Volume I—Social Stratification
Volume II—Marriage/Families
Volume III—Race/Ethnic Relations
Volume IV—Criminology
Volume V—Social Problems
Volume VI—Intro to Sociology I
Volume VII—Intro to Sociology II
Volume VIII—Intro to Sociology III
Volume IX—Social Problems II

Volume X—Marriage/Families II
Volume XI—Race and Ethnic Relations II
Volume XII—Institutions
Volume XIII—Introductory Sociology IV
Volume XIV—Introductory Sociology V

Prentice Hall Introductory Sociology PowerPoint™ Transparencies. Created by Roger J. Eich of Hawkeye Community College, this PowerPoint slide set combines graphics and text in a colorful format to help you convey sociological principles in a new and exciting way. Created in PowerPoint, an easy-to-use, widely available software program, this set contains over 300 slides keyed to each chapter in the text. They are easily downloadable from the *Companion Website™.*

Prentice Hall Color Transparencies: Sociology Series VI. Full-color illustrations, charts, and other visual materials from the text as well as outside sources have been selected to make up this useful in-class tool.

Instructor's Guide to Prentice Hall Color Transparencies: Sociology Series VI. This guide offers suggestions for effectively using each transparency in the classroom.

MEDIA SUPPLEMENTS

Companion Website™. In tandem with the text, students and professors can now take full advantage of the Internet to enrich their study of sociology. The Macionis *Companion Website™* continues to lead the way in providing students with avenues for delving deeper into the topics covered in the text. Features of the *Companion Website™* include chapter objectives, study questions, and faculty resources, as well as links to interesting material and information from other sites on the Web that will reinforce and enhance the content of each chapter. Visit the site at **http://www.prenhall.com/ macionis**, click on the cover of the Sixth Edition, and enter the access code that is packaged with this new textbook. An innovative new feature of the *Companion Website™* is a research database—ContentSelect—developed by Prentice Hall and EBSCO, the world leader in online journal subscription management. With instant access to more than 100 sociological journals and leading popular magazines and newspapers, students have a twenty-four-hour-a-day window into the leading content in sociology from their own home computer.

Online Learning Solutions. Prentice Hall is committed to helping instructors offer courses over the Internet by developing relationships with the leading vendors—Blackboard™ and Web CT™—as well as our own course management system, Course Compass, powered by Blackboard™. Through these relationships, we provide premium, book-specific content in the delivery method of your choice. Please contact your local Prentice Hall representative to find out more about our solutions in this area.

Sociology on the Internet: A Critical Thinking Guide, 2001. This guide focuses on developing the critical thinking skills necessary to evaluate and use online sources. The guide also provides a brief introduction to navigating the Internet, along with references related specifically to the discipline of sociology and instructions on how to use the *Companion Website™* for *Society: The Basics, Sixth Edition.* It is free to students when shrinkwrapped as a package with *Society: The Basics, Sixth Edition.* Please contact your local Prentice Hall representative for your packaging options.

Society: The Basics, Interactive Edition. Believing strongly that equal access to learning resources is as important as ever, *Society: The Basics, Interactive Edition,* offers students review and study material in a rich multimedia environment. The CD-ROM includes multimedia chapter introductions, author's tip videos, video application exercises, interactive U.S. and global maps, substantial portions of the text, review questions, chapter summaries, and text-specific Web links. When purchasing a new textbook, the CD-ROM is free to each student.

FOR THE STUDENT

Study Guide. This complete guide helps students review and reflect on the material presented in *Society: The Basics, Sixth Edition.* Each of the sixteen chapters in the study guide provides an overview of the corresponding chapter in the text, summarizes its major topics and concepts, and offers applied exercises and end-of-chapter tests with solutions.

Seeing Ourselves: Classic, Contemporary, and Cross-Cultural Readings in Sociology, Fifth Edition. Create an even more powerful learning package by combining this text with the fifth edition of the best-selling anthology, *Seeing Ourselves,* edited by John J. Macionis and Nijole V. Benokraitis (University of Baltimore). Instructors favor this reader's unique format: Clusters of readings—classic works, well-rounded contemporary research, and cross-cultural comparisons—correspond to all the major topics included in this text.

The New York Times supplement, Themes of the Times, for Introductory Sociology. *The New York Times* and Prentice Hall are sponsoring *Themes of the Times,* a program designed to enhance student access to current information relevant to the classroom. Through this program, the core subject matter provided in this text is supplemented by a collection of timely articles from one of the world's most distinguished newspapers, *The New York Times.* These articles demonstrate the vital, ongoing connection between what is learned in the classroom and what is happening in the world around us.

To enjoy the wealth of information of *The New York Times* daily, a reduced subscription rate is available. For information, call toll-free 1-800-631-1222. Prentice Hall and *The New York Times* are proud to co-sponsor *Themes of the*

Times. We hope it will make the reading of both textbooks and newspapers a more dynamic and involving process.

IN APPRECIATION

The conventional practice of designating a single author obscures the efforts of dozens of women and men that have resulted in *Society: The Basics, Sixth Edition.* I would like to express my thanks to the Prentice Hall editorial team, including Phil Miller, division president, Laura Pearson, editorial director, Nancy Roberts, publisher, and Chris DeJohn, senior editor for sociology, for their steady enthusiasm and for supporting our pursuit of innovation and excellence. Day-to-day work on the book is shared by the author and the production team. Susanna Lesan, developmental editor-in-chief at Prentice Hall, has played a vital role in the development of all our texts for more than fifteen years, coordinating and supervising the editorial process. Barbara Reilly, production editor at Prentice Hall, is a key member of the team who is responsible for the attractive page layout of the book; indeed, if anyone "sweats the details" more than the author, it is Barbara! Amy Marsh Macionis, the text's "in house" editor, checks virtually everything, untangling awkward phrases and eliminating errors and inconsistencies in all the statistical data. Amy is relentless in her pursuit of quality and it shows.

I also have a large debt to the members of the Prentice Hall sales staff, the men and women who have given this text such remarkable support over the years. Thanks, especially, to Chris Barker and Judie Lamb, who have directed our marketing campaign.

Thanks, too, to Laura Gardner for providing the interior design of the book, which was coordinated in-house by art director Anne Nieglos. Developmental and copy editing of the manuscript was provided by Barbara Reilly, Amy Marsh Macionis, and Mary Louise Byrd. Barbara Salz did the research for this edition's new photographs.

It goes without saying that every colleague knows more about some topics covered in this book than the author does. For that reason, I am grateful to the hundreds of faculty and students who have written to me to offer comments and suggestions. More formally, I am grateful to the following people who have reviewed some or all of the manuscript for this sixth edition:

Pamela Gaiter, Collin County Community College
Fernando Parra, California State Polytechnic
  University, Pomona
Paula Snyder, Columbus Community College
Larry Stern, Collin County Community College

Debbie White, Collin County Community College
Assata Zerai, Syracuse University

I also wish to thank the following colleagues for sharing their wisdom in ways that have improved this book:

Doug Adams (The Ohio State University), Arfa Aflatooni (Linn-Benton Community College), Kip Armstrong (Bloomsburg University), Rose Arnault (Fort Hays State University), Scott Beck (Eastern Tennessee State University), Lois Benjamin (Hampton University), Philip Berg (University of Wisconsin, La Crosse), Janet Carlisle Bogdan (LeMoyne College), Alessandro Bonanno (Sam Houston State University), Charlotte Brauchle (Southwest Texas Junior College), Bill Brindle (Monroe Community College), John R. Brouillette (Colorado State University), Cathryn Brubaker (DeKalb College), Brent Bruton (Iowa State University), Richard Bucher (Baltimore City Community College), Karen Campbell (Vanderbilt University), Cecilia Cantrell (Georgia State University), Harold Conway (Blinn College), Gerry Cox (Fort Hays State University), Lovberta Cross (Shelby State Community College), Robert Daniels (Mount Vernon Nazarene College), James A. Davis (Harvard University), Sumati Devadutt (Monroe Community College), Mary Donaghy (Arkansas State University), Keith Doubt (Northeast Missouri State University), Denny Dubbs (Harrisburg Area Community College), Travis Eaton (Northeast Louisiana State University), Helen Rose Fuchs Ebaugh (University of Houston), John Ehle (Northern Virginia Community College), Roger Eich (Hawkeye Community College), Kevin Everett (Radford University), Heather Fitz Gibbon (The College of Wooster), Kevin Fitzpatrick (University of Alabama-Birmingham), Dona C. Fletcher (Sinclair Community College), Charles Frazier (University of Florida), Karen Lynch Frederick (St. Anselm College), Patricia Gagné (University of Kentucky, Louisville), Jarvis Gamble (Owen's Technical College), Steven Goldberg (City College, City University of New York), Charlotte Gotwald (York College of Pennsylvania), Norma B. Gray (Bishop State Community College), Rhoda Greenstone (DeVry Institute), Jeffrey Hahn (Mount Union College), Harry Hale (Northeast Louisiana State University), Dean Haledjian (Northern Virginia Community College), Dick Haltin (Jefferson Community College), Marvin Hannah (Milwaukee Area Technical College), Charles Harper (Creighton University), Adonna Helmig (Pittsburg State University), Gary Hodge (Collin County Community College), Elizabeth A. Hoisington (Heartland Community College), Sara Horsfall (Stephen F. Austin State University), Peter Hruschka (Ohio Northern University), Glenna Huls (Camden County College), Jeanne Humble (Lexington Community College), Harry Humphries (Pittsburg State University), James Hunter (Indiana University-Purdue University at Indianapolis), Cynthia Imanaka (Seattle Central Community College), Patricia Johnson (Houston Community College), Ed Kain (Southwestern University), Paul Kamolnick (Eastern Tennessee State University), Irwin Kantor (Middlesex County College), Thomas Korllos (Kent State University), Rita Krasnow (Virginia Western Community College), Donald Kraybill (Elizabethtown College), Michael Lacy (Colorado State University), Michael Levine (Kenyon College), George Lowe (Texas Tech University), Don Luidens (Hope College), Larry Lyon (Baylor University), Li-Chen Ma (Lamar University), Karen E. B. McCue (University of New Mexico, Albuquerque), John MacDougal (University of Massachusetts Lowell), Meredith McGuire (Trinity College), Setma Maddox (Texas Wesleyan University), Errol Magidson (Richard J. Daley College), Allan Mazur (Syracuse University), Jack Melhorn (Emporia State University), Ken Miller (Drake University), Richard Miller (Navarro College), Joe Morolla (Virginia Commonwealth University), Craig Nauman (Madison Area Technical College), Toby Parcel (The Ohio State University), Anne Peterson (Columbus State Community College), Marvin Pippert (Roanoke College), Lauren Pivnik (Monroe Community College), Nevel Razak (Fort Hays State College), Jim Rebstock (Broward Community College), George Reim (Cheltenham High School), Virginia Reynolds (Indiana University of Pennsylvania), Laurel Richardson (The Ohio State University), Keith Roberts (Hanover College), Ellen Rosengarten (Sinclair Community College), Howard Schneiderman (Lafayette College), Marvin Scott (Butler University), Ray Scupin (Linderwood College), Steve Severin (Kellogg Community College), Harry Sherer (Irvine Valley College), Walt Shirley (Sinclair Community College), Anson Shupe (Indiana University-Purdue University at Fort Wayne), Ree Simpkins (Missouri Southern State University), Glen Sims (Glendale Community College), Nancy Sonleitner (University of Oklahoma), Randy Ston (Oakland Community College), Verta Taylor (The Ohio State University), Vickie H. Taylor (Danville Community College), Mark J. Thomas (Madison Area Technical College), Kenrick S. Thompson (Arkansas State University at Mountain Home), Len Tompos (Lorain County Community College), Christopher Vanderpool (Michigan State University), Phyllis Watts (Tiffin University), Murray Webster (University of North Carolina, Charlotte), Marilyn Wilmeth (Iowa University), Stuart Wright (Lamar University), William Yoels (University of Alabama, Birmingham), Dan Yutze (Taylor University), Wayne Zapatek (Tarrant County Community College), and Frank Zulke (Harold Washington College).

Finally, I would like to dedicate this edition of *Society* to the thousands of women and men who work in classrooms across the country (and on the Internet) to enrich the lives of their students. I doubt that people in any profession are more committed to what they do or more passionate about making a difference in the lives of others. I am proud to play a small part in your efforts!

SOCIOLOGY:
PERSPECTIVE, THEORY, AND METHOD

On a warm June day in 1999, friends and family gathered to celebrate two graduations in the city of Boston. One was at a school you have probably heard of—Harvard University—which dates back to 1636 and today is a leading university that attracts many of the most well-trained women and men from across the United States and around the world. The other was a school you probably have not heard of—the Pine Street Inn—a Boston homeless shelter and job-training center.

The two schools are close to each other in a physical sense, standing on opposite sides of the Charles River and separated by just a fifteen-minute ride on the Boston subway. But in a social sense, they are worlds apart.

Sarah Martin is typical of the Harvard graduates: This bright, twenty-two-year-old woman completed high school at the top of her class and was voted "Most Likely to Succeed" by her classmates. At Harvard, she continued to earn high grades and won a spot at Harvard Law School, where she enrolled immediately after graduation. After that, she hopes to land a job at one of the city's top law firms. Chances are, she will.

Fred McLemore is typical of the Pine Street Inn graduates: Now thirty-four, he dropped out of school during the eighth grade and lived for years on the streets as a homeless crack addict. Then, two years ago, he walked into the shelter, determined to turn his life around. Now trained to process business accounts on a computer, he is about to begin an internship with a local company. If it works out, his boss promises that in several months he will have a regular job (adapted from Edwards, 1999).

The sharp differences in the lives of Harvard and Pine Street graduates catch our attention and lead us to wonder why people's lives take such different courses. The answer is that our lives do not unfold according to sheer chance; nor do we chart our own futures using what philosophers call "free will." True, we do make many important decisions every day, of course, but we do so within a larger arena called "society"—a family, a campus, a city, a nation, an entire world. The essential wisdom of sociology is that our social world guides our actions and life choices in much the same way that the seasons influence our clothing and activities.

THE SOCIOLOGICAL PERSPECTIVE

Sociology is *the systematic study of human society*. At the heart of this discipline is a distinctive point of view called "the sociological perspective."

SEEING THE GENERAL IN THE PARTICULAR

Peter Berger (1963) characterized the sociological perspective as *seeing the general in the particular*. That is, sociology helps us see *general* patterns in the

We can easily grasp the power of society over the individual by imagining how different our lives would be had we been born in place of any of these children from, respectively, Bolivia, Sri Lanka, Ethiopia, Botswana, the People's Republic of China, and El Salvador.

behavior of *particular* people. Although every individual is unique, society acts differently on various *categories* of people (say, children compared to adults, women versus men, the rich as opposed to the poor). We begin to think sociologically by realizing how the general categories into which we fall shape our particular life experiences.

This text explores the power of society to guide our actions, thoughts, and feelings. The Harvard graduates mentioned in the opening to this chapter, for example, come from more privileged social backgrounds than the graduates of Pine Street Inn. In general, the more privileged people's social background, the more confident and optimistic they are about their own lives. And with good reason, as they are likely to have more opportunities as well as the training and skills to take advantage of them.

SEEING THE STRANGE IN THE FAMILIAR

At first, using the sociological perspective amounts to *seeing the strange in the familiar*. This does not mean that sociologists focus on the bizarre elements of society. Rather, looking at life sociologically requires giving up the familiar idea that human behavior is simply a matter of what people *decide* to do, in favor of the initially strange notion that society has a hand in shaping our lives.

For individualistic North Americans, learning to "see" how society affects us may take a bit of practice. Consider, for example, what seems to be the very personal matter of deciding to change one's name, a practice common among U.S. celebrities. The box on page 4 reveals a general pattern even in these particular choices.

SEEING INDIVIDUALITY IN SOCIAL CONTEXT

Perhaps the most compelling evidence of how social forces affect individual behavior comes from the study of suicide. What could be a more personal choice than taking one's own life? But Emile Durkheim (1858–1917), one of sociology's pioneers, showed that social forces are at work even in the act of self-destruction.

Examining official records in and around his native France, Durkheim found some categories of people were more likely than others to take their own lives. He found that men, Protestants, wealthy people, and the unmarried each had much higher suicide rates than women, Catholics and Jews, the poor, and married people. Durkheim explained the differences in terms of *social integration:* Categories of people with strong social ties had low suicide rates, whereas more individualistic people had high suicide rates.

In the male-dominated societies studied by Durkheim, men certainly had more freedom than women. But despite its advantages, freedom also contributes to social isolation and a higher suicide rate. Likewise, individualistic Protestants were more prone to suicide than traditional Catholics and Jews, whose rituals foster stronger social ties. The wealthy have more freedom than the poor but, once again, at the cost of a higher suicide rate. Finally, can you see why single people, compared to married people, are also at greater risk?

A century later, Durkheim's analysis still holds true (Thorlindsson & Bjarnason, 1998). Figure 1–1 shows suicide rates for four categories of the U.S. population. In 1998, there were 12.4 recorded suicides for every 100,000 white people, which is more than twice the rate for African Americans (5.7). For both races, suicide was more common among men than among women. White men (20.3) are more than four times as likely as white women (4.8) to take their own lives. Among African Americans, the rate for men (10.2) is nearly six times that for women (1.8). Following Durkheim's logic, the higher suicide rate among white people and among men reflects their greater wealth and freedom. Conversely, the lower rate among women and people of color follows from their limited social choices. Just as in Durkheim's day, then, we can see general sociological patterns in the personal actions of particular individuals.

Some situations stimulate sociological insights for everyone. For example, social diversity prompts us to wonder why other people think and act differently than we do. But as we interact with people from social backgrounds that initially seem strange, we grasp the

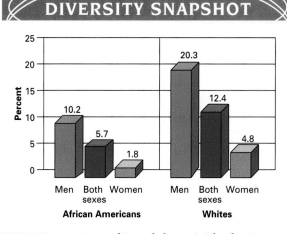

DIVERSITY SNAPSHOT

FIGURE 1–1 Rate of Death by Suicide, by Race and Sex, for the United States

Rates indicate the number of deaths by suicide for every 100,000 people in each category for 1998.

Source: U.S. National Center for Health Statistics (2000).

power of society to shape our lives and find ourselves easing into the role of sociologist.

By the same token, sociological thinking comes easily to people our society tends to label as "different." Those who routinely experience *social marginality*—that is, being excluded as "outsiders"—quickly sense the power of society. Most African Americans, for example, are acutely aware of how much race affects our lives. But because whites are the dominant majority, they think about race only from time to time and often imagine that race affects only people of color rather than themselves as well.

Finally, U.S. sociologist C. Wright Mills (1959) pointed out that periods of social crisis also spark sociological thinking. When, for example, the Great Depression of the 1930s threw one-third of the labor force out of work, unemployed workers could not help but see general social forces at work in their particular lives. Rather than claiming, "Something is wrong with me; I can't find a job," they were likely to say, "We're all out of work because the economy has collapsed!" Of course, just as change stimulates sociological thinking, so does thinking sociologically suggest possibilities for change. The 1930s was also a period of activism directed toward increasing the social security of the U.S. population.

SOCIAL DIVERSITY

What's in a Name?
How Social Forces Affect Personal Choice

Have you ever read "Dear Abby" or "Ann Landers"? These advice columns have been popular in the United States for decades. Not everyone realizes that these two women are sisters (twins, actually), nor that they both changed their names: Abby was born Pauline Friedman and Ann was born Esther Friedman.

Through most of the twentieth century, most people who became celebrities changed their names. Here are a dozen examples. Using the sociological perspective, see if you can detect a pattern to their "old" and "new" names:

1. William Claude Dukenfield
2. Cherilyn Sarkisian
3. Wynona Horowitz
4. George Kyriakou Panayiotou
5. Robert Allen Zimmerman
6. Larry Zeigler
7. Lee Yuen Kam
8. Raquel Tejada
9. Paul Rubenfeld
10. Allen Stewart Konigsberg
11. Henry John Deutschendorf, Jr.
12. Ramon Estevez

Do you see the pattern? In the past, celebrities of various national backgrounds all adopted *English-sounding* names. Why? Because our society has long given high social prestige to people of Anglo-Saxon background. Once again, we see personal choices guided by social forces.

Today, some young actors still adopt English-sounding names—Thomas Mapother, for example, changed his name to Tom Cruise. But the pattern is changing as more of today's film stars are keeping their non-English names. Consider Janeane Garofalo, Gary Sinise, Salma Hayek, Maria Bello, Cameron Diaz, John Malkovich, and Leonardo Di-Caprio. Why the change in trend? Probably because people are now more comfortable with the multicultural mix of U.S. society.

Answers:
1. W. C. Fields; 2. Cher; 3. Wynona Ryder; 4. George Michael; 5. Bob Dylan; 6. Larry King; 7. Bruce Lee; 8. Raquel Welch; 9. Pee Wee Herman; 10. Woody Allen; 11. John Denver; 12. Martin Sheen

BENEFITS OF THE SOCIOLOGICAL PERSPECTIVE

Applying the sociological perspective to our daily lives benefits us in four ways:

1. **The sociological perspective helps us critically assess the truth of "common sense."** Ideas we take for granted are not always true. One good example, noted earlier, is the popular notion that we are free individuals personally responsible for our lives. If we think people decide their own fate, we may be quick to praise successful people as superior and consider people with more modest achievements to be personally deficient. A sociological approach, by contrast, encourages us to think critically, asking whether these beliefs are actually true and, to the extent that they are not, why so many people accept them as fact.

2. **The sociological perspective helps us see the opportunities and constraints in our lives.** Sociological thinking leads us to see that, in the game of life, we have a say in how to play our cards, but it is society that deals us the hand. The more we understand the game, the better players we will be. Sociology helps us "size up" the world around us so we can pursue our goals more effectively.

3. **The sociological perspective empowers us to be active participants in our society.** The more we understand about how society operates, the more active citizens we become. For some, this may mean supporting society as it is; others, however, may attempt nothing less than changing the entire world in some way. Evaluating any aspect of social life—whatever your goal— requires identifying social forces and assessing their consequences.

4. **The sociological perspective helps us live in a diverse world.** North Americans represent a scant 5 percent of the world's population, and, as the remaining chapters of this book explain, much of the other 95 percent lead dramatically different lives from our own. Still, like people everywhere, we tend to view our way of life as "right," "natural," and "better." The sociological perspective prompts us to think critically about the strengths and weaknesses of all ways of life—including our own.

APPLIED SOCIOLOGY

The benefits of sociology go well beyond our personal growth. Sociologists have helped shape public policy and law in countless ways involving issues like school desegregation and busing, pornography, and social welfare. The work that family researcher Lenore Weitzman (1985) did on the financial hardships facing women after divorce "had a real impact on public policy and resulted in the passage of fourteen new laws in California" (1996:538).

Sociology is also good preparation for the working world. According to the American Sociological Association (ASA), sociologists are hired for literally hundreds of jobs in fields such as advertising, banking, criminal justice, education, government, health care, public relations, and research (Billson & Huber, 1993).

Most men and women who continue beyond a bachelor's degree to earn advanced training in sociology go on to careers in teaching and research. But an increasing number of professional sociologists work in all sorts of applied fields. Clinical sociologists, for example, work with troubled clients much as clinical psychologists do. A basic difference, however, is that, while psychologists focus on the individual, sociologists locate difficulties in a person's web of social relationships. Another type of applied sociology is evaluation research. In today's cost-conscious political climate, administrators must evaluate the effectiveness of virtually every program and policy. Sociologists—especially those with advanced research skills—are in high demand for this kind of work.

THE IMPORTANCE OF A GLOBAL PERSPECTIVE

December 10, 1994, Fez, Morocco. This medieval city—a web of narrow streets and

Whenever we come upon people whose habits differ from our own, we become more aware of social patterns. This is why travel is an excellent way to stimulate the sociological perspective. But even within the United States there is striking cultural diversity, which prompts us to become conscious of our social surroundings.

alleyways alive with the sounds of children at play, the silence of veiled women, and the steady gaze of men leading donkeys laden with goods—has changed little over the centuries. We stand in northwest Africa in a strange place that seems lost in time. Never have we had such an adventure! Never have we thought so much about home!

As new communications technology draws even the farthest reaches of the earth closer to each other, many academic disciplines take a **global perspective**, *the study of the larger world and our society's place in it.* What is the importance of a global perspective for sociology?

First, global awareness is a logical extension of the sociological perspective. Sociology shows us that our place in a society profoundly affects our life experiences. It stands to reason, then, that the position of our society in the larger world system affects everyone in the United States.

One important reason to gain a global understanding is that, living in a high-income country, we can scarcely appreciate the suffering that goes on in much of the world. These flood victims in Mozambique are waiting for food. Indeed, throughout Africa, children have only a fifty-fifty chance to grow to adulthood.

Global Map 1–1 shows the relative economic development of the world's countries. **High-income countries** are *nations with very productive economic systems in which most people have relatively high incomes.*[1] High-income countries include the United States and Canada, Argentina, the nations of Western Europe, and Israel, Saudi Arabia, Japan, and Australia. Taken together, these forty nations generate most of the world's goods and services and control most of the planet's wealth. On average, individuals in these countries live well, not because they are smarter than anyone else, but because they had the good fortune to be born in an affluent region of the world.

The world's **middle-income countries** are *nations with moderately productive economic systems in which people's incomes are about the global average.* Individuals living in any of these roughly ninety nations—most of the countries of Eastern Europe, some of southern Africa, and almost all of Latin America—are as likely to live in

villages as in cities, to walk or ride animals, bicycles, scooters, or tractors as they are to drive cars, and are likely to receive only a few years of schooling. As in high-income countries, middle-income countries also have pronounced social inequality, so that while some people are extremely rich, many more lack safe housing and adequate nutrition.

Finally, about half the world's people live in the sixty **low-income countries,** *nations with less productive economic systems in which most people are poor.* As Global Map 1–1 shows, most of the poorest societies in the world are in Africa and Asia. In these nations, a small number of people are rich, but the majority struggle to get by with unclean water, too little food, little or no sanitation, and, perhaps most seriously of all, little chance to improve their lives.

Chapter 9 ("Global Stratification") discusses the causes and consequences of global wealth and poverty. But every chapter highlights life in the world beyond our own borders for three reasons:

1. **Societies the world over are increasingly interconnected.** Historically, the United States has taken only passing notice of the countries beyond its own borders. In recent decades, however, the United States and the rest of the world are becoming linked as never before. Electronic technology now transmits pictures, sounds, and written documents around the globe in seconds.

   One consequence of new technology, as later chapters will explain, is that people all over the world now share many tastes in music, clothing, and food. With their economic clout, high-income countries such as the United States influence other nations, whose people eagerly gobble up our hamburgers, dance to our music, and, more and more, speak the English language.

   We are spreading our way of life around the world; but the larger world, too, has an impact on us. Almost 1 million documented immigrants enter the United States each year, and we are quick to adopt many of their favorite sounds, tastes, and customs as our own, which greatly enhances the cultural diversity of this country.

   Commerce across national borders has also created a global economy. Corporations make and market goods worldwide, just as global financial centers linked by satellite now operate around the clock. Stock traders in New York follow the financial markets in Tokyo and Hong Kong, just as wheat farmers in Kansas watch the price of grain in the former Soviet republic of Georgia. With

[1]This text uses this terminology rather than the traditional but outdated terms "First World," "Second World," and "Third World." Chapter 9 ("Global Stratification") provides a complete discussion of the issue.

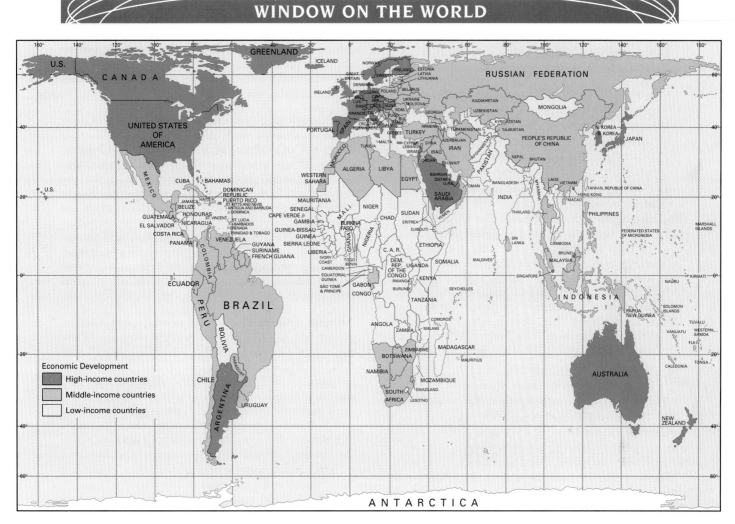

GLOBAL MAP 1–1 Economic Development in Global Perspective

In high-income countries—including the United States, Canada, Argentina, the nations of Western Europe, Israel, Saudi Arabia, Australia, and Japan—a highly productive economy provides people, on average, with material plenty. Middle-income countries—including most of Latin America and the nations of Eastern Europe—are less economically productive, with a standard of living about average for the world as a whole but far below that of most people in the United States. These nations also have a significant share of poor people who barely scrape by with meager housing and diet. In the low-income countries of the world, poverty is severe and extensive. Although small numbers of elites live very well in the poorest nations, most people struggle to survive on a small fraction of the income common in the United States.

Note: Data for this map are provided by the United Nations. High-income countries have a per capita gross domestic product (GDP) of at least $10,000. Many are far richer than this, however; the figure for the United States exceeds $29,000. Middle-income countries have a per capita GDP ranging from $2,500 to $10,000. Low-income countries have a per capita GDP below $2,500. Figures used here reflect the new United Nations "purchasing power parities" system. Rather than directly converting income figures into U.S. dollars, this calculation estimates the local purchasing power of each domestic currency.

Sources: Prepared by the author using data from United Nations Development Programme (2000). Map projection from *Peters Atlas of the World* (1990).

eight out of ten new U.S. jobs involving international trade, gaining greater global understanding has never been more important.

2. **Many social problems that we face in the United States are far more serious elsewhere.** Poverty is a serious problem in this country, but, as Chapter 9 ("Global Stratification") explains, poverty in Latin America, Africa, and Asia is both more widespread and more severe. Similarly, although women have lower social standing than men in the United States, gender inequality is much greater in the world's poor countries.

3. **Thinking globally is a good way to learn more about ourselves.** We cannot walk the streets of a distant city without becoming keenly aware of what it means to live in the United States. Making these comparisons often leads to unexpected lessons. For instance, in Chapter 9, we visit a squatter settlement in Madras, India. There, despite a desperate lack of basic material goods, people thrive in the love and support of family members. Why, then, does poverty in the United States lead to isolation and anger? Are material goods—so crucial to our definition of a "rich" life—the best way to gauge human well-being?

In sum, in an increasingly interconnected world, we can understand ourselves only to the extent that we understand others (Macionis, 1993).

THE ORIGINS OF SOCIOLOGY

Like the "choices" made by individuals, major historical events rarely just "happen." So it was that the birth of sociology resulted from powerful and complex social forces.

SOCIAL CHANGE AND SOCIOLOGY

Striking transformations in eighteenth- and nineteenth-century Europe caused the social ground to tremble under people's feet. Understandably, they focused their attention on society, leading to the rise of the new science of sociology.

Industrial technology. During the Middle Ages, most people in Europe farmed near their homes or engaged in small-scale *manufacturing* (derived from Latin, meaning "to make by hand"). By the end of the eighteenth century, inventors had harnessed new sources of energy—the power of moving water and then steam—to operate large machines in mills and

factories. Now, instead of laboring at home or in tightly knit groups, workers became part of a large and anonymous labor force, toiling for strangers who owned the large factories. This change in the system of production separated families and weakened traditions that had guided members of small communities for centuries.

The growth of cities. Across Europe, factories drew people in need of work. Along with this "pull" came the "push" of the "enclosure movement." Landowners fenced off more and more land, turning farms into grazing land for sheep—the source of wool for the thriving textile mills. Without land, countless tenant farmers left the countryside in search of work in the new factories.

Cities grew to unprecedented size, and streets churned with strangers. Widespread social problems—including pollution, crime, and homelessness—further stimulated development of the sociological perspective.

Political change. Economic development and the growth of cities brought new ways of thinking. In the writings of Thomas Hobbes (1588–1679), John Locke (1632–1704), and Adam Smith (1723–1790), we find less concern with people's moral obligations to God and to political rulers and more focus on pursuing one's own self-interest. Indeed, the key phrases in the new political climate were *individual liberty* and *individual rights*. Echoing the thoughts of Locke, our own Declaration of Independence clearly declares that each citizen has "certain unalienable rights," including "life, liberty, and the pursuit of happiness."

The political revolution in France that began in 1789 symbolized the Western world's break with political and social traditions. As the French social analyst Alexis de Tocqueville (1805–1859) declared after the French Revolution, the change in society amounted to "nothing short of the regeneration of the whole human race" (1955:13; orig. 1856). As the new industrial economy, enormous cities, and fresh political ideas combined to draw attention to society, sociology flowered in precisely those countries—France, Germany, and England—where changes were greatest.

SCIENCE AND SOCIOLOGY

The nature of society fascinated the brilliant minds of the ancient world, including the Chinese philosopher K'ung Fu-tzu or Confucius (551–479 B.C.E.) and the Greek philosophers Plato (427–347 B.C.E.) and

Aristotle (384–322 B.C.E.).[2] Later, the Roman emperor Marcus Aurelius (121–180), the medieval thinkers St. Thomas Aquinas (c. 1225–1274) and Christine de Pizan (c. 1363–1431), and the great English playwright William Shakespeare (1564–1616) took up the question.

Yet these men and women were more interested in envisioning the ideal society than they were in analyzing society as it really was. In creating their new discipline, sociology's pioneers certainly cared how society could be improved, but their major goal was to understand how society actually operates. It was the French social thinker Auguste Comte (1798–1857) who coined the term *sociology* in 1838 to describe this new way of thinking. Thus, sociology is among the youngest academic disciplines—far newer, for example, than history, physics, or economics.

Comte (1975; orig. 1851–54) saw sociology as the product of a three-stage historical development. During the earliest *theological stage*, up to the end of the European Middle Ages, people took a religious view that society expressed God's will. With the Renaissance, this theological approach gradually gave way to a *metaphysical stage* in which people saw society as a natural rather than supernatural phenomenon. The English philosopher Thomas Hobbes (1588-1679), for example, suggested that society reflected not the perfection of God as much as the failings of a selfish human nature.

What Comte called the *scientific stage* began with the work of early scientists such as the Polish astronomer Nicolaus Copernicus (1473–1543), the Italian astronomer and physicist Galileo (1564–1642), and the English physicist and mathematician Isaac Newton (1642–1727). Comte's contribution came in applying the scientific approach—first used to analyze the physical world—to the study of society.

Comte thus favored **positivism**, *a way of understanding based on science.* As a positivist, Comte believed that society operates according to certain laws, just as the physical world operates according to gravity and other laws of nature.

At the beginning of the twentieth century, sociology took hold as an academic discipline in the United

Here we see Copernicus, the sixteenth-century astronomer, taking careful measurements of the world. Just as Copernicus challenged the common sense of his day, sociologists such as Auguste Comte later argued that society is neither fixed by God's will nor set by human nature. On the contrary, Comte claimed, society is a system we can study scientifically, and, based on what we learn, we can act intentionally to improve our lives.

States, strongly influenced by Comte's ideas. Today, most sociologists still consider science a crucial element of sociology. But we now realize that human behavior is far more complex than the movement of planets or the actions of other living things. We are creatures of imagination and spontaneity, so human behavior can never be explained by any rigid "laws of society." In addition, early sociologists like Karl Marx (1818–1883) were deeply troubled by the striking inequality of the new industrial society. Marx wanted the new discipline of sociology not just to understand society but to bring about change toward social justice.

---

[2]Throughout this text, the abbreviation B.C.E. designates "before the common era." We use this terminology in place of the traditional B.C. ("before Christ") in recognition of the religious plurality of our society. Similarly, in place of the traditional A.D. (*anno Domini*, or "in the year of our Lord"), we employ the abbreviation C.E. ("common era").

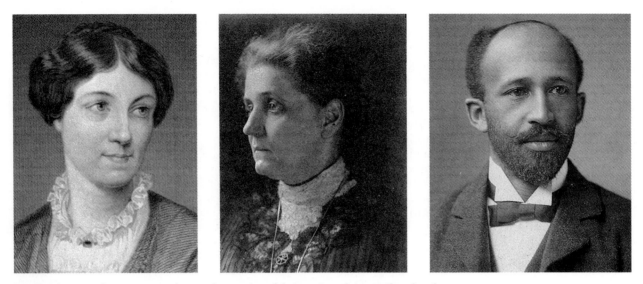

People whose gender or race put them at the margins of their society also contributed to the development of sociology. Harriet Martineau (left), Jane Addams (middle), and W. E. B. Du Bois (right) have only recently been recognized as important founders of the discipline.

MARGINAL VOICES

Auguste Comte and Karl Marx stand among the giants of sociology. But, in recent years, we have come to see the important contributions that others—who were pushed to the margins of society because of their sex or race—have made.

Harriet Martineau (1802–1876), born to a wealthy English family, first made her mark in 1853 by translating the writings of Auguste Comte from French into English. Subsequently, she became a noted scholar in her own right, revealing the evils of slavery and arguing for laws to protect factory workers and to advance the standing of women.

In the United States, Jane Addams (1860–1935) was a sociological pioneer. Trained as a social worker, Addams spoke out on behalf of immigrants who were entering the country at the rate of 1 million per year. In 1889, Addams founded Hull House, a settlement house in Chicago that provided assistance to immigrant families. She also gathered sociologists and politicians to discuss the urban problems of the day. For her work on behalf of immigrants, Addams was awarded the Nobel Peace Prize in 1931.

An important contribution to understanding race in the United States was made by another neglected sociological pioneer, William Edward Burghardt Du Bois (1868–1963). Born to a poor Massachusetts family, Du Bois enrolled at Fisk University in Nashville, Tennessee, and then at Harvard University, where he earned the first doctorate awarded by that university to a person of color. Like Martineau and Addams, Du Bois believed sociologists should try to solve contemporary problems. He therefore studied the black community (1899), spoke out against racial inequality, and served as a founding member of the National Association for the Advancement of Colored People (NAACP).

Widespread belief in the inferiority of women and African Americans kept the work of Martineau, Addams, and Du Bois at the margins of sociology. Looking back with a sociological eye, we can see how the forces of society were at work shaping even the history of sociology itself.

SOCIOLOGICAL THEORY

Weaving observations into understanding brings us to another aspect of sociology: theory. A **theory** is *a statement of how and why specific facts are related.* To illustrate, recall Emile Durkheim's theory that categories of people with low social integration (men, Protestants, the wealthy, and the unmarried) are prone to suicide.

Like all scientists, sociologists conduct research to test and refine their theories. National Map 1–1,

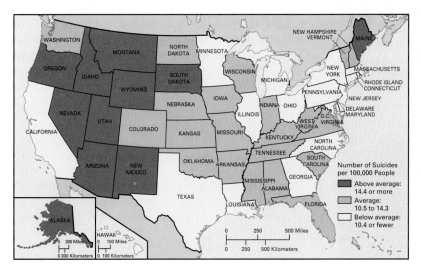

NATIONAL MAP 1–1
Suicide Rates across the United States

This map shows which states have high, average, and low suicide rates. Look for patterns. By and large, high suicide rates occur where people live far apart from one another. More densely populated states, on the other hand, have low suicide rates. Do these data support or contradict Durkheim's theory of suicide? Why?

Source: U.S. National Center for Health Statistics (2000).

which displays the suicide rates for the fifty states, gives you a chance to do some theorizing of your own.

In building theory, sociologists face two basic questions. What issues should we study? How should we connect the facts? In answering these questions, sociologists look to one or more theoretical "roadmaps" or paradigms (Kuhn, 1970). A **theoretical paradigm** is *a basic image of society that guides thinking and research.* Three major paradigms in sociology are the structural-functional paradigm, the social-conflict paradigm, and the symbolic-interaction paradigm.

THE STRUCTURAL-FUNCTIONAL PARADIGM

The **structural-functional paradigm** is *a framework for building theory that sees society as a complex system whose parts work together to promote solidarity and stability.* As its name suggests, this paradigm points to the importance of **social structure,** meaning *any relatively stable pattern of social behavior.* Social structure gives our lives shape in families, the workplace, or the college classroom. Second, this paradigm looks for any structure's **social functions,** or *consequences for the operation of society as a whole.* All social patterns—from a simple handshake to complex religious rituals—function to keep society going, at least in its present form.

The structural-functional paradigm owes much to Auguste Comte, who pointed out the need for social integration during a time of rapid change. Emile

Durkheim, who helped establish sociology in French universities, also based his work on this approach. A third structural-functional pioneer was the English sociologist Herbert Spencer (1820–1903). Spencer compared society to the human body. Just as the structural parts of the human body—the skeleton, muscles, and various internal organs—function together to help the entire organism survive, social structures work together to preserve society. The structural-functional paradigm, then, leads sociologists to identify various structures of society and investigate their functions.

Contemporary U.S. sociologist Robert K. Merton expanded our understanding of social function by pointing out that any social structure probably has many functions, some more obvious than others. He called **manifest functions** *the recognized and intended consequences of any social pattern.* **Latent functions,** by contrast, are *consequences that are largely unintended and unrecognized.* To illustrate, the obvious function of this country's system of higher education is to provide young people with the information and skills they need to perform jobs. Perhaps just as important, although less often acknowledged, is college's function as a "marriage broker," bringing together young people of similar social backgrounds. Another latent function of higher education is keeping millions of people out of the labor market where, presumably, many of them would not find jobs.

The painting Furnishings, *by Paul Marcus, presents the essential wisdom of social-conflict theory: Society operates in a way that conveys wealth, power, and privilege to some at the expense of others. Looking at the painting, what are most of the people doing? What do you make of the head hanging on the wall? The classical scene between the drapes? What categories of people does the artist suggest are disadvantaged?*

© Paul Marcus, *Furnishings*, oil painting on canvas, 64 in. × 48 in. Studio SPM, Inc.

But Merton also recognized that the effects of social structure are not all good—and certainly, not good for everybody (Stern, 1998). Thus, **social dysfunctions** are *a social pattern's undesirable consequences for the operation of society.* People usually disagree on what is beneficial and what is harmful. Moreover, what is functional for one category of people (say, factory owners or landlords) may well be dysfunctional for another category of people (say, factory workers or tenants).

Critical evaluation. The chief characteristic of the structural-functional paradigm is its vision of society as stable and orderly. The main goal of sociologists who use this paradigm, then, is to figure out "what makes society tick."

In the mid-1900s, most sociologists favored the structural-functional paradigm. In recent decades, however, its influence has declined. By focusing attention on social stability and unity, critics point out, structural-functionalism ignores inequalities of social class, race, ethnicity, and gender, which can generate considerable tension and conflict. In general, focusing on stability at the expense of conflict makes this paradigm somewhat conservative. As a critical response to this approach, sociologists developed another theoretical orientation: the social-conflict paradigm.

THE SOCIAL-CONFLICT PARADIGM

The **social-conflict paradigm** is *a framework for building theory that sees society as an arena of inequality that generates conflict and change.* Unlike the structural-functional emphasis on solidarity, this approach highlights inequality. Guided by this paradigm, sociologists investigate how factors such as class, race, ethnicity, gender, and age are linked to the unequal distribution of money, power, education, and social prestige. A conflict analysis rejects the idea that social structure promotes the operation of society as a whole, focusing instead on how any social pattern benefits some people while depriving others.

Sociologists using the social-conflict paradigm look at ongoing conflict between dominant and disadvantaged categories of people—the rich in relation to the poor, white people in relation to people of color, or men in relation to women. Typically, people on top strive to protect their privileges, while the disadvantaged try to gain more for themselves.

A conflict analysis of our educational system would explain how schooling perpetuates inequality by reproducing the class structure in every new generation. That is, secondary schools channel new students into either college-preparatory or vocational training programs. From a structural-functional point of view, such "tracking" benefits everyone by providing schooling that fits students' abilities. But conflict analysis counters that tracking often has less to do with talent than with social background, so that well-to-do students are placed in higher tracks while poor children end up in lower tracks.

In this way, young people from privileged families get the best schooling, which serves as a springboard for high-income careers later on. The children of poor families, on the other hand, are not prepared for college and, like their parents before them, typically enter low-paying jobs. In both cases, the social standing of one generation is passed on to the next, with schools justifying the practice in terms of individual merit (Bowles & Gintis, 1976; Oakes, 1982, 1985).

Many sociologists who use the social-conflict paradigm try not just to understand society but to reduce inequality. This was the goal of W. E. B. Du Bois, who was guided by the social-conflict paradigm to raise the standing of people of color. Likewise, Karl Marx championed the workers against those who owned the factories. In a well-known declaration (inscribed on his monument in London's Highgate Cemetery), Marx declared: "The philosophers have only interpreted the world, in various ways; the point, however, is to change it."

Critical evaluation. The social-conflict paradigm has gained a large following in recent decades, but, like other approaches, it has met with its share of criticism. Because the paradigm focuses on inequality, it largely ignores how shared values and interdependence can unify members of a society. In addition, say critics, to the extent that this paradigm pursues political goals, it cannot claim scientific objectivity. This charge prompts supporters to counter that *all* social approaches have political consequences, albeit different ones.

A final criticism of both the structural-functional and social-conflict paradigms is that they paint society in broad strokes—in terms of "family," "social class," "race," and so on. A third theoretical paradigm views society less in terms of generalizations and more as the everyday experiences of individual people.

THE SYMBOLIC-INTERACTION PARADIGM

The structural-functional and social-conflict paradigms share a **macro-level orientation,** meaning *a concern with broad patterns that shape society as a whole.* Macro-level sociology takes in the big picture, rather like observing a city from a helicopter and seeing how highways help people move from place to place or how housing differs in rich and poor neighborhoods. Sociology also uses a **micro-level orientation,** *a close-up focus on social interaction in specific situations.* Exploring urban life in this way occurs at street level, where perhaps one might watch how children invent games on a school playground or how pedestrians respond to homeless people. The **symbolic-interaction paradigm,** then, is *a framework for building theory that sees society as the product of the everyday interactions of individuals.*

How does "society" result from the ongoing experiences of tens of millions of people? One answer, detailed in Chapter 4 ("Social Interaction in Everyday Life"), is that society is nothing more than the reality

To understand how the symbolic-interaction paradigm views society, consider Emit Bisttram's painting, Domingo Chorus. Society is never at rest; it is an ongoing process by which interacting individuals define and redefine reality.

Emil Bisttram, American (1895–1976). *Domingo Chorus*, 1936, gouache and pencil on paper, 57.8 × 43.5 cm. Christie's Images/The Bridgeman Art Library.

people construct for themselves as they interact. That is, human beings are creatures who live in a world of symbols, attaching *meaning* to virtually everything. "Reality," therefore, is simply how we define our surroundings, our obligations towards others, even our own identities.

The symbolic-interaction paradigm has roots in the thinking of Max Weber (1864–1920), a German sociologist who emphasized understanding a setting from the point of view of the people in it. Since Weber's time, sociologists have taken micro-sociology in a number of directions. Chapter 3 ("Socialization: From Infancy to Old Age") discusses the ideas of George Herbert Mead (1863–1931), who explored how we create our personalities from social experience.

TABLE 1-1 The Three Major Theoretical Paradigms: A Summary

Theoretical Paradigm	Orientation	Image of Society	Core Questions
Structural-functional	Macro-level	A system of interrelated parts that is relatively stable because of widespread agreement on what is morally desirable; each part has a particular function in society as a whole.	How is society integrated? What are the major parts of society? How are these parts interrelated? What are the consequences of each part for the overall operation of society?
Social-conflict	Macro-level	A system based on social inequality; each part of society benefits some categories of people more than others; social inequality leads to conflict which, in turn, leads to social change.	How is society divided? What are the major patterns of social inequality? How do some categories of people try to protect their privileges? How do other categories of people challenge the status quo?
Symbolic-interaction	Micro-level	An ongoing process of social interaction in specific settings based on symbolic communication; individual perceptions of reality are variable and changing.	How is society experienced? How do human beings interact to create, maintain, and change social patterns? How do individuals try to shape the reality that others perceive? How does individual behavior change from one situation to another?

Chapter 4 ("Social Interaction in Everyday Life") presents the work of Erving Goffman (1922–1982), whose *dramaturgical analysis* describes how we resemble actors on a stage as we play out our various roles. Other contemporary sociologists, including George Homans and Peter Blau, have developed *social-exchange analysis*, the idea that interaction is guided by what each person stands to gain and lose from others (Molm, 1997; Mulford et al., 1998). In the ritual of courtship, for example, people seek mates who can offer them at least as much—in terms of physical attractiveness, intelligence, and social background—as they offer in return.

Critical evaluation. Without denying the existence of macro-level social structures such as "the family" and "social class," the symbolic-interaction paradigm reminds us that society basically amounts to *people interacting*. That is, micro-level sociology tries to convey how individuals actually experience society. But the other side of the same coin is that, by emphasizing what is unique in each social scene, this approach risks overlooking the widespread effects of culture, as well as factors such as class, gender, and race.

Table 1–1 summarizes the distinctive features of the structural-functional paradigm, the social-conflict paradigm, and the symbolic-interaction paradigm. As you read the chapters in this book, keep in mind

that each paradigm is helpful in answering particular kinds of questions. As the box about sports on pages 16–17 shows, the fullest understanding of society comes from using all three approaches.

SCIENTIFIC SOCIOLOGY

To test theories, sociologists conduct research. To investigate how and why we behave as we do, they rely on **science,** *a logical system that bases knowledge on direct, systematic observation.* Scientific knowledge is based on *empirical evidence,* meaning facts we verify with our senses.

Sociological research often challenges what we accept as "common sense." Here are three examples of widely held attitudes that are contradicted by scientific evidence:

1. **Differences in the social behavior of women and men reflect "human nature."** Much of what we call "human nature" is constructed by the society in which we live. We know this because researchers have documented how definitions of "feminine" and "masculine" change over time and vary from one society to another (see Chapter 10, "Gender Stratification").

2. **The United States is a middle-class society in which most people are more or less equal.** As Chapter 8 ("Social Stratification") explains, the richest 5 percent of U.S. families control half of the country's wealth, while almost half of all families have scarcely any wealth at all.

3. **People marry because they are in love.** Surprising as it may seem, research indicates that marriages in most societies have little to do with love. Chapter 13 ("Family and Religion") explains why.

These examples confirm the old saying that "It's not what we don't know that gets us into trouble as much as the things we *do* know that just aren't so." Scientific sociology is a useful way to assess many kinds of information.

CONCEPTS, VARIABLES, AND MEASUREMENT

A basic element of science is the **concept,** *a mental construct that represents some part of the world in a simplified form.* Sociologists use concepts to label aspects of social life, including "the family" and "the economy," and to categorize people in terms of their "gender" or "social class."

A **variable** is *a concept whose value changes from case to case.* The familiar variable "price," for example, changes from item to item in a supermarket. Similarly, people use the concept "social class" to size up others as "upper class," "middle class," "working class," or "lower class."

The use of variables depends on **measurement,** *a procedure for determining the value of a variable in a specific case.* Some variables are easy to measure, as when a checkout clerk adds up the cost of our groceries. But measuring sociological variables can be far more difficult. For example, how would you measure a person's "social class"? You might be tempted to look at clothing, listen to patterns of speech, or note a home address. Or, trying to be more precise, you might ask about income, occupation, and education. Since there are many ways to measure almost anything, researchers must *operationalize* their variables, that is, they must specify exactly what they are measuring in each case.

Sociologists also face the problem of dealing with large numbers of people. How, for example, do you report income for thousands or even millions of individuals? Listing streams of numbers would carry little meaning and tell us nothing about the people as a whole. Therefore, sociologists employ *descriptive*

statistics to state what is "average" for a large population. Most commonly used are the *mean* (the arithmetic average of all measures, obtained by adding them up and dividing by the number of cases), the *median* (the middle score that divides a distribution in half), and the *mode* (the single score that appears most often).

Reliability and validity. Beyond carefully operationalizing variables, useful measurement must be reliable and valid. **Reliability** refers to *consistency in measurement.* For measurement to be reliable, in other words, the process must yield the same results when repeated. Even consistent results, however, may not be valid. **Validity** refers to *precision in measuring exactly what one intends to measure.* Valid measurement means more than hitting the same spot on a target again and again—it means hitting the bull's eye.

Say, for example, you want to know how religious people are. You might ask how often your subjects attend religious services. But is going to a church or temple really the same thing as being religious? Maybe not, since people take part in religious rituals for many reasons, not all of them religious; some devout believers, on the other hand, avoid organized religion altogether. Thus, even when a measure yields consistent results (making it reliable), it can still miss the real, intended target (and lack validity). In sum, sociological research depends on careful measurement, which is always a challenge to researchers.

CORRELATION AND CAUSE

The real payoff in sociological research is determining how variables are related. **Correlation** means *a relationship by which two (or more) variables change together.* But sociologists want to know not just *how* variables change but *why.* The scientific ideal, then, is mapping out **cause and effect,** which means *a relationship in which we know that change in one variable causes change in another.* As we noted earlier, Emile Durkheim found that the degree of social integration (the cause) affected the suicide rate (the effect) among categories of people. Scientists refer to the causal factor as the *independent variable,* while calling the effect the *dependent variable.* Understanding cause and effect is valuable because it allows researchers to *predict* how one pattern of behavior will produce another.

Just because two variables change together does not necessarily mean that they have a cause-and-effect relationship. Consider, for instance, that the marriage rate in the United States falls to its lowest point in January, exactly the same month that the

CRITICAL THINKING

Sports: Playing the Theory Game

Who among us doesn't enjoy sports? Soccer moms drive eager eight-year-olds to games, and teens play pick-up basketball after school. Weekend television is filled with sporting events, and whole sections of our newspapers report the scores. What can we learn by applying sociology's three theoretical paradigms to this familiar element of life in the United States?

A structural-functional approach asks what sports do for our society as a whole. The manifest functions include recreation, physical conditioning, and a relatively harmless way to "let off steam." Sports have important latent functions as well, from fostering social relationships to creating countless jobs. Perhaps most important, though, sports encourage competition, which is central to this nation's way of life (Coakley, 1990).

Sports also have dysfunctional consequences, of course. For example, universities intent on fielding winning teams sometimes recruit students for their athletic ability rather than their academic aptitude. This practice not only pulls down a school's academic standards, it shortchanges athletes who devote little time to academic work.

A social-conflict analysis might begin by pointing out how sports are linked to social inequality. Some sports, such as tennis, golf, skiing, and competitive swimming, are expensive, so participation is largely limited to the well-to-do. Football, baseball, and basketball, however, are accessible to people of all income levels. Thus, the games people play are not simply a matter of choice but also a reflection of people's social standing.

Moreover, men dominate sports. The first modern Olympic Games held in 1896, for example, excluded women from competition. In the United States, through most of the twentieth century, even Little League teams barred girls from the playing field on the unfounded notions that girls lack the strength or the stamina to play sports or that they risk losing their

Olympische Spiele München 1972

African American artist Jacob Lawrence recognized that sports are more than mere entertainment. Through sports we acknowledge the importance of individualism and competition to our society's way of life.

Lawrence, Jacob. American, b. 1917. *Munich Olympic Games*, Poster, 1972. Courtesy of the artist and Francine Seders Gallery, Seattle. Photo: Spike Mafford.

femininity if they do participate. Both the Olympics and Little League are now open to females as well as males. But, in the world of sports, women still take a back seat to men, particularly in sports that yield the greatest earnings and social prestige.

Although our society long excluded people of color from professional sports, opportunities have expanded in recent decades. In 1947, Jackie Robinson broke through the "color line" to become the first African American player in Major League Baseball. By 1997 (the year professional baseball retired the legendary Robinson's number 42 on *all* teams), African Americans (13 percent of the U.S. population) accounted for 15 percent of baseball players, 65 percent of National Football League (NFL) players, and 77 percent of National Basketball Association (NBA) players (Center for the Study of Sport in Society, 2000).

One reason for the increasing share of people of African descent in professional sports is the fact that athletic performance—in terms of batting average or number of points scored per game—is measured objectively and is not influenced by racial prejudice. It is also true that some people of color make a special effort to excel in athletics, where they perceive more opportunity than in other careers (Steele, 1990; Hoberman, 1997, 1998). In recent years, in fact, African American athletes have earned higher salaries, on average, than white players.

But racial discrimination still taints professional sports in the United States. For one thing, race is linked to the *positions* athletes play on the field, a pattern called *stacking*. The figure to the right shows the results of a study of race in football. Notice that white players dominate in offense and also play the central positions on both sides of the line. More broadly, African Americans figure prominently in only five sports: basketball, football, baseball, boxing, and track. Across all professional sports, the vast majority of managers, head coaches, and team owners are still white (Gnida, 1995; Smith & Leonard, 1997).

Overall, who benefits most from professional sports? Although individual players may get sky-high salaries, and millions of fans love following their teams, the vast profits sports generate are controlled by a small number of people (predominantly white men). In sum, sports in the United States are bound up with inequalities based on gender, race, and wealth.

At a micro-level, a sporting event is a complex face-to-face interaction. In part, play is guided by assigned positions and, of course, by the rules of the game. But players are also spontaneous and unpredictable. The symbolic-interaction paradigm, then, sees sports less as a system than as an ongoing process. Then, too, we expect each player to understand the game a little differently. Some thrive in a setting of stiff competition, while, for others, love[3] of the

game may be much stronger than the need to win.

Team members also shape their particular realities according to the prejudices, jealousies, and ambitions they bring to the field. Moreover, the behavior of any single player changes over time. A rookie in professional baseball, for example, typically feels self-conscious during the first few games in the big

leagues but goes on to develop a comfortable sense of fitting in with the team. Coming to feel at home on the field was especially difficult for Jackie Robinson in 1947. At first, he was painfully aware that many white players and millions of white fans resented his presence in Major League Baseball. In time, however, his outstanding ability and his confident and cooperative manner won him the respect of the entire nation.

The three theoretical paradigms differ in their approaches to sports, but none is more correct than the others. Applied to any issue, each paradigm generates its own insights so that, to fully appreciate the power of the sociological perspective, you should become familiar with all three.

What do you think?

1. *What does it mean to describe both the structural-functional and social-conflict paradigms as "macro-level" approaches? As a "micro-level" approach, how does the symbolic-interaction paradigm differ?*

2. *Can you devise three additional questions about sports—one that could be answered using each of the three theoretical paradigms?*

3. *How might you apply these three paradigms to other social patterns, such as the workplace or family life?*

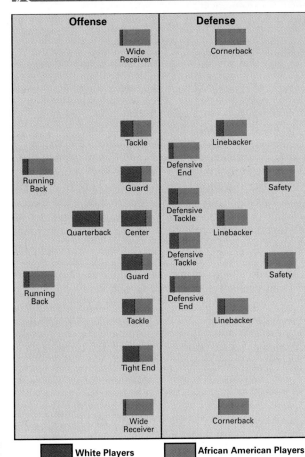

DIVERSITY SNAPSHOT

■ White Players   ■ African American Players

Race and Sport: "Stacking" in Professional Football
Source: Center for the Study of Sport in Society (2000).

[3]The ancient Romans recognized this fact, evident in the Latin root of our word "amateur," literally, "lover," which designates someone who engages in an activity for the sheer love of it.

Myths as well as scientific facts are an important dimension of human existence. In his painting, The Creation of the Earth, *Mexican painter Diego Rivera (1886–1957) offers a mythic account of human origins. A myth (from the Greek, meaning "story" or "word") may or may not be factual in the literal sense. Yet, it conveys some basic truth about the meaning and purpose of life. Indeed, it is science, rather than art, that has no power to address such questions of meaning.*

Diego Rivera, Mexican (1886–1957). *The Creation of the Earth* page from *Popol Vuh,* watercolor on paper. Museo Casa Diego Rivera (INBA), Guanajuato, Mexico. Index/The Bridgeman Art Library. © Banco de Mexico Diego Rivera Museum Trust.

national death rate peaks. This hardly means that people drop dead if they decide not to marry (or that they don't marry because they die). More likely, it is the dreary weather across much of the country during January (perhaps combined with the postholiday "blahs") that causes both the low marriage rate and the high death rate.

When two variables change together but neither one causes the other, sociologists describe the relationship as a *spurious,* or "false," correlation. A spurious correlation between two variables usually results from some third factor. For example, delinquency rates are high where young people live in crowded housing, but both of these factors result from being poor. To be sure of a real cause-and-effect relationship, we must show that (1) the two variables are correlated, (2) the independent (or causal) variable precedes the dependent variable in time, and (3) there is no evidence that the correlation is spurious because of some third variable.

THE IDEAL OF OBJECTIVITY

A guiding principle of scientific study is *objectivity,* or personal neutrality, in conducting research. The ideal of objective inquiry is to allow the facts to speak for themselves and not become colored by the personal values and biases of the researcher. In reality, of course, achieving total neutrality is impossible for anyone. But

carefully adhering to the logic of scientific research will maximize objectivity.

The German sociologist Max Weber expected that people would choose *value-relevant* research topics. But once their work is underway, Weber cautioned researchers to be *value-free.* That is, we must be dedicated to finding truth *as it is* rather than as we think *it should be.* This difference, for Weber, sets science apart from politics. Researchers (unlike politicians) must try to stay open-minded and be willing to accept whatever results come from their work, whether they like them or not.

Weber's argument still carries much weight in sociology, although most researchers concede that we can never be completely value-free or even aware of all our biases (Demerath, 1996). Moreover, sociologists are not "average" people: Most are white people who are highly educated and more politically liberal than the population as a whole (Wilson, 1979). Sociologists need to remember that they, too, are influenced by their social backgrounds.

A SECOND FRAMEWORK: INTERPRETIVE SOCIOLOGY

All sociologists agree that studying social behavior scientifically presents some real challenges. But some sociologists go further, suggesting that science as it is used to study the natural world misses a vital part of the social world: *meaning.*

Human beings do not simply act; we engage in *meaningful* action. Max Weber, the pioneer of this framework, argued that the proper focus of sociology, therefore, is *interpretation*—or understanding the meanings people create in their everyday lives. **Interpretive sociology,** therefore, is *the study of society that focuses on the meanings people attach to their social world.*

Interpretive sociology differs from scientific, or positivist, sociology in three ways. First, scientific sociology focuses on action, what people do; interpretive sociology, by contrast, focuses on the meaning people attach to behavior. Second, while scientific sociology sees an objective reality "out there," interpretive sociology sees reality constructed by people themselves in the course of their everyday lives. Third, while scientific sociology tends to favor *quantitative* data—that is, numerical measurements of social behavior—interpretive sociology favors *qualitative* data, researchers' perceptions of how people understand their surroundings. In sum, the scientific approach is well suited for research in a laboratory, where investigators stand back and take careful measurements. The interpretive approach is better suited for research in a natural setting, where investigators interact with people to learn how they make sense of their everyday lives.

Max Weber claimed the key to interpretive sociology lies in *Verstehen,* the German word for "understanding." It is the interpretive sociologist's job not just to observe *what* people do but to share in their world of meaning, coming to appreciate *why* they act as they do. Subjective thoughts and feelings—which science tends to dismiss as "bias"—now move to the center of the researcher's attention (Berger & Kellner, 1981; Neuman, 1997).

A THIRD FRAMEWORK: CRITICAL SOCIOLOGY

Like the interpretive approach, critical sociology developed in reaction to the limitations of scientific sociology. This time, however, the problem was the foremost principle of scientific research—namely, objectivity.

Scientific sociology holds that reality is "out there" and the researcher's task is to study and document this reality. But Karl Marx, who founded the critical approach, rejected the idea that society exists as a "natural" system with a fixed order. To assume this, he claimed, amounts to saying that society cannot be changed. Scientific sociology, in his view, ends up supporting the status quo.

Critical sociology, then, is *the study of society that focuses on the need for social change.* Rather than asking the scientific question "How does society work?", critical sociologists ask moral and political questions, especially "Should society exist in its present form?" Their answer, typically, is that it should not. The point, said Marx (1972:109; orig. 1845), is not merely to study the world as it is but to *change* it. In making value judgments about how society should be improved, critical sociology rejects Weber's goal that research should be value-free.

Sociologists using the critical approach seek to change not only society but the character of research itself. They consider their research subjects as equals and encourage their participation in deciding what to study and how to do the work. Often, researchers and subjects use their findings to provide a voice for less powerful people and advance the political goal of a more equal society (Nielsen, 1990; Stanley, 1990; Reinharz, 1992; Wolf, 1996; Hess, 1999).

Scientific sociologists object to taking sides in this way, charging that critical sociology (whether feminist, Marxist, or some other critical approach) is political and gives up any claim to objectivity. Critical sociologists respond that all research is political in that either it calls for change or it does not; sociologists thus have no choice about their work being political, but they can choose *which* positions to support. Critical sociology, therefore, is an activist approach tying knowledge to action—seeking not just to understand the world but also to improve it. Generally speaking, scientific sociology tends to appeal to researchers with more conservative political views; critical sociology appeals to those with liberal and radical-left politics.

What about the link between methodological approaches and theory? In general, each of the three methodological approaches is related to one of the theoretical paradigms presented earlier in this chapter. The scientific approach corresponds to the structural-functional paradigm, the interpretive approach to the symbolic-interaction paradigm, and the critical approach to the social-conflict paradigm. Table 1–2 summarizes the differences among the three methodological approaches. Sociologists often favor one approach over another; however, most make use of all three (Gamson, 1999).

TABLE 1-2 Three Methodological Approaches in Sociology			
	Scientific	**Interpretive**	**Critical**
What Is Reality?	Society is an orderly system; reality is "out there."	Society is ongoing interaction; reality is socially constructed meanings.	Society is patterns of inequality; reality is that some dominate others.
How Do We Conduct Research?	Gather empirical data— ideally, quantitative; researcher tries to be an objective observer.	Develop a qualitative account of the subjective sense people make of their world; researcher is a participant.	Research is a strategy to bring about desired change; researcher is an activist.
Corresponding Theoretical Paradigm	Structural-functional paradigm	Symbolic-interaction paradigm	Social-conflict paradigm

GENDER AND RESEARCH

Research is also affected by **gender,** *the personal traits and social positions that members of a society attach to being female and male.* Margrit Eichler (1988) identifies four ways in which gender can influence research:

1. **Androcentricity.** *Androcentricity* (*andro* is the Greek word for "male"; *centricity* refers to "being centered on") means acting as if only the actions of men are important, ignoring what women do. The parallel concept of *gynocentricity*—seeing the world from a female perspective—is a problem, too, but one that occurs less frequently in our male-dominated society.

2. **Overgeneralizing.** This problem occurs when sociologists use data obtained from men to support conclusions about all people. For example, a researcher might gather information from a handful of male public officials and draw conclusions about an entire community.

3. **Gender blindness.** Failing to consider gender at all is termed "gender blindness." A study of growing old in the United States that overlooks the fact that most elderly men live with spouses while elderly women generally live alone would be limited by gender blindness.

4. **Double standards.** Researchers must be careful not to judge men and women differently. For example, a family researcher who labels a couple "man and wife" implies the work of one sex is more significant than that of the other.

5. **Interference.** We can add to Eichler's list the problem of subjects reacting to the sex of the investigator in ways that interfere with the research project. For instance, while conducting research in Sicily, Maureen Giovannini (1992) found many men reacted to her as a *woman* rather than as a *researcher*. Gender dynamics kept her from certain activities, such as private conversations with men, that were deemed inappropriate for single women.

There is nothing wrong with focusing research on one sex or the other. But all sociologists, as well as people who read their work, should be mindful of how gender can affect an investigation.

RESEARCH ETHICS

Like all scientific investigators, sociologists must remember that their work can harm as well as help subjects and communities. For this reason, the American Sociological Association (ASA)—the professional organization of U.S. sociologists—provides formal guidelines for conducting research (1997).

Sociologists must strive to be both technically competent and fair-minded in their work. They must disclose their findings without omitting significant data, and they are ethically bound to share their work with other sociologists who may wish to conduct the same study.

Sociologists must also ensure the safety of subjects taking part in a research project, and must stop work immediately if they suspect that a subject is at risk. Researchers must also protect the privacy of those involved in a research project, even if they come under pressure (perhaps from the police or the courts) to release confidential information. Researchers should obtain the *informed consent* of participants, which means that subjects understand their responsibilities

Conducting Research with Hispanics

Sociological investigators often choose to study people who differ from themselves. Learning—in advance—the cultural traits of research subjects will both speed the work and ensure that no hard feelings arise along the way.

Gerardo Marín and Barbara VanOss Marín have identified five areas of concern when conducting research with Hispanics:

1. **Be careful with terms.** The Maríns point out that "Hispanic" is a label of convenience used by the Census Bureau. Few people of Spanish descent think of themselves as "Hispanic" or "Latino"; most identify with a particular country (generally, with a Latin American nation such as Cuba or Argentina, or with Spain).

2. **Be culturally aware.** By and large, the U.S. population is individualistic and competitive. Many Hispanics, by contrast, have a more collective orientation. An outsider may judge the behavior of a Hispanic subject as conformist or overly trusting when, in fact, the person is simply trying to be courteous. Hispanic respondents might agree with a researcher's statement out of politeness rather than conviction.

3. **Anticipate family dynamics.** Hispanic cultures have strong family loyalties. Asking subjects to reveal information about another family member may make them uncomfortable or even angry. The Maríns add that a researcher's request to speak privately with a Hispanic woman in the home may provoke suspicion or outright disapproval from her husband or father.

4. **Take your time.** Hispanics, the Maríns explain, tend to be more concerned with the quality of

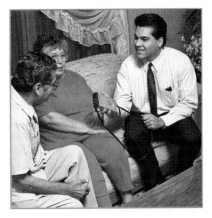

relationships than with simply getting a job done. A non-Hispanic researcher who tries to hurry an interview with a Hispanic family, perhaps wishing not to delay their dinner, may be thought rude for not proceeding at a more sociable and relaxed pace.

5. **Think about personal space.** Finally, the Maríns point out that people of Spanish descent typically maintain closer physical contact than many non-Hispanics. Therefore, researchers who seat themselves across the room from their subjects may come across as "stand-offish." Conversely, researchers may inaccurately label Hispanics "pushy" when they move closer than a non-Hispanic researcher may find comfortable.

Of course, Hispanics differ among themselves just as people in any category do, and these generalizations apply to some more than to others. But investigators should be aware of cultural dynamics when carrying out any research, especially in the United States where hundreds of distinctive categories of people make up this multicultural society.

Source: Marín & Marín (1991).

and risks and agree—before the work begins—to take part in the study.

Another guideline concerns funding. Sociologists must include in their published results any sources of financial support. Furthermore, sociologists must avoid conflicts of interest (or even the appearance of such conflict) that may compromise the integrity of their work. For example, researchers must never accept funding from any organization that seeks to influence the research results for its own purposes.

Finally, there are global dimensions to research ethics. Before beginning work in another nation, investigators must become familiar enough with that society to understand what people *there* are likely to see as a violation of privacy or a source of personal danger. In a multicultural society such as our own, of course, the same rule applies to studying people whose background differs from one's own. The box offers tips about how outsiders can use sensitivity when studying Hispanic communities.

RESEARCH METHODS

A **research method** is *a systematic plan for conducting research*. Here we introduce four widely used methods of sociological investigation: experiments, surveys, participant observation, and use of existing sources. None is better or worse than any other. Rather, in the same way that a carpenter selects a particular tool for a particular task, researchers choose a method according to whom they wish to study and what they wish to learn.

TESTING A HYPOTHESIS: THE EXPERIMENT

The **experiment** is *a research method for investigating cause and effect under highly controlled conditions*. Experiments test a specific *hypothesis*, that is, a statement of a possible relationship between two (or more) variables. A hypothesis is really an educated guess about how variables are linked. An experimenter gathers the evidence needed to accept or reject the hypothesis in three steps: (1) measuring the dependent variable (the "effect"), (2) exposing the dependent variable to the independent variable (the "cause" or "treatment"), and (3) measuring the dependent variable again to see if the predicted change took place. If the expected change took place, the experiment supports the hypothesis; if not, the hypothesis must be modified.

Successful experiments depend on carefully controlling all factors that might affect what is being measured. Control is easiest in a laboratory, an artificial setting specially constructed for this purpose. But experiments in an everyday location—"in the field," as sociologists say—have the advantage of letting researchers observe subjects in their natural settings.

ASKING QUESTIONS: THE SURVEY

A **survey** is *a research method in which subjects respond to a series of statements or questions in a questionnaire or an interview*. The most widely used of all research strategies, the survey is well suited to studying what cannot be observed directly, such as political attitudes or religious beliefs.

A survey targets some *population*, such as unmarried mothers or adults living in rural counties of Wisconsin. Sometimes every adult in the country is the survey population, as in polls taken during national political campaigns. Of course, contacting a vast number of people is all but impossible, so researchers usually study a *sample*, a much smaller number of cases selected to represent the entire population. Surveys commonly provide accurate estimates of national opinions based on samples of only 1,500 people.

The survey must have a specific plan for asking questions and recording answers. The most common way to do this is to give subjects a *questionnaire* with a series of written statements or questions. Often the researcher lets subjects choose possible responses to each item as in a multiple-choice examination. Sometimes, though, a researcher may want subjects to respond freely, as a way of teasing out shades of opinion. Of course, this free-form approach means that the researcher later has to make sense out of what can be a bewildering array of answers.

In an *interview*, a researcher personally asks subjects a series of questions, thereby overcoming one problem typical of the questionnaire method—the failure of some subjects to return the questionnaire to the researcher. A further difference is that interviews afford participants considerable freedom to respond as they wish. Researchers often ask follow-up questions to clarify an answer or to probe a bit more deeply. In doing this, however, a researcher must avoid influencing the subject even in subtle ways, such as by raising an eyebrow as the subject offers an answer.

IN THE FIELD: PARTICIPANT OBSERVATION

Participant observation is *a research method by which investigators systematically observe people while joining in their routine activities*. This strategy lets researchers study social life in any natural setting, from a motorcycle club to a religious seminary. Cultural anthropologists use participant observation to study other societies, calling this method "fieldwork."

Researchers may begin with few specific hypotheses, unsure of what the important questions will turn out to be. Compared to experiments and surveys, participant observation has few hard and fast rules. Flexibility can be an advantage, though, since investigators often must adapt to unexpected circumstances in an unfamiliar environment.

Participant observers try to gain entry into a setting without disturbing the routine behavior of others. To do this, they take on a dual role. On the one hand, to gain an insider's viewpoint, they must become a participant in the setting—"hanging out" for months or even years, trying to act, think, and even feel the same way as the people they are observing. On the other hand, the researcher must remain an "observer," standing back from the action and applying the sociological perspective to social patterns that others take for granted.

TABLE 1–3 Four Research Methods: A Summary			
Method	**Application**	**Advantages**	**Limitations**
Experiment	For explanatory research that specifies relationships among variables; generates quantitative data	Provides the greatest opportunity to specify cause-and-effect relationships; replication of research is relatively easy	Laboratory settings have an artificial quality; unless the research environment is carefully controlled, results may be biased
Survey	For gathering information about issues that cannot be directly observed, such as attitudes and values; useful for descriptive and explanatory research; generates quantitative or qualitative data	Sampling, using questionnaires, allows surveys of large populations; interviews provide in-depth responses	Questionnaires must be carefully prepared and may yield a low return rate; interviews are expensive and time-consuming
Participant observation	For exploratory and descriptive study of people in a "natural" setting; generates qualitative data	Allows study of "natural" behavior; usually inexpensive	Time-consuming; replication of research is difficult; researcher must balance roles of participant and observer
Existing sources	For exploratory, descriptive, or explanatory research whenever suitable data are available	Saves time and expense of data collection; makes historical research possible	Researcher has no control over possible biases in data; data may only partially fit current research needs

Because the personal impressions of a researcher play such a central role, critics claim that participant observation lacks scientific rigor. Yet its personal approach is also a strength: Where a high-profile team of sociologists administering a formal survey might disrupt a setting, a sensitive participant-observer can often gain considerable insight into people's natural behavior.

THE SECOND TIME AROUND: EXISTING SOURCES

Not all research requires collecting new data. In many cases, sociologists save time and money by using existing sources, analyzing data collected by others.

The most widely used data are gathered by government agencies such as the U.S. Census Bureau (for easy access to many data links, visit http://www.thesociologypage.com). Data about other nations in the world are found in various publications of the United Nations and the World Bank.

Drawing on available data is appealing to sociologists with low budgets, and the data are often better than what researchers could hope to obtain on their own. However, data may not be available in the specific form a researcher may wish, and it may be difficult to know how accurate the data are. In his nineteenth-century study of suicide, described earlier,

Emile Durkheim used official records. But Durkheim knew that some recorded suicides were probably really accidents just as some true suicides were never recorded as such.

Characteristics of the four major methods of sociological investigation we have introduced are summarized in Table 1–3.

PUTTING IT ALL TOGETHER: TEN STEPS IN SOCIOLOGICAL RESEARCH

The following ten questions will guide you through a research project in sociology:

1. **What is your topic?** Curiosity—and using the sociological perspective—will generate ideas for social research everywhere. Pick a topic you find important to study.

2. **What have others already learned?** Visit the library and, perhaps, search online to learn what theories and methods others have applied to the topic. What problems did others have studying your topic?

3. **What, exactly, are your questions?** Are you seeking to explore an unfamiliar setting? To describe some category of people? Or to investigate cause and effect among variables? Clearly

CONTROVERSY & DEBATE

Is Sociology Nothing More than Stereotypes?

"Protestants are the ones who kill themselves!"

"People in the United States? They're rich, they love to marry, and they love to divorce!"

"Everybody knows that you have to be black to play professional basketball!"

Everyone—including sociologists—makes generalizations. But many beginning students of sociology may wonder how sociological generalizations differ from simple stereotypes.

The three statements above are examples of a **stereotype,** *an exaggerated description that is applied to every person in some category.* First, rather than describing averages, each statement paints every individual in some category with the same brush; second, each ignores facts and distorts reality (even though many stereotypes do contain an element of truth); third, each sounds more like a "put down" than a fair-minded assertion.

Good sociology, by contrast, involves generalizations, but with three conditions. *First, sociologists do not indiscriminately apply any generalization to all individuals. Second, sociologists are careful that a generalization squares with available facts. Third, sociologists offer generalizations fair-mindedly, with an interest in getting at the truth.*

Earlier in this chapter, we noted that the suicide rate among Protestants is higher than the rate for Catholics or Jews. However, the statement "Protestants are the ones who kill themselves" is not a reasonable generalization because the vast majority of Protestants do no such thing. Furthermore, it would be wrong to assume that a particular friend, since he is a Protestant male, is on the verge of self-destruction. (Imagine yourself refusing to lend some money to him, explaining "Well, given your risk of suicide, I might never get paid back!")

Second, sociologists shape their generalizations to available facts. A more factual version of the second statement is that, by world standards, the U.S. population, on average, has a very high standard of living. It is also true that our marriage rate is one of the highest in the world, and although few people take pleasure in divorcing, so is our divorce rate.

Third, sociologists strive to be fair-minded, and they have a passion for truth. The last of the box-opening statements, about African Americans and basketball, is not good sociology for two reasons. First, it is simply not true, and, second, it seems motivated by bias rather than truth-seeking.

Good sociology, then, stands apart from harmful stereotyping. But a sociology course is an excellent setting for talking over common stereotypes. The classroom encourages discussion and offers the factual information you need to decide if a particular belief is valid or just a stereotype.

Continue the debate . . .

1. *Do people in the United States have stereotypes of sociologists? What are they? Are they valid?*

2. *Do you think taking a sociology course dispels people's stereotypes? Why or why not?*

3. *Can you cite a stereotype of your own that sociology challenges?*

---

state the goals of your research and operationalize all variables.

4. **What will you need to carry out research?** How much time and money are available to you? What special equipment or skills does the research require? Can you do all the work yourself?

5. **Are there ethical concerns?** Can the research harm anyone? How can you minimize the chances for injury? Will you promise your subjects anonymity? If so, how will you ensure that anonymity will be maintained?

6. **What method will you use?** Consider all major research strategies, as well as combinations of approaches. The best method depends on the kinds of questions you are asking as well as the resources available to you.

7. **How will you record the data?** The research method you use guides your data collection. Be sure to record information accurately and in a way that will make sense later on (it may be months before you actually write up the results of your work). Watch out for any bias that may creep into your work.

8. **What do the data tell you?** Study the data in terms of your initial questions and decide how to interpret the data. If your study involves a specific hypothesis, you should be able to confirm, reject, or modify it based on your findings. Keep in mind that there will be several ways to interpret your results, depending on the theoretical paradigm you apply, and you should consider them all.

9. **What are your conclusions?** Prepare a final report indicating what you have learned. Also, evaluate your own work. What problems arose during the research process? What questions were left unanswered?

10. **How can you share what you have learned?** Consider making a presentation to a class, or maybe even to a meeting of professional sociologists. The important point is to share what you have learned with others and to let them respond to your work.

To review many of the issues raised in this chapter, the final box examines how sociological generalizations differ from common stereotypes.

SUMMARY

1. The sociological perspective shows that the general operation of society affects the experiences of particular people. In this way, sociology helps us better understand barriers and opportunities in our lives.

2. Early social thinkers focused on what society *ought to be.* Sociology, named by Auguste Comte in 1838, uses scientific methods to understand society *as it is.*

3. The development of sociology was triggered by the rapid transformation of Europe during the eighteenth and nineteenth centuries. The rise of an industrial economy, the explosive growth of cities, and the emergence of new political ideas combined to weaken tradition and make people more aware of their social world.

4. Theory is the process of linking facts to create meaning. Sociologists use theoretical paradigms to guide theory building.

5. The structural-functional paradigm is a framework for exploring how social structures work together to promote the overall operation of society.

6. The social-conflict paradigm highlights dimensions of social inequality that generate conflict and promote change.

7. In contrast to these macro-level approaches, the symbolic-interaction paradigm is a micro-level framework for studying how people, in everyday interaction, construct reality.

8. Sociological research uses the logic of science, based on empirical evidence we confirm with our senses.

9. Measurement is the process of giving a value to a variable in a specific case. Sound measurement is both reliable and valid.

10. Science seeks to specify the relationships among variables. Ideally, researchers try to identify how one (independent) variable causes change in another (dependent) variable.

11. Although researchers select topics according to their personal interests, the scientific ideal of objectivity demands that they try to suspend personal values and biases as they conduct research.

12. Interpretive sociology is a methodological approach that focuses on the meaning that people attach to behavior. Reality is not "out there" (as scientific sociology claims) but is constructed by people in their everyday interaction.

13. Critical sociology is a methodological approach that uses research to bring about social change. It rejects the scientific principle of objectivity, claiming that all research has a political character.

14. Because their work can harm subjects, professional sociologists must observe ethical guidelines when conducting research.

15. The logic of science is most clearly expressed in the experiment, which investigates cause-and-effect relationships between two (or more) variables under controlled, laboratory conditions.

16. A survey uses either a questionnaire or an interview to gather subjects' responses to a series of questions.

17. Participant observation involves joining with people in a social setting for an extended period of time.

18. Often sociologists use existing sources rather than collect their own data; doing so is attractive to researchers with limited research budgets.

19. Sociologists make generalizations about categories of people. Unlike stereotypes, these sociological statements (1) are not applied indiscriminately to all individuals, (2) are supported by research-based facts, and (3) are put forward in the fair-minded pursuit of truth.

KEY CONCEPTS

sociology (p. 1) the systematic study of human society

global perspective (p. 5) the study of the larger world and our society's place in it

high-income countries (p. 6) nations with very productive economic systems in which most people have relatively high incomes

middle-income countries (p. 6) nations with moderately productive economic systems in which people's incomes are about the global average

low-income countries (p. 6) nations with less productive economic systems in which most people are poor

positivism (p. 9) a way of understanding based on science

theory (p. 10) a statement of how and why specific facts are related

theoretical paradigm (p. 11) a basic image of society that guides thinking and research

structural-functional paradigm (p. 11) a framework for building theory that sees society as a complex system whose parts work together to promote solidarity and stability

social structure (p. 11) any relatively stable pattern of social behavior

social functions (p. 11) the consequences of any social pattern for the operation of society as a whole

manifest functions (p. 11) the recognized and intended consequences of any social pattern

latent functions (p. 11) the unrecognized and unintended consequences of any social pattern

social dysfunctions (p. 12) a social pattern's undesirable consequences for the operation of society

social-conflict paradigm (p. 12) a framework for building theory that sees society as an arena of inequality that generates conflict and change

macro-level orientation (p. 13) a concern with broad patterns that shape society as a whole

micro-level orientation (p. 13) a close-up focus on social interaction in specific situations

symbolic-interaction paradigm (p. 13) a framework for building theory that sees society as the product of the everyday interactions of individuals

science (p. 14) a logical system that bases knowledge on direct, systematic observation

concept (p. 15) a mental construct that represents some part of the world in a simplified form

variable (p. 15) a concept whose value changes from case to case

measurement (p. 15) a procedure for determining the value of a variable in a specific case

reliability (p. 15) consistency in measurement

validity (p. 15) precision in measuring exactly what one intends to measure

correlation (p. 15) a relationship by which two (or more) variables change together

cause and effect (p. 15) a relationship in which we know that change in one (independent) variable causes change in another (dependent) variable

interpretive sociology (p. 19) the study of society that focuses on the meanings people attach to their social world

critical sociology (p. 19) the study of society that focuses on the need for social change

gender (p. 20) the personal traits and social positions that members of a society attach to being female and male

research method (p. 22) a systematic plan for conducting research

experiment (p. 22) a research method for investigating cause and effect under highly controlled conditions

survey (p. 22) a research method in which subjects respond to a series of statements or questions in a questionnaire or an interview

participant observation (p. 22) a research method by which investigators systematically observe people while joining in their routine activities

stereotype (p. 24) an exaggerated description that is applied to every person in some category

CRITICAL-THINKING QUESTIONS

1. In what ways does using the sociological perspective make us seem less in control of our lives? In what ways does it give us greater power over our surroundings?

2. Consider the following argument: Sociology would not have arisen if human behavior were strictly due to biological instincts (as is, say, the highly predictable behavior of ants); nor would sociology exist if human behavior were utterly chaotic. Sociology thrives because humans are partly guided by social structure and partly free.

3. What factors explain why sociology developed where and when it did?

4. Guided by the discipline's three major theoretical paradigms, what kinds of questions might a sociologist ask about (a) television, (b) war, (c) humor, and (d) colleges and universities?

APPLICATIONS AND EXERCISES

1. Packaged in the back of this new textbook is an interactive CD-ROM that offers a variety of study, review, and applications exercises intended to help you better understand the material covered in this chapter. The CD includes an author's tip video for this chapter, interactive maps, video application exercises, Web links, and study questions.

2. Spend several hours exploring your local community. Are there clear residential patterns? That is, do various neighborhoods contain certain categories of people? As best you can, identify who lives where. What social forces explain such patterns?

3. Look ahead to Figure 13–3 on page 347, which shows the U.S. divorce rate over the last century. What societal factors pushed the divorce rate down after 1930, up after 1940, down in 1950, up again after 1960, and down again after 1980?

4. During a class, carefully observe the behavior of the instructor and other students. What patterns do you see in how people use space? Regarding who speaks? Regarding what categories of people are there in the first place?

5. Say you were going to observe your sociology instructor to assess that individual's teaching skills. How would you operationalize the concept "good teaching"? What exactly would you look for? Do you think students are the best judges of good and bad teaching?

6. Conduct a practice interview with a roommate or friend on the topic "What is the value of a college education?" Before the actual interview, prepare a list of specific questions or issues you think are relevant. Afterward, give some thought to why conducting a good interview is much harder than it initially may seem.

 SITES TO SEE

http://www.prenhall.com/macionis

The author and publisher of this book invite you to visit the interactive Web site that accompanies this text. Begin by clicking on the cover of your book. You will find a chapter-by-chapter study guide, practice tests, chat room, and many suggested Web links.

http://www.asanet.org

At the American Sociological Association's Web site, read their "Code of Ethics" to get a better idea of the ethical concerns surrounding sociological research.

http://www.thesociologypage.com
(or http://www.macionis.com)

The author maintains this Web site (use either address) where you will find information about sociology, as well as a Links Library that will connect you with dozens of other interesting sites.

http://www.census.gov/datamap/www

Many kinds of data for any county in the United States are available from the U.S. Census Bureau at this Web site. You can use the data to prepare a sociological profile of your local area.

cyber.scope

WELCOME TO THE INFORMATION REVOLUTION!

Now that we have begun the new century—and a new millennium—we are witnessing astounding changes brought on by a new kind of technology. For the last two centuries, the Industrial Revolution has shaped our society, dictating the kind of work people do and how we think about the world. But now another transformation is underway—dubbed the Information Revolution—that is already redefining our world in novel ways.

At the end of each of the five parts of this text, we present a special section called "cyber.scope." These features highlight how computers and new information technology affect the issues raised in the preceding chapters. In this first cyber.scope, we extend our discussion of the sociological perspective and sociological research (Chapter 1) to explain what the Information Revolution is all about.

The Age of Machines: Industrial Society

The time line found inside the front cover of this book places the onset of the "modern era" about 250 years ago, the dawn of the Industrial Revolution. At that time—first in England then soon after in the United States—new sources of energy led imaginative people to create new products in new ways. First rivers and then steam generated by coal furnaces provided the power to operate large machines. Soon afterward, the Industrial Revolution

was changing all aspects of social life, drawing people away from home to work in the new factories and demanding that they learn the skills needed to operate machinery. As time went on, the increasing size and number of factories encouraged migration from the countryside to rapidly growing cities where most people experienced a faster-paced, more impersonal way of life and, in time, came to enjoy a higher material

Familiarity with computers is far more common among younger members of our society than older generations. Today's young people, who will live out their lives during the twenty-first century, will find computers a natural and indispensable part of day-to-day living.

standard of living. As we have noted, these changes sparked people's interest in studying society and played a key role in the birth of sociology.

The Age of Computers: Information Society

The final decades of the twentieth century witnessed the unfolding of another technological transformation—the Information Revolution—which is changing our world once again. The technology that will define the twenty-first century is based on *information:* the computer and related technology, including the Internet, facsimile machines, modems, hand-held computers, and cellular telephones, as well as fiber optics and satellite communications. We already have shorthand names for such devices—the "Net," "fax," "cell phone," and "dish"—suggesting how quickly they have become an established part of our lives.

The age of the computer began in 1946 when U.S. engineers in a Philadelphia laboratory switched on a room-sized machine stuffed with wires and vacuum tubes. Despite its giant size, this "mother of all computers" could do no more than today's ten-dollar hand-held calculator. No wonder Thomas Watson, head of IBM, thought his company would end up selling "maybe five computers." Thirty years later, Ken Olson, founder of Digital

Equipment Corporation, was just as skeptical, stating that "There is no reason anyone would want a computer in the home" (quoted in Lunsford, 1996).

For better or worse, these two men were quite wrong. In the final decades of the twentieth century, increasingly sophisticated computers quickly became a basic element of our lives. We now find microprocessors at work in virtually all new vehicles as well as in the vast majority of U.S. businesses and households. Surveys show that, in 2000, 56 percent of U.S. households had at least one personal computer, with most of these connected to the Internet. As computers become more numerous—as well as more powerful, smaller, and portable—they will rewrite the rules of social life in the twenty-first century just as monstrous machines defined the industrial era now coming to a close.

What's different about new information technology? Most basically, the change involves the kind of work people do. Yesterday's industrial technology empowered people to create more and more *things;* information technology leads us to work with *ideas,* creating and manipulating symbols. The industrial age was represented by the factory's assembly line, with workers toiling to make steel or to assemble cars. But the typical worker in the information age peers at a computer screen, entering data, writing, calculating, composing, drawing, or designing.

A second key change brought about by the Information Revolution

The earliest computers, including the 1946 ENIAC (Electronic Numerical Integrator and Computer), were monstrous contraptions that filled an entire room. (In fact, in 1949, Popular Mechanics magazine confidently predicted that computers in the future would weigh no more than 1.5 tons!) It wasn't until the development of small, personal computers in the 1980s that the Information Revolution began to change the everyday lives of most people in the United States.

is a declining importance to distance and physical space. Just as industrial technology demands that people work in centralized factories (where the machinery and energy sources are located), information technology allows people to work almost anywhere that they can carry a computer or flip on a cell phone. Note, too, that when we use this technology to communicate with others, we often have no idea where they are. The term *cyberspace* even suggests that our emerging world is less and less bounded by physical dimensions.

Of course, just as we gauge the output of industrial engines with an antiquated reference to the "horsepower" they made obsolete, so we now cling to older, physical images

in describing new cyber-realities: We talk about the "information superhighway,"[1] read "bulletin boards," and enter "chat rooms." Yet these "places" are a "virtual reality," meaning that they are computer simulations that we see and interact with, but they have no physical existence at all. In fact, they exist only in the flow of electrons that illuminates our computer, electrons that can circle the world at the speed of light.

As later chapters of the text explain, this new technology is changing virtually every dimension of our lives: reshaping culture and how we learn about the world, connecting us to people in new ways, generating new kinds of crime as well as new ways of pursuing criminals, and even altering patterns of social inequality. There is little doubt that, as we move through the twenty-first century, we will see more changes that will spark people's sociological interest in the surrounding world.

New Information Technology: Thoughts on Theory

Chapter 1 ("Sociology: Perspective, Theory, and Method") discusses sociology's three major theoretical paradigms. What insights do these paradigms give us into new information technology?

---

[1] The rapidly increasing number of people logging on the Internet has overwhelmed existing telephone lines and sometimes results in long delays in transmitting and receiving information. Until broad-band access is more widespread, the "information superhighway" may remain more of a "dirt road."

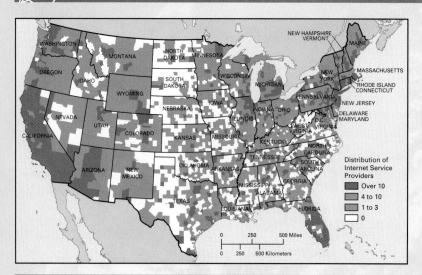

NATIONAL MAP Cyber I–1
Available Internet Service
across the United States

The counties that have the most Internet service providers are those with high population densities and, thus, large markets. These same counties also have a large number of affluent people who can afford to log on to the Information Revolution. Thus, while high technology is transforming the United States, the pace of change is faster in urban than rural areas.

Source: *Time*, March 22, 1999. Copyright © 1999, *Time*, Inc. Reprinted by permission.

Distribution of
Internet Service
Providers

- Over 10
- 4 to 10
- 1 to 3
- 0

A structural-functional analysis would point up the fact that, because society is a system of countless interdependent elements, a new form of technology is likely to affect virtually all aspects of our lives. Since the invention of television in 1939, more than 2 billion TV sets have been built (and their numbers are rising faster than global population). Television has altered what we know, how we learn, patterns of recreation, and even the ways family members interact. The computer will almost certainly change our lives even more. Its manifest (that is, intended and expected) effects will range from decentralizing the workplace to encouraging entire cities to spread outward, since talking to or working with others no longer requires being physically with them. The latent (that is, unintended) effects are certainly harder to foresee, but they may well include new kinds of human communities as people pay less attention to their physical neighbors and spend more time communicating online with like-minded others.

A social-conflict analysis of the rise of new information technology offers other, contrasting insights, especially regarding social inequality. Here, we might note that the spread of new information technology has been rapid among affluent people and those living in densely populated urban areas, but far less among the poor and rural people—a pattern illustrated in National Map Cyber I–1. There is already evidence that the information age will be marked by two distinct classes: educated people with sophisticated symbolic skills (who are likely to prosper) and people without symbolic skills (who are likely to remain in low-income jobs). Statistical comparisons show that, among workers in the same job, those able to use a computer earn 15 percent more than those who cannot (Ratan, 1995).

Finally, the symbolic-interaction paradigm asks questions at the micro-level of analysis. How, for example, does communication via electronic mail differ from face-to-face interaction? Obviously, lacking facial expression or tone of voice, electronic communication cannot convey emotion very well. For this reason, as shown in Figure Cyber I–1, people have creatively turned the characters found on their keyboards into new symbols, generating a new cyber-language.

New Information Technology: What about Research?

How is new information technology changing sociological research? A generation of sociologists has now been trained to use computers to select random samples, to perform complex statistical analysis, and to prepare written reports efficiently. Electronic mail enables researchers to "travel" almost anywhere instantly and with minimal cost. In the coming years, more and more surveys will take place online. Electronic surveys raise some interesting questions: Will this technology improve survey response rates or be discarded as electronic junk mail? Will cyber-surveys end up protecting respondents' anonymity or threatening their privacy?

What seems sure is that new information technology will greatly enhance communication among researchers throughout the world. The Internet, which is highlighted in the next cyber.scope on pages 184–85, now links almost 300 million people in nearly 180 countries. It gives sociologists a powerful tool for building networks, sharing information, and joining together to conduct research. Just as important, faculty and students alike now have ready access to a rapidly increasing amount of statistical information. For example, the U.S. Census Bureau (see its Web site at http://www.census.gov) publishes reports of all kinds online, and will respond to questions from individuals doing research of their own.

Visit Us Online!

Please accept our invitation to visit the Web site that accompanies this text. Travel to the author's home page, which can be found at http://www.thesociologypage.com (or http://www.macionis.com) to review our family of textbooks, read sociological news, view videos, and find a library of links to a wide range of interesting organizations. The author and publisher have prepared an interactive Web site that serves as a study guide to help you throughout this course. Visit it at http://www.prenhall.com/macionis and click on the cover of this book. There you will find learning objectives for each text chapter, self-scoring practice tests, a chat room where you can share ideas and opinions with others, and links to other instructive Web sites. These sites, along with the CD-ROM that is included with your new textbook, are our invitation to you to join the Information Revolution. Welcome, and enjoy!

FIGURE Cyber I–1 Cyber-Symbols: An Emerging Language

It all started with the "smiley" figure that shows one is happy or telling a joke. Now a new language of gestures is emerging as creative people use computer keystrokes to create emoticons, symbols that convey thoughts and emotions. Here is a sampling of the new cyber-language. (Rotate this page 90° to the right to appreciate the emoticon faces below.)

: -)	I'm smiling at you.
: `-)	I'm so happy (laughing so hard) that I'm starting to cry.
: - O	Wow!
: - x	My lips are sealed!
: -||	I'm angry with you!
: - P	I'm sticking my tongue out at you!
: - (	I feel sad.
: - |	Things look grim . . . .
% -}	I think I've had too much to drink . . . .
-:(	Somebody cut my hair into a mohawk!
+O:-)	I've just been elected Pope!
@}——>———	Here's a rose for you!

Computers are as popular in Japan as they are in the United States. The Japanese have their own emoticons:

(^_^)	I'm smiling at you.
(*^o^*)	This is exciting!
(^o^)	I am happy.
\(^o^)/	Banzai! This is wonderful!

How far will this new keyboard language go? If you're creative enough, anything is possible. Here's a routine that has been making the rounds on the Internet. It's called "Mr. Asciihead learns the Macarena"! To see Mr. Asciihead in action, go to one of the "Fun Links" at http://www.thesociologypage.com

```
o       o       o       o       o      <o     <o>     o>      o
.l.     \l.     \l/     //      X       \      l      <l     <l>
/\      >\      /<      >\      /<      >\     /<      >\     /<
```

Sources: Pollack (1996) and Krantz (1997). "Mr. Asciihead" is the creation of Leow Yee Ling.

CULTURE

It all began back in 1971 when Cindy Campbell, a young teen in New York's Bronx, needed some back-to-school money. Cindy had an idea. She asked her big brother Clive to throw a party. In Jamaica, where the two had grown up, Clive had loved music and been fascinated by the happy crowds that filled dance halls.

The party was a smash, lasting until 4:00 in the morning. Clive handled the music; Cindy worked the door, collecting 25 cents from each girl and 50 cents from each boy. The two made a lot more money than they had expected. But Cindy's idea ended up doing far more. She and Clive started a musical revolution that would end up changing our way of life.

In the months after the event, Clive got invitations to do other parties. By 1973, he had taken the name "Kool Herc," and was hosting parties that attracted thousands of people. As the country's first break-beat deejay, he delighted listeners as he recited rhymes over the records he played, beginning a new form of music we now call "rap."

The whole scene caught on. By the end of the 1970s, deejays everywhere were spinning disks, reciting rhymes, and mixing in a distinctive "scratching" sound. In 1979, the Sugarhill Gang performed "Rapper's Delight," rap's first national hit. Rap had arrived coast to coast. Soon after, performers like RUN-D.M.C., Beastie Boys, 2 Live Crew, Sister Souljah, and Snoop Doggy Dogg took up the musical revolution.

How big is rap music now? By the end of the 1990s, based on record sales, rap had surpassed country music and even rock and roll as the most popular form of music

in the United States.[1] Indeed, the entire hip-hop culture— not only music, but fashion and films as well—is now a familiar part of life for most young people.

The United States is clearly a nation with many ways of life. Understanding what we mean by "culture" and how we became a multicultural society is the focus of this chapter. In global perspective, of course, ways of life differ even more. The 6.2 billion people living on the earth are all members of a single biological species: *Homo sapiens*. Even so, differences among people within the United States, and more so around the world, can delight, puzzle, disturb, and sometimes overwhelm us.

Many differences in lifestyle barely matter. Australians, for example, flip switches "down" to put lights "on," whereas North Americans flip them "up." The Australians, British, and Japanese all drive on the left side of the road, while we drive on the right. Some differences are quite charming. Take the practice of kissing: Most people in the United States kiss in public, but the Chinese kiss only in private. The French kiss publicly twice (once on each cheek), while Belgians kiss three times (starting on either cheek). New Zealand Maoris rub noses, while most Nigerians don't kiss at all. In a marriage ceremony, U.S. couples kiss,

---

[1]Opening adapted from Farley (1999).

Human beings around the globe create diverse ways of life. Such differences begin with outward appearance: Contrast the women shown here from Brazil, Kenya, New Guinea, and Morocco, and the men from Taiwan (Republic of China), India, Peru, and New Guinea. Less obvious, but of even greater importance, are internal differences, since culture also shapes our goals in life, our sense of justice, and even our innermost personal feelings.

Koreans bow, and a Cambodian groom touches his nose to the bride's cheek.

Some cultural differences, however, are more profound. The world over, people have many or few children, honor or push aside the elderly, are peaceful or warlike, embrace different religious beliefs, and enjoy different kinds of art and music. In short, although we are the same creatures biologically, human beings have developed very different ideas about what is pleasant and repulsive, polite and rude, beautiful and ugly, right and wrong. This capacity for startling difference is expressed through culture.

WHAT IS CULTURE?

Culture refers to *the values, beliefs, behavior, and material objects that, together, form a people's way of life.* When studying culture, sociologists often distinguish between thoughts and things. *Nonmaterial culture* includes intangible human creations ranging from altruism to zen; *material culture* refers to tangible creations of a society, everything from armaments to zippers. The terms *culture* and *society* obviously go hand in hand, but their precise meanings differ. Culture is a shared way of life or social heritage; **society** refers to *people who interact in a defined territory and share culture.* Neither society nor culture could exist without the other.

Not only does culture shape what we do, it helps form our personalities—what we commonly, but inaccurately, describe as "human nature." The warlike Yąnomamö of the Brazilian rain forest think aggressiveness is natural, while, halfway around the world, the Semai of Malaysia live in peace and cooperation. The cultures of the United States and Japan both stress achievement and hard work; but members of our society value individualism more than the Japanese, who are more traditional and group-oriented.

Given the cultural differences in the world and people's tendency to view their own way of life as "natural," it is no wonder that travelers may experience **culture shock**, *personal disorientation when experiencing an unfamiliar way of life.* The box on page 36 presents one researcher's personal experience of cultural shock.

December 1, 1994, Istanbul, Turkey. Harbors everywhere, it seems, have two things in common: ships and cats. Istanbul, the tenth port on our voyage, is awash with felines, prowling about in search of an easy meal. People certainly change from place to place—but not cats.

Behavior people in one society consider routine can be chilling to members of another culture. In the Russian city of St. Petersburg, this young mother and her six-week-old son brave the 17°F temperatures for a dip in a nearby lake. To Russians, this is something of a national pastime. To some members of our society, however, this practice may seem cruel or even dangerous.

No way of life is "natural" to humanity, even though most people around the world view their own behavior that way. What is natural to our species is the capacity to create culture. Every other form of life—from ants to zebras—behaves in fixed, species-specific ways. To a world traveler, the enormous diversity of human life stands out in contrast to the behavior of, say, cats, which is the same everywhere. This uniformity follows from the fact that most living creatures are guided by *instincts*, biological programming over which animals have no control. A few animals—notably chimpanzees and related primates—have a limited capacity for culture, and researchers have observed them using tools and teaching simple skills to their offspring. But the creative power of humans far exceeds that of any other form of life. In short, *only humans rely on culture rather than instinct to ensure the survival of their kind* (Harris, 1987). To understand how human culture came to be, we need to look back at the history of our species.

GLOBAL SOCIOLOGY

Confronting the Yąnomamö:
The Experience of Culture Shock

A small aluminum motorboat chugged steadily along the muddy Orinoco River, deep within South America's vast tropical rain forest. Anthropologist Napoleon Chagnon was nearing the end of a three-day journey to the home territory of the Yąnomamö, one of the most technologically simple societies on earth.

Some 12,000 Yąnomamö live in villages scattered along the border of Venezuela and Brazil. Their way of life could hardly be more different from our own. The Yąnomamö wear little clothing and live without electricity, cars, or other conveniences most people in the United States take for granted. They use bows and arrows for hunting and warfare, as they have for centuries. Many of the Yąnomamö have had little contact with the outside world, so Chagnon would be as strange to them as they would be to him.

By 2:00 in the afternoon, Chagnon had almost reached his destination. The hot sun and humid air were becoming unbearable. Chagnon's clothes were soaked with perspiration, and his face and hands swelled from the bites of gnats swarming around him. But he scarcely noticed, so preoccupied was he with the fact that in just

a few moments he would be face to face with people unlike any he had ever known.

Chagnon's heart pounded as the boat slid onto the riverbank. He and his guide climbed from the boat and walked toward the Yąnomamö village, stooping as they pushed their way through the dense undergrowth. Chagnon describes what happened next.

> I looked up and gasped when I saw a dozen burly, naked, sweaty, hideous men staring at us down the shafts of their drawn arrows! Immense wads of green tobacco were stuck between their lower teeth and lips, making them look even more hideous, and strands of

dark green slime dripped or hung from their nostrils—strands so long that they clung to their [chests] or drizzled down their chins.

> My next discovery was that there were a dozen or so vicious, underfed dogs snapping at my legs, circling me as if I were to be their next meal. I just stood there holding my notebook, helpless and pathetic. Then the stench of the decaying vegetation and filth hit me and I almost got sick. I was horrified. What kind of welcome was this for the person who came here to live with you and learn your way of life, to become friends with you? (1992:11–12)

Fortunately for Chagnon, the Yąnomamö villagers recognized his guide and lowered their weapons. Reassured that he would survive the afternoon, Chagnon still was shaken by his inability to make any sense of these people. And this was to be his home for a year and a half! He wondered why he had forsaken physics to study human culture in the first place.

Source: Chagnon (1992).

CULTURE AND HUMAN INTELLIGENCE

In a universe 15 billion years old, our planet is a much younger 4.5 billion years of age (see the time lines inside the front cover of this text). Not for a billion years after the planet was formed did life appear. Several billion more years went by before dinosaurs ruled the earth, only to disappear. It was then—some 65

million years ago—that our history took a crucial turn with the appearance of the creatures we call primates.

What sets primates apart is their intelligence: They have the largest brains relative to body size of all living creatures. About 12 million years ago, primates began to develop along two different lines, setting apart humans from the great apes, our closest relatives. But our common lineage is evident in traits that

People throughout the world communicate not just with spoken words but also with bodily gestures, which vary from culture to culture. To most North Americans, there is nothing unusual about the young woman shown in the left-hand photo. But to people living in Muslim societies—who typically use the left hand for bathroom hygiene—eating this way is disturbing, to say the least! Similarly, the familiar "A-OK" gesture, by which we express approval and pleasure, is likely to insult a French person, who "reads" the message as "You're worth zero." Finally, even the commonplace "thumbs up" gesture we take to mean "Good job!" can get you into trouble in Australia, where people take it to mean "Up yours!"

humans share today with chimpanzees, gorillas, and orangutans: great sociability, affectionate and long-lasting bonds for child rearing and mutual protection, the ability to walk upright (normal in humans, but less common among other primates), and hands that manipulate objects with great precision.

Fossil records show that, some 3 million years ago, our distant human ancestors grasped cultural fundamentals like the use of fire, tools, and weapons, and were able to create simple shelters and fashion basic clothing. These Stone Age achievements may seem modest, but they mark the point at which our ancestors embarked on a distinct evolutionary course—making culture their primary strategy for survival.

Culture, then, is relatively recent and was a long time in the making. As culture became a strategy for survival, our forebears descended from the trees into the tall grasses of central Africa. There, they learned the advantages of hunting in groups. As mental capacity expanded, our species emerged as *Homo sapiens*, Latin for "thinking person." Humans became the only species that names itself, and the biological forces we call instincts gave way to a more efficient survival scheme: *Human beings developed the mental power to fashion the natural environment for themselves.* Ever since, humans have made and remade their worlds in countless ways, which explains today's fascinating cultural diversity.

THE COMPONENTS OF CULTURE

Although cultures vary greatly, they all have common components, including symbols, language, values, and norms. We shall begin with the one that underlies all the others: symbols.

SYMBOLS

Like all creatures, human beings sense the surrounding world, but unlike others, we also create a reality of *meaning*. Humans transform the elements of the world into **symbols,** *anything that carries a particular meaning recognized by people who share culture.* A word, a whistle, a wall of graffiti, a flashing red light, a raised fist—all serve as symbols. We see the human capacity to create and manipulate symbols reflected in the variety of meanings associated with the simple act of winking the eye, which can convey interest, understanding, or insult.

For the most part, we are so dependent on our culture's symbols that we take them for granted. We become keenly aware of the importance of a symbol, however, when someone uses it in an unconventional way as, for instance, when a person burns a U.S. flag during a political demonstration. Entering an unfamiliar culture also reminds us of the power of symbols; culture shock is really the inability to "read" meaning in new surroundings. Not understanding the symbols of a culture leaves a person feeling lost and isolated, unsure of how to act and sometimes frightened.

Culture shock is a two-way process. On the one hand, the traveler *experiences* culture shock when meeting people whose way of life is different. For example, North Americans who consider dogs beloved household pets might be put off by the Masai of eastern Africa, who ignore them and never feed them. The same travelers might be horrified to find that in parts of Indonesia and in the northern regions of the People's Republic of China, people roast dogs for dinner!

On the other hand, a traveler *inflicts* culture shock on others by acting in ways that offend them. A North American who asks for a cheeseburger in an Indian restaurant offends Hindus, who consider cows sacred and never to be eaten. Indeed, global travel provides endless opportunities for misunderstanding. When in an unfamiliar setting, we need to remember that even behavior that seems innocent and normal to us can offend others, as the photos on page 37 suggest.

Then, too, symbolic meanings also vary within a single society. In the debate about flying the Confederate flag over the South Carolina state house, some people saw the flag as a symbol of regional pride; most people, however, saw the same flag as a symbol of racial oppression.

LANGUAGE

The heart of a symbolic system is **language,** *a system of symbols that allows people to communicate with one another.* Humans have devised hundreds of alphabets, and even conventions for writing differ: Most people in Western societies write from left to right, while people in northern Africa and western Asia write right to left, and people in eastern Asia write from top to bottom. Global Map 2–1 shows where in the world one finds the three most widely spoken languages.

Language not only facilitates communication, it also ensures the continuity of culture. Language—whether spoken or written—is a cultural heritage in coded form; it is the key to **cultural transmission,** *the process by which one generation passes culture to the next.* Just as our bodies contain the genes of our ancestors, so our cultural heritage contains countless symbols of those who came before us. Language is the key that unlocks centuries of accumulated wisdom.

Language skills may link us to the past, but they also spark the human imagination. Connecting symbols in new ways, we can imagine an almost limitless range of future possibilities. Language sets apart human beings as the only creatures who are self-conscious, aware of our limitations and ultimate mortality, yet able to dream and hope for a future better than the present.

The Sapir-Whorf thesis. Do the Chinese, who think using one language, experience the world differently from North Americans who think in, say, English or Spanish? The answer is yes, because each language has its own distinct symbols that serve as the building blocks of reality.

Edward Sapir and Benjamin Whorf proposed that languages are not just different sets of labels for the same reality (Sapir, 1929, 1949; Whorf, 1956). Rather, each symbolic system is at least partly unique, with words or expressions that have no precise counterpart in another symbolic system. In addition, as multilingual people know, a single idea may "feel" different if spoken in Spanish rather than in English or Chinese (Falk, 1987). Formally, the **Sapir-Whorf thesis** holds that *people perceive the world through the cultural lens of language.*

VALUES AND BELIEFS

What accounts for the popularity of movie characters like James Bond, Dirty Harry, Rambo, and Erin Brockovich? Each is ruggedly individualistic, relying on personal skill and savvy to challenge "the system." In applauding such characters, we are endorsing certain **values,** *culturally defined standards by which people assess desirability, goodness, and beauty, and which serve as broad guidelines for social living.* Values are statements, from the standpoint of a culture, of what ought to be.

Values are broad principles that underlie **beliefs,** *specific statements that people hold to be true.* In other words, values are abstract standards of goodness, while beliefs are particular matters people hold to be true or false. For example, because most U.S. adults share the value of providing equal opportunities for all, they believe that a qualified woman could serve as president (NORC, 1999).

U.S. values. Sociologist Robin Williams (1970) points to the following ten values as central to our way of life:

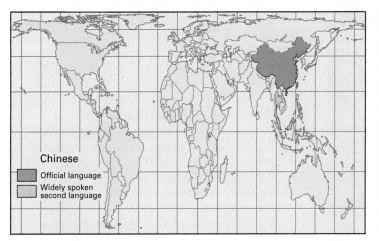

GLOBAL MAP 2–1
Language in Global Perspective

Chinese (including Mandarin, Cantonese, and dozens of other dialects) is the native tongue of one-fifth of the world's people, almost all of whom live in Asia. Although all Chinese people read and write with the same characters, they use several dozen dialects. The "official" dialect, taught in schools throughout the People's Republic of China and the Republic of Taiwan, is Mandarin (the dialect of Beijing, China's historic capital city). Cantonese, the language of Canton, is the second most common Chinese dialect; it differs in sound from Mandarin roughly the way French differs from Spanish.

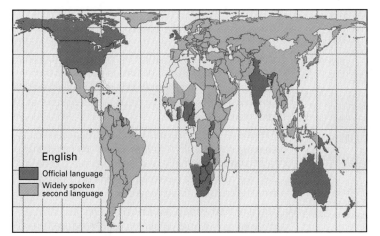

English is the native tongue or official language in several world regions (spoken by 10 percent of humanity) and has become the preferred second language in most of the world.

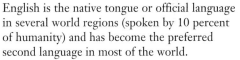

The largest concentration of Spanish speakers is in Latin America and, of course, Spain. Spanish is also the preferred second language of the United States.

Source: *Peters Atlas of the World* (1990).

Australian feminist artist Sally Swain alters a famous artist's painting to make fun of our culture's tendency to ignore the everyday lives of women. This spoof is entitled Mrs. Picasso Dusts the Mantlepiece.

1. **Equal opportunity.** People in the United States endorse not *equality of condition* but *equality of opportunity*. This means that society should provide everyone with the chance to get ahead according to individual talents and efforts.

2. **Achievement and success.** Our way of life encourages competition so that each person's rewards should reflect personal merit. Moreover, success confers worthiness on a person—the mantle of being a "winner."

3. **Material comfort.** Success in the United States generally means making money and enjoying what it will buy. Although people sometimes quip that "money won't buy happiness," most pursue wealth all the same.

4. **Activity and work.** Our heroes, from film's famed archaeologist Indiana Jones to golf champion Tiger Woods, are "doers" who get the job done. Our culture values *action* over *reflection*, and controlling events over passively accepting one's "fate."

5. **Practicality and efficiency.** People in the United States value the practical over the theoretical— "doing" over "dreaming." Activity has value to the extent that it earns money.

6. **Progress.** We are an optimistic people who, despite waves of nostalgia, believe the present is better than the past. We celebrate progress by equating the "latest" with the "best."

7. **Science.** We expect scientists to solve problems and to improve our lives. We believe we are rational people, which probably explains our cultural tendency (especially among men) to devalue emotion and intuition as sources of knowledge.

8. **Democracy and free enterprise.** Members of our society recognize numerous individual rights that cannot be overridden by government. We believe a just political system is based on free elections in which people select their leaders and on an economy that responds to the desires of individual consumers.

9. **Freedom.** Our cultural value of freedom means that we favor individual initiative over collective conformity. We believe that individuals should be free to pursue personal goals with minimal interference from anyone else.

10. **Racism and group superiority.** Despite strong notions about individualism and freedom, most people in the United States still evaluate others according to gender, race, ethnicity, and social class. U.S. culture values males above females, whites above people of color, people with northwestern European backgrounds above those whose ancestors came from other lands, and rich above poor. Although we describe ourselves as a nation of equals, there is little doubt that some of us rank as "more equal than others."

Values: Sometimes in conflict. Looking over Williams's list, we see that some dominant cultural values contradict others (Lynd, 1967; Bellah et al., 1985). For example, people may believe in equality of opportunity, yet they may also degrade others because of their sex or race. Such value conflict inevitably causes strain, leading to awkward balancing acts in our beliefs. Sometimes we decide that one value is more important than another as, for example, by supporting equal opportunity while at the same time opposing acceptance of gays into the U.S. military. In these cases, we simply learn to live with inconsistencies.

NORMS

Most people in the United States are eager to gossip about "who's hot" and "who's not." Members of many Native American societies, however, condemn such behavior as rude and divisive. Both patterns illustrate the operation of **norms,** *rules and expectations by which a society guides the behavior of its members.*

William Graham Sumner (1959; orig. 1906), an early U.S. sociologist, coined the term **mores** (pronounced MORE-ays) to refer to *norms that are widely observed and have great moral significance.* Mores, or *taboos,* include our society's insistence that adults not engage in sexual relations with children.

But people are more casual about **folkways,** *norms for routine, casual interaction.* Examples include notions about appropriate greetings and proper dress. A man who does not wear a tie to a formal dinner party may raise an eyebrow for violating folkways or "etiquette." By contrast, were he to arrive at the dinner party wearing *only* a tie, he would be violating cultural mores and would invite more serious sanctions.

Cultural norms, then, guide individual behavior. Although we sometimes bristle when others pressure us to conform, we can all see that norms make our encounters with others more orderly and predictable.

As we learn cultural norms, we gain the capacity to judge our own behavior. Doing wrong (say, downloading a term paper from the Internet) can cause not only *shame*—the painful sense that others disapprove of our actions—but also *guilt*—a negative judgment we make of ourselves. Only cultural creatures can experience shame and guilt. This is what writer Mark Twain had in mind when he remarked that people "are the only animals that blush . . . or need to."

"IDEAL" AND "REAL" CULTURE

Values and norms do not describe actual behavior as much as they suggest how we *should* behave. We must remember that *ideal culture* always differs from *real culture* that actually occurs in everyday life. To illustrate, most men and women acknowledge the importance of sexual fidelity in marriage. Even so, in a recent study, 25 percent of married men and 10 percent of married women reported having been sexually unfaithful to their spouses at some point in the marriage (Laumann

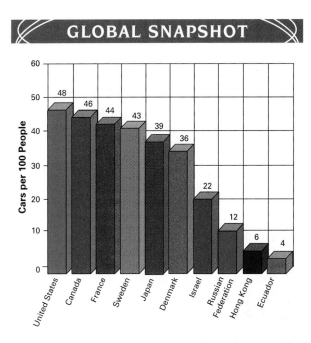

FIGURE 2–1 Car Ownership in Global Perspective
Source: The World Bank (2000).

et al., 1994). But a culture's moral prodding is important all the same, calling to mind the old saying, "Do as I say, not as I do."

TECHNOLOGY AND CULTURE

In addition to intangible elements such as values and norms, every culture includes a wide range of tangible (from the Latin, meaning "touchable") human creations called *artifacts.* The Chinese eat with chopsticks rather than knives and forks, the Japanese place mats rather than rugs on the floor, and many men and women in India prefer flowing robes to the tighter clothing common in the United States. The material culture of a people can seem as strange to outsiders as their language, values, and norms.

A society's artifacts partly reflect underlying cultural values. The warlike Yanomamö carefully craft their weapons and prize the poison tips on their arrows. By contrast, U.S. society's embrace of individuality and independence goes a long way to explain our high regard for the automobile: We own 208 million motor vehicles, one for every licensed driver. Figure 2–1 shows that, compared to other societies, the United States stands out as a car-loving nation.

In addition to reflecting values, material culture also indicates a society's level of **technology,** *knowledge that people apply to the task of living in their surroundings.* The more complex a society's technology, the more its members are able to shape the world for themselves.

Gerhard and Jean Lenski (1995) argue that a society's level of technology is crucial in determining what cultural ideas and artifacts emerge or are even possible. Thus, they see *sociocultural evolution,* or historical change in culture caused by new technology, passing through four levels of development[2]: hunting and gathering, horticulture and pastoralism, agriculture, and industry.

HUNTING AND GATHERING

The oldest and most basic way of living is **hunting and gathering,** *the use of simple tools to hunt animals and gather vegetation.* From the time of our earliest human ancestors 3 million years ago until about 1800, most people in the world lived as hunters and gatherers. Today, however, this technology characterizes only a few societies, including the Kaska Indians of northwest Canada, the Pygmies of central Africa, the Bushmen of southwestern Africa, the Aborigines of Australia, and the Semai of Malaysia. In most cases, hunters and gatherers spend most of their time searching for game and edible plants. Their societies stay small—generally with several dozen people living in a familylike, nomadic group, moving on as they deplete an area's vegetation or pursue migratory animals.

Everyone helps search for food, with the very young and the very old helping as they can. Women usually gather vegetation—the primary food source for these people—while men do most of the hunting. Despite having different roles, the two sexes have rough social parity (Leacock, 1978).

Hunters and gatherers have few formal leaders. They may look to one person as a *shaman,* or priest, but this position does not excuse the person from the daily work of finding food. Overall, hunting and gathering stands as a simple and egalitarian way of life.

Limited technology leaves hunters and gatherers vulnerable to the forces of nature. Storms and droughts can easily destroy their food supply, and they have few effective ways to respond to accident or disease. Not surprisingly, then, many children die in childhood, and only half live to the age of twenty.

Faced with the encroachment of people with powerful technology, hunters and gatherers are fast vanishing from the earth. Fortunately, studying their way of life has already produced valuable information about our sociocultural history as well as our fundamental ties to the natural environment.

HORTICULTURE AND PASTORALISM

Horticulture, *the use of hand tools to raise crops,* first developed 10,000 years ago. The hoe and the digging stick (used to punch holes in the ground for seeds) first appeared in fertile regions of the Middle East and Southeast Asia, and, by 6,000 years ago, these tools were in use from Western Europe to China. Central and South Americans, too, learned to cultivate plants, but rocky soil and mountainous terrain forced people like the Yąnomamö to continue to hunt and gather even as they adopted this new technology (Fisher, 1979; Chagnon, 1992).

In especially dry regions, societies turned not to raising crops but to **pastoralism,** *the domestication of animals.* Throughout the Americas, Africa, the Middle East, and Asia, many societies blend horticulture and pastoralism.

Growing plants and raising animals allow societies to feed hundreds of members. While pastoral peoples remain nomadic, horticulturalists make permanent settlements. There, a material surplus means that not everyone is needed to produce food; some people are then free to make crafts, become traders, or serve as full-time priests. Compared to hunters and gatherers, pastoral and horticultural societies are also more unequal, with some families operating as a ruling elite.

Since hunters and gatherers have little control over nature, they generally believe the world is inhabited by spirits. As they acquire the power to raise plants and animals, however, people come to envision God as creator of the world. The pastoral roots of Judaism and Christianity are evident in the term "pastor" and the common view of God as a "shepherd" who stands watch over us all.

AGRICULTURE

Five thousand years ago, further technological advances led to **agriculture,** *large-scale cultivation using plows harnessed to animals or more powerful energy sources.*

---

[2]This account examines only the major types of societies described by the Lenskis; see Lenski, Nolan, & Lenski (1995).

Hunters and gatherers depend on nature to meet their basic needs. Pastoral peoples have a somewhat higher standard of living based on the ability to domesticate animals. Members of agrarian societies use animal power to plow and irrigate land, boosting their output even more. People in industrial societies are more productive still, utilizing powerful energy sources and huge machinery. Most recently, members of postindustrial societies manipulate symbols in the form of words, images, or music, often using computers.

Agrarian technology first appeared in the Middle East and gradually spread throughout the world. So important were the inventions of the animal-drawn plow, the wheel, writing, numbers, and new metals, that historians call this era "the dawn of civilization" (Lenski, Nolan, & Lenski, 1995:175).

By turning the soil, plows allow land to be farmed for decades, so agrarian people live in permanent settlements. With large food surpluses, which can be transported by animal-powered wagons, populations easily grow into the millions. Members of agrarian societies become ever more specialized in their work so that money is used as a form of common exchange, replacing the earlier system of barter. While the development of agrarian technology expands human choices and fuels urban growth, it also makes social life more individualistic and impersonal.

Agriculture also brings about a dramatic increase in social inequality. While most people live as serfs or slaves, a handful of elites are freed from labor to cultivate a "refined" way of life based on the study of philosophy, art, and literature. At all levels of such a society, men gain pronounced power over women.

People with only simple technology live much the same the world over, with minor differences due to regional variations in climate. But, the Lenskis explain, agrarian technology gives people enough control over the world that cultural diversity increases.

INDUSTRY

Industrialization occurred as societies replaced the muscles of animals and humans with new forms of power. Formally, **industry** is *the production of goods using advanced sources of energy to drive large machinery.* The introduction of steam power, starting in England about 1775, boosted productivity more than ever and transformed culture in the process.

While agrarian people work in or near the home, most people in industrial societies work in large factories, under the supervision of strangers. Thus, industrialization pushes aside the traditional cultural values that guided family-centered agrarian life for centuries.

Industry also made the world seem smaller. During the nineteenth century, railroads and steamships carried people across land and sea, faster and farther than ever before. During the twentieth century, this process continued with the invention of the automobile, radio, and television.

Industrial technology also raises living standards and extends the human lifespan. Schooling becomes the rule, because industrial jobs demand more and more skills. Further, industrial societies steadily extend political rights and somewhat reduce economic inequality.

It is easy to see industrial societies as more "advanced" than those relying on simpler technology. After all, industry raises living standards and stretches life expectancy to seventy-five years—twice that of, say, the Yąnomamö. Even so, industry intensifies individualism, which expands personal freedom but weakens human community. Then, too, industry has led people to abuse the natural environment—at our peril. And while advanced technology gives us work-saving machines and miraculous forms of medical treatment, it also contributes to unhealthy levels of stress and has created weapons capable of destroying in a flash everything that our species has achieved.

POSTINDUSTRIAL INFORMATION TECHNOLOGY

Going beyond the four categories discussed by the Lenskis, we see that all high-income nations, including the United States, have now entered a postindustrial stage of economic development based on new information technology. As the first Cyber.Scope essay (pages 28–31) explained, production in industrial societies centers on factories that make *things*, while postindustrial production centers on computers and other electronic devices that create, process, store, and apply *ideas and information*.

The emergence of an information economy thus changes the skills that define a way of life. No longer are mechanical abilities the only key to success. People find that they must learn to work with symbols by speaking, writing, computing, and creating images and sounds in fields such as art, advertising, and entertainment. The overall effect of this transformation is that our society now has the capacity to generate symbolic culture on an unprecedented scale. The box takes a closer look.

CULTURAL DIVERSITY

As the chapter-opening story about the rise of hip-hop suggests, our nation is becoming more aware of the extent of cultural diversity within its borders. Moreover, this diversity continues to increase as each year almost 1 million people from other lands come to our shores. Thus, while historic isolation makes Japan the most *monocultural* of all high-income nations, heavy

CRITICAL THINKING

Virtual Culture: Is It Good for Us?

The Information Revolution is now generating symbols—words, sounds, and images—faster than ever before and rapidly spreading them across the nation and around the world. What does this new information technology mean for our way of life?

One important trend is that more and more of our cultural symbols are intentionally *created*. In the past, the people talked about culture as a way of life transmitted from generation to generation. In this traditional view, culture is an authentic heritage that belonged to our ancestors. But in the emerging cyber-society, more and more cultural symbols are new, intentionally generated by writers, composers, filmmakers, and others who work within the expanding information economy.

To illustrate this trend, consider our changing cast of cultural heroes, the people who represent some ideal we strive to live up to. Earlier in this century, our heroes were real men and women who made a difference in the life of this nation—George Washington, Abigail Adams, Betsy Ross, Davy Crockett, Daniel Boone, Paul

Bunyon, Abraham Lincoln, and Harriet Tubman. Of course, when we make a hero of someone (almost always long after the person has died), we "clean up" the person's biography, highlighting success and overlooking shortcomings. Nevertheless, although these people may be idealized, they were actual parts of our history.

Today's youngsters, by contrast, are fed a steady diet of *virtual culture*, images that spring from the mind of contemporary culture-makers and that

reach us through a screen—on television, in the movies, or through computer cyber-space. Today's "heroes" are Teletubbies, Rugrats, Pokémon, Barney, Batman, and Barbie, a continuous flow of Disney characters, and the ever-smiling Ronald McDonald. Some of these characters embody values that shape our way of life. But few of them have any historical reality and almost all have come into being for one purpose: to make money.

What do you think?

1. *As the Information Revolution proceeds, do you think virtual culture will become increasingly important? Why or why not?*

2. *Does virtual culture erode or enhance our cultural traditions? Is that good or bad?*

3. *What image of this country do U.S. movies and television shows give to people abroad?*

Source: Thanks to Roland Johnson (1996) for the basic idea for this box.

immigration has made the United States the most *multicultural* of all high-income countries.

Between 1820 (when the government began keeping track of immigration) and 2000, more than 65 million people have added their ways of life to the mix of cultures in the United States. A century ago, as shown in Figure 2–2 on page 46, most immigrants hailed from Europe; today, the majority of newcomers arrive from Latin America and Asia. To understand the reality of life in the United States, then, we must move beyond shared cultural patterns to consider the importance of cultural diversity.

HIGH CULTURE AND POPULAR CULTURE

Cultural diversity often involves social class. In fact, in everyday conversation, we usually reserve the term "culture" for art forms such as literature, music, dance, and painting. We describe people who regularly go to the opera or the theater as "cultured," because they presumably appreciate the "finer things in life."

We speak less generously of ordinary people, assuming that their "everyday" culture is somehow less worthy. So we are tempted to judge the music of Beethoven as "more cultured" than the blues, couscous

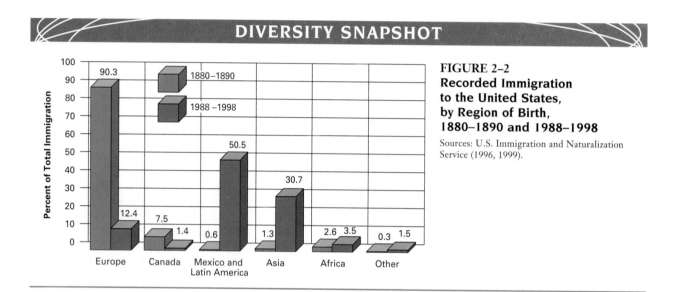

FIGURE 2–2
**Recorded Immigration
to the United States,
by Region of Birth,
1880–1890 and 1988–1998**

Sources: U.S. Immigration and Naturalization
Service (1996, 1999).

as better than cornbread, and polo as more polished than Ping-Pong.

In short, many cultural patterns are readily accessible to only some members of a society (Hall & Neitz, 1993). Sociologists use the shorthand term **high culture**[3] to refer to *cultural patterns that distinguish a society's elite* and **popular culture** to designate *cultural patterns that are widespread among a society's population.* National Map 2–1 looks at preferred alcoholic beverages to show the distribution of high and popular culture across the United States.

Common sense may suggest that high culture is superior to popular culture. But we should resist quick judgments about the merits of high culture over popular culture for two main reasons. First, neither elites nor ordinary people have uniform tastes and interests; people in both categories differ in numerous ways. Second, do we praise high culture because it is inherently better than popular culture, or simply because its supporters have more money, power, and prestige? For example, there is no difference between a violin and a fiddle; however, we name the instrument one way when it is used to produce a type of music typically enjoyed by a person of higher position, and the other

way when it produces music appreciated by people with lower social standing. Sociologists, therefore, are uneasy with distinctions between high and popular culture, preferring the term "culture" to refer to *all* elements of a society's way of life, including patterns of rich and poor alike.

SUBCULTURE

The term **subculture** refers to *cultural patterns that set apart some segment of a society's population.* Young people who enjoy hip-hop music and fashion, as well as Polish Americans, "Yankee" New Englanders, Colorado cowboys, the southern California "beach crowd," campus poets, computer "nerds," and wilderness campers—all display subcultural patterns.

It is easy, but often inaccurate, to put people in subcultural categories, because almost everyone participates in many subcultures without having much commitment to any one of them. In some cases, however, ethnicity and religion do set people apart from one another, with tragic results. Consider the former nation of Yugoslavia in southeastern Europe. The recent civil war there was fueled by astounding cultural diversity. This *one* small country made use of *two* alphabets, embraced *three* major religions, spoke *four* major languages, contained *five* major nationalities, was divided into *six* separate republics, and reflected the cultural influences of *seven* surrounding countries. The cultural conflict that plunged this nation into civil war shows that subcultures are a source not only of

---

[3]The term "high culture" is derived from the term "highbrow." A century ago, people influenced by phrenology—the bogus nineteenth-century theory that personality was affected by the shape of the human skull—praised the tastes of those they termed "highbrows" while dismissing the interests of others they derived as "lowbrows."

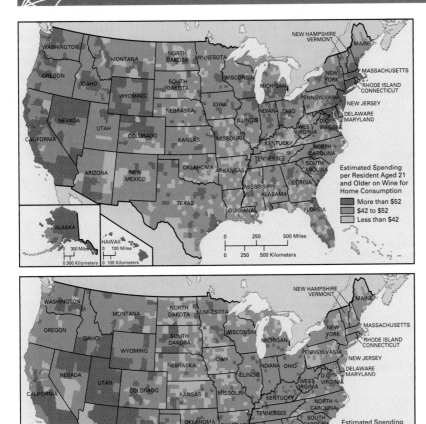

NATIONAL MAP 2–1
What'll Ya Have? Popular Beverages across the United States

What people consume is one mark of their status as a "highbrow" or "lowbrow." Drinking wine at home is an indicator of highbrow standing. These more well-to-do people not only enjoy a glass of wine with dinner, but drink water from bottles rather than the tap, prefer Grey Poupon to Gulden's mustard, and favor Häagen-Daz over the local Tastee-Freeze. Drinking beer, on the other hand, marks a person as a "lowbrow." Such a person has a low to moderate income, consumes a good deal of snack foods, and frequents fast-food restaurants. Looking at the maps, where have the "highbrows" and the "lowbrows" created centers of "high culture" and "popular culture"?

Source: *American Demographics* magazine, March 1998, p. 19. Reprinted with permission. © 1998, *American Demographics* magazine, Ithaca, New York.

pleasing variety but also of tension and outright violence (cf. Sekulic, Massey, & Hodson, 1994).

Historically, we have viewed the United States as a "melting pot" where many nationalities blend into a single "American" culture. But given our cultural diversity, how accurate is the "melting pot" image? For one thing, subcultures involve not just *difference* but *hierarchy*. Too often, what we view as "dominant" or "mainstream" culture are patterns favored by powerful segments of the population, while we view the lives of disadvantaged people as "subculture." Some researchers, therefore, prefer to level the playing field of society by emphasizing multiculturalism.

MULTICULTURALISM

Multiculturalism is *an educational program recognizing the cultural diversity of the United States and promoting the equality of all cultural traditions.* Multiculturalism represents a sharp turn from the past, when our society downplayed cultural diversity, defining itself in terms of its European (and especially English) immigrants. Today, a spirited debate asks whether we should stress past traditions or highlight contemporary diversity (Orwin, 1996; Rabkin, 1996).

E pluribus unum, the Latin phrase that appears on each U.S. coin, means "out of many, one." This motto

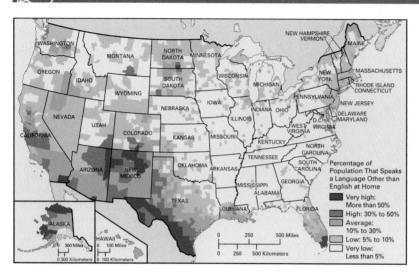

NATIONAL MAP 2–2
Language Diversity across the United States

Of 230 million people over the age of five in the United States, the 1990 census reports that 32 million (14 percent) typically speak a language other than English at home. Of these people, 54 percent speak Spanish, 14 percent use an Asian language, and the remaining 32 percent communicate with some other tongue (the Census Bureau lists 25 languages, each of which is favored by more than 100,000 people in the United States). The map shows that non-English speakers are concentrated in certain regions of the country. Which ones? What do you think accounts for this pattern?

Source: *Time*, January 30, 1995. Copyright © 1995 *Time*, Inc. Reprinted by permission.

symbolizes not only our national political union, but also the idea that the varied experiences of immigrants from around the world come together to form a new way of life. But from the outset, the many cultures did not melt together as much as harden into a hierarchy. At the top were the English who formed a majority and established English as this nation's dominant language. Further down, people of other backgrounds were advised to model themselves after "their betters," so that the "melting" was more accurately a process of Anglicization—adoption of English ways. Thus, early in its history, U.S. society set up the English way of life as an ideal to which all should aspire and by which all should be judged.

Ever since, historians have chronicled events from the point of view of the English and others of European ancestry, paying little attention to the perspectives and accomplishments of Native Americans and people of African and Asian descent. Multiculturalists call this view **Eurocentrism,** *the dominance of European (especially English) cultural patterns.* Molefi Kete Asante, an advocate of multiculturalism, argues that, like "the fifteenth-century Europeans who could not cease believing that the earth was the center of the universe, many today find it difficult to cease viewing European culture as the center of the social universe" (1988:7).

One contested issue involves language. Some people believe that English should be the official language of the United States; by 2000, legislatures in twenty-five states had enacted such laws. Others point out that some 30 million U.S. adults—more than one in six—speak a language other than English in their homes. Spanish is the second most commonly spoken U.S. language, and several hundred other tongues are heard across the country, including Italian, German, French, Filipino, Japanese, Korean, Vietnamese, and a host of Native American languages. National Map 2–2 shows where in the United States large numbers of people speak a language other than English at home.

Proponents also paint multiculturalism as a way of coming to terms with our country's increasing social diversity. With the Asian and Hispanic populations increasing rapidly, some analysts predict that our young children will live to see people of African, Asian, and Hispanic ancestry become the *majority* of this country's population.

Proponents also claim that multiculturalism is a good way to strengthen the academic achievement of African American children. To offset Eurocentrism, some multicultural educators are calling for **Afrocentrism,** *the dominance of African cultural patterns,* which they see as a strategy for correcting centuries of overlooking the achievements of African societies and African Americans.

Although multiculturalism has found favor in recent years, it has provoked criticism as well. Opponents say it encourages divisiveness rather than unity, because it urges people to identify with only their own category rather than with the nation as a whole. Moreover, critics doubt that multiculturalism actually benefits minorities as its supporters claim. Some multicultural policies (from African American studies departments to all-black dorms) seem to endorse precisely the kind of racial separation that our nation has struggled so long to end. Then too, an Afrocentric curriculum may well deny children important knowledge and skills by forcing them to study only certain topics from a single point of view. Historian Arthur Schlesinger, Jr. (1991), puts the matter bluntly: "If a Kleagle of the Ku Klux Klan wanted to use the schools to handicap black Americans, he could hardly come up with anything more effective than the 'Afrocentric' curriculum.'"

Is there any common ground in this debate? Almost everyone agrees that we need greater appreciation of our cultural diversity. But precisely where the balance is to be struck—between the *pluribus* and the *unum*—is likely to remain an issue for some time to come.

COUNTERCULTURE

Cultural diversity also includes outright rejection of conventional ideas or behavior. **Counterculture** refers to *cultural patterns that strongly oppose those widely accepted within a society.*

In many societies, counterculture is linked to youth (Spates, 1976, 1983; Spates & Perkins, 1982). The youth-oriented counterculture of the 1960s, for example, rejected mainstream culture as overly competitive, self-centered, and materialistic. Instead, hippies and other counterculturalists favored a collective and cooperative lifestyle in which "being" took precedence over "doing," and personal growth—or "expanded consciousness"—was prized over material possessions like homes and cars. Such differences led some people to "drop out" of the larger society.

Countercultures are still flourishing. Today, militaristic bands of men and women, deeply suspicious of the federal government, advocate dropping out of the political system. Countercultural extremism of this kind led to the bombing of the Oklahoma City federal building in 1995, killing 168 people.

TABLE 2–1 Attitudes among Students Entering U.S. Colleges, 1968 and 2000				
Life Objectives ("Essential" or "Very Important")		**1968***	**1999**	*Change*
Develop a philosophy of life	Men	79%	43%	–36%
	Women	87	42	–45
Keep up with political affairs	Men	52	32	–20
	Women	52	25	–27
Help others in difficulty	Men	50	53	+ 3
	Women	71	69	– 2
Raise a family	Men	64	73	+ 9
	Women	72	73	+ 1
Be successful in my own business	Men	55	45	–10
	Women	32	35	+ 3
Be very well off financially	Men	51	76	+25
	Women	27	71	+44

*To allow comparisons, data from the early 1970s rather than 1968 are used for some items.

Sources: Richard G. Braungart and Margaret M. Braungart, "From Yippies to Yuppies: Twenty Years of Freshmen Attitudes," *Public Opinion*, vol. 11, no. 3 (September–October 1988): 53–56; Linda J. Sax, Alexander W. Astin, William S. Korn, and Kathryn M. Mahoney, *The American Freshman: National Norms for Fall 2000* (Los Angeles: UCLA Higher Education Research Institute, 2000).

CULTURAL CHANGE

Perhaps the most basic human truth is that "All things shall pass." Even the dinosaurs, which thrived on this planet for 160 million years (see the time line), exist today only as fossils. Will humanity survive for millions of years to come? All we can say with certainty is that, given our reliance on culture, the human record will be one of continuous change.

Table 2–1 shows changes in student attitudes between 1968 (the height of the 1960s counterculture) and 2000. Some things have changed only slightly: Today, as a generation ago, most men and women look forward to raising a family. But today's students are much more interested in making money than developing a philosophy of life.

Change in one dimension of a cultural system usually sparks changes in others. For example, women's increased participation in the labor force parallels changing family patterns, including later first marriages and a rising divorce rate. Such connections illustrate the principle of **cultural integration,** *the close relationship among various elements of a cultural system.*

Most people in the affluent United States take for granted that childhood should be a carefree time of life devoted to learning and play. In low-income societies of the world, however, poor families depend on the income earned by children, some of whom perform long days of heavy physical labor. We may not want to accept all cultural practices as "natural" just because they exist. But what universal standards can be used to judge social patterns as either right or wrong?

Some parts of a cultural system change more quickly than others. William Ogburn (1964) observed that technology moves quickly, generating new elements of material culture (like test-tube babies) faster than nonmaterial culture (such as ideas about parenthood) can keep up with them. Ogburn called this inconsistency **cultural lag,** *the fact that some cultural elements change more quickly than others, which may disrupt*

a cultural system. To illustrate, consider this dilemma: How are we to apply traditional notions about motherhood and fatherhood in a culture where one woman now can give birth to a child by using another woman's egg, which has been fertilized in a laboratory with the sperm of a total stranger?

Cultural changes are set in motion in three ways. The first is *invention,* the process of creating new cultural elements such as the telephone (1876), the airplane (1903), and the computer (the late 1940s). The process of invention goes on constantly, as indicated by the thousands of applications submitted annually to the U.S. Patent Office. The time line shows other inventions that have helped change our way of life.

Discovery, a second cause of change, involves recognizing and understanding something already in existence—from a distant star, to the foods of a foreign culture, to the athletic prowess of women. Many discoveries result from painstaking scientific research, and others happen by a stroke of luck, as when Marie Curie unintentionally left a rock on a piece of photographic paper in 1898 and thus discovered radium.

The third cause of cultural change is *diffusion,* the spread of objects or ideas from one society to another. The ability of new information technology to send information around the world in seconds means that the level of cultural diffusion has never been greater than it is today.

Certainly our own society has contributed many significant cultural elements to the world, ranging from computers to jazz music. Sometimes, though, we forget that diffusion works the other way, so that much of what we assume is "American" actually comes from elsewhere. Most clothing, furniture, clocks, newspapers, money, and even the English language are derived from other cultures (Linton, 1937a).

ETHNOCENTRISM AND CULTURAL RELATIVITY

December 10, 1994, a small village in rural Morocco. Watching many of our shipmates browsing through this tiny ceramic factory, one can hardly doubt that North Americans are among the world's greatest shoppers. They delight in surveying handwoven carpets in China or India, inspecting finely crafted metals in Turkey, or collecting beautifully colored porcelain tiles here in Morocco. And, of course,

The View from "Down Under"

North America should be "up" and South America "down," or so we think. But, because we live on a globe, such notions are conventions rather than absolutes. The reason this map of the Western Hemisphere looks wrong to us is not that it is geographically inaccurate; it simply violates our ethnocentric assumption that the United States should be "above" the rest of the Americas.

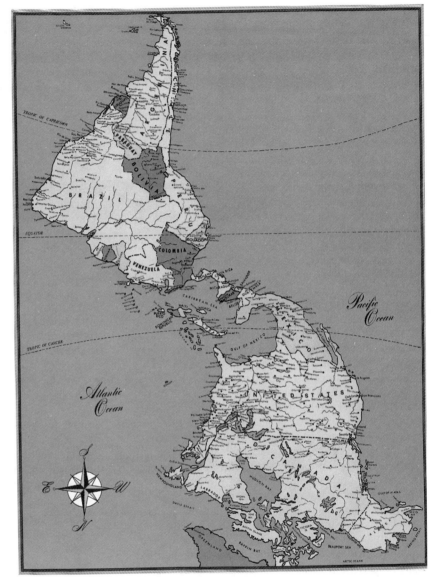

all these items are wonderful bargains. But the major reason for the low prices is unsettling: Many products from the world's low- and middle-income countries are produced by children—some as young as five or six—who work long days for pennies per hour.

We think of childhood as a time of innocence and freedom from adult burdens like work. In poor countries throughout the world, however, families depend on income earned by children. So what people in one society think of as right and natural, people elsewhere find puzzling and even immoral. Perhaps the Chinese philosopher Confucius had it right when he noted that "All people are the same; it's only their habits that are different."

Just about every imaginable idea or behavior can be found somewhere around the world, and this cultural variation causes travelers equal measures of excitement and distress. For instance, the tradition in Japan is to name intersections rather than streets, a practice that regularly confuses North Americans who do just the opposite. Egyptians move very close to others in conversation, which irritates North Americans used to maintaining several feet of "personal space." Bathrooms lack toilet paper in much of rural Morocco, causing great agitation among Westerners unaccustomed to using the left hand for bathroom hygiene.

Given that a particular culture is the basis for everyone's reality, it is no wonder that people everywhere exhibit **ethnocentrism,** *the practice of judging another culture by the standards of one's own culture.* Some ethnocentrism is necessary if people are to be emotionally attached to a cultural system. But ethnocentrism also generates misunderstanding and conflict.

Even our language is culturally biased. People in North America or Europe refer to China as the "Far East." Such a term, which has little meaning to the Chinese, is an ethnocentric expression for a region that is far east *of us.* For their part, the Chinese name their country using a word translated as "Central Kingdom," suggesting that they, too, see their society as the center of the world. The map on page 51 challenges our ethnocentrism by presenting a "down under" view of the Western Hemisphere.

The logical alternative to ethnocentrism is **cultural relativism,** *the practice of evaluating a culture by its own standards.* Cultural relativism is a difficult attitude to adopt, since it requires understanding unfamiliar values and norms and also suspending cultural standards we have known all our lives. But, as people of the world come into increasing contact with one another, the importance of understanding other cultures becomes even greater.

Businesses in the United States are learning that success in the global economy depends on cultural sophistication. General Motors, for example, learned the hard way that its Nova wasn't selling well in Spanish-speaking nations because the name in Spanish means "No Go." Coors's phrase "Turn It Loose" startled Spanish-speaking customers by proclaiming that the beer would cause diarrhea. Braniff Airlines turned "Fly in Leather" into clumsy Spanish reading "Fly Naked," and Eastern Airlines translated its slogan "We Earn Our Wings Daily" into "We Fly Every Day to Heaven." Even Frank Purdue fell victim to poor marketing when his pitch "It Takes a Tough Man to Make a Tender Chicken" ended up in Spanish reading "A Sexually Excited Man Will Make a Chicken Affectionate" (Helin, 1992).

But cultural relativity introduces problems of its own. If almost any behavior is the norm *somewhere* in the world, does that mean everything is equally right? Does the fact that some Indian and Moroccan families benefit from their children working long hours justify such child labor?

Since we are all members of a single human species, surely there must be some universal standards of proper conduct. But what are they? And, in trying to identify them, how can we avoid imposing our own standards on others? There are no simple answers. But when confronting an unfamiliar cultural practice, resist making judgments before grasping what "they" think of the issue. Remember, in addition, to think about your own way of life as others might see it. After all, what we gain most from studying others is insight into ourselves.

A GLOBAL CULTURE?

Today, more than ever before, we see many of the same cultural patterns the world over. Walking the streets of Seoul (South Korea), Kuala Lumpur (Malaysia), Madras (India), Cairo (Egypt), and Casablanca (Morocco), we find jeans, hear well-known pop music, and see advertising for many of the same products we use at home. Recall, too, from Global Map 2–1 that English is rapidly becoming the second language of most of the world. Are we witnessing the birth of a single global culture?

It is true that societies around the world now have more contact with one another than ever before, thanks to the flow of goods, information, and people.

1. **The global economy: the flow of goods.** There has never been more international trade. The global economy has spread many consumer goods (from cars and TV shows to music and fashion) throughout the world.

2. **Global communications: the flow of information.** Satellite-based communications enable people throughout the world to experience the sights and sounds of events taking place thousands of miles away—often, even as they are happening.

3. **Global migration: the flow of people.** Knowing about the rest of the world motivates people to move where they imagine life will be better. Moreover, today's transportation technology— especially air travel—makes moving about faster than ever before. As a result, in most nations, significant numbers of people have been born elsewhere (including some 26 million people

Following the structural-functional paradigm, what do you make of the Amish practice of "barn raising," by which everyone in a community joins together to raise a family's new barn in a day? Why is such a ritual almost unknown in rural areas outside of Amish communities?

who are now in the United States, about 10 percent of the population).

These global links have made the cultures of the world more similar. But there are three important limitations to the global culture thesis. First, the flow of information, goods, and people is uneven. Generally speaking, urban areas (centers of commerce, communication, and people) have stronger ties to one another, while rural villages remain more isolated. Then, too, the greater economic and military power of North America and Western Europe means that nations in these regions influence the rest of the world more than happens the other way around.

Second, the global culture thesis assumes people everywhere are able to afford the new goods and services. As Chapter 9 ("Global Stratification") explains, desperate poverty in much of the world deprives people of even the basic necessities of a safe and secure life.

Third, although many cultural elements have now spread throughout the world, people everywhere do not attach the same meanings to them. Do teenagers in Tokyo understand hip-hop the way their counterparts in New York or Los Angeles do? Similarly, although we may enjoy foods from around the world, we probably know little or nothing about the lives of the people who created them. In short, people everywhere look at the world through their own cultural lenses (Featherstone, 1990; Hall & Neitz, 1993).

THEORETICAL ANALYSIS OF CULTURE

Culture helps us make sense of ourselves and the surrounding world. Sociologists, however, have the special task of understanding culture. They use several theoretical approaches.

STRUCTURAL-FUNCTIONAL ANALYSIS

The structural-functional paradigm depicts culture as a complex strategy for meeting human needs. Borrowing from the philosophical doctrine of *idealism*, this approach considers values to be the core of a culture (Parsons, 1966; Williams, 1970). Cultural values, in other words, give meaning to life and bind people together. Countless other cultural traits each have various functions that support a way of life.

Thinking functionally helps us make sense of an unfamiliar way of life. Take, for example, the Amish farmer plowing hundreds of acres of an Ohio farm with a team of horses. His farming methods may violate our cultural value of efficiency but, from the Amish point of view, hard work functions to develop the discipline necessary for a highly religious way of life. Long days of working together not only make the Amish self-sufficient but unify families and local communities.

Of course, Amish practices have dysfunctions as well. The hard work and strict religious discipline is too demanding for some, who end up leaving the community. Then, too, religious devotion sometimes prevents compromise, resulting in lasting divisions within the Amish world (Hostetler, 1980; Kraybill, 1989; Kraybill & Olshan, 1994).

If cultures are strategies for meeting human needs, we would expect to find many common patterns around the world. The term **cultural universals** refers to *traits that are part of every known culture*. Comparing hundreds of cultures, George Murdock (1945) identified dozens of cultural universals. One common element is the family, which functions everywhere to control sexual reproduction and to oversee the care and upbringing of children. Funeral rites, too, are found everywhere, because all human communities cope with death. Jokes are another cultural universal, serving as a safe means of releasing social tensions.

Critical evaluation. The strength of structural-functional analysis lies in showing how culture operates to meet human needs. Yet by emphasizing a society's dominant cultural patterns, this approach overlooks cultural diversity. Moreover, because this approach emphasizes cultural stability, it downplays the importance of change. In short, cultural systems are neither as stable nor a matter of as much agreement as structural-functional analysis leads us to believe.

SOCIAL-CONFLICT ANALYSIS

The social-conflict paradigm draws attention to the link between culture and inequality. Any cultural trait, from this point of view, benefits some members of society at the expense of others.

We might begin a conflict analysis of culture by asking why certain values dominate a society in the first place. Many conflict theorists, especially Marxists, argue that culture is shaped by a society's system of economic production. "It is not the consciousness of men that determines their being," Marx asserted, "it is their social being that determines their consciousness" (Marx & Engels, 1978:4; orig. 1859). Social-conflict theory, then, is rooted in the philosophical doctrine of *materialism*, which holds that a society's system of material production (such as our own industrial-capitalist economy) has a powerful effect on the rest of a culture. This materialist approach contrasts with the idealist leanings of structural-functionalism.

Social-conflict analysis ties our competitive values to our society's capitalist economy, which serves the interests of the nation's wealthy elite. The culture of capitalism further teaches us that rich and powerful people have more energy and talent than others, and therefore deserve their wealth and privilege. Viewing capitalism as somehow "natural" also discourages efforts to reduce economic disparity in the United States.

Eventually, however, the strains of inequality erupt into movements for social change. Two recent examples in the United States are the civil rights movement and the women's movement. Both seek greater equality and both, too, encounter opposition from defenders of the status quo.

Critical evaluation. The social-conflict paradigm suggests that cultural systems do not address human needs equally, and that they allow some people to dominate others. This inequity, in turn, generates pressure toward change.

Yet by stressing the divisiveness of culture, this paradigm understates ways in which cultural patterns integrate members of a society. Thus we should consider both social-conflict and structural-functional insights for a fuller understanding of culture.

SOCIOBIOLOGY

We know culture is a human creation, but does our biological existence influence how this process unfolds? A third theoretical paradigm, standing with one leg in biology and the other in sociology, is **sociobiology,** *a theoretical paradigm that explores ways in which human biology affects how we create culture.*

Sociobiology rests upon the theory of evolution proposed by Charles Darwin (1859) in his book *On the Origin of Species.* Darwin asserted that living organisms change over long periods of time as a result of *natural selection,* a matter of four simple principles. First, all living things live to reproduce themselves. Second, the blueprint for reproduction is in the genes, the basic units of life that carry traits of one generation into the next. Third, some random variation in genes allows each species to "try out" new life patterns in a particular environment. This variation enables some organisms to survive better than others and to pass on their advantageous genes to their offspring. Fourth and finally, over thousands of generations, the genes that promote reproduction survive and become dominant. In this way, as biologists say, a species *adapts* to its environment, and dominant traits emerge as the "nature" of the organism.

Sociobiologists claim that the large number of cultural universals reflects the fact that all humans are members of a single biological species. It is our

Using an evolutionary perspective, sociobiologists point to a double standard by which men treat women as sexual objects more than women treat men that way. While this may be so, many sociologists counter that behavior—such as that shown in Ruth Orkin's photograph, American Girl in Paris—*is more correctly understood as resulting from a culture of male domination.*
Copyright 1952, 1980 Ruth Orkin.

common biology that underlies, for example, the apparently universal "double standard." As sex researcher Alfred Kinsey put it, "Among all people everywhere in the world, the male is more likely than the female to desire sex with a variety of partners" (quoted in Barash, 1981:49). But why?

We all know that a child results from joining a woman's egg with a man's sperm. But the biological significance of a single sperm is very different from that of a single egg. For healthy men, sperm represents a "renewable resource" produced by the testes throughout most of the life course. A man releases hundreds of millions of sperm in a single ejaculation—technically, enough to fertilize every woman in North America (Barash, 1981:47). A newborn female's ovaries, however, contain her entire lifetime allotment of immature eggs. A woman's ovaries release a single egg cell each month. So, while men are biologically capable of fathering thousands of offspring, a woman is able to bear a relatively small number of children.

Given this biological difference, the two sexes have distinctive strategies for reproduction. Men reproduce their genes most efficiently by being promiscuous—engaging in sex readily and often. But this scheme opposes the reproductive interests of women. Each of a woman's relatively few pregnancies demands that she carry the child, give birth, and provide care for some time afterward. Thus, efficient reproduction on the part of the woman depends on selecting a man whose qualities (beginning with the

likelihood that he will simply stay around) will contribute to her child's survival and, later, successful reproduction (Remoff, 1984).

The "double standard" certainly involves more than biology; it is also a product of the historical domination of women by men (Barry, 1983). But sociobiology suggests that this cultural pattern, like many others, has an underlying bio-logic. Simply put, the "double standard" exists around the world because women and men everywhere tend toward distinctive reproductive strategies.

Critical evaluation. Sociobiology has generated intriguing insights into the biological roots of some cultural patterns. But this paradigm remains controversial for two main reasons.

First, some critics fear that sociobiology may revive the biological arguments of a century ago that claimed the superiority of one race or sex. But defenders counter that sociobiology rejects the past pseudo-science of racial superiority. In fact, sociobiology unites all humanity because all people share a single evolutionary history. Sociobiology does assert that men and women differ biologically in some ways that culture may not overcome. But, far from asserting that males are somehow more important than females, sociobiology emphasizes that both sexes are vital to human survival.

Second, say the critics, sociobiologists have little evidence to support their theories. Research to date

What Are the "Culture Wars"?

"Hi, there, this is WYMI's 'Open Line' talk show. This afternoon, we are debating the question 'Should gay partners be permitted by law to marry?' I have Rhonda from the East Side on the line; Rhonda, what do you think . . . ?"

The easy rhythm of radio talk shows is familiar to just about everyone all across the country. But there is nothing easy about the questions being asked and, more often than not, little agreement about the answers. Indeed, on a host of issues—including gay rights, gender equality, affirmative action, the welfare system, abortion, single parenting, prayer in schools, multiculturalism, and government funding to the arts—there now seems to be a wide and angry gulf in U.S. society. On both sides, people are thoughtful, committed to their principles, and concerned about the future of their country. They are fighting the "culture wars."

Today's "culture wars" represent our nation's latest round of **cultural conflict**, *political differences, often expressed with hostility, based on disagreement over cultural values.* There is nothing new about cultural conflict; throughout much of the nineteenth century, for example, Protestants and Catholics clashed over the direction of U.S. society. Today, the issues in the "culture wars" are new, but as sociologist James Davison Hunter explains, the struggle to define our way of life is still going on.

Hunter offers several insights into the current cultural conflict. First, he notes that people's positions on various issues are consistent. That is, knowing someone's view on one issue is likely to predict the person's view on another. This connection stems from the fact that most individuals fall into one of two major camps—"traditionalists" or "progressives"—that have different cultural orientations.

Traditionalists, explains Hunter, see the world as a moral system. That is, they recognize "an external, definable, and transcendent authority" that clearly defines right and wrong and to whom everyone is responsible. For many—

suggests that biological forces do not *determine* human behavior in any rigid sense. Rather, humans *learn* behavior within a cultural system. The contribution of sociobiology, then, lies in explaining why some cultural patterns seem "easier to learn" than others (Barash, 1981).

CULTURE AND HUMAN FREEDOM

Underlying the discussion throughout this chapter is an important question: To what extent are human beings, as cultural creatures, free? Does culture bind us to each other and force us to relive the past? Or does culture enhance our capacity for individual thought and independent choice?

Humans cannot live without culture. But living as symbolic creatures does have some drawbacks. We may be the only animals able to name ourselves, but living in a symbolic world also means that we are also the only creatures who experience alienation. Then, too, culture is largely a matter of habit, which limits our choices and drives us to repeat troubling patterns, such as racial prejudice and sex discrimination, in each new generation. In addition, in this age of new information technology and virtual reality, we may wonder about the extent to which business-dominated media manipulate our culture in pursuit of profits.

Moreover, our insistence on competitive achievement urges us toward excellence, yet often at the cost of isolating us from one another. Material comforts do make life easy but divert us from close relationships and spiritual strength.

For better and worse, human beings are cultural creatures, just as ants and bees are prisoners of their biology (Berger, 1967). But there is a crucial difference. Biological instincts create a ready-made world; culture, by contrast, forces us to choose as we make and remake a world for ourselves. No better evidence of this freedom exists than the cultural diversity of our own society and the even greater human diversity around the world.

Furthermore, culture is ever-changing as the result of human imagination. For this reason, as the final box explains, members of our society hotly debate the future direction of our way of life. But, whatever one's politics, the better we understand the workings of our culture, the better prepared we are to use the freedom it offers us.

whether they are Christians, Jews, or Muslims—God is this authority. For others, this authority is the cultural heritage of strong families and local communities that has guided this country for centuries. Traditionalists, then, are conservatives: They are patriotic, religious, and believe in "old-fashioned family values." They oppose gay rights, condemn abortion, and think that today's public schools have abandoned moral teaching in favor of tolerance for every imaginable lifestyle. From a traditionalist's point of view, the growing tide of violence, divorce, and out-of-wedlock births stems from too little moral responsibility and too much personal freedom.

For progressives, on the other hand, a just world is composed of thoughtful people free to make their own choices. Progressives see no clear line between right and wrong. Indeed, they believe

that our country deliberately removed religion from public life in order to make it clearly a matter of individual belief. Certainly, some progressives are religious, but they tend to see the Bible or other religious texts as a source of historical wisdom that people must interpret for themselves in light of our lives today. Progressives oppose prejudice against gay people, support a woman's right to abortion, and see no place for religious observance in public schools. From their point of view, social problems like poverty and racial discrimination are best remedied not with greater moral discipline but by making everyone more equal.

One reason this country's "culture wars" generate so much heated discussion, claims Hunter, is that media coverage focuses on people taking extreme positions on one side or the other of various issues. In addition, many people find

compromise difficult not just because they hold deep beliefs but because what one side sees as the "solution," the other views as the "problem."

Continue the debate . . .

1. *Do you agree that people find it hard to compromise on most "culture wars" issues, such as gay rights and abortion? Why?*

2. *Are the "culture wars" evident on your campus? If so, how?*

3. *In your opinion, which side in the "culture wars" has the upper hand? Why?*

Sources: Adapted, in part, from Hunter (1991); see also Davis & Robinson (1996), DiMaggio, Evans, & Bryson (1996), Nolan (1996), and Evans (1997).

SUMMARY

1. Culture is a way of life shared by members of a society. Several species display limited capacity for culture, but only human beings rely on culture for survival.

2. As the human brain evolved, the first elements of culture appeared some 3 million years ago. Culture steadily increased in importance, replacing biological instincts as the foundation of behavior.

3. Culture relies on symbols. Language is the symbolic system by which one generation transmits culture to the next.

4. Values are culturally defined standards of what ought to be; beliefs are statements that people who share a culture hold to be true. Norms, which guide human behavior, are of two kinds: mores, which have great moral significance, and folkways, which are everyday matters of politeness.

5. Culture is shaped by technology. We understand technological development in terms of stages of sociocultural evolution: hunting and gathering,

horticulture and pastoralism, agriculture, industry, and the postindustrial information age.

6. High culture refers to patterns that distinguish a society's elites; popular culture includes patterns widespread in a society.

7. The United States stands among the most culturally diverse nations due to its historically high levels of immigration. A subculture is a distinctive set of traits that characterizes a segment of society; counterculture refers to patterns strongly at odds with a conventional way of life. Multiculturalism refers to efforts to enhance appreciation of cultural diversity.

8. Invention, discovery, and diffusion all generate cultural change. Cultural lag results as some parts of a cultural system change faster than others.

9. Ethnocentrism involves judging others using the standards of one's own culture. By contrast, cultural relativism means evaluating another culture according to its own standards.

10. Global cultural patterns result from the worldwide flow of goods, information, and people.

11. Structural-functional analysis views culture as a relatively stable system built on core values. Cultural traits function to maintain the overall system.

12. The social-conflict paradigm envisions culture as a dynamic arena of inequality and conflict. Cultural traits benefit some categories of people more than others.

13. Sociobiology studies how evolution shapes the human creation of culture.

14. The concept of cultural conflict refers to political debate ("culture wars") on the direction of cultural change in the United States.

15. Culture can constrain social possibilities; yet, as cultural creatures, we have the capacity to shape and reshape our world to meet our needs and pursue our dreams.

KEY CONCEPTS

culture (p. 35) the values, beliefs, behavior, and material objects that, together, form a people's way of life

society (p. 35) people who interact in a defined territory and share culture

culture shock (p. 35) personal disorientation when experiencing an unfamiliar way of life

symbol (p. 37) anything that carries a particular meaning recognized by people who share culture

language (p. 38) a system of symbols that allows people to communicate with one another

cultural transmission (p. 38) the process by which one generation passes culture to the next

Sapir-Whorf thesis (p. 38) the assertion that people perceive the world through the cultural lens of language

values (p. 38) culturally defined standards by which people assess desirability, goodness, and beauty, and which serve as broad guidelines for social living

beliefs (p. 38) specific statements that people hold to be true

norms (p. 41) rules and expectations by which a society guides the behavior of its members

mores (p. 41) norms that are widely observed and have great moral significance

folkways (p. 41) norms for routine, casual interaction

technology (p. 42) the knowledge that people apply to the task of living in their surroundings

hunting and gathering (p. 42) the use of simple tools to hunt animals and gather vegetation

horticulture (p. 42) the use of hand tools to raise crops

pastoralism (p. 42) the domestication of animals

agriculture (p. 42) large-scale cultivation using plows harnessed to animals or more powerful energy sources

industry (p. 44) the production of goods using advanced sources of energy to drive large machinery

high culture (p. 46) cultural patterns that distinguish a society's elite

popular culture (p. 46) cultural patterns that are widespread among a society's population

subculture (p. 46) cultural patterns that set apart some segment of a society's population

multiculturalism (p. 47) an educational program recognizing the cultural diversity of the United States and promoting the equality of all cultural traditions

Eurocentrism (p. 48) the dominance of European (especially English) cultural patterns

Afrocentrism (p. 48) the dominance of African cultural patterns

counterculture (p. 49) cultural patterns that strongly oppose those widely accepted within a society

cultural integration (p. 49) the close relationship among various elements of a cultural system

cultural lag (p. 50) the fact that some cultural elements change more quickly than others, which may disrupt a cultural system

ethnocentrism (p. 52) the practice of judging another culture by the standards of one's own culture

cultural relativism (p. 52) the practice of evaluating a culture by its own standards

cultural universals (p. 54) traits that are part of every known culture

sociobiology (p. 54) a theoretical paradigm that explores ways in which human biology affects how we create culture

cultural conflict (p. 56) political differences, often expressed with hostility, based on disagreement over cultural values

CRITICAL-THINKING QUESTIONS

1. Many people in the United States pay careful attention to their lawns. What is the cultural significance of a carefully manicured lawn in a largely anonymous society? What does a well-tended (or untended) front yard say about a person?

2. How does a schoolroom activity such as a "spelling bee" embody U.S. cultural values? What cultural values are expressed by children's stories such as *The Little Engine That Could*, or popular board games like "Monopoly" and "Risk"?

3. Do you identify with one or more subcultures? If so, which? How are they distinctive?

4. To what extent, in your opinion, is a global culture emerging? Do you regard the prospect of a global culture as positive or negative? Why?

APPLICATIONS AND EXERCISES

1. Try to find someone on campus who has lived in another country. Ask for a chance to discuss how the culture of that society differs from the way of life here. Look for ways in which the other person sees U.S. culture differently from most people.

2. Make a list of words with the prefix "self" (self-service, self-esteem, self-image, self-destructive, and so on); there are hundreds of them. What does this fact suggest about our way of life?

3. Watch a Disney video like *The Little Mermaid*, *Aladdin*, *Pocahontas*, or *Mulan*. All of these films share cultural themes, which is one reason for their popularity. According to these films, how should young people behave toward their parents? What makes these films especially "American"?

4. An easy way to study popular culture is to read a number of super-hero comic books. Decide why some people are defined as heroes and others as villains. Does gender figure in this process? (Cf. Hall & Lucal, 1999.)

5. Install the CD-ROM packaged in the back of this new textbook to access a variety of study, review, and applications exercises designed to help you better understand the material covered in this chapter. The CD includes an author's tip video, as well as interactive maps, video application exercises, Web links, and study questions.

 SITES TO SEE

http://www.prenhall.com/macionis

Visit the interactive Web site that accompanies this text. Begin by clicking on the cover of your book. You will find a chapter-by-chapter study guide, practice tests, chat room, and many suggested Web links.

http://www.macionis.com
(or http://www.thesociologypage.com)

Visit this Web site to view several short videos in which the author describes the excitement and challenges of traveling through other cultures.

http://www.nationalgeographic.com

The National Geographic Society offers information on world cultures, including search engines, and a library of maps.

http://www.gorilla.org

What does a 450-pound gorilla say? Anything she wants! The Gorilla Foundation offers a look at the sign language used by a 450-pound gorilla named Koko.

SOCIALIZATION:
FROM INFANCY TO OLD AGE

Andrew Macara
Footballers, Kos 1993
Oil on canvas, 63.5 × 76.2 cm. Private Collection/The Bridgeman Art Library.

On a cold winter day in 1938, a social worker walked quickly to the door of a rural Pennsylvania farmhouse. Investigating a case of possible child abuse, the social worker soon discovered a five-year-old girl hidden in a second-floor storage room. The child, whose name was Anna, was wedged into an old chair with her arms tied above her head so that she couldn't move. Her clothes were filthy, and her arms and legs were as thin as matchsticks (Davis, 1940:554).

Anna's situation can only be described as tragic. She was born in 1932 to an unmarried and mentally impaired woman of twenty-six who lived with her strict father. Enraged by his daughter's "illegitimate" motherhood, the grandfather did not even want the child in his house. For her first six months, Anna was shuttled among various welfare agencies. But when her mother was no longer able to pay for care, Anna returned to the hostile home of her grandfather.

To lessen the grandfather's anger, Anna's mother kept the child in the storage room, giving her just enough milk to keep her alive. There she stayed—day after day, month after month, with almost no human contact—for five long years.

Learning of the discovery of Anna, sociologist Kingsley Davis (1940) immediately went to see the child. He found her with local authorities at a county home. Davis was appalled by the emaciated girl, who could not laugh, speak, or even smile. Anna was completely unresponsive, as if alone in an empty world.

SOCIAL EXPERIENCE: THE KEY TO OUR HUMANITY

Here is a terrible case of a child deprived of social contact. Although physically alive, Anna hardly seemed human. Her plight reveals that, without social experience, a child is incapable of thought, emotion, or meaningful action, more an *object* than a *person*.

Sociologists use the term **socialization** to refer to *the lifelong social experience by which individuals develop their human potential and learn culture.* Unlike other living species, whose behavior is biologically set, humans need social experience to learn their culture and survive. Social experience is also the basis of **personality,** *a person's fairly consistent patterns of acting, thinking, and feeling.* We build a personality by internalizing—or taking in—our surroundings. But without social experience, as Anna's case shows, personality does not develop at all.

HUMAN DEVELOPMENT: NATURE AND NURTURE

Helpless at birth, the human infant depends on others to provide the nourishment and care needed for development. Anna's case makes these facts clear; but, a century ago most people mistakenly believed that human behavior was the product of biology.

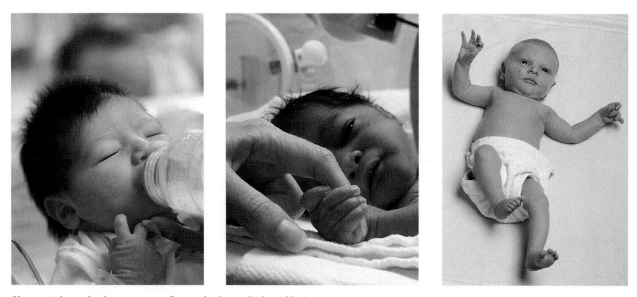

Human infants display various reflexes—biologically based behavior patterns that enhance survival. The sucking reflex, which actually begins before birth, enables the infant to obtain nourishment. The grasping reflex, triggered by placing a finger on the infant's palm causing the hand to close, helps the infant to maintain contact with a parent and, later on, to grasp objects. The Moro reflex, activated by startling the infant, has the infant swinging both arms outward and then bringing them together across the chest. This action, which disappears after several months of life, probably developed among our evolutionary ancestors so that a falling infant could grasp the body hair of a parent.

Charles Darwin's groundbreaking study of evolution, described in the last chapter, led people to think that human behavior was instinctive, simply our "nature." Such notions led some people to claim, for example, that the U.S. economic system reflects "instinctive human competitiveness," that some people are "born criminals," or that women are innately emotional while men are inherently more rational (Witkin-Lanoil, 1984).

People trying to understand cultural diversity also misunderstood Darwin's thinking. Centuries of world exploration had taught Western Europeans that people around the world display very different behavior. But Europeans linked these differences to biology rather than culture. It was an easy, although very damaging, step to claim that members of technologically simple societies were biologically less evolved and, thus, less human than their Western counterparts. But this ethnocentric view helped justify colonialism: Why not exploit others if they seem not to be human in the same sense that you are?

In the twentieth century, biological explanations of human behavior came under fire. Psychologist John B. Watson (1878–1958) developed a theory called *behaviorism*, which held that behavior is not instinctive but learned. Thus people everywhere are equally human, differing only in their cultural patterns. Watson, in short, rooted human behavior not in nature but in *nurture*.

Today, social scientists are cautious about describing *any* human behavior as instinctive. This does not mean that biology plays no part in human behavior. Human life, after all, depends on the functioning of the body. We also know that children often share biological traits (like height and hair color) with their parents, and that heredity plays a part in intelligence, musical and artistic aptitude, and personality (such as how one reacts to frustration). However, whether anyone *realizes* an inherited potential depends on the chance to develop it. In fact, unless children use their brains early in life, the brain itself does not fully develop (Plomin & Foch, 1980; Goldsmith, 1983; Begley, 1995).

Without denying the importance of nature, then, nurture matters more in shaping human behavior. More precisely, as cultural creatures, *nurture is our nature.*

The personalities we develop depend largely on the environment in which we live. When a child's world is shredded by violence, the damage can be profound and lasting. This drawing was made by a youngster growing up in the midst of the recent conflict in Yugoslavia. What are the likely effects of such experiences on a young person's self-confidence and ability to form trusting ties with others?

From the exhibition, *Far from Homeland: Refugee Children's Art from around the World*, London International Gallery of Children's Art.

SOCIAL ISOLATION

Of course, researchers must never experiment on human beings by placing people in total isolation. But, in the past, they did study the effects of social isolation on nonhuman primates.

Research with monkeys. Psychologists Harry and Margaret Harlow (1962) placed rhesus monkeys—whose behavior is in some ways surprisingly similar to that of human beings—in various conditions of social isolation. They found that complete isolation (with adequate nutrition) for even six months seriously disturbed the monkeys' development. When returned to their group, these monkeys were passive, anxious, and fearful.

The Harlows then placed infant rhesus monkeys in cages with an artificial "mother" made of wire mesh with a wooden head and the nipple of a feeding tube where the breast would be. These monkeys, too, survived but later were unable to interact with others.

But when the Harlows covered the artificial "mother" with soft terry cloth, the infant monkeys would cling to it. The monkeys benefited from the closeness, the Harlows concluded, because they showed less developmental damage than earlier monkeys. The experiment confirmed how important it is that adults cradle infants affectionately.

Finally, the Harlows discovered that infant monkeys could recover from as much as three months of isolation. But by about six months, isolation caused irreversible emotional and behavioral damage.

Isolated children. The rest of Anna's story squares with the Harlows' findings. After her discovery, Anna received extensive social contact and soon showed improvement. When Kingsley Davis (1940) revisited her after ten days, he found her more alert and even smiling with obvious pleasure. Over the next year, Anna made slow but steady progress, showing more interest in other people and gradually learning to walk. After a year and a half, she could feed herself and play with toys.

As the Harlows might have predicted, however, Anna's five years of social isolation had caused permanent damage. At age eight, her mental development was still less than that of a two-year-old. Not until she was almost ten did she begin to use words. Since Anna's mother was mentally retarded, perhaps Anna was similarly challenged. The riddle was never solved, however, because Anna died at age ten of a blood disorder, possibly related to years of abuse (Davis, 1940, 1947).

A more recent case of childhood isolation involves a California girl abused by her parents (Curtiss, 1977; Pines, 1981; Rymer, 1994). From about age two, Genie was tied to a potty chair in a dark garage. In 1970, when she was rescued at age thirteen, Genie weighed only fifty-nine pounds and had the mental development of a one-year-old. With intensive treatment, she became physically healthy, but her language ability remains that of a young child. Genie lives today in a home for developmentally disabled adults.

All evidence points to the crucial role of social experience in forming personality. Human beings can

Society, according to Sigmund Freud, is an ongoing battle between the moral forces of culture and the often aggressive impulses of individual human beings. Salvador Dalí (1904–1989), perhaps the best known Surrealist painter, created Premonition of Civil War in which a grossly distorted human figure rises up in a threatening way—foretelling the civil war that would shatter the nation of Spain, his homeland, between 1936 and 1940.

Salvador Dalí (Spanish, 1904–1989) *Soft Construction with Boiled Beans* (*Premonition of Civil War*), 1936, oil on canvas, 39⁵⁄₁₆ × 39³⁄₈ in. 50-134-41. Philadelphia Museum of Art: The Louise and Walter Arensberg Collection. © 2002, Kingdom of Spain, Gala—Salvador Dalí Foundation/Artists Rights Society (ARS), New York.

sometimes recover from abuse and isolation. But there is a point—precisely where is unclear from the small number of cases studied—at which isolation in infancy causes permanent developmental damage.

UNDERSTANDING SOCIALIZATION

Socialization is a complex, lifelong process. The following sections highlight the work of six researchers who made lasting contributions to our understanding of human development.

SIGMUND FREUD: THE ELEMENTS OF PERSONALITY

Sigmund Freud (1856–1939) lived in Vienna at a time when most Europeans considered human behavior biologically fixed. Trained as a physician, Freud soon turned to the analysis of personality and eventually developed the celebrated theory of psychoanalysis.

Basic needs. Freud claimed that biology plays a major part in human development, although not in terms of specific instincts as in other species. He theorized that

humans have two basic needs or drives. First is a need for bonding, which he termed the life instinct, or *eros* (from the Greek god of love). Second, we share an aggressive drive he called the death instinct, or *thanatos* (derived from Greek meaning "death"). To Freud, these opposing forces, operating at an unconscious level, generate deep inner tension.

Freud's personality model. Freud incorporated basic drives and the influence of society into a model of personality with three parts: id, ego, and superego. The **id** (the Latin word for "it") represents *the human being's basic drives*, which are unconscious and demand immediate satisfaction. Rooted in biology, the id is present at birth, making a newborn a bundle of demands for attention, touching, and food. But society opposes the self-centered id, which is why one of the first words a child usually learns is "no."

To avoid frustration, a child must learn to approach the world realistically. This is done through the **ego** (Latin for "I"), which represents *a person's conscious efforts to balance innate pleasure-seeking drives with the demands of society.* The ego arises as we gain awareness of our distinct existence and face up to the fact that we cannot have everything we want.

In the human personality, **superego** (Latin, meaning "above" or "beyond" the ego) is *the operation of culture within the individual.* The superego operates as our conscience, telling us *why* we cannot have everything we want. The superego begins to form as a child becomes aware of parental demands, and matures as the child comes to understand that everyone's behavior should take account of cultural norms.

To the id-centered child, the world is a bewildering array of physical sensations that bring either pleasure or pain. As the superego develops, however, the child learns the moral concepts of right and wrong. Initially, in other words, children can feel good only in a physical way, but, after three or four years, they feel good or bad as they judge their behavior against cultural norms.

The id and the superego remain in conflict, but, in a well-adjusted person, the ego manages these opposing forces. But when conflicts are not resolved during childhood, they may surface as personality disorders later on.

Culture, in the form of the superego, serves to *repress* the selfish demands of individuals. Often the competing demands of self and society result in a compromise Freud called *sublimation,* which changes selfish drives into socially acceptable behavior. Sexual urges, for example, may lead to marriage, and aggression often finds expression through competitive sports.

Critical evaluation. In Freud's time, few people were ready to accept sex as a basic drive. More recently, critics charge that Freud's work presents humans in male terms and devalues women (Donovan & Littenberg, 1982). But Freud influenced everyone who later studied human personality. Of special importance to sociology are his ideas that we internalize social norms and that childhood experiences have a lasting impact on our personalities.

JEAN PIAGET: COGNITIVE DEVELOPMENT

Swiss psychologist Jean Piaget (1896–1980) studied human *cognition*—how people think and understand. As Piaget watched his own three children grow, he wondered not only *what* they knew, but *how* they made sense of the world. Piaget went on to identify four stages of cognitive development.

The sensorimotor stage. Stage one is the **sensorimotor stage**, *the level of human development at which individuals experience the world only through their senses.* For about the first two years of life, infants know the world only by touching, tasting, smelling, looking, and

In a well-known experiment, Jean Piaget demonstrated that children over the age of seven had entered the concrete operational stage of development because they could recognize that the quantity of liquid remained the same when poured from a wide beaker into a tall one.

listening. "Knowing" to young children amounts to sensory experience.

The preoperational stage. About age two, children enter the **preoperational stage**, *the level of human development at which individuals first use language and other symbols.* Now children begin to think about the world mentally and begin to use their imagination. But "pre-op" children attach meanings only to specific experiences and objects. They can identify a special toy, for example, but they cannot describe what *kinds* of toys they like.

Lacking abstract concepts, a child cannot judge size, weight, or volume. In one of his best-known experiments, Piaget placed two identical glasses containing equal amounts of water on a table. He asked several five- and six-year-olds whether the amount in each was the same. They nodded that it was. The children then watched Piaget take one of the glasses and pour its contents into a taller, narrower glass, raising the level of the water. He asked again whether each glass held the same amount. The typical five- or six-year-old now insisted that the taller glass held more water. But, by age seven, children were able to think more abstractly and realized that the amount of water stayed the same.

The concrete operational stage. Next comes the **concrete operational stage**, *the level of human development at which individuals first perceive causal connections in their surroundings.* Between ages seven and eleven, children focus on how and why things happen. In addition, children now attach more than one symbol to an event or object. If, for example, you say to a child of five, "Today is Wednesday," she might respond, "No, it's my birthday," indicating that she can use just one symbol at a time. But an older child at the concrete operational stage would be able to respond, "Yes, and this Wednesday is my birthday."

The formal operational stage. The last step in Piaget's model is the **formal operational stage**, *the level of human development at which individuals think abstractly and critically*. At about age twelve, young people begin to reason abstractly, rather than think only of concrete situations. If, for example, you ask a child of seven "What would you like to be when you grow up?" you will get a concrete response such as "a teacher." But most teenagers can consider the question more abstractly, and might respond, "I would like a job that helps others." As they gain the capacity for abstract thought, young people also learn to comprehend metaphors. Hearing the phrase "A penny for your thoughts" might lead a child to ask for a coin, but a teenager will recognize a gentle invitation to intimacy.

Critical evaluation. While Freud saw human beings passively torn by opposing forces of biology and culture, Piaget saw the mind as active and creative. He saw the ability to engage the world unfolding in stages as the result of both biological maturation and social experience.

But do people in all societies pass through all four of Piaget's stages? In fact, living in a traditional society that changes slowly probably limits the capacity for abstract, critical thought. Even in the United States, perhaps 30 percent of people never reach the formal operational stage (Kohlberg & Gilligan, 1971).

LAWRENCE KOHLBERG: MORAL DEVELOPMENT

Lawrence Kohlberg (1981) built on Piaget's work to study moral reasoning, that is, how individuals come to judge situations as right or wrong. Here, again, development occurs in stages.

Young children who experience the world in terms of pain and pleasure (Piaget's sensorimotor stage) are at the *preconventional* level of moral development. At first, then, "rightness" amounts to "what feels good to me."

The *conventional* level, Kohlberg's second stage, appears by the teens (corresponding to Piaget's final,

formal operational stage). At this point, young people shed some of their selfishness as they learn to define right and wrong in terms of what pleases parents and conforms to cultural norms.

In the final stage of moral development, the *postconventional* level, individuals move beyond their society's norms to consider abstract ethical principles. Now they think about liberty, freedom, or justice, perhaps arguing that what is lawful still may not be right.

Critical evaluation. Like the work of Piaget, Kohlberg's model explains moral development in terms of distinct stages. But, here again, whether this model applies to people in all societies remains unclear. Then, too, many people in the United States apparently never reach the postconventional level of moral reasoning, although exactly why is still an open question.

Another problem with Kohlberg's research is that all his subjects were boys. Thus Kohlberg commits a research error, described in Chapter 1 ("Sociology: Perspective, Theory, and Method"), by generalizing the results of male subjects to all people. This problem led a colleague, Carol Gilligan, to investigate how gender affects moral reasoning.

CAROL GILLIGAN: THE GENDER FACTOR

Carol Gilligan (1982) set out to compare the moral development of girls and boys and concluded that the two sexes use different standards of rightness. Males, she contends, have a *justice perspective*, relying on formal rules to define right and wrong. Girls, on the other hand, have a *care and responsibility perspective*, judging a situation with an eye toward personal relationships and loyalties. For example, as boys see it, stealing is wrong because it breaks the law. Girls, however, are more likely to wonder why someone would steal, and to be sympathetic toward someone who steals, say, to feed a hungry child.

Kohlberg treats rule-based male reasoning as morally superior to the person-based female perspective. But Gilligan notes that impersonal rules have long governed men's lives in the workplace, whereas personal relationships are more relevant to women's lives as mothers and caregivers. Why, then, Gilligan asks, should we set up male patterns as the standards by which to judge everyone?

Critical evaluation. Gilligan's work sharpens our understanding of both human development and gender issues in research. Yet, what accounts for the differences she documents between females and males?

Is it nature or nurture? In Gilligan's view, cultural conditioning is at work. Thus we might predict that as more women organize their lives around the workplace, the moral reasoning of women and men will become more similar.

GEORGE HERBERT MEAD: THE SOCIAL SELF

George Herbert Mead (1863–1931) developed a theory of *social behaviorism* to explain how social experience develops an individual's personality (1962; orig. 1934).

The self. Mead's central concept is the **self**, *that part of an individual's personality composed of self-awareness and self-image.* Mead's genius lay in seeing the self as the product of social experience.

First, said Mead, *the self develops only with social experience.* The self is not part of the body and does not exist at birth. Mead rejected the idea that personality is guided by biological drives (as Freud asserted) or even biological maturation (as Piaget claimed). For Mead, self develops only as the individual interacts with others. In the absence of interaction—as we see from isolated children—the body grows but no self emerges.

Second, Mead explained, *social experience is the exchange of symbols.* Only people use words, a wave of the hand, or a smile to create meaning. We can train a dog using reward and punishment, but the dog attaches no meaning to its actions. Human beings, by contrast, find meaning in action by imagining people's underlying intentions. In short, a dog responds to *what you do*, but a human responds to *what you have in mind* as you do it. Thus you can train a dog to go to the hallway and bring back an umbrella. But, without understanding intention, if the dog cannot find the umbrella, it is incapable of the *human* response: to look for a raincoat instead.

Third, Mead continues, *to understand intention, you must imagine a situation from the other's point of view.* Using symbols, we imagine ourselves in another person's shoes and see ourselves as that person does. This capacity lets us anticipate how others will respond to us even before we act. A simple toss of a ball, for example, requires stepping outside ourselves to imagine how the other will catch our throw. All symbolic interaction, then, involves seeing ourselves as others see us—a process Mead termed *taking the role of the other.*

The looking-glass self. In effect, others represent a mirror (which people used to call a "looking glass") in

George Herbert Mead wrote: *"No hard-and-fast line can be drawn between our own selves and the selves of others." The painting* Manyness *by Rimma Gerlovina and Valeriy Gerlovin conveys this important truth. Although we tend to think of ourselves as unique individuals, each person's characteristics develop in an ongoing process of interaction with others.*

Rimma Gerlovina & Valeriy Gerlovin, *Manyness*, 1990. © the artists, New City, N.Y.

which we see ourselves. What we think of ourselves, then, depends on what we think others think of us. If we think others see us as clever or clumsy, in other words, we will think of ourselves in the same way. Charles Horton Cooley (1864–1929) used the phrase **looking-glass self** to mean *a self-image based on how we think others see us.*

The I and the me. Mead's fourth point is that, *by taking the role of another, we become self-aware.* The self, then, has two parts. As subject, the self is active and spontaneous. Mead called the subjective side of the self the *I* (the subjective form of the personal pronoun). But the self is also an object, as we imagine ourselves as others see us. Mead called the objective side of the self the *me* (the objective form of the personal pronoun). All social experience has both components: We initiate action (the I-phase of the self), and we continue the action based on how others respond to us (the me-phase of the self).

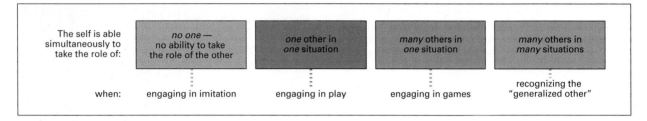

The self is able simultaneously to take the role of:	*no one* — no ability to take the role of the other	*one* other in *one* situation	*many* others in *one* situation	*many* others in *many* situations
when:	engaging in imitation	engaging in play	engaging in games	recognizing the "generalized other"

FIGURE 3–1 Building on Social Experience

George Herbert Mead described the development of the self as a process of gaining social experience. That is, the self develops as we expand our capacity to take the role of the other.

Stages of development. The key to developing the self, then, is learning to take the role of the other. With limited social experience, infants cannot do this and respond to others only through *imitation*. That is, they mimic behavior without understanding underlying intention and, so, have no self.

As children learn to use language and other symbols, the self emerges in the form of *play*. Play involves assuming roles modeled on important people—such as parents—who are sometimes termed *significant others*. Playing "mommy" or "daddy" (often putting themselves, literally, in the shoes of a parent) begins to teach children to imagine the world from a parent's point of view.

Gradually, children learn to take the roles of several others at once. This skill lets them move from simple play (say, playing catch) involving one other person to complex *games* (like baseball) involving many others. By about age seven, most children have the social experience needed to engage in team sports.

Figure 3–1 charts the progression from imitation to play to games. But a final stage in the development of the self remains. Games involve dealing with a limited number of other people in one specific situation, but social life demands that we see ourselves in terms of cultural norms as *anyone* else might. Mead used the term *generalized other* to refer to widespread cultural norms and values we use as a reference in evaluating ourselves.

As life goes on, the self continues to change along with our social experiences. But no matter how much events change us, we remain creative beings. Thus, Mead concluded, we play a key role in our own socialization.

Critical evaluation. Mead's work explores the character of social experience itself. In the symbolic interaction of human beings, Mead found the root of both self and society.

Some critics say Mead's view is completely social, allowing no biological element at all. In this, he stands apart from Freud (who identified general human drives) and Piaget (whose stages of development are tied to biological maturation).

Be careful not to confuse Mead's concepts of the I and the me with Freud's terms id and superego. Freud rooted the id in the biological organism, while Mead rejected any biological element of the self (although he never clearly spelled out the origin of the I). Moreover, while the superego and id are locked in continual combat, the I and the me work cooperatively together (Meltzer, 1978).

ERIK H. ERIKSON: EIGHT STAGES OF DEVELOPMENT

All of the thinkers we have discussed so far point to childhood as the crucial time when personality takes shape. Erik H. Erikson (1902–1994) took a broader view of socialization. He explained that we face challenges throughout the life course (1963; orig. 1950).

Stage 1 Infancy: the challenge of trust (versus mistrust). Between birth and about eighteen months, infants face the first of life's challenges: to gain a sense of trust that their world is a safe place. Family members play a key role in how any infant meets this challenge.

Stage 2 Toddlerhood: the challenge of autonomy (versus doubt and shame). The next challenge up to age three is to learn skills to cope with the world in a confident way. Failure to gain self-control leads children to doubt their abilities.

Stage 3 Pre-school: the challenge of initiative (versus guilt). Four- and five-year-olds must learn to engage their surroundings—including people outside the family—or experience guilt at having failed to meet the expectations of parents and others.

Stage 4   Pre-adolescence: the challenge of industriousness (versus inferiority). Between ages six and thirteen, children enter school, make friends, and strike out on their own more and more. They feel proud of their accomplishments or, at times, fear that they do not measure up.

Stage 5   Adolescence: the challenge of gaining identity (versus confusion). During the teenage years, young people struggle to establish their own identity. In part, teens identify with others close to them, but they also see themselves as unique. Almost all teens experience some confusion as they struggle to establish an identity.

Stage 6   Young adulthood: the challenge of intimacy (versus isolation). The challenge for young adults is to form and keep intimate relationships with others. Falling in love (as well as making close friendships) involves balancing the need to bond with the need to have a separate identity.

Stage 7   Middle adulthood: the challenge of making a difference (versus self-absorption). The challenge of middle age is to contribute to the lives of others in the family, at work, and in the larger world. Failing at this, people stagnate, trapped in their own limited concerns (think of Scrooge in Dickens's classic *A Christmas Carol*).

Stage 8   Old age: the challenge of integrity (versus despair). Near the end of their lives, Erikson explains, people hope to look back on what they have accomplished with a sense of integrity and satisfaction. For those who have been self-absorbed, old age brings only a sense of despair over missed opportunities.

Critical evaluation. Erikson's theory views personality formation as a lifelong process. Further, success at one stage (say, an infant gaining trust) prepares us for meeting the next challenge.

One problem with this model is that not everyone confronts these challenges in the exact order presented by Erikson. Nor is it clear that failure to meet a challenge at one stage of life means that a person is doomed to fail later on. A broader question, raised earlier in our discussion of Piaget's ideas, is whether people in other cultures and at other times in history would define a successful life in the same terms as Erikson.

In sum, Erikson's model helps us make sense of socialization and points out how the family, school, and other settings shape us. We now take a close look at these agents of socialization.

Sociological research indicates that affluent parents tend to encourage creativity in their children while poor parents tend to foster conformity. While this general difference may be valid, parents at all class levels can and do provide loving support and guidance by simply involving themselves in their children's lives. Henry Ossawa Tanner's painting The Banjo Lesson *stands as a lasting testament to this process.*

Henry Ossawa Tanner, *The Banjo Lesson*, 1893. Oil on canvas. Hampton University Museum, Hampton, Virginia.

AGENTS OF SOCIALIZATION

Every social experience we have affects us in at least a small way. However, several familiar settings have special importance to the socialization process.

THE FAMILY

The family has the greatest impact on socialization. Infants are totally dependent on others, and responsibility for their care typically falls on parents and other family members. In addition, at least until children

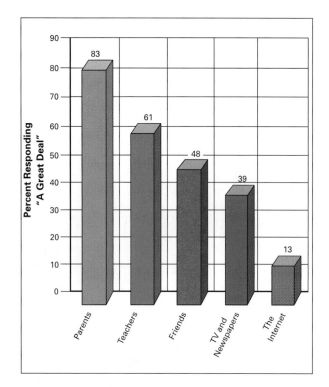

FIGURE 3–2 Whom Do You Trust?

Survey Question: "How much do you trust the information you get from . . . ?"

Sample = 409 U.S. teens, ages 13 to 17, 341 (83%) responding using the Internet. Survey taken April 1999 by Yankelovich Partners, Inc.

Source: Data from Okrent (1999).

begin school, the family has the job of teaching children skills, values, and beliefs.

Family learning is not all intentional. Children also learn from the kind of environment adults create. Whether children learn to see themselves as strong or weak, smart or stupid, loved or simply tolerated, and, as Erik Erikson suggests, whether they see the world as trustworthy or dangerous, largely depend on their surroundings.

The family also gives children a social position in terms of race, religion, ethnicity, and class. In time, all these elements become part of the child's self-concept.

Research in the United States shows that the class position of parents influences how they raise their children (Ellison, Bartowski, & Segal, 1996). Social class affects not just how much money parents have to spend, but what they expect of their children. Surveys show that, when asked to pick from a list of traits that are most desirable in a child, lower-class people in the United States favor obedience and conformity. Well-to-do people, by contrast, tend to select good judgment and creativity (NORC, 1999).

Why the difference? Melvin Kohn (1977) explains that people of lower social standing usually have limited education and perform routine jobs under close supervision. Expecting that their children will hold similar positions, they encourage obedience and may even use physical punishment like spanking to get it. Well-off parents, with more schooling, usually have jobs that demand imagination and provide more personal freedom. These parents, therefore, try to inspire the same qualities in their children. All parents, then, act in ways that encourage their children to follow in their footsteps.

THE SCHOOL

Schooling enlarges children's social world to include people with backgrounds different from their own. In the process, they learn the importance that society attaches to race and gender. Studies document that children tend to cluster in play groups made up of one race and gender (Lever, 1978; Finkelstein & Haskins, 1983).

Schooling teaches children a wide range of knowledge and skills. But schools informally convey other value-lessons, known as a *hidden curriculum*. Activities such as spelling bees and sports, for example, foster the value of competition and showcase success. Children also receive countless subtle lessons that their society's way of life is morally good.

School is also most children's first experience with bureaucracy. The school day runs on impersonal rules and a strict time schedule. Not surprisingly, these are also the traits of the large organizations that will employ them later in life.

Finally, schools socialize children into gender roles. Raphaela Best (1983) notes that at school boys engage in more physical activities and spend more time outdoors, while girls are more likely than boys to help teachers with various housekeeping chores in the classroom. Gender differences continue through college, where women tend to major in the arts or humanities, while men lean toward economics, the physical sciences, and computing.

THE PEER GROUP

By the time they enter school, children have also discovered the **peer group,** *a social group whose members have interests, social position, and age in common.* Unlike the family and the school, the peer group allows children to escape the direct supervision of adults. Among their peers, children learn how to form relationships on their own. Peer groups also offer the chance to discuss interests that adults may not share (such as clothes and popular music) or tolerate (such as drugs and sex).

Not surprisingly, then, parents express concern about who their children's friends are. In a rapidly changing society, peer groups have great influence, and the attitudes of young and old may be separated by a "generation gap." The importance of peer groups typically peaks during adolescence, when young people begin to break away from their families and think of themselves as adults.

Even during adolescence, however, parental influence on children remains strong. Peers may guide short-term choices in dress and music, but parents retain more sway over long-term goals such as going to college (Davies & Kandel, 1981). Figure 3–2 shows the results of a recent survey of teenagers confirming that teens still place their greatest trust in their parents.

Finally, any neighborhood or school is a social mosaic of many peer groups. As Chapter 5 ("Groups and Organizations") explains, individuals tend to view their own group in positive terms and discredit others. Moreover, people are also influenced by peer groups they would like to join, a process sociologists call **anticipatory socialization,** *learning that helps a person achieve a desired position.* In school, for example, young people may mimic the styles and slang of the group they hope will accept them. Or, later in life, a young lawyer may conform to the attitudes and behavior of the firm's partners in order to assure career advancement.

THE MASS MEDIA

`September 29, 1994, the Pacific Ocean, nearing Japan.` We have been out of sight of land for two weeks now, which makes this ship our entire social world. But more than land, many of the students miss television! Tapes of "Beverly Hills 90210" are a hot item.

The **mass media** are *impersonal communications aimed at a vast audience.* The term "media" comes from Latin, meaning "middle," suggesting that media serve to connect people. *Mass* media occur as communications technology (first newspapers, then radio and television) spreads information on a *mass* scale.

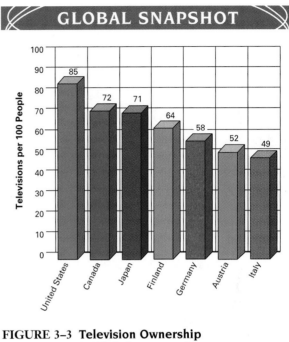

FIGURE 3–3 Television Ownership in Global Perspective

Source: The World Bank (2000).

In the United States, the mass media have an enormous effect on our attitudes and behavior. Television, introduced in 1939, soon became the dominant medium, and 98 percent of U.S. households have at least one set (by comparison, just 94 percent of households have telephones). Two of three households also have cable television. As Figure 3–3 indicates, the United States has the highest rate of television ownership in the world.

Just how "glued to the tube" are we? Government statistics show that the average household has at least one set turned on for seven hours each day, and people spend almost half their free time watching television (Nielsen, 1997; Seplow & Storm, 1997). National Map 3–1 shows where in the country people are more likely to be television watchers and where they are more likely to spend their leisure time reading newspapers.

Years before children learn to read, television watching is a regular routine. As they grow, children spend as many hours in front of a television as they do in school or interacting with their parents. This is so despite research that suggests television makes children more passive and less likely to use their imagination (Singer & Singer, 1983; APA, 1993; Fellman, 1995).

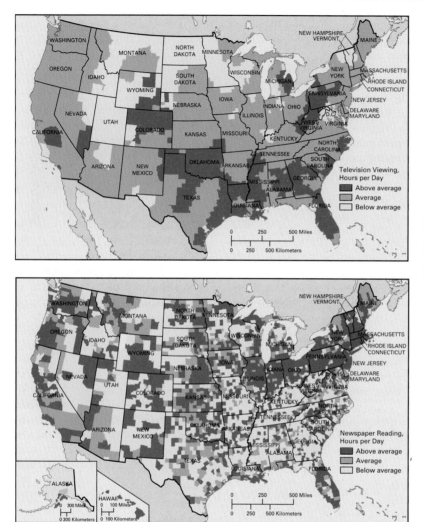

NATIONAL MAP 3–1
Television Viewing and Newspaper Reading across the United States

The map on the left identifies U.S. counties where television watching is above average, average, and below average. The map below provides comparable information for time devoted to reading newspapers. What do you think accounts for the high level of television viewing across much of the South and in rural West Virginia? Does your theory also account for patterns of newspaper reading?

Source: *American Demographics* magazine, August 1993, p. 64; *American Demographics* magazine, November 1998, p. 46. Reprinted with permission from American Demographics. © 1998 by Intertec Publishing, a Primedia Company.

Comedian Fred Allen once quipped that we call television a "medium" because it is rarely well done. For a variety of reasons, television (like other media) provokes plenty of criticism. Some liberal critics argue that television shows mirror our society's patterns of social inequality and rarely challenge the status quo. Most programs involve men in positions of power over women. Moreover, although racial and ethnic minorities watch about 40 percent more television than white people, they are largely absent from programming (Gans, 1980; Cantor & Pingree, 1983; Ang,

1985; Parenti, 1986; Brown, 1990). The box asks how the U.S. entertainment industry ought to characterize minorities.

On the other side of the fence, conservative critics charge that the television and film industries are dominated by a liberal "cultural elite." In recent years, they claim, "politically correct" media have advanced liberal causes including feminism and gay rights (Lichter, Rothman, & Rothman, 1986; Woodward, 1992b; Prindle, 1993; Prindle & Endersby, 1993; Rothman, Powers, & Rothman, 1993).

SOCIAL DIVERSITY

How Do the Media Portray Minorities?

On an old "Saturday Night Live" sketch, actor and director Ron Howard tells comedian Eddie Murphy about a new film, *Night Shift*, in which two mortuary workers decide to open a prostitution ring as a side-line. Murphy asks if there are any black actors in the film; Howard shakes his head "no." Murphy then thunders, "A story about two pimps and there wasn't no brothers in it? I don't know whether to thank you or punch you in the mouth, man!"

Murphy's response points to twin criticisms of the U.S. mass media: Films and television have portrayed minorities in stereotypical fashion or ignored them altogether (Press, 1993:219). Back in the 1950s, minorities were all but absent from television and films. Even the wildly successful 1950s comedy "I Love Lucy," which is still popular today, initially was turned down by every major television studio because it featured Desi Arnaz—a Cuban—in a starring role. Since that time, the media have steadily included more minorities. But, despite top-rated programs like "The Cosby Show" in the 1980s, *visibility* remains

Does a television show like "The Hughleys," which depicts a successful family, improve popular perceptions among whites of African Americans, or does it hide the real problems many black families face?

an issue: The 1990s came to an end with just a handful of African American stars on prime-time television.

And what about *how* the media portray minorities? The few African Americans who managed to break into television in the 1950s (for example, "Amos 'n' Andy" and Jack Benny's butler "Rochester") were stereotypical low-status characters. Today, many television shows feature African American stars, but most are situation comedies ("sitcoms") filled with crude humor and bumbling characters.

Certainly, the image of minorities in the mass media is better than it used to be. But how minorities should be portrayed is still a matter of debate (cf. MacDonald, 1992). Should the mass media portray disadvantaged minorities *as they are*, which risks perpetuating stereotypes? Should shows present minorities *as they should be*, which risks being unrealistic about this nation's problems? Or should the television industry be guided by ratings, giving the public "what sells"?

A final issue concerns violence and the mass media. In 1996, the American Medical Association (AMA) declared violence in the mass media a hazard to this country's health. An AMA survey (1996) found that three-fourths of U.S. adults have either walked out of a movie or turned off television because of too much violence. A more recent national study found that almost two-thirds of television shows contain violence and that, in most scenes, violent characters show no remorse and are not punished (Wilson, 1998).

In 1997, the television industry adopted a rating system for programs. But larger questions remain: Does viewing violent programming hurt people as much as critics say it does? More important, why do the mass media contain so much violence (and sex) in the first place?

In sum, television and other mass media have enriched our lives with entertaining and educational programming. The media also increase our exposure to diverse cultures and provoke discussion of current issues. At the same time, the power of the media—especially television—to shape how we think remains highly controversial.

Finally, other spheres of life beyond family, school, peer group, and the media also play a part in social learning. For most people in the United States, these include religious organizations, the workplace,

In recent decades, some analysts suggest that U.S. society is shortening childhood by pushing children to grow up faster and faster. What role do you think the mass media have in this process? What about the rising number of children left to fend for themselves while their parents work? What other factors are affecting the experience of childhood today?

the military, and social clubs. As a result, socialization is an uneven process as we absorb different information from different sources. In the end, socialization is not a simple learning process but a complex balancing act. In the process of sorting and weighing all the information we encounter, we form our own distinctive personalities and world views.

SOCIALIZATION AND THE LIFE COURSE

Although childhood has special importance to socialization, this process continues throughout our lives. An overview of the life course reveals that our society organizes human experience according to age—childhood, adolescence, adulthood, and, finally, old age.

CHILDHOOD

In recent years, the Nike corporation, maker of popular athletic shoes, has come under fire. Their shoes are made in Taiwan and Indonesia, in many cases by young children who work in factories rather than go to school. In all, some 200 million of the world's children work full time, earning about fifty cents an hour (Gibbs, 1996). Global Map 3–1 shows that child labor is most common in the nations of Africa and Asia.

Criticism of Nike springs from the fact that most North Americans think of *childhood*—roughly the first twelve years of life—as a carefree time of learning and play. In fact, explains historian Philippe Ariès (1965), the whole idea of "childhood" is fairly new. During the Middle Ages, children of four or five were treated like adults and expected to fend for themselves. Even a century ago, children in North America and Europe had much the same life as children in poor countries today: Many worked long hours, often under dangerous conditions, for little pay.

We may be tempted to defend our idea of childhood because youngsters are biologically immature. But a look back in time and around the world shows that the concept of "childhood" is grounded in culture. In rich countries, not everyone has to work. In addition, societies such as our own extend childhood to allow time for young people to learn the skills they will need in a high-technology workplace. Thus, we construct childhood and adulthood in contrasting ways, with "irresponsible" children looked after by "capable" adults (Benedict, 1938).

ADOLESCENCE

As industrialization created childhood as a distinct stage of life, adolescence emerged as a buffer between childhood and adulthood. We generally link

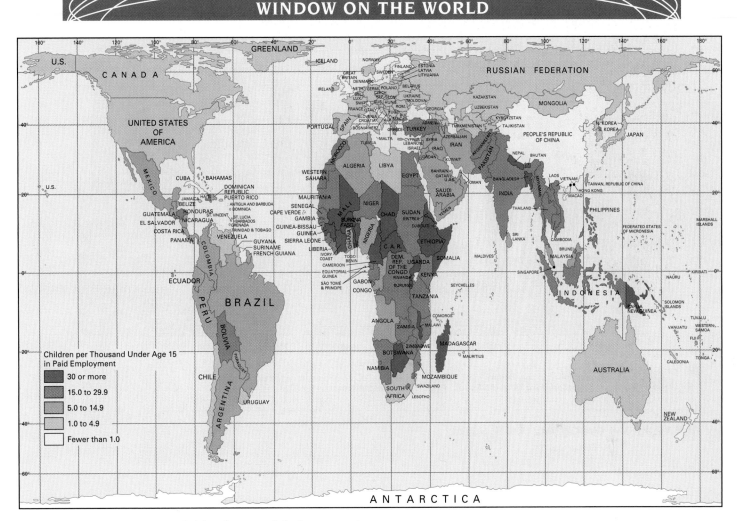

GLOBAL MAP 3–1 Child Labor in Global Perspective

Industrialization prolongs childhood and discourages children from work and other activities deemed suitable only for adults. Thus, child labor is relatively uncommon in the United States and other high-income countries. In less economically developed nations of the world, however, children are a vital economic asset, and they typically begin working as soon as they are able.

Source: *Peters Atlas of the World* (1990).

adolescence, or the teenage years, with emotional and social turmoil as parents spar with young people trying to develop their own identities. Here, again, we are tempted to attribute teenage turbulence to the biological changes of puberty. But this turmoil more correctly reflects cultural inconsistency. For example, the mass media glorify sex, and schools hand out condoms, even as parents urge restraint. Consider, too, that an eighteen-year-old male may in the United States face the adult duty of going to war, but he lacks the adult right to drink alcohol. In this society, then, adolescence is a time of social contradictions, when people are no longer children but are not yet adults.

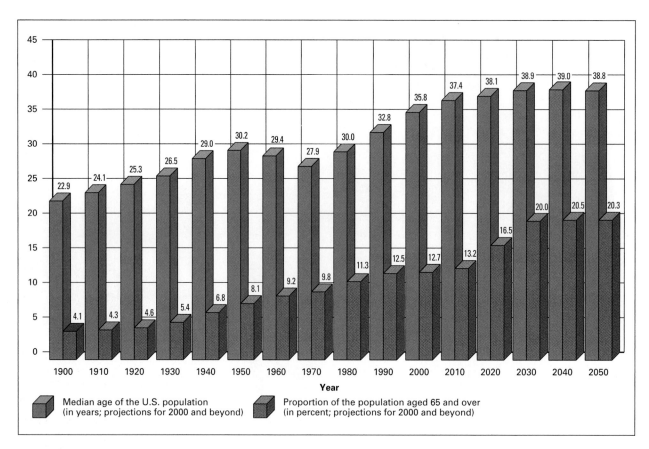

FIGURE 3–4 The Graying of U.S. Society

Source: U.S. Census Bureau (2000).

As is true of all stages of life, adolescence varies according to social background. Most young people from working-class families move right from high school to the adult world of work and parenting. Wealthier teens, however, have the resources to attend college and perhaps graduate school, thereby stretching adolescence to the late twenties and perhaps even the thirties.

ADULTHOOD

Adulthood, which begins between the late teens and early thirties depending on social background, is the time of life when most accomplishments occur. Having completed their schooling, people embark on careers and raise families of their own. Personalities are now largely formed, although marked change in a person's environment—such as unemployment, divorce, or serious illness—may result in significant change to the self.

During early adulthood—until about age forty—young adults learn to manage day-to-day affairs for themselves, often juggling conflicting priorities: parents, partner, children, schooling, and work (Levinson et al., 1978). Women especially often try to "do it all," since our culture gives them major responsibility for child rearing and household chores, even if they have demanding jobs outside the home (Hochschild, 1989).

In middle adulthood—roughly between the ages of forty and sixty—people sense that their life circumstances are pretty well set. They also become more aware of the fragility of health, which the young typically take for granted. Women who have devoted many years to raising a family can find middle adulthood emotionally trying. Children grow up and require less attention, and husbands become absorbed in their careers, leaving some women with spaces in their lives that are difficult to fill. Many women who divorce during middle adulthood also face serious financial problems (Weitzman, 1985, 1996). For all these reasons, an increasing number of women in middle adulthood return to school and seek new careers.

For everyone, growing older means facing physical decline, a prospect our culture makes more painful for women. Because good looks are considered more important for women, wrinkles, added weight, and graying hair can be traumatic. Men, of course, have their own particular difficulties as they grow older. Some must admit that they are never going to reach their career goals. Others realize that the price of career success has been neglect of family or personal health (Farrell & Rosenberg, 1981; Wolf, 1990).

OLD AGE

Old age—the later years of adulthood and the final stage of life itself—begins about the mid-sixties. With people living longer, the elderly population in the United States is growing twice as fast as the population as a whole. As Figure 3–4 shows, about one in eight people is over age sixty-five, and the elderly now outnumber teenagers. By 2050, the number of seniors will more than double (to at least 82 million), and almost half the country's people will be over forty (U.S. Census Bureau, 2000).

We can only begin to imagine the full consequences of the "graying of the United States." As more and more people retire from the labor force, the share of nonworking adults—already ten times greater than in 1900—will go up, fueling demand for health care and other social resources. But, perhaps most important, elderly people will be more visible in everyday life. In the twenty-first century, the young and the old will interact far more.

The aging of the U.S. population is one focus of **gerontology** (from the Greek word *geron*, meaning "old person"), *the study of aging and the elderly*. Gerontologists study both the physical and social dimensions of growing old.

Aging and biology. For most of our population, gray hair, wrinkles, and declining vitality begin in middle age. After about age fifty, bones become more brittle so that injuries take longer to heal, and the risks of chronic illnesses (such as arthritis and diabetes) and life-threatening conditions (such as heart disease and cancer) rise steadily. Sensory abilities—taste, sight, touch, smell, and especially hearing—become less

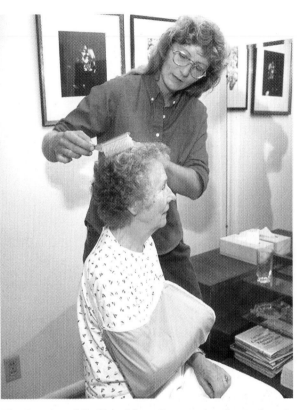

The "graying of the United States" means that the number of elders is increasing much faster than the population as a whole. This trend has increased the importance of caregiving: Many middle-aged people (typically, women) will spend as much time caring for aging parents (and in-laws) as they do raising their young children.

keen with age (Colloway & Dollevoet, 1977; Treas, 1995).

Even so, the vast majority of older people are neither disabled nor discouraged by their physical condition. Only one in ten seniors reports trouble walking, and fewer than one in twenty needs care in a hospital or nursing home. Overall, while 27 percent of people over age sixty-five characterize their health as "fair" or "poor," 73 percent consider their overall condition "good" or "excellent." Moreover, on average, the health of U.S. seniors is steadily improving (*Population Today*, 1997; U.S. National Center for Health Statistics, 1999).

Aging and culture. Culture shapes how we understand growing old. In low-income countries, old age confers on people great influence and respect, because

The reality of growing old is as much a matter of culture as it is of biology. In the United States, being elderly often means being inactive; yet, in rural regions of Iraq and other more traditional societies, old people commonly continue many familiar and productive routines.

elders control the most land and have wisdom gained over a lifetime (Sheehan, 1976; Hareven, 1982). A preindustrial society, then, is usually a **gerontocracy,** *a form of social organization in which the elderly have the most wealth, power, and prestige.*

But industrialization lessens the social standing of the elderly. Older people typically live apart from their grown children, and rapid social change renders much of what seniors know obsolete, at least from the point of view of the young. A problem of technologically advanced societies, then, is **ageism,** *prejudice and discrimination against the elderly.*

November 1, 1994, approaching Kandy, Sri Lanka. Our little van struggles up the steep mountain incline. Breaks in the lush vegetation offer spectacular views that interrupt our conversation about growing old. "Then there are no old age homes in your country?" I ask. "In Colombo and other cities, I am sure," our driver responds, "but not many. We are not like you Americans." "And how is that?" I counter, stiffening a bit. His eyes remain fixed on the road: "We would not leave our fathers and mothers to live alone."

Not surprisingly, growing old in the United States is challenging. Early in life, advancing in years means taking on new roles and responsibilities. In old age, by contrast, aging means leaving behind roles that have provided social identity and prestige. Removed from familiar work routines, some people view retirement as restful recreation, but others lose their self-worth and suffer outright boredom.

Reaching old age also means living with less income. But, today, the U.S. elderly population is doing better than ever. In 1960, 35 percent of the elderly were poor; in 1999, this figure fell to 9.7 percent—below the poverty rate of 11.8 percent for the population as a whole (U.S. Census Bureau, 2000). Put differently, a generation ago, old age carried the highest risk of poverty; today, the same is true of childhood.

Why the change? Better health, which allows older people to continue to work for income, is one reason. Another is more generous pension programs for retirees. Government programs also play a big part, with almost half of all government spending now assisting the elderly, even as spending on children has remained more or less flat.

Since 1980, on average, seniors have posted a 31 percent increase in income (in constant dollars), while the income of people under twenty-five has actually declined (U.S. Census Bureau, 2001). A reasonable question, then, is whether we should continue to favor the oldest members of our society and risk slighting the youngest—those who now suffer most from poverty.

DEATH AND DYING

Through most of human history, low living standards and limited medical technology meant that death—caused most often by disease or accident—came at any stage of life. Today, however, 85 percent of people in the United States die after the age of fifty-five (U.S. National Center for Health Statistics, 1999).

After observing many dying people, Elisabeth Kübler-Ross (1969) described death as an orderly transition involving five stages. Typically, a person first reacts to the prospect of dying with *denial*. The second phase is *anger*, as the person facing death sees it as a gross injustice. Third, anger gives way to *negotiation*, as the person imagines avoiding death by striking a bargain with God. The fourth stage, *resignation*, is often accompanied by psychological depression. Finally, a complete adjustment to death requires *acceptance*. At this point, no longer paralyzed by fear and anxiety, the person whose life is ending sets out to make the most of whatever time remains.

As the share of women and men in old age increases, we can expect our culture to become more comfortable with the idea of death. In recent years, for example, people in the United States and elsewhere are discussing death more openly, and the trend is to view dying as better than painful or prolonged suffering. Moreover, more married couples now prepare for death with legal and financial planning; this openness may ease somewhat the pain of the surviving spouse, a consideration for women who, more often than not, outlive their husbands.

THE LIFE COURSE: AN OVERVIEW

This brief examination of the life course points to two major conclusions. First, although each stage of life reflects the biological process of aging, the life course is largely a social construction. For this reason, people in various societies may experience a stage of

In many traditional societies, people express great respect not only for elders but also for their ancestors. Dani villagers in New Guinea mummified the body of this elder in a sitting position so that they could continue to honor him and feel his presence in their daily lives.

life quite differently or, for that matter, not at all. Second, in any society, the stages of the life course present characteristic problems and transitions that involve learning something new and, in many cases, unlearning familiar routines.

Note, too, that the experience of growing older varies according to class, race, ethnicity, and gender. Thus, the general patterns we have described are all subject to modification as they apply to various categories of people (Duncan et al., 1998).

Finally, people's life experiences also vary depending on when, in the history of a society, they are born. A **cohort** is *a category of people with a common characteristic, usually their age*. Age-cohorts are likely to be influenced by the same economic and cultural trends, so members have similar attitudes and values (Riley, Foner, & Waring, 1988). Women and men born in the 1940s and 1950s grew up during an economic expansion that gave them a sense of optimism. Today's college students, who have grown up in an age of economic uncertainty, are less confident about the future.

The penal system's requirement that new inmates suffer the indignity of having their heads shaved is more than a matter of hair style; such a degrading ritual is also the first stage in the process by which a total institution attempts to break down an individual's established social identity.

RESOCIALIZATION: TOTAL INSTITUTIONS

A final type of socialization, experienced by more than 2 million people in the United States at any one time, involves being confined—often against their will—in prisons or mental hospitals. This is the special world of the **total institution,** *a setting in which people are isolated from the rest of society and manipulated by an administrative staff.*

According to Erving Goffman (1961), total institutions have three distinctive characteristics. First, staff members supervise all spheres of daily life, including where residents (often called "inmates") eat, sleep, and work. Second, the environment of a total institution is highly standardized, with institutional food, uniforms, and one set of activities for everyone. Third, rules and schedules dictate when, where, and how inmates perform their daily routines.

The purpose of such regimentation is **resocialization,** *radically changing an inmate's personality through carefully controlling the environment.* Prisons and mental hospitals physically isolate inmates behind fences, barred windows, and locked doors, and control their access to the telephone, mail, and visitors. The institution becomes the inmate's entire world, making it easier for the staff to produce lasting change—or at least immediate compliance—in the inmate.

Resocialization is a two-part process. First, the staff breaks down a new inmate's existing identity using what Goffman (1961:14) describes as "abasements, degradations, humiliations, and profanations of self." For example, an inmate must surrender personal possessions, including clothing and grooming articles used to maintain a distinctive appearance. Instead, the staff provides standard-issue clothes so everyone looks alike. The staff subjects new inmates to "mortifications of self," including searches, medical examinations, head shaving, and fingerprinting, and then assigns each a serial number. Once inside the walls, individuals also give up their privacy as guards routinely monitor their living quarters.

In the second part of the resocialization process, the staff tries to build a new self in the inmate through a system of rewards and punishments. Having a book to read, watching television, or accessing the Internet may seem trivial to the outsider, but in the rigid environment of the total institution, these simple privileges can be a powerful motivation to conform. In the end, the length of incarceration typically depends on how well the inmate cooperates with the staff.

Resocialization can bring about considerable change in an inmate, but total institutions affect people in different ways. While some inmates are considered "rehabilitated" or "recovered," others may change little, and still others may become hostile and bitter. Furthermore, over a long period of time, the rigidly controlled environment can leave some *institutionalized,* without the capacity for independent living.

But what about the rest of us? Does socialization crush our individuality or empower us? The final box takes a closer look at this vital question.

CONTROVERSY & DEBATE

Are We Free within Society?

Throughout this chapter, we have stressed one key theme: Society shapes how we think, feel, and act. If this is so, then in what sense are we free? To answer this important question, consider the Muppets, puppet stars of television and film. Watching the antics of Kermit the Frog, Miss Piggy, and the rest of the troupe, we almost believe they are real, not objects animated from backstage. As the sociological perspective points out, human beings are like puppets in that we, too, respond to backstage forces. Society, after all, gives us a culture and shapes our lives according to class, race, and gender. In the face of such social constraints, are we ever really free?

Sociologists speak with many voices when addressing this question. One response, with politically liberal overtones, is that individuals are *not* free of society—in fact, as social creatures, we never could be. But if we are condemned to live in a society with power over us, it is important to do what we can to make our home as just as possible. That is, we

should work to lessen class differences and other barriers to opportunity for minorities, including women. Another approach, this time with conservative overtones, is that we *are* free because society can never dictate our dreams. Our history as a nation—right from the revolutionary act that led to its founding—is one story after another of individuals pursuing personal goals in spite of great odds.

We find both attitudes in George Herbert Mead's analysis of socialization. Mead recognized that society makes demands on us, sometimes setting itself before us as a barrier. But he also reminded us that human beings are spontaneous and creative, capable of continually acting back—individually and collectively—on society. Thus Mead noted the power of society while still affirming the human capacity to evaluate, criticize, and, ultimately, to choose and to change.

In the end, then, we may resemble puppets, but only on the surface. A crucial

difference—one that gives us a large measure of freedom—is that we can stop and look up at the "strings" that animate much of our action, and even yank on them defiantly at times (Berger, 1963:176). If our pull is persistent and powerful enough, we may accomplish more than we might imagine. As anthropologist Margaret Mead once mused, "Do not make the mistake of thinking that concerned people cannot change the world; it's the only thing that ever has."

Continue the debate . . .

1. *Do you think our society affords more freedom to males than to females? Why or why not?*

2. *What about modern, high-income countries compared to the world's traditional, low-income nations: Are some of the world's people more free than others?*

3. *Does an understanding of sociology increase your freedom? Why?*

SUMMARY

1. Socialization is the way individuals develop their humanity and particular identities. Through socialization, one generation transmits culture to the next.

2. A century ago, people thought most human behavior was guided by biological instinct. Today, we recognize human behavior results mostly from nurture rather than nature.

3. The permanently damaging effects of social isolation reveal that social experience is essential to human development.

4. Sigmund Freud's model of human personality has three parts. The id expresses innate human needs

or drives (the life and death instincts); the superego represents internalized cultural values and norms; the ego resolves competition between the demands of the id and the restraints of the superego.

5. Jean Piaget believed that human development reflects both biological maturation and increasing social experience. He identified four stages of cognitive development: sensorimotor, preoperational, concrete operational, and formal operational.

6. Lawrence Kohlberg applied Piaget's approach to moral development. Individuals first judge rightness in preconventional terms, according to their individual needs. Next, conventional moral

reasoning takes account of parents' attitudes and cultural norms. Finally, postconventional moral reasoning allows people to criticize society itself.

7. Carol Gilligan discovered that while males rely on abstract standards of rightness, females look at the effect of decisions on interpersonal relationships.

8. To George Herbert Mead, social experience generates the self, which Mead characterized as partly autonomous (the I) and partly guided by society (the me). Infants engage in imitation; children engage in play and games and eventually recognize the "generalized other."

9. Charles Horton Cooley used the term "looking-glass self" to explain that we see ourselves as we imagine others see us.

10. Erik H. Erikson identified characteristic challenges that individuals face at each stage of life from infancy to old age.

11. Usually the first setting of socialization, the family is the greatest influence on a child's attitudes and behavior.

12. Schools expose children to greater social diversity and introduce them to impersonal performance evaluations.

13. Peer groups free children from adult supervision and take on special significance during adolescence.

14. The mass media, especially television, also shape the socialization process. The average U.S. child spends as much time watching television as attending school or interacting with parents.

15. Each stage of the life course—from childhood to old age—is socially constructed in ways that vary from society to society.

16. People in high-income countries typically fend off death until old age. Accepting death is part of socialization for the elderly.

17. Total institutions such as prisons and mental hospitals try to resocialize inmates—that is, to radically change their personalities.

18. Socialization demonstrates the power of society to shape our thoughts, feelings, and actions. Yet, as humans we have the ability to act back, shaping both ourselves and our social world.

KEY CONCEPTS

socialization (p. 61) the lifelong social experience by which individuals develop their human potential and learn culture

personality (p. 61) a person's fairly consistent patterns of acting, thinking, and feeling

id (p. 64) Freud's term for the human being's basic drives

ego (p. 64) Freud's term for a person's conscious efforts to balance innate pleasure-seeking drives with the demands of society

superego (p. 65) Freud's term for the operation of culture within the individual in the form of internalized values and norms

sensorimotor stage (p. 65) Piaget's term for the level of human development at which individuals experience the world only through their senses

preoperational stage (p. 65) Piaget's term for the level of human development at which individuals first use language and other symbols

concrete operational stage (p. 65) Piaget's term for the level of human development at which individuals first perceive causal connections in their surroundings

formal operational stage (p. 66) Piaget's term for the level of human development at which individuals think abstractly and critically

self (p. 67) George Herbert Mead's term for that part of an individual's personality composed of self-awareness and self-image

looking-glass self (p. 67) Charles Horton Cooley's term referring to a self-image based on how we think others see us

peer group (p. 70) a social group whose members have interests, social position, and age in common

anticipatory socialization (p. 71) learning that helps a person achieve a desired position

mass media (p. 71) impersonal communications aimed at a vast audience

gerontology (p. 77) the study of aging and the elderly

gerontocracy (p. 78) a form of social organization in which the elderly have the most wealth, power, and prestige

ageism (p. 78) prejudice and discrimination against the elderly

cohort (p. 79) a category of people with a common characteristic, usually their age

total institution (p. 80) a setting in which people are isolated from the rest of society and manipulated by an administrative staff

resocialization (p. 80) radically changing an inmate's personality through carefully controlling the environment

CRITICAL-THINKING QUESTIONS

1. What do cases of social isolation teach us about the importance of social experience to humans?

2. State the two sides of the "nature-nurture" debate. In what sense are human nature and nurture not opposed to one another?

3. We have all seen young children place their hands in front of their faces and exclaim, "You can't see me!" They assume that if they cannot see you, then you cannot see them. What does this behavior suggest about a young child's ability to "take the role of the other"? Can a parent expect a young child to "see things from *my* point of view"?

4. What are the common themes in the ideas of Freud, Piaget, Kohlberg, Gilligan, Mead, and Erikson? In what ways do their theories differ?

APPLICATIONS AND EXERCISES

1. Working with several members of your sociology class, gather data by asking several classmates and friends to name traits they consider elements of "human nature." Then compare notes and discuss the extent to which these traits are the product of nature or nurture.

2. Find a copy of the book or video *Lord of the Flies*, a tale by William Golding based on a Freudian model of personality. Jack (and his hunters) represent the power of the id; Piggy consistently opposes them as the superego; Ralph stands between the two as the ego, the voice of reason. Golding was inspired to write the book by participating in the bloody D-Day landing in France during World War II. Do you agree with his belief that violence is part of human nature?

3. Make a list of the personality traits you think characterize you. If you have the courage, ask several others who know you well what they think. Can you explain where these traits came from?

4. Watch several hours of prime-time programming on network or cable television. Keep track of all the violence you see. Assign each program a "YIP rating," for the number of Years In Prison a person would serve for committing all the violent acts you witness (Fobes, 1996). On the basis of observing this small (and unrepresentative) sample of programs, what are your conclusions?

5. Install the CD-ROM packaged in the back of this new textbook to access a variety of study, review, and applications exercises designed to help you better understand the material covered in this chapter. The CD includes an author's tip video, as well as interactive maps, video application exercises, Web links, and study questions.

 SITES TO SEE

http://www.prenhall.com/macionis
Visit the interactive Web site that accompanies this text. Begin by clicking on the cover of your book. You will find a chapter-by-chapter study guide, practice tests, chat room, and many suggested Web links.

http://www.macionis.com
(or http://www.thesociologypage.com)
At the author's Web site, you can find brief biographies of George Herbert Mead, Charles Horton Cooley, and other sociologists.

http://www.nypsa.org
Learn more about Sigmund Freud and his work at the "Freud Net" site.

http://www.piaget.org/
The Jean Piaget Society hosts this Web site, which presents the work of this celebrated social psychologist.

http://www.nd.edu/~rbarger/kohlberg.html
This Web site is dedicated to the ideas and research of Lawrence Kohlberg.

SOCIAL INTERACTION IN EVERYDAY LIFE

Harold and Sybil are on their way to another couple's home in an unfamiliar section of Rochester, New York. They are now late because for the last twenty minutes they have traveled in circles looking for Monroe Avenue. Harold, gripping the wheel ever more tightly, is doing a slow burn. Sybil, sitting next to him, looks straight ahead, afraid to utter a word. Both realize that the evening is off to a bad start (Tannen, 1990:62).

Harold and Sybil are lost in more ways than one: They are unable to understand why they are growing enraged at their situation and at each other. Consider their plight from Harold's point of view: Like most men, Harold cannot tolerate getting lost, and, the longer he drives around, the more incompetent he feels. Sybil, on the other hand, cannot understand why Harold does not pull over and ask someone where Monroe Avenue is. If she were driving, she fumes to herself, they would already have arrived and would now be comfortably settled with drink in hand.

Why don't men like to ask for directions? Because men value their independence, they are uncomfortable asking for help (and also reluctant to accept it). To ask someone for assistance is the same as saying, "You know something I don't." If it takes Harold a few more minutes to find Monroe Avenue on his own—and keep his self-respect in the process—he thinks it's a good bargain.

If men pursue self-sufficiency and are aware of hierarchy, women are more attuned to others and strive for connectedness. From Sybil's point of view, asking for help is right because sharing information reinforces social bonds. Asking for directions seems as natural to her as searching on his own is to Harold. Obviously, getting lost is sure to generate conflict as long as neither one understands the other's point of view.

Such everyday social patterns are the focus of this chapter. We begin by presenting the building blocks of common experience and then explore the almost magical way in which face-to-face interaction generates reality. The central concept is **social interaction,** *the process by which people act and react in relation to others.* Through social interaction, we create the reality we perceive. Social structure, in turn, guides our interaction.

SOCIAL STRUCTURE: A GUIDE TO EVERYDAY LIVING

October 21, 1994, Ho Chi Minh City, Vietnam. This morning we leave the ship and make our way along the docks toward the center of Ho Chi Minh City—known to an earlier generation as Saigon. The government security officers wave us through the heavy iron gates. Pressed against the fence are dozens of men who operate cyclos (bicycles that push a small carriage attached to the front), the Vietnamese equivalent of taxicabs. We wave them off, but spend the next twenty minutes shaking our heads at several persistent drivers, who pedal alongside pleading for our business. The pressure is uncomfortable. We decide to cross the street but realize suddenly that there are no stop signs or signal lights—and the street is

In any rigidly ranked setting, no interaction can proceed until people assess each other's social standing. Thus, military personnel wear clear insignia to designate their level of authority. Don't we size up one another in much the same way in routine interactions, noting a person's rough age, quality of clothing, and manner for clues about social position?

```
an unbroken stream of bicycles, cyclos,
motorbikes, and small trucks. What to do?
The locals don't bat an eye—they just walk
at a steady pace across the street, part-
ing waves of vehicles that immediately
close in again behind them. Walk right
into traffic? With our small children on
our backs? Yup, we did it; that's the way
it works in Vietnam.
```

Members of every society rely on social structure to make sense out of daily situations. As one family's introduction to the streets of Vietnam suggests, the world can be disorienting—even frightening—when cultural norms are unclear. So what, then, are the building blocks of our daily lives?

STATUS

One building block of social organization is **status,** *a social position that an individual occupies.* Sociologists do not use the term "status" in its everyday meaning of "prestige," as when a bank president has more "status" than a bank teller. Sociologically, both "president" and "teller" are statuses or positions within the bank organization.

Every status is part of our social identity and defines our relationship to others. In the college classroom, for example, professors and students have distinct, well-defined responsibilities. Of course, we occupy many statuses at once. The term **status set** refers to *all the statuses a person holds at a given time.* A teenage girl is a *daughter* to her parents, a *sister* to her brother, a *student* at her college, and a *goalie* on her hockey team. Just as status sets branch out in many directions, they also change over the life course. A child turns into a parent, a student becomes a lawyer, and people marry to become husbands and wives, sometimes becoming single again as a result of divorce or death. Joining an organization or finding a job enlarges our status set; retirement or withdrawing from activities makes it smaller. Over a lifetime, individuals gain and lose dozens of statuses.

ASCRIBED AND ACHIEVED STATUS

Sociologists analyze statuses in terms of how people attain them. An **ascribed status** is *a social position a person receives at birth or assumes involuntarily later in life.* Examples of ascribed statuses are being a daughter, a Cuban, a teenager, or a widower. Ascribed statuses are matters about which people have little or no choice.

By contrast, an **achieved status** refers to *a social position a person assumes voluntarily and that reflects personal ability and choice.* Examples of achieved statuses are being an honors student, an Olympic athlete, a spouse, or a computer programmer or thief.

In practice, of course, most statuses involve a combination of ascription and achievement. That is, people's ascribed statuses influence the statuses they achieve. People who achieve the status of lawyer, for example, are likely to share the ascribed trait of having been born into well-off families. By the same token, many less desirable statuses, such as criminal, drug addict, or being out of work are more easily "achieved" by people born into poverty.

MASTER STATUS

Some statuses matter more than others. A **master status** is *a status that has special importance for social identity, often shaping a person's entire life.* For most people, occupation is a master status because it conveys a great deal about social background, education, and income.

Role models teach us that any one person can truly make a difference for our world. In December, 1955, the driver of a city bus in Montgomery, Alabama, asked passenger Rosa Parks to give up her seat, as required by law, so a white man could sit down. She refused and was arrested, fingerprinted, and later fined $14 for the offense. This courageous act prompted Birmingham's African American population to boycott city buses, leading to the repeal of the bus-segregation law.

In a negative sense, serious disease can also operate as a master status. Sometimes even lifelong friends avoid cancer patients or people with acquired immune deficiency syndrome (AIDS) simply because of their illness. Most societies of the world also limit opportunities for women, whatever their abilities, making gender a master status (Webster & Hysom, 1998).

ROLE

A second component of social interaction is **role**, *behavior expected of someone who holds a particular status.* Individuals *hold* a status and *perform* a role (Linton, 1937b). Holding the status of student, for example, leads one to attend classes and complete assignments and, more broadly, devote much of one's time to personal enrichment through academic study.

Both statuses and roles vary by culture. In the United States, the status "uncle" refers to a sibling of either mother or father; in Vietnam, however, the word for "uncle" is different on the mother's and father's sides of the family, and the two men have different responsibilities. In every society, actual role performance varies according to an individual's unique personality, although some societies permit more individual expression than others.

Because we occupy many statuses at once—a status set—everyday life is a mix of multiple roles. Robert Merton (1968) introduced the term **role set** to identify *a number of roles attached to a single status.*

Figure 4–1 shows four statuses of one individual, with each status linked to a different role set. First, the woman occupies the status of "wife," with a conjugal role (such as confidante and sexual partner) toward her husband, with whom she shares a domestic role toward the household. Second, she also holds the status of "mother," with routine responsibilities for her children (the maternal role) as well as their school and other organizations (the civic role). Third, as a professor, she interacts with students (the teacher role) and other academics (the colleague role). Fourth, as a researcher she gathers data (the laboratory role) that lead to publications (the author role).

A global perspective shows us that the roles people use to define their lives differ from society to society. In low-income countries, for example, most people work in agriculture or factories; postindustrial nations, by contrast, offer a greater range of occupational choices. Another dimension of difference is housework. As Global Map 4–1 on page 89 shows, especially in poor nations of the world, housework falls heavily on women.

ROLE CONFLICT AND ROLE STRAIN

People in high-income countries juggle many responsibilities demanded by their various statuses and roles. As most mothers can testify, both parenting and working outside the home are physically and emotionally draining. Sociologists thus recognize **role conflict** as *conflict among roles corresponding to two or more statuses.*

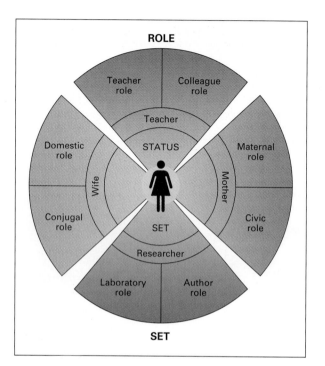

FIGURE 4–1 Status Set and Role Set

Even roles linked to a single status can make competing demands on us. **Role strain** refers to *tension among roles connected to a single status.* A plant supervisor may enjoy being friendly with other workers. At the same time, however, the supervisor has production goals and must maintain the personal distance needed to evaluate employees. In short, performing the roles of even a single status can be something of a balancing act (Gigliotti & Huff, 1995).

One strategy for minimizing role conflict is "compartmentalizing" our lives so that we perform roles for one status at one time and place, and carry out roles for another status in a completely different setting. A familiar example of this scheme is deciding to "leave the job at work" before heading home to one's family.

ROLE EXIT

After she herself left the life of a Catholic nun to become a university sociologist, Helen Rose Fuchs Ebaugh (1988) began to study *role exit,* the process by which people disengage from important social roles. In studying a range of "exes," including ex-nuns, ex-doctors, ex-husbands, and ex-alcoholics, Ebaugh saw a pattern in the process of "becoming an 'ex'."

According to Ebaugh, the process begins as people come to doubt their ability to continue in a certain role. As they imagine alternative roles, they ultimately reach a tipping point when they decide to pursue a new life. Even at this point, however, a past role can continue to influence our lives. "Exes" carry with them a self-image shaped by an earlier role, which can interfere with building a new sense of self. An ex-nun, for example, may hesitate to wear stylish clothing and makeup.

"Exes" must also rebuild relationships with people who knew them in their earlier life. Learning new social skills is another challenge. For example, Ebaugh reports, nuns who begin dating after decades in the church are often startled to learn that today's sexual norms are vastly different from those they knew as teenagers.

THE SOCIAL CONSTRUCTION OF REALITY

More than fifty years ago, the Italian playwright Luigi Pirandello wrote a play titled *The Pleasure of Honesty,* centered on a character named Angelo Baldovino—a brilliant man with a rather checkered past. Baldovino enters the fashionable home of the Renni family and introduces himself in a most peculiar way:

> Inevitably we construct ourselves. Let me explain. I enter this house and immediately I become what I have to become, what I can become: I construct myself. That is, I present myself to you in a form suitable to the relationship I wish to achieve with you. And, of course, you do the same with me. (1962:157–58)

Baldovino's introduction suggests that, while behavior is guided by status and role, we also have considerable ability to shape what happens moment to moment. "Reality," in other words, is not as fixed as we may think.

The phrase **social construction of reality** describes *the process by which people creatively shape reality through social interaction.* This idea is the familiar foundation of the symbolic-interaction paradigm, detailed in Chapter 1 ("Sociology: Perspective, Theory, and Method"). As Angelo Baldovino's remark suggests, quite a bit of "reality" remains unclear in everyone's mind, especially in unfamiliar situations. So we present ourselves in terms that suit the setting and our purposes, and, as others do the same, reality emerges.

Social interaction, then, amounts to a complex negotiation of reality. Most everyday situations involve

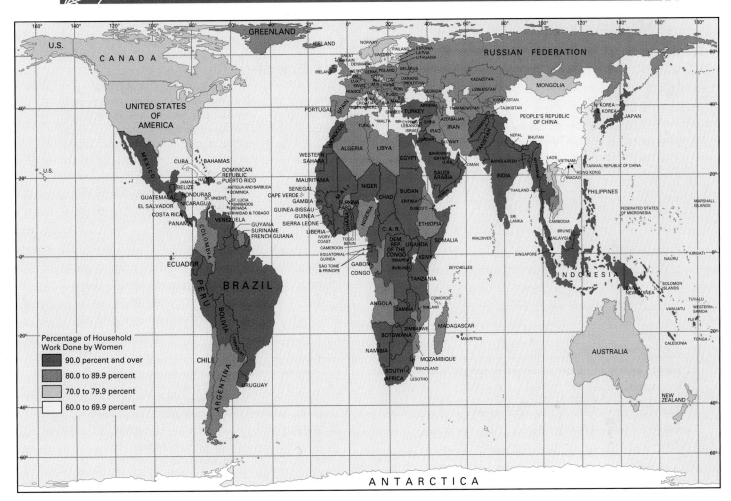

GLOBAL MAP 4–1 Housework in Global Perspective

Throughout the world, housework is a major component of women's routines and identities. This is especially true in poor societies of Latin America, Africa, and Asia, where women are not generally in the paid labor force. But our society, too, defines housework and child care as "feminine" activities, even though a majority of U.S. women work outside the home.

Source: *Peters Atlas of the World* (1990); updated by the author.

at least some agreement about what's going on, but participants share different perceptions of events to the extent that they are motivated by different interests and intentions.

Our very choice of words is one way we put a "spin" on events. The box on page 90 provides examples of language used by the military to create (or conceal?) reality.

"STREET SMARTS"

What people commonly call "street smarts" is actually a form of constructing reality. In his autobiography, *Down These Mean Streets*, Piri Thomas recalls moving to a new apartment in Spanish Harlem. Returning home one evening, young Piri found himself cut off by

CRITICAL THINKING

The "Spin" Game:
Choosing Our Words Carefully

Military organizations choose their words carefully to mask the horrors of war and make military action seem necessary and good.

William Lutz, an English professor at Rutgers University, collected examples of language used by U.S. military officers in the 1991 Persian Gulf War.

Read the following military terminology and the straight-talk translations. How do these terms put a "spin" on reality?

What do you think?

1. *Why, in your opinion, does the military "spin" reality in this way? Is this in the nation's interest or not?*

2. *What does this example suggest about the role of power in reality construction? Do large organizations have the power to shape the reality experienced by individuals?*

3. *Can you think of other examples of organizations shaping the reality we experience?*

Military language	Everyday meaning
Incontinent ordinance	Bombs or shells that miss their targets and hit civilians
Area denial weapons	Cluster bombs that kill and destroy anything within a particular area
Coercive potential	The capacity of bombs and shells to kill and injure the enemy
Suppressing assets	Reducing the enemy's ability to fight by killing people and destroying equipment
Ballistically induced aperture	Bullet hole
Scenario-dependent, post-crisis environment	Whether we win or lose

Waneko, the leader of the local street gang, who was flanked by a dozen others.

"Whatta ya say, Mr. Johnny Gringo," drawled Waneko.

Think man, I told myself, *think your way out of a stomping. Make it good.* "I hear you 104th Street coolies are supposed to have heart," I said. "I don't know this for sure. You know there's a lot of streets where a whole 'click' is made out of punks who can't fight one guy unless they all jump him for the stomp." I hoped this would push Waneko into giving me a fair one. His expression didn't change.

"Maybe we don't look at it that way."

Crazy, man, I cheer inwardly, *the cabron is falling into my setup.* . . . "I wasn't talking to you," I said. "Where I come from, the pres is president 'cause he got heart when it comes to dealing."

Waneko was starting to look uneasy. He had bit on my worm and felt like a sucker fish. His boys were now light on me. They were no longer so much interested in stomping me as seeing the outcome between Waneko and me. "Yeah," was his reply. . . .

I knew I'd won. Sure, I'd have to fight; but one guy, not ten or fifteen. If I lost, I might still get stomped, and if I won I might get stomped. I took care of this with my next sentence. "I don't know you or your boys," I said, "but they look cool to me. They don't feature as punks."

I had left him out purposely when I said "they." Now his boys were in a separate class. I had cut him off. He would have to fight me on his own, to prove his heart to himself, to his boys, and most important, to his turf. He got away from the stoop and asked, "Fair one, Gringo?" (1967:56–57)

This situation reveals the drama—sometimes subtle, sometimes savage—by which human beings creatively build reality. But, of course, not everyone enters a situation with equal standing. Should a police officer have come upon the fight that ensued between Piri and Waneko, both young men might well have ended up in jail.

Flirting is an everyday experience in reality construction. Each person offers information to the other, and hints at romantic interest. Yet the interaction proceeds with a tentative and often humorous air so that either individual can withdraw at any time without further obligation.

THE THOMAS THEOREM

By displaying his wits and boxing with Waneko until they both tired, Piri Thomas won acceptance by the gang. What took place that evening in Spanish Harlem is an example of the **Thomas theorem,** named after W. I. Thomas (1966:301; orig. 1931): *Situations that are defined as real become real in their consequences.*

Applied to social interaction, Thomas's theorem means that although reality, as it is fashioned, is initially "soft," it can become "hard" in its effects. In the case we have described, local gang members saw Piri Thomas act in a worthy way, so, in their eyes, he *became* worthy.

ETHNOMETHODOLOGY

Rather than assume that reality is something "out there," the symbolic-interaction paradigm states that people create reality in everyday encounters. But how, exactly, do we define reality for ourselves? Answering this question is the objective of *ethnomethodology,* a specialized approach within the symbolic-interaction paradigm.

The term itself has two parts: The Greek *ethno* refers to people and how they understand their surroundings; "methodology" designates a set of methods or principles. Combining them makes **ethnomethodology,** *the study of the way people make sense of their everyday surroundings.*

Ethnomethodology is largely the creation of Harold Garfinkel (1967), who challenged the then-dominant view of society as a broad, abstract "system."

Garfinkel wanted to explore how we make sense of countless familiar situations. Our talk and behavior, explained Garfinkel, rest on deeper assumptions about the world that, typically, we take quite for granted.

Consider, for a moment, how much about human behavior we assume in asking someone the simple question, "How are you?" Do we mean physically? mentally? spiritually? financially? Do we even want an answer, or are we "just being polite"?

Ethnomethodology, then, explores the process of making sense in social encounters. Garfinkel argues that the only way to discover how we make sense of events is to purposely *break the rules.* By deliberately ignoring conventional norms and observing how people respond, we tease out how people build a reality. Thus, Garfinkel (1967) directed his students to refuse to "play the game" in a wide range of situations. Some students living with their parents started acting as if they were boarders rather than children; others entered stores and insisted on bargaining for items; others engaged people in simple games (like tic-tac-toe) only to ignore the rules; still others began conversations while slowly moving closer and closer to the other person.

The students then reported on people's reactions. Typically, the "victims" became annoyed, which suggests how important our everyday reality is to us. Trying to identify exactly *why* people were disturbed led students to consider the unspoken social agreements that underlie family life, shopping, fair play, and the like.

Some sociologists view ethnomethodology as less-than-serious research because it focuses on commonplace experiences and employs unusual—even

How people construct reality has much to do with the society in which they live. For example, major political events, such as a nation going to war, reshape the lives of just about everyone. Imagine the effects of losing homes—and loved ones—on people living in the Balkans during the recent conflict there. Indeed, such tragic events may continue to shape people's lives for generations.

bizarre—methods. Nevertheless, ethnomethodology heightens our awareness of the unnoticed patterns of everyday life.

REALITY BUILDING: CLASS AND CULTURE

People do not build everyday experience "out of thin air." In part, how we act or what we see in our surroundings depends on our interests. Scanning the sky on a starry night, for example, lovers discover romance, while scientists view the same stars as hydrogen atoms fusing into helium. Social background also directs our perceptions, so that residents of, say, Spanish Harlem experience the world somewhat differently than people living on Manhattan's affluent East Side.

In truth, there are few common elements to the reality construction that goes on across the United States. Take baseball, the activity long described as our "national pastime." Only about one-third of U.S. adults describe themselves as "fans" and, as National Map 4–1 indicates, they are concentrated in particular regions of the country.

In global perspective, reality construction is even more variable. Consider these everyday situations: People waiting for a bus in London typically "queue up" in a straight line; people in New York are rarely so orderly. The law in Saudi Arabia forbids women to drive cars, a constraint unheard of in the United States. Fear of crime in our big cities is much greater than it is elsewhere—including London, Paris, Rome, Calcutta, and Hong Kong—and this sense of public danger shapes the daily realities of tens of millions of our citizens.

The general conclusion is that people build reality from the surrounding culture. Chapter 2 ("Culture") explained how people the world over find different meanings in specific gestures, so travelers can find themselves building a most unexpected reality. Similarly, what we see in a book or a film also depends on the assumptions we hold about the world. In a study of popular culture, JoEllen Shively (1992) screened "western" films to men of European descent and to Native American men. The men in both categories claimed to enjoy the films but for different reasons. White men interpreted the films as praising rugged people striking out for the West to impose their will on nature. Native American men, by contrast, saw in the same films a celebration of land and nature apart from any human ambitions.

If people in different societies construct different realities, what about human feelings? Are emotions much the same everywhere? Or are our deepest feelings a product of culture? Cross-cultural research, described in the box on pages 94–95, indicates that emotions are rooted in both biology and culture.

DRAMATURGICAL ANALYSIS: "THE PRESENTATION OF SELF"

Erving Goffman (1922–1982) analyzed social interaction, explaining how people in their everyday behavior are very much like actors performing on a stage. If we imagine ourselves as directors observing what goes on in the "theater" of everyday life, we engage in what

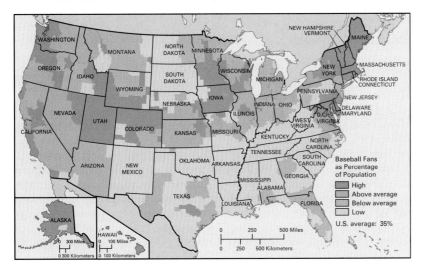

NATIONAL MAP 4–1
Baseball Fans
across the United States

One in three U.S. adults claims to follow baseball. The map shows that fans are concentrated in the northern states from New England to the Pacific Northwest. Why? What categories of people have a world view that celebrates this kind of activity? (Hint: Baseball is more likely to appeal to white males over forty years of age who were born in the United States.)

Source: From Michael J. Weiss, *Latitudes & Attitudes: An Atlas of American Tastes, Trends, Politics, and Passions.* Copyright © 1994 by Michael J. Weiss. Reprinted by permission of the author.

Goffman called **dramaturgical analysis,** *the study of social interaction in terms of theatrical performance.*

Dramaturgical analysis offers a fresh look at the concepts of status and role. A status is like a part in a play, and a role serves as a script, supplying dialogue and action for the characters. Goffman described each person's performance as the **presentation of self,** *an individual's efforts to create specific impressions in the minds of others.* This process, sometimes called *impression management,* has several distinctive elements (Goffman, 1959, 1967).

PERFORMANCES

As we present ourselves in everyday situations, we convey information—consciously and unconsciously—to others. An individual's performance includes dress (costume), objects carried along (props), and tone of voice and gestures (manner). In addition, people craft their performances according to the setting. We may joke loudly in a restaurant, for example, but assume a reverent manner upon entering a church. Individuals design settings, such as homes or offices, to bring about desired reactions in others.

An illustration: the doctor's office. Consider how a physician's office conveys information to an audience of patients. Physicians enjoy high prestige and power in the United States, a fact evident on entering the doctor's office. First, the physician is nowhere to be seen. Instead, in what Goffman describes as the "front region" of the setting, the patient encounters a receptionist who functions as a gatekeeper, deciding if and when the patient can see the physician. Who waits to see whom is, of course, a power game. A simple survey of the doctor's waiting room, with patients (often impatiently) waiting to gain entry to the inner sanctum, leaves little doubt that the physician controls events.

The physician's private office and examination room are the "back region" of the setting. Here, the patient confronts a wide range of props, such as medical books and framed degrees, that reinforce the impression that the physician has the specialized knowledge necessary to call the shots. In the office, the physician usually remains seated behind a desk—the larger and grander the desk, the greater the statement of power—while the patient is provided with only a chair.

The physician's appearance and manner convey still more information. The usual costume of white lab coat may have the practical function of keeping clothes from becoming soiled, but its social function is to let others know at a glance the physician's status. A stethoscope around the neck or a black medical bag in hand has the same purpose. A doctor's highly technical language—frequently mystifying to the patient—also emphasizes the hierarchy in the situation. Finally,

GLOBAL SOCIOLOGY

The Sociology of Emotions: Do People Everywhere Feel the Same?

On a busy New York sidewalk, a woman reacts angrily to an in-line skater who zooms past her. Her facial expression, accompanied by a few choice words, broadcasts a strong emotion that North Americans easily recognize. But would an observer from Nigeria, Nicaragua, or New Guinea be able to interpret her gestures? In short, do people everywhere have similar feelings and express them in the same way?

Paul Ekman and his colleagues studied emotional life in a number of countries, including a small society in New Guinea. From this research, they concluded that people around the world share six basic emotions: anger, fear, disgust, happiness, surprise, and sadness. Moreover, people everywhere express these feelings using the same distinctive facial gestures. To Ekman, this commonality points to the fact that much of our emotional life is universal—rather than culturally variable—and that the display of emotion is biologically rooted in our

facial features, muscles, and central nervous system.

But Ekman notes three ways in which emotional life differs according to culture. First, *what triggers an emotion differs from one society to another.* Whether a particular situation is defined as an insult (causing anger), a loss (producing sadness), or a mystical event (provoking surprise) depends on culture. In other words, people in various societies around the world react quite differently to the same event.

Second, *people display emotions according to the norms of their culture.* Every society has its own rules about when, where, and to whom people may exhibit certain emotions. Members of our society, for example, typically express emotions more freely at home among family members than in the workplace among colleagues. Similarly, we expect children to show emotion to parents, although parents are taught to carefully guard their emotions in front of their children.

Third, *societies differ in terms of how people cope with emotions.* Some societies encourage the expression of feelings, while others belittle emotion and demand that people keep their feelings to themselves. Societies also display significant gender differences in this regard. Our culture tends to label emotional expression as feminine, expected of women but a sign of weakness among men. In other societies, however, the link between gender and emotions is less pronounced or even reversed.

In sum, Ekman's research leads us to conclude that people the world over experience the same basic emotions. But what sparks a particular emotion, how and where a person expresses it, and how people define emotions in general all vary as matters of culture.

Sources: Ekman (1980a, 1980b), Lutz & White (1986), and Lutz (1988).

---

patients use the title "doctor," but they, in turn, are frequently addressed only by their first names, which further underscores the physician's dominant position. The overall message of a doctor's performance is clear: "I will help you, but you must allow me to take charge."

NONVERBAL COMMUNICATION

Novelist William Sansom describes the performance of a fictional Mr. Preedy—an English vacationer on a beach in Spain:

> He took care to avoid catching anyone's eye.
> First, he had to make it clear to those potential

companions of his holiday that they were of no concern to him whatsoever. He stared through them, round them, over them—eyes lost in space. The beach might have been empty. If by chance a ball was thrown his way, he looked surprised; then let a smile of amusement light his face (Kindly Preedy), looked around dazed to see that there were people on the beach, tossed it back with a smile to himself and not a smile *at* the people. . . .

> [He] then gathered together his beach-wrap and bag into a neat sand-resistant pile (Methodical and Sensible Preedy), rose slowly to stretch his huge frame (Big-Cat Preedy), and

To most people in the United States, these expressions convey anger, fear, disgust, happiness, surprise, and sadness. But do people elsewhere in the world define them in the same way? Research suggests that all human beings experience the same basic emotions and display them to others in the same basic ways. But culture plays a part by specifying the situations that trigger one emotion or another.

tossed aside his sandals (Carefree Preedy, after all). (1956; quoted in Goffman, 1959:4–5)

Without uttering a single word, Mr. Preedy offers a great deal of information about himself to anyone observing him. This illustrates the process of **nonverbal communication,** *communication using body movements, gestures, and facial expressions rather than speech.*

Many parts of the body can be used to generate *body language,* that is, to convey information to others. Facial expressions are the most significant form of body language. Smiling, for example, expresses pleasure, although we distinguish between the deliberate smile of Kindly Preedy on the beach, a spontaneous smile of joy

at seeing a friend, a pained smile of embarrassment, and the full, unrestrained smile of self-satisfaction we often associate with the "cat who ate the canary."

Eye contact is another crucial element of nonverbal communication. Generally, we use eye contact to invite social interaction. Someone across the room "catches our eye," sparking a conversation. Avoiding another's eyes, by contrast, discourages communication. Hands, too, speak for us. Common hand gestures within our culture convey, among other things, an insult, a request for a ride, an invitation for someone to join us, or a demand that others stop in their tracks. Gestures also supplement spoken words. Pointing in a menacing way at someone, for example, gives greater

When we enter the presence of others, we "construct" ourselves and begin a "presentation of self" that has much in common with a dramatic performance. Such a presentation involves clothing (costume), other objects (props), certain typical behavior (script), and it takes place in a particular setting (stage). No wonder the ancient Greeks, who understood the element of acting in everyday life, used the same word for "person" and "mask."

emphasis to a word of warning, as shrugging the shoulders adds an air of indifference to the phrase "I don't know," and rapidly waving the arms lends urgency to the single word "Hurry!"

As any actor knows, it is very difficult to pull off a "perfect performance" in front of others. In everyday performances, unintended body language can contradict our planned meaning: A teenage boy explains why he is getting home so late, for example, but his mother doubts his words because he avoids looking her in the eye; the movie star on a television talk show claims that her recent flop at the box office is "no big deal," but the nervous swing of her leg suggests otherwise. Because nonverbal communication is hard to control, it provides clues to deception, in much the same way that a lie detector records telltale changes in breathing, pulse rate, perspiration, and blood pressure.

Detecting lies is difficult, because no single bodily gesture directly indicates deceit the way, say, a smile indicates pleasure. Even so, because a performance involves so many expressions, few people can lie without

allowing some piece of contradictory information to slip by, thereby arousing the suspicions of a careful observer. Thus, the key to detecting deceit is to scan the whole performance with an eye for inconsistencies (Ekman, 1985).

GENDER AND PERFORMANCES

Because women are socialized to be less assertive than men, they tend to be especially sensitive to nonverbal communication. In fact, gender is a central element in personal performances. Based on the work of Nancy Henley, Mykol Hamilton, and Barrie Thorne (1992), we can extend our discussion of personal performances to spotlight the importance of gender.

Demeanor. Demeanor—general conduct or deportment—is a clue to social power. Simply put, powerful people enjoy more personal freedom in how they act. Off-color remarks, swearing, or removing shoes and putting one's feet up on a desk may be acceptable for the boss, but rarely for employees. Similarly, powerful people can interrupt others whenever they wish, while subordinates are expected to display deference through silence (Smith-Lovin & Brody, 1989; Henley, Hamilton, & Thorne, 1992).

Since women generally occupy positions of lesser power, demeanor is a gender issue as well. As Chapter 10 ("Gender Stratification") explains, about half of all working women in the United States hold clerical or service jobs under the control of supervisors, who are usually men. Women, then, must craft their personal performances more formally than men and defer more often in everyday interaction.

Use of space. How much space does a personal performance require? Power plays a key role here, also, because using more space is a sign of personal importance. According to Henley, Hamilton, and Thorne (1992), men typically command more space than women, whether pacing back and forth before an audience or casually sitting on a bench. Why? Our culture traditionally has measured femininity by how *little* space women occupy (the standard of "daintiness") and masculinity by how *much* territory a man controls (the standard of "turf").

For both sexes, **personal space** refers to *the surrounding area over which a person makes some claim to privacy.* In the United States, people generally position themselves several feet apart when speaking; throughout the Middle East, by contrast, people stand much closer. But just about everywhere, men routinely

Near the end of his life, Erving Goffman (1979) studied the place of gender in advertising—that is, how advertising portrays the relative social position of men and women. Look at this Pepsi ad from an earlier era: What messages does it convey about women and men? Do you think today's advertising is different in this regard?

intrude into women's personal space. If a woman moves into a man's personal space, however, he is likely to take it as a sexual overture, a fact that helps keep women "in their place."

Staring, smiling, and touching. Eye contact encourages interaction. In conversations, women more than men work to sustain eye contact. But men have their own distinctive brand of eye contact: *staring*. When men stare at women, they are claiming social dominance and defining women as sexual objects.

Although frequently conveying pleasure, smiling is also a symbol of appeasement or submission. In a male-dominated world, say Henley, Hamilton, and Thorne, women smile more than men.

Finally, mutual touching conveys intimacy and caring. Apart from close relationships, however, touching is generally something men do to women (and rarely, in our culture, to other men). A male physician touches the shoulder of his female nurse as they examine a report, a young man touches the back of his woman friend as he guides her across the street, or a male instructor touches young women as he teaches them to ski. In such examples, the touching may evoke little response, but it amounts to a subtle ritual by which men claim dominance over women.

IDEALIZATION

Complex motives underlie human behavior. Even so, Goffman suggests, we construct performances to *idealize* our intentions. That is, we try to convince others (and perhaps ourselves) that our actions reflect ideal cultural standards rather than selfish motives.

Idealization is easily illustrated by returning to the world of physicians and patients. In a hospital, physicians engage in a performance known as "making rounds." Entering a patient's room, the physician often stops at the foot of the bed and silently examines the patient's chart. Afterwards, physician and patient talk briefly. In ideal terms, this routine involves a physician making a personal visit to inquire about a patient's condition.

In reality, the picture is not so perfect. A physician may see dozens of patients a day and remember little about many of them, so that reading the chart is a chance to recall the patient's name and medical problems. Revealing the impersonality of much medical care would undermine the cultural ideal of the physician as deeply concerned about the welfare of others.

Physicians, college professors, and other professionals typically idealize their motives for entering their chosen careers. They describe their work as "making a contribution to science," perhaps "serving the community," or even "answering a call from God." Rarely do people admit the less honorable, although common, motives—namely, the income, power, prestige, and leisure that these occupations provide.

More generally, idealization is part of civility, since we all smile and make polite remarks to people we do not like. Such little lies ease our way through social interactions. Even when we suspect that others are putting on an act, we are unlikely to challenge their performance, for reasons that we shall explain next.

Hand gestures vary widely from one culture to another. Yet people everywhere define a chuckle, grin, or smirk in response to someone's performance as an indication that one does not take another person seriously. Therefore, the world over, people who cannot restrain their mirth tactfully cover their faces.

EMBARRASSMENT AND TACT

The famous professor keeps mispronouncing the dean's name; the ambassador rises from the table to speak, unaware of the napkin that still hangs from her neck; the president becomes ill at a state dinner. As carefully as individuals may craft their performances, slip-ups of all kinds occur. The result is *embarrassment*, or discomfort following a spoiled performance. Goffman describes embarrassment as "losing face."

Embarrassment is an ever-present danger because, first, idealized performances typically contain some deception. Second, most performances involve juggling so many elements that one thoughtless moment can shatter the intended impression.

A curious fact is that an audience often overlooks flaws in a performance, allowing the actor to avoid embarrassment. If we do point out a misstep ("Excuse me, but do you know your fly is open?"), we do it discreetly and only to avoid some even greater loss of face. In Hans Christian Andersen's classic fable, "The Emperor's New Clothes," the child who blurts out that the emperor is naked tells the truth, but is scolded for being rude.

Often, too, members of an audience help the performer recover from a flawed performance. *Tact*, then, amounts to helping someone "save face." After hearing a supposed expert make an embarrassingly inaccurate remark, for example, people may tactfully ignore the comment, as if it had never been spoken. Or mild laughter may indicate they wish to treat what was said as a joke. Or a listener may simply respond, "I'm sure

you didn't mean that," noting the statement but not allowing it to destroy the actor's performance.

Why is tact so common? Because embarrassment provokes discomfort not simply for the actor but for *everyone*. Just as the entire audience feels uneasy when an actor forgets a line, people who observe awkward behavior are reminded of how fragile their own performances often are. Socially constructed reality thus functions like a dam holding back a sea of chaos. Should one person's performance spring a leak, others tactfully help make repairs. Everyone, after all, lends a hand in building reality, and no one wants it to be suddenly swept away.

In sum, Goffman's research shows that, although behavior is spontaneous in some respects, it is more patterned than we like to think. Almost 400 years ago, William Shakespeare captured this idea in memorable lines that still ring true:

> All the world's a stage,
> And all the men and women merely players.
> They have their exits and their entrances,
> And one man in his time plays many parts.
> (*As You Like It*, II)

INTERACTION IN EVERYDAY LIFE: TWO APPLICATIONS

We have now examined the major elements of social interaction. The final sections of this chapter illustrate these lessons by focusing on two important dimensions of everyday life: language and humor.

LANGUAGE: THE GENDER ISSUE

As Chapter 2 ("Culture") explains, language is the thread that joins members of a society in the symbolic web we call culture. Language conveys not only a surface message, but also deeper levels of meaning. One level involves gender. Language defines men and women differently in at least three ways—in terms of power, value, and attention.[1]

Language and power. A young man astride his new motorcycle rolls proudly up his friend's driveway and eagerly asks, "Isn't she a beauty?" On the surface, the question has little to do with gender. Yet, why does the fellow use the pronoun "she" rather than "he" to refer to his prized possession?

The answer is that language helps men to establish control over their surroundings. That is, a man attaches a female pronoun to a motorcycle (or car, boat, or other object) because it reflects *ownership*.

Another control function of language relates to people's names. Traditionally in the United States and in many other parts of the world, a woman takes the family name of the man she marries. While few today consider this an explicit statement of a man's ownership of a woman, many think it reflects male dominance. For this reason, an increasing share of married women (about 15 percent) have kept their own names or merged two family names (Brightman, 1994).

Language and value. The English language usually treats as masculine whatever has greater value, force, or significance. For instance, the adjective "virtuous," meaning "morally worthy" or "excellent," is derived from the Latin word *vir* meaning "man." Contrarily, the disparaging adjective "hysterical," meaning "uncontrollable emotion," comes from the Greek word *hyster*, meaning "uterus."

In many familiar ways, language also confers different value upon the two sexes. Traditional masculine terms such as "king" or "lord" have retained their positive meaning, while some comparable terms, such as "queen," "madam," or "dame," have acquired negative connotations. Thus, language both mirrors social attitudes and helps to perpetuate them.

Language and attention. Language also shapes reality by directing attention to masculine activity. In

Why do we associate ownership with men and characterize what is owned as feminine? How easily can you imagine renaming this boat with the gender reversed?

the English language, the plural pronoun "they" is gender-neutral. But the corresponding singular pronouns "he" and "she" specify gender. According to traditional grammatical practice, "he" along with the possessive "his" and objective "him" refer to *all people*. Thus, we assume that the bit of wisdom "He who hesitates is lost" refers to women as well as men. But this practice also reflects the cultural pattern of neglecting the existence of women.

The English language has no gender-neutral third-person singular pronoun. In recent years, however, the plural pronouns "they" and "them" have increasingly gained currency as singular pronouns ("A person should do as they please"). This usage violates grammatical rules, yet there is no doubt that English is changing to accept such gender-neutral constructions.

Grammar aside, the mix of gender and language is likely to remain a source of miscommunication between women and men. In the box, Harold and Sybil—whose misadventures finding a friend's home opened this chapter—return to illustrate how the two sexes often seem to be speaking different languages.

---

[1] The following sections draw primarily on Henley, Hamilton, & Thorne (1992). Additional material is drawn from Thorne, Kramarae, & Henley (1983), MacKay (1983), and others as noted.

SOCIAL DIVERSITY

Gender and Language:
"You Just Don't Understand!"

In the story that opened this chapter, a couple faces a situation that rings all too true to many people: When they are lost, men grumble to themselves, and perhaps blame their partners, but avoid asking for directions. For their part, women can't understand such behavior.

Deborah Tannen, who has studied the language differences between the sexes, explains why. Men, she claims, see almost all everyday encounters as competitive, so getting lost is bad enough without asking for help and thereby letting someone else get "one up." By contrast, because women have a generally subordinate position, they are socialized to ask for help. Sometimes, Tannen points out, women will ask for assistance even when they don't need it.

A similar gender-linked problem common to couples involves what men call "nagging." Consider the following exchange (Adler, 1990:74):

SYBIL: What's wrong, honey?

HAROLD: Nothing . . .

SYBIL: Something is bothering you. I can tell.

HAROLD: I told you nothing is bothering me. Leave me alone.

SYBIL: But I can see that something is wrong.

HAROLD: OK. Just why do you think something is bothering me?

SYBIL: Well, for one thing, you're bleeding all over your shirt.

HAROLD [*now irritated*]: It doesn't bother me.

SYBIL [*losing her temper*]: WELL, IT SURE IS BOTHERING ME!

HAROLD: I'll go change my shirt.

The problem couples face in communicating is that what one partner *intends* by a comment is not always what the other *hears* in the words. To Sybil, her opening question is an effort at

cooperative problem solving. She can see that something is wrong with Harold (who has carelessly cut himself while doing yard work), and she wants to help him. But Harold interprets her pointing out his problem as belittling him, and tries to close off the discussion. Sybil, confident that Harold would be more positive towards her if he just understood that she only wants to be helpful, repeats herself. This sets in motion a vicious circle in which Harold, thinking his wife is trying to make him feel incapable of looking after himself, responds by digging in his heels. This, in turn, makes his wife all the more sure that she needs to do something. And round it goes until somebody loses patience.

In the end, Harold gives in only to the extent that he agrees to change his shirt. Notice he still refuses to discuss the original problem. Misunderstanding his wife's motives, Harold just wants Sybil to leave him alone. For her part, Sybil fails to understand her husband's view of the situation and walks away convinced that he is a stubborn grouch.

Sources: Adler (1990) and Tannen (1990).

HUMOR: PLAYING WITH REALITY

Humor plays a vital part in everyday life. But, while everyone laughs at a joke, few people think about what makes something funny or why humor is a part of everyday life around the world. We can apply many of the ideas developed in this chapter to explore the character of humor.[2]

The foundation of humor. Humor is a product of reality construction; specifically, it stems from the con-

trast between two different realities. Generally, one reality is *conventional*, that is, what people expect in some situation. The other reality is *unconventional*, an unexpected violation of cultural patterns. Humor, therefore, arises from contradiction, ambiguity, and

---

[2]The ideas contained in this discussion are those of the author (1987), except as otherwise noted. The general approach draws on work presented earlier in this chapter, especially on the ideas of Erving Goffman.

"double meanings" found in differing definitions of the same situation. Note how this principle works in the newspaper headlines presented in the box on page 102.

Of course, there are countless ways to mix realities and, thereby, generate humor. Contrasting realities emerge from statements that contradict themselves, like "Nostalgia is not what it used to be." Switching words, too, can create humor, as in Oscar Wilde's line that "Work is the curse of the drinking class," and even reordering syllables does the trick, as in the case of the (probably fictitious) country song "I'd rather have a bottle in front of me than a frontal lobotomy."

Of course, a joke can be built the other way around, so that the comic leads the audience to *expect* an unconventional answer and then delivers a very ordinary one. When a reporter asked the famous desperado Willy Sutton why he robbed banks, for example, he replied dryly: "Because that's where the money is." However a joke is constructed, the greater the opposition or incongruity between the two definitions of reality, the greater the potential for humor.

When telling jokes, the comedian can strengthen this opposition in various ways. One common technique used on the stage is to present the first, conventional remark in conversation with another actor, then turn toward the audience (or the camera) to deliver the second, unexpected line. In one of his films, Groucho Marx swaggers in front of a young woman and brags, "This morning I shot a lion in my pajamas." Then, dropping his voice and turning to the camera, he adds, "What the lion was doing in my pajamas, I'll *never* know." Such "changing channels" underscores the incongruity of the two parts. Following the same logic, many stand-up comedians also "reset" the audience to conventional expectations by interjecting "But, seriously, folks . . ." after one joke and before the next one.

To construct the strongest contrast in meaning, comedians pay careful attention to their performances—the precise words they use, as well as the timing of their delivery. A joke is "well told" if the comic creates the sharpest possible opposition between the realities; in a careless performance, the humor falls flat. Since the key to humor lies in the opposition of realities, we can see why the climax of a joke is termed the "*punch* line."

The dynamics of humor: "Getting it." Someone who does not understand either the expected or unexpected realities embedded in a joke may complain, "I don't get it." To "get" humor, members of an audience must understand the two realities involved well enough to appreciate their difference.

But comics may make getting the joke harder still by leaving out some important information. The audience, in other words, must pay attention to the *stated* elements of the joke and fill in the missing pieces on their own. As a simple case, consider the comment of movie producer Hal Roach upon reaching his one-hundredth birthday:

"If I had known I would live to be one hundred, I would have taken better care of myself!"

Here, "getting" the joke depends on realizing the unstated fact that Roach *must* have taken pretty good care of himself since he made it to one hundred in the first place. Or take one of W. C. Fields's lines: "Some weasel took the cork out of my lunch!" To finish the joke, we think to ourselves, "Some lunch!"

Here is a more complex joke, found on the wall of a college restroom:

Dyslexics of the World, Untie!

To get this one, you must know, first, that people with dyslexia reverse letters; second, you must recognize the line as a play on Karl Marx's call to the world's workers to unite; third, you must recognize "untie" as an anagram of "unite," as a disgruntled dyslexic person might write it.

Why would a comic ask an audience to make such an effort to understand a joke? Simply because our enjoyment of a joke is heightened by the pleasure of having completed the puzzle necessary to "get it." In addition, "getting" the joke confers a favored insider status. We can also understand the frustration of *not* getting a joke: fear of being judged stupid, coupled with a sense of being excluded from the pleasure shared by others. Not surprisingly, outsiders in such a situation sometimes fake "getting" the joke, or someone may tactfully explain a joke so a person doesn't feel left out.

But, as the old saying goes, if a joke has to be explained, it won't be very funny. Besides taking the edge off the language and timing on which the *punch* depends, an explanation removes the mental involvement and greatly reduces the listener's pleasure.

The topics of humor. People throughout the world smile and laugh, making humor a universal human trait. But the world's people differ in what they find funny, so humor does not travel well.

October 1, 1994, Kobe, Japan. Can you share a joke with people who live halfway around the world? At dinner, I ask two Japanese college women to tell me a joke.

CRITICAL THINKING

Double Take:
Real Headlines That Make People Laugh

Humor is generated by mixing together two opposing realities. Here are several actual headlines from recent newspapers. Read each one and identify the conventional meaning intended by the writer as well as the unconventional interpretation that generates humor.

"Police Begin Campaign to Run Down Jaywalkers"

"Drunk Gets Nine Months in Violin Case"

"Iraqi Head Seeks Arms"

"Stud Tires Out"

"Survivor of Siamese Twins Joins Parents"

"Prostitutes Appeal to Pope"

"Panda Mating Fails: Veterinarian Takes Over"

"Soviet Virgin Lands Short of Goal Again"

"Teacher Strikes Idle Kids"

"Squad Helps Dog Bite Victim"

"Miners Refuse to Work after Death"

"Killer Sentenced to Die for Second Time in Ten Years"

"War Dims Hope for Peace"

"British Left Waffles on Falkland Islands"

"Stolen Painting Found by Tree"

What do you think?

1. For each headline, do you see the "expected" and "unexpected" meaning?

2. Which headlines are most funny? Why?

3. Can you think of other everyday examples of humor?

Source: Thanks to Kay Fletcher.

"You know 'crayon'?" Asako asks. I nod. "How do you ask for a crayon in Japanese?" I respond that I have no idea. She laughs as she says what sounds like "crayon crayon." Her companion Mayumi laughs, too. My wife and I sit awkwardly straight-faced. Asako relieves some of our embarrassment by explaining that the Japanese word for "give me" is <u>kureyo</u>, which sounds like "crayon." I force a smile.

What is humorous to the Japanese, then, may be lost on the Chinese, Iraqis, or people in the United States. To some degree, too, the social diversity of our own country means that people will find humor in different situations. New Englanders, southerners, and westerners have their own brands of humor, as do Latinos and Anglos, fifteen- and fifty-year-olds, Wall Street bankers and southwestern rodeo riders.

But, for everyone, humor deals with topics that lend themselves to double meanings or *controversy*. For example, the first jokes many of us learned as children concerned the cultural taboo, sex. The mere mention of "unmentionable acts" or even certain parts of the body can dissolve young faces in laughter. Are there

jokes that can break through the cultural barrier? Yes, but they must touch upon universal human experiences such as, say, turning on a friend.

I think of a number of jokes, but none seems to work. Understanding jokes about the United States is difficult for people who have never been there. Is there something more universal? Inspiration: "Two fellows are walking in the woods and come upon a huge bear. One guy leans over and tightens up the laces on his running shoes. 'Jake,' says the other, 'what are you doing? You can't outrun this bear!' 'I don't have to outrun the bear' responds Jake, 'I just have to outrun <u>you</u>!'" Smiles all around.

The controversy inherent in humor often walks a fine line between what is funny and what is considered "sick." During the Middle Ages, the word *humors* (derived from the Latin *humidus*, meaning "moist") referred to a balance of bodily fluids that regulated a person's health. Researchers today document the power of humor to reduce stress and improve health, confirming the old saying, "Laughter is the best medicine" (Robinson, 1983; Haig, 1988). At the extreme, however, people who always take conventional reality lightly risk being defined as deviant or even mentally ill (a common stereotype depicts insane people laughing uncontrollably, and we have long dubbed mental hospitals "funny farms").

Then, too, every social group considers certain topics too sensitive for humorous treatment. Of course, one can joke about such things, but doing so courts criticism for telling a "sick" joke (and, therefore, *being* sick). People's religious beliefs, tragic accidents, or appalling crimes are the stuff of "sick" jokes.

The functions of humor. Humor is found everywhere because it acts as a safety valve to vent potentially disruptive sentiments. Put another way, humor provides a way to discuss an opinion on a sensitive topic without being serious. Having said something controversial, a person can also use humor to diffuse the situation by simply stating, "I didn't mean anything by what I said—it was just a joke!" Likewise, an audience may use humor as a form of tact, smiling, as if to say, "We could be angry at this, but we'll assume you were only kidding."

Similarly, people use humor to relieve tension in uncomfortable situations. One study of medical examinations found most patients begin to joke with doctors to ease their own nervousness (Baker et al., 1997).

Humor and conflict. If humor holds the potential to liberate those who laugh, it can also be used to oppress others. Men who tell jokes about women, for example, typically are voicing some hostility towards them (Benokraitis & Feagin, 1986; Powell & Paton, 1988). Similarly, jokes at the expense of gay people reveal tensions surrounding sexual orientation in the United States. Humor is often a sign of real conflict in situations where one or both parties choose not to bring the conflict out into the open (Primeggia & Varacalli, 1990).

"Put-down" jokes make one category of people feel good at the expense of another. After analyzing jokes from many societies, Christie Davies (1990) confirmed that ethnic conflict is a driving force behind humor almost everywhere. The typical ethnic joke makes fun of some disadvantaged category of people, thereby making the jokester and the audience feel superior. Given the Anglo-Saxon traditions of U.S. society, Poles and other ethnic and racial minorities have long been the butt of jokes, as have Newfoundlanders in eastern Canada, the Scots in England, the Irish in Scotland, the

Because humor involves challenging established conventions, most U.S. comedians—including Margaret Cho—have been social "outsiders," members of racial and ethnic minorities.

Sikhs in India, the Hausas in Nigeria, the Tasmanians in Australia, and the Kurds in Iraq.

Disadvantaged people, of course, also make fun of the powerful, although usually more discreetly. Women in the United States joke about men, just as African Americans find humor in white people's ways, and poor people poke fun at the rich. Throughout the world, people target their leaders with humor, and officials in some countries take such jokes seriously enough to suppress them (Speier, 1998).

In sum, the significance of humor is much greater than we may think. Humor amounts to a means of mental escape from a conventional world that is never entirely to our liking (Flaherty, 1984, 1990; Yoels & Clair, 1995). Indeed, this idea would explain why so many of our nation's comedians come from the ranks of historically oppressed peoples, including Jews and African Americans. As long as we maintain a sense of humor, we assert our freedom and are never prisoners of reality. By putting a smile on our faces, we change ourselves and the world just a little.

SUMMARY

1. Social structure provides guidelines for behavior, making everyday life understandable and predictable.

2. A major component of social structure is status. Within an entire status set, a master status has special importance for a person's identity.

3. Ascribed statuses are involuntary, whereas achieved statuses are earned. In practice, most statuses are both ascribed and achieved.

4. Role is the dynamic expression of a status. Incompatible roles corresponding to two or more statuses generate role conflict. Likewise, incompatible roles linked to a single status cause role strain.

5. The "social construction of reality" refers to the idea that we build the social world through our interactions with others.

6. The Thomas theorem states, "Situations defined as real become real in their consequences."

7. Ethnomethodology seeks to reveal the assumptions and understandings people have of their social world.

8. Dramaturgical analysis views everyday life as theatrical performance, noting how people try to create particular impressions in the minds of others.

9. Social power affects performances, which is one reason that men's behavior typically differs from women's.

10. Everyday behavior carries the ever-present danger of embarrassment. People use tact to prevent others' performances from breaking down.

11. Language is vital to the process of socially constructing reality. In various ways, language defines women and men differently, generally to the advantage of men.

12. Humor stems from the difference between conventional and unconventional definitions of a situation. Because humor is an element of culture, people throughout the world find different situations funny.

KEY CONCEPTS

social interaction (p. 85) the process by which people act and react in relation to others

status (p. 86) a social position that an individual occupies

status set (p. 86) all the statuses a person holds at a given time

ascribed status (p. 86) a social position a person receives at birth or assumes involuntarily later in life

achieved status (p. 86) a social position a person assumes voluntarily and that reflects personal ability and choice

master status (p. 86) a status that has special importance for social identity, often shaping a person's entire life

role (p. 87) behavior expected of someone who holds a particular status

role set (p. 87) a number of roles attached to a single status

role conflict (p. 87) conflict among roles corresponding to two or more statuses

role strain (p. 88) tension among roles connected to a single status

social construction of reality (p. 88) the process by which people creatively shape reality through social interaction

Thomas theorem (p. 91) the assertion that situations defined as real become real in their consequences

ethnomethodology (p. 91) the study of the way people make sense of their everyday surroundings

dramaturgical analysis (p. 93) the study of social interaction in terms of theatrical performance

presentation of self (p. 93) Goffman's term for an individual's efforts to create specific impressions in the minds of others

nonverbal communication (p. 95) communication using body movements, gestures, and facial expressions rather than speech

personal space (p. 96) the surrounding area over which a person makes some claim to privacy

CRITICAL-THINKING QUESTIONS

1. Consider ways in which a physical disability can serve as a master status. What assumptions do people commonly make about the mental ability of someone with a physical disability such as cerebral palsy? What assumptions are made about the person's sexuality?

2. How do people on a first date present themselves to each other and, in the process, construct reality? What kind of information does each offer? Why do people in such a situation often begin with "small talk"?

3. George Jean Nathan once quipped, "I only drink to make other people interesting." What does this mean in terms of reality construction? Can you identify the elements of humor in this comment?

4. Here is a joke about sociologists: "Question—How many sociologists does it take to change a light bulb? Answer—None. There is nothing wrong with the light bulb; it's *the system* that needs to be changed!" What makes this joke funny? What sort of people are likely to "get it"? What kind of people probably won't? Why?

APPLICATIONS AND EXERCISES

1. Write down as many of your own statuses as you can. Do you consider any statuses to be a master status? To what extent are each of your statuses ascribed or achieved?

2. During the next twenty-four hours, every time people ask "How are you?" stop and actually give a full and truthful answer. What happens when you respond to a polite question in an unexpected way? (Watch people's body language as well as note what they say.) What does this experience suggest about everyday interactions?

3. This chapter illustrated Erving Goffman's ideas with a description of a physician's office. Investigate the offices of several professors in the same way. What furniture is there and how is it

arranged? What "props" do professors use? How are the offices of physicians and professors different? Which are tidier? Why?

4. Spend an hour or two walking around the businesses of your town (or shops at a local mall). Observe the number of women and men in each business. Based on your observations, would you conclude that physical space is "gendered"?

5. Install the CD-ROM packaged in the back of this new textbook to access a variety of study, review, and applications exercises designed to help you better understand the material covered in this chapter. The CD includes an author's tip video, as well as interactive maps, video application exercises, Web links, and study questions.

 SITES TO SEE

http://www.prenhall.com/macionis

Visit the interactive Web site that accompanies this text. Begin by clicking on the cover of your book. You will find a chapter-by-chapter study guide, practice tests, chat room, and many suggested Web links.

http://www.census.gov/geneaology/www/

Many interesting patterns of everyday life involve names. This Census Bureau Web site has a search engine for names. Study the frequency of different last names (or investigate first names) in the U.S. population. What patterns can you find? How many others share your own name?

http://www.ai.mit.edu/projects/kismet

Is it possible to build a machine capable of human interaction? That is the goal of robotics engineers at the Massachusetts Institute of Technology; this Web site provides details and photographs. Look over their work and think about issues raised in this chapter. In what ways are machines able, and unable, to mimic human behavior?

CHAPTER 5

GROUPS AND ORGANIZATIONS

*B*ack in 1948, people in Pasadena, California, paid little attention to the opening of a new restaurant. Yet this one small business—owned by brothers Maurice and Richard McDonald—would not only transform the restaurant industry but introduce a new organizational model copied by countless businesses of all kinds.

The McDonald brothers' basic concept—which we now call "fast food"—was to serve meals quickly and cheaply to large numbers of people. The brothers trained employees to perform highly specialized jobs, so that one person grilled hamburgers while others "dressed" them, made French fries, whipped up milkshakes, and presented the food to the customers in assembly-line fashion.

As the years went by, the McDonald brothers prospered, and they decided to move their restaurant from Pasadena to San Bernardino. It was there, in 1954, that Ray Kroc, a traveling blender and mixer merchant, paid them a visit.

Kroc was fascinated by the efficiency of the brothers' system and saw the potential for a whole chain of fast-food restaurants. The three launched the plan as partners. Soon, however, Kroc bought out the McDonalds and went on to become one of the greatest success stories of all time. Today, almost 30,000 McDonald's restaurants have served more than 150 billion hamburgers to people throughout the United States and in 119 countries around the world.

McDonald's success is evidence of more than the popularity of hamburgers. The larger importance of McDonald's lies in the extent to which the principles that guide this company are coming to dominate social life in the United States and elsewhere (Ritzer, 1993, 1998).

We begin with an examination of *social groups*, the clusters of people with whom we interact in much of our daily lives. As we shall see, the scope of group life expanded greatly during the twentieth century. From a world of families, local neighborhoods, and small businesses, our society now turns on the operation of huge businesses and other bureaucracies that sociologists describe as *formal organizations*. Understanding how this expanding scale of life came to be, and appreciating what it means for us as individuals, are this chapter's main objectives.

SOCIAL GROUPS

Virtually everyone seeks a sense of belonging, which is the experience of group membership. A **social group** is *two or more people who identify and interact with one another.* Human beings come together in couples, families, circles of friends, churches, clubs, businesses, neighborhoods, and large organizations. Whatever the form, groups contain people with shared experiences, loyalties, and interests. In short, while keeping their individuality, members of social groups also think of themselves as a special "we."

Not every collection of individuals forms a group. People with a status in common, such as women, homeowners, soldiers, millionaires, and Roman Catholics,

As human beings, we live our lives as members of groups. Such groups may be large or small, temporary or long-lasting, and can be based on kinship, cultural heritage, or some shared interest.

are not a group but a *category*. While they know that others hold the same status, the vast majority are strangers to one another. Likewise, students sitting together in a large lecture hall interact to a very limited extent; thus, they are a very loosely formed group that is better termed a *crowd*.

The right circumstances, however, could turn a crowd into a group. People riding on an elevator that stalls between floors become keenly aware of their common plight and turn to each other for help. Sometimes out of accidents and disasters, people form lasting relationships.

PRIMARY AND SECONDARY GROUPS

Friends often greet one another with a smile and the simple phrase "Hi! How are you?" The response is usually, "Just fine, thanks. How about you?" This answer, of course, is often more scripted than truthful. Telling how you *really* are doing might well make many people feel so awkward they would beat a hasty retreat.

Social groups fall into one of two types based on their members' degree of genuine personal concern towards each other. According to Charles Horton Cooley (1864–1929), a **primary group** is *a small social group whose members share personal and enduring relationships*. Joined by *primary relationships*, people spend a great deal of time together, engage in a wide range of activities, and feel that they know one another pretty well. In short, they display real concern for each

other's welfare. The family is every society's most important primary group.

Cooley called personal and tightly integrated groups *primary* because they are among the first groups we experience in life. In addition, family and friends have primary importance in the socialization process, shaping attitudes, behavior, and social identity.

Members of primary groups help one another in many ways, but they generally think of their group as an end in itself rather than as a means to other ends. In other words, we prefer to think that kinship and friendship link people who "belong together." Moreover, members of a primary group tend to view each other as unique and irreplaceable. Especially in the family, we are bound to others by emotion and loyalty. Brothers and sisters may not always get along, but they always remain siblings.

In contrast to the primary group, the **secondary group** is *a large and impersonal social group whose members pursue a specific goal or activity*. In most respects, secondary groups have precisely the opposite characteristics of primary groups. *Secondary relationships* involve weak emotional ties and little personal knowledge of one another. Many secondary groups are short term, beginning and ending with no particular significance. Students in a college course, for example, who may or may not see each other after the semester ends, exemplify the secondary group.

Secondary groups include many more people than primary groups. For example, dozens or even hundreds of people may work together in the same company, yet most of them pay only passing attention to one another. Sometimes time transforms a group from secondary to primary, as with co-workers who share an office for many years. But, generally, members of a secondary group do not think of themselves as "we."

Whereas members of primary groups display a *personal orientation*, people in secondary groups have a *goal orientation*. Secondary ties need not be hostile or cold, of course. Interaction among students, co-workers, and business associates is often quite pleasant even if it is impersonal. But while primary group members define each other according to *who* they are in terms of kinship or personal qualities, people in secondary groups look to one another for *what* they are, that is, what they can do for each other. In secondary groups, we tend to "keep score," mindful of what we give others and what we receive in return. This goal orientation means that secondary group members usually remain formal and polite. The secondary relationship, therefore, is one in which we ask the question "How are you?" without expecting a detailed, or even truthful, answer.

Table 5–1 summarizes the characteristics that distinguish primary and secondary groups. Keep in mind that these traits define two ideal types of groups; most real groups contain elements of both. But placing these concepts at opposite ends of a continuum helps us describe and analyze group life.

Many people think that small towns and rural areas emphasize primary relationships, while large cities are characterized by secondary ties. This generalization holds some truth, but some urban neighborhoods—especially those populated by people of a single ethnic or religious category—are quite tightly knit. National Map 5–1 on page 110 presents one state-by-state indicator of the primary or secondary character of social ties, namely, how likely people are to resolve disputes personally or to seek redress formally in court.

GROUP LEADERSHIP

How do groups operate? One important dimension of group dynamics is leadership. Though a small circle of friends may have no leader at all, most large, secondary groups place leaders in a formal chain of command.

Instrumental and expressive leaders. Groups typically benefit from two kinds of leadership. **Instrumental leadership** refers to *group leadership that emphasizes the completion of tasks.* Members look to instrumental leaders to "get things done." **Expressive**

TABLE 5–1 Primary Groups and Secondary Groups: A Summary		
	Primary ←→ Secondary **Group** **Group**	
Quality of Relationships	Personal orientation	Goal orientation
Duration of Relationships	Usually long term	Variable; often short term
Breadth of Relationships	Broad; usually involving many activities	Narrow; usually involving few activities
Subjective Perception of Relationships	As ends in themselves	As means to an end
Typical Examples	Families; circles of friends	Co-workers; political organizations

leadership, on the other hand, *focuses on collective well-being.* Expressive leaders take less of an interest in achieving the goals of a group than in raising group morale and minimizing tension and conflict among members.

Because they concentrate on performance, instrumental leaders usually have formal, secondary relationships with other members. These leaders give orders and reward or punish people according to their contribution to the group's efforts. Expressive leaders, however, cultivate more primary ties. They offer sympathy to a member going through a tough time, keep the group united, and lighten serious moments with humor. While successful instrumental leaders enjoy more *respect* from other members, expressive leaders generally receive more personal *affection*.

In the traditional North American family, the two types of leadership are linked to gender. Historically, cultural norms bestowed instrumental leadership on men, who, as fathers and husbands, assumed primary responsibility for earning income and making major family decisions. Traditionally, women exercised expressive leadership: As mothers and wives, they encouraged supportive and peaceful relationships among family members. One result of this division of labor was that many children had greater respect for their fathers but closer personal ties with their mothers (Parsons & Bales, 1955; Macionis, 1978a).

Greater equality between men and women has blurred the gender-based distinction between

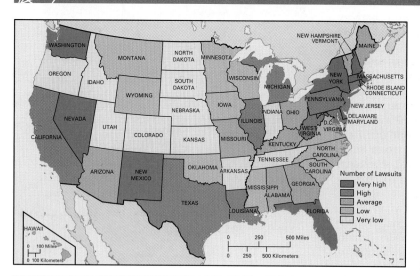

NATIONAL MAP 5–1
The Quality of Relationships: Lawsuits across the United States

Social conflicts are found everywhere, but whether people tend to resolve them informally or resort to legal action varies from state to state. It stands to reason that, in regions of the country where litigation is least common, people's social ties are typically more primary. By contrast, where people are most likely to turn to lawyers, social ties would seem to be more secondary. Looking at the map, what do the states with high (or low) levels of litigation have in common?

Source: Prepared by the author using data from Frum & Wolfe (1994).

instrumental and expressive leadership. In most group settings, women and men now assume both leadership roles.

Leadership styles. Sociologists also characterize leadership in terms of its decision-making style. *Authoritarian leadership* focuses on instrumental concerns, takes personal charge of decision making, and demands strict compliance from subordinates. Although this leadership style may win little affection from the group, a fast-acting authoritarian leader is appreciated in a crisis.

Democratic leadership is more expressive, making a point of including everyone in the decision-making process. Although less successful in a crisis situation, where there is little time for discussion, democratic leaders generally draw on the ideas of all members to develop creative solutions to problems.

Laissez-faire leadership (a French phrase meaning roughly "to leave alone") allows the group to function more or less on its own. This style typically is the least effective in promoting group goals (White & Lippitt, 1953; Ridgeway, 1983).

GROUP CONFORMITY

Groups influence the behavior of their members, often promoting conformity. "Fitting in" provides a secure feeling of belonging, but, at the extreme, group pressure

can be unpleasant and even dangerous. Moreover, even strangers can foster conformity, as experiments by Solomon Asch and Stanley Milgram showed.

Asch's research. Asch (1952) recruited students allegedly to study visual perception. Before the experiment began, he explained to all but one member of a small group that their real purpose was to put pressure on the remaining person. Placing six to eight students around a table, Asch showed them a "standard" line, as drawn on Card 1 in Figure 5–1, and asked them to match it to one of the three lines on Card 2.

Anyone with normal vision can see that the line marked "A" on Card 2 is the correct choice. Initially, as planned, everyone made the correct matches. But then Asch's accomplices began answering incorrectly, leaving the naive subject (seated at the table in order to answer next to last) bewildered and uncomfortable.

What happened? Asch found that one-third of all subjects chose to conform by answering incorrectly. Apparently, many of us are willing to compromise our own judgment to avoid the discomfort of being different, even from people we do not know.

Milgram's research. Stanley Milgram, a former student of Solomon Asch, conducted conformity experiments of his own. In Milgram's controversial study (Milgram, 1963, 1965; Miller, 1986), a researcher explained to male recruits that they would be taking part in a study of how punishment affects learning. One by one, he assigned them to the role of teacher and placed another individual—actually an accomplice of Milgram's—in a connecting room to pose as a learner.

The teacher watched the learner sit down in a contraption resembling an electric chair. As the teacher looked on, the researcher applied electrode paste to the learner's wrist, explaining that this would "prevent blisters and burns." The researcher then attached an electrode to the learner's wrist and fastened the leather straps, explaining that these would "prevent excessive movement while the learner was being shocked." Although the shocks would be painful, the researcher reassured the teacher, they would cause "no permanent tissue damage."

The researcher then led the teacher back into the adjoining room, pointing out that the "electric chair" was connected to a "shock generator," actually a phony but realistic-looking piece of equipment with a label that read "Shock Generator, Type ZLB, Dyson Instrument Company, Waltham, Mass." On the front was a dial that supposedly regulated electric current beginning with 15 volts (labeled "Slight Shock"), going up to 300 volts ("Intense Shock"), and, finally, to 450 volts (marked "Danger: Severe Shock").

Seated in front of the "shock generator," the teacher was told to read aloud pairs of words. Then the teacher was to repeat the first word of each pair and wait for the learner to recall the second word. Whenever the learner failed to answer correctly, the teacher was instructed to apply an electric shock.

The researcher directed the teacher to begin at the lowest level (15 volts) and to increase the shock by another 15 volts every time the learner made a mistake. And so they did. At 75, 90, and 105 volts, the teacher heard moans from the learner; at 120 volts, shouts of pain; by 270 volts, screams; at 315 volts, pounding on the wall; after that, deadly silence. None of the forty subjects assigned to the role of teacher during the initial research even questioned the procedure before reaching 300 volts, and twenty-six of the subjects—almost two-thirds—went all the way to 450 volts. Even Milgram was surprised at how readily people obeyed authority figures.

Milgram (1964) then modified his research to see if Solomon Asch had documented such a high degree of group conformity only because the task—matching lines—was a trivial one. What if groups could also pressure people to administer electrical shocks?

This time, Milgram formed a group of three teachers, two of whom were his accomplices. Each of

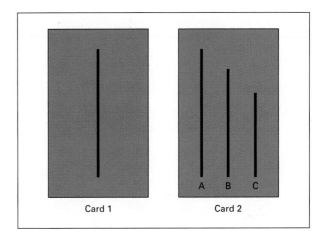

FIGURE 5–1 Cards Used in Asch's Experiment in Group Conformity

Source: Asch (1952).

the teachers was to suggest a shock level when the learner made an error; the rule was that the group would then administer the lowest of the three suggestions. This arrangement gave the naive subject the power to deliver a lesser shock regardless of what the others proposed.

The accomplices suggested increasing the shock level with each error, putting pressure on the subject to do the same. The subjects in these groups applied voltages three to four times higher than other subjects acting alone. Thus, Milgram's research suggests that people are surprisingly likely to follow the directions of not only "legitimate authority figures," but also of groups of ordinary individuals, even when it means inflicting harm on another person.

Janis's research. Experts, too, cave in to group pressure, says Irving L. Janis (1972, 1989). Janis contends that a number of U.S. foreign policy blunders, including the failure to foresee the Japanese attack on Pearl Harbor during World War II and our ill-fated involvement in the Vietnam War, resulted from group conformity among our highest-ranking political leaders.

Common sense tells us that group discussion improves decision making. Janis counters that group members often seek consensus that closes off alternative points of view. Janis called this process **groupthink,** *the tendency of group members to conform, resulting in a narrow view of some issue.*

A classic example of groupthink resulted in the disastrous 1961 invasion of the Bay of Pigs in Cuba.

In many nonindustrial societies, young people of the same age participate in rituals that forge bonds among them and teach them a way of life. Here, young women in the African nation of Swaziland who are reaching adulthood perform a traditional reed dance.

Looking back, Arthur Schlesinger, Jr., an advisor to President Kennedy, confessed to feeling guilty "for having kept so quiet during those crucial discussions in the Cabinet Room," adding that the group discouraged anyone from challenging what, in hindsight, Schlesinger considered "nonsense" (quoted in Janis, 1972:30, 40).

REFERENCE GROUPS

How do we assess our own attitudes and behavior? Frequently, we use a **reference group**, *a social group that serves as a point of reference in making evaluations and decisions.*

A young man who imagines his family's response to a woman he is dating is using his family as a reference group. Similarly, a supervisor who tries to gauge her employees' reaction to a new vacation policy is

using them as a standard of reference. As these examples suggest, reference groups can be primary or secondary. In either case, our need to conform means that others' attitudes greatly affect us.

We also use groups we do *not* belong to for reference. Being well prepared for a job interview means showing up dressed the way people in that company dress for work. Conforming to groups we do not belong to is a strategy to win acceptance and illustrates the process of *anticipatory socialization*, discussed in Chapter 3 ("Socialization: From Infancy to Old Age").

Stouffer's research. Samuel A. Stoufer (1949) conducted a classic study of reference groups during World War II. Researchers asked soldiers to rate their own, or any competent soldier's, chances of promotion in their branch of the Army. One might guess that soldiers serving in outfits with high promotion rates would be optimistic about advancement. Yet Stouffer's research pointed to the opposite conclusion: Soldiers in Army assignments with low promotion rates were actually more positive about their chances to move ahead.

The key to understanding Stouffer's results lies in the groups against which soldiers measured themselves. Those assigned to units with lower promotion rates looked around them and saw people making no more headway than they were. That is, although they had not been promoted, neither had many others, so they did not feel deprived.

Soldiers in units with a higher promotion rate, however, could easily think of people who had been promoted sooner or more often than they had. With such people in mind, even soldiers who had been promoted themselves were likely to feel shortchanged.

The point of Stouffer's research is that we do not make judgments about ourselves in isolation, nor do we compare ourselves with just anyone. Regardless of our situation in *absolute* terms, we form a subjective sense of our well-being by looking at ourselves *relative* to specific reference groups (Merton, 1968; Mirowsky, 1987).

INGROUPS AND OUTGROUPS

Everyone favors some groups over others, whether due to political outlook, social prestige, or just manner of dress. On the college campus, for example, left-leaning student activists may look down on fraternity members, whom they view as conservative; the Greeks, in turn, may snub the computer "nerds" and "grinds," who work too hard. People in virtually every social setting develop such positive and negative evaluations.

Such judgments illustrate another key element of group dynamics: the opposition of ingroups and outgroups. An **ingroup** is *a social group commanding a member's esteem and loyalty.* An **outgroup,** by contrast, is *a social group toward which one feels competition or opposition.* Ingroups and outgroups are based on the idea that "we" have valued traits that "they" lack.

Tensions among groups sharpen the groups' boundaries and give people a clearer social identity. However, members of ingroups generally hold overly positive views of themselves and unfairly negative views of various outgroups (Tajfel, 1982).

Power also shapes intergroup relations. A powerful ingroup can define others as a lower-status outgroup. Historically, for example, white people have viewed people of color as an outgroup and subordinated them socially, politically, and economically. Internalizing these negative attitudes, minorities often struggle to overcome negative self-images. In this way, ingroups and outgroups foster loyalty but also generate conflict (Bobo & Hutchings, 1996).

GROUP SIZE

If you are the first person to arrive at a party, you are in a position to observe some fascinating group dynamics. Until about six people enter the room, everyone generally shares a single conversation. But as more people arrive, the group soon divides into two or more clusters. Size plays a crucial role in how group members interact.

To understand why, note the mathematical number of relationships possible among two to seven people. As shown in Figure 5–2, two people form a single relationship; adding a third person results in three relationships; a fourth person yields six. Increasing the number of people, then, boosts the number of relationships much more rapidly, because every new individual can interact with everyone already there. Thus, by the time seven people join one conversation, twenty-one "channels" connect them. With so many open channels, at this point the group usually divides.

German sociologist Georg Simmel (1858–1918) explored the dynamics of the smallest social groups. Simmel (1950; orig. 1902) used the term **dyad** (from the Greek word for *pair*) to designate *a social group with two members.*

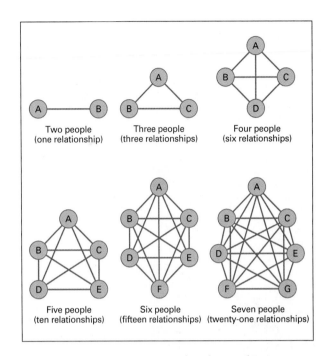

Two people (one relationship)
Three people (three relationships)
Four people (six relationships)
Five people (ten relationships)
Six people (fifteen relationships)
Seven people (twenty-one relationships)

FIGURE 5–2 Group Size and Relationships

Simmel explained that social interaction in a dyad is typically more intense than in larger groups because neither member shares the other's attention with anyone else. In the United States, love affairs, marriages, and the closest friendships are dyadic.

But, like a stool with only two legs, dyads are unstable. Both members of a dyad must work to keep the relationship going; if either member withdraws, the group immediately collapses. Because the stability of marriage is important to society, the marital dyad is supported with legal, economic, and often religious ties.

A **triad** is *a social group with three members.* A triad contains three relationships, each uniting two of the three people. A triad is more stable than a dyad because one member can act as a mediator if relations between the other two become strained. This bit of group dynamics explains why members of a dyad (say, a married couple) often seek out the help of a third person (such as a counselor) to air tensions between them.

On the other hand, two members of the triad can pair up to press their views on the third, or two may intensify their relationship, leaving the other feeling left out. For example, when two of the three develop a romantic interest in each other, they discover the

The triad, illustrated by Jonathan Green's painting Friends, *includes three people. A triad is more stable than a dyad because conflict between any two persons can be mediated by the third member. Even so, should the relationship between any two become more intense in a positive sense, those two are likely to exclude the third.*

Jonathan Green, *Friends*, 1992. Oil on masonite, 14 in. × 11 in.
© Jonathan Green, Naples, Florida. Collection of Patric McCoy.

meaning of the old saying, "Two's company, three's a crowd."

As groups grow beyond three people, they become more stable and capable of withstanding the loss of even several members. At the same time, increases in group size reduce the intense interaction possible in only the smallest groups. Larger groups are thus based less on personal attachments and more on formal rules and regulations. Such formality helps a group persist over time, though the group is not immune to change. After all, their membership gives large groups more contact with the outside world, opening the door to new attitudes and behavior (Carley, 1991).

SOCIAL DIVERSITY: RACE, CLASS, AND GENDER

Race, ethnicity, class, and gender also affect group dynamics. Peter Blau (1977; Blau, Blum, & Schwartz, 1982; South & Messner, 1986) points out three ways in which social diversity influences intergroup contact:

1. **Large groups turn inward.** Blau explains that the larger a group, the more likely its members will concentrate relationships among themselves. Say a college is trying to enhance social diversity by admitting more international students. These students may add a dimension of difference, but, as their numbers rise, they become more likely to form their own social group. Thus, efforts to promote social diversity may have the unintended effect of promoting separatism.

2. **Heterogeneous groups turn outward.** The more internally diverse a group is, the more likely its members are to interact with outsiders. Campus groups that recruit people of both sexes and various class positions typically have more intergroup contact than those with members of one particular type.

3. **Physical boundaries foster social boundaries.** To the extent that a social group is physically segregated from others (by having its own dorm or dining area, for example), its members are less likely to associate with other people.

NETWORKS

A **network** is *a web of weak social ties.* Think of a network as a "fuzzy" group containing people who come into occasional contact but lack a sense of boundaries and belonging. If we think of a group as a "circle of friends," then, we might think of a network as a "social web" expanding outward, often reaching great distances and including large numbers of people.

Some networks come close to being groups, as is the case with college friends who stay in touch years after graduation by e-mail and telephone. More commonly, however, a network includes people we *know of*—or who *know of us*—but with whom we interact rarely if at all. As one woman with a reputation as a community organizer puts it, "I get calls at home, someone says, 'Are you Roseann Navarro? Somebody told me to call you. I have this problem . . .'" (Kaminer, 1984:94).

Networks may contain weak ties, but they can be a powerful resource. For immigrants seeking to

GLOBAL SOCIOLOGY

The Internet: A Global Network

Its origins seem right out of the 1960s cold war film *Dr. Strangelove*. Back then, government officials and scientists were trying to figure out how to run the country after an atomic attack, which, they assumed, would knock out telephones and television. The solution was brilliant: Devise a communication system with no central headquarters, no one in charge, and no main power switch—in short, an electronic web that would link the country in one vast network.

By 1985, the federal government was installing high-speed data lines around the country, and the Internet was about to be born. Today, thousands of colleges and universities across the United States, as well as tens of thousands of government offices, are joined by the Internet and share in the cost of its operation. Individuals can connect their home computers to the "information superhighway" using a telephone-line modem and a subscription to an Internet "gateway."

How many people use the Internet? A rough estimate is that, in 2002, almost 300 million people in nearly 180 (of 191) countries around the world are connected by the largest network in history.

What is available on the Internet? Popular "search engines" such as YAHOO! (http://www.yahoo.com) list sites for just about any topic you can imagine. The Internet also allows you to send e-mail: You can start a cyber-romance with a pen-pal, write to your textbook author (macionis@kenyon.edu), or even send a message to the president of the United States (president@whitehouse.gov). Through the Internet, you can join in discussion groups, visit museums through "virtual tours," locate data from government agencies (a good starting point is http://www.census.gov), explore sites of sociological interest (try the author's Web site at http://www.thesociologypage.com), or review for exams in this course (http://www.prenhall.com/macionis).

With no formal rules for its use, the Internet's potential is limited only by our own imaginations.

Ironically, perhaps, it is precisely this freedom that disturbs some people. Critics claim that "electronic democracy" threatens our political system, parents fear that their children will access sexually explicit "adult sites," and purists bristle as the Internet becomes ever more flooded with advertising.

In its "anything goes" character, of course, the Internet is like the real world. Not surprisingly, then, a recent trend is that more and more users now employ passwords, fees, and other "gates" to create subnetworks limited to people like themselves. From one vast network, then, is emerging a host of social groups.

Sources: Based, in part, on Elmer-DeWitt (1993, 1994b), Hafner (1994), and O'Connor (1997).

become established in a new community, business-people seeking to expand their operations, or anyone looking for a job, *whom you know* is often just as important as *what you know* (Luo, 1997; Hagan, 1998).

Networks are based on peoples' colleges, clubs, neighborhoods, political parties, and personal interests. Obviously, some networks are made up of people with considerably more wealth, power, and prestige than others, which is what the expression "well connected" means. Some people also have denser networks than others—that is, they are connected to more people. Typically, the most extensive social networks are maintained by people who are young, well educated, and living in large cities (Markovsky et al., 1993; Kadushin, 1995; O'Brien, Hassinger, & Dershem, 1996; Fernandez & Weinberg, 1997; Podolny & Baron, 1997).

Gender, too, shapes networks. Although the networks of men and women are typically the same size, women include more relatives (and women) in their networks, while men include more co-workers (and men). Women's ties, therefore, may not carry quite the same clout as the "old boy" networks. Even so, research suggests that as gender inequality lessens in the United States, the networks of men and women are becoming more alike (Moore, 1991, 1992; Wright, 1995).

Finally, new information technology has generated a global network of unprecedented size in the form of the Internet. The box takes a closer look at this twenty-first century form of communication, and Global Map 5–1 on page 116 shows where around the world people are most likely to have access to personal computers.

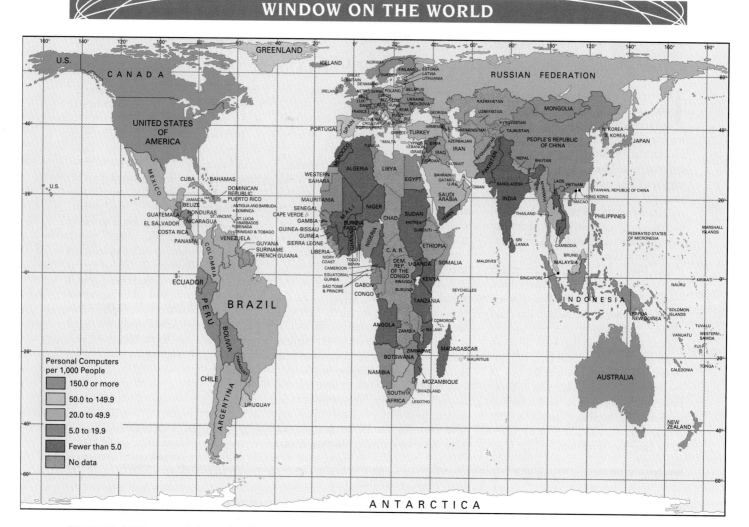

GLOBAL MAP 5–1 High Technology in Global Perspective

The Information Revolution may be sweeping the United States, but, so far, its effect on much of the rest of the world is far more limited. This map shows that access to personal computers is relatively common in high-income countries, including the United States, Canada, the nations of Western Europe, Australia, and Japan. By contrast, in low-income countries—especially those in much of Africa and Asia—personal computers are unknown to most people. What effect do you think a lack of computer access has on economic development? On education? On health care?

Source: The World Bank (2000).

FORMAL ORGANIZATIONS

A century ago, most people lived in small groups of family, friends, and neighbors. Today, our lives revolve more and more around **formal organizations,** *large secondary groups that are organized to achieve their goals* *efficiently.* Formal organizations such as corporations and government offices differ from small primary groups in their impersonality and planned atmosphere.

When you think about it, organizing some 280 million people is a remarkable feat involving countless jobs, from collecting taxes to delivering the mail. To carry out most of these tasks, we rely upon large formal organizations, which develop lives and cultures of their own so that, as members come and go, their operation can stay much the same over many years.

TYPES OF FORMAL ORGANIZATIONS

Amitai Etzioni (1975) identified three types of organizations distinguished by the reasons people participate in them. Just about everyone who works for income belongs to a *utilitarian organization*. Joining a utilitarian organization is usually a matter of individual choice, although, obviously, most people must join one or another such organization to make a living.

People join *normative organizations* not for income but to pursue some goal they think is morally worthwhile. Sometimes called *voluntary associations*, these include community service groups (such as the PTA, the Lions Club, the League of Women Voters, and the Red Cross), political parties, and religious organizations. In global perspective, people in the United States are especially likely to be members of voluntary associations (Curtis, Grabb, & Baer, 1992). Figure 5–3 provides a comparative glance at membership in arts-related organizations for selected countries.

Coercive organizations have an involuntary membership. That is, people are forced to join these organizations as a form of punishment (prisons) or treatment (psychiatric hospitals). Coercive organizations have special physical features, such as locked doors and barred windows, and are supervised by security personnel. They isolate people as "inmates" or "patients" for a period of time and sometimes radically alter their attitudes and behavior (Goffman, 1961).

From differing points of view, a formal organization may fall into *all* of these categories. A mental hospital, for example, serves as a coercive organization for a patient, a utilitarian organization for a psychiatrist, and a normative organization for a part-time hospital volunteer.

ORIGINS OF BUREAUCRACY

Formal organizations date back thousands of years. Elites who governed early empires relied on government officials to collect taxes, undertake military campaigns, and construct monumental structures, from the Great Wall of China to the pyramids of Egypt.

The efficiency of early organizations was limited, however, in two ways. First, people lacked the

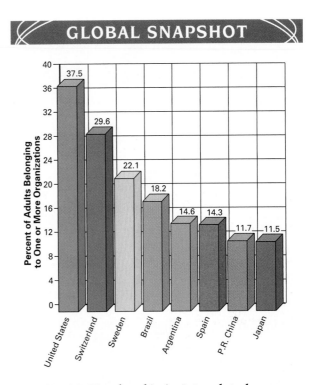

GLOBAL SNAPSHOT

FIGURE 5–3 Membership in Arts-related Organizations

Source: Inglehart et al. (2000).

technology to travel over large distances, to communicate quickly, and to collect and store information on a large scale. Second, preindustrial societies usually have a traditional character. **Tradition,** according to German sociologist Max Weber, is *sentiments and beliefs about the world passed from generation to generation.* Tradition makes a society conservative, Weber explained, because it limits an organization's efficiency and ability to change.

By contrast, Weber characterized the modern worldview as **rationality,** *deliberate, matter-of-fact calculation of the most efficient means to accomplish a particular task.* A rational worldview pays little attention to the past and is open to change in whatever way seems likely to get the job done better or more quickly.

The rise of the "organizational society" rests on what Weber termed **rationalization,** *change from tradition to rationality as the dominant mode of human thought.* Modern society, he claimed, becomes "disenchanted" as sentimental ties give way to a rational focus on science, complex technology, and the organizational structure called *bureaucracy.*

Although formal organization is vital to modern, high-income nations, it is far from new. Twenty-five centuries ago, the Chinese philosopher and teacher K'ung Fu-Tzu (known to Westerners as Confucius) endorsed the idea that government offices should be filled by the most talented young men. This led to what was probably the world's first system of civil service examinations. Here, would-be bureaucrats compose essays to demonstrate their knowledge of Confucian texts.

CHARACTERISTICS OF BUREAUCRACY

Bureaucracy is *an organizational model rationally designed to perform tasks efficiently.* Bureaucratic officials regularly enact and revise policy to increase efficiency. To appreciate the power and scope of bureaucratic organization, consider that any one of nearly 300 million phones in the United States can connect you within seconds to any other phone in a home, business, automobile, or even a hiker's backpack on an Adirondack mountain trail. Such instant communication is beyond the imagination of people who lived in the ancient world.

Of course, the telephone system depends on technology such as electricity, fiber optics, and computers. But the system could not exist without the organizational capacity to keep track of every telephone call—recording which phone called which other phone, when, and for how long—and presenting all this information to more than 100 million telephone users in the form of monthly bills.

What specific traits promote organizational efficiency? Max Weber (1978; orig. 1921) identified six key elements of the ideal bureaucratic organization:

1. **Specialization.** Our ancestors spent most of their time looking for food and finding shelter. Bureaucracy, by contrast, assigns individuals highly specialized duties.

2. **Hierarchy of offices.** Bureaucracies arrange personnel in a vertical ranking of offices. Each person is thus supervised by "higher-ups" in the organization while, in turn, supervising others in lower positions. Usually, with few people at the top and many at the bottom, bureaucratic organizations take the form of a pyramid.

3. **Rules and regulations.** Rationally enacted rules and regulations guide a bureaucracy's operation. Ideally, a bureaucracy seeks to operate in a completely predictable fashion.

4. **Technical competence.** Bureaucratic officials have the technical competence to carry out their

duties. Bureaucracies typically recruit new members according to set criteria and, afterward, monitor their performance. Such impersonal evaluation contrasts with the ancient custom of favoring relatives—whatever their talents—over strangers.

5. **Impersonality.** Bureaucracy puts rules ahead of personal whim so that clients as well as workers are all treated uniformly. From this detached approach comes the notion of the "faceless bureaucrat."

6. **Formal, written communications.** Someone once said that the heart of bureaucracy is not people but paperwork. Rather than casual, face-to-face talk, bureaucracy relies on formal written memos and reports, which accumulate in vast files.

Bureaucratic organization promotes efficiency by carefully recruiting personnel and limiting the unpredictable effects of personal taste and opinion. Table 5–2 summarizes the differences between small social groups and large formal organizations.

ORGANIZATIONAL ENVIRONMENT

No organization operates in a vacuum. How any organization performs depends not only on its own goals and policies but also the **organizational environment,** *a range of factors outside the organization that affects its operation.* These factors include technology, economic and political trends, and the available work force, as well as other organizations.

Modern organizations are shaped by the *technology* of computers, telephone systems, and copiers. Computers give employees access to more information and people than ever before. At the same time, computer technology allows managers to closely monitor the activities of workers (Markoff, 1991).

Economic and political trends affects organizations. All organizations are helped or hindered by periodic economic growth or recession. Most industries also face competition from abroad as well as government regulation and changes in law (such as new environmental standards) at home.

Population patterns, such as the size and composition of the surrounding populace, also affect organizations. The average age, typical education, and social diversity of a local community determine the available work force and sometimes the market for an organization's products or services.

Fourth, *other organizations* also contribute to the organizational environment. To be competitive, a

TABLE 5–2 Small Groups and Formal Organizations: A Comparison		
	Small Groups	**Formal Organizations**
Activities	Members typically engage in many of the same activities	Members typically engage in distinct, highly specialized activities
Hierarchy	Often informal or nonexistent	Clearly defined, corresponding to offices
Norms	Informal application of general norms	Clearly defined rules and regulations
Criteria for Membership	Variable, often based on personal affection or kinship	Technical competence to carry out assigned tasks
Relationships	Variable; typically primary	Typically secondary, with selective primary ties
Communications	Typically casual and face to face	Typically formal and in writing
Focus	Person-oriented	Task-oriented

hospital must be responsive to the insurance industry and organizations representing doctors, nurses, and other workers. It must also keep abreast of the equipment and procedures available at nearby facilities, as well as their prices.

THE INFORMAL SIDE OF BUREAUCRACY

Weber's ideal bureaucracy deliberately regulates every activity. In actual organizations, however, human beings are creative (and stubborn) enough to resist bureaucratic blueprints. Informality may amount to simply cutting corners on the job, but it also can provide necessary flexibility (Scott, 1981).

In part, informality comes from the varying personalities of organizational leaders. Studies of U.S. corporations document that the qualities and quirks of individuals—including personal charisma and interpersonal skills—greatly affect organizational outcomes (Halberstam, 1986).

Authoritarian, democratic, and laissez-faire types of leadership (described earlier in this chapter) reflect individual personality as much as any organizational plan. Then, too, in the "real world" of organizations,

According to Max Weber, bureaucracy is an organizational strategy that promotes efficiency. Impersonality, however, also fosters alienation among employees, who may become indifferent to the formal goals of the organization. The behavior of this municipal employee in Bombay, India, is understandable to members of formal organizations almost anywhere in the world.

leaders and their cronies sometimes seek to benefit personally through abuse of organizational power. Perhaps even more commonly, leaders take credit for the efforts of their subordinates. Many secretaries, for example, have far more authority and responsibility than their official job titles and salaries suggest.

Communication offers another example of organizational informality. Memos and other written documents are the formal way to spread information through the organization. Typically, however, people create informal networks, or "grapevines," that spread information quickly, if not always accurately. Grapevines—using word-of-mouth and e-mail—are particularly important to rank-and-file workers because higher-ups often attempt to keep important information from them.

The spread of e-mail has "flattened" organizations somewhat, allowing even the lowest-ranking

employee to bypass immediate superiors in order to communicate directly with the organization's leader or all fellow employees at once. Some organizations consider such "open-channel" communication unwelcome and limit the use of e-mail. Leaders also may seek to protect themselves from a flood of messages each day. Microsoft Corporation (whose leader, Bill Gates, has an "unlisted" address yet still receives hundreds of e-mail messages a day) has developed "screens" that allow messages from only approved people to reach a particular computer terminal (Gwynne & Dickerson, 1997).

Despite the highly regulated nature of bureaucracy, members of formal organizations still find ways to personalize their work and surroundings. Such efforts suggest that we now take a closer look at some of the problems of bureaucracy.

PROBLEMS OF BUREAUCRACY

We rely on bureaucracy to manage countless dimensions of everyday life, but many people are, at best, uneasy about large organizations. Bureaucracy can dehumanize as well as manipulate us, and some say it poses a threat to political democracy.

Bureaucratic alienation. Max Weber touted bureaucracy as a model of productivity. Yet, Weber was keenly aware of bureaucracy's potential to *dehumanize* the people it is supposed to serve. The same impersonality that fosters efficiency simultaneously keeps officials and clients from responding to each other's unique, personal needs. Typically, officials treat each client impersonally as a standard "case."

Formal organizations create *alienation*, according to Weber, by reducing the human being to "a small cog in a ceaselessly moving mechanism" (1978:988; orig. 1921). Although formal organizations are designed to serve humanity, Weber feared that people might well end up serving formal organizations.

Bureaucratic ritualism. *Inefficiency,* the failure of a formal organization to carry out the work it exists to perform, is a familiar problem. According to one report, the government agency that buys equipment for federal workers takes up to three years to process a request for a new computer. This ensures that, by the time the computer arrives, it is already out of date (Gwynne & Dickerson, 1997).

The problem of inefficiency is captured in the concept of *red tape,* a term derived from the red tape used by eighteenth-century English administrators to wrap official parcels and records (Shipley, 1985). To

George Tooker's painting Government Bureau *is a powerful statement about the human costs of bureaucracy. The artist depicts members of the public in monotonous similitude—reduced from human beings to mere "cases" to be disposed of as quickly as possible. Set apart from others by their positions, officials are "faceless bureaucrats" concerned more with numbers than with providing genuine assistance (notice that the artist places the fingers of the officials on calculators).*

George Tooker, *Government Bureau*, 1956. Egg tempera on gesso panel, 19⅝ x 29⅝ inches. The Metropolitan Museum of Art, George A. Hearn Fund, 1956 (56.78). Photograph © 1984 The Metropolitan Museum of Art.

Robert Merton (1968), red tape amounts to a new twist to the familiar concept of group conformity. He coined the term **bureaucratic ritualism** to describe *a preoccupation with rules and regulations to the point of thwarting an organization's goals.*

Bureaucratic inertia. If bureaucrats sometimes have little reason to work efficiently, they have every reason to protect their jobs. Thus, officials typically strive to keep their organization going even when its goal has been realized. As Weber put it, "once fully established, bureaucracy is among the social structures which are hardest to destroy" (1978:987; orig. 1921).

Bureaucratic inertia refers to *the tendency of bureaucratic organizations to perpetuate themselves.* Formal organizations tend to take on a life of their own beyond their formal objectives. For example, the U.S. Agriculture Department still has offices in almost all U.S. counties, even though only one in seven has working farms (Littman, 1992). Usually, an organization stays in business by redefining its goals; the Agriculture Department, for example, now performs a broad range of work not directly related to farming, including nutritional and environmental research.

Oligarchy. Early in the twentieth century, Robert Michels (1876–1936) pointed out the link between bureaucracy and political **oligarchy,** *the rule of the many by the few* (1949; orig. 1911). According to what Michels called "the iron law of oligarchy," the pyramid shape of bureaucracy places a few leaders in charge of organizational resources.

Max Weber credited a strict hierarchy of responsibility with superior organizational efficiency. But Michels countered that hierarchy also undermines democracy because officials can—and often do—use their access to information, resources, and the media to promote their personal interests.

Furthermore, bureaucracy helps insulate officials from the public, as in the case of the corporate president or public official who is "unavailable for comment" to the local press, or the national president who claims "executive privilege" when withholding documents from Congress. Oligarchy, then, thrives in the hierarchical structure of bureaucracy and reduces the accountability of leaders to the people (Tolson, 1995).

Political competition, term limits, and a system of checks and balances prevent the U.S. government from becoming an out-and-out oligarchy. Even so, incumbents enjoy a significant advantage in U.S. politics. In the 2000 congressional elections, only 15 of 437 congressional officeholders running for reelection were defeated by their challengers.

THE EVOLUTION OF FORMAL ORGANIZATIONS

The problems of bureaucracy—especially the alienation it produces and its tendency toward oligarchy—stem from two organizational traits: hierarchy and rigidity. To Weber, bureaucracy was a top-down system: Rules and regulations made at the top guide every facet of people's work down the chain of command. A

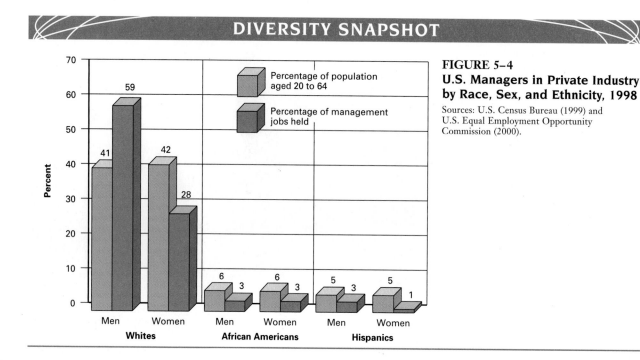

FIGURE 5–4
U.S. Managers in Private Industry by Race, Sex, and Ethnicity, 1998
Sources: U.S. Census Bureau (1999) and U.S. Equal Employment Opportunity Commission (2000).

century ago in the United States, Weber's ideas took hold in an organizational model called "scientific management." We begin with a look at this model, and then describe three challenges over the course of the twentieth century that gradually led to a new model—the "flexible organization."

SCIENTIFIC MANAGEMENT

Frederick Winslow Taylor (1911) had a simple message: Most businesses in the United States were sadly inefficient. Most managers had little idea of how to increase their business's output, and workers relied on the same tired skills of earlier generations.

To increase efficiency, Taylor explained, business should apply the principles of science. **Scientific management,** then, is *the application of scientific principles to the operation of a business or other large organization.*

Scientific management involves three steps. First, managers carefully observe the task performed by each worker, identifying all the operations involved and measuring the time needed for each. Second, managers then analyze their data, trying to discover ways for workers to perform each task more efficiently. Managers, for example, might decide to provide workers with different tools, or reposition various work operations within the factory. Third, management provides guidance and incentives for workers to do

their jobs more efficiently. If a factory worker moves twenty tons of pig iron in one day, for example, management would show the worker how to do the job more efficiently, and then provide higher wages as the worker's productivity rises. Applying scientific principles in this way, Taylor concluded, companies become more profitable, workers earn higher wages, and, in the end, consumers end up paying lower prices. Auto pioneer Henry Ford, who was enthusiastic in his support of scientific management, put it this way: "Save ten steps a day for each of 12,000 employees, and you will have saved fifty miles of wasted motion and misspent energy" (Allen & Hyman, 1999:209).

In the early 1900s, the Ford Motor Company and many other businesses followed Taylor's lead and improved their efficiency. As time went on, however, formal organizations faced three new challenges, involving race and gender, rising competition from abroad, and changes in the nature of work itself. We look briefly at each in turn.

THE FIRST CHALLENGE:
RACE AND GENDER

During the 1960s, critics pointed out that big businesses and other organizations were inefficient—and also unfair—in their hiring practices. Rather than hiring on the basis of competence, as Weber had proposed, they routinely excluded women and other minorities. As a result, the vast majority of managers were white men.

Patterns of exclusion. Even by the end of the twentieth century, as shown in Figure 5–4, white men in the United States (41 percent of the working-age population) still held 59 percent of management jobs. White women made up about the same share of the population, but they held just 28 percent of managerial positions (U.S. Equal Employment Opportunity Commission, 2000). The members of other minorities lagged further behind.

Rosabeth Moss Kanter (1977; Kanter & Stein, 1979) points out that excluding women and minorities from the workplace ignores the talents of more than half the population. Furthermore, underrepresented people in an organization often feel like socially isolated outgroups—uncomfortably visible, taken less seriously, and given fewer chances for promotion.

"Opening up" an organization, Kanter claims, improves everyone's on-the-job performance by motivating employees to become fast-trackers who work harder and are more committed to the company. By contrast, an organization with many dead-end jobs turns workers into unproductive "zombies." Open organizations also encourage leaders to seek out the input of everyone, which benefits the whole organization. It is officials in rigid organizations—those who have little reason themselves to be creative—who jealously guard their privileges and ride herd over their employees.

The "female advantage." Some organizational researchers argue that including more women, in particular, brings special management skills that strengthen an organization. Deborah Tannen (1994) claims, for example, that women have a greater "information focus," and more readily ask questions to understand an issue. Men, on the other hand, have an "image focus" that makes them wonder how asking questions in a particular situation will affect their reputation.

In another study of women executives, Sally Helgesen (1990) found three additional gender-linked patterns. First, women place greater value on communication skills and share information more than men do. Second, women are more flexible leaders who typically give their employees greater autonomy. Third, compared to men, women tend to emphasize the interconnectedness of all organizational operations. Thus, women bring a "female advantage" to companies striving to be more flexible and democratic.

In sum, one challenge to conventional bureaucracy is becoming more open and flexible in order to

During the last fifty years in the United States, women have moved into management positions throughout the corporate world. While some men initially opposed women's presence in the executive office, it is now clear that women bring particular strengths to the job, including leadership flexibility and communication skills. Thus, some analysts speak of women offering a "female advantage."

take advantage of everyone's experience, ideas, and creativity. The result goes right to the bottom line: greater profits.

THE SECOND CHALLENGE: THE JAPANESE ORGANIZATION

In 1980, the corporate world in the United States was shaken to discover that the most popular automobile model sold in this country was not a Chevrolet, Ford, or Plymouth, but the Honda Accord, made in Japan. To people old enough to remember back to the 1950s, the words "made in Japan" generally meant a cheap, poorly made product. But times had changed. The success of the Japanese auto industry (and, shortly thereafter, companies making electronics, cameras, and other products) soon had analysts buzzing about the "Japanese organization." How else could so small a country challenge the world's economic powerhouse?

Japanese organizations reflect that nation's strong collective spirit. That is, while most members of our society prize rugged individualism, the Japanese value cooperation. In effect, then, formal organizations in Japan are like very large primary groups. William Ouchi (1981) highlights five differences between formal organizations in Japan and in the United States:

1. **Hiring and advancement.** U.S. organizations hold out promotions and raises as prizes for individual achievement. Japanese companies, however, hire new school graduates together, and all in the group receive the same salary and responsibilities. Only after several years is anyone likely to be singled out for special advancement.

2. **Lifetime security.** Employees in the United States expect to move from one company to another to advance their careers. U.S. companies are also quick to lay off employees during an economic setback. By contrast, most Japanese firms hire workers for life, fostering strong mutual loyalties. If jobs become obsolete, Japanese companies avoid layoffs by retraining workers for new positions.

3. **Holistic involvement.** While we tend to see the home and the workplace as distinct spheres, Japanese companies play a much larger role in workers' lives. They provide home mortgages, sponsor recreational activities, and schedule social events. Such interaction beyond the workplace strengthens collective identity and offers the respectful Japanese employees a chance to voice suggestions and criticisms informally.

4. **Broad-based training.** U.S. workers are highly specialized, and many spend an entire career doing one thing. But a Japanese organization trains workers in all phases of its operation, again with the idea that employees will remain with the company for life.

5. **Collective decision making.** In the United States, key executives make the important decisions. Although Japanese leaders also take ultimate responsibility for their organization's performance, they involve workers in "quality circles" to discuss decisions that affect them. A closer working relationship is also encouraged by Japan's lower salary difference between executives and workers—about 10 percent of the difference typical in the United States.

These characteristics give the Japanese a strong sense of organizational loyalty. Because their personal interests are tied to company interests, workers realize their ambitions through the organization. Japanese *groupism* is thus the cultural equivalent of our society's emphasis on *individualism*.

Many U.S. companies have been influenced by Japanese organizations. But "transplanting" an organizational system from one culture to another is not easy, as the box explains.

THE THIRD CHALLENGE: THE CHANGING NATURE OF WORK

Beyond rising global competition, pressure to modify conventional organizations is also coming from changes in the nature of work itself. In recent decades, the U.S. economy has moved from industrial to postindustrial production. In other words, rather than working in factories using heavy machinery to make *things*, more people are using computers and other electronic technology to create or process *information*. A postindustrial society, then, is characterized by information-based organizations.

Frederick Taylor developed his concept of "scientific management" at a time when jobs involved tasks that, while often backbreaking, were routine. Workers shoveled coal, poured liquid iron into molds, attached body panels to automobiles on an assembly line, or shot hot rivets into steel girders to build skyscrapers. In addition, a large part of the U.S. labor force in Taylor's day was immigrants, most of whom had little schooling and many of whom knew little English. The routine nature of industrial jobs, coupled with the limited skills of the labor force, led Taylor to treat work as a series of fixed tasks set down by management and followed by employees.

Many of today's information-age jobs are very different: The work of designers, artists, consultants, writers, editors, composers, programmers, business owners, and others now demands creativity and imagination. What does this mean for formal organizations? Here are several ways in which today's organizations differ from those of a century ago:

1. **Creative autonomy.** Organizations know that employees with information-age skills are a vital resource. Executives can set production goals, but cannot dictate how to accomplish tasks involving imagination and discovery. Thus, highly skilled workers have *creative autonomy*, which means they are subject to less day-to-day supervision as long as they generate good ideas in the long run.

2. **Competitive work teams.** Many organizations give several groups of employees the freedom to work on a problem simultaneously, offering the

The Japanese Model: Will It Work in the United States?

What the company wants is for us to work like the Japanese. Everybody go out and do jumping jacks in the morning and kiss each other when they go home at night. You work as a team, rat on each other, and lose control of your destiny. That's not going to work in this country.

> John Brodie
> President, United Paperworkers
> Local 448
> Chester, Pennsylvania

Competition—from Asia and, increasingly, from Europe—is forcing U.S. companies to rethink how corporate organizations should operate in a global marketplace. Business leaders are looking, for example, at the Japanese manufacturing plants built here in the United States. These "transplant organizations" operated in the United States by Honda, Nissan, and Toyota have adapted well to a new environment, achieving the same level of efficiency and quality that won these companies praise in Japan. They have also provided more than 250,000 jobs for U.S. workers.

Yet, some voices in this country—from the ranks of workers, union leaders, and managers—

speak as bitterly about importing Japanese organizational techniques as they do about importing Japanese cars. Our corporate culture still favors hierarchy, praises individualism, and remembers its long history of labor-management conflict. As a result, workers and managers are wary of traditional Japanese practices such as worker participation.

Some employees in the United States think worker participation ends up increasing their workload. While still responsible for building cars, for instance, workers also have to worry about quality control, unit costs, and overall efficiency—concerns usually shouldered by management. Moreover, some employees see the broad training

From Japanese organizations, U.S. companies have learned the value of building team spirit.

favored by the Japanese as meaning that they will be moving endlessly from job to job, always having to learn new skills. Many union leaders fear that any alliance of workers and managers undermines union strength. Some managers, too, look warily on worker participation programs: Sharing the power to set production goals or schedule vacations does not come easily to them. Finally, U.S. corporations have a short-term outlook on profits, which discourages investing time and money in organizational restructuring.

But the pressure of rising global competition is slowly changing U.S. organizations. The government reports that 70 percent of large businesses have begun at least some reforms of this kind. The fact is that productivity and profits are usually higher when workers have a say in decision making. Moreover, most employees in worker participation programs—even those who may not want to sign up for morning jumping jacks—seem happier about their jobs. Workers who have long used only their bodies are now enjoying the opportunity to use their minds as well.

Sources: Hoerr (1989) and Florida & Kenney (1991).

greatest rewards to those who come up with the best solution. Competitive work teams—a strategy first used by Japanese organizations—draw out the creative contributions of everyone and, at the same time, reduce the alienation often found in conventional organizations (Yeatts, 1991, 1994; Maddox, 1994).

3. A flatter organization: from pyramid to football. By spreading responsibility for creative problem solving throughout the work force, organizations take on a flatter shape. That is, the pyramid shape of conventional bureaucracy is replaced by a new organizational form with fewer levels in the chain of command, as shown in Figure 5–5.

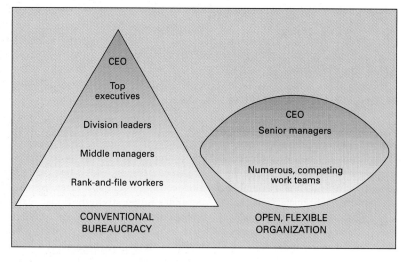

FIGURE 5–5 Two Organizational Models

The conventional model of bureaucratic organizations has a pyramid shape, with a clear chain of command. Directives flow from the top down, while reports of performance flow from the bottom up. Such organizations have extensive rules and regulations, and their workers have highly specialized jobs. More open and flexible organizations have a flatter shape, more like a football. With fewer levels in the hierarchy, responsibility for generating ideas and making decisions is shared throughout the organization. Many workers do their jobs in teams and have a broad knowledge of the entire organization's operation.

Source: Created by the author.

4. **Greater flexibility.** The typical industrial-age organization was a rigid structure guided from the top. Such organizations may accomplish a good deal of work, but they are not especially creative or able to respond quickly to changes in their larger environment. The ideal model in the information age is a *flexible* organization, one that both generates new ideas and, in a rapidly changing global marketplace, adapts quickly.

As important as these changes are, bear in mind that many of today's jobs *do not* involve creative work at all. In reality, the postindustrial economy has created two very different types of work: highly skilled, creative work and low-skilled, service work. Work in the fast-food industry, for example, is routine and highly supervised, and thus has much more in common with factory work of a century ago than with the work of teams in information organizations. Therefore, at the same time that some organizations have taken on a flexible, flatter form, others continue to use a rigid chain of command, as we now explain.

THE "McDONALDIZATION" OF SOCIETY[1]

As noted in the opening to this chapter, McDonald's has enjoyed enormous success, now operating almost 30,000 restaurants in the United States and around the world. There are more than 850 Golden Arches in

[1]Much of the material in this section is based on Ritzer (1993, 1998).

Japan, for example, and the world's largest McDonald's recently opened in China's capital city of Beijing.

October 9, 1994, Macau. Here we are, halfway around the world, in the Portuguese colony of Macau—a little nub jutting from the Chinese coast. Few people speak English, and life on the streets seems a world apart from the urban rhythms of New York, Chicago, or Los Angeles. Then I turn the corner and stand face to face with (who else?) Ronald McDonald! After eating who-knows-what for many days, forgive me for giving in to the lure of the Big Mac. But the most amazing thing is that the food—the burger, fries, and drinks—looks, smells, and tastes exactly the same as it does back home 10,000 miles away!

McDonald's can be found almost everywhere these days, and, in the United States, it is more than a restaurant—it has become a symbol of our way of life. Not only do people around the world associate McDonald's with the United States, but, here at home, one poll found that 98 percent of school children could identify Ronald McDonald, making him as well known as Santa Claus.

Even more important, the organizational principles that underlie McDonald's are coming to dominate our entire society. Our culture is becoming "McDonaldized," an awkward way of saying that many aspects of life are modeled on the famous restaurant chain. Parents buy toys at worldwide chain stores like Toys 'Я' Us; we drive in to Jiffy Lube for a ten-minute oil change; face-to-face communication is sliding more and more toward voice mail, e-mail, and junk mail; more vacations take the form of resort and tour packages; television presents news in the form of ten-second sound bites; college admission officers size up students they have never met by glancing at their GPA and SAT scores; and professors assign ghost-written textbooks[2] and evaluate students with tests mass-produced for them by publishing companies. The list goes on and on.

Basic principles. What do all these developments have in common? According to George Ritzer (1993), the McDonaldization of society involves four basic organizational principles:

1. **Efficiency.** Ray Kroc, the marketing genius behind McDonald's, set out with one goal: to serve a hamburger, French fries, and milkshake to a customer in fifty seconds or less. Today, one of the company's most popular items is the Egg McMuffin, an entire breakfast in a single sandwich. In the restaurant, customers bus their own trays or, better still, drive away from the pick-up window taking whatever mess they make with them.

   Efficiency is a value virtually without criticism in our society. We tend to think that anything done quickly is, for that reason alone, good.

2. **Calculability.** The first McDonald's operating manual declared the weight of a regular raw hamburger to be 1.6 ounces, its size to be 3.875 inches across, and its fat content to be 19 percent. A slice of cheese weighs exactly half an ounce, and French fries are cut precisely 9/32 of an inch thick.

   Think about how many objects around the home, the workplace, or the campus are designed and mass-produced uniformly according to a standard plan. Not just our environment but our life experiences—from traveling the nation's interstates to sitting at home viewing television—are now more deliberately planned than ever before.

3. **Uniformity and predictability.** An individual can walk into a McDonald's restaurant almost anywhere and buy the same sandwiches, drinks, and desserts prepared in precisely the same way.[3] Uniformity results from a highly rational system that specifies every action and leaves nothing to chance.

4. **Control through automation.** The most unreliable element in the McDonald's system is human beings. People, after all, have good and bad days, sometimes let their minds wander, or decide to try something a different way. To minimize the unpredictable human element, McDonald's has automated their equipment to cook food at fixed temperatures for set lengths of time. Even the cash register at a McDonald's is keyed to pictures of the items, so that ringing up a customer's order is as simple as possible.

   Similarly, automatic teller machines are replacing banks, highly automated bakeries produce bread with scarcely any human intervention, and chickens and eggs (or is it eggs and chickens?) emerge from automated hatcheries. In supermarkets, laser scanners are phasing out human checkers. Most of our shopping now occurs in malls, where everything from temperature and humidity to the kinds of stores and products are subject to continuous control and supervision (Ide & Cordell, 1994).

Can rationality be irrational? There can be no argument about the popularity or efficiency of McDonald's. But there is another side to the story.

Max Weber was alarmed at the increasing rationalization of the world, fearing that formal organizations would cage our imagination and crush the human spirit. As he saw it, rational systems were efficient but dehumanizing. McDonaldization bears him out. Each of the four principles just discussed limits human creativity, choice, and freedom. Echoing Weber, George Ritzer states that "the ultimate irrationality of McDonaldization is that people could lose control over the system and it would come to control us" (1993:145).

---

[2]Half a dozen popular sociology texts were not authored by the person or persons whose names appear on the cover. This book is not one of them.

[3]As McDonald's has "gone global," a few products have been added or modified according to local tastes. For example, in Uruguay, customers enjoy the McHuevo (hamburger with poached egg on top); Norwegians can buy McLaks (grilled salmon sandwiches); the Dutch favor the Groenteburger (vegetable burger); in Thailand, McDonald's serves Samurai pork burgers (pork burgers with teriyaki sauce); the Japanese can purchase Chicken Tatsuta Sandwich (chicken seasoned with soy and ginger); Filipinos eat McSpaghetti (spaghetti with tomato sauce and bits of hot dog); and, in India, where Hindus eat no beef, McDonald's sells a vegetarian Maharaja Mac (Sullivan, 1995).

Are Large Organizations a Threat to Personal Privacy?

Joe finishes dressing and dials a 1-800 number to check the pollen count. As he listens to a recorded message, a Caller I.D. computer identifies Joe and pulls up his profile from a public records database. The profile, to which is now added the fact that Joe suffers from allergies, is sold to a drug company, which sends Joe a free sample of a new allergy medication.

At a local department store, Nina uses her American Express card to buy an expensive new watch and some sleepwear. The store's computer adds Nina's name to its databases of "buyers of expensive jewelry" and "buyers of sexy lingerie." The store trades this database with other companies and within a month Nina receives four jewelry catalogues and a brochure advertising "adult" videos (Bernstein, 1997).

Are these organizations providing consumers with helpful products or violating people's privacy? The answer, of course, is both: The same systems that help organizations operate efficiently also let them invade our lives and manipulate us. So, as bureaucracy has expanded in the United States, privacy has declined.

Small-town life in the past, of course, gave people little privacy. But at least if people knew something about you, you were just as likely to know something about them. Today, unknown people "out there" can access information about any of us at any time.

This loss of privacy reflects the enormous power of large organizations, their tendency to treat people impersonally, and their appetite for information. In recent decades, the danger to privacy has increased with the spread of computers that store and share information.

Consider some of the obvious ways in which organizations compile personal information. As they issue driver's licenses, state motor vehicle agencies generate files that they can dispatch at the touch of a button to other officials, including police. Similarly, the Internal Revenue Service and the Social Security Administration, as well as other government agencies that benefit veterans, students, the unemployed, and the poor, all collect extensive information.

Businesses in the private sector do much the same thing, although, as the examples above show, people are usually not aware that their everyday choices and activities are ending up in the companies' databases. Most people find the use of credit cards a great convenience (the U.S. population now holds more than 1 billion of them, averaging more than five per adult), but few of us stop to think that our credit card purchases are automatically generating records that can end up almost anywhere. Indeed, every time we log on to the Internet, computers track every site we visit; in this way, companies can build a profile of our activities and interests, which they use to target us with customized advertising.

As concern about the loss of privacy in the United States has increased, many states have enacted laws that give citizens

THE FUTURE OF ORGANIZATIONS: OPPOSING TRENDS

Early in the twentieth century, ever-larger organizations arose in the United States, most taking on the bureaucratic form described by Max Weber. In many respects, these organizations resembled armies led by powerful generals who issued orders to their captains and lieutenants. Foot soldiers—working in the factories—did what they were told.

With the emergence of a postindustrial economy after mid-century, as well as rising competition from abroad, many organizations evolved toward the flatter, more flexible model that prizes communication and creativity. Such "intelligent organizations" (Gifford & Pinchot, 1993) have become more productive than ever. Just as important, for highly skilled people who enjoy "creative autonomy," these organizations create less of the alienation that so worried Max Weber.

But this is only half the story. Though the postindustrial economy created many highly skilled jobs, it created even more routine service jobs, as exemplified by McDonald's, where one in eight U.S. adults has worked at some time (Ritzer, 1998). Work of this kind—which Ritzer terms "McJobs"—offers few of

the right to examine some of the records about themselves, especially those kept by employers, banks, and credit bureaus. The U.S. Privacy Act of 1974 also limits the exchange of personal information among government agencies and permits citizens to examine and correct most government files. But the fact is that so many organizations now have so much information about us—experts estimate that 90 percent of U.S. households are profiled in databases somewhere—that current laws simply cannot address the full scope of the problem. In addition, as computer technology becomes more complex, the privacy problem only grows worse.

Across the United States, who is most concerned about the growing assault on privacy? National Map 5–2 provides some insights.

Continue the debate . . .

1. *Look at National Map 5–2. Where are people most concerned about losing their privacy? Can you explain this pattern?*

2. *Internet search engines such as YAHOO! (http://www.yahoo.com) have "people search" programs that let you locate almost anyone. See if you are listed. Do you think such programs, on balance, help or harm the public?*

3. *Looking ahead, in light of the rapid development of new computer technology, do you think the privacy problem will get better or worse? Why?*

SEEING OURSELVES

NATIONAL MAP 5–2 Concerns about Privacy across the United States

Source: *Business Geographics* © 1994 GIS World, Inc., 2101 S. Arlington Heights Boulevard, Arlington Heights, Ill., 60005-4185.

Sources: Dunn (1991), Miller (1991), Bernstein (1997), and Wright (1998).

the benefits that today's highly skilled workers enjoy. On the contrary, the automated routines that define work in the fast-food industry, telemarketing, and similar fields are very much the same as Frederick Taylor described a century ago.

Moreover, the organizational "flexibility" that gives better-off workers more autonomy carries, for rank-and-file employees, the ever-present threat of "downsizing" (Sennett, 1998). That is, organizations facing global competition are eager to attract creative employees, but they are just as eager to cut costs by eliminating as many routine jobs as possible. The net result is that some people are better off than ever, while others worry about holding their jobs and struggle to make ends meet, a trend that Chapter 8 ("Social Stratification") explores in detail.

In sum, many analysts conclude that U.S. organizations remain the envy of the world for their productive efficiency. Indeed, there are few places on earth where the mail arrives as quickly and dependably as it does in the United States (Wilson, 1991). But we should remember that the future is far brighter for some than for others. In addition, as the final box explains, organizations pose an increasing threat to our privacy—something to keep in mind as we envision our organizational future.

SUMMARY

1. Social groups are building blocks of society that join members as well as perform various tasks.

2. Primary groups tend to be small and person-oriented; secondary groups are typically large and goal-oriented.

3. Instrumental leadership is concerned with realizing a group's goals; expressive leadership focuses on members' morale and well-being.

4. Because group members often seek consensus, groups can pressure members toward conformity.

5. Individuals use reference groups—both ingroups and outgroups—to form attitudes and make evaluations.

6. Georg Simmel characterized the dyad as intense but unstable; a triad, he added, can easily dissolve into a dyad by excluding one member.

7. Peter Blau explored how group size, internal homogeneity, and physical segregation of groups all affect members' behavior.

8. Social networks are relational webs that link people who have little common identity and limited interaction. The Internet is a vast electronic network linking millions of people worldwide.

9. Formal organizations are large secondary groups that try to perform complex tasks efficiently. They are classified as normative, coercive, or utilitarian based on their members' reasons for joining.

10. Bureaucratic organization expands in modern societies to perform complex tasks efficiently. Bureaucracy is based on specialization, hierarchy, rules and regulations, technical competence, impersonal interaction, and formal written communications.

11. Technology, economic and political trends, population patterns, and other organizations all combine to form the environment in which a particular organization must operate.

12. Ideal bureaucracy promotes efficiency, but bureaucracy may generate alienation and oligarchy, and contributes to the erosion of personal privacy.

13. Frederick Taylor's "scientific management" shaped U.S. organizations a century ago. Since then, organizations have evolved toward a more open and flexible form as they have (a) included a larger share of women and other minorities, (b) responded to global competition, especially from Japan, and (c) shifted their focus from industrial production to postindustrial information processing.

14. Reflecting the collective spirit of Japanese culture, formal organizations in Japan are based more on personal ties than their U.S. counterparts.

15. The "McDonaldization" of society involves increasing automation and impersonality.

16. The future of organizations will likely involve opposing trends: toward more creative autonomy for highly skilled, information workers and toward supervision and discipline for less-skilled, service workers.

KEY CONCEPTS

social group (p. 107) two or more people who identify and interact with one another

primary group (p. 108) a small social group whose members share personal and enduring relationships

secondary group (p. 108) a large, impersonal social group whose members pursue a specific goal or activity

instrumental leadership (p. 109) group leadership that emphasizes the completion of tasks

expressive leadership (p. 109) group leadership that focuses on collective well-being

groupthink (p. 111) the tendency of group members to conform, resulting in a narrow view of some issue

reference group (p. 112) a social group that serves as a point of reference in making evaluations and decisions

ingroup (p. 113) a social group commanding a member's esteem and loyalty

outgroup (p. 113) a social group toward which one feels competition or opposition

dyad (p. 113) a social group with two members

triad (p. 113) a social group with three members

network (p. 114) a web of weak social ties

formal organization (p. 116) a large secondary group that is organized to achieve its goals efficiently

tradition (p. 117) sentiments and beliefs about the world passed from generation to generation

rationality (p. 117) deliberate, matter-of-fact calculation of the most efficient means to accomplish a particular task

rationalization (p. 117) Max Weber's term for the change from tradition to rationality as the dominant mode of human thought

bureaucracy (p. 118) an organizational model rationally designed to perform tasks efficiently

organizational environment (p. 119) a range of factors outside the organization that affects its operation

bureaucratic ritualism (p. 121) a preoccupation with rules and regulations to the point of thwarting an organization's goals

bureaucratic inertia (p. 121) the tendency of bureaucratic organizations to perpetuate themselves

oligarchy (p. 121) the rule of the many by the few

scientific management (p. 122) Frederick Taylor's term for the application of scientific principles to the operation of a business or other large organization

CRITICAL-THINKING QUESTIONS

1. How do primary groups differ from secondary groups? Identify examples of each in your own life.
2. According to Max Weber, what are the six characteristic traits of bureaucracy? In what ways do new, "flexible" organizations differ?
3. George Ritzer (1996:1), a critic of McDonaldization, suggests that fast-food restaurants should carry the following label: "Sociologists warn us that habitual use of McDonald's systems are destructive to our physical and psychological well-being as well as to society as a whole." Do you agree? Why or why not?
4. The twentieth century saw the widespread use of initials, such as IRS, IRA, IMF, IBM, WPA, CIA, PLO, NATO, CNN, CDC, and so on. What does this suggest about social trends?

APPLICATIONS AND EXERCISES

1. Visit a large public building with an elevator. Observe groups of people as they approach the elevator, and enter the elevator with them. Watch their behavior: What happens to the conversations? Where do people fix their eyes? Can you account for these patterns?
2. Make a list of ingroups and outgroups on your campus. What traits account for groups' falling into each category? Ask several other people to see whether they agree with your classifications.
3. Spend several hours observing customers at a fast-food restaurant. Think about ways in which not just employees but *customers* are trained to behave in certain ways. For example, customer norms include lining up to order and finding one's own table. What other norms are at work?
4. Using available publications (and some assistance from an instructor), try to draw an "organizational pyramid" for your college or university, showing the key officials and how they supervise and report to one other.
5. Install the CD-ROM packaged in the back of this new textbook to access a variety of study, review, and applications exercises designed to help you better understand the material covered in this chapter. The CD includes an author's tip video, as well as interactive maps, video application exercises, Web links, and study questions.

 SITES TO SEE

http://www.prenhall.com/macionis
Visit the interactive Web site that accompanies this text. Begin by clicking on the cover of your book. You will find a chapter-by-chapter study guide, practice tests, chat room, and many suggested Web links.

http://www.saturnbp.com
Visit the Saturn car company Web site to read about Saturn's "flatter" organizational structure.

http://www.mte.com/webcam
This site connects you to a camera placed at New York City's Fifth Avenue at Forty-fifth Street. Do you think new Internet technology of this kind threatens people's privacy? Why or why not?

http://www.egroups.com
At this site, people build their own social groups to chat and exchange personal information. Take a look and see what you think about "virtual groups."

DEVIANCE

Dear Family,

For some reason, I've sat here and prayed to the Lord for answers on why this is happening. Since Ms. Babin took the stand, I knew I was gonna get found guilty. Down in my heart, I truly believe the Gerardi family knew I didn't do it, and I know I didn't do it, the Lord knows, y'all know, my defense team knows, the State knows, and everyone else. But that's not the answer. We will never get an answer as to why this is happening to us.

Shareef Cousin wrote this letter to his family from a prison cell. The incident that landed him in jail occurred on May 2, 1995, when Michael Gerardi and Connie Babin were leaving a restaurant in the French Quarter of New Orleans at about 10:30 P.M. Three young men approached the couple on the street as they were about to enter their car. Sensing an attack, Gerardi told Babin to run. She began to flee, but turned to see one of the young men walk right up to Gerardi and shoot him in the face, killing him.

Charged with the crime, Cousin sat in the courtroom as Babin testified she was there that night and that he was the one who fired the gun. The jury convicted Cousin

of murder, and soon after, the court handed down the death sentence. At age sixteen, he was sent to the Louisiana State Prison at Angola, one of the youngest people on death row in the United States.

Cousin continued to declare his innocence. A year later, during the appeals process, sufficient doubt was raised about his guilt that his murder conviction was set aside. As part of the deal, however, Cousin said that he did take part in the robbery. At first elated to be off death row, Cousin soon realized he would still spend years behind bars. He continues to maintain his innocence, and hopes for a new trial (Farley & Willwerth, 1998; Shareef-Cousin.com, 1999).

This chapter explores the problem of violent crime and other offenses, profiles offenders, and looks at the criminal justice system. First, however, we tackle the broader issue of why societies develop standards of right and wrong in the first place. As we shall see, the law is simply one part of a complex system of social control: Society teaches us all to conform, at least most of the time, to countless rules. We begin our investigation by defining several basic concepts.

The kind of deviance people create reflects the moral values they embrace. The Berkeley campus of the University of California has long celebrated its open-minded tolerance of sexual diversity. Thus, in 1992, when Andrew Martinez decided to attend classes wearing virtually nothing, people were reluctant to accuse "The Naked Guy" of immoral conduct. However, in Berkeley's politically correct atmosphere, it was not long before school officials banned Martinez from campus—charging that his nudity constituted a form of sexual harassment.

WHAT IS DEVIANCE?

Deviance is *the recognized violation of cultural norms.* Norms guide virtually all human activities, so the concept of deviance is quite broad. One category of deviance is **crime,** *the violation of a society's formally enacted criminal law.* Even criminal deviance spans a wide range, from minor traffic violations to sexual assault to murder.

Most familiar examples of nonconformity are negative cases of rule breaking, such as stealing from a convenience store, abusing a child, or driving while intoxicated. But we also define especially righteous people—students who volunteer too much in class or people who are overly enthusiastic about new computer technology—as deviant, even if we accord them a measure of respect (Huls, 1987). What all deviant actions or attitudes have in common is some element of *difference* that causes us to regard another person as an "outsider" (Becker, 1966).

Not all deviance involves action or even choice. The very *existence* of some categories of people can be troublesome to others. To the young, elderly people may seem hopelessly "out of it"; and to some whites, the mere presence of people of color may cause discomfort. Able-bodied people often view individuals with disabilities as an outgroup, just as affluent people may shun the poor for falling short of their standards.

All of us are subject to **social control,** *attempts by society to regulate people's thought and behavior.* Often, this process is informal, as when parents praise or scold their children or when friends make fun of someone's musical taste. Cases of serious deviance, however, may provoke action by the **criminal justice system,** *a formal response by police, courts, and prison officials to alleged violations of the law.*

In sum, deviance is much more than a matter of individual choice or personal failing. *How* a society defines deviance, *who* is branded as "deviant," and *what* people decide to do about deviance are all issues of social organization. Only gradually, however, have people recognized this fact, as we shall now explain.

THE BIOLOGICAL CONTEXT

Chapter 3 ("Socialization: From Infancy to Old Age") explained that a century ago most people understood—or, more correctly, misunderstood—human behavior to be the result of biological instincts. Early interest in criminality thus focused on biological causes. In 1876, Caesare Lombroso (1835–1909), an Italian physician who worked in prisons, theorized that criminals stand out physically, with low foreheads, prominent jaws and cheekbones, protruding ears, hairiness, and unusually long arms, all characteristics that made them look like humans' apelike ancestors.

But Lombroso's work was flawed, since the physical features he attributed to prisoners could be found throughout the entire population. We now know that no physical attributes, of the kind described by Lombroso, set off criminals from noncriminals (Goring, 1972; orig. 1913).

At midcentury, William Sheldon (Sheldon, Hartl, & McDermott, 1949) took a different tack, suggesting that body structure might predict criminality. He cross-checked hundreds of young men for body type and criminal history and concluded that delinquency was most likely among boys with muscular, athletic builds. Sheldon Glueck and Eleanor Glueck (1950) confirmed Sheldon's conclusion, but cautioned that a powerful build does not necessarily *cause* or even predict criminality. Parents, they suggested, tend to be more distant from powerfully built sons who, in turn, grow up to display less sensitivity toward others. Moreover, in a self-fulfilling prophecy, people who expect muscular boys to be bullies may act in ways that provoke the aggressive behavior they expect.

Today, genetics research seeks possible links between biology and crime. Though no conclusive evidence connects criminality to any specific genetic trait, people's overall genetic composition, in combination with social influences, probably accounts for some tendency toward criminality. In other words, biological factors may have a real, but modest, effect on whether or not an individual becomes a criminal (Rowe, 1983; Rowe & Osgood, 1984; Wilson & Herrnstein, 1985; Jencks, 1987).

Critical evaluation. At best, biological theories offer a very limited explanation of crime. Recent sociobiological research—noting, for example, that violent crime is overwhelmingly male and that parents are more likely to abuse foster children than natural children—is promising, but we know too little about the links between genes and human behavior to draw firm conclusions (Daly & Wilson, 1988).

Then, too, because a biological approach looks at the individual, it offers no insight as to how some kinds of behaviors come to be defined as deviant in the first place. Therefore, although there is much to learn about how human biology may affect behavior, research currently places far greater emphasis on social influences (Gibbons & Krohn, 1986; Liska, 1991).

PERSONALITY FACTORS

Like biological theories, psychological explanations of deviance focus on individual abnormality. Some personality traits are hereditary, but most psychologists think temperament is primarily shaped by social experience. Deviance, then, is viewed as the result of "unsuccessful" socialization.

Research by Walter Reckless and Simon Dinitz (1967) illustrates the psychological approach. Reckless and Dinitz began by asking teachers to categorize twelve-year-old male students as either likely or unlikely to get into trouble with the law. They then interviewed both the boys and their mothers to assess each boy's self-concept and how he related to others. Analyzing their results, the researchers found that the "good boys" displayed a strong conscience (or superego, in Freud's terminology), could handle frustration, and identified with cultural norms and values. The "bad boys," by contrast, had a weaker conscience, displayed little tolerance for frustration, and felt out of step with conventional culture.

As we might expect, the "good boys" went on to have fewer run-ins with the police than the "bad boys." Since all the boys lived in areas where delinquency was widespread, the investigators attributed staying out of trouble to a personality that reined in deviant impulses. Based on this conclusion, Reckless and Dinitz call their analysis *containment theory*.

Critical evaluation. Psychologists have shown that personality patterns bear some connection to deviance. However, the fact is that most serious crimes are committed by people whose psychological profiles are *normal*.

Overall, both biological and psychological research views deviance as an individual trait, without exploring how conceptions of right and wrong initially arise, why people define some rule breakers—but not others—as deviant, and what role power plays in shaping a society's system of social control. To explore these issues, we now turn to a sociological analysis of deviance.

THE SOCIAL FOUNDATIONS OF DEVIANCE

Although we tend to view deviance as the free choice or personal failings of individuals, all behavior—deviance as well as conformity—is shaped by society. Three *social* foundations of deviance, identified here, will be detailed later in this chapter:

I. **Deviance varies according to cultural norms.** No thought or action is inherently deviant; it becomes deviant only in relation to particular norms. The law in certain parts of Nevada permits prostitution, although the practice is outlawed in the rest of the United States. Casinos in Atlantic City, Las Vegas, and on Mississippi river boats and numerous Indian reservations beckon high rollers, but everywhere else in the United States gambling is illegal. Further, most cities

AN AGED VICTIM OF SUPERSTITION.

Emile Durkheim's important insight is that no society can exist without deviance. Thus, after arriving in New England in the early seventeenth century, the very religious Puritans soon found themselves accusing some of their members of serious wrongdoing. The best known Puritan "crime wave" climaxed in the Salem witch trials of 1692, which led to two dozen executions of women and men thought to be doing the work of the devil.

and towns have at least one unique statute: South Padre Island, Texas, bans wearing ties; Mount Prospect, Illinois, has a law against keeping pigeons or bees; Los Angeles bans gas-powered leaf blowers; and Beverly Hills regulates the number of tennis balls allowed on the court at one time (Sanders & Horn, 1998).

Around the world, deviance is even more diverse. Albania outlaws any public display of religious faith, such as "crossing" oneself; Cuba and Vietnam can prosecute citizens for meeting with foreigners; Singapore prohibits the sale of chewing gum; police in Iran can arrest a woman wearing makeup; and U.S. citizens risk arrest for traveling to Libya or Iraq.

2. **People become deviant as others define them that way.** Each of us violates cultural norms, occasionally to the extent of breaking the law. For example, most of us at some time or other have walked around talking to ourselves or "borrowed" a pen from our workplace. Whether such activities are sufficient to define us as mentally ill or criminal depends on how others perceive, define, and respond to our behavior.

3. **Both norms and the way people define situations involve social power.** The law, declared Karl Marx, is the means by which powerful people protect their interests. A homeless person who stands on a street corner denouncing the government risks arrest for disturbing the peace; a mayoral candidate during an election campaign does exactly the same thing and gets police protection. In short, norms and how we apply them reflect social inequality.

THE FUNCTIONS OF DEVIANCE: STRUCTURAL-FUNCTIONAL ANALYSIS

The key insight of the structural-functional paradigm is that deviance is a necessary element of social organization. This point was made a century ago by Emile Durkheim.

DURKHEIM'S BASIC INSIGHT

In his pioneering study of deviance, Emile Durkheim (1964a, orig. 1895; 1964b, orig. 1893) made the surprising statement that there is nothing abnormal about deviance. In fact, it performs four essential functions:

1. **Deviance affirms cultural values and norms.** As moral creatures, people must prefer some attitudes and behaviors to others. But any conception of virtue rests upon an opposing notion of vice: There can be no good without evil and no justice without crime. Deviance, then, is needed to define and sustain morality.

2. **Responding to deviance clarifies moral boundaries.** By defining some individuals as deviant, people draw a boundary between right and wrong. For example, a college marks the line between academic honesty and cheating by disciplining students who plagiarize.

3. Responding to deviance brings people together.
People typically react to serious deviance with collective outrage. In doing so, Durkheim explained, they reaffirm the moral ties that bind them. For example, after the Columbine High School shooting in 1999, feelings of anguish and outrage were shared not just by that Colorado community but by the entire nation.

4. Deviance encourages social change. Deviant people push a society's moral boundaries; their lives suggest alternatives to the status quo and may encourage change. Today's deviance, declared Durkheim, can become tomorrow's morality (1964a:71). Look, for example, at how rock and roll—condemned as morally degenerate in the 1950s—became a mainstream, multibillion-dollar industry just a few years later.

MERTON'S STRAIN THEORY

Some deviance may be necessary for a society to function, but Robert Merton (1938, 1968) argued that excessive deviance arises from particular social arrangements. Specifically, the extent and kind of deviance depends on whether a society provides the *means* (such as schooling and job opportunities) to achieve cultural *goals* (such as financial success).

Conformity, Merton begins, lies in pursuing conventional goals through approved means. Thus, the U.S. "success story" is someone who acquires wealth and prestige through talent, schooling, and hard work. But not everyone who desires conventional success has the opportunity to attain it. People raised in poverty, for example, may see little hope of becoming successful if they play by the rules. As a result, they may try to make money through crime—say, by dealing cocaine. Merton called this type of deviance *innovation*—the use of unconventional means (drug sales) to achieve a culturally approved goal (wealth). Figure 6–1 shows that innovation involves accepting the cultural goal (financial success) but rejecting the conventional means (hard work at a "straight" job).

According to Merton, the strain between our culture's emphasis on wealth and the limited opportunities to get rich gives rise, especially among the poor, to theft, the sale of illegal drugs, and other forms of street crime. The inability to succeed by normative means may also prompt another type of deviance that Merton calls *ritualism* (see Figure 6–1). Lower-level bureaucrats, for example, may know they will achieve

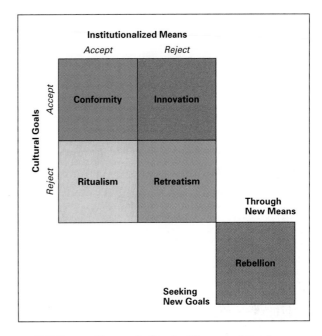

FIGURE 6–1 Merton's Strain Theory of Deviance
Source: Merton (1968).

only limited financial success, so they obsessively stick to the rules in order to at least feel respectable.

A third response to the inability to succeed is *retreatism*—rejection of both cultural goals and means so that one, in effect, "drops out." Some alcoholics, drug addicts, and street people are retreatists. The deviance of retreatists lies in their unconventional lifestyles and, perhaps more seriously, in their apparent willingness to live that way.

The fourth response to failure is *rebellion*. Like retreatists, rebels reject both the cultural definition of success and the normative means of achieving it. Rebels—such as radical "survivalists"—go one step further by forming a counterculture and advocating alternatives to the existing social order.

DEVIANT SUBCULTURES

Richard Cloward and Lloyd Ohlin (1966) extended Merton's theory, proposing that crime results not simply from limited legitimate (legal) opportunity but also from readily accessible illegitimate (illegal) opportunity. In short, deviance or conformity depends upon the *relative opportunity structure* that frames a person's life.

In Kosovo, as in the United States, young people (especially males) cut off from legitimate opportunity may form deviant subcultures as a strategy to gain the prestige denied them by the larger society.

The life of Al Capone, a notorious gangster of the Prohibition era (which ran from 1920 to 1933), illustrates Cloward and Ohlin's theory. As a poor immigrant with no hope of getting a college education, Capone saw few legitimate ways to succeed. Yet he did see illegitimate opportunity for success as a bootlegger. Where relative opportunity favors criminal activity, Cloward and Ohlin predict the development of *criminal subcultures*. Gangs, for example, may specialize in one or another type of crime, depending on available opportunities (Sheley et al., 1995).

But what happens when people are unable to find *any* kinds of opportunities, legal or illegal? Then delinquency may take the form of *conflict subcultures* (armed street gangs) where violence is ignited by frustration and a desire for respect. Alternatively, those who fail to achieve success, even through crime, may fall into *retreatist subcultures*, dropping out and abusing alcohol or other drugs.

Albert Cohen (1971) suggests that criminality is most common among lower-class youths because they have the least opportunity to achieve conventional success. Neglected by society, they seek self-respect by creating a delinquent subculture that "defines as meritorious the characteristics [these youths] *do* possess, the kinds of conduct of which they *are* capable" (1971:66). Being feared on the street, for example,

may win few points with society as a whole, but it may satisfy a youth's desire to "be somebody" in a local neighborhood.

Walter Miller (1970) adds that deviant subcultures are characterized by (1) *trouble*, arising from frequent conflict with teachers and police; (2) *toughness*, the value placed on physical size, strength, and agility, especially among males; (3) *smartness*, the ability to succeed on the streets, to out-smart or "con" others; (4) *a need for excitement*, the search for thrills, risk, or danger; (5) *a belief in fate*, a sense that people lack control over their own lives; and (6) *a desire for freedom*, often expressed as hostility toward all authority figures.

Finally, Elijah Anderson (1994) explains that, in poor urban neighborhoods, most people manage to conform to conventional ("decent") values. Yet, faced with the dangers of crime and violence, hostility from police, and sometimes even neglect from their own parents, some young men adopt a "street code," which stresses their ability to take care of themselves and their willingness to stand up to any threat. According to this code, even a violent death, explains Anderson, is better than being "dissed" (disrespected) by others. Some manage to escape the dangers, but the risk of ending up in jail—or worse—is very high for these young men pushed to the margins of our society.

Critical evaluation. Durkheim made an important contribution by pointing out the functions of deviance. There is, however, evidence that a community does not always come together in reaction to crime; sometimes fear of crime drives people to withdraw from public life (Liska & Warner, 1991).

Merton's strain theory also has been criticized for explaining some kinds of deviance (theft, for example) better than others (crimes of passion or mental illness). Moreover, not everyone seeks success in conventional terms of wealth, as strain theory implies.

The general argument of Cloward and Ohlin, Cohen, and Miller—that deviance reflects the opportunity structure of society—has been confirmed by subsequent research (cf. Allan & Steffensmeier, 1989). However, these theories, too, fall short by assuming that everyone shares the same cultural standards for judging right and wrong. Moreover, we must be careful not to define deviance in terms that unfairly focus attention on poor people. If crime is defined to include stock fraud as well as street theft, then more affluent people will be counted among criminals. Finally, all structural-functional theories imply that everyone who breaks the rules will be labeled deviant. Becoming deviant, however, is actually a highly complex process, as the next section explains.

LABELING DEVIANCE: THE SYMBOLIC-INTERACTION APPROACH

The symbolic-interaction paradigm explains how people define deviance in everyday situations. From this point of view, definitions of deviance and conformity are surprisingly flexible.

LABELING THEORY

The central contribution of symbolic-interaction analysis is **labeling theory,** *the assertion that deviance and conformity result, not so much from what people do, as from how others respond to those actions.* Labeling theory stresses the relativity of deviance, meaning that people may define the same behavior in any number of ways. Howard S. Becker claims that deviance is, therefore, nothing more than behavior that people define as deviant (1966:9).

Consider these situations: A woman takes an article of clothing from a roommate's drawer; a married man at a convention in a distant city has sex with a prostitute; a

mayor gives a big city contract to a major campaign contributor. We might define the first situation as carelessness, borrowing, or theft. The consequences of the second situation depend largely on whether the man's behavior becomes known back home. In the third situation, is the official choosing the best contractor or paying off a political debt? The social construction of reality, then, is a highly variable process of detection, definition, and response.

At a broader level, since "reality" depends on time and place, it is no surprise that one society's conformity may be another's deviance. Consider, for example, cockfighting, described in the box on page 140. Is this popular sport an important cultural ritual or a vicious abuse of animals?

PRIMARY AND SECONDARY DEVIANCE

Edwin Lemert (1951, 1972) observed that some norm violations—say, skipping school or underage drinking—provoke slight reaction from others and have little effect on a person's self-concept. Lemert calls such passing episodes *primary deviance.*

But what happens if people take notice of someone's deviance and make something of it? If, for example, people begin to describe a young man as a "boozer" and evict him from their social circle, he may become embittered, drink even more, and seek the company of those who approve of his behavior. So the response to initial deviance can set in motion *secondary deviance,* by which an individual repeatedly violates a norm and begins to take on a deviant identity. The development of secondary deviance is one application of the Thomas theorem (see Chapter 4, "Social Interaction in Everyday Life"), which states that situations people define as real become real in their consequences.

STIGMA

Secondary deviance marks the start of what Erving Goffman (1963) called a *deviant career.* As individuals acquire a stronger commitment to deviant behavior, they typically acquire a **stigma,** *a powerfully negative label that greatly changes a person's self-concept and social identity.* Stigma operates as a master status (see Chapter 4), overpowering other dimensions of identity so that a person is discredited in the minds of others and, consequently, becomes socially isolated. Sometimes an entire community stigmatizes an individual through what Harold Garfinkel (1956) calls a

GLOBAL SOCIOLOGY

Cockfighting:
Cultural Ritual or Abuse of Animals?

You won't see it on television, but one of the world's most popular sports—from North America to Europe to Asia—is cockfighting. Legal in parts of Louisiana, Texas, New Mexico, and Arizona, cockfighting is big business in Mexico, and is something of a national pastime in the Philippines. There, the local cock pit is as important as the town square in the U.S. Midwest: Every village has one, and it draws a crowd on weekends and fiesta days.

On the surface, cockfights are about gambling. An afternoon or evening event might include ten fights. A fight begins with the cock owners displaying their birds to one another, calling out for bets as to which is the stronger bird. Members of the audience weigh in with cash. Keeping track of the bets is the "cristo," someone who stands, arms extended, taking money.

With the odds of winning set and the money on the table, the actual combat begins. Each rooster is outfitted with a small, sharp blade strapped to the rear of its left leg. The cocks need little encouragement to fight, but the owners do a bit of strutting themselves, swinging their birds in front of each other

before dropping them on lines drawn in the pit sand. Upon hitting the ground, the birds fly at one another, merging in a blur of legs and feathers.

Within minutes, one bird may collapse from exhaustion; the owner steps in to revive his cock, and the process is repeated. Before long, however, a blade finds its mark. The victor, the bird that will live to fight another day, perches on the vanquished, which will not.

In many parts of the world, cockfighting is an important male ritual. Men raise their roosters for about two years, often at considerable expense, giving them as good care as they offer to their sons. Then, through the ritual of the cockfight, men test their own claims to manhood, establish their standing in the community pecking order, and pass on to their sons lessons about honor, competition, and masculinity.

Many outside observers are repulsed by the spectacle. But cockfighting is obviously deeply important to insiders. Should an outsider, then, condemn it as brutality or respect it as ceremony?

Sources: Based on *The Economist* (1994), Harris (1994), and the author's research in the Philippines.

---

degradation ceremony. A criminal prosecution is one example, operating much like a high school graduation in reverse: In this instance, a person stands before the community to be labeled in a negative rather than a positive way.

Once people stigmatize a person, they may engage in *retrospective labeling*, a reinterpretation of a person's past in light of some present deviance (Scheff, 1984). For example, after discovering that a priest has sexually molested a child, others rethink his past,

perhaps musing, "He always did want to be around young children." Retrospective labeling distorts a person's biography by being highly selective, a process that can deepen a deviant identity.

Similarly, people may engage in *projective labeling* of a stigmatized person. That is, people use a deviant identity to predict future action. Regarding the priest, people might say, "He's never going to change." The more people think such things, of course, the greater the chance that they will come true.

LABELING AND MENTAL ILLNESS

Is a woman who believes that Jesus rides the bus to work with her every day seriously deluded or merely expressing her religious faith in a symbolic way? Is a homeless man who refuses to allow police to take him to a city shelter on a cold night mentally ill or simply trying to live independently?

Psychiatrist Thomas Szasz charges that people apply the label "insanity" to what is actually only "difference." Therefore, he concludes, we should abandon the notion of mental illness entirely (1961, 1970, 1994, 1995). Illness, Szasz continues, is physical and afflicts only the body; mental illness, then, is a myth. The world is full of people whose differences in thought or action may irritate others, but such differences are no grounds for defining someone as sick. Such labeling, Szasz claims, simply enforces conformity to the standards created by people powerful enough to impose their will on others.

Many of Szasz's colleagues reject the notion that all mental illness is a fiction. But some hail his work for pointing out the danger of using medical practice to promote conformity. Most of us, after all, experience periods of extreme stress or other mental instability from time to time. Such episodes, although upsetting, are usually of passing importance. If, however, others respond with labeling that forms the basis of a social stigma, the long-term result may be further deviance as a self-fulfilling prophecy (Scheff, 1984; Rosenfeld, 1997).

THE MEDICALIZATION OF DEVIANCE

Labeling theory, particularly the ideas of Szasz and Goffman, helps explain an important shift in the way our society understands deviance. Over the last fifty years, the growing influence of psychiatry and medicine has led to the **medicalization of deviance,** *the transformation of moral and legal deviance into a medical condition.*

Medicalization amounts to swapping one set of labels for another. In moral terms, we evaluate people or their behavior as "bad" or "good." However, the scientific objectivity of medicine passes no moral judgment, instead using clinical diagnoses such as "sick" or "well."

To illustrate, until the middle of this century, most people viewed alcoholics as morally weak people easily tempted by the pleasure of drink. Gradually, however, medical specialists redefined alcoholism so that most people now consider it a disease, rendering individuals

When people step out of line, should we consider their behavior "bad" or "sick"? In 2000, Atlanta Braves pitcher John Rocker made comments about minorities that many considered offensive. Rocker was reprimanded, and was also required to undergo psychological testing, suggesting that he has an illness. Do you think these kinds of cases warrant "treatment," or is "punishment" more appropriate? Why?

"sick" rather than "bad." In the same way, obesity, drug addiction, child abuse, promiscuity, and other behaviors that used to be strictly moral matters are widely defined today as illnesses for which people need help rather than punishment. National Map 6–1 on page 142 suggests where in the United States this transformation has been most pronounced.

Whether we define deviance as a moral or medical issue has three consequences. First, it affects *who responds* to deviance. An offense against common morality typically provokes a reaction from members of the community or the police. Applying medical labels, however, transfers the situation to the control of clinical specialists, including counselors, psychiatrists, and physicians.

A second issue is *how people respond* to a deviant. A moral approach defines the deviant as an "offender" subject to punishment. Medically, however, "patients" need treatment (for their own good, of course). Therefore, while punishment is designed to fit the crime, treatment programs are tailored to the patient and may involve virtually any therapy that a specialist thinks might prevent future illness (von Hirsh, 1986).

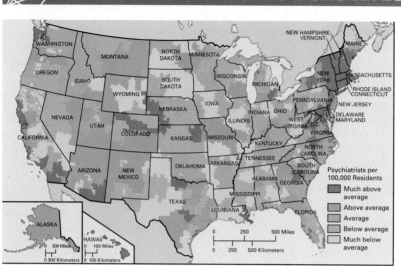

Third, and most important, the two labels differ on the issue of *the personal competence of the deviant person.* From a moral standpoint, whether we are right or wrong, at least we take responsibility for our own behavior. Once defined as sick, however, we are seen as unable to control (or, if "mentally ill," even understand) our actions. People who are incompetent are, in turn, subject to treatment, often against their will. For this reason alone, defining deviance in medical terms should be done with extreme caution.

SUTHERLAND'S DIFFERENTIAL ASSOCIATION THEORY

Learning any social pattern—whether conventional or deviant—is a process that takes place in groups. Therefore, according to Edwin Sutherland (1940), a person's tendency toward conformity or deviance depends upon the amount of contact with others who encourage—or reject—conventional behavior. This is Sutherland's theory of *differential association.*

We can illustrate Sutherland's theory with a study of drug and alcohol use among young adults in the United States (Akers et al., 1979). Questionnaires completed by junior and senior high school students showed a close connection between the extent of alcohol and drug use and the degree to which peer groups encouraged such activity. The investigators concluded

that young people embrace delinquent patterns to the degree that they are rewarded for defining deviance—rather than conformity—in positive terms.

HIRSCHI'S CONTROL THEORY

Sociologist Travis Hirschi (1969; Gottfredson & Hirschi, 1995) developed *control theory,* which states that social control depends on anticipating the consequences of one's behavior. Hirschi assumes that everyone finds at least some deviance tempting. But imagining the reactions of family and friends deters most people; almost everyone else would stop at the prospect of a ruined career. On the other hand, individuals who think that they have little to lose from deviance are likely to become rule-breakers.

Specifically, Hirschi links conformity to four different types of social control:

1. **Attachment.** Strong social attachments encourage conformity; weak relationships in the family, peer group, and school leave people freer to engage in deviance.

2. **Opportunity.** The greater a person's access to legitimate opportunity, the greater the advantages of conformity. By contrast, someone with little confidence in future success is freer to drift toward deviance.

Artist Frank Romero was one of the founders of the Chicano movement in the late 1960s. Drawing on his own childhood in East Los Angeles, his art depicts the importance of cars, gangs, and violence in young people's efforts to gain a sense of importance and belonging in a society that has pushed them to its margins.

Frank Romero, *Freeway Wars*, 1990, Serigraph (edition of 99), 31½ × 38 inches. © Frank Romero. Nicolas and Cristina Hernandez Trust Collection, Pasadena, California.

3. **Involvement.** Extensive involvement in legitimate activities—such as holding a job, going to school, or playing sports—inhibits deviance. By contrast, people who simply "hang out" waiting for something to happen have time and energy for deviant activity.

4. **Belief.** Strong beliefs in conventional morality and respect for authority figures restrain tendencies toward deviance. By contrast, people with a weak conscience (and who are left unsupervised) are more vulnerable to temptation (Osgood et al., 1996).

Hirschi's analysis draws together a number of earlier ideas about the causes of deviant behavior. Note that both a person's relative social privilege as well as strength of moral character are crucial in generating a stake in conformity to conventional norms (Wiatrowski, Griswold, & Roberts, 1981; Sampson & Laub, 1990; Free, 1992).

Critical evaluation. The various symbolic-interaction theories all see deviance as process. Labeling theory links deviance not to *action* but to the *reaction* of others. Thus some people are defined as deviant while others who think or behave in the same way are not. The concepts of secondary deviance, deviant careers, and stigma demonstrate how being labeled a deviant can become a lasting self-concept.

Yet labeling theory has several limitations. First, because it takes a highly relative view of deviance, labeling theory ignores the fact that some kinds of behavior—such as murder—are condemned virtually everywhere (Wellford, 1980). Labeling theory, therefore, is most usefully applied to less serious deviance, such as sexual promiscuity or mental illness. Second, research on the consequences of deviant labeling is inconclusive (Smith & Gartin, 1989; Sherman & Smith, 1992). Does deviant labeling produce further deviance or discourage it? Third, not everyone resists being labeled as deviant; some people actually seek it out (Vold & Bernard, 1986). For example, people engage in civil disobedience and willingly subject themselves to arrest in order to call attention to social injustice.

Both Sutherland's differential association theory and Hirschi's control theory have had considerable influence in sociology. But they provide little insight into why society's norms and laws define certain kinds of activities as deviant in the first place. This important question is addressed by social-conflict analysis, the focus of the next section.

DEVIANCE AND INEQUALITY: SOCIAL-CONFLICT ANALYSIS

The social-conflict paradigm links deviance to social inequality. That is, *who* or *what* is labeled "deviant" depends on which categories of people hold power in a society.

DEVIANCE AND POWER

Alexander Liazos (1972) points out that everyday conceptions of deviants—"nuts, sluts, and 'preverts'"—all share the trait of powerlessness. Bag ladies (not corporate polluters) and unemployed men on street corners (not arms dealers) carry the stigma of deviance.

Social-conflict theory explains this pattern in three ways. First, the norms—and especially laws—of any society generally reflect the interests of the rich and powerful. People who threaten the wealthy, either by taking their property or by advocating a more egalitarian society, are often defined as "common thieves" or "political radicals." Karl Marx, a major architect of the social-conflict approach, argued that the law (and all social institutions) support the interests of the rich. Or, as Richard Quinney puts it: "Capitalist justice is by the capitalist class, for the capitalist class, and against the working class" (1977:3).

Second, even if their behavior is called into question, the powerful have the resources to resist deviant labels. Corporate executives or government officials who might order or condone the dumping of hazardous wastes are rarely held personally accountable. Moreover, as the O. J. Simpson trial made clear, even when charged with violent crimes, the rich have the resources to vigorously resist being labeled as criminal.

Third, the widespread belief that norms and laws are natural and good masks their political character. For this reason, we may condemn the *unequal application* of the law but give little thought to whether the *laws themselves* are inherently unfair (Quinney, 1977).

DEVIANCE AND CAPITALISM

In the Marxist tradition, Steven Spitzer (1980) argues that deviant labels are applied to people who interfere with the operation of capitalism. First, because capitalism is based on private control of property, people who threaten the property of others—especially the poor who steal from the rich—are prime candidates for being labeled deviant. Conversely, the rich who exploit the poor are less likely to be labeled deviant. Landlords, for example, who charge poor tenants high rents

and evict those who cannot pay are not considered a threat to anyone; they are simply "doing business."

Second, because capitalism depends on productive labor, people who cannot or will not work risk being labeled deviant. Many members of our society think people who are out of work—even if through no fault of their own—are somehow deviant.

Third, capitalism depends on respect for authority figures, so people who resist authority are labeled deviant. Examples are children who skip school or talk back to parents and teachers and adults who do not cooperate with employers or police.

Fourth, anyone who directly challenges the capitalist status quo is likely to be defined as deviant. In this category are antiwar activists, radical environmentalists, and labor organizers.

On the other side of the coin, society positively labels whatever enhances the operation of capitalism. Winning athletes, for example, enjoy celebrity status because they make money and express the values of individual achievement and competition vital to capitalism. Additionally, Spitzer notes, we condemn using drugs of escape (marijuana, psychedelics, heroin, and crack) as deviant, but promote drugs that encourage adjustment to the status quo (alcohol and caffeine).

The capitalist system also strives to control people who don't fit into the system. The elderly, people with mental or physical disabilities, and Robert Merton's "retreatists" (including people addicted to alcohol or other drugs) represent a "costly yet relatively harmless burden" on society. Such people, claims Spitzer, are subject to control by social welfare agencies. But people who directly challenge the capitalist system, including the inner-city "underclass" and revolutionaries—Merton's "innovators" and "rebels"—are controlled by the criminal justice system or, in times of crisis, military forces such as the National Guard.

Note that both the social welfare and criminal justice systems blame individuals—not the system—for social problems. Welfare recipients are deemed unworthy freeloaders; poor people who vent rage at their plight are labeled rioters; anyone who actively challenges the government is branded a radical or a Communist; and those who attempt to gain illegally what they will never acquire legally are rounded up as common criminals.

WHITE-COLLAR CRIME

In 1987, a Wall Street stockbroker named Michael Milken made headlines for becoming the highest paid U.S. worker in half a century. His yearly salary and

Businesses can engage in wrongdoing, just as individuals can. Yet, as social-conflict analysis points out, rich and powerful people who head up corporations charged with law-breaking, such as Microsoft, rarely are considered to be criminals, and rarely are they subject to the kinds of punishment accorded to ordinary people who break the law.

bonuses totaled $550 million—*about $1.5 million a day.* Such a sum placed Milken right behind Al Capone, whose earnings in 1927 reportedly exceeded $600 million in current dollars (Swartz, 1989). Milken had something else in common with Capone: He was jailed—in his case, for business fraud.

Milken's activities exemplify **white-collar crime,** defined by Edwin Sutherland in 1940 as *crime committed by people of high social position in the course of their occupations* (Sutherland & Cressey, 1978). As the Milken case suggests, white-collar crimes do not involve violence and rarely bring police with guns drawn to the scene. Rather, white-collar criminals use their powerful occupational offices to illegally enrich themselves or others, often causing significant public harm in the process (Hagan & Parker, 1985; Vold & Bernard, 1986). For this reason, sociologists sometimes call white-collar offenses *crime in the suites* as opposed to *crime in the streets.*

The most common white-collar crimes are bank embezzlement, business fraud, bribery, and antitrust violations. Certainly, some white-collar crime causes only limited harm. But many white-collar crimes— like the savings and loan scandal a few years ago— attract a great deal of attention and cause great loss to the public (Weisburd et al., 1991). The government program to bail out the savings and loan industry ended up costing U.S. taxpayers $600 billion dollars, which amounts to $2,500 per person.

Sutherland (1940) explains that white-collar offenses typically end up in a civil hearing rather than a criminal courtroom. *Civil law* regulates economic affairs between private parties, while *criminal law* defines every individual's moral responsibilities to society. In practice, then, the loser in a civil case pays for damages or injury, but is not labeled a criminal. Further, corporate officials are protected by the fact that most charges of white-collar crime target the organization rather than individuals.

In the rare cases in which white-collar criminals are charged and convicted, the odds are only about fifty-fifty that they will go to jail. One accounting shows that just 54 percent of the embezzlers convicted in U.S. federal courts served prison sentences; the rest were put on probation and/or were fined (U.S. Bureau of Justice Statistics, 2000).

CORPORATE CRIME

Sometimes whole companies, not just individuals, break the law. **Corporate crime** refers to *the illegal actions of a corporation or people acting on its behalf.*

Corporate crime ranges from knowingly selling faulty or dangerous products to deliberately polluting the environment (Benson & Cullen, 1998). As is the case with white-collar crime, most such cases go unpunished, and many are never a matter of public record. But the cost of corporate crime goes beyond dollars to human lives. For example, coal mining companies have hidden the dangers of bad air in the mines, so that hundreds of people die annually from "black lung" disease. The death toll from all job-related hazards known to companies probably reaches more than 100,000 annually (Reiman, 1998; Carroll, 1999; Jones, 1999b).

TABLE 6–1 Sociological Explanations of Deviance: A Summary	
Theoretical Paradigm	Major Contributions
Structural-functional analysis	What is deviant may vary, but deviance is found in all societies; deviance and the social response it provokes sustain the moral foundation of society; deviance may also guide social change.
Symbolic-interaction analysis	Nothing is inherently deviant but may become defined as such through the response of others; the reactions of others are highly variable; labeling someone deviant may lead to the development of secondary deviance and deviant careers.
Social-conflict analysis	Laws and other norms reflect the interests of powerful members of society; those who threaten the status quo generally are defined as deviant; social injury caused by powerful people is less likely to be considered criminal than is social injury caused by people who have little social power.

When corporations are accused of wrong-doing, they have the resources to fight back. In 1998, a federal judge concluded that software giant Microsoft had committed anti-trust violations, meaning that it had knowingly established such tight control over a market that it could just about set its own prices. The corporation has vigorously defended itself, however, and the civil proceedings are expected to continue for some time (Cohen, 2000). Whatever the outcome, it is the company as a whole that is on the line; individuals who lead the corporation are not subject to criminal prosecution.

ORGANIZED CRIME

Organized crime is *a business supplying illegal goods or services.* Sometimes organized crime forces people to do business with them, as when a gang extorts money from shopkeepers for "protection." In most cases, however, organized crime involves selling illegal goods and services—including sex, drugs, or gambling—to a willing public.

For more than a century, organized crime has flourished in the United States. The scope of its operations expanded among immigrants who found that this society was not willing to share its opportunities with them. Thus, some ambitious minorities (such as Al Capone, described earlier) made their own success, especially during Prohibition (1919–1933), when the government banned alcohol coast to coast.

The Italian Mafia is a well-known example of organized crime. But other criminal organizations involve African Americans, Chinese, Colombians, Cubans, Haitians, and Russians, as well as others of almost every racial and ethnic category. Moreover, today's organized crime involves a wide range of activities, from selling illegal drugs to prostitution to credit card fraud and marketing false identification papers to illegal immigrants (Valdez, 1997).

Critical evaluation. According to social-conflict theory, a capitalist society's inequality in wealth and power guides the creation and application of laws and other norms. The criminal justice and social welfare systems thus act as political agents, controlling categories of people who threaten the capitalist system.

Like other approaches to deviance, however, social-conflict theory has its critics. First, this approach implies that laws and other cultural norms are created directly by the rich and powerful. At the very least, this is an oversimplification, since laws also protect workers, consumers, and the environment, sometimes opposing the interests of the rich.

Second, social-conflict analysis implies that criminality springs up only to the extent that a society treats its members unequally. However, as Durkheim noted, deviance exists in all societies, whatever their economic system.

The sociological explanations for crime and other types of deviance that we have discussed are summarized in Table 6–1.

DEVIANCE AND SOCIAL DIVERSITY

What people consider deviant reflects the relative power and privilege of different categories of people. The following sections offer two examples: how racial and ethnic hostility motivate hate crimes and how gender is linked to deviance.

HATE CRIMES

The term **hate crime** refers to *a criminal act against a person or a person's property by an offender motivated by racial or other bias.* A hate crime may express hostility toward someone based on race, religion, ancestry, sexual orientation, or physical disability.

Most people were stunned by the brutal killing in 1998 of Matthew Shepard—a gay student at the University of Wyoming—by two men filled with hate toward homosexuals. The National Gay and Lesbian Task Force reports that one in five lesbians and gay men has been physically assaulted and more than 90 percent have been verbally abused because of sexual orientation (cited in Berrill, 1992:19–20). Victims of hate-motivated violence are especially likely to be people who contend with multiple stigmas, such as gay men of color. The federal government records nearly 8,000 hate crimes each year.

By 1999, forty-two states and the federal government had enacted legislation that raises penalties for crimes motivated by hatred. Supporters are gratified but opponents charge that such laws punish thoughts, not actions. Legal scholar Alan Dershowitz cautions, "As much as I hate bigotry, I fear much more [government] attempting to control the minds of its citizens" (Greenhouse, 1993:1, 8).

DEVIANCE AND GENDER

Virtually every society in the world applies more stringent normative controls to women than to men. Historically, our society has centered women's lives around the home. In the United States even today, women's opportunities in the workplace, in politics, and in the military are limited. Elsewhere in the world, the normative constraints on women are greater still. In Saudi Arabia, women cannot vote or legally operate motor vehicles; in Iran, women who expose their hair or wear makeup in public can be whipped.

Gender also figures into the theories about deviance noted earlier. Robert Merton's strain theory, for example, seems masculine in that it defines cultural goals in terms of financial success. Traditionally at least, this goal has had more to do with the lives of men, while women have been socialized to define success in terms of relationships, particularly marriage and motherhood (Leonard, 1982). A more woman-focused theory might recognize the "strain" that results from the cultural ideal of equality clashing with the reality of gender-based inequality.

In labeling theory, too, gender influences how we define deviance, because people commonly use different standards to judge the behavior of females as opposed to males. Further, because society puts men in positions of power over women, men often escape direct responsibility for actions that victimize women. In the past, at least, men who sexually harassed or assaulted women were labeled only mildly deviant, if they were punished at all.

By contrast, women who are victimized may have to convince an unsympathetic audience that they are not to blame for their own sexual harassment. Research confirms an important truth: Whether people define a situation as deviance—and, if so, whose deviance it is—depends on the sex of both the audience and the actors (King & Clayson, 1988).

Finally, in spite of its focus on social inequality, much social-conflict analysis does not address the issue of gender. If, as conflict theory suggests, economic disadvantage is a primary cause of crime, why do women (whose economic position is much worse than men's) commit far *fewer* crimes than men?

CRIME

Crime is the violation of criminal laws enacted by a locality, state, or the federal government. Technically, all crimes are composed of two distinct elements: an *act* (or, in some cases, the failure to do what the law requires) and *criminal intent* (in legal terminology, *mens rea*, or "guilty mind"). Intent is a matter of degree, ranging from willful conduct to negligence. Someone who is negligent does not set out deliberately to hurt anyone but acts (or fails to act) in such a way that results in harm. Prosecutors weigh the degree of intent in determining whether, for example, to charge someone with first-degree murder, second-degree murder, or negligent manslaughter. Alternatively, they may consider a killing justifiable, as in self-defense.

TYPES OF CRIME

In the United States, the Federal Bureau of Investigation (FBI) gathers information on criminal offenses and regularly reports the results in a publication called *Crime in the United States.* Two major types of crimes make up the FBI "crime index."

Crimes against the person are *crimes that direct violence or the threat of violence against others.* Violent crimes include murder and manslaughter (legally defined as "the willful killing of one human being by another"), aggravated assault ("an unlawful attack by one person on another for the purpose of inflicting severe or aggravated bodily injury"), forcible rape ("the carnal knowledge of a female forcibly and against her will"), and robbery ("taking or attempting to take anything of value from the care, custody, or control of a person or persons, by force or threat of force or violence and/or putting the victim in fear").

Crimes against property are *crimes that involve theft of property belonging to others.* Property crimes include burglary ("the unlawful entry of a structure to commit a [serious crime] or a theft"), larceny-theft ("the unlawful taking, carrying, leading, or riding away of property from the possession of another"), auto theft ("the theft or attempted theft of a motor vehicle"), and arson ("any willful or malicious burning or attempt to burn the personal property of another").

A third category of offenses, not included in major crime indexes, is **victimless crimes,** *violations of law in which there are no readily apparent victims.* Also called "crimes without complaint," they include illegal drug use, prostitution, and gambling. The term "victimless crime" is misleading, however. How victimless is a crime when young drug users embark on a life of crime to support their drug habit? What about a pregnant woman who, by smoking crack, permanently harms her baby? Perhaps it is more correct to say that people who commit such crimes are themselves both offenders and victims.

Because public views of victimless crime vary greatly, laws differ from place to place. In the United States, gambling is legal only in a few locations within twenty-three states (in Nevada, on some Indian reservations, and on river boats in some areas); prostitution is lawful only in one (part of Nevada). Yet both activities are commonplace across the country. Homosexual (and some heterosexual) behavior among consenting adults is legally restricted in about half the states; where such laws exist, enforcement is light and selective.

CRIMINAL STATISTICS

Statistics gathered by the FBI show crime rates rising from 1960 to 1990 but declining over the last decade. Even so, police still tally more than 11 million serious crimes each year. Figure 6–2 shows the trends for various serious crimes.

One should always read crime statistics with caution, however, since they include only crimes known to the police. Almost all homicides are reported, but other assaults—especially among acquaintances—often are not. Police records include an even smaller proportion of property crime, especially when the losses are small.

Researchers check official crime statistics by conducting *victimization surveys,* in which they ask a representative sample of people about their experience with crime. According to these surveys, the overall crime rate is about three times higher than official reports indicate (Russell, 1995b).

THE "STREET" CRIMINAL: A PROFILE

Using government crime reports, we can draw some general descriptions of people arrested for violent and property crimes.

Age. Official crime rates rise sharply during adolescence and peak in the late teens, falling thereafter. People between the ages of fifteen and twenty-four represent just 14 percent of the U.S. population, but, in 1999, they accounted for 38.9 percent of all arrests for violent crimes and 45.9 percent of arrests for property crimes.

A disturbing trend today is that young people are responsible for a larger share of serious crimes. During the 1990s, juveniles accounted for a rising share of arrests for rape, robbery, and assault (U.S. Federal Bureau of Investigation, 2000).

Gender. Although each sex makes up roughly half of the population, police collared males in 70.4 percent of all property crime arrests in 1999. In other words, men are arrested more than twice as often as women for property crimes. In the case of violent crimes, the disparity is even greater: 83 percent of arrests involved males but just 17 percent were females (a five-to-one ratio).

One reason for this disparity is that law enforcement officials are reluctant to define women as criminals. Even so, the difference in arrest rates for women and men has been narrowing in recent years, which probably indicates increasing sexual equality in our society. Between 1990 and 1999, the *increase* in arrests of women (18 percent) contrasted to a *drop* of 5 percent in arrests of men (U.S. Federal Bureau of Investigation, 2000). A similar pattern holds globally, with the greatest gender difference in crime rates occurring in societies that most severely limit the opportunities of women.

Social class. The FBI does not assess the social class of arrested persons, so no statistical data of the kind given above are available. But research has long indicated that criminality is more widespread among people of lower social position (Wolfgang, Figlio, &

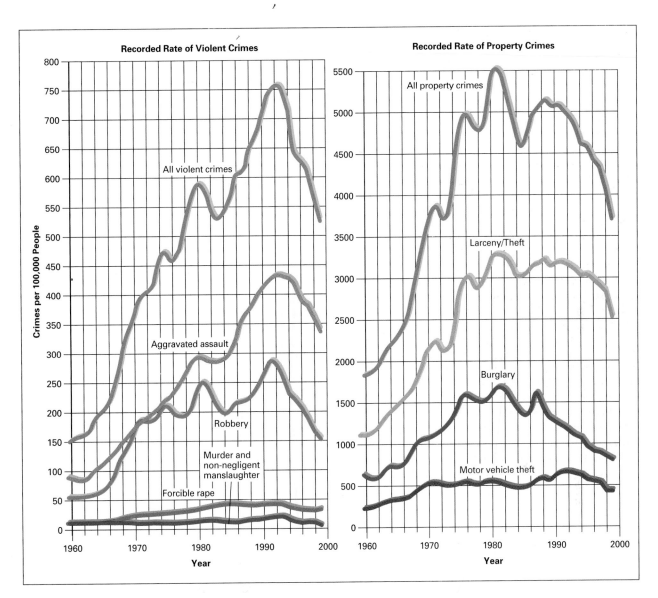

FIGURE 6–2 Crime Rates in the United States, 1960–1999

The graphs represent crime rates for various violent crimes and property crimes during recent decades.

Source: U.S. Federal Bureau of Investigation (2000).

Sellin, 1972; Clinard & Abbott, 1973; Braithwaite, 1981; Thornberry & Farnsworth, 1982; Wolfgang, Thornberry, & Figlio, 1987).

Yet the connection between class and crime is more complicated than it appears on the surface. For one thing, many people look upon the poor as less worthy than the rich, whose wealth and power confer "respectability" (Tittle & Villemez, 1977; Tittle, Villemez, & Smith, 1978; Elias, 1986). Moreover, while crime—especially violent crime—is a serious problem in the poorest inner-city neighborhoods, most of these crimes are committed by a few hard-core offenders. The majority of poor people who live in these neighborhoods have no criminal records at all (Wolfgang,

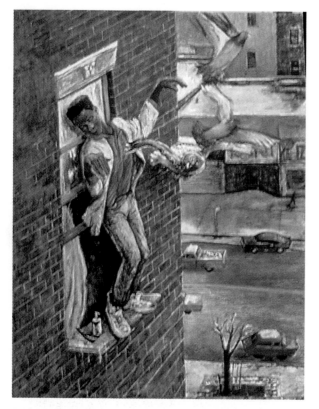

In the United States, African Americans contend with higher rates of poverty, which goes a long way to explaining their proportionately higher involvement in crime—as victims as well as offenders. Especially in inner cities, where there is little available work, young people can be consumed by despair and anger, perhaps turning to crime or drugs. Paul Marcus captures one man's self-defeating efforts to escape his situation in the painting Cracked-up.

© Paul Marcus, *Cracked-up*, oil on panel, 24 in. × 30 in. Studio SPM Inc.

Figlio, & Sellin, 1972; Elliott & Ageton, 1980; Harries, 1990).

Moreover, the connection between social standing and criminality depends on what kind of crime one is talking about (Braithwaite, 1981). If we expand our definition of crime beyond street offenses to include white-collar crime, the "common criminal" suddenly looks much more affluent.

Race and ethnicity. Both race and ethnicity are strongly correlated to crime rates, although the reasons are many and complex. Official statistics indicate that 64 percent of arrests for index crimes in 1999 involved white people. However, arrests of African Americans were higher than for whites in proportion to their representation in the general population. African Americans constitute 12.2 percent of the population but 31.4 percent of arrests for property crimes (versus 65.7 percent for whites) and 38.7 percent of arrests for violent crimes (59.2 percent for whites) (U.S. Federal Bureau of Investigation, 2000).

What accounts for the disproportionate number of arrests among African Americans? First, to the degree that prejudice prompts white police to arrest black people more readily and leads citizens to report African Americans more willingly, people of color are overly criminalized (Liska & Tausig, 1979; Unnever, Frazier, & Henretta, 1980; Smith & Visher, 1981; Holmes et al., 1993; Covington, 1995).

Second, race in the United States closely relates to social standing, which, as we have already explained, affects the likelihood of engaging in street crimes. Poor people living in the midst of affluence come to see society as unjust and, thus, are more likely to turn to crime (Blau & Blau, 1982; Anderson, 1994).

Third, black and white family patterns differ: Two-thirds of black children (compared to one-fourth of white children) are born to single mothers. In general, single-parenting means that children get less supervision and the family is at a higher risk for being poor. With one-third of African American children growing up in poverty (in contrast to about one in eight white children), no one should be surprised at proportionately higher crime rates for African Americans (Sampson, 1987; Courtwright, 1996; Jacobs & Helms, 1996).

Fourth, remember that the official crime index does not include arrests for many offenses, ranging from drunk driving to white-collar violations. This omission contributes to the view of the typical criminal as a person of color. If we broaden our definition of crime to include driving while intoxicated, business fraud, embezzlement, and cheating on income tax returns, the proportion of white criminals rises dramatically.

Finally, some categories of the population have unusually low rates of arrest. People of Asian descent, who account for about 4 percent of the population, figure in only 1.1 percent of all arrests. As Chapter 11 ("Race and Ethnicity") explains, Asian Americans enjoy higher-than-average educational achievement and income. Moreover, Asian American culture emphasizes family solidarity and discipline, both of which keep criminality down.

CRIME IN GLOBAL PERSPECTIVE

By world standards, the crime rate in the United States is high. Although recent crime trends are downward, there were 15,533 murders in the United States in 1999, which amounts to one every half-hour around the clock. In large cities such as New York, rarely does a day pass with no murder; in fact, more New Yorkers are hit with stray bullets than are deliberately gunned down in most large cities elsewhere in the world.

Overall, the U.S. violent crime rate is five times greater than Europe's, and the U.S. property crime rate is twice as high. The contrast is even greater between our country and the nations of Asia, including India and Japan, where violent and property crime rates are among the lowest in the world.

Elliott Currie (1985) suggests that crime stems from our culture's emphasis on individual economic success, frequently at the expense of strong families and neighborhoods. The United States also has extraordinary cultural diversity, a result of centuries of immigration. Moreover, economic inequality is higher in this country than in most other high-income nations. Thus, our society's relatively weak social fabric, combined with considerable frustration among the have-nots, generates widespread criminal behavior.

Another factor adding to violence in the United States is extensive private ownership of guns. About two-thirds of murder victims in the United States die from shootings. Since the early 1990s, in Texas and several other southern states, shooting deaths have exceeded automobile-related fatalities. As Figure 6–3 shows, the United States is the runaway leader in handgun deaths among industrial societies.

Surveys suggest that almost half of U.S. households have at least one gun (Gallup, 1993; Wright, 1995; NORC, 1999). Put differently, there are more guns than adults in this country, and one-third of these weapons are handguns that figure in violent crime. In large part, gun ownership reflects people's fear of crime; yet easy availability of guns in this country also makes crime more deadly.

But, as critics of gun control point out, waiting periods and background checks at retail gun stores (mandated by the 1993 "Brady bill") do not keep guns out of the hands of criminals, who almost always obtain guns illegally (Wright, 1995). Moreover, we should be cautious about assuming that gun control would be a magic bullet in the war on crime. Elliott Currie (1985) notes, for example, that the number of Californians killed each year by knives alone exceeds the number of Canadians killed by weapons of all kinds. Most experts

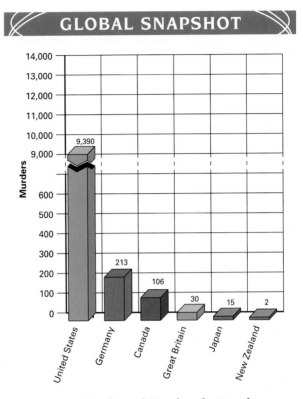

GLOBAL SNAPSHOT

FIGURE 6–3 Number of Murders by Handguns, 1996

Source: Handgun Control, Inc. (2001).

do think, however, that stricter gun control laws would reduce the level of deadly violence.

Crime rates are soaring in some of the largest cities of the world like Manila, Philippines, and São Paulo, Brazil, which have rapid population growth and millions of desperately poor people. Outside of big cities, however, the traditional character of low-income societies and their strong family structure allow local communities to control crime informally (Clinard & Abbott, 1973; *Der Spiegel*, 1989).

Some kinds of crime have always been multinational, such as terrorism, espionage, and arms dealing (Martin & Romano, 1992). But, today, the globalization we are seeing on many fronts also extends to crime. A recent case in point is the illegal drug trade. In part, the problem of illegal drugs in the United States is a "demand" issue. That is, the demand for cocaine and other drugs in this country is high, and many young people are willing to risk arrest or even

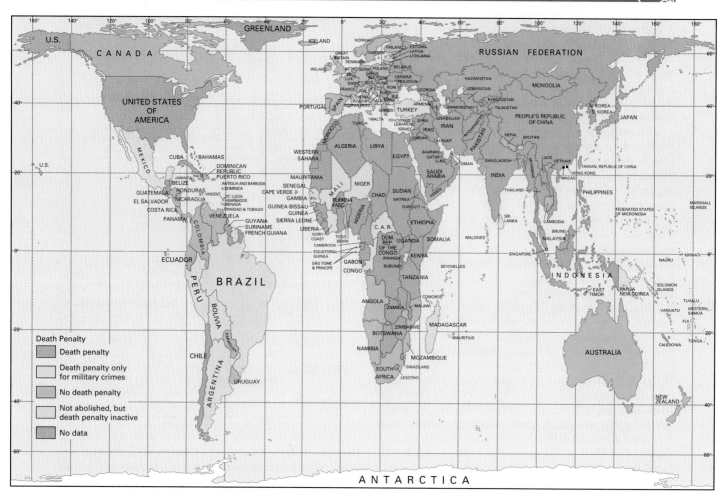

GLOBAL MAP 6–1 Capital Punishment in Global Perspective

The map identifies ninety countries and territories in which the law provides for the death penalty for ordinary crimes; in thirteen more, the death penalty is reserved for exceptional crimes under military law or during times of war. The death penalty does not exist in seventy countries and territories; in twenty-three more, although the death penalty remains in law, no execution has taken place in more than a decade. Compare rich and poor nations: What general pattern do you see? In what way do the United States and Japan stand out?

Source: Amnesty International, "The Death Penalty: List of Abolitionist and Retentionist Countries." Revised 18 December 1999, http://www.amnesty.org/ailib/inteam/dp/abrelist.htm

violent death to enter the lucrative drug trade. But the "supply" side of the issue is just as important. In the South American nation of Colombia, at least 20 percent of the people depend on cocaine production for their livelihood. Furthermore, not only is cocaine Colombia's most profitable export, but it outsells all other exports—including coffee—combined. Clearly, then, understanding drug dealing and many other crimes requires analyzing social conditions both in this country and elsewhere.

During the 1990s, the United States built prisons at an unprecedented rate. There are now twice as many people in jail—more than 2 million—than there were in 1990. The public's "get tough with criminals" attitude has also led to the spread of "road gangs"—a return of the "chain gangs" common in the early decades of the twentieth century. As some see it, putting criminals to work along busy highways reminds the public of the consequences of law-breaking.

Countries have different strategies for dealing with crime. The use of the death penalty provides a case in point. Global Map 6–1 identifies countries that employ capital punishment and those that do not. The global trend is toward abolition of the death penalty: Amnesty International (2000) reports that, since 1980, more than forty nations have ended this practice.

THE CRIMINAL JUSTICE SYSTEM

December 10, 1994, Casablanca, Morocco. Casablanca! An exciting mix of African, European, and Middle Eastern cultures. Returning from a stroll through the medina, the medieval section of this coastal, north African city, we confront lines of police along a boulevard, standing between us and our ship in the harbor. The police are providing security for many important leaders attending an Islamic conference at a nearby hotel. Are the streets closed? No one asks, but people stop short of an invisible line some fifty feet from the police officers. I play the brash North American and start across the street to inquire (in broken French) if we can pass by; but I stop cold as several officers draw a bead on me with their eyes. Their fingers nervously tap at the grips on their automatic weapons. This is no time to strike up a conversation.

The criminal justice system is a society's formal response to crime. In some of the world's countries, military police keep a tight rein on people's behavior; in others, including the United States, police have more limited powers and only respond to violations of criminal law. We shall briefly introduce the key elements of the criminal justice system: police, courts, and the punishment of convicted offenders.

POLICE

The police generally serve as the point of contact between a population and the criminal justice system. In principle, the police maintain public order by enforcing the law. Of course, there is only so much 637,551 full-time police officers in the United States (in 1999) can do to monitor the activities of 280 million people. As a result, the police exercise considerable discretion about which situations warrant their attention and how to handle them.

How, then, do police carry out their duties? In a study of police behavior in five cities, Douglas Smith and Christy Visher (1981; Smith, 1987) concluded that, because they must act swiftly, police quickly size up situations in terms of six factors. First, the more serious they think the situation is, the more likely they

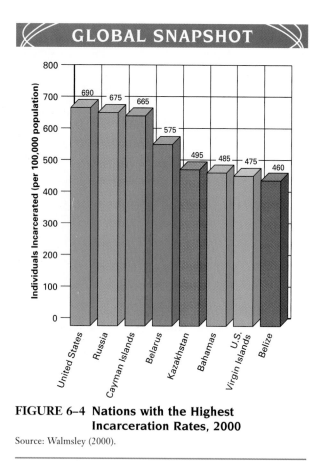

FIGURE 6–4 Nations with the Highest Incarceration Rates, 2000

Source: Walmsley (2000).

are to make an arrest. Second, police take account of the victim's desire in deciding whether or not to make an arrest. Third, the odds of arrest go up the more uncooperative a suspect is. Fourth, police are more likely to take into custody someone they have arrested before, presumably because this suggests guilt. Fifth, the presence of bystanders increases the chances of arrest. According to Smith and Visher, the presence of observers prompts police to take stronger control of a situation, if only to move the encounter from the street (the suspect's turf) to the police department (where law officers have the edge). Sixth, all else being equal, police are more likely to arrest people of color than whites, perceiving people of African or Latino descent as either more dangerous or more likely to be guilty.

COURTS

After arrest, a court determines a suspect's guilt or innocence. In principle, our courts rely on an adversarial

process involving attorneys—one representing the defendant and another the state—in the presence of a judge who monitors legal procedures.

In practice, however, about 90 percent of criminal cases are resolved prior to court appearance through **plea bargaining**, *a legal negotiation in which a prosecutor reduces a charge in exchange for a defendant's guilty plea.* For example, the state may offer a defendant charged with burglary a lesser charge, perhaps possession of burglary tools, in exchange for a guilty plea.

Plea bargaining is widespread because it spares the system the time and expense of trials. A trial is usually unnecessary if there is little disagreement as to the facts of the case. Moreover, since the number of cases entering the system doubled over the last decade, prosecutors cannot possibly bring every one to trial. By quickly resolving most of their work, then, the courts channel their resources into the most important cases.

But plea bargaining pressures defendants (who are presumed innocent) to plead guilty. A person can exercise the right to a trial, but only at the risk of receiving a more severe sentence if found guilty. Furthermore, low-income defendants enter the process relying on a public defender—an attorney, often overworked and usually underpaid, who may devote little time to even a serious case (Novak, 1999). Overall, plea bargaining may be efficient but at the cost of undercutting the adversarial process as well as the rights of defendants.

PUNISHMENT

When a young man is shot dead on the street after leaving a restaurant—as in the case of Michael Gerardi featured in the opening to this chapter—almost everyone believes that someone should have to "pay" for the crime. Indeed, sometimes the desire to punish is so great that justice may be lost.

Such cases force us to ask *why* a society should punish its wrongdoers. Over many years, scholars have pointed to four basic reasons to punish: retribution, deterrence, rehabilitation, and societal protection.

Retribution. The oldest justification for punishment is to satisfy a society's need for **retribution**, *an act of moral vengeance by which society inflicts on the offender suffering comparable to that caused by the offense.* Retribution rests on a view of society as a moral balance. When criminality upsets this balance, punishment enacted in comparable measure restores the moral order, as suggested by the biblical dictum "an eye for an eye."

During the Middle Ages, most people viewed crime as sin—an offense against God as well as society—that warranted a harsh response. Today, although critics point out that retribution does little to reform the offender, many people consider vengeance reason enough for punishment.

Deterrence. A second justification for punishment is **deterrence**, *the use of punishment to discourage criminality.* Deterrence is based on the eighteenth-century Enlightenment idea that, as calculating and rational creatures, humans will not break the law if they think that the pains of punishment outweigh the pleasures of crime.

Deterrence emerged as a reform measure in response to the harsh punishments based on retribution. Why put someone to death for stealing, reformists reasoned, if theft can be discouraged by a prison sentence? As the concept of deterrence gained widespread acceptance, execution and physical mutilation of criminals in most industrial societies were replaced by milder forms of punishment such as incarceration.

Punishment may deter crime in two ways. *Specific deterrence* convinces an individual offender that crime does not pay. Through *general deterrence*, punishing one person serves as an example to others.

Rehabilitation. The third justification for punishment, **rehabilitation,** is *a program for reforming the offender to prevent subsequent offenses.* Rehabilitation arose along with the social sciences in the nineteenth century. Since then, sociologists have claimed that crime and other deviance spring from a social environment marked by poverty or lack of parental supervision. Logically, then, if offenders learn to be deviant, they can also learn to obey the rules; the key is controlling the environment. *Reformatories* or *houses of correction* provided controlled settings where people could learn proper behavior (recall the description of total institutions in Chapter 3, "Socialization").

Like deterrence, rehabilitation motivates the offender to conform. But rehabilitation emphasizes constructive improvement while deterrence and retribution simply make the offender suffer. In addition, while retribution demands that the punishment fit the crime, rehabilitation tailors treatment to each offender. Thus, identical crimes would prompt similar acts of retribution but different rehabilitation programs.

Societal protection. A final justification for punishment is **societal protection,** *a means by which society renders an offender incapable of further offenses, either temporarily through incarceration or permanently by execution.*

TABLE 6–2	**Four Justifications for Punishment: A Summary**
Retribution	The oldest justification for punishment. Punishment is atonement for a moral wrong; in principle, punishment should be comparable in severity to the deviance itself.
Deterrence	An early modern approach. Deviance is considered social disruption, which society acts to control. People are viewed as rational and self-interested; deterrence works because the pains of punishment outweigh the pleasures of deviance.
Rehabilitation	A modern strategy linked to the development of social sciences. Deviance is viewed as the product of social problems (such as poverty) or personal problems (such as mental illness). Social conditions are improved; treatment is tailored to the offender's condition.
Societal Protection	A modern approach easier to implement than rehabilitation. If society is unable or unwilling to rehabilitate offenders or reform social conditions, people are protected by incarcerating or executing the offender.

Like deterrence, societal protection is a rational approach to punishment and seeks to protect society from crime.

Currently, more than 2 million people are incarcerated in the United States and another 4 million are on parole and probation. In response to tougher public attitudes and an increasing number of drug-related arrests, the U.S. prison population has tripled since 1980. As Figure 6–4 shows, the United States incarcerates a larger share of its population than all other countries of the world.

Critical evaluation. Table 6–2 summarizes the four justifications for punishment. Assessing the actual consequences of punishment, however, is no simple task.

The value of retribution lies in Durkheim's contention that punishing the deviant person increases society's moral awareness. For this reason, punishment was traditionally a public event. Although the last public execution in the United States took place in Kentucky in 1937, today's mass media ensure public awareness of executions carried out inside prison walls (Kittrie, 1971).

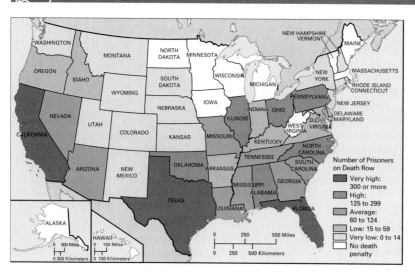

The United States and Japan are the only high-income nations in which the government imposes the death penalty. Yet, within the United States, the fifty states have broadly divergent capital punishment laws: Half of the 3,527 prisoners on death row are in five states. What regional pattern do you see in the map? Can you account for this pattern?

Source: U.S. Bureau of Justice Statistics (2000).

Number of Prisoners on Death Row
- Very high: 300 or more
- High: 125 to 299
- Average: 60 to 124
- Low: 15 to 59
- Very low: 0 to 14
- No death penalty

Certainly, punishment deters some crime. Yet our society has a high rate of **criminal recidivism,** *subsequent offenses committed by people previously convicted of crimes.* About three-fourths of state prisoners have been jailed before and, once released, about half will be back within a few years (McNulty, 1994; Petersilia, 1997). In light of such patterns, we may well wonder about the extent to which punishment really deters crime. Then, too, only about one-third of all crimes are known to police, and of these, only about one in five results in an arrest. The old saying "crime doesn't pay" rings hollow when we consider that only a small share of offenses are ever punished.

General deterrence is even more difficult to investigate scientifically, since we have no way of knowing how people might act if they were unaware of punishments meted out to others. In the debate over capital punishment, opponents point to research suggesting that the death penalty has limited value as a general deterrent. Moreover, the United States is the only Western, high-income nation that routinely executes serious offenders. Even more troubling is the fact that some death sentences turn out to be flawed. The case of Shareef Cousin is just one example. Between 1973 and 2000, in fact, eighty-six people have been released from death row, indicating that punishment itself can sometimes be unjust (Sellin, 1980; van den Haag & Conrad, 1983; Lester, 1987; Archer & Gartner, 1987; Bailey & Peterson, 1989; Bailey, 1990; Bohm, 1991; Tanber, 1998; CBS, 2000). National Map 6–2

identifies the thirty-eight states that have the death penalty and shows that half of all prisoners on death row are in just five of these states.

Prisons provide short-term societal protection by keeping offenders off the streets, but they do little to reshape attitudes or behavior in the long term (Carlson, 1976; Wright, 1994). Perhaps rehabilitation is an unrealistic expectation, since according to Sutherland's theory of differential association, locking up criminals together for years probably strengthens criminal attitudes and skills. Incarceration also severs whatever social ties inmates may have in the outside world which, following Hirschi's control theory, leaves individuals prone to commit more crime upon their release.

Finally, the stigma of being an ex-convict can be a powerful barrier to building a new life. One study of young offenders in Philadelphia found that boys who were sentenced to long prison terms—those most likely to acquire a criminal stigma—went on to commit both more crimes and more serious ones (Wolfgang, Figlio, & Sellin, 1972).

Ultimately, we should never assume that the criminal justice system—the police, courts, and prisons—can eliminate crime. As the final box explains, police, courts, and prisons have played a part in the recent downturn in crime rates. But more is involved. As this chapter has explained, crime and other deviance result not just from the acts of "bad people" but from the operation of society itself.

Violent Crime Is Down—But Why?

During the 1980s, crime rates went up rapidly. Just about everyone lived in fear of violent crime, and, in many larger cities, the numbers killed and wounded made whole neighborhoods seem like war zones. There seemed to be no solution to the problem.

Then, in the 1990s, something good and unexpected happened—serious crime rates began to fall until, by 2000, they were at levels not seen in more than a generation. Why? Applying the perspectives and theories presented in this chapter, we can identify several reasons:

1. **Changes in policing.** Much of the drop in crime (as well as the earlier rise in crime) has taken place in large cities. New York City, where the number of murders fell from 2,245 in 1990 to just 671 in 1999, has adopted a policy of *community policing,* which means that police are concerned not just with making arrests but in preventing crime before it happens. Officers get to know better the areas they patrol and frequently stop young men for jaywalking or other minor infractions so they can check them for concealed weapons (the word has gotten around that you risk arrest for carrying a gun). Moreover, there are *more* police at work in large cities. Los Angeles, for example, added more than 2,000 police during the 1990s, and it, too, has seen its violent crime rate fall.

2. **More prisons.** From 1985 to 2000, the number of

inmates in U.S. jails and prisons soared from 750,000 to 2 million. The main reason for this increase is new, tough laws that demand prison time for many crimes, especially drug offenses. As one analyst put it, "When you lock up an extra million people, it's got to have some effect on the crime rate" (Zimring, cited in Witkin, 1998:31).

3. **A better economy.** The U.S. economy has boomed during the last ten years. With unemployment down, more people are working, which reduces the likelihood that some will turn to crime out of economic desperation. The logic here is simple: More jobs, fewer crimes.

4. **The declining drug trade.** Many analysts agree that the most important factor in reducing rates of violent crime is the decline of crack cocaine. Crack came on the scene around 1985, and violence spread

One reason that crime has gone down is that there are more than 2 million people incarcerated in this country. This has caused severe overcrowding of facilities such as this Huntsville, Texas, prison with makeshift outdoor sleeping shelters.

as young people—especially in the inner cities and increasingly armed with guns—became part of a booming drug trade. With legitimate job opportunities low, and rising opportunity to make money illegally, a generation of young people became part of a wave of violence. Widespread crack cocaine use also explains the trend, noted earlier, of the younger age of violent criminals.

By the early 1990s, however, the popularity of crack began to fall as people saw the damage the drug was causing to entire communities. This realization, coupled with steady economic improvement and stiffer sentences for drug offenses, brought the turnaround in violent crime.

Keep in mind that the current picture looks better *relative* to what it was a decade ago. The crime problem, says one researcher, "looks better, but only because the early 1990s were so bad. So let's not fool ourselves into thinking everything is resolved. It's not."

What do you think?

1. *Do you support the policy of community policing? Why or why not?*

2. *What are the pros and cons of building more prisons?*

3. *Of all the factors mentioned here, which do you think is the most important in crime control? Why?*

Sources: Based on Boggess & Bound (1997), Blumstein & Rosenfeld (1998), Fagan, Zimring, & Kim (1998), and Witkin (1998).

SUMMARY

1. Deviance refers to norm violations ranging from mild breaches of etiquette to serious violence.

2. Biological research, from Lombroso's nineteenth-century observations of convicts to recent genetic studies, has yet to offer much insight into the causes of deviance.

3. Psychological study links deviance to abnormal personality resulting from either biological or environmental causes. Psychological theories help explain some kinds of deviance.

4. Deviance has societal roots because it (a) varies according to cultural norms, (b) is socially defined, and (c) reflects patterns of social power.

5. Using the structural-functional paradigm, Durkheim explained that deviance serves to affirm norms and values, clarify moral boundaries, promote social unity, and encourage social change.

6. The symbolic-interaction paradigm is the basis of labeling theory, which holds that deviance lies in people's reaction to a person's behavior, not in the behavior itself. Acquiring the stigma of deviance can lead to secondary deviance and a deviant career.

7. Based on Karl Marx's ideas, social-conflict theory holds that laws and other norms reflect the interests of powerful members of society. Although white-collar and corporate crime cause extensive social harm, offenders are rarely branded as criminals.

8. Hate crimes and the application of stricter normative controls to women represent two examples of how deviance reflects the social standing of different categories of people.

9. Official statistics indicate that arrest rates peak in late adolescence, then drop steadily with advancing age. Seventy percent of those arrested for property crimes and 83 percent of those arrested for violent crimes are males.

10. People of lower social position commit more street crime than those with greater social privilege. When white-collar crimes are included among criminal offenses, however, this disparity in criminal activity goes down.

11. More whites than African Americans are arrested for street crimes. However, African Americans are arrested more often than whites in proportion to their respective populations. Asian Americans have lower-than-average rates of arrest.

12. Police use considerable discretion in their work. Arrest is more likely if an offense is serious, bystanders are present or the accused is African American.

13. Although ideally an adversarial system, U.S. courts resolve most cases through plea bargaining. While efficient, this method puts less powerful people at a disadvantage.

14. Justifications of punishment include retribution, deterrence, rehabilitation, and societal protection. Because its consequences are difficult to evaluate scientifically, punishment—like deviance itself—sparks considerable controversy.

KEY CONCEPTS

deviance (p. 134) the recognized violation of cultural norms

crime (p. 134) the violation of a society's formally enacted criminal law

social control (p. 134) attempts by society to regulate people's thought and behavior

criminal justice system (p. 134) a formal response by police, courts, and prison officials to alleged violations of the law

labeling theory (p. 139) the assertion that deviance and conformity result, not so much from what people do, as from how others respond to those actions

stigma (p. 139) a powerfully negative label that greatly changes a person's self-concept and social identity

medicalization of deviance (p. 141) the transformation of moral and legal deviance into a medical condition

white-collar crime (p. 145) crime committed by people of high social position in the course of their occupations

corporate crime (p. 145) the illegal actions of a corporation or people acting on its behalf

organized crime (p. 146) a business supplying illegal goods or services

hate crime (p. 146) a criminal act against a person or a person's property by an offender motivated by racial or other bias

crimes against the person (violent crimes) (p. 147) crimes that direct violence or the threat of violence against others

crimes against property (property crimes) (p. 148) crimes that involve theft of property belonging to others

victimless crimes (p. 148) violations of law in which there are no readily apparent victims

plea bargaining (p. 154) a legal negotiation in which the prosecutor reduces a charge in exchange for a defendant's guilty plea

retribution (p. 154) an act of moral vengeance by which society inflicts on the offender suffering comparable to that caused by the offense

deterrence (p. 155) the use of punishment to discourage criminality

rehabilitation (p. 155) a program for reforming the offender to prevent subsequent offenses

societal protection (p. 155) a means by which society renders an offender incapable of further offenses, either temporarily through incarceration or permanently by execution

criminal recidivism (p. 156) subsequent offenses committed by people previously convicted of crimes

CRITICAL-THINKING QUESTIONS

1. How does a sociological view of deviance differ from the common-sense notion that bad people do bad things?
2. List Durkheim's functions of deviance. From his point of view, can society ever be free from deviance? Why or why not?
3. An old saying is that "Sticks and stones can break my bones, but names can never hurt me." Explain how labeling theory contradicts this statement.
4. A recent study found that one in three African American men between the ages of twenty and twenty-nine is in jail, on probation, or on parole (The Sentencing Project, 2000). Based on the material in this chapter, what factors help explain this pattern?

APPLICATIONS AND EXERCISES

1. Research computers and crime. What new types of crime, as well as methods of tracking down lawbreakers, are emerging in the information age?
2. Rent a wheelchair from a local pharmacy or medical supply store and use it for a day or two. Not only will you gain a firsthand understanding of the physical barriers to getting around, but you will discover that people respond to you in new ways.
3. Watch an episode of the real-action police show "COPS." Based on this program, how would you profile the people who commit crimes?
4. Install the CD-ROM packaged in the back of this new textbook to access a variety of study, review, and applications exercises. The CD includes an author's tip video, interactive maps, video application exercises, Web links, and study questions.

SITES TO SEE

http://www.prenhall.com/macionis
Visit the interactive Web site that accompanies this text to find a chapter-by-chapter study guide, practice tests, chat room, and many suggested Web links.

http://www.Nashville.Net/~police/risk/
This site, run by the Nashville Police Department, rates your chances of becoming a victim of a serious crime.

http://www.civilrights.org/
The Leadership Conference on Civil Rights site deals with hate crimes and other issues of civil rights.

http://www.igc.apc.org/spr/
The organization "Stop Prisoner Rape" hosts this site to increase awareness of the problem of rape in U.S. prisons.

http://www.ncadp.org
http://www.uaa.alaska.edu/just/death/intl.html
These sites provide information on the death penalty. The first presents the views of the National Coalition to Abolish the Death Penalty. The second looks at the death penalty in global perspective.

http://www.cybercrime.gov
This site, operated by the U.S. Department of Justice, provides a great deal of information on cyber-crime and protecting intellectual property.

SEXUALITY

As the old saying goes, birds do it and so do bees. So do frogs, chimps, and even the great elephants. Indeed, biologists tell us that the animal world contains countless fascinating mating rituals. Take, for example, scorpions: The couple engages in a deadly dance, round and round, locked face to face with their mouths and claws. As the mating proceeds, the male repeatedly stings the female as she clings to him. In the end, however, it is the larger female that prevails. Once fertilized, she turns on her mate and, in a burst of strength and ferocity, devours him.

Nature offers many strange stories about animal mating. However, the most fascinating of all must be about human beings. Humans—most people, at least—like to "do it," too. But, as the only creatures who attach meaning to all behavior, what humans "do" when it comes to sex varies quite a bit from culture to culture as well as over time. Moreover, we are the only species whose members think about the purpose of sex, encourage some forms of sex while outlawing others, and, in an effort to learn more, even conduct research about our own sexuality.

This chapter presents some of what we have learned about human sexuality. From a sociological point of view, the main question is how society shapes our sexuality.

UNDERSTANDING SEXUALITY

How much of the day goes by without your giving any thought to sexuality? If you are like most people, the answer is "not very much." That is because sexuality is not just about "having sex." Sexuality is a theme found throughout society—apparent on campus, in the workplace, and especially in the mass media. In addition, the sex industry, including pornography and prostitution, is a multibillion-dollar business in its own right. Then, too, sexuality is an important part of how we think about ourselves as well as how we evaluate others. In truth, there are few areas of life in which sexuality does *not* play some part.

But, in spite of its importance, few people really understand sexuality. Throughout much of our history, sex has been a cultural taboo, so, at least in polite conversation, people do not talk about it. As a result, while sex can produce much pleasure, it also causes confusion, anxiety, and sometimes outright fear. Even scientists long considered sex research "off limits." It was not until the middle of the twentieth century that researchers turned attention to this pervasive dimension of social life. Since then, as this chapter reports, we have learned a great deal about human sexuality.

SEX: A BIOLOGICAL ISSUE

Sex refers to *the biological distinction between females and males.* From a biological point of view, sex is the means by which humans reproduce. A female ovum and a male sperm, each containing twenty-three chromosomes (biological codes that guide physical development), combine to form a fertilized embryo. One of these chromosome pairs determines the child's sex. To this pair, the mother contributes an X chromosome and the father contributes either an X or a Y. An X from the father produces a female (XX) embryo; a

We claim that beauty is in the eye of the beholder, which suggests the importance of culture in setting standards of attractiveness. All of the people pictured here—from Morocco, South Africa, Nigeria, Myanmar (Burma), Japan, and Ecuador—are beautiful to members of their own society. At the same time, in every society on earth, people are attracted to youthfulness. The biological reason is that attractiveness underlies our choices about reproduction, which is most readily accomplished in early adulthood.

Y from the father produces a male (XY) embryo. A child's sex, then, is determined at conception.

Within weeks, the sex of an embryo starts to guide its development. If the embryo is male, testicular tissue starts to produce testosterone, a hormone that triggers the development of male genitals. If no testosterone is present, the embryo develops female genitals. In the United States, about 105 boys are born for every 100 girls, but a higher death rate among males makes females a slight majority by the time people reach their mid-thirties (U.S. Census Bureau, 2000; U.S. National Center for Health Statistics, 1999).

SEX AND THE BODY

What sets females and males apart are differences in the body. Right from birth, the two sexes have different **primary sex characteristics,** namely, *the genitals, organs used for reproduction.* At puberty, as individuals reach sexual maturity, additional sex differentiation takes place. At this point, individuals develop **secondary sex characteristics,** *bodily development, apart from the genitals, that distinguishes biologically mature females and males.* Mature females have wider hips for giving birth, breasts for nurturing infants, and soft

Transsexuals who alter their sex surgically provoke controversy because they challenge conventional norms about what is feminine and masculine. Here, high school students demonstrate in support of Dana Rivers (formerly David Warfield), a teacher who was suspended from her duties after she underwent medical procedures to become a woman.

fatty tissue that provides a reserve supply of nutrition during pregnancy and breast-feeding. Mature males, on the other hand, typically develop more muscle in the upper body, more extensive body hair, and deeper voices. Of course, these are general differences, since some males are smaller and have less body hair and higher voices than some females.

Hermaphrodites. Sex is not always as clear-cut as we have just described. In rare cases, a hormone imbalance before birth produces a **hermaphrodite** (a word derived from Hermaphroditus, the offspring of the mythological Greek gods Hermes and Aphrodite who embodied both sexes), *a human being with some combination of female and male genitalia.*

Because our culture is uneasy about sexual ambiguity, some people respond to hermaphrodites with confusion or even disgust. But other cultures lead people to respond quite differently: The Pokot of eastern Africa, for example, pay little attention to what they consider a simple biological error, and the Navajo look on hermaphrodites with awe, seeing in them the full potential of both the female and the male (Geertz, 1975).

Transsexuals. Some hermaphrodites undergo genital surgery to appear (and even function) as a sexually normal female or male. Other people, however, deliberately change their sex: **Transsexuals** are *people who feel they are one sex even though biologically they are the other.* Tens of thousands of transsexuals in the United States have surgically changed their genitals because they feel "trapped in the wrong body" (Restak, 1979, cited in Offir, 1982:146; Gagné, Tewksbury, & McGaughey, 1997).

SEX: A CULTURAL ISSUE

Sexuality has a biological foundation. But, like all dimensions of human behavior, sexuality is also very much a cultural issue. Biology may be sufficient to explain the strange mating ritual of scorpions, described in the opening to this chapter, but humans have no similar biological program. Though there is a biological "sex drive" in the sense that people find sex pleasurable and may desire to engage in sexual activity, our biology does not dictate any specific ways of being sexual any more than our desire to eat dictates any particular foods or table manners.

Cultural variation. Almost any sexual practice shows considerable variation from one society to another. In his pioneering study of sexuality in the United States, Alfred Kinsey (1948) found that most couples in the

One sign of the growing openness about sexuality in the United States after World War II was the 1953 publication of the first issue of Playboy. *Back then, it was conservatives who objected to the magazine on moral grounds; by the 1970s, many liberals also opposed such publications as demeaning to women.*

United States reported having intercourse in a single position—face to face, with the woman on the bottom and the man on top. Halfway around the world, in the South Seas, most couples *never* have sex in this way. In fact, when the people of the South Seas learned of this practice from missionaries, they poked fun at it as the strange "missionary position."

As noted in Chapter 2 ("Culture"), even the simple practice of displaying affection shows extensive cultural variation. While most people in the United States readily kiss in public, the Chinese kiss only in private. The French kiss publicly, often twice (once on each cheek), while Belgians go them one better, kissing three times (starting on either cheek). For their part, the Maoris of New Zealand rub noses, while most people in Nigeria don't kiss at all.

Modesty, too, is culturally variable. If a woman entering a bath is disturbed, what body parts does she cover? Helen Colton (1983) reports that an Islamic woman covers her face, a Laotian woman covers her breasts, a Samoan woman her navel, a Sumatran woman her knees, and a European woman covers her breasts with one hand and her genital area with the other.

Around the world, some societies restrict sexuality, while others are more permissive. In China, for example, societal norms closely regulate sexuality, so that few people have sexual intercourse before they marry. In the United States, however—at least in recent decades—intercourse prior to marriage has become the norm, and people may choose to have sex even when there is no strong commitment between them.

THE INCEST TABOO

Are any cultural views of sex the same everywhere? The answer is yes. One cultural universal—an element found in every society the world over—is the **incest taboo**, *a norm forbidding sexual relations or marriage between certain relatives.* In the United States, the law, as well as cultural mores, prohibits close relatives (including brothers and sisters, parents and children) from having sex or marrying. But exactly which family members are included in a society's incest taboo varies from one place to another. Some societies (such as the North American Navajo) apply incest taboos to the mother and others on her "side" of the family. There are also societies on record (including ancient Peru and Egypt) that have approved brother-sister marriages among the nobility (Murdock, 1965).

Why does the incest taboo exist everywhere? Biology is part of the reason: Reproduction between close relatives of any species risks offspring with mental or physical problems. But this fact does not explain why, of all living species, only humans observe an incest taboo. In other words, controlling sexuality among close relatives seems to be a necessary element of social organization. For one thing, the incest taboo limits sexual competition in families by restricting sex to spouses (ruling out, for example, sex between parent and child). Second, since family ties define people's rights and obligations toward each other, reproduction among close relatives would hopelessly confuse kinship (if a mother and son had a daughter, for example, what would the child's relationship be to the other two?). Third, by requiring people to marry outside of their immediate families, the incest taboo integrates the larger society as people look widely for partners to form new families.

The incest taboo has been an enduring sexual norm in the United States and elsewhere. But in this country, many other sexual norms have changed over time. During the twentieth century, as we now explain, our society experienced both a sexual revolution and, later, a sexual counterrevolution.

SEXUAL ATTITUDES IN THE UNITED STATES

What do people in the United States think about sex? Our cultural orientation toward sexuality has been inconsistent. On the one hand, most of the Europeans who came to this continent held rigid notions that, ideally, sex was only for the purpose of reproduction within marriage. The early Puritan settlers of New England demanded conformity in all attitudes and behavior, and they imposed severe penalties for any misconduct—even if the sexual "misconduct" took place in the privacy of one's home. Efforts to regulate sexuality continued well into the twentieth century; as late as the 1960s, for example, some states legally banned the sale of condoms in stores. Even today, in a number of states, laws banning homosexuality and various "unnatural" acts are still on the books.

But this is just one side of the story of sexuality in the United States. As Chapter 2 ("Culture") explains, our culture is also individualistic, and many believe in giving people freedom to do pretty much as they wish, as long as they cause no direct harm to others. Such thinking—that what people do in the privacy of their own homes is *their* business—makes sex a matter of individual freedom and personal choice.

So which is it? Is the United States a restrictive or a permissive society when it comes to sexuality? The answer is that it is both. On the one hand, many people in the United States still view sexual conduct as an important indicator of personal morality. On the other, sex is exploited and glorified everywhere in our culture—and strongly promoted by the mass media—as if to say that "anything goes."

Within this general framework, we turn now to changes in sexual attitudes and behavior over the course of the twentieth century.

THE SEXUAL REVOLUTION

During the last century, people witnessed profound changes in sexual attitudes and practices. The first indications of this change occurred in the 1920s, as millions from farms and small towns migrated to the rapidly growing cities. There, living apart from their families and meeting in the workplace, young men and

The sexual revolution was well underway by the late 1960s, when the youth counterculture embraced the idea of "free love." This term is something of an exaggeration, but many people did enter into more casual sexual relationships.

women enjoyed considerable sexual freedom. Indeed, this is one reason the decade became known as the "Roaring Twenties."

In the 1930s and 1940s, the Great Depression and World War II slowed the rate of change. But in the postwar period, after 1945, Alfred Kinsey set the stage for what later came to be known as the *sexual revolution*. Kinsey and his colleagues published their first study of sexuality in the United States in 1948, and it raised eyebrows everywhere. It was not so much what Kinsey said about sexual behavior (although he did present some surprising results) but simply the fact that scientists were studying *sex*, that set off a national conversation. At that time, after all, many people were uneasy talking about sex even privately at home.

But Kinsey's two books (1948 and 1953) became best-sellers because they revealed that people in the

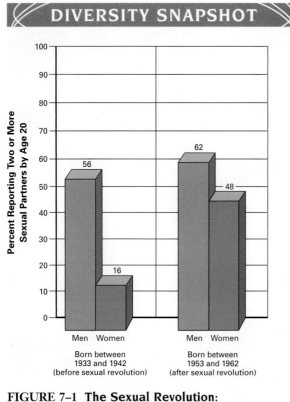

FIGURE 7–1 The Sexual Revolution: Closing the Double Standard

Source: Laumann et al. (1994:198).

According to the so-called "double standard," society allows (and even encourages) men to be sexually active, while it expects women to remain chaste before marriage and faithful to their husbands afterwards. The sexual revolution, then, had special significance for women because, historically, women were subject to greater sexual regulation than men. Survey data shown in Figure 7–1 support this conclusion. Among people born in the United States between 1933 and 1942 (that is, people in their sixties today), 56 percent of men but just 16 percent of women report having had two or more sexual partners by the time they were age twenty. Compare this wide gap to the pattern among the baby boomers born between 1953 and 1962 (people now in their forties), who came of age after the sexual revolution. In this category, 62 percent of men and 48 percent of women say they had two or more sexual partners by age twenty (Laumann et al., 1994:198). Thus, while the sexual revolution advanced the principle of sexual freedom, it changed behavior among women more than among men.

THE SEXUAL COUNTERREVOLUTION

The sexual revolution made sex a topic of everyday discussion and sexual activity more a matter of individual choice. But given that U.S. society has always had two minds about sex, the sexual revolution was highly controversial. By 1980, the climate of sexual freedom that had marked the late 1960s and 1970s was criticized by some as evidence of our country's moral decline. Thus the *sexual counterrevolution* began.

Politically speaking, the sexual counterrevolution was a conservative call for a return to "family values" and for an abandonment of sexual freedom in favor of sexual responsibility. In practice, this meant moving sex back within marriage. Critics objected not just to the idea of "free love" but to trends such as cohabitation (living together) and having children out of wedlock.

Looking back, we can see that the sexual counterrevolution did not greatly change the idea that individuals should decide for themselves when and with whom to have a sexual relationship. What did happen, however, is that more people began choosing to limit the number of their sexual partners or to abstain from sex entirely. In many cases, such decisions are made on moral grounds. For others, however, the decision to limit sexual activity reflects a fear of sexually transmitted diseases (STDs). As Chapter 14 ("Education and Medicine") explains, although rates of most infectious

United States, on average, were far less conventional in sexual matters than most had thought. Thus, these books fostered a new openness toward sexuality, which helped move along the sexual revolution.

In the late 1960s, the sexual revolution truly came of age. Youth culture dominated public life, and expressions like "if it feels good, do it" and "sex, drugs, and rock 'n' roll" summed up a new freedom in sexual behavior. Some people were turned off by the idea of "turning on," of course, but the baby boom generation, born between 1945 and 1960, became the first cohort in U.S. history to grow up with the idea that sex was part of everyone's life, married or not.

Technology, too, played a part in the sexual revolution. "The pill," introduced in 1960, not only prevented pregnancy, it made sex more convenient. Unlike a condom or diaphragm, which has to be used at the time of intercourse, the pill could be taken any time during the day. Now women as well as men could engage in sex without any special preparation.

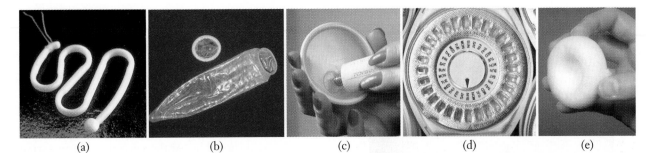

(a)   (b)   (c)   (d)   (e)

Contraception has a long history, beginning with the intrauterine device or IUD (a) in ancient times (originally, stones were used); by 1500, men employed condoms (b), more to prevent disease than pregnancy; the early 1600s saw the invention of the diaphragm (c), later used with spermicidal jelly; the birth control pill (d) came on the scene in 1960; sponges (e) were first licensed in 1983; the Norplant skin implant (f) debuted in 1990, followed by the RU-486 "morning after" pill (g) in 2000.

(f)   (g)

diseases fell after 1960, rates of STDs rose sharply. Moreover, the fact that some STDs (such as genital herpes) are incurable and others (AIDS) are deadly has given individuals good reason to consider carefully their sexual choices.

PREMARITAL SEX

In light of the sexual revolution and the sexual counterrevolution, how much has sexual behavior in the United States really changed? One interesting trend involves premarital sex—that is, the likelihood that young people will have sexual intercourse before marriage.

Consider, first, what U.S. adults *say* about premarital intercourse. Table 7–1 shows that about 35 percent characterize sexual relations before marriage as "always wrong" or "almost always wrong." Another 20 percent consider premarital sex "wrong only sometimes," while more than 40 percent say premarital sex is "not wrong at all." Public opinion is more accepting of premarital sex today than a generation ago, but even so, our society remains divided on this issue.

Now consider what young people *do* regarding premarital intercourse. For women, there has been marked change over time. The Kinsey studies (1948, 1953; see also Laumann et al., 1994) reported that for people born in the early 1900s, about 50 percent of men but just 6 percent of women had premarital

sexual intercourse before age nineteen. Studies of baby boomers born after World War II show a slight increase in premarital intercourse among men but a large increase—to about one-third—among women. The most recent studies, targeting men and women born in the 1970s, show that 76 percent of men and 66 percent of women had premarital sexual intercourse

TABLE 7–1 How We View Premarital and Extramarital Sex

Survey Question: "There's been a lot of discussion about the way morals and attitudes about sex are changing in this country. If a man and a woman have sexual relations before marriage, do you think it is always wrong, almost always wrong, wrong only sometimes, or not wrong at all? What about a married person having sexual relations with someone other than the marriage partner?"

	Premarital Sex	Extramarital Sex
"Always wrong"	25.4%	77.9%
"Almost always wrong"	8.9	12.3
"Wrong only sometimes"	20.2	5.7
"Not wrong at all"	41.9	2.3
"Don't know"/No answer	3.6	1.8

Source: *General Social Surveys, 1972–1998: Cumulative Codebook* (Chicago: National Opinion Research Center, 1999), p. 235.

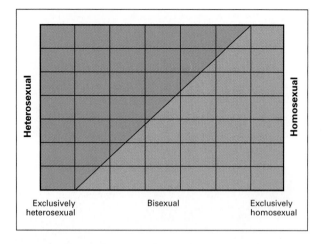

FIGURE 7–2 The Sexual Orientation Continuum

Source: Adapted from Kinsey et al. (1948).

by their senior year in high school (Laumann et al., 1994:323–24). Thus, although general public attitudes remain divided on premarital sex, this behavior is widely accepted among young people.

SEX AMONG ADULTS

To hear the mass media tell it, people in the United States are very active sexually. But do popular images exaggerate reality? The Laumann study (1994) found that frequency of sexual activity varies widely in the U.S. population. The patterns break down like this: One-third of adults report having sex with a partner a few times a year or not at all; another one-third have sex once or several times a month; the remaining one-third have sex with a partner two or more times a week. In short, no single stereotype accurately describes sexual activity in the United States.

Moreover, despite the widespread image of "swinging singles," it is married people who have sex with partners the most. In addition, married people report the highest level of satisfaction—both emotional and physical—with their partners (Laumann et al., 1994).

EXTRAMARITAL SEX

What about married people having sex with someone other than their marriage partner? What people commonly call "adultery" (sociologists prefer the more neutral-sounding term "extramarital sex") is widely condemned. Table 7–1 shows that more than 90 percent of U.S. adults consider a married person having sex with someone other than the marital partner to be "always wrong" or "almost always wrong." The norm of sexual fidelity within marriage has been, and remains, a strong element of U.S. culture.

But in terms of behavior, the cultural ideal often differs from real life. It probably comes as no surprise that extramarital sexual activity is more common than people say it should be. At the same time, extramarital sex is not as frequent as many believe. The Laumann study reports that about 25 percent of married men and 10 percent of married women have had at least one extramarital sexual experience. Or, the other way around, 75 percent of men and 90 percent of women have remained sexually faithful to their partners (Laumann et al., 1994:214; NORC, 1999:996).

SEXUAL ORIENTATION

Sexual orientation refers to *a person's romantic and emotional attraction to another person.* The norm in all human societies is **heterosexuality** (*hetero* is a Greek word meaning "the other of two"), *sexual attraction to someone of the other sex.* Yet, in every society a significant share of people favor **homosexuality** (*homo* is the Greek word for "the same"), *sexual attraction to someone of the same sex.* When thinking about these categories, keep in mind that homosexuality and heterosexuality are not mutually exclusive. People do not necessarily fall into one category or the other, but may have both sexual orientations to varying degrees. Figure 7–2 presents these two sexual orientations as a continuum, indicating that most people actually experience at least some degree of sexual attraction to people of both sexes.

The fact that sexual orientation is often not clear-cut points to the importance of a third category: **bisexuality,** which refers to *sexual attraction to people of both sexes.* Some bisexual people are attracted equally to males and females; many others, however, are attracted more to one sex than the other. Finally, one additional sexual orientation is **asexuality,** *no sexual attraction to people of either sex.*

It is also important to note that sexual *attraction* is not the same thing as sexual *behavior.* Many people, no doubt, have experienced some attraction to someone of the same sex, but fewer ever actually engage in same-sex behavior. This is in large part due to cultural constraints on our actions.

Cultural systems do not accept all sexual orientations equally. In the United States, as well as the rest of the world, heterosexuality is the norm because heterosexual relations permit human reproduction. Even so, most societies tolerate homosexuality. In fact, among the ancient Greeks, upper-class men considered homosexuality the highest form of relationship, partly because they looked down on women as their intellectual inferiors. "Real" men preferred other men as sexual partners, and engaged in heterosexual relations only in order to have children (Kluckhohn, 1948; Ford & Beach, 1951; Greenberg, 1988).

WHAT GIVES US A SEXUAL ORIENTATION?

The question of *how* people come to have a particular sexual orientation in the first place is vigorously debated. But the arguments cluster around two general, opposite positions: (1) that sexual orientation is a product of society, and (2) that sexual orientation is a product of biology.

Sexual orientation: A product of society. This approach argues that people in any society construct a set of meanings that lets them make sense of sexuality. Understanding of sexuality, therefore, differs from place to place and over time. As Michel Foucault (1990) points out, there was no distinct category of people called "homosexuals" until a century ago when scientists and, eventually, the public as a whole began labeling people that way. Throughout most of history, in other words, some people no doubt had what we would call "homosexual experiences." But neither they nor others saw in this behavior the basis for any special identity.

Anthropologists provide further evidence that sexual orientation is socially constructed. Studies show that patterns of homosexuality differ greatly among societies. In Siberia, for example, the Chukchee Eskimo perform a ritual during which one man dresses like a female and does a woman's work. The Sambia of the Eastern Highlands of New Guinea have a ritual in which young boys perform oral sex on older men in the belief that ingesting semen will enhance their masculinity (Herdt, 1993). The existence of such diverse patterns in societies around the world seems to indicate that sexual orientation and sexual expression have much to do with society itself.

Sexual orientation: A product of biology. A growing body of evidence suggests that sexual orientation is innate, that it is rooted in human biology, in much the same way that people are born right-handed or left-handed. Arguing this position, Simon LeVay (1993)

This gathering took place on June 27, 1999, at New York's Stonewall Inn to celebrate the thirtieth anniversary of the so-called "Stonewall Riot" in 1969, when gay people first fought back against harassment by the police, sparking the gay rights movement.

links sexual orientation to the structure of an individual's brain. LeVay studied the brains of both homosexual and heterosexual men and found a small but important difference in the size of the hypothalamus, a part of the brain that regulates hormones. Such an anatomical difference, he claims, plays a part in shaping one's sexual orientation.

Genetics, too, may influence sexual orientation. One study of forty-four pairs of brothers—all homosexual—found that thirty-three pairs had a distinctive genetic pattern involving the X chromosome inherited from their mothers. Moreover, the gay brothers had an unusually high number of gay male relatives—but only on their mother's side. Such evidence leads

FIGURE 7–3 Sexual Orientation in the United States: Survey Data

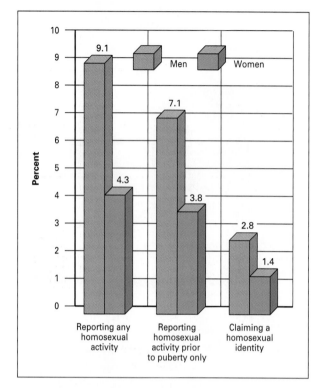

(a) How Many Gay People?

Source: Adapted from Laumann et al. (1994).

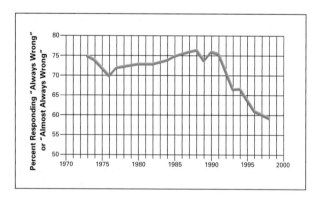

(b) Attitudes toward Homosexual Relations, 1973–1998

Survey Question: "What about sexual relations between two adults of the same sex—do you think it is always wrong, almost always wrong, wrong only sometimes, or not wrong at all?"

Source: NORC (1999).

some researchers to think there may be a "gay gene" (Hamer & Copeland, 1994).

Critical evaluation. Mounting evidence supports the conclusion that sexual orientation is rooted in biology, although the best guess at present is that it is derived from *both* society and biology (Gladue, Green, & Hellman, 1984; Weinrich, 1987; Troiden, 1988; Isay, 1989; Puterbaugh, 1990; Angier, 1992; Gelman, 1992). But we need to bear in mind that sexual orientation is not a matter of neat categories. That is, most people who think of themselves as homosexual have had some heterosexual experiences, just as many people who think of themselves as heterosexual have had some homosexual experiences. Thus, the task of explaining sexual orientation is extremely complex.

There is also a political issue here with great importance for gay men and lesbians. To the extent that sexual orientation is based in biology, homosexuality is not a matter of choice any more than, say, skin color. If this is so, shouldn't gay men and lesbians expect the same legal protection from discrimination as African Americans? (Herek, 1991)

HOW MANY GAY PEOPLE?

What share of our population is gay? This is a hard question to answer because, as we have explained, sexual orientation is not a matter of neat categories. Moreover, people are not always willing to discuss their sexuality with strangers or even family members. Pioneering sex researcher Alfred Kinsey (1948, 1953) estimated that about 4 percent of males and 2 percent of females have an exclusively same-sex orientation, although his research suggested that at least one-third of men and one-eighth of women have had at least one homosexual experience leading to orgasm.

In light of the Kinsey studies, many social scientists put the gay share of the population at 10 percent. But a more recent national survey of sexuality in the United States indicates that how one operationalizes "homosexuality" makes a big difference in the results (Laumann et al., 1994). As Part (a) of Figure 7–3 shows, around 9 percent of men and 4 percent of women between ages eighteen and fifty-nine reported homosexual activity *at some time* in their lives. The second set of numbers shows that a significant share of men (less so, women) have a homosexual experience during childhood but not after puberty. And 2.8 percent of men and 1.4 percent of women define themselves as "partly" or "entirely" homosexual.

170   CHAPTER 7 Sexuality

Finally, Kinsey treated sexual orientation as an "either/or" trait: To be more homosexual was, by definition, to be less heterosexual. But same-sex and other-sex attractions can operate independently. At one extreme, then, bisexual people feel strong attractions to people of both sexes; at the other, asexual people experience little sexual attraction to people of either sex.

In the national survey just noted, less than 1 percent of adults described themselves as bisexual. But bisexual experiences appear to be fairly common (at least for a time) among younger people, especially on college campuses (Laumann et al., 1994; Leland, 1995). Many bisexuals, then, do not think of themselves as either gay or straight, and their behavior reflects elements of both gay and straight living.

THE GAY RIGHTS MOVEMENT

In the long term, the public's attitude toward homosexuality has been moving toward greater acceptance. Back in 1973, as shown in Part (b) of Figure 7–3, about three-fourths of U.S. adults claimed homosexual relations were "always wrong" or "almost always wrong." While that percentage changed little during the 1970s and 1980s, by 1998 it had dropped to less than 60 percent (NORC, 1999:236).

In large measure, this change of thinking came about as a result of the gay rights movement that gained strength after the tumultuous decade of the 1960s (Chauncey, 1994). Up to that time, most people did not discuss homosexuality, and it was common for companies (including the federal government and the armed forces) to fire anyone who was accused of being gay. Mental health professionals, too, took a hard line, describing homosexuals as "sick," and sometimes placing them in mental hospitals where, presumably, they might be cured. In this climate of intolerance, most lesbians and gay men remained "in the closet"—closely guarding the secret of their sexual orientation.

As the gay rights movement gained strength over the years, however, the climate changed. One early milestone occurred in 1973 when the American Psychiatric Association declared that homosexuality was not an illness but simply "a form of sexual behavior." The gay rights movement also began using the term **homophobia** to describe *the dread of close personal interaction with people thought to be gay, lesbian, or bisexual* (Weinberg, 1973). The concept of homophobia (literally, "fear of sameness") turns the tables on society: Instead of asking "What's wrong with gay people?" the question becomes "What's wrong with people who can't accept a different sexual orientation?"

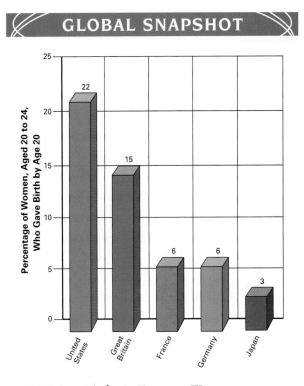

FIGURE 7–4 **Births to Teenage Women**
Source: The Alan Guttmacher Institute (2000).

SEXUAL CONTROVERSIES

Sexuality lies at the heart of a number of controversies in the United States. Here we take a look at four issues: teen pregnancy, pornography, prostitution, and sexual violence.

TEEN PREGNANCY

Being sexually active—especially having intercourse—demands a high level of responsibility, because it carries the risk of pregnancy. Teenagers may be biologically mature, but many are not emotionally mature and may not appreciate all the consequences of their actions. Indeed, surveys indicate that while 1 million U.S. teens become pregnant each year, most of them do not intend to. Not only does pregnancy mean that many young women (and, sometimes, young fathers-to-be) cannot finish school, but they are at high risk of poverty. Figure 7–4 shows that this country's rate of teen pregnancy is higher than that of other high-income countries.

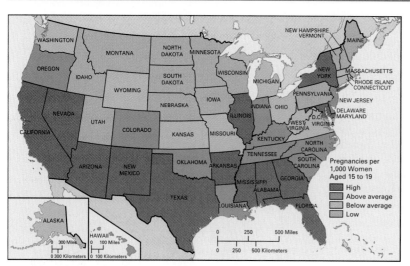

NATIONAL MAP 7–1
Teenage Pregnancy Rates across the United States

The map shows pregnancy rates in the mid-1990s for women aged fifteen to nineteen. In what regions of the country are rates high? Where are they low? What explanation can you offer for these patterns?

Source: The Alan Guttmacher Institute (1999).

Pregnancies per 1,000 Women Aged 15 to 19

- High
- Above average
- Below average
- Low

Did the sexual revolution raise the level of teenage pregnancy? Surprisingly, the answer is no. The rate of pregnancy among teens in 1950 was actually higher than it is today, but this is because people back then married at a younger age. In fact, many pregnancies led to quick marriages. As a result, there were many pregnant teenagers, but most were married women. Today, by contrast, most teenagers who become pregnant are not married. In about half of such cases, these women have abortions; in the other half, they keep their babies (Voydanoff & Donnelly, 1990; Holmes, 1996a). National Map 7–1 shows the distribution of births to females between the ages of fifteen and seventeen in the United States.

Concern about the high rate of teenage pregnancy has led to sex education programs in schools. But such programs are controversial, as the box explains.

PORNOGRAPHY

In general terms, **pornography** refers to *sexually explicit material that causes sexual arousal.* But what, exactly, is or is not pornographic has long been a matter of debate. Recognizing that people view the portrayal of sexuality differently, the U.S. Supreme Court gives local communities the power to decide for themselves what violates "community standards" of decency and lacks any redeeming social value.

Definitions aside, pornography is certainly popular in the United States: X-rated videos, 1-900 telephone "sex lines," and a host of sexually explicit movies and magazines together constitute almost a $10-billion-a-year industry. And that figure is rising, as people buy more and more pornography from thousands of sites on the Web.

Traditionally, people have criticized pornography on *moral* grounds. As national surveys confirm, 60 percent of U.S. adults are concerned that "sexual materials lead to a breakdown of morals" (NORC, 1999:237). Today, however, pornography is also seen as a *power* issue because it depicts women as the sexual playthings of men.

Some critics also claim that pornography is a cause of violence against women. While it is difficult to document a scientific cause-and-effect relationship between what people view and how they act, the public shares a concern about pornography and violence, with almost half of adults holding the opinion that pornography encourages people to commit rape (NORC, 1999:237).

Though people everywhere object to sexual material they find offensive, many also value free speech and want to protect artistic expression. Nevertheless, pressure to restrict pornography is building from an unlikely coalition of conservatives (who oppose pornography on moral grounds) and progressives (who condemn it for political reasons).

CRITICAL THINKING

Sex Education: Solution or Problem?

Most schools today have sex education programs that teach the basics of sexuality. Instructors explain to young people how their bodies grow and change, how reproduction occurs, and how to avoid pregnancy by using birth control or abstaining from sex.

Because half of U.S. teenage boys report having sex by the time they reach sixteen, and half of girls report doing so by seventeen, "sex ed" programs seem to make sense. But critics point out that as the scope of sex education programs has expanded, the level of teenage sexual activity has actually gone *up*. This trend seems to suggest that sex education may not be discouraging sex among youngsters; on the contrary, learning more about sex may encourage young people to become sexually active sooner. Critics also say that it is parents who should be instructing their children about sex, since, at the same time, they can also teach their beliefs about what is right and wrong.

But supporters of sex education counter that it is unrealistic to expect that in a culture that celebrates sexuality, children will not become sexually active. If this is the case, the sensible strategy is to ensure that they understand what they are doing and take reasonable precautions to protect themselves from unwanted pregnancy and sexually transmitted diseases.

What do you think?

1. *Schools can teach the facts about sexuality. But do you think they can address the emotional issues that often accompany sex? What about the moral issues? Why or why not?*

2. *What about parents? Are they doing their job as far as instructing children about sex? Ask members of your class how many of them received instruction in sexual matters from their parents.*

3. *Overall, do you think young people today know too little about sexuality? Or, do you think they might know too much? What specific changes would you suggest to address the problem of unwanted pregnancy among teens?*

Sources: Gibbs (1993) and Stodghill (1998).

PROSTITUTION

Prostitution is *the selling of sexual services*. Often called "the world's oldest profession," prostitution has always been widespread, and about one in five adult men in the United States reports having paid for sex at some time (NORC, 1999:996). Even so, to the extent that people think of sex as an expression of interpersonal intimacy, they find the idea of sex for money disturbing. As a result, prostitution is against the law everywhere in the United States except for parts of Nevada.

Around the world, prostitution is greatest in poor countries where patriarchy is strong and traditional cultural norms limit women's ability to earn a living. Global Map 7–1 on page 174 shows where in the world prostitution is most widespread.

Types of prostitution. While most prostitutes (many prefer the morally neutral term "sex workers") are women, they fall into different categories. *Call girls* are elite prostitutes, typically women who are young, attractive, and well-educated and arrange their own "dates" with clients by telephone. The classified pages of any large city newspaper contain numerous ads for "escort services," by which women (and sometimes men) offer both companionship and sex for a fee.

A middle category of prostitutes works in "massage parlors" or brothels under the control of managers. These sex workers have less choice about their clients, receive less money for their services, and get to keep no more than half of what they make.

At the bottom of the sex-worker hierarchy are *street walkers*, women and men who "work the streets" of large cities. Typically, female street walkers are under the control of male pimps who take most of their earnings. Many street walkers fall victim to violence from pimps and clients (Gordon & Snyder, 1989).

Most, but not all, prostitutes offer heterosexual services. Gay prostitutes, too, trade sex for money. Researchers report that many gay prostitutes have suffered rejection by family and friends because of their sexual orientation (Weisberg, 1985; Boyer, 1989; Kruks, 1991).

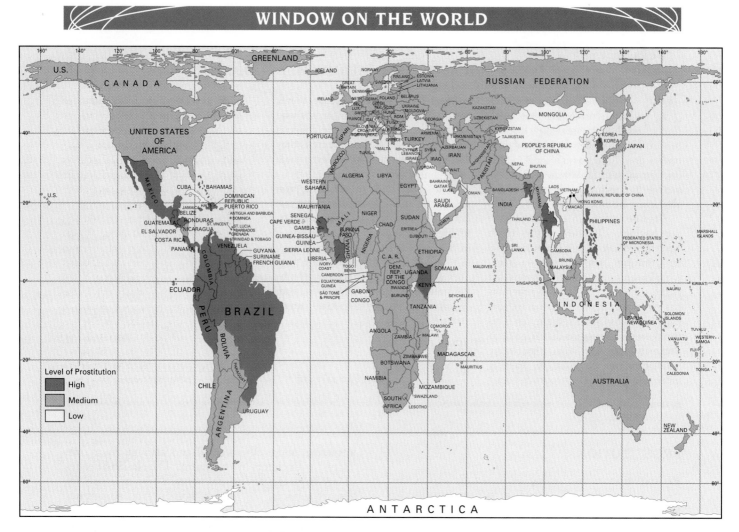

GLOBAL MAP 7–1 Prostitution in Global Perspective

Generally speaking, prostitution is widespread in societies of the world where women have low standing in relation to men. Officially, at least, the People's Republic of China boasts of gender equality, including the elimination of "vice," such as prostitution, which oppresses women. By contrast, in much of Latin America, a region of pronounced patriarchy, prostitution is commonplace. In many Islamic societies patriarchy is also strong, but religion is a counterbalance so prostitution is limited. Western, high-income nations display a moderate amount of prostitution.

Source: *Peters Atlas of the World* (1990); updated by the author.

A victimless crime? Prostitution is against the law almost everywhere, but many people consider it a victimless crime (see Chapter 6, "Deviance"). Consequently, instead of enforcing prostitution laws all the time, police stage only occasional crackdowns. This policy reflects a desire to control prostitution while assuming that nothing will totally eliminate it.

Is selling sex a victimless crime that hurts no one? Certainly, many people who take a "live and let live" attitude about prostitution would say "yes." But it is

Thailand

GLOBAL SOCIOLOGY

Sexual Slavery: A Report from Thailand

Around the world, poverty forces many women and children into prostitution as a means of survival. Nowhere is this trend more evident than in Southeast Asia. Recent decades have witnessed an explosion of what amounts to sexual slavery that exploits women and attracts men from rich nations as "sex tourists."

Sex-tourism districts can be found in many large cities throughout Africa, Eastern Europe, and, especially, Southeast Asia. Bangkok, Thailand—called the sex-tourism capital of the world—receives tens of thousands of visitors from Japan, Western Europe, and North America each year. Thailand has some 2 million prostitutes, with 10 percent of the female Thai population working in the sex industry.

Almost all of these women are poor, and many come from rural regions where people struggle to survive. Some girls who see little future

in a rural village make their own way to the city, hoping to find work. With few skills and little awareness of the dangers they face, most fall under the control of pimps and end up working in brothels, soliciting in bars, or performing in sex shows. In some cases, desperate parents even sell their female infants to agents who promise to see that the girls get work in the city. The agents take the girls, pay others to raise them, and then "harvest

Young girls await customers in a Bangkok brothel.

their crop" years later when the girls are old enough (sometimes just twelve or thirteen) to work the sex trade. In fact, prostitutes on average are getting younger and younger, because it is the younger girls who can earn the most money from sex tourists fearful of contracting sexually transmitted diseases.

Once they work in the sex industry, the future for women is bleak. Pimps provide girls with clothes and housing, but usually at a cost that exceeds the girls' salaries. The result is a system of debt bondage that keeps them virtual prisoners. To make matters worse, most sex workers suffer from diseases brought on by abuse and neglect. Worst of all, estimates suggest that about half are infected with the virus that causes AIDS.

Sources: Based, in part, on Santoli (1994) and Remy (1996).

also true that prostitution subjects many women to abuse and outright violence and plays a part in spreading sexually transmitted diseases, including AIDS. In addition, many poor women become trapped in a life of selling sex, especially in low-income nations. The box offers a closer look at the flourishing sex trade in Southeast Asia.

SEXUAL VIOLENCE AND ABUSE

Ideally, sexual activity occurs within a loving relationship; but sex can sometimes be twisted by hate and violence. Sexual violence, which ranges from verbal abuse to rape and assault, is widespread in the United States.

Rape. Although some people think rape is motivated solely by a desire for sex, it is actually an expression of power—a violent act that uses sex to hurt, humiliate,

or control another person. The U.S. Federal Bureau of Investigation reports that about 90,000 women are raped each year. This number, though, reflects only the reported cases, and the actual number of rapes is several times this number (McCormick, 1994; U.S. Federal Bureau of Investigation, 2000).

The official definition of rape according to the federal government is "the carnal knowledge of a female forcibly and against her will." Thus, official rape statistics include only victims who are women. But men, too, are raped—in perhaps 10 percent of all cases. Most men who rape men are not homosexual. They are heterosexuals who are motivated by a desire not for sex but to dominate another person (Groth & Birnbaum, 1979; Gibbs, 1991a).

Date rape. A common myth is that rape involves strangers. In reality, most rapes involve people who

Date Rape: Exposing Dangerous Myths

April Sanders was beside herself with excitement: She had a date with Bob Thomas, a smooth-talking senior she had admired all semester. On Saturday night, she met Bob at 10 o'clock at the south end of the Arts Quad, and they talked easily as they walked across campus to a party. The more Bob talked, the more April liked him.

The music was live and loud as they joined the crowd at a favorite campus hangout, and the beer was flowing freely. They had a few beers and danced. Then they joined some of Bob's friends at a table where everyone was downing shots of hard liquor. Bob handed April a glass. She paused, but then smiled and drank it down. He kept refilling her glass and soon April's head was spinning. She knew she had drunk too much and needed to lie down. Embarrassed, she announced she had better go back to her dorm room. "No problem," Bob responded, insisting on walking her home.

When they reached her room, April let Bob in while she went to the bathroom to look for an aspirin. When she returned to the room, Bob walked toward her and tried to kiss her. At that point, he seemed to change, forcibly pushing April into having sex. "Bob, no!" April pleaded, overcome with fear. But Bob was determined as well as strong, and she simply could not stop him.

Ten minutes later, the attack was over, and Bob got up and left. April's first reaction was to take a shower. "I felt so filthy," she recalled later. "I washed myself over and over." For hours, she sat crying, trying to make sense of a night that had gone terribly wrong. "Was I raped?" she asked herself, "I told him 'no,' I tried to stop him." But she also worried, "Who will believe me? We were out drinking together. . . . I let him into my room. . . ."

In the morning, April Sanders went to the dean's office to report the attack. Later that day, she spoke with two sheriff's deputies. The police conducted an investigation, but they were reluctant to act because Bob claimed the sex was consensual, and there was no other evidence such as bruises, a medical examination, or torn clothes to back up April's story.

The case of April Sanders is all too typical. In fact, at least half of all victims of sexual attack make no report to police. One reason is that many women and men do not understand what rape is. In fact, three wrong ideas about rape are so common in the United States that they might be called "rape myths":

Myth #1: Rape involves strangers. A sexual attack brings to mind a strange man lurking in the shadows who suddenly springs on an unsuspecting victim. In four out of five rapes, however, the victim knows the offender. For this reason, it is more realistic to speak of *acquaintance rape* or *date rape*.

Myth #2: Women provoke their attackers. Many people think a woman who has been raped must have done *something* to make the man think she wanted to have sex. In the case described above,

know one another, and they usually take place in familiar surroundings, especially the home. For this reason, the term "date rape" or "acquaintance rape" refers to sexual violence against women by men they know.

Many victims of date rape do not report the crime. Some believe that because they know the offender, the attack could not really have been rape. But the tide is turning, with more and more women speaking out. The box takes a closer look.

THEORETICAL ANALYSIS OF SEXUALITY

We can better understand human sexuality by using sociology's theoretical paradigms. In the following sections, we apply the three major paradigms in turn.

STRUCTURAL-FUNCTIONAL ANALYSIS

The structural-functional approach highlights the contribution of any social pattern to the overall operation of society. Because sexuality is an important dimension of social life, society regulates sexual behavior.

The need to regulate sexuality. From a biological point of view, sex allows our species to reproduce. But culture and social institutions regulate *with whom* and *when* people reproduce. For example, most societies condemn married people for having sex with someone other than their spouse. To do otherwise—to give the forces of sexual passion free rein—would threaten family life and, especially, the raising of children.

Another example, discussed earlier, is the incest taboo. The fact that this norm exists everywhere

didn't April Sanders agree to go drinking? Didn't she let Bob into her room late at night? Such self-doubt often paralyzes victims. But going out with a man—or even inviting him into her room—is not consent to have sex with him any more than it is consent to have him beat her with a club.

Myth #3: Rape is simply sex.
If there is no knife held to a woman's throat or if she is not bound and gagged, what's the crime? The answer is that under the law, forcing a woman to have sex without her consent is a *violent crime.* "Having sex" implies intimacy, caring, and, most important of all, consent—none of which is present in rape. Beyond the brutality of being physically violated, date rape also undermines a victim's sense of trust. Psychological scars are especially serious among the half of rape victims who are under eighteen; one-third of these young victims are attacked by their own fathers or stepfathers (Greenfield, 1996).

The ancient Babylonians stoned married women who had been raped, convinced that they had committed adultery. Ideas about rape have changed little over thousands of years, which helps explain why—even today—only

Is a person who drinks alcohol to excess capable of making a responsible decision about having sex? What role does alcohol play in date rape on the campus?

about one in twenty rapes results in an offender being sent to jail.

Nowhere has the issue of date rape been more widely discussed than on the campus. The collegiate environment promotes easy friendships and encourages trust. At the same time, many young students have much to learn about relationships and about themselves. So, while college life encourages communication, it also invites sexual violence.

To counter the problem, many schools now actively address myths about rape and the place of alcohol in campus life. College men and women alike need to understand two simple truths: Sex without a woman's consent is rape, and when a woman says "no," she means just that.

What do you think?
1. *Why, in your opinion, are myths about rape so widespread?*
2. *What programs or policies exist on your campus to address sexual assault?*
3. *What else needs to be done?*

Sources: Gibbs (1991a, 1991b) and Gilbert (1992).

---

shows clearly that no society is willing to permit completely free choice in sexual partners. Reproduction resulting from sex between family members other than married partners would break down the system of kinship and hopelessly confuse human relationships.

Historically, the social control of sexuality was strong, mostly because sex inevitably led to childbirth. We see this in the traditional distinction between "legitimate" reproduction (within marriage) and "illegitimate" reproduction (out of wedlock). But once a society develops the technology to control births, its sexual norms become more permissive. This occurred in the United States where, over the course of the twentieth century, sex moved beyond its basic reproductive function and became a form of intimacy and even recreation (Giddens, 1992).

Latent functions: The case of prostitution. It is easy to see that prostitution is harmful because it spreads disease and exploits women. But Kingsley Davis (1971) explains that prostitution performs several latent functions—the reason it exists everywhere despite society's attempts to limit it. Prostitution is one way to meet the sexual needs of a large number of people who do not have ready access to sex, including soldiers, travelers, and people who have trouble establishing relationships. Moreover, adds Davis, the availability of sex without commitment may even help to stabilize some loveless marriages that might otherwise collapse.

Critical evaluation. The structural-functional paradigm helps us appreciate the important role sexuality plays in how society is organized. The incest taboo

Europeans developed the concept of virginity during the Middle Ages with the rise of feudal estates. With property and titles to pass on, males needed to be certain of their heirs and, thus, desired to marry a woman who had never had sex to ensure she was not pregnant with another man's child. The loss of virginity became a significant life-course event for women, a fact captured in Jean-Baptiste Greuze's painting, The Broken Jug *(1773).*

Jean-Baptiste Greuze (1725–1805), *The Broken Jug* 1772–1773 (*La cruche cassée*). Rococo painting, canvas, 85 × 86.5 cm. Louvre, Dpt. des Peintures, Paris, France. © Photograph by Erich Lessing/Art Resource, N.Y.

and other cultural norms also suggest that society has always paid attention to who has sex with whom and, especially, who reproduces with whom.

At the same time, this approach pays little attention to the great diversity of sexual ideas and practices found within every society. Moreover, sexual patterns change over time, just as they differ in remarkable ways around the world. To appreciate the varied and changeable character of sexuality, we turn to the symbolic-interaction paradigm.

SYMBOLIC-INTERACTION ANALYSIS

The symbolic-interaction paradigm highlights how, as people interact, they construct everyday reality. As Chapter 4 ("Social Interaction in Everyday Life") explains, the process of reality construction is highly variable, so that one group's or society's views of sexuality may well differ from another's. In the same way, how people understand sexuality can and does change over time.

The social construction of sexuality. Almost all social patterns involving sexuality have seen considerable change over the course of the twentieth century. One good illustration is the changing importance of virginity. A century ago, our society's norm—for women, at least—was virginity until marriage. This norm was strong because there was no effective means of birth control, and virginity was the only assurance a man had that his bride-to-be was not carrying another man's child. Today, however, we have gone a long way toward separating sex from reproduction, and the virginity norm has weakened. In the United States, among those born between 1963 and 1974, just 16.3 percent of men and 20.1 percent of women report being virgins at first marriage (Laumann et al., 1994:503).

Another example of our society's construction of sexuality involves young people's awareness of sex. A century ago, childhood was a time of innocence in sexual matters. In recent decades, however, thinking has changed. Though few people condone sexual activity among children, most people believe children should be educated about sex so that they can make intelligent choices about their own behavior as they grow older.

Global comparisons. The broader our view, the more variation we see in the meanings people attach to sexuality. In global perspective, differences can be striking, indeed. Anthropologists report that people in some societies are far more accepting of childhood sexuality than people in the United States. Studying the Melanesian people of southeast New Guinea, anthropologist Ruth Benedict (1938) concluded that adults paid little attention when young children engaged in sexual experimentation with one another. Parents in Melanesia shrugged off such activity because, before puberty, sex cannot lead to reproduction.

Critical evaluation. The strength of the symbolic-interaction paradigm lies in revealing the constructed character of familiar social patterns. Understanding that people "construct" sexuality, we can better appreciate the variety of sexual practices found over history and around the world.

One limitation of this approach, however, is that not everything is so variable. Throughout our own history—and around the world—men are more likely to see women in sexual terms than vice versa. If this pattern is widespread, some broader social structure must be at work, as we shall see in the next section.

SOCIAL-CONFLICT ANALYSIS

The social-conflict paradigm highlights dimensions of inequality. This approach, therefore, shows how sexuality reflects patterns of social inequality and also how it helps perpetuate them.

Sexuality: Reflecting social inequality. Recall our discussion of prostitution, a practice outlawed almost everywhere. Even so, enforcement is uneven at best, especially when it comes to who is and is not likely to be arrested. Although two parties are involved, the record shows that police are far more likely to arrest (less powerful) female prostitutes than (more powerful) male clients. Similarly, of all women engaged in prostitution, it is street walkers—women with the least income and those most likely to be minorities—who face the highest risk of arrest (COYOTE, 2000). Then, too, we might wonder if so many women would be involved in prostitution at all if they had legitimate economic opportunities equal to those of men.

Sexuality: Creating social inequality. Social-conflict theorists, especially feminists, point to sexuality as being at the root of inequality between women and men. How can this be? Defining women in sexual terms amounts to devaluing them from full human beings into objects of men's interest and attention.

Is it any wonder, then, that the word "pornography" comes from the Greek word *porne*, meaning "a man's sexual slave"? If men define women in sexual terms, it is easy to see why many people consider pornography—almost all of which is consumed by males—a power issue. Since pornography typically depicts women seeking to please men, it supports the idea that men have power over women.

Some radical critics doubt that this element of power can ever be removed from heterosexual relations (Dworkin, 1987). While most social-conflict theorists do not reject heterosexuality, they do agree that sexuality can and does degrade women. They point out that our culture often depicts sexuality in terms of sport (men "scoring" with women) and also violence ("slamming," "banging," and "hitting on," for example, are verbs used for both fighting and sex).

Queer theory. Finally, social-conflict theory has taken aim not only at men dominating women but also at heterosexuals dominating homosexuals. In recent years, just as many lesbians and gay men have sought

Prostitution involves two people, but far more female prostitutes than male "Johns" face arrest for this crime. Moreover, of all categories of prostitutes, low-income street walkers are at the highest risk of arrest, disease, and violence.

public acceptance, so have some sociologists tried to add a gay voice to their discipline. The term **queer theory** refers to *a growing body of knowledge that challenges the heterosexual bias in U.S. society.*

Queer theory begins with the assertion that our society is characterized by **heterosexism,** *a view stigmatizing anyone who is not heterosexual as "queer."* Our heterosexual culture victimizes a wide range of people, including gay men, lesbians, bisexuals, transsexuals, and even asexual people. Further, although most people agree that bias against women (sexism) and people of color (racism) is wrong, heterosexism is widely tolerated and sometimes well within the law. This country's military forces, for example, cannot legally discharge a female soldier for "acting like a woman,"

CONTROVERSY & DEBATE

The Abortion Controversy

A black van pulls up to a storefront in a busy section of the city. Two women get out of the front seat and cautiously scan the sidewalk. After a moment, one nods to the other and they open the rear door to let a third young woman out of the van. Standing to the right and left of their charge, the two quickly whisk her inside the building.

Is this a description of two federal marshals escorting a convict to a police station? It might be. But it is actually an account of two clinic workers escorting a young woman who has decided to have an abortion. Why must they be so cautious? Anyone who has read the papers in recent years knows about the heated confrontations at abortion clinics across North America. In fact, some opponents have even targeted and killed several doctors who perform abortions. Overall, abortion is probably the most hotly contested issue in the United States today.

Abortion has not always been so controversial. During the colonial era, midwives and other healers performed abortions with little community opposition and with full approval of the law. But controversy arose about 1850, when early medical doctors sought to eliminate the competition they faced from midwives and other traditional health providers, whose income was derived largely from terminating pregnancies. By 1900, medical doctors succeeded in getting every state to pass a law banning abortion.

Such laws did not end abortion, but they greatly reduced the numbers. In addition, these laws drove abortion underground, so that many women—especially those who were poor—had little choice but to seek help from unlicensed "back alley" abortionists, sometimes with tragic results.

By the 1960s, opposition to abortion laws was rising. In 1973, the U.S. Supreme Court rendered a landmark decision (in the cases of *Roe* v. *Wade* and *Doe* v. *Bolton*), striking down all state laws banning abortion. In effect, this action by the High Court established a woman's legal access to abortion. As a result, about 1.3 million abortions are performed in the United States each year.

Even so, the abortion controversy continues. On one side of the issue are people who describe themselves as "pro-choice," supporting a woman's right to choose abortion. On the other side are those who call themselves "pro-life," opposing abortion as morally wrong; these people would like to see the Supreme Court reverse its 1973 decision.

How strong is the support for each side of the abortion controversy? A recent national survey asked a sample of adults the question: "Should it be possible for a pregnant woman to obtain a legal abortion if the woman wants it for any reason?" In response, 42.6 percent said "yes" (placing them in the pro-choice camp) and 52.1 percent say "no" (the pro-life position); the remaining 5.3 percent offered no opinion (NORC, 1999:209).

A closer look, however, shows that particular circumstances make a big difference in how people see this issue. The figure shows that a large majority of U.S.

---

because that would be a clear case of gender discrimination. But the military forces can discharge her for homosexuality if she is a sexually active lesbian.

Heterosexism also exists at a more subtle level in our everyday understanding of the world. When we describe something as "sexy," for example, don't we really mean attractive to *heterosexuals*?

Critical evaluation. Applying the social-conflict paradigm shows how sexuality is both a cause and effect of inequality. In particular, this paradigm helps us understand men's power over women and heterosexual people's domination of homosexual people.

At the same time, this approach overlooks the fact that sexuality is not a power issue for everyone: Many couples enjoy a vital sexual relationship that deepens their commitment to one another. In addition, the social-conflict paradigm pays little attention to strides our society has made toward reducing inequality. Men today, in public at least, are less likely to describe women as sex objects than a few decades ago; moreover, our rising public concern about sexual harassment (see Chapter 10, "Gender Stratification") has had some effect in reducing sexuality in the workplace. Likewise, there is ample evidence that the gay rights movement has secured greater opportunities and social acceptance for gay people.

We bring this chapter to a close with a look at what is perhaps the most divisive sexuality issue of all: **abortion,** *the deliberate termination of a pregnancy.* The issue cuts to the heart of just about everyone's sense of justice, as described in the box.

adults favor legal abortion if a pregnancy seriously threatens a woman's health, if the woman became pregnant as a result of rape, or if a fetus is very likely to have a serious defect. The bottom line, then, looks like this: About 40 percent support access to abortion under *any* circumstances, but about 80 percent support access to abortion under *some* circumstances.

Many pro-life people feel strongly that abortion is nothing more than killing unborn children. To them, people never have the right to end innocent life in this way. But pro-choice people are no less committed to their position. As they see it, the abortion debate is really about the standing of women in society. Why? Because, they believe, women must have control over their own sexuality. If pregnancy dictates the course of women's lives, women will never be able to compete with men on equal terms, whether it is on campus or in the workplace. Thus, the pro-life position concludes, women must have access to legal, safe abortion as a necessary condition to full participation in society.

Continue the debate . . .

1. *The more conservative pro-life people see abortion as a moral issue, while more liberal pro-choice people see abortion as a power issue. Can you see a parallel to how conservatives and liberals view the issue of pornography?*

2. *Surveys show that men and women have almost the same opinions about abortion. Does this surprise you? Why?*

3. *Why do you think the abortion controversy is often so bitter? Why has our nation been unable to find a middle ground on which all can agree?*

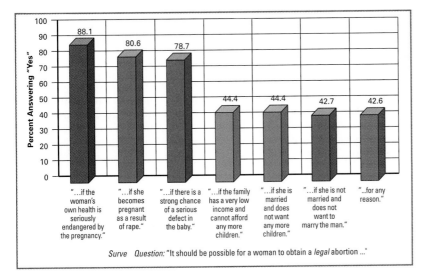

Surve Question: "It should be possible for a woman to obtain a *legal* abortion ..."

When Should the Law Allow a Woman to Choose Abortion?
Source: NORC (1999).

Source: Based, in part, on Luker (1984), Tannahill (1992), and various news reports.

SUMMARY

1. U.S. culture has long defined sex as a taboo topic. The Kinsey studies (1948, 1953) were among the first surveys of human sexuality by social scientists.

2. Sex refers to the biological distinction between females and males, which is determined at conception as a male sperm joins a female ovum.

3. Males and females are distinguished not only by their genitals (primary sex characteristics) but also by bodily development as they mature (secondary sex characteristics). Hermaphrodites have some combination of both male and female genitalia. Transsexuals are people who feel they are one sex although, biologically, they are the other.

4. For most species, sex is rigidly directed by biology; for human beings, sex is a matter of cultural definition as well as personal choice. Patterns of kissing, modesty, and beauty vary around the world, revealing the cultural foundation of sexual practices.

5. Although, early in its history, U.S. society held rigid attitudes toward sexuality, these attitudes have become more permissive over time.

6. The sexual revolution, which came of age in the 1960s and 1970s, brought a far greater openness in matters of sexuality. Research shows that changes in sexuality were greater for women than for men. By 1980, a sexual counterrevolution was

taking form, condemning permissiveness and urging a return to more conservative "family values."

7. The share of people in the United States who have premarital sexual intercourse increased over the course of the twentieth century. Research shows that about three-fourths of young men and two-thirds of young women do so by their senior year in high school.

8. The level of sexual activity varies within the population of U.S. adults: One-third report having sex with a partner a few times a year or not at all; another one-third have sex once or several times a month; the remaining one-third have sex with a partner two or more times a week.

9. Although extramarital sex is widely condemned, about 25 percent of married men and 10 percent of married women report being sexually unfaithful to their spouses at some time.

10. Sexual orientation refers to a person's romantic and emotional attraction to another person. Four major orientations are heterosexuality, homosexuality, bisexuality, and asexuality. Sexual orientation reflects both biological and cultural factors.

11. The share of the population that is homosexual depends on how researchers define "homosexuality." About 9 percent of adult men and 4 percent of adult women report having had some homosexual experience, compared with 2.8 percent of men and 1.4 percent of women who say they have a homosexual identity.

12. The gay rights movement has worked to gain greater acceptance for gay people. Largely due to this movement, the share of the U.S. population condemning homosexuality as morally wrong has steadily decreased and stands now at about half.

13. Some 1 million teenagers become pregnant each year in the United States. The rate of teenage pregnancy has dropped since 1950, when many teens married and had children. Today, most pregnant teens are not married and, especially if they drop out of school, are at high risk of poverty.

14. With no universal definition of pornography, the law allows local communities to set standards of decency. Conservatives condemn pornography as immoral; liberals, by contrast, condemn it as demeaning to women.

15. Prostitution, the selling of sexual services, is illegal almost everywhere in the United States. Although many people think of prostitution as a victimless crime, others point out that it victimizes women and spreads sexually transmitted diseases.

16. Some 90,000 rapes are reported each year, but the actual number is several times greater. Although many people think of rape as a sexual act, rape is really a violent expression of power. Most rapes involve people who know one another.

17. Structural-functional theory highlights society's need to regulate sexual activity. A universal norm in this regard is the incest taboo, which keeps kinship relations clear.

18. The symbolic-interaction paradigm points up how people attach various meanings to sexuality. Thus, societies differ from one another in terms of sexual attitudes and practices; similarly, sexual patterns change within any one society over time.

19. Social-conflict theory links sexuality to inequality. From this point of view, men dominate women in part by devaluing them as sexual objects.

KEY CONCEPTS

sex (p. 161) the biological distinction between females and males

primary sex characteristics (p. 162) the genitals, organs used for reproduction

secondary sex characteristics (p. 162) bodily development, apart from the genitals, that distinguishes biologically mature females and males

hermaphrodite (p. 163) a human being with some combination of female and male genitalia

transsexuals (p. 163) people who feel they are one sex even though biologically they are the other

incest taboo (p. 164) a norm forbidding sexual relations or marriage between certain relatives

sexual orientation (p. 168) a person's romantic and emotional attraction to another person

heterosexuality (p. 168) sexual attraction to someone of the other sex

homosexuality (p. 168) sexual attraction to someone of the same sex

bisexuality (p. 168) sexual attraction to people of both sexes

asexuality (p. 168) no sexual attraction to people of either sex

homophobia (p. 171) the dread of close personal interaction with people thought to be gay, lesbian, or bisexual

pornography (p. 172) sexually explicit material that causes sexual arousal

prostitution (p. 173) the selling of sexual services

queer theory (p. 179) a growing body of knowledge that challenges the heterosexual bias in U.S. society

heterosexism (p. 179) a view stigmatizing anyone who is not heterosexual as "queer"

abortion (p. 180) the deliberate termination of a pregnancy

CRITICAL-THINKING QUESTIONS

1. What do sociologists mean by the *sexual revolution*? What did the sexual revolution change? Can you suggest some of the reasons that these changes occurred?

2. What is sexual orientation? Why is this characteristic difficult for researchers to measure?

3. Do you think laws should regulate the portrayal of sex in books, films, or on the Internet? Why or why not?

4. Overall, do you think sexuality plays too great a role in the mass media and other dimensions of everyday life? Why or why not?

APPLICATIONS AND EXERCISES

1. The most complete study of sexual patterns in the United States to date is *The Social Organization of Sexuality: Sexual Practices in the United States* by Edward Laumann and others. You can find this book in your campus or community library.

2. Contact your school's student services office and ask what information there is about the extent of sexual violence on your campus. Do people report such crimes? What policies and procedures does your school have to respond to sexual violence?

3. In the past, state and local laws permitted prostitution much more widely than they do today. Do some research on the history of prostitution laws in your state or community.

4. Install the CD-ROM packaged in the back of this new textbook to access a variety of study, review, and applications exercises designed to help you better understand the material covered in this chapter. The CD includes an author's tip video, as well as interactive maps, video application exercises, Web links, and study questions.

 SITES TO SEE

http://www.prenhall.com/macionis

Visit the Interactive Web site that accompanies this text. Begin by clicking on the cover of your book. You will find a chapter-by-chapter study guide, practice tests, chat rooms, and many suggested Web links.

http://www.teenpregnancy.org

Visit the Web site of The National Campaign to Prevent Teen Pregnancy, an organization formed to guide teens toward responsible sexual behavior. You can find data for your state at this site. What are the key parts of this organization's program? How effective would you imagine it is? Why?

http://www.qrd.org

This Web site, the Queer Resource Directory, looks at a wide range of issues—including family, religion, education, and health—from a queer theory perspective. Visit this site to see in what ways various social institutions can be considered "heterosexist." Do you agree? Why?

http://www.gay.com

This is a search engine for all sorts of information highlighting issues involving homosexuality.

cyber.scope

How New Technology Is Changing Our Way of Life

Marshall McLuhan (1969) summed up his pioneering research in the study of communications this way: "Any new technology tends to create a new human environment." In other words, technology affects not just how we work, but it shapes and colors our entire way of life. In this second cyber.scope, we pause to reflect on some of the ways the Information Revolution is changing our culture and society.

The Information Revolution and Cultural Values

Chapter 2 ("Culture") noted the importance members of our society attach to material comfort. Throughout our history, many people have defined "success" to mean earning a good income and enjoying the things money will buy, including a home, car, and fashionable clothing.

But there are signs that, as we move through this new century, our values may shift from a single-minded focus on the accumulation of "things" (the products of industrial technology) to an appreciation of "ideas" (the product of information technology). Such "new age" ideas range from experiences, including both travel and countless experiences with virtual reality,[1] to well-being, including the self-actualization that has become popular in recent decades.

Socialization in the Computer Age

Half a century ago, television rewrote the rules for socialization in the United States and, as Chapter 3

[1]For example, "travel" to an Adirondack mountaintop and enjoy the view (http://www.adirondack.net/adnet/bluemt/bluemt1.html), or wander through the Tower of London (http://www.toweroflondontour.com).

("Socialization") explained, young people now spend more time watching TV than talking to their parents. Today, in the new information society, screens are not just for television; they are our windows into a cyber-world in which we look to computers to link, entertain, and educate us. But this trend toward cyber-socialization raises several important questions.

First, will the spread of computer-based information erode the regional diversity that has marked this country's history, setting off New England from the Deep South and the Midwest from the West Coast? We know that new information technology is linking our nation and the world, so that we might well expect to see a more national culture emerge and, with time, a more global culture as well.

Second, how will this cyber-culture affect our children? Is having computers at the center of their lives good for them? For most children, at least, computer-based images and information play a significant role in teaching them about themselves and the world. Is this trend reducing the importance of parents in children's lives, as

Almost unlimited access to information can be a mixed blessing, as parents can well understand. How can we prevent children from gaining access to pornography or other objectionable material on the Internet? Or, should we?

television did? Cyber-socialization can certainly entertain and instruct, but can it meet the emotional needs of children? Will it contribute to their moral development? After all, there is nothing more important to a child—and more *low tech*—than a warm hug.

Third, who will control cyber-socialization? Just as parents have long expressed concerns about what their children watch on television, they now worry about what kids encounter as they "surf the Net." To date, the federal courts have taken the position that the Internet should operate with minimal government interference. Do we—as citizens and as parents—have expectations for the content of virtual culture? Should the information industry operate for profit? With standards to ensure some measure of educational content? Who should decide?

The Cyber-Self

A person using the name "VegDiet" enters one of thousands of chat rooms found on the Internet, the vast global network described in Chapter 5 ("Groups and Organizations"). Within a few seconds, "VegDiet" is actively debating the state of the world with three other people: "MrMaine," "Ferret," and "RedWine."

The growing popularity of computer-chat gives us a chance to highlight ways in which online interaction differs from more conventional modes of interaction. After studying online interaction, Dennis Waskul (1997) described the self we transmit via a computer as "disembodied." Using Erving Goffman's dramaturgical approach (see Chapter 4), Waskul notes that computer technology screens out a host of "cues" about people's identities—where they are, what they look like, how they dress, and their age and sex—and conveys only the identities they choose to present.

Cyberspace thus affords us great freedom to "try on" identities with few, if any, lasting consequences. As one chat-room participant explained, "Online is a game.... Only here, I play with who I am" (Waskul, 1997:21).

But Wait A Minute . . .
The Neo-Luddites

In the eighteenth century, groups of English weavers who opposed the Industrial Revolution traveled about demolishing new machinery whenever they could gain access to a factory. The Luddites (named after Ned Ludd, their leader) were convinced that the new technology of their day would end up eliminating jobs and, generally, make life worse (Zachary, 1997).

Although the Luddites lost their battle to stem the tide of change, their spirit lives on today in people opposed to the Information Revolution. These neo-Luddites, as they are called, speak with many voices. But they agree that we should not race headlong into a cyber-future without thinking critically about how new technology is likely to make our lives better and worse.

The neo-Luddites remind us, first, that technology is never socially neutral. That is, technology does not simply exist *in* the world, it *changes* the world, pushing human lives in one direction while closing off other alternatives. By venerating technology as good in and of itself, Theodore Roszak (1986) points out, we give up the power to decide for ourselves how we should live. Is putting computers in the classroom a substitute for good teaching? We might well remember that no computer ever created a painting, penned a poem, or composed a symphony. Perhaps most important, computers have no capacity to address ethical questions about right and wrong.

Living in a forward-looking culture, we easily imagine the benefits of new technology. But we need to remember that, just as technology can serve us, it also can diminish us and even destroy us. After all, the Luddites were not anti-technology; they simply wanted to be sure that technology responded to human needs—and not the other way around.

"*On the Internet, nobody knows you're a dog.*"

Peter Steiner © 1993 from The New Yorker Collection. All rights reserved.

How New Technology Is Changing Our Way of Life **185**

SOCIAL STRATIFICATION

Paul Marcus, *The New Nanny*
© Paul Marcus, oil painting on wood, 48 × 72 in. Studio SPM, Inc.

O*n April 10, 1912, the ocean liner* Titanic *slipped away from the docks of Southampton, England, on its maiden voyage across the North Atlantic to New York. A proud symbol of the new industrial age, the towering ship carried 2,300 passengers, some enjoying more luxury than most travelers today could imagine. Poor people, however, crowded the lower decks, journeying to what they hoped would be a better life in the United States.*

Two days out, the crew received reports of icebergs in the area, but paid little notice. Then, near midnight, as the ship steamed swiftly westward, a stunned lookout reported a massive shape rising out of the dark ocean directly ahead. Moments later, the Titanic *collided with a huge iceberg, as tall as the ship itself, that split open its side as if the grand vessel were just a giant tin can.*

Seawater flooded into the ship's lower levels, pulling the ship down by the bow. Within twenty-five minutes of impact, people were rushing for the lifeboats. By 2:00 A.M., the bow was completely submerged and the stern rose high above the water. Clinging to the deck, quietly observed by those in lifeboats, hundreds of helpless passengers and crew solemnly passed their final minutes before the ship disappeared into the frigid Atlantic (Lord, 1976).

The tragic loss of more than 1,600 lives made news around the world. Looking back on this terrible event with a sociological eye, however, we see that some categories of passengers had much better odds of survival than others. In an age of conventional gallantry, women and children boarded the lifeboats first, so that 80 percent of the casualties were men. Class, too, was at work. More than 60 percent of those holding first-class tickets were saved because they were on the upper decks where warnings were sounded first and lifeboats were accessible. Only 36 percent of the second-class passengers survived, and of the third-class passengers on the lower decks, only 24 percent escaped drowning. On board the *Titanic*, class turned out to mean more than the quality of accommodations. Class was a matter of life or death.

The fate of those aboard the *Titanic* dramatically illustrates how social inequality affects the way people live—and sometimes whether they live at all. This

The personal experience of poverty is captured in Sebastiao Salgado's haunting photograph, which stands as a universal portrait of human suffering. The essential sociological insight is that, however strongly individuals feel its effects, our social standing is largely a consequence of the way in which a society (or a world of societies) structures opportunity and reward. To the core of our being, then, we are all the products of social stratification.

chapter explores the important concept of social stratification and surveys social inequality in the United States.

WHAT IS SOCIAL STRATIFICATION?

Every society is marked by inequality, with some people having more money, schooling, health, and power than others. **Social stratification** refers to *a system by which a society ranks categories of people in a hierarchy.* Social stratification involves four basic principles:

1. **Social stratification is a trait of society, not simply a reflection of individual differences.** Many of us tend to think of social standing in terms of personal talent and effort, and as a result we often exaggerate the extent to which we control our own destinies. Did a higher percentage of the first-class passengers on the *Titanic* survive because they were better swimmers than second- and third-class passengers? Hardly. They fared better because of their privileged position on the ship. Similarly, children born into wealthy families are more likely than children born into poverty to enjoy good health, do well in school, succeed in a career, and live a long life. Neither

the rich nor the poor are responsible for creating social stratification, yet this system shapes the lives of us all.

2. **Social stratification persists over generations.** To see that stratification is a trait of societies rather than individuals, we have only to look at how inequality persists from generation to generation as parents pass their social position on to their children.

    Some individuals, especially in industrial societies, do experience **social mobility,** *change in one's position in the social hierarchy.* For most people, however, social standing remains much the same over a lifetime.

3. **Social stratification is universal but variable.** Social stratification is found everywhere. Yet *what* is unequal and *how* unequal it is vary from one society to another. In some societies inequality is mostly a matter of prestige, while in others wealth or power is the key dimension of difference. Moreover, some societies display more inequality than others.

4. **Social stratification involves not just inequality but beliefs.** Any system of inequality not only gives some people more than others, it defines these arrangements as fair. Just as *what* is unequal differs from society to society, then, so does the explanation of *why* people should be unequal.

CASTE AND CLASS SYSTEMS

Sociologists distinguish between "closed" systems, which allow for little change in social position, and "open" systems, which permit some social mobility (Tumin, 1985).

THE CASTE SYSTEM

A **caste system** amounts to *social stratification based on ascription, or birth.* A pure caste system is "closed" because birth alone determines one's destiny with little or no social mobility based on individual effort. In caste systems, then, people are ranked in rigid categories, where they live out their lives.

An illustration: India. Many of the world's societies—most of them agrarian—approximate caste systems. One example is India, or at least India's traditional villages, where most of the country's people still live. The Indian system identifies four major castes (or *varna,* a Sanskrit word that means "color"): Brahmin,

In India, the traditional caste system still guides people's choice of work, especially in rural areas. Below the four basic castes are the Harijans, people defined as "outcasts" or "untouchables." These people perform jobs, such as turning leather into shoes, defined as unclean for others of higher social position.

Kshatriya, Vaishya, and Shudra. On the local level, however, each of these is composed of hundreds of subcaste (or *jati*) groups.

From birth, caste position determines the direction of people's lives. First, families in each caste perform one type of work. Some work (like farming) is open to all, but castes are known for the jobs their members do (as priests, barbers, leather workers, sweepers, and so on).

Second, a caste system demands that people marry others of the same ranking. If people married outside their castes, what rank would their children hold? Sociologists call this pattern *endogamous* marriage (*endo* stems from the Greek, meaning "within"). According to tradition, Indian parents select their children's marriage partners, often before the children reach their teens.

Third, caste systems shape people's beliefs. Indian culture is built on the Hindu tradition that accepting one's parents' choice of spouse, as well as one's life work, is a moral duty.

Fourth, caste guides everyday life by keeping people in the company of "their own kind." Norms reinforce this practice by teaching, for instance, that a ritually "pure" person of higher caste position is "polluted" by contact with someone of lower standing.

Caste systems are typical of agrarian societies because agriculture demands a lifelong routine of hard work; by instilling a sense of moral duty, a caste system ensures that people are disciplined for a lifetime of

work and are willing to perform the same jobs as their parents. Thus, caste hangs on in rural India more than half a century after being formally outlawed. People living in the industrial cities of India, on the other hand, have far more choice about their work and marriage partners.

Another country dominated by caste is South Africa, although that nation's racial system of *apartheid* is now in decline. The box on page 190 takes a closer look.

THE CLASS SYSTEM

Farming, by its nature, demands the kind of lifelong discipline created by caste systems. But a modern economy depends on developing people's talents, which gives rise to a **class system,** *social stratification based on both birth and individual achievement.*

Class systems are more "open," so that individuals who gain schooling and skills may be socially mobile in relation to their parents and siblings. Such mobility, in turn, blurs class distinctions, so that even blood relatives may have different social standing. Categorizing people according to their color, sex, or social background comes to be seen as wrong in modern societies, as all people acquire political rights and, in principle, equal standing before the law. Moreover, work is no longer fixed at birth, but involves some personal choice. Greater individuality also translates into more freedom in selecting a marital partner.

GLOBAL SOCIOLOGY

Race as Caste: A Report from South Africa

At the southern tip of the African continent lies South Africa, a country about the size of Alaska and with a population of about 43 million in 2000. Long inhabited by people of African descent, the region attracted Dutch traders and farmers in the mid-seventeenth century. Early in the nineteenth century, a second wave of British colonization pushed the Dutch inland. By the early 1900s, the British had taken over the country, proclaiming it the Union of South Africa. In 1961, the Republic of South Africa declared its independence.

But freedom was a reality only for the white minority. To ensure their control over the black majority, whites relied on a policy of *apartheid*, or racial separation. Apartheid, formalized as law in 1948, denied blacks citizenship, ownership of land, and any voice in the government. As a subordinate caste, blacks received little schooling and performed menial, low-paying jobs. Even middle-class white people had at least one black household servant.

The white minority defended apartheid by claiming that blacks threatened white cultural traditions or, more simply, were inferior beings. But resistance to apartheid rose steadily, prompting whites to resort to brutal military repression to maintain their power.

Steady resistance—primarily from younger blacks impatient for political and economic opportunity—gradually forced change. Adding to the internal pressure was criticism from other industrial nations, including the United States. By the mid-1980s, the tide began to turn as the South African government granted some rights to people of mixed race and Asian ancestry. Then came the right for all people to form labor unions, to enter various occupations once restricted to whites, and to own property. Officials also repealed laws that separated the races in public places, such as beaches and hospitals.

The pace of change increased in 1990 with Nelson Mandela's release

from prison. In 1994, the first national election open to all races named Mandela president, ending centuries of white minority rule.

Despite this dramatic political change, social position in South Africa is still based on race. Even with the right to own property, about one-third of black South Africans have no work, and the majority remain dirt poor. The worst off are the 7 million *ukuhleleleka*, which means "marginal people" in the Xhosa language. Soweto-by-the-Sea may sound like a summer getaway, but it is home to thousands of people crammed into shacks made from packing cases, corrugated metal, cardboard, and other discarded materials. There is no electricity for lights or refrigeration. Without plumbing, people use buckets to haul sewerage; women line up to take a turn at a single water tap that serves more than 1,000 people. Jobs are hard to come by, and those who do find work are lucky to earn $200 a month.

South Africa's new president, Thabo Mbeki, elected in 1999, leads a nation still twisted by its history of racial caste. Tourism is up and holds out promise of an economic boom in years to come. But the country can only shed its past by providing real opportunity to all its people.

Sources: Fredrickson (1981), Wren (1991), Hawthorne (1999), and Mabry & Masland (1999).

Meritocracy. Compared to agrarian societies where caste is the rule, industrial societies move toward **meritocracy**, *social stratification based on personal merit*. Because industrial societies need to develop a broad range of abilities (beyond farming), stratification is based not just on the accident of birth but also on "merit"—that is, what job one does and how well one does it. To advance meritocracy, industrial societies expand equality of opportunity, although people expect inequality of outcomes.

In a pure meritocracy, social position would depend entirely on a person's ability and effort. Such a system would have ongoing social mobility, blurring social categories as individuals continuously move up or down in the system depending on their most recent performance.

Caste societies define "merit" (from the Latin, meaning "worthy of praise") as dutifully performing whatever job comes with a person's birth. Caste systems waste human potential, of course, but they are very orderly. And herein lies the answer to an important question: Why do modern, industrial societies keep some elements of caste—such as letting wealth pass from generation to generation—rather than becoming complete meritocracies? Simply because a pure meritocracy erodes families and other social groupings. Economic performance is not *everything*, after all. Would we want to evaluate our family members solely on their jobs? Probably not. Therefore, class systems in industrial societies move toward meritocracy to promote productivity and efficiency but retain some caste elements to maintain order and social cohesion.

Status consistency. **Status consistency** refers to *the degree of consistency in a person's standing across various dimensions of social inequality*. A caste system has little social mobility and high status consistency, so the typical person has the same relative standing with regard to wealth, power, and prestige. The greater mobility of class systems, however, produces less status consistency. In the United States, then, a college professor with an advanced degree might enjoy high social prestige but earn only a modest income. Because of lower status consistency in modern societies, *classes* are less well-defined than *castes*.

An illustration: The United Kingdom. The mix of meritocracy and caste in class systems is well illustrated by the United Kingdom (composed of England, Wales, Scotland, and Northern Ireland), an industrial nation with a long agrarian history.

In the Middle Ages, England had a castelike system of three *estates*. The *first estate* was a hereditary nobility composed of 5 percent of the population who controlled most of the land, which was the chief form of wealth (Laslett, 1984). Most nobles had no occupation at all, since they deemed engaging in trade or doing other work for income "beneath" them. Well-tended by servants, nobles used their leisure time to develop refined tastes in art, music, and literature.

To prevent vast landholdings from being divided by heirs, the law of *primogeniture* (from the Latin,

meaning "first born") stated that all landholdings pass to the oldest son or other male relation. Younger sons had to find other means of support. Some entered the clergy—the *second estate*—where spiritual power was supported by the church's extensive landholdings. Other men of high birth became military officers or lawyers, professions considered honorable for gentlemen. In an age when no woman could inherit her father's property and few women had the chance to earn a living on their own, a noble daughter depended for her security on marrying well.

Below the nobility and the clergy, the vast majority of men and women formed the *third estate*, or commoners. Most commoners were serfs who worked the land owned by nobles. Unlike nobles or clergy, most commoners had little schooling and were illiterate.

As the Industrial Revolution expanded England's economy, some commoners living in cities made enough money to challenge the nobility. More emphasis on meritocracy, the growing importance of money, and the expansion of schooling and legal rights eventually blurred social rankings and gave rise to a class system.

Perhaps it is a sign of the times that, these days, traditional titles are put up for sale by nobles who need money. In 1996, for example, the title "Lord of Wimbledon" was put on the block by Earl Spencer—Princess Diana's brother—to raise the $300,000 he needed to redo the plumbing in one of his large homes (McKee, 1996).

Yet the legacy of England's feudal past remains evident. A small cluster of families still holds considerable inherited wealth and enjoys the highest prestige, admission to elite universities, and political influence. A traditional monarch stands as head of state, and Parliament's House of Lords is composed of "peers," most of noble birth. Even so, actual control of government resides in the House of Commons, where the prime minister and other ministers typically reach their positions through achievement—by winning an election—rather than ascription.

Further down, roughly one-fourth of the British people fall into the "middle class." Some earn comfortable incomes from professions and business and are among the 10 to 15 percent of Britons who own stocks and bonds. Below the middle class, perhaps half of all Britons consider themselves "working class," earning modest incomes through manual work. The remaining one-fourth of the British people make up the lower class, the poor who lack steady work. They are concentrated in the nation's northern and western regions, which are plagued by closings of mines and factories.

After the collapse of the Soviet Union in 1991, that nation began a transition toward a market economy. Since then, some people have become quite rich, but others have lost their jobs as old, inefficient factories closed. As a result, the problem of poverty has become widespread, affecting perhaps one-third of the Russian people. Scenes like this one—a Moscow woman begging for money—have become all too common.

Today's British class system mixes caste elements and meritocracy, producing a highly stratified society with opportunity to move upward or downward. One legacy of the historical estate system, however, is that social mobility occurs less frequently in the United Kingdom than in the United States (Kerckhoff, Campbell, & Winfield-Laird, 1985). The difference in mobility between the two countries is reflected in the importance attached to accent. Distinctive patterns of speech develop when people are set off from one another over many generations. Whereas people in this country treat accent as a clue to where one lives (there is little mistaking a midwestern "twang" or a southern "drawl"), Britons recognize accent as a mark of social class (elites speak the "King's English," while most people speak like "commoners"). So different are these two accents that the British seem to be, as the saying goes, a single people divided by a common language.

CLASSLESS SOCIETIES?

Nowhere in the world do we find a society without some degree of social inequality. Yet some nations have claimed that they are classless.

An illustration: The former Soviet Union. The Union of Soviet Socialist Republics (U.S.S.R.), which has rivaled the United States as a military superpower since the middle of the twentieth century, was born out of revolution in 1917. The Russian Revolution ended the feudal estate system ruled by a hereditary nobility and transferred most farms, factories, and other productive property from private ownership to state control. Following the lead of Karl Marx, who believed that private ownership of property was the basis for social classes, Soviet leaders boasted of becoming a classless society.

Yet high government officials, or *apparatchiks*, ranked highest in the social order, followed by intellectuals and other professionals, manual workers, and, at the lowest level, rural peasantry. The fact that these rankings had very different living standards shows that the former Soviet Union never really became classless.

In 1985, Mikhail Gorbachev came to power with a new economic program known as *perestroika*, meaning "restructuring." Gorbachev saw that, while the Soviet system had reduced economic inequality, everyone was relatively poor and living standards lagged far behind those of other industrial nations. Gorbachev tried to generate economic expansion by reducing inefficient centralized control of the economy.

Gorbachev's reforms turned into one of the most dramatic social movements in history. People throughout Eastern Europe toppled their socialist governments, and, in 1991, the Soviet Union itself collapsed. People blamed their poverty as well as their lack of basic freedoms on a repressive ruling class of Communist party officials. In the Soviet Union, for example, just 6 percent of the population formed the Communist party, which ran the whole country.

The Soviet story shows that social inequality involves more than economic resources. Soviet society may not have had the extremes of wealth and poverty found in Great Britain, Japan, and the United States. But an elite class existed all the same, one based on power rather than wealth.

What about social mobility in so-called classless societies? During the twentieth century, there was as much upward social mobility in the Soviet Union as in Great Britain or the United States. Rapidly expanding industry and government drew many poor rural peasants into factories and offices. This trend illustrates what sociologists call **structural social mobility**, *a shift in the social position of large numbers of people due more to changes in society itself than to individual efforts.*

November 24, 1994, Odessa, Ukraine. The first snow of our voyage flies over the decks as our ship puts in at Odessa, the former Soviet Union's southern port on the Black Sea. Not far from the dock, we gaze up at the Potemkin Steps—the steep stairway up to the city, where the first shots of the Russian Revolution rang out. It has been six years since our last visit and much has changed; indeed, the Soviet Union itself has collapsed. Has life improved? For some people, certainly. There are now chic boutiques in which well-dressed shoppers buy fine wines, designer labels, and imported perfumes. Outside, shiny new Volvos, Mercedes, and even a few Cadillacs stand out against the small Ladas from the "old days." But for most, life seems much worse. Flea markets line the curbs as families sell their home furnishings. When meat sells for $4 a pound and the average person earns just $30 a month, people become desperate. Even the city has to save money by turning off street lights after 8:00 p.m. The spirits of most people seem as dim as Odessa's streets.

During the 1990s, structural social mobility in the Russian Federation turned downward. In fact, between 1990 and 1998, the average life span for Soviet men declined by eight years and for women, two years. Many factors are involved, including Russia's poor health care system, but the Russian people clearly are suffering from a turbulent period of economic change (Róna-Tas, 1994; Specter, 1997b; Bohlen, 1998; Gerber & Hout, 1998).

In the long run, closing inefficient state industries may improve the nation's economic performance. In the short run, however, most citizens face hard times as living standards fall. Moreover, as businesses become privately owned once again, the gulf between rich and poor grows, a trend reflected in Figure 8–1. While some praise the recent changes, others hang on, patiently hoping for a higher standard of living.

IDEOLOGY:
THE POWER BEHIND STRATIFICATION

Noting the extent of social inequality around the world, we might wonder how societies persist without sharing resources more equally. The British estate system lasted for centuries, and for 2,000 years, people in

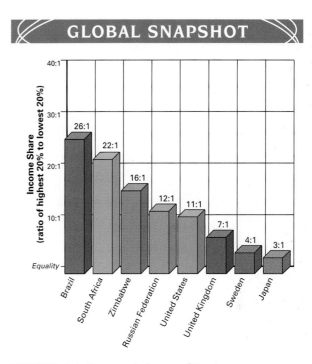

FIGURE 8–1 Economic Inequality in Selected Countries, 1990–1999

These data are the most recent available, representing income share for various years between 1990 and 1999.
Sources: U.S. Census Bureau (2000) and The World Bank (2000).

India accepted the idea that they should be privileged or poor due to the accident of birth.

A major reason that social hierarchies endure is **ideology,** *cultural beliefs that justify social stratification.* Any beliefs—for example, the idea that the rich are smart and the poor are lazy—are ideological to the extent that they define the wealthy as worthy and suggest that poor people deserve their plight.

The ancient Greek philosopher Plato (427–347 B.C.E.) defined *justice* as agreement about who should have what. Every culture, Plato explained, considers some type of inequality "fair." Karl Marx, too, understood this fact, although he was far more critical of inequality than Plato. Marx took capitalist societies to task for defending wealth and power in the hands of a few as a "law of the marketplace." Capitalist law, Marx continued, defines the right to own property and ensures that money stays within the same families from one generation to the next. In short, Marx concluded, culture and institutions combine to shore up a

Medieval Europeans accepted rigid social differences as part of a divine plan for the world. This fifteenth-century painting by the Limbourg brothers shows peasants toiling in the fields while the nobles, who are not to be seen, reside in the castle well-attended by servants.

September: *Harvesting Grapes*, by the Limbourg Brothers. *Très riches heures du duc de Berry* (early 15th century). Victoria and Albert Museum, London, UK. The Bridgeman Art Library.

society's elite, which is why established hierarchies last a long time.

Ideology changes along with a society's economy and technology. Because agrarian societies depend on the routine labor of their people, they develop caste systems that make performing the duties of one's

"station" a moral responsibility. With the rise of industrial capitalism, an ideology of meritocracy arises, defining wealth and power as prizes to be won by those who perform the best. This change means that the poor—often the recipients of charity under feudalism—are scorned under industrial capitalism as personally undeserving. This harsh view is linked with the work of Herbert Spencer, as explained in the box.

History shows how difficult it is to change social stratification. However, challenges to the status quo always arise. Traditional notions about "a woman's place," for example, are losing their power to deprive women of economic opportunity. The continuing struggle for racial equality in South Africa, too, demonstrates widespread rejection of the ideology of apartheid.

THE FUNCTIONS OF SOCIAL STRATIFICATION

Why does social stratification exist at all? According to the structural-functional paradigm, social stratification plays a vital part in the operation of society. This argument was presented more than fifty years ago by Kingsley Davis and Wilbert Moore (1945).

THE DAVIS-MOORE THESIS

The **Davis-Moore thesis** states that *social stratification has beneficial consequences for the operation of a society.* How else, ask Davis and Moore, can we explain the fact that some form of social stratification has been found in every known society?

Davis and Moore note that modern societies have hundreds of occupational positions of varying importance. Certain jobs—say, washing windows or answering a telephone—are fairly easy and can be performed by almost anyone. Other jobs—such as designing new generations of computers—are very difficult and demand the scarce talents of people with extensive (and expensive) training.

Therefore, Davis and Moore explain, the greater the functional importance of a position, the more rewards a society attaches to it. This strategy promotes productivity and efficiency, since rewarding important work with income, prestige, power, or leisure encourages people to do these things, and to work better, longer, and harder. In short, unequal rewards—which is what social stratification is—benefits society as a whole.

Davis and Moore concede that any society can be egalitarian, but only to the extent that people are

CRITICAL THINKING

Is Getting Rich "The Survival of the Fittest"?

"The survival of the fittest"—we have all heard these words used to describe society as a competitive jungle. The phrase was coined by one of sociology's pioneers, Herbert Spencer (1820–1903), whose ideas about social inequality are still widespread today.

Spencer, who lived in England, eagerly followed the work of the natural scientist Charles Darwin (1809–1882). Darwin's theory of biological evolution held that individual members of any species are born with particular traits or characteristics that make them better able to survive and reproduce; through this process of "natural selection," a species changes physically over many generations as it adapts to the natural environment. Spencer, however, distorted Darwin's theory, applying it to the operation of society: Society became the "jungle," with the "fittest"

people rising to wealth and the more deficient gradually sinking into miserable poverty.

It is no surprise that Spencer's views were popular among the rising U.S. industrialists of the day. John D. Rockefeller (1839–1937), who made a vast fortune building the oil industry, recited Spencer's "social gospel" to young children in Sunday school. As Rockefeller saw it, the growth of giant corporations—and the astounding wealth of their owners—was merely the result of the "survival of the fittest," a basic fact of nature. Neither Spencer nor Rockefeller had much sympathy for the poor, seeing poverty as evidence of not measuring up in a competitive world. Spencer opposed social welfare programs for allegedly penalizing society's "best" people (through taxes) and rewarding its "worst" members (through welfare benefits).

Today's sociologists are quick to point out that society is far from a meritocracy, as Spencer contended. Moreover, it is not the case that companies or individuals who generate lots of money necessarily benefit society. Yet, Spencer's view that people more or less get what they deserve in life remains part of our individualistic culture.

What do you think?

1. *What did Herbert Spencer mean when he said that society encourages "the survival of the fittest"?*

2. *Does Spencer's idea square with the fact that about half of rich people gain their wealth through inheritance?*

3. *In what sense do highly paid people benefit society? In what ways do they not?*

willing to let *anyone* perform *any* job. Equality also demands that someone who does a job poorly be rewarded on a par with someone who performs well. Such a system clearly offers little incentive for people to try their best and thereby reduces a society's productive efficiency.

The Davis-Moore thesis suggests why *some* form of stratification exists everywhere; it does not state precisely what rewards a society should give to any occupational position or how unequal rewards should be. Davis and Moore merely point out that positions a society considers crucial must yield sufficient rewards to draw talented people away from less important work.

Critical evaluation. Although the Davis-Moore thesis is an important contribution to sociological analysis, it has provoked criticism. Melvin Tumin (1953) wondered, first, how we assess how important any occupation really is. Perhaps the high rewards our society gives to, say, physicians partly results from deliberate efforts

by medical schools to limit the supply of physicians and thereby increase the demand for their services. Moreover, do rewards actually reflect the contribution one makes to society? With income approaching $100 million per year, television personality Oprah Winfrey earns more in two days than the president of the United States earns all year. Would anyone argue that hosting a talk show is more important than leading a country?

Second, Tumin claimed that Davis and Moore ignore how the caste elements of social stratification can *prevent* the development of individual talent. Born to inequality, rich children may develop their abilities, something many gifted poor children can never do.

Third, by suggesting that social stratification benefits all of society, the Davis-Moore thesis ignores how social inequality promotes conflict and even outright revolution. This criticism leads to the social-conflict paradigm, which provides a very different explanation for social hierarchy.

STRATIFICATION AND CONFLICT

Social-conflict analysis argues that, rather than benefiting society as a whole, stratification provides some people with advantages over others. This analysis draws heavily on the ideas of Karl Marx, with contributions from Max Weber.

KARL MARX: CLASS CONFLICT

As Marx saw it, the Industrial Revolution promised humanity a society free from want. Yet the capitalist economy had done little to improve the lives of most people. Marx devoted his life to explaining a glaring contradiction: how, in a society so rich, so many could be so poor.

In Marx's view, social stratification is rooted in people's relationships to the means of production. Individuals either (1) own productive property or (2) labor for others. In feudal Europe, the nobility and the church owned the productive land; the peasants toiled as farmers. Under industrial capitalism, the nobility was replaced by **capitalists** (sometimes termed the *bourgeoisie*, a French word meaning "of the town"), *people who own factories and other businesses in pursuit of profits.* Serfs became **proletarians**, *people who sell their productive labor for wages.* Capitalists and proletarians have opposing interests, and they are separated by a vast gulf of wealth and power, making class conflict inevitable.

Marx's analysis reflects the capitalism he observed in the nineteenth century, when industry had raised some individuals to great wealth while the vast majority made do with low wages. During this era, wealthy U.S. capitalists like Andrew Carnegie, J. P. Morgan, and John Jacob Astor (one of the few rich passengers to drown on the *Titanic*) lived in fabulous mansions filled with priceless art and staffed by dozens of servants. Even by today's standards, their incomes were staggering. Carnegie, for example, earned more than $20 million in 1900 (the equivalent of more than $100 million in today's dollars), when the average worker's wages totaled perhaps $500 a year (Baltzell, 1964; Pessen, 1990).

In time, Marx believed, the working majority would overthrow the capitalists once and for all. Capitalism would bring about its own downfall, Marx reasoned, by making workers poorer and poorer and giving them little control over the workplace or what they made. Under capitalism, work produces only **alienation**, *the experience of isolation and misery resulting from powerlessness.*

To replace capitalism, Marx imagined a *socialist* system to meet the needs of all rather than just the few. Thus, Marx looked to the future with hope: "The proletarians have nothing to lose but their chains. They have a world to win" (Marx & Engels, 1972:362; orig. 1848).

Critical evaluation. There is no doubt that Marx has had enormous influence on sociological thinking. But seen as a revolutionary—calling for the overthrow of capitalist society—Marx is also highly controversial.

One of the strongest criticisms of the Marxist approach is that it ignores a central idea of the Davis-Moore thesis: that motivating people to do their work well requires a system of unequal rewards. Marx separated reward from performance; his egalitarian ideal was based on the principle "from each according to ability, to each according to need" (Marx & Engels, 1972:388). But severing rewards from performance may be precisely what resulted in the low productivity of the former Soviet Union and other socialist economies around the world. Even so, defenders respond by asking why we assume humanity is inherently selfish rather than social; that is, individual rewards should not be the only way to motivate people to perform their social roles (Clark, 1991; Fiske, 1991).

A second problem is that the revolutionary change Marx predicted has failed to happen, at least in advanced capitalist societies. The next section takes a closer look at this issue.

WHY NO MARXIST REVOLUTION?

Despite Marx's prediction, capitalism is still thriving. Why have industrial workers not overthrown capitalism? Ralf Dahrendorf (1959) proposed four reasons:

1. **The fragmentation of the capitalist class.**
   Today, tens of millions of stockholders rather than single families own most large companies. Moreover, day-to-day corporate operations are in the hands of a large managerial class, whose members may or may not be major stockholders. With stock so widely held—by 2000, about 50 percent of the U.S. population was "in the market"—more and more people have a direct stake in the capitalist system.

2. **A higher standard of living**. As Chapter 12 ("Economics and Politics") explains, a century ago most U.S. workers were in factories or on

TABLE 8–1 Two Explanations of Social Stratification: A Summary

Structural-Functional Paradigm	Social-Conflict Paradigm
Social stratification keeps society operating. Linking greater rewards to more important social positions benefits society as a whole.	Social stratification is the result of social conflict. Differences in social resources serve the interests of some and harm others.
Social stratification matches talents and abilities to appropriate occupational positions.	Social stratification ensures that much talent and ability in society will not be developed at all.
Social stratification is both useful and inevitable.	Social stratification is useful only to some people; it is not inevitable.
The values and beliefs that legitimize social inequality are widely shared throughout society.	Values and beliefs tend to be ideological; they reflect the interests of the more powerful members of society.
Because systems of social stratification are useful to society as a whole and are supported by cultural values and beliefs, they are usually stable over time.	Because systems of social stratification reflect the interests of only part of society, they are unlikely to remain stable over time.

Source: Adapted, in part, from Arthur L. Stinchcombe, "Some Empirical Consequences of the Davis-Moore Theory of Stratification," *American Sociological Review*, Vol. 28, No. 5 (October 1963):808.

farms performing **blue-collar occupations,** *lower-prestige work that involves mostly manual labor.* Today, most workers hold **white-collar occupations,** *higher-prestige work that involves mostly mental activity.* These jobs are in sales, management, and other service fields. Most of today's white-collar workers do not think of themselves as an "industrial proletariat." Just as important, the average income in the United States rose almost tenfold over the course of the twentieth century, even allowing for inflation, and the workweek decreased. As a result, most workers see themselves as better off than their parents and grandparents, a case of structural mobility helping people accept the status quo (Edwards, 1979; Gagliani, 1981; Wright & Martin, 1987).

3. **More worker organizations.** Employees have an organizational clout that they lacked a century ago. Workers have the right to form labor unions that, backed by threats of work slowdowns and strikes, make demands of management. In other words, worker-management disputes are settled without threatening the capitalist system.

4. **More extensive legal protections.** During the twentieth century, new laws made the workplace safer, and unemployment insurance, disability protection, and Social Security now provide workers with greater financial security.

A counterpoint. These developments suggest that our society has smoothed many of capitalism's rough edges. Yet, many claim that Marx's analysis of

capitalism is still largely valid (Miliband, 1969; Edwards, 1979; Giddens, 1982; Domhoff, 1983; Stephens, 1986). First, wealth remains highly concentrated, with about 40 percent of all property owned by 1 percent of our population (Keister, 2000). Second, many of today's white-collar jobs offer no more income, security, or satisfaction than factory work did a century ago. Third, many benefits enjoyed by today's workers came about through the class conflict Marx described, and workers still struggle to hold on to what they have. Fourth, while workers have gained legal protections, the law has not helped ordinary people use the legal system as effectively as the rich use it. Therefore, social-conflict theorists conclude, the absence of a socialist revolution in the United States does not necessarily negate Marx's analysis of capitalism.

Table 8–1 summarizes the two contrasting explanations of social stratification.

MAX WEBER: CLASS, STATUS, AND POWER

Max Weber agreed with Karl Marx that social stratification causes social conflict, but he viewed Marx's two-class model as simplistic. Instead, he thought social stratification resulted from the interplay of three distinct kinds of inequality.

The first dimension is economic inequality—the issue so vital to Marx—which Weber termed *class* position. Weber did not think of "classes" as well-defined categories but as a continuum ranging from high to low. Weber's second dimension is *status*, or social prestige, and the third is *power*.

The early industrial era, according to Simon Kuznets, is marked by extreme social inequality that affords aristocratic people a life of leisure while others toil at manual labor for pennies a day. U.S. artist Ford Madox Brown (1821–1893) captures such class distinctions in his painting, Work. *Today, more than a century after Brown lived, do you think class differences in the United States have become smaller or greater? Why?*

Ford Madox Brown (1821–1893), *Work*, Superstock, Inc.

The socioeconomic status hierarchy. Marx viewed prestige and power as simple reflections of economic position, and did not treat them as distinct dimensions of inequality. But Weber noted that status consistency in modern societies is often quite low: A local official, say, might wield considerable power yet have little wealth or social prestige.

Weber's contribution, then, is characterizing stratification in industrial societies as a multidimensional ranking rather than a hierarchy of clearly defined classes. In line with Weber's thinking, sociologists use the term **socioeconomic status (SES)** to refer to *a composite ranking based on various dimensions of social inequality.*

Inequality in history. Weber observed that each of his three dimensions of social inequality stands out at a different time in the evolution of human societies.

Status, or social prestige, is the main dimension of difference in agrarian societies, taking the form of honor. Members of these societies gain prestige by conforming to cultural norms corresponding to their rank.

Industrialization and the development of capitalism level traditional rankings based on birth but generate striking financial inequality. Thus, Weber argued, the crucial difference among industrial people is the economic dimension of class.

Over time, industrial societies witness the growth of a bureaucratic state. Bigger government and the spread of all kinds of other organizations make power more important in the stratification system. Especially in socialist societies, where government regulates many aspects of life, high-ranking officials become the new ruling elite.

This historical analysis points to a final difference between Weber and Marx. Marx thought societies could eliminate social stratification by abolishing private ownership of productive property. Weber doubted that overthrowing capitalism would significantly diminish social stratification. It might lessen economic disparity, he reasoned, but socialism would increase inequality by expanding government and concentrating power in the hands of a political elite. Popular uprisings against entrenched bureaucracies in Eastern Europe and the former Soviet Union support Weber's position.

Critical evaluation. Weber's multidimensional view of social stratification has enormously influenced sociologists. But critics (particularly those who favor Marx's ideas) argue that, although social class boundaries may have blurred, all industrial nations still show striking patterns of social inequality. Moreover, as we shall see presently, economic inequality has increased recently in the United States. Thus, while some people favor Weber's multidimensional hierarchy, others think that Marx's view of the rich versus the poor is closer to the mark.

STRATIFICATION AND TECHNOLOGY: A GLOBAL PERSPECTIVE

We can weave together a number of observations made in this chapter by considering the relationship between a society's technology and its type of social stratification. This analysis draws on Gerhard Lenski and Jean Lenski's model of sociocultural evolution discussed in Chapter 2 ("Culture").

With simple technology, hunters and gatherers produce only what is necessary for day-to-day living. Some people may produce more than others, but the group's survival depends on all sharing what they have. Thus, no categories of people emerge as better off than others.

But as technological advances generate a surplus, social inequality increases. In horticultural and pastoral societies, a small elite controls most of the surplus. Larger-scale agriculture is more productive still, and striking inequality—as great as any time in history—places the nobility in an almost godlike position over the masses.

Industrialization turns the tide, nudging inequality downward. Prompted by the need to develop people's talents, meritocracy takes hold and erodes the power of traditional elites. Industrial productivity also raises the living standards of the historically poor majority. Furthermore, specialized work demands schooling for all, sharply reducing illiteracy. A literate population, in turn, presses for a greater voice in political decision making, reducing social inequality and lessening male domination of women.

Over time, wealth becomes less concentrated, countering the trend predicted by Marx. In the 1920s, the richest 1 percent of the U.S. population owned about 36 percent of all wealth, a figure that fell to 30 percent by the 1980s (Williamson & Lindert, 1980; Beeghley, 1989; *1991 Green Book*). This trend helps explain why Marxist revolutions took place in *agrarian* societies—such as Russia (1917), Cuba (1959), and Nicaragua (1979)—where economic inequality is much greater, rather than in *industrial* societies as Marx predicted. Worth noting, however, is that wealth inequality turned up again after 1990 (Keister, 2000).

In human history, then, technological advance first increases but then moderates the intensity of social stratification. Greater inequality is functional for agrarian societies, but industrial societies benefit

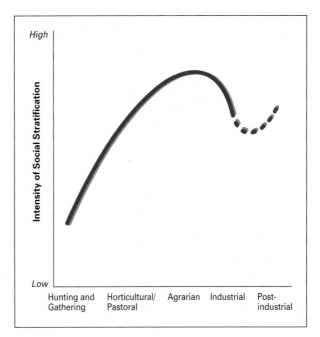

FIGURE 8–2 Social Stratification and Technological Development: The Kuznets Curve

The Kuznets curve shows that greater technological sophistication is generally accompanied by more pronounced social stratification. The trend reverses itself, however, as industrial societies relax rigid castelike distinctions in favor of greater opportunity and equality under the law. Political rights are more widely extended, and there is even some leveling of economic differences. The Kuznets curve may also be usefully applied to the relative social standing of the two sexes. The emergence of postindustrial society, however, has brought an upturn in economic inequality, as indicated by the broken line added by the author.

Source: Created by the author, based on Kuznets (1955) and Lenski (1966).

from a less unequal system. This historical pattern, recognized by the Nobel Prize–winning economist Simon Kuznets (1955, 1966), is illustrated by the Kuznets curve, shown in Figure 8–2.

Patterns of global inequality square with the Kuznets curve. Global Map 8–1 shows that industrial nations have somewhat less income inequality than predominantly agrarian countries (common in Latin America and Africa). Of course, income disparity reflects not just technology but also political and economic priorities. Countries that have had socialist economies (including the People's Republic of China)

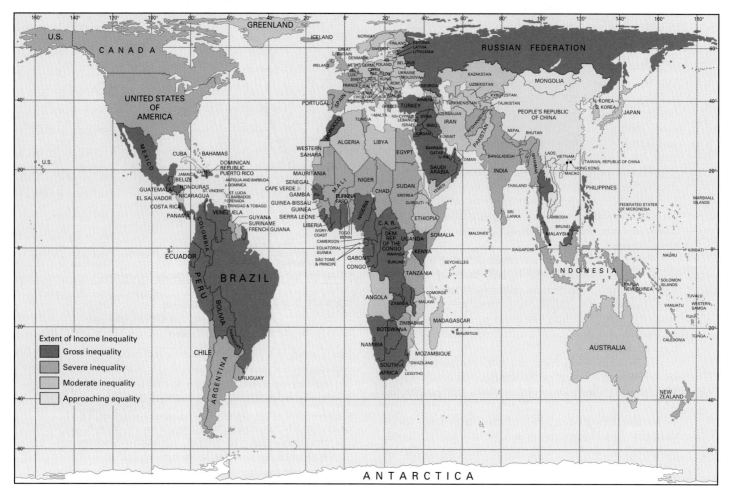

GLOBAL MAP 8–1 Income Disparity in Global Perspective

Societies throughout the world differ in the rigidity and extent of social stratification as well as in overall standard of living. This map highlights income inequality. Generally speaking, countries that have centralized, socialist economies (including the People's Republic of China and Cuba) display the least income inequality, although their standard of living is relatively low. Postindustrial societies with predominantly capitalist economies, including the United States and most of Western Europe, have higher overall living standards accompanied by severe income disparity. The less economically developed countries of Latin America and Africa (including Mexico, Brazil, and the Democratic Republic of the Congo), as well as the Russian Federation and much of the Arab world, exhibit the most pronounced inequality of income.

Sources: *Peters Atlas of the World* (1990); updates by the author from United Nations Development Programme (1999).

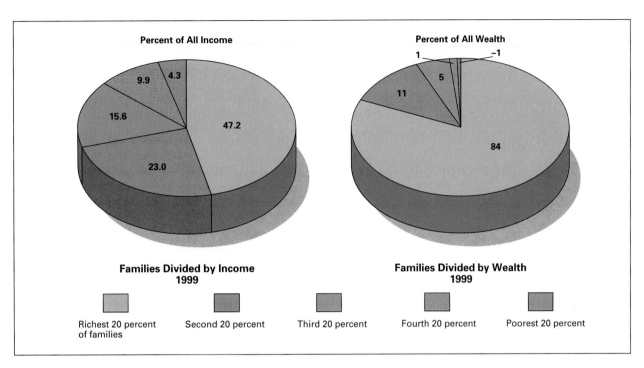

Percent of All Income

9.9   4.3
15.6
47.2
23.0

**Families Divided by Income
1999**

Percent of All Wealth

1 ⎯   ⎯ –1
5
11
84

**Families Divided by Wealth
1999**

☐ Richest 20 percent of families ☐ Second 20 percent ☐ Third 20 percent ☐ Fourth 20 percent ☐ Poorest 20 percent

FIGURE 8–3 Distribution of Income and Wealth in the United States

Sources: Income data from U.S. Census Bureau (2000); wealth data are author estimates based on Keister (2000) and Russell & Mogelonsky (2000).

display less income inequality, albeit with a rather low standard of living overall. They also have pronounced inequality on noneconomic dimensions such as political power.

And what of the future? Notice that in Figure 8–2 we extend the trend described by Kuznets to the postindustrial era (the broken line) to show social inequality on the upswing once again. That is, as the Information Revolution moves ahead, we are experiencing some economic polarization, suggesting that the long-term trend may differ from what Kuznets observed half a century ago (Nielsen & Alderson, 1997).

INEQUALITY IN THE UNITED STATES

The United States stands apart from most European nations in never having had a titled aristocracy. With the significant exception of our racial history, we have never known a caste system that rigidly ranks categories of people.

Even so, U.S. society is highly stratified. Not only do the rich have most of the money, they also receive the most schooling, enjoy the best health, and consume the lion's share of goods and services. Such

privilege contrasts sharply with the poverty of millions of women and men who worry about paying next month's rent or a doctor's bill if a child becomes ill. Many people think the United States is a middle-class society, but is this really the case?

INCOME, WEALTH, AND POWER

One important dimension of economic inequality is **income,** *wages or salary from work and earnings from investments.* The Census Bureau reports median U.S. family income in 1999 as $49,940. The first part of Figure 8–3 shows the distribution of income among all U.S. families.[1] The richest 20 percent of families (those earning at least $88,082 annually, with a mean

---

[1]The Census Bureau reports both mean and median incomes for families ("two or more persons related by blood, marriage, or adoption") and households ("two or more persons sharing a living unit"). In 1999, mean family income was $63,522, higher than the median because high-income families pull the mean (but not the median) upward. For households, these figures are somewhat lower—a mean of $54,842 and a median of $40,816—largely because families average 3.2 persons while households average 2.6.

TABLE 8-2 U.S. Family Income, 1999	
Highest paid . . .	Annually earns at least . . .
0.5%	$1,400,000
1	320,000
5	155,000
10	105,000
20	88,000
30	70,000
40	59,000
50	50,000
60	40,000
70	30,000
80	23,000
90	10,000

Sources: Kennickell, Starr-McCluer, & Surette (2000), U.S. Census Bureau (2000), and author calculations.

of $147,779) received 47.2 percent of all income, while the bottom 20 percent (those earning less than $22,826, with a mean of $13,320) received only 4.3 percent.

Table 8–2 takes a closer look at income distribution. In 1999, the highest-paid 5 percent of U.S. families earned six-figure incomes (averaging $254,840), or 20.3 percent of all income, more than the total earnings of the lowest-paid 40 percent. At the very top of the pyramid, the richest half of 1 percent earned at least $1.4 million. In short, while a small number of people earn very high incomes, the majority make do with far less.

Income is only one component of a person's or family's **wealth,** *the total value of money and other assets, minus outstanding debts.* Wealth—including stocks, bonds, and real estate—is distributed even less equally than income.

The second part of Figure 8–3 shows the approximate distribution of wealth in the United States. The richest 20 percent of U.S. families own roughly four-fifths of the country's entire wealth. High up in this privileged category are the top 5 percent of families—the "very rich," who own 60 percent of all property. Richer still—with wealth into the tens of millions—are the 1 percent of families that qualify as "super rich" and possess about 40 percent of this nation's privately held resources (Keister, 2000). And capping the wealth pyramid, the one dozen richest U.S. families have a combined net worth exceeding $330 billion (*Forbes,* 2000). This equals the total property of 4.5 million average families, including enough people to fill the cities of Chula Vista, California; Colorado

Springs, Colorado; Chicago, Illinois; Cleveland, Ohio; Chattanooga, Tennessee; Charlotte, North Carolina; and Clearwater, Florida.

The wealth of the average U.S. household, currently about $71,600, rose throughout the 1990s. This figure reflects the total value of homes, cars, investments, insurance policies, retirement pensions, furniture, clothing, and all other personal property, minus a home mortgage and other debts. The wealth of average people is not only less than that of the rich, however, it is also different in kind. While most people's wealth centers on a home and a car—property that generates no income—the greater wealth of the rich is mostly in the form of stocks and other income-producing investments.

When financial assets are balanced against debits, the lowest-ranking 40 percent of families have virtually no wealth at all. The negative percentage shown in Figure 8–3 for the poorest 20 percent means that these families actually live in debt.

In the United States, wealth is an important source of power. Therefore, the small proportion of families that controls most of the wealth also has the ability to shape the agenda of the entire society. As explained in Chapter 12 ("Economics and Politics"), some sociologists argue that such concentrated wealth undermines democracy because the political system serves the interests of the "super rich" families.

OCCUPATIONAL PRESTIGE

Beyond generating income, work is also an important source of prestige. We commonly evaluate each other according to the kind of work we do, respecting those who do what we consider important work and looking down on others with less prestigious jobs.

Sociologists monitor the relative social prestige of various occupations (Counts, 1925; Hodge, Treiman, & Rossi, 1966; NORC, 1999). Table 8–3 shows that people accord high prestige to occupations—such as physicians, lawyers, and engineers—that require extensive training and generate high income. By contrast, less prestigious work—as a waitress or janitor, for example—not only pays less but requires less ability and schooling. Occupational prestige rankings are much the same in all industrial societies (Ma, 1987; Lin & Xie, 1988).

In any society, high-prestige occupations go to privileged categories of people. In Table 8–3, for example, the highest-ranking occupations are dominated by men. Only thirteen jobs down the list do we find "registered nurse," where most workers are women.

TABLE 8–3 The Relative Social Prestige of Selected Occupations in the United States

White-collar Occupations	Prestige Score	Blue-collar Occupations	White-collar Occupations	Prestige Score	Blue-collar Occupations
Physician	86		Funeral director	49	
Lawyer	75		Realtor	49	
College/university professor	74		Bookkeeper	47	
Architect	73			47	Machinist
Chemist	73			47	Mail carrier
Physicist/astronomer	73		Musician/composer	47	
Aerospace engineer	72			46	Secretary
Dentist	72		Photographer	45	
Member of the clergy	69		Bank teller	43	
Psychologist	69			42	Tailor
Pharmacist	68			42	Welder
Optometrist	67			40	Farmer
Registered nurse	66			40	Telephone operator
Secondary-school teacher	66			39	Carpenter
Accountant	65			36	Brick/stone mason
Athlete	65			36	Child-care worker
Electrical engineer	64		File clerk	36	
Elementary-school teacher	64			36	Hairdresser
Economist	63			35	Baker
Veterinarian	62			34	Bulldozer operator
Airplane pilot	61			31	Auto body repairperson
Computer programmer	61		Retail apparel salesperson	30	
Sociologist	61			30	Truck driver
Editor/reporter	60		Cashier	29	
	60	Police officer		28	Elevator operator
Actor	58			28	Garbage collector
Radio/TV announcer	55			28	Taxi driver
Librarian	54			28	Waiter/waitress
	53	Aircraft mechanic		27	Bellhop
	53	Firefighter		25	Bartender
Dental hygienist	52			23	Farm laborer
Painter/sculptor	52			23	Household laborer
Social worker	52			22	Door-to-door salesperson
	51	Electrician		22	Janitor
Computer operator	50			09	Shoe shiner

Source: Adapted from *General Social Surveys 1972–1998: Cumulative Codebook* (Chicago: National Opinion Research Center, 1999), pp. 1223–41.

Similarly, many of the lowest-prestige jobs are commonly performed by people of color.

SCHOOLING

Industrial societies expand opportunities for schooling, but some people still receive much more than others. Table 8–4 on page 204 shows the schooling for U.S. women and men aged twenty-five and over. In 1999, while 84 percent had completed high school, only about 26 percent were college graduates.

Schooling affects both occupation and income, since most (but not all) of the better-paying, white-collar jobs shown in Table 8–3 require a college degree or other advanced study. By contrast, most blue-collar jobs, which bring lower income and social prestige, require less schooling.

ANCESTRY, RACE, AND GENDER

A class system rewards individual talent and effort. But nothing affects one's social standing as much as birth into a particular family. Ancestry has a strong bearing on future schooling, occupation, and income. Research suggests that at least half of our country's richest individuals—those with hundreds of millions of dollars in wealth—derived their fortunes mostly from inheritance (Thurow, 1987; Queenan, 1989). By

TABLE 8–4 Schooling of U.S. Adults, 1999 (aged 25 and over)		
	Women	**Men**
Not a high school graduate	**16.0%**	**15.8%**
8 years or less	6.8	7.1
9–11 years	9.2	8.7
High school graduate	**84.0**	**84.2**
High school only	34.3	31.9
1–3 years college	26.1	24.5
College graduate or more	23.6	27.8

Source: U.S. Census Bureau (2000).

the same token, inherited poverty just as surely shapes the future of many others.

Race, too, is closely linked to social position in the United States. White people have a higher overall occupational standing than African Americans, and also receive more schooling. Thus, the median African American family income was $33,805 in 1999, just 65 percent of the $51,912 earned by white families. This disparity makes a real difference in people's lives. White families, for example, are more likely to own their homes (70 percent do) than black families (46 percent) (U.S. Census Bureau, 2000).

Much of the racial disparity in income is due to the larger proportion of single-parent families among African Americans. Comparing only families that include a married couple, African American families earned 89 percent as much as white families.

Over time, as Figure 8–4 shows, this income differential builds into a considerable "wealth gap." A recent survey of households by the Federal Reserve found that median wealth for minorities, including African Americans, Hispanics, and Asian Americans ($16,400), is just 17 percent of the median ($94,900) for whites.

Social ranking involves ethnicity as well. Historically, people of English ancestry have enjoyed the most wealth and wielded the greatest power in the United States. The rapidly growing Latino population, by contrast, has long been disadvantaged. In 1999, median income among Hispanic families was $33,077, 64 percent of the comparable figure for all white families. A detailed examination of how race and ethnicity affect social standing is presented in Chapter 11 ("Race and Ethnicity").

Of course, both men and women are found in families at every social level. Yet, on average, women have less income, wealth, and occupational prestige than men. Even more important, households headed by women are ten times more likely to be poor than those headed by men. Chapter 10 ("Gender Stratification") fully examines the link between gender and social stratification.

SOCIAL CLASSES IN THE UNITED STATES

As we have explained, rankings in a caste system are rigid and obvious to all. Defining the social categories in a more fluid class system, however, is not so easy. Followers of Karl Marx see two major social classes—capitalists and proletariat. Other sociologists, however, find as many as six classes (Warner & Lunt, 1941) or even seven (Coleman & Rainwater, 1978). Still others side with Max Weber, believing that people form not clear-cut classes but a multidimensional status hierarchy.

Defining classes in the United States is difficult because of the relatively low level of status consistency. Especially toward the middle of the hierarchy, people's social position on one dimension may contradict their standing on another. A government official, for example, may have the power to administer a multimillion-dollar budget yet earn a modest personal income. Similarly, many members of the clergy enjoy ample prestige but only moderate power and low pay. Or consider a lucky day trader in the stock market who wins no special respect but makes a lot of money.

Finally, the social mobility characteristic of class systems—again, most pronounced near the middle—means that social position may change during a person's lifetime, further blurring class boundaries. With these problems in mind, we can describe four general rankings: the upper class, the middle class, the working class, and the lower class.

THE UPPER CLASS

Families in the upper class—5 percent of the U.S. population—earn at least $155,000 annually, and some earn ten times that much. As a general rule, the more a family's income comes from inherited wealth in the form of stocks and bonds, real estate, and other investments, the stronger a family's claim to being upper class.

In 2000, *Forbes* magazine profiled the richest 400 people in the United States, noting that they had a *minimum* net worth of $725 million and included 284 billionaires. The upper class are Karl Marx's "capitalists"—those who own the means of production and, thus, most of the nation's private wealth. Many upper-class people work as top executives in large corporations and as senior government officials. Historically, though less so today, the upper class has been composed of white Anglo-Saxon Protestants (WASPs) (Baltzell, 1964, 1976, 1988).

Upper-uppers. The *upper-upper class*, sometimes called "blue bloods" or simply "society," includes less than 1 percent of the U.S. population (Warner & Lunt, 1941; Coleman & Neugarten, 1971; Baltzell, 1995). Membership is almost always the result of birth, as suggested by the quip that the easiest way to become an upper-upper is to be born one. Most of these families possess enormous wealth that is primarily inherited. For this reason, members of the upper-upper class are said to have *old money*.

Set apart by their wealth, upper-uppers live in exclusive neighborhoods, such as Beacon Hill in Boston, the Rittenhouse Square section of Philadelphia, the Gold Coast of Chicago, and Nob Hill in San Francisco. Their children typically attend private schools with others of similar background and complete their formal education at high-prestige colleges and universities. In the historical pattern of European aristocrats, they study liberal arts rather than vocational skills. Women of the upper-upper class often do volunteer work for charitable organizations; while helping the larger community, these activities also build networks that broaden this elite's power (Ostrander, 1980, 1984).

Lower-uppers. Most upper-class people actually fall into the *lower-upper class*. To most of us, the 3 or 4 percent of the U.S. population in this category seem every bit as privileged as the upper-upper class. The major difference is that lower-uppers are the "working rich"; earnings rather than inherited wealth are the primary source of their income. While so-called "new rich" families generally live in expensive neighborhoods, most do not gain entry into the clubs and associations of "old money" families.

THE MIDDLE CLASS

Including 40 to 45 percent of the U.S. population, the large middle class has a tremendous influence on our culture. Television and movies usually show middle-class people, and most commercial advertising is directed at these average consumers. The middle class contains far more ethnic and racial diversity than the upper class.

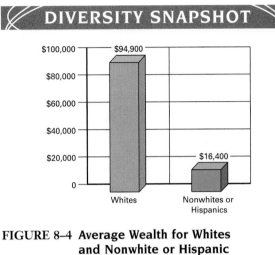

DIVERSITY SNAPSHOT

FIGURE 8–4 Average Wealth for Whites and Nonwhite or Hispanic Minorities, 1998

Source: Kennickell, Starr-McCluer, & Surette (2000).

Upper-middles. The top half of this category is termed the *upper-middle class*, based on their above-average income in the range of $80,000 to $140,000 a year. Such income allows upper-middle-class families to accumulate considerable property—a comfortable house in a fairly expensive area, several automobiles, and investments. Two-thirds of upper-middle-class children receive college educations, and postgraduate degrees are common. Many go on to high-prestige occupations as physicians, engineers, lawyers, accountants, or business executives. Lacking the power of the richest people to influence national or international events, upper-middles often play an important role in local political affairs.

Average-middles. The rest of the middle class falls close to the center of the U.S. class structure. *Average-middles* typically work in less prestigious white-collar occupations as bank tellers, middle managers, or sales clerks or in highly skilled blue-collar jobs such as electrical work and carpentry. Household income falls between $40,000 and $60,000 a year, which is roughly the national average.

Middle-class people generally accumulate a small amount of wealth over the course of their working lives, mostly in the form of a house and a retirement account. Most middle-class men and women are likely to be high school graduates, but the odds are just fifty-fifty that they will complete a college degree, usually at a less expensive, state-supported school.

Sometimes whole neighborhoods rise or fall due to a changing economy. The photo on the left, taken in 1979, shows Fern Street in Camden, New Jersey, as a stable though modest urban neighborhood. A decade later after several major industries closed their doors, the same neighborhood has the look of a ghost town.

THE WORKING CLASS

About one-third of the population is working class (sometimes called the *lower-middle class*). In Marxist terms, the working class forms the core of the industrial proletariat. Their blue-collar occupations generally yield a family income of between $20,000 and $40,000 a year, somewhat below the national average, and they have little or no wealth. Working-class families, thus, are vulnerable to financial problems caused by unemployment or illness.

Many working-class jobs provide little personal satisfaction—requiring discipline but rarely imagination—and subject workers to continual supervision. These jobs also offer fewer benefits, such as medical insurance and pension plans. About half of working-class families own their homes, usually in lower-cost neighborhoods. College is a goal that only about one-third of working-class children realize.

THE LOWER CLASS

The remaining 20 percent of our population make up the lower class. Low income makes their lives insecure and difficult. In 1999, the federal government classified 32.3 million people (11.8 percent of the population) as poor. Millions more—called the "working poor"—are just slightly better off, holding low-prestige jobs that provide little satisfaction and minimal income. Barely

half manage to complete high school, and only one in four ever reaches college.

Society segregates the lower class, especially when the poor are racial or ethnic minorities. About 40 percent of lower-class families own their own home, typically in the least desirable neighborhoods. Although poor neighborhoods are found in inner cities, lower-class families also live in rural areas, especially across the South.

THE DIFFERENCE CLASS MAKES

September 2, 1995, Mount Vernon, Ohio. My bike leans right, leaving the trail for the rest station that offers a stretch and a drink of water. Here I encounter Linda, a thirty-something woman having trouble with her roller blades. Eye contact and a perplexed look are a call for help, so I walk over to see what I might offer. Several of her boot buckles require adjustment. Close up, she doesn't look well. "Are you OK?" I inquire. "Very tired," Linda responds, and goes on to explain why. Now divorced, she cannot pay off her debts with one low-income job, an 11 A.M. to 7 P.M. shift as a computer clerk at a bank in town. Catching four hours of sleep after work, she then drives an hour to Columbus, where she sits at another computer, processing catalog orders from 2 a.m. until 10 a.m. That leaves just enough time to drive back to Mount Vernon to start all over again at the bank.

HEALTH

Health is closely related to social standing. Children born into poor families are three times more likely to die from disease, neglect, accidents, or violence during their first year of life than children born into privileged families. Among adults, people with above-average incomes are twice as likely as low-income people to describe their health as excellent. Moreover, richer people live, on average, seven years longer because they eat more nutritious foods, live in safer and less stressful environments, and receive better medical care (U.S. National Center for Health Statistics, 1999).

VALUES AND ATTITUDES

Some cultural values, too, vary from class to class. The "old rich" have an unusually strong sense of family history since their position is based on wealth passed down from generation to generation (Baltzell, 1979). Secure in their birthright privileges, upper-uppers also favor understated manners and tastes, while many "new rich" people practice *conspicuous consumption*, using homes, cars, and even airplanes as *status symbols* that make a statement about their social position.

Affluent people with greater education and financial security are also more tolerant of controversial behavior such as homosexuality. Working-class people, who grow up in an atmosphere of greater supervision and discipline and are less likely to attend college, tend to be less tolerant (Kohn, 1977; NORC, 1999).

Political affiliations, too, flow along class lines. By and large, more privileged people support the Republican party while those with fewer advantages favor the Democrats. But, issue by issue, the pattern is more complex. A desire to protect wealth prompts well-off people to take a more conservative approach to *economic* issues, favoring, for example, lower taxes. But on *social* matters—such as abortion and gay rights—highly educated, more affluent people are

Compared to high-income people, low-income people are half as likely to report good health and, on average, live about seven fewer years. The toll of low income—played out in inadequate nutrition, little medical care, and high stress— is easy to see on the faces of the poor, who look old before their time.

more liberal. People of lower social standing, on the other hand, tend to be economic liberals, favoring government social programs, but support a more conservative social agenda (Erikson, Luttbeg, & Tedin, 1980; NORC, 1999).

FAMILY AND GENDER

Finally, social class also shapes family life. Generally, lower-class families are somewhat larger than middle-class families, due to earlier marriage and less use of birth control. In addition, working-class parents encourage children to conform to conventional norms and respect authority figures. Parents of higher social standing transmit a different "cultural capital" to their children, teaching them to express their individuality

Industrial class systems provide the opportunity for social mobility—both upward and downward. Typically, social mobility is modest and gradual. Sociologists track this change by comparing the social standing of people in different generations of the same family—for example, in the achievement of a son that makes his father proud.

and imagination more freely (Kohn, 1977; McLeod, 1995).

Of course, the more money a family has, the better parents can develop their children's talents and abilities. For example, an affluent family earning $92,700 a year will spend $233,850 raising a child born in 1999 to the age of eighteen. Middle-class people, with income of $49,000 a year, will spend $160,140, and families earning less than $36,800 will spend $117,390 (Lino, 2000). Privilege, then, tends to beget privilege as family life reproduces the class structure in each generation.

Class also shapes our world of relationships. Elizabeth Bott (1971) found that most working-class couples divide their responsibilities according to gender roles; middle-class couples, by contrast, are more egalitarian, sharing more activities and expressing greater intimacy. More recently, Karen Walker (1995) discovered that working-class friendships typically provide material assistance; middle-class friendships, however, are likely to involve shared interests and leisure pursuits.

SOCIAL MOBILITY

Ours is a dynamic society marked by significant social movement. Earning a college degree, landing a higher-paying job, or marrying someone who earns a high income contribute to *upward social mobility*, while dropping out of school, losing a job, or becoming divorced (especially for women) may signal *downward social mobility*.

Over the long term, though, social mobility is not so much a matter of individual changes as changes in society itself. During the first half of the twentieth century, for example, industrialization expanded the U.S. economy, pushing up living standards. Even without being very good swimmers, so to speak, people rode a rising tide of prosperity. More recently, structural social mobility in a downward direction has dealt many people economic setbacks.

Sociologists distinguish between shorter- and longer-term changes in social position. **Intragenerational social mobility** refers to *a change in social position occurring during a person's lifetime.* **Intergenerational social mobility,** *upward or downward social mobility of children in relation to their parents,* is important because it reveals long-term changes in society that affect almost everyone.

MYTH VERSUS REALITY

In few societies do people think about "getting ahead" as much as in the United States. Moving up, after all, is the American Dream. But is there as much social mobility as we like to think?

Studies of intergenerational mobility (almost all of which, unfortunately, have focused exclusively on men) show that almost 40 percent of the sons of blue-collar workers attained white-collar jobs and about 30 percent of sons born into white-collar families ended up doing blue-collar work. *Horizontal social mobility*—changing occupation at one class level—is even more common so that, overall, about 80 percent of sons showed some type of social mobility in relation to their fathers (Blau & Duncan, 1967; Featherman & Hauser, 1978; Hout, 1998).

Research points to four general conclusions about social mobility in the United States:

1. **Social mobility, at least among men, has been fairly high.** The widespread notion that the United States has a lot of social mobility is true. Mobility is what we would expect in an industrial class system.

2. **The long-term trend in social mobility has been upward.** Industrialization, which greatly expanded the U.S. economy, and the growth of white-collar work over the course of the twentieth century, have boosted living standards.

3. **Within a single generation, social mobility is usually small.** Most young families increase their income over time (Duncan et al., 1998). Yet very few people move from "rags to riches." While sharp rises or falls in individual fortunes may attract public attention, most social mobility involves limited movement *within* one class level rather than dramatic moves *between* classes.

4. **Social mobility since the 1970s has been uneven.** Real income (that is, adjusted for inflation) rose during the twentieth century until the 1970s, when it hit a plateau. During the 1980s, real income remained stagnant for many people, rising again by the end of the 1990s. But these general trends mask the experiences of different categories of people, as the next section explains.

MOBILITY BY INCOME LEVEL

In Figure 8–5, we see how U.S. families at different income levels fared between 1980 and 1999. Well-to-do families (the highest 20 percent, but not all the same families over the entire period) saw their incomes jump 48 percent, from an average $99,693 in 1980 to $147,779 in 1999. People in the middle of the population also had gains, albeit more modest ones. The lowest-income 20 percent saw only a 2.6 percent increase in earnings.

For families at the top of the income scale (the highest 1 percent), the last fifteen years have been a windfall. These families, with average income of $132,451 in 1980, were making $500,000 in 1999—almost four times as much (Edmondson, 1995; Nielsen & Alderson, 1997; U.S. Census Bureau, 2000).

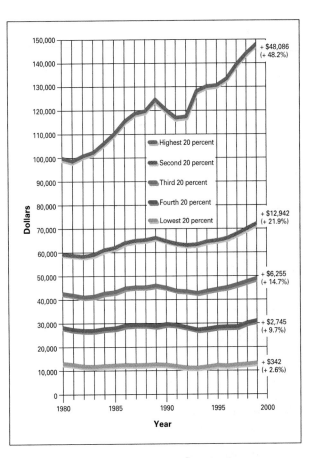

FIGURE 8–5 Mean Income, U.S. Families, 1980–1999 (in 1999 dollars, adjusted for inflation)

Source: U.S. Census Bureau (2000).

MOBILITY: RACE, CLASS, AND GENDER

White people, in a more privileged position to begin with, have been more upwardly mobile in recent decades than people of African or Hispanic ancestry. Through the economic expansion of the 1980s and 1990s, more African Americans entered the ranks of the wealthy. But, overall, the real income of African Americans has changed little in two decades. African Americans earned nearly the same percentage of white family income in 1999 (65 percent) as in 1970 (61 percent). Compared to white families, Latinos lost ground between 1975 (when their average income was 67 percent of white family income) and 1999 (when it had fallen to 64 percent) (Featherman & Hauser, 1978; Pomer, 1986; U.S. Census Bureau, 2000).

Historically, women have had less chance for upward mobility than men, since most working women hold clerical jobs (such as secretary) and service positions (like waitress) that offer few promotions. In addition, when marriages end in divorce (as almost half do), women commonly experience downward social mobility, since they may lose not only income but a host of benefits, including health care and insurance coverage (Weitzman, 1996).

Over time, however, the earnings gap between women and men has been narrowing. Women working full time in 1980 earned 60 percent as much as men working full time; by 1999, women earned 72 percent as much. Unfortunately, much of this change was due to a *drop* in men's earnings through the 1980s, while the income of women stayed about the same (U.S. Census Bureau, 2000).

THE AMERICAN DREAM: STILL A REALITY?

The expectation of upward social mobility is deeply rooted in our culture. Through much of our history, economic expansion fulfilled this promise by raising living standards. But, about 1970, this upward trend leveled off, beginning a period of "income stagnation" for many families that has shaken our national confidence. Note these disturbing trends:

1. **For many workers, earnings have stalled.** The annual income of a fifty-year-old man working full time climbed by 50 percent between 1958 and 1974 (from $22,500 to $34,000 in constant 1998 dollars). But between 1974 and 1998, this worker's income rose only slightly, even as the number of hours worked increased and the cost of necessities like housing, education, and medical care went up (Russell, 1995a; U.S. Census Bureau, 2000).

2. **Multiple-job holding is up.** According to the Bureau of Labor Statistics, 4.7 percent of the U.S. labor force worked at two or more jobs in 1975; by 2000, the proportion had risen to 5.6 percent.

3. **More jobs offer little income.** In 1979, the Census Bureau classified 12 percent of full-time workers as "low-income earners" because they earned less than $6,905; by 1998, this segment of the labor force had increased to 15.4 percent,

earning less than the comparable figure of $15,208.

4. **Young people are remaining at home.** Fully 53 percent of young people aged eighteen to twenty-four are now living with their parents. Since 1975, the average age at marriage has moved upward three years (to 25.0 years for women and 26.7 years for men).

In sum, over the last generation, the rich have become richer. Moreover, the number of rich people has increased, with at least 5 million millionaires in the United States, four times the number a decade ago (D'Souza, 1999). So, for some at least, the American Dream is alive and well. But most are less optimistic about the future, and a significant share worry that the chance for a middle-class life is slipping away (Kerckhoff, Campbell, & Winfield-Laird, 1985; Newman, 1993).

Dubbed the *middle-class slide*, this downward structural mobility came about as more new jobs offered lower pay. As Figure 8–6 shows, although median family income grew by almost 65 percent between 1950 and 1973, it has moved up only 15 percent since then (U.S. Census Bureau, 2000).

THE GLOBAL ECONOMY AND THE U.S. CLASS STRUCTURE

Underlying these shifts in the U.S. class structure is global economic change. Much of the industrial production that gave U.S. workers high-paying jobs a generation ago has moved overseas. With less industry at home, the United States now serves as a vast market for industrial goods such as cars, stereos, cameras, and computers produced in Japan, South Korea, and elsewhere.

High-paying jobs in manufacturing, held by 26 percent of U.S. workers in 1960, support only 15 percent of workers today. In their place, the economy offers "service work," which often pays far less. Thus, traditionally high-paying corporations like USX (formerly United States Steel) now employ fewer people than the ever-expanding McDonald's restaurant chain, and fast-food clerks make only a fraction of what steel workers earn.

The global reorganization of work is not bad news for everyone. On the contrary, the global economy is driving upward social mobility for educated people who specialize in law, finance, marketing, and computer technology. Moreover, global economic expansion has helped push up the stock market almost

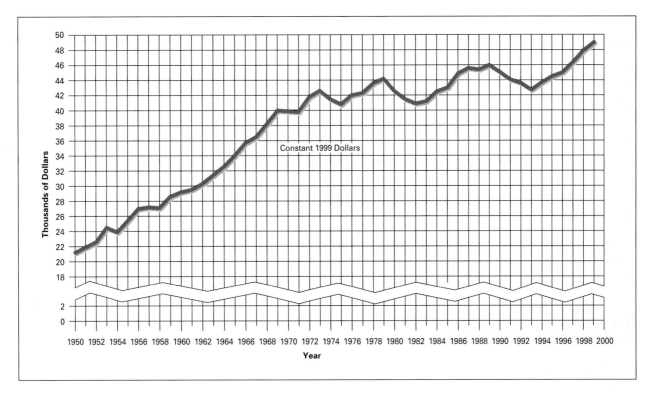

FIGURE 8–6 Median Income, U.S. Families, 1950–1999
Source: U.S. Census Bureau (2000).

tenfold between 1980 and 2000, reaping huge profits for families with money to invest.

But the same trend has hurt many average workers who have seen their factory jobs relocate overseas. Moreover, many companies have downsized—cutting the ranks of their work force—in order to become competitive in world markets. As a result, although 45 percent of all households contain two or more workers—double the share in 1950—many families are working harder simply to hold onto what they have (Reich, 1989, 1991; Nelson, 1998; Schlesinger, 1998; Sennett, 1998).

POVERTY IN THE UNITED STATES

Social stratification creates both "haves" and "have-nots." All systems of social inequality, then, generate poverty—or at least **relative poverty,** *the deprivation of some people in relation to those who have more.* A more serious but preventable problem is **absolute poverty,** *a deprivation of resources that is life-threatening.*

As Chapter 9 ("Global Stratification") explains, upwards of 1 billion human beings around the world—one in six—are at risk of absolute poverty. Even in the affluent United States, families go hungry, live in inadequate housing, and suffer poor health because of wrenching poverty.

THE EXTENT OF POVERTY

In 1999, the government tallied 32.3 million men, women, and children—11.8 percent of the population—as poor. This count of relative poverty refers to families with income below an official poverty line, which, for a nonfarm family of four, was $17,029 in 1999. The poverty line represents a figure that is about three times what the government estimates a family will spend for food. But not all poor families are even this well off since the income of the typical poor family was nearly $6,700 *below* the poverty threshold. This means that, in 1999, the typical poor family struggled to get by on no more than about $10,300 (U.S. Census Bureau, 2000).

In the 1952 painting Laundress, *U.S. artist George Tooker captures the humanity and humility of impoverished people. This message—that the poor are human beings, most doing the best they can to get by—is important to remember in a society that tends to define poor people as morally unworthy and deserving of their bitter plight.*

George Tooker (b. 1920), *Laundress*, 1952. Oil on gesso panel, 23 1/2 × 24 in. (59.7 × 61 cm.). Christie's Images, NY. © George Tooker.

WHO ARE THE POOR?

Although there is no single profile of poor people, poverty is pronounced among certain categories of our population. Where these categories overlap, the problem is especially serious.

Age. A generation ago, the elderly were at greatest risk for poverty, but no longer. Thanks to the better retirement programs offered today by private employers and government, the poverty rate for seniors over the age of sixty-five has plummeted from 30 percent in 1967 to 9.7 percent—well below the national average—in 1999. Even so, with the number of older people increasing, about 10 percent (3.2 million) of the poor are still elderly people.

Today, the burden of poverty falls most heavily on children. In 1999, 16.9 percent of people under age eighteen (12.1 million children) were poor. Tallied another way, four in ten of the U.S. poor are children under eighteen.

Race and ethnicity. Two-thirds of all poor people are white; 26 percent are African Americans. But in relation to their overall numbers, African Americans are about three times as likely as whites to be poor. In 1999, 23.6 percent of African Americans (8.4 million

people) lived in poverty, compared to 22.8 percent of Latinos (7.4 million), 10.7 percent of Asians and Pacific Islanders (1.2 million), and 7.7 percent of non-Hispanic whites (14.9 million). The poverty gap between whites and minorities has changed little since 1975 (U.S. Census Bureau, 2000).

Gender and family patterns. Of all poor people over age eighteen in the United States, 62 percent are women and 38 percent are men. This disparity reflects the fact that women who head households bear the brunt of poverty. Of all poor families, 53 percent are headed by women with no husband present, while just 7 percent of poor families are headed by single men.

The term **feminization of poverty** describes *the trend by which women represent an increasing proportion of the poor.* In 1960, only 25 percent of all poor households were headed by women; the majority of poor families had both wives and husbands in the home. By 1999, however, the proportion of poor households headed by single women had more than doubled to 53 percent. The feminization of poverty is thus part of a larger change: the rapidly increasing number of households—at all class levels—headed by single women. This trend, coupled with the fact that households headed by women are at high risk of poverty,

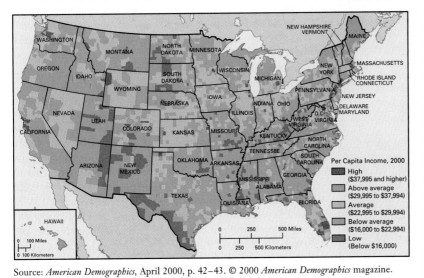

NATIONAL MAP 8-1
Per Capita Income
across the United States, 2000

This map shows the median per-person income (that is, how much money, on average, a person has to spend) for the more than 3,000 counties that make up the United States for the year 2000. The fifty richest counties, shown in dark green, are not spread randomly across the country. Nor are the poorest U.S. counties, which are shown in dark red. Looking at the map, what patterns do you see in the distribution of wealth and poverty across the United States? Do these patterns support our assertion linking affluence to urban living and poverty to rural places?

Per Capita Income, 2000
- High ($37,995 and higher)
- Above average ($29,995 to $37,994)
- Average ($22,995 to $29,994)
- Below average ($16,000 to $22,994)
- Low (Below $16,000)

Source: *American Demographics*, April 2000, p. 42–43. © 2000 *American Demographics* magazine.

explains why women (and their children) represent an increasing share of the U.S. poor.

Urban and rural poverty. The greatest concentration of poverty is found in central cities, where the 1999 poverty rate stood at 16.4 percent. Suburbs, too, have destitute people, but their poverty rate is just 8.2 percent. Thus, the poverty rate for urban areas as a whole is 11.2 percent, lower than the 14.3 percent found in rural areas. National Map 8–1 shows where poverty is most pronounced.

EXPLAINING POVERTY

For the richest nation on earth to contain tens of millions of poor people raises serious questions. It is true, as some analysts remind us, that most poor people in the United States are far better off than the poor in other countries—41 percent of U.S. poor families own their home, for example, 70 percent own a car, and only a few percent report often going without food (Rector, 1998). Nevertheless, poverty harms the overall well-being of millions of people in this country.

What, then, are the causes of poverty? One approach holds that *the poor are primarily responsible for their own poverty.* Throughout our history, people in the United States have valued self-reliance, convinced that social standing is mostly a matter of individual talent and effort. This view sees society as offering plenty of opportunity to anyone able and willing to take advantage of it. From this point of view, the poor are those who cannot or will not work, women and men with fewer skills, less schooling, and little motivation.

In his study of Latin American cities, the anthropologist Oscar Lewis (1961) concluded that the poor become trapped in a *culture of poverty,* a lower-class subculture that can destroy people's ambition to improve their lives. Socialized in poor families, children become resigned to their plight, producing a self-perpetuating cycle of poverty.

In 1996, hoping to break the cycle of poverty in the United States, Congress changed the welfare system that had provided a federal guarantee of financial assistance to poor people since 1935. Now the federal government sends money to the states to distribute to needy people, but benefits carry strict limits: in most cases, no more than two years at a stretch and a total of five years if an individual moves in and out of the welfare system. The purpose of this reform is to force people to be self-supporting and move them away from dependence on government.

An alternative position, argued by William Julius Wilson (1996a, 1996b), holds that *society is primarily responsible for poverty.* Wilson points to the loss of jobs in our inner cities as the primary cause of poverty, claiming there is simply not enough work to support families.

About 2.5 million people in the United States work full time yet do not earn enough to escape poverty. These laundry workers in San Francisco's Chinatown earn $7 per hour, about $14,500 per year, in one of the most expensive cities in the country.

at all during 1999, and an additional 40 percent worked only part time (U.S. Census Bureau, 2000). Such facts seem to support the "blame the poor" position since a major cause of poverty is *not holding a job*.

But the *reasons* that people do not work are more in step with the "blame society" position. Middle-class women may be able to combine working and child rearing, but this is much harder for poor women who cannot afford child care, and few employers provide child-care programs for their employees. Moreover, as William Julius Wilson explains, many people are idle not because they are avoiding work but because there are not enough jobs to go around. In short, most poor people in the United States find few opportunities to improve their lives (Popkin, 1990; Schiller, 1994; Edin & Lein, 1996; Wilson, 1996a; Pease & Martin, 1997).

But not all poor people are jobless, and the *working poor* command the sympathy and support of people on both sides of the poverty debate. In 1999, 21 percent of heads of poor families (1.2 million women and men) worked at least fifty weeks of the year and yet could not escape poverty. Another 40 percent of these heads of families (2.4 million people) remained poor despite part-time employment. Put differently, about 3.1 percent of full-time workers earn so little that they remain poor (U.S. Census Bureau, 2000). A key cause for "working poverty" is that a full-time worker earning a minimum wage—in 2000, $5.15 per hour—cannot keep a family of four above the poverty line.

To sum up, individual ability and personal initiative do play a part in shaping everyone's social position. However, the weight of sociological evidence points toward society—not individual character traits—as the primary source of poverty. Society must be at fault because the poor are *categories* of people—women heads of families, people of color, people in inner-city neighborhoods isolated from the larger society—who face special barriers and limited opportunities.

Thus, Wilson sees any apparent lack of trying on the part of the poor as a *result of little opportunity* rather than a *cause of poverty*. From this point of view, Oscar Lewis's analysis amounts to "blaming the victims" for their own suffering (Ryan, 1976). To combat poverty and reduce the need for welfare, Wilson argues, the government should fund jobs and provide affordable child care for low-income mothers and fathers.

Critical evaluation. The U.S. public is evenly divided over whether government or people themselves should take responsibility for reducing poverty (NORC, 1999), and both sides have evidence to support their positions. Government statistics show that 40 percent of the heads of poor families did not work

HOMELESSNESS

Many low-income people in the United States cannot afford even basic housing. There is no precise count of homeless people. Fanning out across the United States on the night of March 20, 1991, Census Bureau officials tallied 178,828 people at shelters and 49,793 people on streets where the poor are known to congregate. But experts estimate that a full count of the homeless would probably reach 500,000 *on any given night* and perhaps 1.5 million people homeless *at some time during the course of a year* (Kozol, 1988; Wright, 1989).

The familiar stereotypes of homeless people—men sleeping in doorways and women carrying everything they own in shopping bags—have been replaced by the "new homeless": people thrown out of work because of plant closings, people forced out of apartments by rent increases, and others who cannot meet mortgage or rent payments because of low wages or no work at all. Today, no stereotype paints a complete picture of the homeless.

But virtually all homeless people have one thing in common: *poverty*. For that reason, the explanations of poverty already offered also apply to homelessness. Some blame the *personal traits* of the homeless themselves. One-third of homeless people are substance abusers and one-fourth are mentally ill. More broadly, it should not be surprising that, for one reason or another, a fraction of 1 percent of our population cannot cope with our complex and highly competitive society (Bassuk, 1984; Whitman, 1989).

Others, however, see homelessness resulting from *societal factors*, including low wages and a lack of low-income housing (Kozol, 1988; Schutt, 1989; Bohannan, 1991). Supporters of this position point out that one-third of all homeless people are entire families, and children are the fastest-growing category of the homeless.

No one disputes that a large proportion of homeless people are personally impaired to some degree, although how much is cause and how much is effect is difficult to untangle. But structural changes in the U.S. economy, coupled with reduced aid to low-income people and a real estate market that puts housing out of reach of the poorest members of U.S. society, all contribute to homelessness (Ratnesar, 1999).

CLASS AND WELFARE, POLITICS AND VALUES

We have presented many facts about social inequality. In the end, however, what we think about wealth and poverty depends not just on facts but also on our politics and values. As we might expect, the idea that social standing reflects personal merit is popular among well-off people. The opposing idea, that society should spread wealth more equally, finds favor among those who are less well-off (NORC, 1999).

Figure 8–7 shows that people in the United States are more likely than people in other high-income countries to blame individuals rather than society for poverty. Our cultural emphasis on individual responsibility encourages us to see successful people as personally worthy and the poor as personally lacking. Such attitudes go a long way toward explaining why

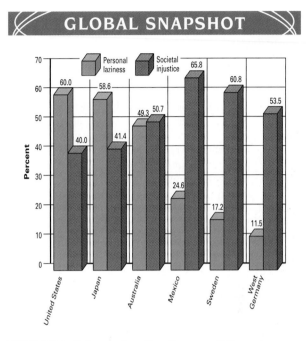

GLOBAL SNAPSHOT

FIGURE 8–7 Assessing the Causes of Poverty

Survey Question: "Why are there people in this country who live in need?" Percentages reflect respondents' identification of either "personal laziness" or "societal injustice" as the primary cause of poverty.

Percentages for each country may add up to 100 because less frequently identified causes of poverty were omitted from this figure.

Source: Inglehart et al. (2000).

our society spends much more than other high-income nations on education (to promote opportunity) but much less on public assistance programs (which directly support the poor).

Most members of our society accept a high level of income disparity, and many hold a harsh view of the poor. Moreover, to the extent that we define poor people as undeserving, we perceive public assistance programs as, at best, a waste of money and, at worst, a threat to personal initiative. The final box takes a closer look at recent welfare reforms.

Finally, the drama of social stratification extends far beyond the borders of the United States. The most striking social inequality is found not by looking inside one country but by comparing living standards in various parts of the world. In Chapter 9, we broaden our focus by investigating global stratification.

CONTROVERSY & DEBATE

The Welfare Dilemma

In 1996, Congress ended federal public assistance, which guaranteed some income to all poor people. The new state-run programs require people who receive aid to get training or find work—or have the benefits cut off.

Almost no one likes "welfare." Liberals criticize welfare for doing too little to help the poor; conservatives charge that it hurts the people it is supposed to help; and the poor themselves find welfare a complex and often degrading program.

So what, exactly, *is* "welfare"? The term *welfare* refers to a host of policies and programs designed to improve the well-being of some of the U.S. population. Until the welfare reform of 1996, most people used the term to refer to one part of the overall system—Aid for Dependent Children (AFDC), a program of monthly financial support to parents (mostly single women) to care for themselves and their children. In 1996, some 5 million households received AFDC for some part of the year.

Did AFDC help or hurt the poor? There are two sides to the debate. Conservative critics charge that, rather than reducing child poverty, AFDC actually made the problem worse, for two reasons. First, this form of welfare weakened families, they say, because for years after the program began, public assistance regulations provided benefits to poor mothers *only if no husband lived in the home*. As conservatives see it, AFDC operated as an economic incentive to women to have children outside of marriage, and they blamed it for the rapid rise in out-of-wedlock births among poor people. To

Do welfare programs such as food stamps do too much, or too little, to help the poor?

conservatives, the connection between being poor and not being married is clear: Fewer than one in ten married-couple families were poor, while more than nine out of ten AFDC families were headed by an unmarried woman.

Second, conservatives also believe that welfare encouraged poor people to become dependent on government handouts. This, they say, is the main reason that eight out of ten poor heads of households did not have full-time jobs. Furthermore, more than half of non-poor, single mothers worked full time, compared to only 5 percent of single mothers receiving AFDC. Conservatives thus claim that welfare strayed far from its original purpose of short-term help to nonworking women with children (typically, after the death or divorce of a husband) and became a way of life. Once trapped in dependency, poor women are likely to raise children who will, themselves, be poor as adults.

Liberals charge that their opponents use a double standard in evaluating government programs. Why, they ask, does our

SUMMARY

1. Social stratification refers to categories of people ranked in a hierarchy. Caste systems, common in agrarian societies, are based on ascription and permit little or no social mobility. Class systems, with an element of meritocracy, are found in high-income countries and allow social mobility based on individual achievement.

2. The Davis-Moore thesis states that social stratification is universal because it is useful to a society.

In class systems, unequal rewards attract the most able people to the most important jobs.

3. For Karl Marx, conflict in industrial societies places the capitalists, who own the means of production and seek profits, in opposition to the proletariat, who provide labor in exchange for wages.

4. Max Weber identified three distinct dimensions of social stratification: economic class, social

national dander rise at the thought of government money going to poor mothers and children when most "welfare" actually goes to relatively rich people? The AFDC budget was around $25 billion annually—no small sum, to be sure—but just half of the $50 billion in home mortgage deductions that homeowners pocket each year. And it pales in comparison to the $300 billion in annual Social Security benefits Uncle Sam provides to senior citizens, most of whom are relatively well-off. And what about "corporate welfare" to big companies? Their tax write-offs and other benefits run into hundreds of billions of dollars per year. As liberals see it, "wealthfare" is far greater than "welfare."

Second, liberals claim that conservatives have a distorted picture of public assistance. The popular images of do-nothing "welfare queens" mask the fact that most poor families who turn to public assistance are truly needy. Moreover, the typical household receiving AFDC received barely $400 per month, hardly enough to attract people to a life of welfare dependency. In constant dollars, in fact, AFDC payments actually declined over recent decades. Thus, liberals fault public assistance as a "Band-Aid approach" to the serious social problems of too few jobs and too much income inequality in the United States.

As for the charge that public assistance undermines families, liberals concede that the proportion of single-parent families has risen, but they dispute that AFDC was to blame. Rather, they maintain, single parenting is a broad cultural trend found at all class levels in many countries.

Thus, liberals conclude, programs such as AFDC were not attacked because they have failed, but because they benefited a part of the population many consider undeserving. Our cultural tradition of equating wealth with virtue and poverty with vice allows rich people to display privilege as a badge of ability, while poverty is a sign of personal failure. According to Richard Sennett and Jonathan Cobb (1973), the negative stigma of poverty is the "hidden injury of class."

A look back at Figure 8–7 shows that people in the United States, more than people in other high-income countries, tend to see poverty as a mark of laziness and personal failure. It should not be surprising, then, that Congress replaced the federal AFDC program with state-run programs called Temporary Assistance for Needy Families (TANF). States can set their own qualification requirements and benefits, but they must limit benefits to two consecutive years (with a lifetime limit of five years).

By 2002, TANF expects to move half of single parents on welfare into jobs or job training. By 1999, three years after the welfare reform bill took effect, the welfare rolls had shrunk by 56 percent, with the number of people receiving benefits falling from 14.1 million to 6.3 million. Half of those who have left welfare have found jobs; others are in school or job-training programs. Supporters declare the reforms successful. Opponents, however, fear that many families will end up worse off than before.

Continue the debate . . .

1. *How does our cultural emphasis on self-reliance help explain the controversy surrounding public assistance? Why do people not criticize benefits (like home mortgage deductions) for more well-to-do people?*

2. *Do you think public assistance has become a way of life and eroded the family? Why or why not?*

3. *Do you approve of the time limits built into the new TANF program? Why or why not?*

Sources: Katz (1986), Mead (1989), Ehrenreich (1991), Weidenbaum (1991), Jensen, Eggebeen, & Lichter (1993), Shapiro (1995), Church (1996), Murray (1996), Broder (1997), Dervarics (1998), Jones (1999a), and U.S. Department of Health and Human Services (2000).

status or prestige, and power. Together, these form a multidimensional hierarchy of socioeconomic standing (SES).

5. Gerhard and Jean Lenski explained that, historically, advancing technology tends to increase social inequality. Some reversal of this trend occurs in industrial societies, as represented by the Kuznets curve; even so, the new postindustrial society shows an increase in economic inequality.

6. The upper class (5 percent of the population) includes this country's richest and most powerful individuals. Members of the upper-upper class, or the "old rich," typically inherit great wealth; those in the lower-upper class, or "new rich," depend on earned income.

7. The middle class (40 to 45 percent) enjoys reasonable financial security, but only some of these people (the upper-middle class) have significant

wealth. With below-average incomes, members of the working class or lower-middle class (33 percent) typically perform blue-collar work, and only one-third of their children reach college.

8. About one-fifth of the U.S. population belongs to the lower class; about half of these people live below the government's poverty line. People of African and Latino descent, as well as women, are disproportionately represented in the lower class.

9. Social mobility is common in the United States, as it is in other high-income countries; typically, however, there are only small changes from one generation to the next.

10. The growing global economy has increased the wealth of rich families in the United States, but stalled or even lowered the standard of living of low-income families.

11. The government classifies 32.3 million people as poor. About 40 percent of the poor are under the age of eighteen.

12. The "culture of poverty" thesis suggests that poverty is caused by shortcomings in the poor themselves. An alternative approach claims that poverty is caused by a society's unequal distribution of income and wealth.

13. The U.S. cultural emphasis on individual responsibility helps explain why public assistance for the poor is controversial.

KEY CONCEPTS

social stratification (p. 188) a system by which a society ranks categories of people in a hierarchy

social mobility (p. 188) change in one's position in the social hierarchy

caste system (p. 188) social stratification based on ascription, or birth

class system (p. 189) social stratification based on both birth and individual achievement

meritocracy (p. 190) social stratification based on personal merit

status consistency (p. 191) the degree of consistency in a person's standing across various dimensions of social inequality

structural social mobility (p. 192) a shift in the social position of large numbers of people due more to changes in society itself than to individual efforts

ideology (p. 193) cultural beliefs that justify social stratification

Davis-Moore thesis (p. 194) the assertion that social stratification is a universal pattern because it benefits the operation of a society

capitalists (p. 196) people who own factories and other businesses in pursuit of profits

proletarians (p. 196) people who sell their productive labor for wages

alienation (p. 196) the experience of isolation and misery resulting from powerlessness

blue-collar occupations (p. 197) lower-prestige work that involves mostly manual labor

white-collar occupations (p. 197) higher-prestige work that involves mostly mental activity

socioeconomic status (p. 198) a composite ranking based on various dimensions of social inequality

income (p. 201) wages or salary from work and earnings from investments

wealth (p. 202) the total value of money and other assets, minus outstanding debts

intragenerational social mobility (p. 208) a change in social position occurring during a person's lifetime

intergenerational social mobility (p. 208) upward or downward social mobility of children in relation to their parents

relative poverty (p. 211) the deprivation of some people in relation to those who have more

absolute poverty (p. 211) a deprivation of resources that is life-threatening

feminization of poverty (p. 212) the trend by which women represent an increasing proportion of the poor

CRITICAL-THINKING QUESTIONS

1. How is social stratification a creation of society rather than simply an expression of individual differences?

2. How do caste and class systems differ? What do they have in common?

3. Would you be in favor of class-based affirmative action? That is, should U.S. society give people born to lower-class families an edge in college admissions and company hiring? Why or why not?

4. Our society is always ready to assist the "worthy" poor, including elderly people who we do not expect to fend for themselves. At the same time, we are less generous toward the "unworthy poor," able-bodied people who, we think, could take care of themselves but do not. If this is so, why has U.S. society not done more to reduce poverty among children, who surely fall into the "worthy" category?

APPLICATIONS AND EXERCISES

1. Sit down with parents, grandparents, or other relatives and try to assess the social position of your family over the last three generations. Has social mobility taken place? Why or why not?

2. Develop several simple questions that, taken together, would let you measure someone's social class position. The trick is to decide exactly what you think social class really means. Then try your questions on several adults, refining the questions as you proceed.

3. Visit the social services office that oversees financial assistance to people with low incomes in your community. See what you can learn about the effect of the 1996 welfare reforms.

4. Install the CD-ROM packaged in the back of this new textbook to access a variety of study, review, and applications exercises designed to help you better understand the material covered in this chapter. The CD includes an author's tip video, as well as interactive maps, video application exercises, Web links, and study questions.

 SITES TO SEE

http://www.prenhall.com/macionis

Visit the interactive Web site that accompanies this text. Begin by clicking on the cover of your book. You will find a chapter-by-chapter study guide, practice tests, chat room, and many suggested Web links.

http://www.census.gov/datamap/www/
http://www.bea.doc.gov

These two sites, the first run by the Census Bureau and the second by the government's Bureau of Economic Analysis, provide state-by-state and county-by-county income data. Visit these sites and see what you can learn about social standing in your part of the country.

http://www.ssc.wisc.edu/irp
http://www.jcpr.org
http://www.nber.org

Here are three Web sites that are worth a visit to learn more about poverty in the United States. The first is operated by the Institute for Research on Poverty, the second by the Joint Center for Poverty Research, and the third by the National Bureau of Economic Research.

http://www.researchforum.org
http://www.childrensdefense.org/states/data.html

In the United States, children are at high risk of poverty. The two sites noted here introduce you to the National Center on Children in Poverty and the Children's Defense Fund, organizations concerned with child poverty.

http://www.iwpr.org

The Institute for Women's Policy Research investigates the interplay of gender and poverty.

GLOBAL STRATIFICATION

"I am going to America!" Twenty-six-year-old Li Li *was elated at what seemed to be the chance of a life-time—to leave the poverty she had known in China and start a new life in the United States. A Chinese clothing company had recruited Li Li with the promise of a job, but only if she agreed to pay them her first $2,800 in earnings to cover her transportation to "American soil."*

Amid great excitement, Li Li and hundreds of other poor people set sail from China. But two days later, the ship docked and they stepped off not in California but in Saipan, the largest of the Northern Mariana Islands, some 1,500 miles southeast of her homeland. Technically speaking, Saipan is "American soil" because the islands are a U.S. territory. Li Li's dream soon became a night-mare. The company put her to work for eighteen hours a day cutting fabric in its clothing factory. At night, she and 700 other workers were herded into rat-infested barracks where they shared just twelve toilets. Guards patrolled the borders of the camp, giving people only one hour of freedom on Sundays.

Being paid about two dollars an hour, Li Li soon real-ized that she would have to work for months under these terrible conditions just to pay off her "loan." This system of indentured service, common in poor countries around the world, comes very close to out-and-out slavery.

How did such a system come to be in a place that flies the flag of the United States of America? In 1975, the United States agreed to allow the Northern Mariana Islands to control their own labor practices, which, local officials claimed, would allow them to keep out low-wage foreign workers. But the opposite has happened, and today 40,000 workers from China, South Korea, the Philippines, and Bangladesh now make up 90 percent of the islands' labor force. The Chinese and South Korean companies that operate there make millions exporting clothing to U.S. retail stores—all familiar brands with "MADE IN THE USA" labels. For Li Li and thousands upon thousands of workers like her, this story has no happy ending (adapted from McCarthy, 1998).

The fact is that billions of people in the world work hard every day and are miserably poor. As this chapter explains, while poverty is a reality in the United States, this problem is both more severe and more widespread in the poor countries of the world.

GLOBAL STRATIFICATION: AN OVERVIEW

Chapter 8 ("Social Stratification") described inequality in the United States. In global perspective, however, social stratification is far more pronounced. Figure 9–1 on page 222 divides the world's total income by fifths of the population. Recall that the richest 20 percent of the U.S. population earns about 47 percent of the national income (see Figure 8–3 on page 201). The richest 20 percent of the global population, however, receives about 80 percent of world income. At the other extreme, the poorest 20 percent of the U.S. pop-ulation earns 4 percent of our national income; the poorest fifth of the world's people, by contrast, strug-gles to survive on just 1 percent of global income.

Because global income is so concentrated, even people in the United States with income below the government's poverty line live far better than the majority of people elsewhere. The average person in a rich nation such as the United States is quite well-off by world standards. At the top of the pyramid, the wealth of the world's three richest *individuals* roughly equals the annual economic output of the world's forty-eight poorest *countries* (Annan, 1998).

A WORD ABOUT TERMINOLOGY

A familiar model for describing global stratification, developed after World War II, labeled the rich, indus-trial countries the "First World," the less industrial-ized, socialist countries the "Second World," and the

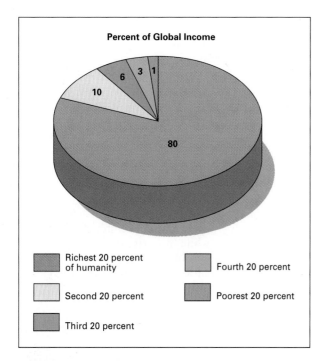

Percent of Global Income

Richest 20 percent of humanity

Second 20 percent

Third 20 percent

Fourth 20 percent

Poorest 20 percent

FIGURE 9–1 Distribution of World Income

Sources: Calculated by the author based on United Nations Development Programme (2000) and The World Bank (2001).

nonindustrialized, poor countries the "Third World." But the "Three Worlds" model is now less useful. For one thing, the term was a product of cold war politics by which the capitalist West (the First World) faced off against the socialist East (the Second World), while other nations (the Third World) remained more or less on the sidelines. But the sweeping changes in Eastern Europe and the collapse of the former Soviet Union mean that a distinctive Second World no longer exists.

A second problem is that the "Three Worlds" model lumped together more than 100 countries as the Third World. In reality, some relatively better off nations of the Third World (such as Chile in South America) have twenty times the per-person productivity seen in the poorest countries of the world (including Ethiopia in eastern Africa).

These facts call for a revised system of classification. Here, we define *high-income countries* as the richest forty nations with the highest overall standard of living. Next, the world's ninety *middle-income countries* are somewhat poorer, with economic development more or less typical for the world as a whole.

Finally, the remaining sixty *low-income countries* have the lowest productivity and the most severe and extensive poverty.

This new model has two advantages over the older "Three Worlds" system. First, it focuses on economic development rather than whether societies are capitalist or socialist. Second, it gives a better picture of the relative economic development of various countries because it does not lump together all less industrialized nations into a single "Third World."

Still, classifying the 191 nations on earth into any three categories ignores many striking differences. These nations have rich and varied histories, speak different languages, and take pride in their distinctive cultures.

Keep in mind, too, that every country on earth is also internally stratified. Thus, the extent of global inequality is actually greater than national comparisons suggest, since the most well-off people in rich countries (such as the United States) live worlds apart from the poorest people in low-income countries (such as Haiti, Sudan, and India).

HIGH-INCOME COUNTRIES

In nations where the Industrial Revolution first took place more than two centuries ago, productivity increased one-hundredfold. To understand the power of industrialization, consider that the small European nation of Holland is more productive than the vast continent of Africa south of the Sahara; likewise, tiny Belgium outproduces all of India.

A look back at Global Map 1–1 on page 7 identifies the forty high-income countries of the world. They include the United States and Canada, Argentina, the nations of Western Europe, Israel, Saudi Arabia, Singapore, Japan, Australia, and New Zealand.

Taken together, countries with the most developed economies cover roughly 25 percent of the earth's land area—including parts of five continents—and lie mostly in the Northern Hemisphere. In 2000, the population of these nations was slightly more than 900 million, or 15 percent of the earth's people. About three-fourths of the people in high-income countries live in or near cities.

Significant cultural differences exist among high-income countries; the nations of Europe, for example, recognize more than thirty official languages. But these societies share an industrial capacity that generates, on average, a rich material life for their people. Per capita income ranges from about $10,000 annually

Japan represents the world's high-income countries, in which industrial technology and economic expansion have produced material prosperity. The presence of market forces is evident in this view of downtown Tokyo (above, left). The Russian Federation represents the middle-income countries of the world. Industrial development and economic performance were sluggish under socialism; as a result, Moscow residents had to wait in long lines for their daily needs (above, right). The hope is that the introduction of a market system will raise living standards, although in the short run, Russian citizens must adjust to increasing economic disparity. Bangladesh (right) represents the world's low-income countries. As the photograph suggests, these nations have limited economic development and rapidly increasing populations. The result is widespread poverty.

(in Hungary and Saudi Arabia) to more than $25,000 annually (in the United States and Norway).[1] In fact, people in high-income countries enjoy more than half the world's total income.

Production in rich nations is capital-intensive, based on factories, big machinery, and advanced technology. High-income countries also stand at the forefront of the Information Revolution, and have most of the largest corporations that design and market

computers, as well as most of the world's computer users. High-income countries also control the world's financial markets, so that daily events in the stock exchanges of New York, London, and Tokyo affect people throughout the world.

MIDDLE-INCOME COUNTRIES

Middle-income countries have per capita income ranging between $2,500 and $10,000, roughly the median for the world's nations. Two-thirds of the people live in cities, with one-third residing in rural areas where most are poor and lack schooling, medical care, adequate housing, and even safe drinking water.

Looking back at Global Map 1–1 (page 7), about ninety of the world's nations fall into the middle-income category. At the high end are Chile (Latin America), South Africa (Africa), and Malaysia (Asia),

[1]High-income countries have per capita annual income of at least $10,000. For middle- and low-income countries, the comparable figures are $2,500 to $10,000, and $2,500 and less. All data reflect the United Nations' concept of "purchasing power parities," which avoids distortion caused by exchange rates when converting all currencies to U.S. dollars. Instead, the data represent the local purchasing power of each nation's currency.

When natural disasters strike high-income countries, such as Hurricane Andrew that devasted much of southern Florida in 1992, property loss is great but the loss of life is low. In low-income countries, by contrast, the converse is true; the death toll from Hurricane Mitch's rampage through Honduras in 1998 reached 5,000.

where annual income is about $8,500. At the low end are Ecuador (Latin America), Ukraine (Europe), Egypt (Africa), and China (Asia), with roughly $3,000 annually in per capita income.

One cluster of middle-income countries includes the former Soviet Union and the nations of Eastern Europe (in the past, known as the Second World). These countries had mostly socialist economies until popular revolts between 1989 and 1991 swept aside their governments. Since then, these nations have begun to introduce market systems but, so far, the results have been uneven. Some (including Slovakia) have improving economies, while living standards in others (including Russia) have actually fallen.

A second category of less developed countries are the oil-producing nations of the Middle East (or, less ethnocentrically, western Asia). These nations—including Oman and Iran—are very rich, but their wealth is so concentrated in the hands of a small elite that most of the people do not benefit and remain poor.

The third, and largest, category of middle-income nations includes Chile and Brazil in South America, as well as Algeria and Botswana in Africa. Although South Africa's white minority lives as well as people in the United States, it, too, must be considered less developed because its majority black population has far less income.

Taken together, middle-income countries span roughly 47 percent of the earth's land area and include about 3.3 billion people, or more than one-half of humanity. Some countries (like Russia) are far less crowded than others (like El Salvador), but compared to high-income countries, these societies on the whole are densely populated.

LOW-INCOME COUNTRIES

Low-income countries, where most people are very poor, are largely agrarian societies with some industry. Most of these sixty nations, identified in Global Map 1–1, are found in Africa and southern Asia. Low-income countries cover 28 percent of the planet's land area and are home to 28 percent of its people. Population density is generally high, although greater in Asian countries (such as Bangladesh and India) than in central African nations (like Chad and the Democratic Republic of Congo).

In poor countries, 31 percent of the people live in cities; most inhabit villages and farms, as their ancestors have done for centuries. In fact, half the world's people are peasants, who, by and large, follow cultural traditions. Without industrial technology, peasants are not very productive, one reason that many endure severe poverty. Hunger, disease, and

By and large, rich nations such as the United States wrestle with the problem of relative poverty, meaning that poor people get by with less than we think they should have. In poor countries such as Ethiopia, absolute poverty means that people lack what they need to survive. What kind of diet, medical care, and access to clean water do you think families like this one have?

unsafe housing frame the lives of the world's poorest people.

People living in affluent nations such as the United States find it hard to grasp the scope of want in much of the world. From time to time, televised pictures of famine in very poor countries such as Ethiopia and Bangladesh give us a shocking glimpse of the poverty that makes every day a life-and-death struggle. Behind these images lie cultural, historical, and economic forces that we shall explore in the remainder of this chapter.

GLOBAL WEALTH AND POVERTY

October 14, 1994, Manila, the Philippines. What caught my eye was how clean she was—a girl no more than seven or eight years old, wearing a freshly laundered dress and her hair carefully combed. She followed us with her eyes: Camera-toting Americans stand out in this, one of the poorest neighborhoods in the entire world.

Fed by methane from the decomposing garbage, the fires never go out on Smokey Mountain, the vast garbage dump on the north side of Manila. The smoke envelops the hills of refuse like a thick fog. But

Smokey Mountain is more than a dump; it is a neighborhood that is home to thousands of people. The residents of Smokey Mountain are the poorest of the poor. It is hard to imagine a setting more hostile to human life. Amidst the smoke and the squalor, men and women do what they can to survive. They pick plastic bags from the garbage and wash them in the river, and collect cardboard boxes or anything else they can sell. And all over Smokey Mountain are children who must already sense the enormous odds against them. What chance do they have, living in families that earn scarcely a few hundred dollars a year? With barely any opportunity for schooling? Year after year, breathing this air?

Against this backdrop of human tragedy, one lovely little girl has put on a fresh dress and gone out to play. . . .

Now our taxi driver threads his way through heavy traffic as we head for the other side of Manila. The change is amazing: The smoke and smell of the dump give way to neighborhoods that could be in Miami or Los Angeles. On the bay in the distance floats a cluster of yachts. No

TABLE 9–1 Wealth and Well-Being in Global Perspective, 1998

Country	Gross Domestic Product ($ billion)	GDP per Capita (PPP$)*	Quality of Life Index
High Income			
Canada	581	23,582	.935
Norway	146	26,342	.934
United States	8,230	29,605	.929
Australia	362	22,452	.929
Sweden	227	20,659	.926
Japan	3,783	23,257	.924
United Kingdom	1,357	20,336	.918
France	1,427	21,175	.917
South Korea	321	13,478	.854
Middle Income			
Eastern Europe			
Poland	159	7,619	.814
Lithuania	11	6,436	.789
Russian Federation	277	6,460	.771
Ukraine	44	3,194	.744
Latin America			
Mexico	394	7,704	.784
Venezuela	95	5,808	.770
Brazil	778	6,625	.747
Asia			
Malaysia	73	8,137	.772
Thailand	111	5,456	.745
China, P.R.	959	3,105	.706
Middle East			
Oman	15	9,960	.730
Iran	113	5,121	.709
Africa			
Algeria	47	4,792	.683
Botswana	5	6,103	.593
Low Income			
Latin America			
Honduras	5	2,433	.653
Haiti	4	1,383	.440
Asia			
India	430	2,077	.563
Bangladesh	43	1,361	.461
Africa			
Democratic Republic of the Congo	7	822	.430
Guinea	4	1,782	.394
Ethiopia	7	574	.309
Sierra Leone	1	458	.252

* These data are the United Nations' "purchasing power parity" calculations that avoid currency rate distortion by showing the local purchasing power of each domestic currency.

Source: United Nations Development Programme, *Human Development Report, 2000* (New York: Oxford University Press, 2000).

more rutted streets; now we glide quietly along wide boulevards lined with trees and filled with expensive Japanese cars. We pass shopping plazas, upscale hotels, and high-rise office buildings. Every block or so we see the gated entrance to an exclusive residential enclave with security guards standing watch. Here, in large, air-conditioned homes, the rich of Manila live and many of the poor work.

Low-income nations are home to some rich and many poor people. For most, an income of barely several hundred dollars a year means the burden of poverty is far greater than among the poor of the United States. This does not mean that poverty here is a minor problem. In so rich a country, too little food, substandard housing, and no medical care for tens of millions of people—almost half of them children—amounts to a national tragedy. Yet, poverty in poor counties is both *more severe* and *more extensive* than in the United States.

THE SEVERITY OF POVERTY

Poverty in poor countries is more severe than it is in rich countries. The data in Table 9–1 show why. The first column of figures gives, for countries at each level of economic development, gross domestic product (GDP).[2] A large industrial nation like the United States had a 1998 GDP of more than $8 trillion; Japan's GDP was nearly $4 trillion. A comparison of GDP figures shows that the world's richest nations are thousands of times more productive than the poorest countries.

The second column of figures in Table 9–1 indicates per capita GDP in terms of what the United Nations (1995) calls "purchasing power parities"— what people can buy using their income in the local economy. The per capita GDP for rich countries like the United States, France, and Canada is very high—

[2]Gross domestic product (GDP) includes all the goods and services on record as produced by a country's economy in a given year, excluding income earned outside the country by individuals or corporations. Gross national product (GNP) adds in the foreign earnings. For countries that invest heavily abroad (Kuwait, for example), GDP is much smaller than GNP; for countries in which other nations invest heavily (Hong Kong), GDP is much bigger than GNP. For countries that both invest heavily abroad and have high foreign investment at home (including the United States), the two measures are about the same.

more than $20,000. For middle-income countries, such as Brazil and Lithuania, the figures are much lower—in the $6,500 range. In the world's low-income countries, per capita annual income is just a few hundred dollars. In the Democratic Republic of the Congo or in Ethiopia, for example, a typical person labors all year to make what the average worker in the United States earns in several days.

The last column of Table 9–1 provides a measure of quality of life in the various nations. This index, calculated by the United Nations, combines income, education (extent of adult literacy and average years of schooling), and longevity (how long people typically live). Index values are decimals that fall between hypothetical extremes of 1 (highest) and zero (lowest). By this calculation, Canadians enjoy the highest quality of life (.935), with residents of the United States close behind (.929). At the other extreme, people in the African nation of Sierra Leone have the lowest quality of life (.252).

A key reason that quality of life differs so much around the world is that economic productivity is lowest in precisely those regions where population growth is highest. Figure 9–2 shows the division of global population and global income for countries at each level of economic development. High-income countries are by far the most advantaged, with 79 percent of global income supporting just 18 percent of humanity. In middle-income nations, 54 percent of the world's people earn 18 percent of global income. This leaves 28 percent of the planet's population with just 3 percent of global income. In short, for every dollar received by individuals in a low-income country, someone in a high-income nation takes home $41.

Relative versus absolute poverty. The distinction between relative and absolute poverty, made in the last chapter, has an important application to global inequality. People living in rich countries generally focus on *relative poverty*, meaning that some people lack resources that are taken for granted by others. Relative poverty, by definition, cuts across every society, whether rich or poor.

More important in a global perspective, however, is *absolute poverty*, a lack of resources that is life-threatening. Human beings in absolute poverty lack the nutrition necessary for health and long-term survival. To be sure, some absolute poverty exists in the United States; but such immediately life threatening poverty strikes only a small proportion of the U.S. population. In low-income countries, by contrast, one-third or more of the people are in desperate need.

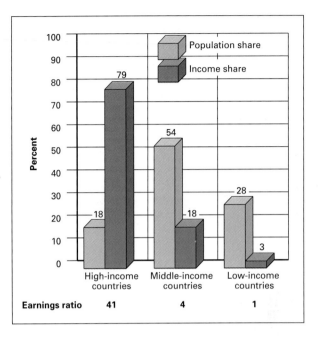

FIGURE 9–2 The Relative Share of Income and Population by Level of Economic Development

Sources: Calculated by the author based on United Nations Development Programme (2000) and The World Bank (2001).

Since absolute poverty is deadly, one global indicator of this problem is the median age at death. Global Map 9–1 on page 228 identifies the age by which half of all people born in a nation die. In rich societies, most people die after the age of seventy-five, but in poor countries, half of all deaths occur among children under the age of ten.

THE EXTENT OF POVERTY

Poverty in poor countries is more extensive than it is in rich nations such as the United States. Chapter 8 ("Social Stratification") indicated that the U.S. government officially classifies about 12 percent of the population as poor. In low-income countries, however, most people live no better than the poor in the United States, and many are far worse off. As Global Map 9–1 shows, the high death rates among children in Africa indicate that absolute poverty is greatest there, where half the population is malnourished. In the world as a whole, at any given time, 15 percent of the people (about 1 billion) suffer from chronic hunger, which leaves them less able to work and puts them at high risk of disease

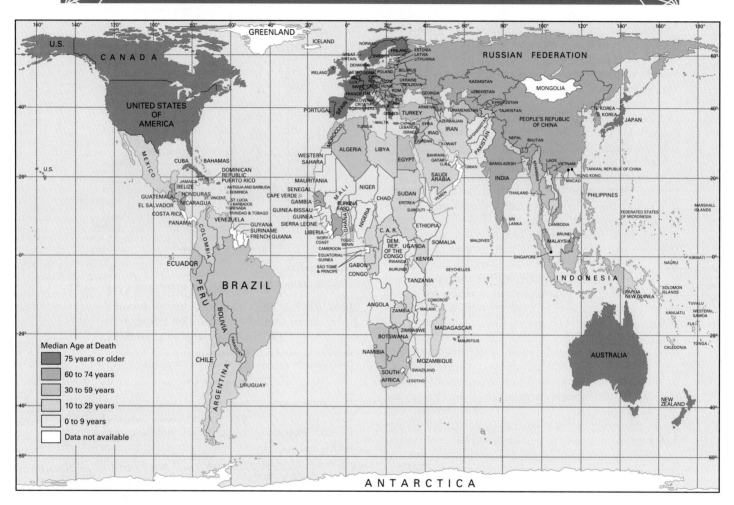

GLOBAL MAP 9–1 Median Age at Death in Global Perspective

This map identifies the age below which half of all deaths occur in any year. In the high-income countries of the world, including the United States, it is mostly the elderly who face death—that is, people age seventy-five or older. In middle-income countries, including most of Latin America, most people die years or even decades earlier. In low-income countries, especially in Africa and parts of Asia, it is children who die, half of them never reaching their tenth birthday.

Sources: The World Bank (1993); map projection from *Peters Atlas of the World* (1990).

(Kates, 1996; United Nations Development Programme, 2000).

The typical adult in a rich nation such as the United States consumes about 3,500 calories a day, too much for optimal health. The typical adult in a low-income country not only does more physical labor but consumes just 2,000 calories a day. The result is undernourishment: too little food or not enough of the right kinds of food.

In the ten minutes it takes to read through this section of the chapter, about 300 people in the world who are sick and weakened from hunger will die. This amounts to about 40,000 people a day, or 15 million people each year. Clearly, easing world hunger is one of the most serious challenges facing humanity in the twenty-first century.

POVERTY AND CHILDREN

Death comes early in poor societies, where families lack adequate food, safe drinking water, secure housing, and access to medical care. Organizations combating child poverty estimate that at least 100 million city children in poor countries beg, steal, sell sex, or work for drug gangs to provide income for their families. Such a life almost always means dropping out of school, and places children at high risk of disease and violence. Many girls, with little or no access to medical assistance, become pregnant: a case of children who cannot support themselves being forced to have still more children.

Perhaps 100 million of the world's children leave their families altogether, sleeping and living on the streets as best they can. Roughly half of all street children are found in Latin America (United Nations Development Programme, 2000). Some 10,000 homeless children roam throughout Mexico City (Ross, 1996). In Brazil, millions of street children live in makeshift huts, under bridges, or in alleyways. In Rio de Janeiro, known to many in the United States as Brazil's seaside resort, police try to keep the numbers of street children in check; at times, death squads may sweep through a neighborhood in a bloody ritual of "urban cleansing." Several hundred street children are murdered in that city each year (Larmer, 1992; U.S. House of Representatives, 1992).

POVERTY AND WOMEN

In rich societies, the work women do is typically unrecognized, undervalued, and underpaid. In poor societies, this is even more the case. Workers in the sweatshops found in poor countries—including Li Li, whose eighteen-hour days were described in the opening to this chapter—are mostly women.

Families in poor societies depend on women's income. At the same time, tradition bars many women from attending school, and gives them primary responsibility for child rearing and maintaining the household. The United Nations estimates that, in poor countries, men own 90 percent of the land, a far greater gender disparity in wealth than is found in industrial nations. Thus, about 70 percent of the

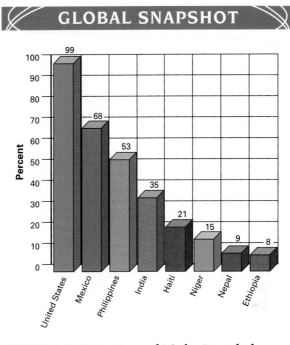

FIGURE 9–3 Percentage of Births Attended by Trained Health Personnel

Source: The World Bank (2000).

world's 1 billion people living near absolute poverty are women (Hymowitz, 1995).

Women in poor countries have limited access to birth control (which raises the birth rate), and they typically give birth without the assistance of any trained health personnel. Figure 9–3 draws a stark contrast between high- and low-income countries in this regard.

SLAVERY

Poor societies are vulnerable to many problems: hunger, illiteracy, warfare, and slavery. The British Empire banned slavery in 1833; the United States followed suit in 1865. But, according to Anti-Slavery International (ASI), as many as 400 million men, women, and children (almost 7 percent of humanity) live today in conditions that amount to slavery (Janus, 1996).

ASI distinguishes four types of slavery. First is *chattel slavery* in which one person owns another. The number of chattel slaves is difficult to estimate because this practice is against the law almost everywhere. But

Mauritania

GLOBAL SOCIOLOGY

"God Made Me to Be a Slave"

Fatma Mint Mamadou is a young woman who lives in North Africa's Islamic Republic of Mauritania. Asked her age, she pauses and smiles. She has no idea when she was born. Nor can she read or write. What she knows is tending camels, herding sheep, hauling bags of water, sweeping, and serving tea to her owners. This young woman is one of perhaps 90,000 slaves in Mauritania.

In the central region of this nation, having dark brown skin almost always means being a slave to an Arab owner. Fatma has always accepted her situation; she has known nothing else. She explains in a matter-of-fact voice that she is a slave as was her mother before her. And her grandmother before that. "Just as God created a camel to be a camel," she shrugs, "he created me to be a slave."

Fatma, her mother, and her brothers and sisters live together in a squatter settlement on the edge of Nauakchott, Mauritania's capital city. Their home is a nine-by-twelve-foot hut they built from wood scraps and other building materials taken from construction sites. The roof is nothing more than a piece of cloth; there is no plumbing, not even any furniture. The nearest water comes from a well a mile down the road.

In this region, slavery began 500 years ago, about the time Columbus sailed west toward the New World. As Arab and Berber tribes moved across the continent spreading Islam, they raided local villages and made slaves of the people. So it has been for dozens of generations ever since. In 1905, the French colonial rulers of Mauritania banned slavery. After the nation gained independence in 1961, the new government reaffirmed the ban. But such proclamations have done little to change strong traditions. Indeed, people like Fatma have no idea what freedom to choose means.

The next question is more personal: "Are you and other girls ever raped?" Again, Fatma hesitates. With no hint of emotion, she responds, "Of course, in the night the men come to breed us. Is that what you mean by rape?"

Human slavery continues to exist in the twenty-first century.

Source: Based on Burkett (1997).

the buying and selling of slaves still takes place in many countries in Asia, the Middle East, and, especially, in Africa. The box describes the reality of one slave's life in the African nation of Mauritania.

A second, more common form of bondage is *child slavery*, in which desperately poor families let their children take to the streets to do what they can to survive. Perhaps 100 million children—many in poor countries of Latin America—fall into this category.

Third, *debt bondage* refers to the practice by which employers hold workers captive by paying them too little to pay for their debts. In this case, workers do receive a wage, but not enough to pay for the food and housing provided by an employer. Thus, for practical purposes, they are enslaved. The story of Li Li working in Saipan, which opens this chapter, is one example of debt bondage.

Fourth, *servile forms of marriage* may also amount to slavery. In India, Thailand, and some African nations, families marry off women against their will. Many end up as slaves performing work for their husband's family; some are forced into prostitution.

In 1948, the United Nations issued a Universal Declaration of Human Rights, which states: "No one shall be held in slavery or servitude; slavery and the slave trade shall be prohibited in all their forms." Unfortunately, more than fifty years later, the social evil persists.

Brazil's Rio de Janeiro is known the world over as a spectacular resort city. The other side of Rio is poverty, which forces thousands of children and young people to live on the streets. These young people are vulnerable to hunger, disease, and violence. Here a seventeen-year-old victim of a gunshot lies dead in the streets in the Lapa district near the center of Rio.

CORRELATES OF GLOBAL POVERTY

What accounts for severe and extensive poverty throughout much of the world? The rest of this chapter weaves together explanations from the following facts about poor societies:

1. **Technology.** About one-fourth of people in low-income countries farm the land using human muscles or beasts of burden. Since this energy falls far short of the force of steam, oil, or nuclear power, there is little use of complex machinery.

2. **Population growth.** As Chapter 15 ("Population, Urbanization, and Environment") explains, the poorest countries have the world's highest birth rates. Despite the death toll from poverty, the populations of poor countries in Africa, for example, double every twenty-five years. In these countries, half the people are teenagers or younger. With such numbers entering their childbearing years, a wave of population growth will roll into the future. In recent years, for example, the population of Chad swelled by 3.3 percent annually, so that even with economic development, living standards have fallen.

3. **Cultural patterns.** Poor societies are usually traditional. Adhering to long-established ways of life, people resist innovations, even those that

promise a richer material life. The box on page 232 explains why traditional people in India respond to their poverty differently than poor people in the United States.

4. **Social stratification.** Low-income societies distribute their wealth very unequally. Chapter 8 ("Social Stratification") explained that social inequality is more pronounced in agrarian societies than in industrial societies. In Brazil, for example, half of all farmland is owned by just 1 percent of landowners (Bergamo & Camarotti, 1996).

5. **Gender inequality.** Extreme gender inequality in poor societies means that women lack opportunities, so they have many children. An expanding population, in turn, slows a society's economic development. Thus, many analysts conclude, raising living standards in much of the world depends on improving the social standing of women.

6. **Global power relationships.** A final cause of global poverty lies in the relationships among the nations of the world. Historically, wealth flowed from poor societies to rich nations through **colonialism,** *the process by which some nations enrich themselves through political and economic control of other nations.* The countries of Western Europe colonized much of Latin America and Africa beginning roughly 500 years ago. Such

A Different Kind of Poverty: A Report from India

Most North Americans know that India is one of the poorest nations on earth. A vast country with per capita gross domestic product (GDP) of only $2,077 a year (see Table 9–1), India is home to one-third of the world's hungry people.

But most North Americans do not readily understand the reality of poverty in India. Most of the country's 1 billion people live in conditions far worse than those our society labels "poor." A traveler's first experience of Indian life can be shocking. Madras, one of India's largest cities with 7 million inhabitants, seems chaotic to the newly arrived outsider, with streets choked by motorbikes, trucks, carts pulled by oxen, and waves of people. Along the roadway, vendors sit on burlap cloth and hawk fruits, vegetables, and cooked food, while people a few yards away work, talk, bathe, and sleep.

Madras is dotted by more than a thousand shanty settlements, where half a million people from rural villages have come in search of a better life. Shantytowns are clusters of huts built with branches, leaves, and pieces of discarded cardboard

and tin. These dwellings offer little privacy and lack refrigeration, running water, and bathrooms. The visitor from the United States may feel uneasy in such an area, knowing that the poorest sections of our own inner cities seethe with frustration and sometimes explode with violence.

But India's people understand poverty differently than we do. No restless young men hang out on the corners, no drug dealers work the streets, and there is little danger of violence. In the United States, poverty often means anger and isolation; in India, even shantytowns are organized around

strong families—children, parents, and often grandparents—who offer a smile and a welcome to a stranger.

For traditional people in India, life is shaped by *dharma*, the Hindu concept of duty and destiny that teaches people to accept their fate, whatever it may be. Mother Teresa, who worked among the poorest of India's people, goes to the heart of the cultural differences: "Americans have angry poverty," she explains. "In India, there is worse poverty, but it is a happy poverty."

Perhaps we should not describe anyone who clings to the edge of survival as happy. But poverty in India is eased by the strength and support of families and communities, a sense that existence has a purpose, and a worldview that encourages each person to accept whatever life offers. As a result, a visitor may well come away from a first encounter with Indian poverty in confusion: "How can people be so poor, and yet apparently content, active, and *joyful*?"

Source: Based on the author's research in Madras, India, November 1988.

global exploitation of resources allowed some nations to develop economically at the expense of other nations.

Although 130 former colonies gained their independence during the twentieth century, exploitation continues through **neocolonialism** (*neo* is a Greek word for "new"), *a new form of global power relationships that involves not direct*

political control but economic exploitation by multinational corporations. **Multinational corporations—** *huge businesses that operate in many countries*—wield tremendous economic power in today's world. Corporate decision makers can impose their will on countries where they do business to create favorable economic conditions, just as colonizers did in the past.

In rich nations such as the United States, most parents expect their children to enjoy years of childhood, largely free from the responsibilities of adult life. This is not the case in poor nations across Latin America, Africa, and Asia. Poor families depend on whatever income their children can earn, and many children as young as six or seven work full days weaving or performing other kinds of manual labor. Child labor lies behind the low prices of many products imported for sale in this country.

GLOBAL STRATIFICATION: THEORETICAL ANALYSIS

There are two major explanations for the unequal distribution of the world's wealth and power—*modernization theory* and *dependency theory*. Each theory suggests a different path toward relieving the suffering of hungry people in much of the world.

MODERNIZATION THEORY

Modernization theory is *a model of economic and social development that explains global inequality in terms of technological and cultural differences among societies.* Modernization theory emerged in the 1950s, a time when U.S. society was fascinated with new technology. To counter the growing influence of the Soviet Union in much of the world, U.S. policymakers drafted a foreign policy that was pro-market and has been with us ever since.[3]

Historical perspective. Modernization theorists point out that as recently as several centuries ago, the entire world was poor. Because poverty is the norm

_____
[3]The following discussion of modernization theory draws primarily on Rostow (1960, 1978), Bauer (1981), and Berger (1986); see also Firebaugh (1996) and Firebaugh & Sandu (1998).

throughout human history, it is *affluence* that demands an explanation.

Affluence came within reach of a growing share of people in Western Europe during the late Middle Ages as the scope of world exploration and trade expanded. Soon, the Industrial Revolution was underway, transforming first Western Europe, then North America. Industrial technology, coupled with the spirit of capitalism, created new wealth on an unprecedented scale. At the outset, this new wealth benefited only a few. But industrial technology was so productive that gradually the living standard of even the poorest people began to improve. The specter of absolute poverty, which had cast a menacing shadow over humanity throughout history, was finally being routed.

During the twentieth century, the standard of living in high-income countries, where the Industrial Revolution began, jumped at least fourfold. Many middle-income nations in Asia and Latin America are now industrializing, and they, too, are becoming richer. But those low-income countries where many people remain in agriculture have changed little.

The importance of culture. Why didn't the Industrial Revolution sweep away poverty the world over? Modernization theory points out that not every society has been eager to seek out new technology. Doing so requires a cultural environment that emphasizes the benefits of materialism and innovation.

Modernization theory identifies *tradition* as the greatest barrier to economic development. In societies with strong family systems and a reverence for the past, "cultural inertia" discourages people from adopting new technologies that would raise their living standards. Even today, many people—from the North American Amish, to Islamic people of Iran, to the Semai of Malaysia—oppose technological advances as a threat to their family relationships, customs, and religious beliefs.

Max Weber (1958; orig. 1904–5) found that at the end of the Middle Ages, the cultural environment of Western Europe was quite another story. As explained in Chapter 13 ("Family and Religion"), the Protestant Reformation had reshaped traditional Catholicism to generate a progress-oriented way of life. Wealth, regarded with suspicion by the Catholic church, became a sign of personal virtue, and the growing importance of individualism steadily replaced the traditional emphasis on kinship and community. Taken together, these new cultural patterns nurtured the Industrial Revolution, which propelled one segment of humanity from poverty to prosperity.

Rostow's stages of modernization. Modernization theory holds that the door to affluence is open to all. Indeed, as technological advances diffuse around the world, all poor societies are gradually industrializing. According to W. W. Rostow (1960, 1978), modernization occurs in four stages:

1. **Traditional stage.** Socialized to venerate the past, people in traditional societies cannot easily imagine how life could be very different. Therefore, they build their lives around families and local communities and follow well-worn paths that allow for little individual freedom or change. Life is often spiritually rich but lacking in material abundance.

   A century ago, much of the world was in this initial stage of economic development. Bangladesh, Niger, and Somalia are still at the traditional stage and remain impoverished.

2. **Take-off stage.** As a society shakes off the grip of tradition, people start to use their talents and imagination, sparking economic growth. A market emerges as people produce goods not just for their own consumption but in order to trade with others for profit. Greater individualism, a willingness to take risks, and a desire for material goods also take hold, often at the expense of family ties and time-honored norms and values.

   Great Britain reached take-off by about 1800, the United States by 1820. Thailand, a middle-income country in eastern Asia, is now within this stage. Such development typically is speeded by progressive influences from rich nations—including foreign aid, the availability of advanced technology and investment capital, and opportunities for schooling abroad.

3. **Drive to technological maturity.** As this stage begins, "growth" is a widely accepted concept that fuels a society's pursuit of higher living standards. A diversified economy drives a population eager to enjoy the benefits of industrial technology. At the same time, however, people begin to realize (and sometimes lament) that industrialization is eroding traditional family and local community life. Great Britain entered this stage by about 1840, the United States by 1860. Today, Mexico, the U.S. territory of Puerto Rico, and South Korea are among the nations driving to technological maturity.

   Societies in stage three have greatly reduced absolute poverty. Cities swell with people who leave rural villages in search of economic opportunity; occupational specialization makes relationships less personal, and heightened individualism generates social movements demanding greater political rights. Societies approaching technological maturity also provide basic schooling to all their people and advanced training for some. The newly educated tend to consider tradition "backward," which opens the door to further change. The social position of women steadily becomes more equal to that of men. Even so, in the short term, the process of development may subject women to new and unexpected problems, as the box explains.

4. **High mass consumption.** Economic development driven by industrial technology steadily raises living standards, as mass production stimulates mass consumption. Simply put, people soon learn to "need" the expanding array of goods that their society produces.

   The United States, Japan, and other rich nations entered this stage of development by 1900. Approaching this level of economic prosperity today are two former British colonies in East Asia: Hong Kong (now part of the People's

Modernization: New Challenges for Women

Around the world, gender inequality is greatest where people are poorest. Economic development, then, depends on giving women opportunities for schooling and for work outside the home, which helps to reduce birth rates and, in the process, weakens traditional male domination.

But modernization also poses dangers for women. Investigating the lives of women in a poor, rural district of Bangladesh, Sultana Alam (1985) reports several hazards.

First, as economic opportunity draws men from rural areas to cities in search of work, women and children must fend for themselves. Some men sell their land and simply abandon their wives, who are left with nothing but their children.

Second, the eroding strength of the family and neighborhood leaves women who are deserted in this way with little assistance. The same holds true for women who become single through divorce or the death of a spouse. In the past,

Alam reports, kin or neighbors readily took in a Bangladeshi woman who found herself alone. Today, as Bangladesh seeks to advance economically, the number of households headed by women is increasing, and most are poor. Rather than enhancing women's autonomy, Alam argues, a new spirit of individualism has lowered the social standing of women.

In Rajshahi, Bangladesh, women meet to address their common problems.

Third, economic development—as well as the growing influence of Western movies and mass media—undermines women's traditional roles as wives, sisters, and mothers, defining them instead as objects of sexual attention. A new cultural emphasis on sexuality now encourages men in poor countries to abandon their aging spouses and take on younger, more physically attractive partners. The same emphasis contributes to the world's rising tide of prostitution.

Modernization, then, does not affect men and women in the same ways. In the long run, the evidence suggests, modernization does give the sexes more equal standing. In the short run, however, women may endure setbacks as they face new challenges virtually unknown in traditional societies.

Sources: Based on Alam (1985) and Mink (1989).

Republic of China) and Singapore (independent since 1965).

The role of rich nations. Modernization theory claims that high-income countries play four important roles in global economic development:

1. **Helping control population.** Since population growth is greatest in the poorest societies, rising population can overtake economic advances. Rich nations can help limit population growth by exporting birth control technology and promoting its use. Once economic development is underway, birth rates should decline, as they have in high-income nations, because children will no longer be an economic asset.

2. **Increasing food production.** Rich nations can export "high-tech" farming methods to poor nations to help raise agricultural yields. Such techniques—collectively referred to as the "Green Revolution"—include using new hybrid seeds, modern irrigation methods, chemical fertilizers, and pesticides for insect control.

3. **Introducing industrial technology.** Rich nations can accelerate economic growth in poor societies by introducing machinery and information technology, which raise productivity. Industrialization also shifts the labor force from farming to skilled industrial and service jobs.

4. **Providing foreign aid.** Investment capital from rich nations can boost the prospects of poor

societies striving to reach Rostow's "take-off" stage. Foreign aid can help raise agricultural productivity by enabling poor countries to purchase more fertilizer and build irrigation systems. In addition, financial and technical assistance to build power plants and factories improves industrial output.

Critical evaluation. Modernization theory has many influential supporters among social scientists (Parsons, 1966; Moore, 1977, 1979; Bauer, 1981; Berger, 1986; Firebaugh & Beck, 1994; Firebaugh, 1996; Firebaugh & Sandu, 1998). Moreover, for decades it has shaped the foreign policy of the United States and other rich nations. Proponents point to rapid economic development in Asia—including South Korea, Taiwan, Singapore, and Hong Kong—as proof that the affluence created in Western Europe and North America is within reach of all countries.

But modernization theory comes under fire from socialist countries (and also from left-leaning analysts in the West) as a thinly veiled defense of capitalism. Its most serious flaw, according to critics, is that modernization simply has not occurred in many poor countries. The United Nations recently reported that living standards in a number of nations, including Haiti and Nicaragua in Latin America, and Sudan, Ghana, and Rwanda in Africa, are actually lower than they were in 1960 (United Nations Development Programme, 1996).

A second criticism lodged against modernization theory is that it fails to recognize how rich nations, which benefit from the status quo, often block paths to development for poor countries. Centuries ago, critics charge, rich countries industrialized from a position of global *strength*. Can we expect poor countries today to do so from a position of global *weakness*?

Third, critics continue, modernization theory treats rich and poor societies as separate worlds, ignoring how international relations have affected all nations. To begin with, it was colonization that boosted the fortunes of Europe. This same economic windfall has left countries in Latin America and Asia reeling to this day.

Fourth, critics contend that modernization theory holds up the world's most developed countries as the standard for judging the rest of humanity, thus revealing an ethnocentric bias. We need to remember that our Western conception of "progress" has caused us to degrade the physical environment throughout the world and to rush headlong into a competitive, materialistic way of life.

Fifth, and finally, modernization theory draws criticism for suggesting that the causes of global poverty lie almost entirely within the poor societies themselves. Critics see this analysis as little more than "blaming the victims" for their own plight. Instead, they argue, an analysis of global inequality should focus as much on the behavior of *rich* nations as poor nations (Wiarda, 1987).

Such concerns reflect a second major approach to understanding global inequality. We now turn to dependency theory.

DEPENDENCY THEORY

Dependency theory is *a model of economic and social development that explains global inequality in terms of the historical exploitation of poor societies by rich ones.* This analysis puts primary responsibility for global poverty on rich nations. It holds that rich countries have systematically impoverished low-income countries, making poor nations *dependent* on rich ones. This destructive process extends back for centuries and persists today.

Historical perspective. Everyone agrees that before the Industrial Revolution, there was little affluence in the world. Dependency theory asserts, however, that people living in poor countries were actually better off economically in the past than their descendants are now. André Gunder Frank (1975), a noted proponent of this theory, argues that the colonial process that helped develop rich nations also *underdeveloped* poor societies.

Dependency theory is based on the idea that the economic positions of the rich and poor nations of the world are linked and cannot be understood in isolation from one another. Poor nations are not simply lagging behind rich ones on the "path of progress"; rather, the prosperity of the most developed countries came largely at the expense of less developed ones. In short, then, some nations became rich only because others became poor. Both are products of the onset of global commerce beginning five centuries ago.

The importance of colonialism. Late in the fifteenth century, Europeans began surveying the Americas to the west, Africa to the south, and Asia to the east in order to establish colonies. They were so successful in their efforts that, a century ago, Great Britain controlled about one-fourth of the world's land, boasting that "the sun never sets on the British Empire." The United States, itself originally thirteen small British colonies on the eastern seaboard, soon

Was the arrival of Europeans in the Western Hemisphere a tale of brave explorers or greedy conquerors? The painting Colonial Domination, *a mural by Mexican artist Diego Rivera, clearly presents the artist's point of view.*

Diego Rivera, *Colonial Domination.* The Granger Collection. © Banco de Mexico Diego Rivera Museums Trust.

pushed across the North American continent, purchased Alaska, and gained control of Haiti, Puerto Rico, Guam, the Philippines, the Hawaiian Islands, and part of Cuba.

Meanwhile, Europeans and Africans engaged in a brutal form of human exploitation—the slave trade—from about 1500 until 1850. But even as the world was rejecting slavery, Europeans took control of Africa itself, as Figure 9–4 on page 238 shows. European powers dominated most of the continent until the early 1960s.

Formal colonialism has almost disappeared from the world. However, according to dependency theory, political liberation has not meant economic autonomy. Far from it: The economic relationship between poor and rich nations continues the colonial pattern of domination. This neocolonialism is the essence of the capitalist world economy.

Wallerstein's capitalist world economy. Immanuel Wallerstein (1974, 1979, 1983, 1984) explains global stratification using a model of the "capitalist world economy." Wallerstein's term *world economy* suggests that the prosperity or poverty of any country is the product of a global economic system. He traces the roots of the global economy to the onset of colonization 500 years ago, when Europeans began gathering wealth from the rest of the world. Since the global economy is based in high-income countries, it is capitalist in character.[4]

Wallerstein calls the rich nations the *core* of the world economy. Colonialism enriched this core by funneling raw materials from around the world to Western Europe, where they fueled the Industrial Revolution. Today, multinational corporations operate profitably worldwide, channeling wealth to North America, Western Europe, Australia, and Japan.

Low-income countries, on the other hand, represent the *periphery* of the world economy. Drawn into the world economy by colonial exploitation, poor nations continue to support rich ones by providing inexpensive labor and a vast market for industrial products. The remaining countries are considered the *semiperiphery* of the world economy. They include middle-income countries like Mexico and South Africa that have closer ties to the global economic core.

---

[4]While based on Wallerstein's ideas, this section also reflects the work of Frank (1980, 1981), Delacroix & Ragin (1981), Bergesen (1983), Dixon & Boswell (1996), and Kentor (1998).

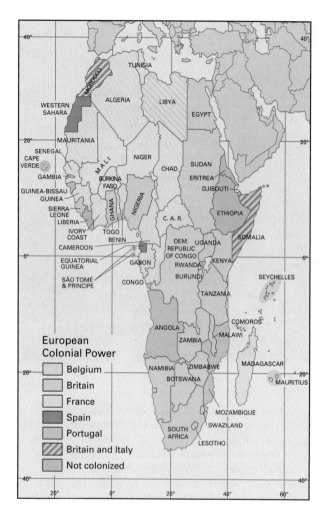

FIGURE 9–4 Africa's Colonial History

According to Wallerstein, the world economy benefits rich societies (by generating profits) and harms the rest of the world (by perpetuating poverty). The world economy thus makes poor nations dependent on rich ones. This dependency involves three factors:

1. **Narrow, export-oriented economies.** Poor nations produce only a few crops for export to rich countries. Examples include coffee and fruits from Latin American nations, oil from Nigeria, hardwoods from the Philippines, and palm oil from Malaysia.

    Today's multinational corporations purchase raw materials cheaply in poor societies and transport them to core nations where factories process them for profitable sale. Thus, poor nations develop few industries of their own.

2. **Lack of industrial capacity.** Without an industrial base, poor societies face a double bind: They both depend on rich nations to buy their inexpensive raw materials and look to rich nations to sell them whatever expensive manufactured goods they can afford. In a classic example of this dependency, British colonialists encouraged the people of India to raise cotton, but prevented them from weaving their own cloth. Instead, the British shipped Indian cotton to English textile mills in Birmingham and Manchester, manufactured the cloth, and shipped finished goods back for profitable sale in India.

    Dependency theorists claim the Green Revolution—widely praised by modernization theorists—works the same way. Poor countries sell cheap raw materials to rich nations and then try to buy expensive fertilizers, pesticides, and mechanical equipment in return. Typically, rich countries profit from this exchange more than poor nations.

3. **Foreign debt.** Unequal trade patterns have plunged poor countries into debt. Collectively, the poor nations of the world owe rich countries more than $2.5 trillion, including hundreds of billions of dollars owed to the United States. Such staggering debt paralyzes a country with high unemployment and rampant inflation (Walton & Ragin, 1990; World Bank, 2001).

The role of rich nations. Nowhere is the difference between modernization theory and dependency theory drawn more sharply than in the role each assigns to rich nations. Modernization theory maintains that rich societies *produce wealth* through capital investment and technological innovation. Accordingly, as poor nations adopt pro-growth policies and more productive technology, they, too, will prosper. By contrast, dependency theory views global inequality in terms of how countries *distribute wealth*, arguing that rich nations have *over*developed themselves as they have *under*developed the rest of the world.

Dependency theorists dismiss the idea that strategies by rich countries to control population and boost agricultural and industrial output will help raise living standards in poor countries. Instead, they contend, such programs actually benefit rich nations and only the ruling elites, not the poor majority, in low-income countries (Lappé, Collins, & Kinley, 1981).

Hunger activists Frances Moore Lappé and Joseph Collins (1986) maintain that the capitalist culture of the United States encourages people to think of poverty as somehow inevitable. Following this line of reasoning, poverty results from "natural" processes, including having too many children, and from natural disasters such as droughts. But global poverty is far from inevitable; it results from deliberate policies. Lappé and Collins point out that the world already produces enough food to allow every person on the planet to become quite fat. Moreover, India and most of Africa actually *export* food, even though many of their own people go hungry.

According to Lappé and Collins, the contradiction of poverty amid plenty stems from the rich-nation policy of producing food for profits, not people. That is, corporations in rich nations cooperate with elites in poor countries to grow and export profitable crops such as coffee, which means using land that could otherwise produce staples such as beans and corn for local families. Governments of poor countries support the practice of "growing for export" because they need food profits to repay massive foreign debt. At the core of this vicious cycle, according to Lappé and Collins, is the capitalist corporate structure of the global economy.

Critical evaluation. The main idea of dependency theory is that no nation develops (or fails to develop) in isolation, because the global economy shapes the destiny of all nations. Citing Latin America and other poor regions of the world, dependency theorists claim that development simply cannot proceed under the constraints presently imposed by rich countries. Rather, they call for radical reform of the entire world economy so that it operates in the interests of the majority of people.

Critics, however, charge that dependency theory wrongly treats wealth as a zero-sum commodity, as if no one gets richer without someone else getting poorer. Not so, critics continue, since corporations, small business owners, and farmers can and do create new wealth through their drive and imaginative use of new technology. After all, they point out, the entire world's wealth has swelled sixfold since 1950.

Second, critics continue, dependency theory is wrong in blaming rich nations for global poverty because many of the world's poorest countries (like Ethiopia) have had little contact with rich nations. On the contrary, a long history of trade with rich countries has dramatically improved the economies of nations such as Sri Lanka, Singapore, and Hong Kong

Hong Kong—until 1998 a British colony—falls within the "semiperiphery" category in Wallerstein's model of the world economy. Although some districts of this city are centers for international business and playgrounds for the rich, other areas—such as this squatter settlement in the foreground—contain thousands of poor people.

(all former British colonies), as well as South Korea and Japan. In short, say the critics, most evidence shows that foreign investment by rich nations fosters economic growth, as modernization theory claims, not economic decline, as dependency theorists assert (Vogel, 1991; Firebaugh, 1992).

Third, critics contend that dependency theory is simplistic for pointing the finger at a single factor—world capitalism—as the cause of global inequality (Worsley, 1990). Dependency theory casts poor societies as passive victims and ignores factors inside these countries that contribute to their economic plight. Sociologists have long recognized the vital role of culture in shaping people's willingness to embrace or resist change. Iran's brand of fundamentalist Islam, for example, has deliberately discouraged economic ties with other countries. Capitalist societies, then, need hardly accept the blame for Iran's economic stagnation.

TABLE 9–2 Modernization Theory and Dependency Theory: A Summary

	Modernization Theory	Dependency Theory
Historical Pattern	The entire world was poor several centuries ago; the Industrial Revolution brought affluence to high-income countries; as industrialization gradually transforms poor societies, all nations are likely to become more equal and alike.	Global parity was disrupted by colonialism, which made some countries rich while simultaneously making others poor; barring radical change in the world capitalist system, rich nations will grow richer and poor nations will become poorer.
Primary Causes of Global Poverty	Characteristics of poor societies cause their poverty, including lack of industrial technology, traditional cultural patterns that discourage innovation, and rapid population growth.	Global economic relations—historical colonialism and now multinational corporations—have enriched high-income countries while making low-income nations economically dependent.
Role of Rich Nations	Rich countries can and do assist poor nations through population control programs, technology transfers that increase food production and stimulate industrial development, and capital investment in the form of foreign aid.	Rich countries have concentrated global resources, conferring advantages on themselves while generating massive foreign debt in low-income countries; rich nations impede the economic development of poor nations.

Nor can rich societies be saddled with responsibility for the reckless behavior of foreign leaders whose corruption and militaristic campaigns impoverish their countries (examples include the regimes of Ferdinand Marcos in the Philippines, François Duvalier in Haiti, Manuel Noriega in Panama, Mobutu Sese Seko in Zaire, and Saddam Hussein in Iraq). Some leaders even use food supplies as a weapon in internal political struggles, leaving the masses starving in the African nations of Ethiopia, Sudan, and Somalia. Other regimes throughout the world have done little to improve the status of women or to control population growth.

Fourth, critics chide dependency theorists for downplaying the economic dependency fostered by the former Soviet Union. The Soviet army seized control of most of Eastern Europe during World War II and then politically and economically dominated these countries. Many see the uprisings between 1989 and 1991 as a wholesale rejection of the Soviet Union's socialist colonial system.

Fifth, critics fault this approach for offering only vague solutions to global poverty. Most dependency theorists urge poor nations to end all contact with rich countries, and some call for nationalizing foreign-owned industries. In other words, dependency theory amounts to a thinly disguised call for some sort of world socialism. In light of the difficulties socialist societies have had in meeting the needs of their own people, critics ask, should we really expect such a system to rescue the entire world from poverty?

GLOBAL STRATIFICATION: LOOKING AHEAD

Among the most important trends of recent decades is the development of a global economy. Increased production and sales abroad have brought record profits to many corporations and their stockholders. At the same time, the global economy has cut factory jobs in this country, hurting many average workers. The net result: economic polarization in the United States.

As this chapter has noted, however, social inequality is far more striking in a global context. The concentration of wealth among high-income countries, coupled with the grinding poverty typical of low-income nations, may well be the biggest problem facing humanity in the twenty-first century.

Finding answers to questions about global poverty, therefore, takes on great urgency. Both modernization theory and dependency theory have their merits and their limitations. Table 9–2 summarizes important arguments of each approach.

In searching for truth, we must consider empirical evidence. According to a recent survey of the world conducted by the United Nations (1996), people in about one-third of the world's countries are living far better than they have in the past. These nations—identified in Global Map 9–2—include most of the high-income countries but also dozens of poorer countries, especially in Asia. These prospering nations stand as evidence that the market forces endorsed by modernization theory can raise living standards.

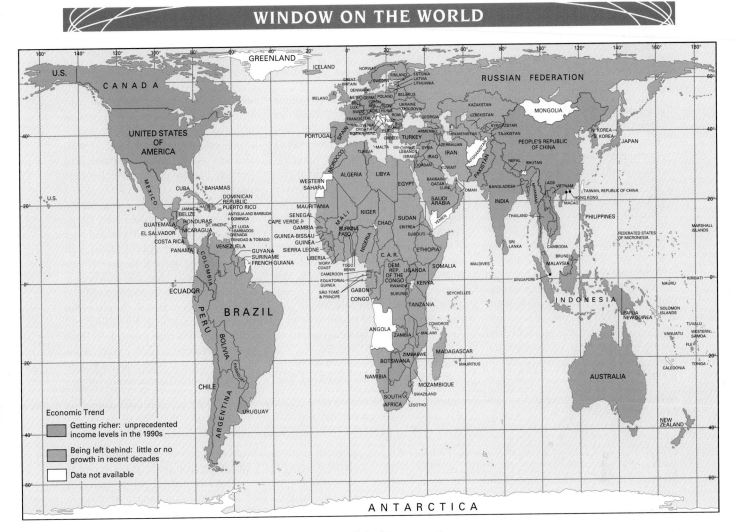

GLOBAL MAP 9–2 Prosperity and Stagnation in Global Perspective

In about sixty nations of the world, people are enjoying a higher standard of living than ever before. These prospering countries include some rich nations (such as the United States) and some poor nations (especially in Asia). For most countries, however, living standards have remained steady or even slipped in recent decades. Especially in Eastern Europe and the Middle East, some nations have experienced economic setbacks since the 1980s. And in sub-Saharan Africa, some nations are no better off than they were in 1960. The overall pattern is economic polarization, with an increasing gap between rich and poor nations.

Source: United Nations Development Programme (1996); updates by the author.

In another one-third of the world's countries, however, living standards were actually lower in 1996 than they were in 1980. A rising wave of poverty, especially in the nations of sub-Saharan Africa, supports the dependency theory assertion that current economic arrangements are leaving hundreds of millions of people behind.

The picture now emerging from this evidence calls into question both modernization and dependency theories, and both camps are revising their

Will the World Starve?

The animals' feet leave their prints
  on the desert's face.
Hunger is so real, so very real,
that it can make you walk around a
  barren tree looking for
  nourishment.
Not once,
Not twice,
Not thrice . . .

These lines, by Indian poet Amit Jayaram, describe the appalling hunger found in Rajasthan, in northwest India. As this chapter has explained, however, hunger casts its menacing shadow not only over Asia but also regions of Africa, Latin America, and even North America. Throughout the world, hundreds of millions of adults do not eat enough food to enable them to work. Most tragically, some 10 million children die each year because of hunger. As we begin the twenty-first century, what are the prospects for ending the wretched misery of daily hunger?

Pessimists point out that the population of poor countries is currently increasing by about 74 million people annually—equivalent to adding another Egypt to the world every year. Poor countries can scarcely feed the people they have now; how will they ever feed *twice* as many people a generation in the future?

In addition, hunger forces poor people to exploit the earth's resources by using short-term strategies for food production, which leads to long-term disaster. For example, farmers are cutting rain forests in order to increase their farmland. But, without the protective canopy of trees, it is only a matter of time before much of this land turns to desert. Taken together, rising populations and shortsighted policies raise the specter of unprecedented hunger, human misery, and political calamity.

But there are also some grounds for optimism. Thanks to the Green Revolution, food production the world over is up sharply over the last fifty years, well outpacing the growth in population. Taking a broader view, the world's economic productivity has risen steadily, so that the average person on the planet has more income now to purchase food and other necessities than ever before. This growth has increased daily calorie intake as well as life expectancy, access to safe water, and adult literacy, while, around

views of proper "paths to development." On the one hand, few societies seeking economic growth now favor a market economy completely free of government control; this fact challenges orthodox modernization theory and its free-market approach to development. On the other hand, the upheavals in the former Soviet Union and Eastern Europe demonstrate that a global reevaluation of socialism is currently underway. Since these uprisings followed decades of poor economic performance and political repression, many poor societies are reluctant to consider a government-controlled path to development. Because dependency theory has historically supported socialist economic systems, changes in world socialism will generate new thinking here as well.

Perhaps the basic problem for everyone to face is hunger. As the final box explains, many analysts wonder if we have the determination to provide for everyone on the planet.

Although the world's future is uncertain, we have learned a great deal about global stratification. One major insight, offered by modernization theory, is that poverty is partly a *problem of technology*. A higher standard of living for a surging world population depends on raising agricultural and industrial productivity. A second insight, derived from dependency theory, is that global inequality is also a *political issue*. Even with higher productivity, the human community must address crucial questions concerning how resources are distributed—both within societies and around the globe.

Note, too, that while economic development increases living standards, it also places greater strains on the natural environment. Imagine, for example, if the 1 billion people in India were suddenly to become middle class, all owning automobiles that guzzle gasoline and spew hydrocarbons into the atmosphere.

Finally, the vast gulf that separates the world's richest and poorest people puts everyone at greater risk of war, as the most impoverished people act to challenge the social arrangements that threaten their very existence. In the long run, we can achieve peace on this planet only by ensuring that all people live with dignity and security.

the world, infant mortality is half of what it was in 1960.

So what are the prospects for eradicating world hunger? Overall, we see less hunger in both rich and poor countries, and a smaller *share* of the world's people are hungry now than back in 1960. But as global population increases, with 96 percent of children born in middle- and low-income countries, the *number* of lives at risk is as great today as ever before. Thus, many low-income countries have made solid gains, but many more are stagnating or even losing ground.

The best-case region of the world is eastern Asia, where incomes, controlled for inflation, have tripled over the last generation. Optimists in the global hunger debate point to Asia for evidence that poor countries can and do raise living standards and reduce hunger. The worst-case region of the world is sub-Saharan Africa, where living standards have fallen over the last decade. It is here that high technology is least evident and birth rates are highest. Pessimists typically look to Africa when they argue that poor countries are losing ground in the struggle to feed their people.

In the cities of India and other poor nations, poor people routinely approach foreigners traveling by car in the hopes of receiving money in return.

Television brings home the tragedy of hunger when news cameras focus on starving people in places like Ethiopia and Somalia. But hunger—and early deaths from illness—is the plight of millions all year round. The world has the technical means to feed everyone; the question is, do we have the moral determination?

Continue the debate . . .

1. In your opinion, what are the primary causes of global hunger?

2. Do you place more responsibility for solving this problem on poor countries or rich ones? Why?

3. Do you consider yourself an "optimist" or a "pessimist" about the problem of global hunger? Why?

Sources: United Nations Development Programme (1994, 1995, 1996, 1997, 1998, 1999, 2000).

SUMMARY

1. In the world as a whole, social stratification is more pronounced than it is in the United States. About 18 percent of the world's people live in postindustrial, high-income countries such as the United States and receive 79 percent of the world's income. Another 54 percent of humanity live in middle-income countries with significant industrialization and receive about 18 percent of all income. Twenty-eight percent of the world's population live in low-income countries with limited industrialization and earn only 3 percent of global income.

2. While relative poverty is found everywhere, poor societies grapple with widespread, absolute poverty. Worldwide, the lives of some 1 billion people are at risk due to poor nutrition. About 15 million people, most of them children, die annually from various causes because they lack adequate nourishment.

3. Women are more likely than men to be poor nearly everywhere in the world. Gender bias against women is greatest in poor, agrarian societies.

4. The poverty found in much of the world is a complex problem reflecting limited industrial technology, rapid population growth, traditional cultural patterns, internal social stratification, male domination, and global power relationships.

5. Modernization theory maintains that successful development hinges on breaking out of traditional cultural patterns to acquire advanced technology.

6. Modernization theorist W. W. Rostow identifies four stages of development: traditional, take-off, drive to technological maturity, and high mass consumption.

7. Arguing that rich societies hold the keys to creating wealth, modernization theory claims rich nations can assist poor nations by providing (a)

population control programs; (b) agricultural technology such as hybrid seeds and fertilizers to increase food production; (c) industrial technology, including machinery and information technology; and (d) foreign aid to help pay for power plants and factories.

8. Critics of modernization theory say that rich nations do not spread economic development around the world. Further, they claim, poor nations cannot follow the path to development taken by rich nations centuries ago.

9. Dependency theory claims global wealth and poverty are the historical products of the capitalist world economy, first because of colonialism and, more recently, the operation of multinational corporations.

10. Immanuel Wallerstein views the high-income countries as the advantaged "core" of the capitalist world economy; middle-income nations are the "semiperiphery," and poor societies form the global "periphery."

11. Three key factors—export-oriented economies, a lack of industrial capacity, and foreign debt—perpetuate poor countries' dependency on rich nations.

12. Critics of dependency theory argue that this approach overlooks the sixfold increase in the world's wealth since 1950. Furthermore, the world's poorest societies are not those with the strongest ties to rich countries.

13. Both modernization and dependency approaches offer useful insights into the development of global inequality. Some evidence supports each view. Less controversial is the urgent need to address the various problems caused by worldwide poverty.

KEY CONCEPTS

colonialism (p. 231) the process by which some nations enrich themselves through political and economic control of other nations

neocolonialism (p. 232) a new form of global power relationships that involves not direct political control but economic exploitation by multinational corporations

multinational corporation (p. 232) a huge business that operates in many countries

modernization theory (p. 233) a model of economic and social development that explains global inequality in terms of technological and cultural differences among societies

dependency theory (p. 236) a model of economic and social development that explains global inequality in terms of the historical exploitation of poor societies by rich ones

CRITICAL-THINKING QUESTIONS

1. Based on what you have read here and elsewhere, what is your prediction about the extent of global hunger fifty years from now? Will the problem be more or less serious? Why?

2. What is the difference between relative and absolute poverty? Use these two concepts to describe social stratification in the United States and around the world.

3. Why do many analysts argue that economic development in low-income countries depends on raising the social standing of women?

4. State the basic tenets of modernization theory and dependency theory. Spell out several criticisms of each approach.

APPLICATIONS AND EXERCISES

1. Keep a log book of mass media advertising mentioning low-income countries (selling, say, coffee from Colombia or exotic vacations to a Caribbean island). What image of life in low-income countries does the advertising present? In light of this chapter, do you think this image is accurate?

2. Millions of students from abroad study on U.S. campuses. See if you can identify a woman and a man on your campus raised in a poor country. Approach them, explain your interest in global stratification, and ask if they are willing to share what life is like back home. You may be able to learn quite a bit from them.

3. By comparing the Global Maps in this text, identify social traits associated with the world's richest and poorest nations. Try to use both modernization theory and dependency theory to build theoretical explanations of the patterns you find.

4. Install the CD-ROM packaged in the back of this new textbook to access a variety of study, review, and applications exercises designed to help you better understand the material covered in this chapter. The CD includes an author's tip video, as well as interactive maps, video application exercises, Web links, and study questions.

 SITES TO SEE

http://www.prenhall.com/macionis

Visit the interactive Web site that accompanies this text. Begin by clicking on the cover of your book. You will find a chapter-by-chapter study guide, practice tests, chat room, and many suggested Web links.

http://members/aol.com/casmasalc

This is the Web site for the Coalition against Slavery in Mauritania and Sudan. This site provides information about the problem of slavery as well as links to similar organizations.

http://www.oneworld.net

This site highlights a variety of issues and controversies relating to global stratification.

http://www.fh.org
http://www.worldconcern.org
http://www.worldvision.org
http://www.care.org

These are the sites for various organizations active in the struggle to reduce global inequality. The first is operated by Food for the Hungry International; the second takes you to the home page for World Concern; the third organization is World Vision; the fourth is CARE. Visit them all and watch for differences in the focus and strategies of the various organizations.

http://www.census.gov/ipc/www/idbnew.html
http://www.prb.org/index.html

These two sites—operated by the U.S. Census Bureau and the Population Reference Bureau—offer a statistical profile of world nations.

http://www.fao.org/NEWS/1999/img/SOFI99–E.PDF

Read the United Nations report titled *The State of Food Insecurity in the World 1999*, which surveys the extent of poverty in low-, middle-, and high-income countries.

http://www.worldbank.org/poverty/data/index.htm

This site, operated by the World Bank, provides data and analysis of global poverty.

http://www.globalexchange.org/education/
speakers/CarmencitaAbad.html

Read about a woman who spent six years working in a sweatshop in Saipan producing clothing sold by Gap in the United States.

http://www.un.org/rights/50/decla.htm

More than fifty years ago, the United Nations published the Universal Declaration of Human Rights. What does this document say about social inequality in the world?

GENDER STRATIFICATION

At first we traveled quite alone . . . but before we had gone many miles, we came on other wagon-loads of women, bound in the same direction. As we reached different cross-roads, we saw wagons coming from every part of the country and, long before we reached Seneca Falls, we were a procession.

So wrote Charlotte Woodward in her journal as she made her way along the rutted dirt roads leading to Seneca Falls, a small town in upstate New York. The year was 1848, a time when slavery was legal in much of the United States and the social standing of all women—regardless of color—was subordinate to that of men. Back then, in much of the United States, women could not own property or keep their wages if they were married; women could not draft a will or file lawsuits in a court (including suits seeking custody of their own children); women could not attend college; and husbands could legally beat their wives, as long as the stick they used was no wider than a thumb (the origin of today's phrase "the rule of thumb").

Nor could women express their disapproval of such conditions. In this "land of the free," more than seventy years would pass before women gained the right to vote.

At Wesleyan Chapel in Seneca Falls, some 300 women gathered to challenge this second-class citizenship. They listened as their leader Elizabeth Cady Stanton called for expanding women's rights and opportunities, including the right to vote. At that time, most people considered such a proposal absurd and outrageous. Even many attending the conference were shocked by the idea: Stanton's husband, Henry, rode out of town in protest (Gurnett, 1998).

Much has changed in the century and a half since the Seneca Falls convention, and many of the proposals made by Stanton are now accepted as matters of basic fairness. But, as this chapter explains, women and men still lead different lives in the United States, as well as elsewhere in the world, and, in most respects, men still dominate. This chapter explores the importance of gender and explains how, like class position, gender is a major dimension of social stratification.

GENDER AND INEQUALITY

Chapter 7 ("Sexuality") explained that biological differences divide the human population into categories of female and male. **Gender** refers to *the personal traits and social positions that members of a society attach to being female and male.* Gender, then, is a dimension of social organization, shaping how we interact with others and even how we think about ourselves. More important, gender also involves *hierarchy*, placing men and women in different positions in terms of power, wealth, and other resources. This is why sociologists speak of **gender stratification**, *the unequal distribution of wealth, power, and privilege between men and women.* In short, gender affects the opportunities and constraints each of us faces throughout our lives (Ferree & Hall, 1996; Riley, 1997).

MALE-FEMALE DIFFERENCES

Many people think there is something "natural" about gender distinctions, since, after all, biological factors make one sex different from the other. But we must be

Sex is a biological distinction that develops prior to birth. Gender is the meaning that a society attaches to being female or male. Gender differences are a matter of power, as what is masculine typically has social priority over what is feminine. The importance of gender is not evident among infants, of course, but the ways in which we think of boys and girls set in motion patterns that will continue for a lifetime.

careful not to think of social differences in biological terms. In 1848, for example, women were denied the vote because many people assumed that women "naturally" lacked sufficient intelligence and political interest. Such attitudes had nothing to do with biology but, rather, reflected the *cultural conventions* of that time and place.

Figure 10–1 presents another example—athletic performances. In 1925, most people would have doubted that the best women runners could ever finish a marathon in anywhere near the time that men could. Today, as the figure shows, the best women routinely post better times than the fastest men of decades past, and the performance gap between the sexes has narrowed greatly. Here, again, most of the differences between men and women turn out to be socially created.

True, there are some differences in physical ability between the sexes. On average, males are 10 percent taller, 20 percent heavier, and 30 percent

stronger, especially in their upper bodies (Ehrenreich, 1999). On the other hand, women outperform men in the ultimate game of life itself: While life expectancy for men is 73.8 years, women can expect to live 79.5 years (U.S. National Center for Health Statistics, 2001).

In adolescence, males show greater mathematical ability, while adolescent females excel in verbal skills, a difference that reflects both biology and the socialization process (Maccoby & Jacklin, 1974; Baker et al., 1980; Lengermann & Wallace, 1985). However, research points to no overall differences in intelligence between males and females.

Biologically, then, men and women differ in limited ways, with neither one naturally superior. But culture can define the two sexes differently, as the global study of gender shows.

The Israeli kibbutzim. In Israel, collective Jewish settlements are called *kibbutzim*. The *kibbutz* (the singular form) is important for gender research because gender equality is one of its goals, with men and women sharing in both work and decision making.

Members of kibbutzim consider gender irrelevant to most of everyday life. Both men and women take care of children, cook and clean, repair buildings, and make day-to-day decisions concerning life in the kibbutz. Girls and boys are raised in the same way and, from the first weeks of life, children live together in dormitories. Women and men in the kibbutzim have achieved remarkable (although not complete) social equality. Thus, kibbutzim are evidence of the wide latitude that cultures have in defining what is feminine and what is masculine.

Margaret Mead's research. Anthropologist Margaret Mead carried out groundbreaking research on gender. To the extent that gender reflects the biological facts of sex, she reasoned, people everywhere should define "feminine" and "masculine" in the same way; if gender is cultural, these conceptions should vary.

Mead studied three societies in New Guinea (1963; orig. 1935). In the mountainous home of the Arapesh, Mead observed men and women with remarkably similar attitudes and behavior. Both sexes, she reported, were cooperative and sensitive to others—in short, what our culture would label "feminine."

Moving south, Mead studied the Mundugumor, whose head-hunting and cannibalism stood in striking contrast to the gentle ways of the Arapesh. Both sexes were typically selfish and aggressive, traits we define as more "masculine."

Finally, traveling west to the Tchambuli, Mead discovered a culture that, like our own, defined females and males differently. But, Mead reported, the Tchambuli *reversed* many of our notions of gender: Females were dominant and rational, while males were submissive, emotional, and nurturing toward children. Based on her observations, Mead concluded that culture is the key to gender since what one society defines as masculine, another may see as feminine.

Some critics consider Mead's findings "too neat," as if she saw in these societies just the patterns she was looking for. Deborah Gewertz (1981) challenged Mead's "reversal hypothesis," claiming that Tchambuli males are really the more aggressive sex and Tchambuli females the more submissive. Gewertz explains that Mead visited the Tchambuli (who actually call themselves the Chambri) during the 1930s, after they had lost much of their property in tribal wars, and observed men rebuilding their homes. Men working in the home, she claims, was a temporary role for Chambri men.

George Murdock's research. In a broader study of more than 200 preindustrial societies, George Murdock (1937) found some global agreement on which tasks are feminine and which, masculine. Hunting and warfare, Murdock observed, generally fall to men, while home-centered tasks such as cooking and child care tend to be women's work. With their simple technology, preindustrial societies apparently assign roles reflecting men's and women's physical attributes. With their greater size and strength, men hunt game and protect the group; because women bear children, they assume domestic duties.

But beyond this general pattern, Murdock found significant variation. Consider agriculture: Women did the farming in about the same number of societies as men; in most societies, the two sexes divided this work. When it came to many other tasks—from building shelters to tattooing the body—Murdock found societies of the world were as likely to turn to one sex as the other.

In sum: Gender and culture. Global comparisons show that, by and large, societies vary widely in defining tasks as either feminine or masculine. With industrialization, moreover, the importance of muscle power declines, reducing gender differences (Lenski, Nolan, & Lenski, 1995). In sum, gender is too variable to be a simple expression of biology. Instead, as with many other elements of culture, what it means to be female and male is mostly a creation of society.

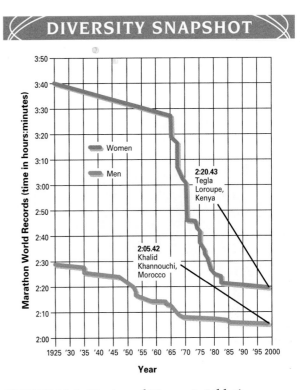

DIVERSITY SNAPSHOT

FIGURE 10–1 Men's and Women's Athletic Performance

Do men naturally outperform women in athletic competition? The answer is not obvious. Early in the twentieth century, men outdistanced women by many miles in marathon races. But as opportunities for women in athletics increased, women have been closing the performance gap. Fifteen minutes separate the current world marathon records for women and for men (both set in 1999).

Sources: *The Christian Science Monitor* (1995) and www.marathonguide.com (2000). Reprinted with permission of *The Christian Science Monitor.* All rights reserved.

PATRIARCHY AND SEXISM

Although conceptions of gender vary, everywhere in the world we find some degree of **patriarchy** (literally, "the rule of fathers"), *a form of social organization in which males dominate females.* Despite mythical tales of societies run by female "Amazons," **matriarchy,** *a form of social organization in which females dominate males,* has never been documented in human history (Gough, 1971; Harris, 1977; Lengermann & Wallace, 1985).

In every society, people assume certain jobs, patterns of behavior, and ways of dressing are "naturally" feminine while others are just as obviously masculine. But, in global perspective, we see remarkable variety in such social definitions. These men, Wodaabe pastoral nomads who live in the African nation of Niger, are proud to engage in a display of beauty most people in our society would consider feminine.

But while some degree of patriarchy may be universal, Global Map 10–1 shows great variation in the relative power and privilege of women around the world. According to the United Nations, three Nordic countries—Norway, Sweden, and Finland—afford women the highest social standing; by contrast, in the Asian nations of Pakistan and Afghanistan and the East African nation of Djibouti, women have the lowest social standing compared to men. Out of the 116 countries surveyed in the United Nations study, which took into account women's portion of national income and their representation in national legislatures as well as their share of managerial, professional, and technical jobs, the United States ranked eighth in terms of gender equality (United Nations, 1995).

Sexism, *the belief that one sex is innately superior to the other,* is the ideological basis of patriarchy. Sexism is not just a matter of individual attitudes; it is built into the institutions of our society. *Institutional sexism* pervades the economy, for example, with women highly concentrated in low-paying jobs. Similarly, the legal system has long excused violence against women, especially on the part of boyfriends, husbands, and fathers (Landers, 1990).

The costs of sexism. Sexism stunts the talents and limits the ambitions of women, who are half the population. And although men benefit in some respects from sexism, their privilege comes at a high price.

Masculinity in our culture calls for men to engage in many high-risk behaviors, including using tobacco and alcohol, playing dangerous sports, and even driving recklessly (motor-vehicle accidents are the leading cause of death among young males). Moreover, as Marilyn French (1985) argues, patriarchy compels men to relentlessly seek control—not only of women but also of themselves and their world. Thus, masculinity is linked not only to accidents but also to suicide, violence, and stress-related diseases. The Type A personality—marked by chronic impatience, driving ambition, competitiveness, and free-floating hostility—is a recipe for heart disease and almost perfectly matches the behavior our culture considers masculine (Ehrenreich, 1983).

Finally, insofar as men seek control over others, they lose opportunities for intimacy and trust. As one researcher put it, competition is supposed to separate "the men from the boys." In practice, however, it separates men from men and everyone else (Raphael, 1988).

Is patriarchy inevitable? In preindustrial societies, women have little control over pregnancy and childbirth, which limits the scope of their lives. Similarly, men's greater height and physical strength are valued resources. But industrialization—including birth control technology—gives people choices about how to live. In societies like our own, then, biological differences offer little justification for patriarchy.

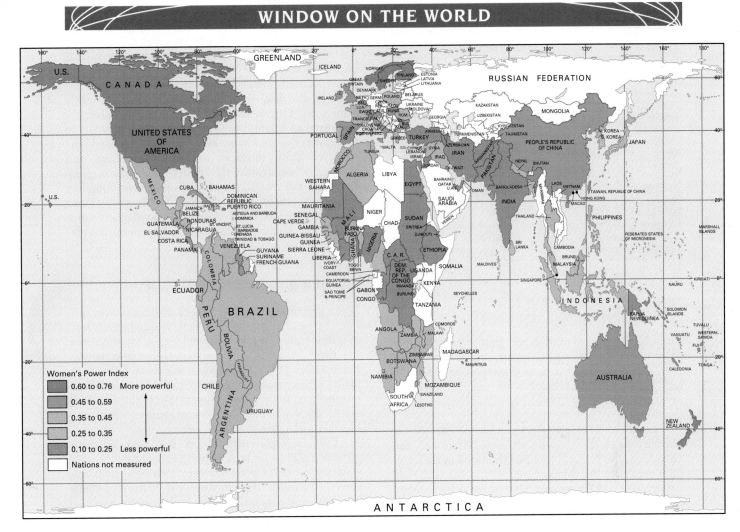

GLOBAL MAP 10–1 Women's Power in Global Perspective

A United Nations study ranked 116 nations on a scale of 0 (women have no power) to 1 (women have as much power as men). In general, women fare better in rich nations than in poor countries. Yet some countries stand out: Nordic societies lead the world in promoting women's power.

Source: *The Christian Science Monitor* (1995). Reprinted with permission of *The Christian Science Monitor*. All rights reserved.

But, legitimate or not, male dominance persists in the United States and elsewhere. Does this mean that patriarchy is inevitable? Some sociologists claim that biological factors "wire" the sexes with different motivations and behaviors—especially, aggressiveness in males—making patriarchy difficult, perhaps even impossible, to eliminate (Goldberg, 1974, 1987; Rossi, 1985; Popenoe, 1993b). Most sociologists, however, believe that gender is a social construct that *can* be changed. Just because no society has yet eliminated patriarchy does not mean that we must stay prisoners of the past.

To understand the persistence of patriarchy, we need to examine how gender is rooted and reproduced in society, a process that begins in childhood and continues throughout our lives.

CHAPTER 10 Gender Stratification **251**

TABLE 10–1 Traditional Notions of Gender Identity	
Feminine Traits	**Masculine Traits**
Submissive	Dominant
Dependent	Independent
Unintelligent and incapable	Intelligent and competent
Emotional	Rational
Receptive	Assertive
Intuitive	Analytical
Weak	Strong
Timid	Brave
Content	Ambitious
Passive	Active
Cooperative	Competitive
Sensitive	Insensitive
Sex object	Sexually aggressive
Attractive because of physical appearance	Attractive because of achievement

GENDER AND SOCIALIZATION

From birth right up until death, gender has a hand in shaping human feelings, thoughts, and actions. Children quickly learn that their society defines females and males as different kinds of people; by about age three, they begin to apply gender standards to themselves.

Table 10–1 presents traits that people in the United States traditionally link to "feminine" and "masculine" behavior. Note that the traits in each column are direct opposites of each other; this is so even though research shows that most young people do not develop consistently feminine or masculine personalities (Bernard, 1980; Bem, 1993).

Just as gender affects how we think of ourselves, so it teaches us to *act* in normative ways. **Gender roles** (or sex roles) are *attitudes and activities that a society links to each sex.* Insofar as our culture defines males as ambitious and competitive, we expect them to play team sports and aspire to positions of leadership. To the extent that we define females as deferential and emotional, we expect them to be supportive helpers and quick to cry.

GENDER AND THE FAMILY

The first question people usually ask about a newborn—"Is it a boy or a girl?"—looms large because the answer involves not just sex but the likely direction of a child's life.

In fact, gender is at work even before a child is born, since, especially in lower-income nations, parents hope their first-born will be a boy rather than a girl. Soon after birth, family members usher infants into the "pink world" of girls or the "blue world" of boys (Bernard, 1981). Parents even send gender messages in the way they handle daughters differently from sons. One researcher at an English university presented an infant dressed as either a boy or a girl to a number of women; her subjects handled the "female" child tenderly, with frequent hugs and caresses, while treating the "male" child more aggressively, often lifting him up high in the air or bouncing him on the knee (Bonner, 1984). The lesson is clear: The female world revolves around passivity and emotion, while the male world places a premium on independence and action.

GENDER AND THE PEER GROUP

About the time they enter school, children move outside the family, making friends with others their own age. Peer groups teach additional lessons about gender.

After spending a year watching children at play, Janet Lever (1978) concluded that boys favor team sports with complex rules and clear objectives such as scoring a run or a touchdown. Such games nearly always involve winners and losers, reinforcing masculine traits of aggression and control.

Girls, too, play team sports. But, Lever explains, girls also play hopscotch or jump rope, or simply talk, sing, or dance. These activities have few rules and rarely is "victory" the ultimate goal. Instead of teaching girls to be competitive, Lever explains, female peer groups promote interpersonal skills of communication and cooperation—presumably the basis for girls' future roles as wives and mothers.

Lever's observations recall Carol Gilligan's (1982) gender-based theory of moral reasoning. Boys, Gilligan contends, reason according to abstract principles. For them, "rightness" amounts to "playing by the rules." Girls, by contrast, consider morality a matter of responsibility to others. Thus, the games we play have serious implications for our later lives.

GENDER AND SCHOOLING

In high school, more girls than boys learn secretarial skills and take vocational classes such as cosmetology and food services. Classes in woodworking and auto mechanics, conversely, attract mostly young men.

Pretty Is as Pretty Does: The Beauty Myth

The Duchess of Windsor once quipped, "A woman cannot be too rich or too thin." The first half of her observation might apply to men as well, but certainly not the second. It is no surprise that the vast majority of advertisements placed by the $20-billion-a-year U.S. cosmetics industry and the $40-billion diet industry target women.

According to Naomi Wolf (1990), certain cultural patterns create a "beauty myth" that is damaging to women. The beauty myth arises, first, because society teaches women to measure themselves in terms of physical appearance (Backman & Adams, 1991). Yet, the standards of beauty (such as the *Playboy* centerfold or the 100-pound New York fashion model) are unattainable for most women.

The way society teaches women to prize relationships with men, whom they presumably attract with their beauty, also contributes to the beauty myth.

Striving for beauty not only drives women to be extremely disciplined; it also forces them to be highly attuned and responsive to men. Beauty-minded women, in short, try to please men and avoid challenging male power.

The beauty myth affects males as well: Men should want to possess beautiful women. Thus, our ideas about beauty reduce women to objects and motivate men to possess women as if they were dolls rather than human beings.

Wolf stresses that the beauty myth is not so much about appearance as about behavior. It should not be surprising, therefore, that the beauty myth surfaced in our culture during the 1890s, the 1920s, and the 1980s—all decades of heightened debate about the social standing of women.

Source: Based on Wolf (1990).

In college, the pattern continues, with men disproportionately represented in mathematics and the sciences—including physics, chemistry, and biology. Women cluster in the humanities (such as English), the fine arts (painting, music, dance, and drama), and the social sciences (including anthropology and sociology). New areas of study are also likely to be gender-typed. Computer science, for example, enrolls mostly men, while courses in gender studies tend to enroll more women.

GENDER AND THE MASS MEDIA

Since television first captured the public imagination in the 1950s, white males have held center stage, and racial and ethnic minorities were all but absent from television until the early 1970s. Even when both sexes appear on camera, men generally play the brilliant detectives, fearless explorers, and skilled surgeons. Women, by contrast, play the less capable characters, unnecessary except for the sexual interest they add to the story.

Historically, ads have presented women in the home, cheerfully using cleaning products, serving food, trying out appliances, and modeling clothes. Men, on the other hand, predominate in ads for cars, travel, banking services, industrial companies, and alcoholic beverages. The authoritative "voiceover"—the faceless voice that describes a product in television and radio advertising—is almost always male (Courtney & Whipple, 1983; Davis, 1993).

Advertising also perpetuates what Naomi Wolf called the "beauty myth." The box takes a closer look at how this myth affects women.

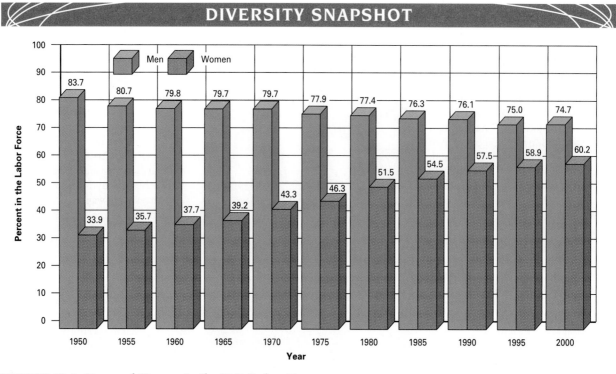

FIGURE 10–2 Men and Women in the U.S. Labor Force
Source: U.S. Department of Labor (2001).

GENDER AND SOCIAL STRATIFICATION

Gender implies more than how people think and act. It is also about social hierarchy. The reality of gender stratification can be seen, first, in the world of work.

WORKING WOMEN AND MEN

Back in 1900, just one-fifth of women were in the labor force. In 2000, 60 percent of women aged sixteen and over worked for income, and three-fourths of working women did so full time. The traditional view that earning an income is exclusively a "man's role" no longer holds true, as Figure 10–2 shows.

Factors that have changed the U.S. labor force include the decline of farming, the growth of cities, a shrinking family size, and a rising divorce rate. Thus, the United States, along with most other nations of the world, considers women working for income to be the rule rather than the exception. In fact, 62 percent

of U.S. married couples now depend on two incomes. As Global Map 10–2 shows, women represent almost half the work force in the United States; this is not the case in many of the poorer societies of the world.

In the past, many women in the labor force were childless. But today, 62 percent of married women with children under age six work for income, as do 77 percent of married women with children between six and seventeen years of age. For divorced women with children, the comparable figures are 77 percent of women with younger children and 82 percent of women with older children (U.S. Census Bureau, 2000).

Gender and occupations. While the shares of women and men in the labor force have been converging, the work they do remains different. The U.S. Department of Labor (2001) reports that nearly half of working women have one of just two job types. Administrative support work draws 23 percent of working women, most of whom are secretaries or other office workers. These are often called "pink-collar" jobs

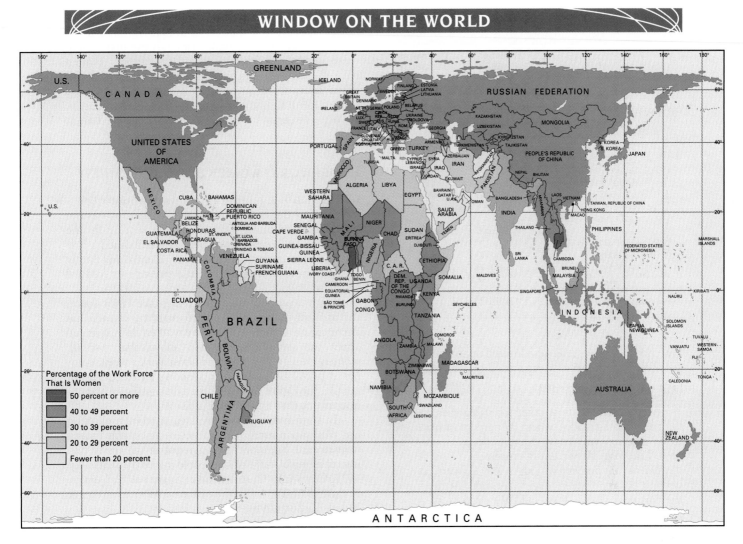

GLOBAL MAP 10–2 Women's Paid Employment in Global Perspective

This map shows, for the world's nations, the percentage of the labor force made up of women. A country's level of technological development plays an important part here. In 2000, women were 47 percent of the labor force in the United States—up almost 10 percent over the last generation. Throughout the industrialized world, nearly one-half of the labor force is made up of women. In poor societies, however, women work even harder than in this country, but they are less likely to be paid for their efforts. In Latin America, for example, women represent about one-third of the paid labor force; in Islamic societies of northern Africa and the Middle East, the figure is significantly lower.

Source: *Peters Atlas of the World* (1990); updated by the author from The World Bank (2000).

because 79 percent are filled by women. Another 16 percent of employed women perform service work. Most of these jobs are in food-service industries, in child care, and health care.

Table 10–2 on page 256 shows the ten occupations with the highest concentrations of women. Overall, although more women now work for pay, they remain segregated in the labor force in jobs at the

TABLE 10-2	Jobs with the Highest Concentrations of Women, 2000	
Occupation	Number of Women Employed	Percent in Occupation Who Are Women
1. Secretary	2,594,000	98.9%
2. Dental hygienist	110,000	98.5
3. Prekindergarten and kindergarten teacher	617,000	98.5
4. Family child-care provider	446,000	97.7
5. Private household child-care worker	268,000	97.5
6. Receptionist	983,000	96.7
7. Dental assistant	210,000	96.4
8. Early childhood teacher's assistant	457,000	95.2
9. Private household cleaner/servant	474,000	94.8
10. Stenographer	146,000	94.7

Source: U.S. Department of Labor, Bureau of Labor Statistics, *Employment and Earnings*, vol. 48, no. 1, January 2001, pp. 178–83.

low end of the pay scale, with limited opportunities for advancement and usually supervised by men (Charles, 1992; Bianchi & Spain, 1996; U.S. Department of Labor, 2001).

Men dominate most other job categories, including the building trades, where 99 percent of brick and stone masons and heavy-equipment mechanics are men. Likewise, 90 percent of engineers, 72 percent of physicians, 70 percent of judges and lawyers, and 55 percent of corporate managers are men. At the top of the business world, men hold 94 percent of senior management jobs in this country's 1,000 largest companies. Just six of these largest U.S. corporations have a woman as their chief executive officer (Catalyst, 2001; U.S. Department of Labor, 2001).

Gender stratification in the workplace is easy to see: Female nurses assist male physicians, female secretaries serve male executives, and female flight attendants are under the command of male airline pilots. Moreover, in any field, the greater a job's income and prestige, the more likely it is held by a man. For example, women represent 98 percent of kindergarten teachers; 83 percent of elementary school teachers; 58 percent of secondary school educators; 42 percent of professors in colleges and universities; and 16 percent of college and university presidents (U.S. Department of Labor, 2001).

But one challenge to male domination in the workplace comes from women who are entrepreneurs.

Women now own more than 9 million small businesses—double the number a decade ago and more than one-third of the total. Although the majority of these businesses are one-person operations, women have shown they can make opportunities for themselves apart from large, male-dominated companies (Ando, 1990; O'Hare & Larson, 1991; Mergenhagen, 1996c; Winters, 1999; U.S. Department of Labor, 2001).

HOUSEWORK: WOMEN'S "SECOND SHIFT"

Global Map 4–1, on page 89, shows that housework—maintaining the home and caring for children—is the province of women throughout the world. In the United States, housework has always embodied a cultural contradiction: We claim it is essential for family life, but housework carries little prestige or reward (Bernard, 1981).

With women's rapid entry into the labor force, the amount of housework performed by women has declined; nevertheless, the *share* women do has stayed about the same. Figure 10–3 shows that, overall, women average 16.5 hours of housework a week, compared to 9.2 hours for men. Among all categories of people, the figure shows, women do significantly more housework than men (Stapinski, 1998).

In sum, men support the idea of women entering the paid labor force, and most count on the money women earn. But more, although not all, men resist taking on an equal share of household duties (Komarovsky, 1973; Cowan, 1992; Robinson & Spitze, 1992; Lennon & Rosenfeld, 1994; Heath & Bourne, 1995; Harpster & Monk-Turner, 1998).

GENDER, INCOME, AND WEALTH

In 1999, the median earnings for women working full time were $27,370, while men working full time earned $37,574. This means that, for every dollar earned by men, women earned about 72 cents.

Among full-time workers, 42 percent of women earned less than $25,000 in 1999, compared to 26 percent of comparable men. At the upper end of the income scale, men were three times more likely than women (14.9 percent versus 5.0 percent) to earn more than $75,000 (U.S. Census Bureau, 2000).

The main reason women earn less is the *kind* of work they do: largely clerical and service jobs. In effect, jobs and gender interact. People still perceive jobs with less clout as "women's work," just as people

FIGURE 10–3 Housework: Who Does How Much?

Overall, women average 16.5 hours of housework per week, compared to 9.2 hours for men. This pattern holds whether people are employed or not, married or not, and parenting or not.

Source: Adapted from Stapinski (1998).

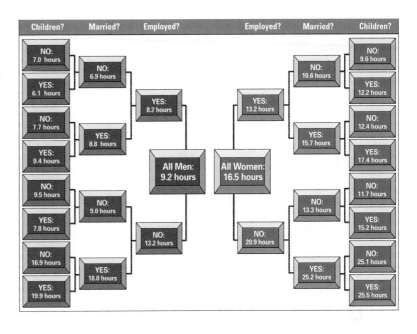

devalue work simply because it is performed by women (Parcel, Mueller, & Cuvelier, 1986; Blum, 1991; England, 1992; Bellas, 1994; Huffman, Velasco, & Bielby, 1996).

In recent decades, proponents of gender equality proposed a policy of "comparable worth." That is, people should be paid not according to the historical double standard but according to the worth of what they do. Several nations, including Great Britain and Australia, have adopted comparable worth policies, but these policies have found limited acceptance in the United States. As a result, women in this country lose as much as $1 billion annually.

A second cause of this gender-based income disparity has to do with the family. Both men and women have children, of course, but our culture defines parenting as more of a woman's responsibility than a man's. Pregnancy and raising small children keep many younger women out of the labor force altogether at a time when their male peers are making significant career advancements. When women workers return to the labor force, they have less job seniority than their male counterparts (Fuchs, 1986; Stier, 1996; Waldfogel, 1997).

Moreover, women who choose to have children may be reluctant or unable to maintain fast-paced jobs that tie up their evenings and weekends. To avoid role strain, they may take jobs that offer a shorter commuting distance, more flexible hours, and employer child-care services. Women pursuing both a career and a family are torn between their dual responsibilities in ways that men are not. Consider this: At age forty, 90 percent of men—but only 35 percent of women—in executive positions have at least one child (F. Schwartz, 1989).

The two factors noted so far—type of work and family responsibilities—account for about two-thirds of the earnings disparity between women and men. A third factor—discrimination against women—accounts for most of the remainder (Pear, 1987; Fuller & Schoenberger, 1991). Because discrimination is illegal, it is practiced in subtle ways (Benokraitis & Feagin, 1995). Corporate women often encounter a *glass ceiling*, a barrier that is invisible because it is denied by company officials but that effectively prevents women from rising above middle management.

For all these reasons, then, women earn less than men in all major occupational categories. As shown in Table 10–3 on page 258, this disparity varies from job to job, but in only two of the major job classifications do women earn more than 75 percent as much as men.

Finally, perhaps because women typically outlive men, many people think that women own most of the country's wealth. Government statistics tell a different story: Fifty-three percent of individuals with $1 million or more in assets are men, although widows are highly represented in this elite club (U.S. Internal Revenue Service, 1993). Just 12 percent of the individuals identified in *Forbes* and *Fortune* magazines as the richest people in the United States are women.

TABLE 10–3 Earnings of Full-Time U.S. Workers,* by Sex, 1999

Selected Occupational Categories	Median Income		Women's Income as a Percentage of Men's
	Men	Women	
Executives, administrators, and managers	$55,261	$36,141	65%
Professional specialties	54,616	37,533	69
Technical workers	41,700	30,001	72
Sales	38,267	23,778	62
Clerical and other administrative support workers	31,767	24,581	77
Precision production, craft, and repair workers	34,429	24,946	72
Machine operators, assemblers, and inspectors	29,156	18,928	65
Transportation and material movers	30,754	20,720	67
Handlers, equipment cleaners, helpers, and laborers	21,206	18,432	87
Service workers	24,289	16,306	67
Farming, forestry, and fishing workers	18,949	13,230	70
All occupations listed above	36,476	26,324	72

*Workers aged 15 and over.

Source: U.S. Bureau of the Census, *Money Income in the United States: 1999*, Current Population Reports, ser. P-60, no. 206 (Washington, D.C.: U.S. Government Printing Office, 2000).

GENDER AND EDUCATION

In the past, our society thought schooling was irrelevant for women because their lives revolved around the home. But times have changed. By 1980, women earned a majority of all associate's and bachelor's degrees; in 1998, that proportion stood at 56 percent (U.S. National Center for Education Statistics, 2001).

College doors have opened to women, and differences in men's and women's majors are becoming smaller. In 1970, for example, women earned just 17 percent of bachelor's degrees in natural sciences, computer science, and engineering; by 1998, the proportion had increased to 31 percent.

In 1993, for the first time, women earned a majority of postgraduate degrees, which are often a springboard to high-prestige jobs. In all areas of study in 1998, women earned 57 percent of master's degrees and 42 percent of all doctorates (including 56 percent of all Ph.D.s in sociology). Women have also broken into many graduate fields that used to be almost all male. For example, in 1970 only a few hundred women received a master's of business administration (M.B.A.) degree, compared to more than 39,000 in 1998 (39 percent of all such degrees) (U.S. National Center for Education Statistics, 2001).

Men continue to dominate some professional fields, however. In 1998, men received 56 percent of law degrees (LL.B. and J.D.), 58 percent of medical degrees (M.D.), and 62 percent of dental degrees (D.D.S. and D.M.D.) (U.S. National Center for Education Statistics, 2001). Our society still defines high-paying professions (and the drive and competitiveness needed to succeed in them) as masculine; this fact helps explain why, although just as many women as men begin most pre-professional graduate programs, women are less likely to complete their degrees (Fiorentine, 1987; Fiorentine & Cole, 1992). Even so, the proportion of women in all these professions is steadily rising.

GENDER AND POLITICS

A century ago, virtually no women held elected office in the United States. In fact, women were legally barred from voting in national elections until the passage of the Nineteenth Amendment to the Constitution in 1920. A few women, however, were candidates for political office even before they could vote. The Equal Rights party supported Victoria Woodhull for the U.S. presidency in 1872; perhaps it was a sign of the times that she spent election day in a New York City jail. Table 10–4 identifies subsequent milestones in women's gradual movement into political life.

Today, thousands of women serve as mayors of cities and towns across the United States, and tens of thousands more hold responsible administrative posts in the federal government. At the state level, 23 percent of state legislators in 2000 were women (up from just 6 percent in 1970). National Map 10–1 on page 260 shows where in the United States women have made the greatest political gains.

Less change has occurred at the highest levels of power, although a majority of U.S. adults claim they would support a qualified woman for any office, including the presidency. After the 2000 national elections,

5 of the 50 state governors were women (10 percent) and, in Congress, women held 59 of 435 seats in the House of Representatives (14 percent) and 13 of 100 seats (13 percent) in the Senate.

In global perspective, although women are half the earth's population, they hold just 11.7 percent of seats in the world's 179 parliaments. While this represents a rise from 3 percent fifty years ago, only in the Nordic nations (Norway, Sweden, Finland, and Denmark) and the Netherlands does the share of parliamentary seats held by women (36.4 percent) even approach their share of the population (Inter-Parliamentary Union, 1997).

GENDER AND THE MILITARY

A small number of women have served in the U.S. armed forces since colonial times. Yet, in 1940, at the outset of World War II, just 2 percent of armed forces personnel were women. In the 1991 Persian Gulf War, 35,000 women represented 6.5 percent of a total deployment of 540,000 U.S. troops. Five of the 148 Gulf War casualties were women.

In 2000, women represented 15 percent of all armed forces personnel. But only the Coast Guard makes all assignments available to women. At the other extreme, the Marine Corps denies women access to two-thirds of its jobs. Those who defend limited roles for women in the military claim that, on average, women lack the physical strength of men. Critics counter that military women are better educated and score higher on intelligence tests than their male counterparts. But the heart of the issue is our society's deeply held view of women as *nurturers*—people who give life and help others—which clashes intolerably with the image of women trained to kill.

Although integrating women into military culture has been difficult, women in all branches of the armed forces are taking on more and more assignments. One reason is that high technology blurs the distinction between combat and noncombat personnel. A combat pilot can fire missiles at a radar-screen target miles away, while nonfighting medical evacuation teams perform their duties at the battle site (McNeil, Jr., 1991; May, 1991; Segal & Hansen, 1992; Wilcox, 1992; Kaminer, 1997).

ARE WOMEN A MINORITY?

A **minority**[1] is *any category of people, characterized by physical or cultural difference, that a society sets apart and subordinates.* Given the clear economic disadvantage of

TABLE 10–4 Significant "Firsts" for Women in U.S. Politics	
1869	Law allows women to vote in Wyoming territory; Utah follows suit in 1870.
1872	First woman to run for the presidency (Victoria Woodhull) represents the Equal Rights party.
1917	First woman elected to the House of Representatives (Jeannette Rankin of Montana).
1924	First women elected state governors (Nellie Taylor Ross of Wyoming and Miriam ["Ma"] Ferguson of Texas); both followed their husbands into office. First woman to have her name placed in nomination for vice-presidency at the convention of a major political party (Lena Jones Springs).
1931	First woman to serve in the Senate (Hattie Caraway of Arkansas); completed the term of her husband upon his death and won reelection in 1932.
1932	First woman appointed to the presidential cabinet (Frances Perkins, secretary of labor in the cabinet of President Franklin D. Roosevelt).
1964	First woman to have her name placed in nomination for the presidency at the convention of a major political party (Margaret Chase Smith, a Republican).
1972	First African American woman to have her name placed in nomination for the presidency at the convention of a major political party (Shirley Chisholm, a Democrat).
1981	First woman appointed to the U.S. Supreme Court (Sandra Day O'Connor).
1984	First woman to be successfully nominated for the vice-presidency (Geraldine Ferraro, a Democrat).
1988	First woman chief executive to be elected to a consecutive third term (Madeleine Kunin, governor of Vermont).
1992	Political "Year of the Woman" yields record number of women in the Senate (six) and the House (forty-eight), as well as (1) first African American woman to win election to U.S. Senate (Carol Moseley-Braun of Illinois); (2) first state (California) to be served by two women senators (Barbara Boxer and Dianne Feinstein); (3) first woman of Puerto Rican descent elected to the House (Nydia Valasquez of New York).
1996	First woman appointed secretary of state (Madeleine Albright).
2000	Record number of women in the Senate (thirteen) and the House (fifty-nine).
2000	First "First Lady" to win elected political office (Hillary Rodham Clinton, senator from New York).

Sources: Based on data compiled from Sandra Salmans, "Women Ran for Office before They Could Vote," *New York Times*, July 13, 1984, p. A11; and news reports.

[1]We use the term *minority* instead of *minority group* because, as explained in Chapter 5 ("Groups and Organizations"), a minority is a category, not a group.

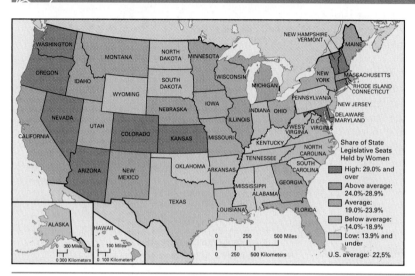

NATIONAL MAP 10–1
Women in State Government across the United States

Although women represent half of U.S. adults, just 23 percent of seats in state legislatures are held by women. Look at the state-by-state variation in the map. In which regions of the country have women gained the greatest political power? What factors do you think account for this pattern?

Source: Center for American Women and Politics, Eagleton Institute of Politics, Rutgers University, "Women in State Legislatures 2000." [Online] Available http://www.rci.rutgers.edu/~cawp/pdf/stleg.pdf, January 5, 2001.

being a woman in our society, it seems reasonable to say that U.S. women are a minority.

Even so, most white women do *not* think of themselves this way (Hacker, 1951; Lengermann & Wallace, 1985). This is partly because, unlike racial minorities (including African Americans) and ethnic minorities (say, Hispanics), white women are well represented at all levels of the class structure, including the very top.

Bear in mind, however, that at every class level, women typically have less income, wealth, education, and power than men. In fact, patriarchy makes women dependent for much of their social standing on men—first their fathers and later their husbands (Bernard, 1981).

MINORITY WOMEN

If women are defined as a minority, what about minority women? Are they doubly handicapped? Generally speaking, the answer is yes, as we can show with some income comparisons. Looking first at race and ethnicity, the median income in 1999 for African American women working full time was $25,142, which is 90 percent as much as the $28,023 earned by white women; Hispanic women earned $20,052, just 72 percent as much as their white counterparts. In regard to gender, African American women earned 83 percent as much as African American men, while Hispanic women earned 86 percent as much as Hispanic men.

With these disadvantages combined, African American women earned 64 percent as much as white men, and Hispanic women earned 51 percent as much (U.S. Census Bureau, 2000). These disparities reflect minority women's lower positions in the occupational and educational hierarchies compared to white women (Bonilla-Santiago, 1990). These data confirm that, while gender has a powerful effect on our lives, it never operates alone. Class position, race and ethnicity, and gender form a multilayered system of disadvantage for some and privilege for others (Ginsburg & Tsing, 1990; St. Jean & Feagin, 1998).

VIOLENCE AGAINST WOMEN

The phrase "rule of thumb" entered our language about 150 years ago when common decency of the day demanded that a man should not beat his wife with a stick thicker than his thumb. Even today, a great deal of "manly" violence is still directed against women. A government report estimates 383,000 sexual assaults against women annually, including 201,000 rapes or attempted rapes. To this number can be added perhaps 2 million physical assaults (Goetting, 1999; U.S. Bureau of Justice Statistics 2000).

Most gender-linked violence occurs where men and women interact most—in the home. Richard Gelles (cited in Roesch, 1984) argues that, except for the police and the military, the family is the most violent organization in the United States. Both sexes

Many private companies and public organizations have adopted policies to discourage forms of behavior that might create a "hostile or intimidating environment." In practice, such policies seek to remove sexuality from the workplace so that employees can do their jobs while steering clear of traditional notions about female and male relationships. The hope is that sexual harassment policies will develop a comfortable informal atmosphere in which people can interact freely and easily.

suffer from family violence, although, by and large, women sustain more serious injuries than men (Straus & Gelles, 1986; Schwartz, 1987; Shupe, Stacey, & Hazlewood, 1987; Gelles & Cornell, 1990; Smolowe, 1994).

Violence toward women also occurs in casual relationships. As noted in Chapter 6 ("Deviance"), most rapes involve not strangers but men known, and often trusted, by their victims. Dianne Herman (2001) argues that the extent of sexual abuse shows that at least some tendency toward sexual violence is built into our way of life. All forms of violence against women—from the wolf whistles that intimidate women on city streets, to a pinch in a crowded subway, to physical assaults that occur at home—express what she calls a "rape culture" of men trying to dominate women. In fact, sexual violence is fundamentally about *power,* not sex, and therefore should be understood as a dimension of gender stratification.

Sexual harassment. The term **sexual harassment** refers to *comments, gestures, or physical contact of a sexual nature that are deliberate, repeated, and unwelcome.* During the 1990s, sexual harassment became a national issue that rewrote the rules for workplace interaction.

Most (but not all) victims of sexual harassment are women. This is because, first, our culture encourages men to be sexually assertive and to perceive women in sexual terms. As a result, social interaction in the workplace, on campus, and elsewhere can readily take on sexual overtones. Second, most individuals in positions of power—including business executives,

physicians, bureau chiefs, assembly line supervisors, professors, and military officers—are men who oversee the work of women. Surveys carried out in widely different work settings show that half of women respondents receive unwanted sexual attention (Loy & Stewart, 1984; Paul, 1991; NORC, 1999).

Sexual harassment is sometimes blatant and direct: A supervisor may solicit sexual favors from an employee and threaten reprisal if the advances are refused. Courts have declared such *quid pro quo* sexual harassment (the Latin phrase means "one thing in return for another") to be a violation of civil rights.

More often, however, the problem of unwelcome sexual attention is a matter of subtle behavior—sexual teasing, off-color jokes, pin-ups displayed in the workplace—that may not even be *intended* to harass anyone. But, based on the *effect* standard favored by many feminists, such actions add up to creating a *hostile environment* (Cohen, 1991; Paul, 1991). Incidents of this kind are far more complex because they involve very different perceptions of the same behavior. For example, a man may think that complimenting a co-worker on her appearance is simply a friendly gesture; she, on the other hand, may feel his behavior hinders her job performance.

Pornography. Chapter 7 ("Sexuality") defined *pornography* as sexually explicit material that causes sexual arousal. Keep in mind, however, that people take different views of exactly what is or is not pornographic, and the law gives local municipalities the power to draw the lines that define what sexually explicit

In the 1950s, Talcott Parsons proposed that sociologists interpret gender as a matter of differences. *As he saw it, masculine men and feminine women formed strong families and made for an orderly society. In recent decades, however, social-conflict theory has reinterpreted gender as a matter of* inequality. *From this point of view, U.S. society places men in a position of dominance over women.*

material violates "community standards" of decency and lacks any redeeming social value.

Traditionally, U.S. society has raised concerns about pornography on *moral* grounds. But pornography also plays a part in gender stratification. From this point of view, pornography is really a *power* issue because most pornography dehumanizes women as the playthings of men. Put otherwise, pornography rests on the assumptions that both sexuality and women should fall under the control of men. Worth noting, in this context, is that the term *pornography* is derived from the Greek word *porne*, meaning a harlot who acts as a man's sexual slave.

In addition, there is widespread concern that pornography promotes violence against women. Depicting women as merely the playthings of men amounts to defining women as weak and undeserving of respect. Men show contempt for women defined in this way by striking out against them. National surveys show that about half of U.S. adults think that pornography encourages people to commit rape (NORC, 1999:237).

Like sexual harassment, pornography raises complex and conflicting concerns. While everyone objects to offensive material, many also endorse rights of free speech and artistic expression. Nevertheless, pressure to restrict pornography has increased, reflecting both the long-standing concern that pornography undermines morality and the more recent concern that it is demeaning and threatening to women.

THEORETICAL ANALYSIS OF GENDER

Each of sociology's major theoretical paradigms addresses the significance of gender in social organization.

STRUCTURAL-FUNCTIONAL ANALYSIS

The structural-functional paradigm views society as a complex system of many separate but integrated parts. From this point of view, gender serves as a means to organize social life.

As Chapter 2 ("Culture") explained, the earliest hunting and gathering societies had little power over the forces of biology. Lacking effective birth control, women were frequently pregnant, and the responsibilities of child care kept them close to home. At the same time, men's greater strength made them better suited for warfare and hunting game. Over the centuries, this sex-based division of labor became institutionalized and largely taken for granted (Lengermann & Wallace, 1985).

Industrial technology, however, opens up a vastly greater range of cultural possibilities. With human muscle power no longer the main energy source, the physical strength of men becomes less significant. In addition, the ability to control reproduction gives women greater choice in shaping their lives. Modern societies relax traditional gender roles as people come to recognize the enormous amount of human talent they waste; yet change comes slowly because gender is deeply embedded in culture.

Talcott Parsons: gender and complementarity. As Talcott Parsons (1942, 1951, 1954) observed, gender helps integrate society—at least in its traditional form. Gender forms a *complementary* set of roles that link women and men into family units for carrying out various important tasks. Women take primary responsibility for managing the household and raising children. Men connect the family to the larger world as they participate in the labor force.

Parsons further argued that distinctive socialization teaches the two sexes their appropriate gender identity and skills needed for adult life. Thus, society teaches boys—presumably destined for the labor force—to be rational, self-assured, and competitive. This complex of traits Parsons termed *instrumental*. To prepare girls for child rearing, socialization stresses *expressive* qualities, such as emotional responsiveness and sensitivity to others.

Society, explains Parsons, encourages gender conformity by instilling in men and women a fear that straying too far from accepted standards of masculinity or femininity courts rejection by the opposite sex. In simple terms, women learn to view nonmasculine men as sexually unattractive, while men learn to shun unfeminine women.

Critical evaluation. Structural functionalism puts forward a theory of complementarity by which gender integrates society both structurally (in terms of what people do) and morally (in terms of what they believe). Influential at midcentury, this approach has lost much of its standing today.

First, functionalism assumes a singular vision of society that is not shared by everyone. For example, historically many women have worked outside the home because of economic necessity, a fact not reflected in Parsons's conventional, middle-class view of social life. Second, Parsons's analysis ignores personal strains and social costs of rigid gender roles (Giele, 1988). Third, to those who seek sexual equality, what Parsons describes as gender "complementarity" amounts to little more than women submitting to male domination.

SOCIAL-CONFLICT ANALYSIS

From a social-conflict point of view, gender involves not just differences in behavior but in power. Consider the striking parallel between the ways ideas about gender have benefited men and the way oppression of racial and ethnic minorities has benefited whites (Hacker, 1951, 1974; Collins, 1971; Lengermann & Wallace, 1985). That is, conventional ideas about gender promote not cohesion but division and tension, with men seeking to protect their privileges as women challenge the status quo.

As earlier chapters noted, the social-conflict paradigm draws heavily on the ideas of Karl Marx. Yet Marx was a product of his times, insofar as his writings focused almost exclusively on men. His friend and collaborator Friedrich Engels, however, did develop a theory of gender stratification (1902; orig. 1884).

Friedrich Engels: gender and class. Looking back through history, Engels saw that in hunting and gathering societies the activities of women and men, while different, had the same importance. A successful hunt brought men great prestige, but the vegetation gathered by women provided most of a group's food supply. As technological advances led to a productive surplus, however, social equality and communal sharing gave way to private property and, ultimately, a class hierarchy. At this point, men gained pronounced power over women. With surplus wealth to pass on to heirs, upper-class men wanted to be sure of paternity, which led them to control the sexuality of women. The desire to control property, then, prompted the creation of monogamous marriage and the family. Women were taught to remain virgins until marriage, to remain faithful to their husbands thereafter, and to build their lives around bearing and raising one man's children.

Furthermore, said Engels, capitalism intensifies this male domination. For one thing, capitalism creates more wealth, which confers greater power on men as owners of property and as primary wage earners. Second, an expanding capitalist economy depends on turning people, especially women, into consumers who seek personal fulfillment through buying and using products. Third, to free men to work in factories, society assigns women the task of maintaining the home. The double exploitation of capitalism, as Engels saw it, lies in paying low wages for male labor and no wages for female work (Eisenstein, 1979; Barry, 1983; Jagger, 1983; Vogel, 1983).

Critical evaluation. Social-conflict analysis of gender highlights how society places the two sexes in unequal positions of wealth, power, and privilege. It is decidedly critical of conventional ideas about gender, claiming that society would be better off if we minimized or even eliminated this dimension of social structure.

But social-conflict analysis, too, has its critics. One problem is that this approach sees conventional families—defended by traditionalists as morally good—as a social evil. Second, from a more practical point of view, social-conflict analysis minimizes the extent to which women and men live together cooperatively, and often happily, in families. A third problem with this approach lies in its assertion that capitalism is the root of gender stratification. In fact, agrarian societies are typically more patriarchal than industrial-capitalist societies, and socialist nations—including the People's Republic of China and the former Soviet Union—are strongly patriarchal (Moore, 1992; Rosendahl, 1997).

These three women made enormous contributions to the women's movement during the twentieth century. Margaret Higgins Sanger (1883–1966) was a pioneer activist in the crusade for women's reproductive rights. Margaret Mead (1901–1978), probably the best known anthropologist of all time, showed how definitions of femininity and masculinity are rooted in culture rather than biology. In 1949, Simone De Beauvoir (1908–1986) published The Second Sex, *one of the first books to explore systematically the importance of gender to social life.*

FEMINISM

Feminism is *the advocacy of social equality for men and women, in opposition to patriarchy and sexism.* The "first wave" of the feminist movement in the United States began in the 1840s, as women opposed to slavery, including Elizabeth Cady Stanton and Lucretia Mott, drew parallels between the oppression of African Americans and the oppression of women. Their primary objective was securing the right to vote, which was finally achieved in 1920. But other disadvantages persisted, and a "second wave" of feminism arose in the 1960s and continues today.

BASIC FEMINIST IDEAS

Feminism views the personal experiences of women and men through the lens of gender. How we think of ourselves (gender identity), how we act (gender roles), and our sex's social standing (gender stratification) are all rooted in the operation of society. Although people who consider themselves feminists disagree about many things, most support five general principles:

1. **The importance of change.** Feminist thinking is decidedly political; it relates ideas to action. It is also critical of the status quo, advocating change toward social equality for women and men.

2. **Expanding human choice.** Feminists argue that cultural conceptions of gender divide the full range of human qualities into two opposing

spheres: the female world of emotion and cooperation and the male world of rationality and competition. As an alternative, feminists propose a "reintegration of humanity" by which *all* individuals develop *all* human traits (French, 1985).

3. **Eliminating gender stratification.** Feminism opposes laws and cultural norms that limit the education, income, and job opportunities of women. For this reason, feminists have long advocated passage of the Equal Rights Amendment (ERA) to the U.S. Constitution, which states:

   Equality of rights under the law shall not be denied or abridged by the United States or any State on account of sex.

   The ERA, first proposed in Congress in 1923, has the support of two-thirds of U.S. adults (NORC, 1999:258). Even so, it has yet to become law, which probably reflects the fact that men dominate state legislatures around the country and most of them oppose the amendment.

4. **Ending sexual violence.** Today's women's movement seeks to eliminate sexual violence. Feminists argue that patriarchy distorts the relationships between women and men, encouraging violence against women in the form of rape, domestic abuse, sexual harassment, and pornography (Millet, 1970; J. Bernard, 1982, orig. 1973; Dworkin, 1987).

5. **Promoting sexual freedom.** Finally, feminism advocates women's control over their sexuality and reproduction. Feminists support the free availability of birth control information. As Figure 10–4 shows, contraceptives are much less available in most of the world than in the United States. Most feminists also support a woman's right to choose whether to bear children or to terminate a pregnancy, rather than allowing men—as fathers, husbands, physicians, and legislators—to control their reproduction. Many feminists also support gay people's efforts to overcome prejudice and discrimination in a predominantly heterosexual culture (Deckard, 1979; Barry, 1983; Jagger, 1983).

TYPES OF FEMINISM

Although feminists agree on the importance of gender equality, they disagree on how to achieve it—through liberal feminism, socialist feminism, and radical feminism (Barry, 1983; Jagger, 1983; Stacey, 1983; Vogel, 1983).

Liberal feminism is rooted in classic liberal thinking that individuals should be free to develop their own talents and pursue their own interests. Liberal feminism accepts the basic organization of our society, but seeks to expand the rights and opportunities of women, in part by passage of the Equal Rights Amendment.

Liberal feminists endorse reproductive freedom for all women. They respect the family as a social institution but seek changes in society, including more widely available maternity and paternity leave and child care for parents who work.

Socialist feminism evolved from the ideas of Karl Marx and Friedrich Engels, in part as a critical response to Marx's inattention to gender. From this point of view, capitalism increases patriarchy by concentrating wealth and power in the hands of a small number of men. Socialist feminists do not think the reforms sought by liberal feminism go far enough. The bourgeois family fostered by capitalism must change if we are to replace "domestic slavery" with some collective means of carrying out housework and child care. Moreover, replacing the traditional family can come about only through a socialist revolution that creates a state-centered economy to meet the needs of all.

Radical feminism, too, finds liberal feminism inadequate. Moreover, radical feminists do not believe that even a socialist revolution would end patriarchy.

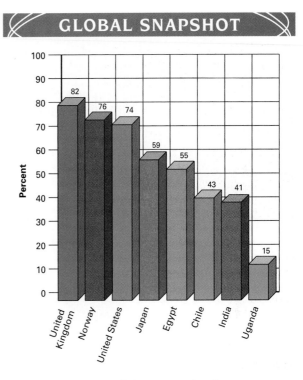

FIGURE 10–4 Use of Contraception by Women of Childbearing Age
Source: United Nations Development Programme (2000).

Instead, to attain gender equality, society must eliminate gender itself. One possible way to achieve this goal is to use new reproductive technology (see Chapter 13, "Family and Religion") to separate women's bodies from the process of childbearing. With an end to motherhood, radical feminists reason, society could leave behind the entire family system, liberating women, men, and children from the tyranny of family, gender, and sex itself (Dworkin, 1987). Thus, radical feminism envisions an egalitarian and gender-free society—a revolution much more broad-sweeping than that sought by Marx.

OPPOSITION TO FEMINISM

Feminism provokes criticism and resistance from men and women who hold conventional ideas about gender. Some men oppose sexual equality for the same reason that many white people have historically opposed social equality for people of color: They do not want to give up their privileges. Other men and women,

As a general rule, patriarchy is strongest in nations with traditional cultures and less economic development. Here we see a husband dragging his wife through the streets of Dhaka, Bangladesh, reportedly because she did not do the cooking on time. But, while violence against women in the United States may not be so public, it remains a serious problem linked to women's subordination here as well.

including those who are neither rich nor powerful, distrust a social movement (especially its radical forms) that attacks the traditional family and rejects patterns that have guided male-female relations for centuries.

Further, for some men, feminism threatens the basis of their status and self-respect: their masculinity. Men who have been socialized to value strength and dominance may feel uneasy about feminist ideals of men as gentle and warm (Doyle, 1983). Similarly, women who have built their lives around husbands and children may see feminism as disparaging the social roles that give meaning to their lives (Marshall, 1985).

Resistance to feminism also comes from academic circles. Some sociologists charge that feminism ignores a growing body of evidence that men and women do think and act in somewhat different ways, which may make gender equality impossible. Furthermore, say critics, with its drive to enhance women's presence in the workplace, feminism belittles the crucial and unique contribution women make to the development

of children—especially in the first years of life (Baydar & Brooks-Gunn, 1991; Popenoe, 1993b).

Finally, there is the question of *how* women should go about improving their social standing. A large majority of U.S. adults think that women should have equal rights, but 70 percent also say women should advance individually, according to their training and abilities; only 10 percent favor women's rights groups or collective action (NORC, 1999:355).

In sum, most opposition to feminism is directed toward its socialist and radical forms, while support for liberal feminism is widespread. Moreover, we are seeing an unmistakable trend toward gender equality. In 1977, 65 percent of all adults endorsed the statement "It is much better for everyone involved if the man is the achiever outside the home and the woman takes care of the home and family." By 1999, however, the share supporting this statement had dropped sharply to 34 percent (NORC, 1999:257).

LOOKING AHEAD: GENDER IN THE TWENTY-FIRST CENTURY

At best, predictions about the future are informed speculation. Just as economists disagree about the likely inflation rate a year from now, so sociologists offer only general observations about the likely future of gender and society.

To begin, change so far has been remarkable. A century ago, women occupied a position of striking subordination. Husbands controlled property in marriage and laws barred women from most jobs, from holding political office, and from voting. Although women remain socially disadvantaged, the movement toward equality has surged ahead. Two-thirds of people entering the work force during the 1990s were women, and, in 2000, for the first time, a majority of families had both husband and wife in the labor force. Clearly, today's economy *depends* on the earnings of women.

Many factors have contributed to this transformation. Perhaps most important, industrialization as well as the more recent Information Revolution have shifted the nature of work from physically demanding tasks that favored male strength to jobs that require thought and imagination. This change puts women and men on a more even footing. In addition, since we have control over reproduction, women's lives are less constrained by unwanted pregnancies.

Many women and men have also deliberately pursued social equality. Sexual harassment complaints are now taken seriously in the workplace. And as more

A Closer Look:
Are Males Really So Privileged?

Anti-male discrimination has become far greater in scope, in degree, and in damage than any which may exist against women.
—*Men's rights advocate Richard F. Doyle*

It is men, this chapter argues, who dominate society. Men enjoy higher earnings, control more wealth, exercise more power, do less housework, and get more respect than women. But Doyle's assertion is an important counterpoint advanced by the "men's rights" movement—that the male world is not nearly as privileged as some people think.

If men are so privileged in our society, why do they turn to crime more often than women? Moreover, the criminal justice system does not give men any special privileges. Probably most people would not be surprised to learn that police are reluctant to arrest a woman, especially if she has children. This fact helps explain why 80 percent of arrests for serious crime put the handcuffs on a male. Neither do men get a break from the courts, since males make up 95 percent of the U.S. prison population. And, despite the fact that women, too, can and do kill, all but two of the roughly 400 offenders executed during the last several decades have been men.

Culture is not always generous to men either. Our way of life praises as "real men" males who work and play hard, and who drink, smoke, and speed on the highways. Given this view of maleness, is it any wonder that men are twice as likely as women to suffer serious assault, three times more likely to fall victim to homicide, and four times more likely to commit suicide? In light of these statistics, how do we explain our society's attention to violence against *women*? Perhaps, critics suggest, we are in the grip of a cultural double standard: We accept harm that comes to males while showing sympathy for the far fewer cases of violence against women. It is this same double standard, the argument continues, that moves women and children out of harm's way and expects men to "go down with the ship" or die defending their country on the battlefield.

Child custody is another sore point from the perspective of many men. Despite decades of consciousness-raising in pursuit of gender fairness, and clear evidence that men earn more than women, courts across the United States routinely award primary care of children to mothers. To make matters worse, men separated from their children by the courts are often stigmatized as "runaway fathers" or "dead-beat dads," even though government statistics show that *women* are more likely to refuse to pay court-ordered child support (in 37 percent of cases) than men (24 percent of cases).

Finally, male advocates point out that affirmative action laws now cover three-fourths of the population, but notably exclude white males. Therefore, in today's affirmative action climate, women have the inside track to college (where they now outnumber men) as well as the work force (where businesses expect they will be called to account for hiring practices).

Even nature seems to plot against men, as, on average, women live six years longer. The controversial question is this: When society plays favorites, who is favored?

Continue the debate . . .

1. *Do you think the criminal justice system favors women over men? Or do men simply get what they deserve? Why, in your opinion, are so many more men than women in prison?*

2. *On your campus, do male organizations (such as fraternities and athletic teams) enjoy special privileges? What about women's organizations?*

3. *On balance, do you agree or disagree with the "men's rights" perspective? What specific points do you find convincing or wrong? Why?*

Sources: Based on Doyle (1980), Scanlon (1992), Rosenfeld (1998), and Kleinfeld (1999).

women assume positions of power in the corporate and political worlds, social change in the new century may be as great as what we have already witnessed.

Gender is an important part of personal identity and family life. It is deeply woven into the moral fabric of our society. Therefore, efforts to change our ideas will continue to provoke opposition, as the final box illustrates. On balance, however, we are seeing movement toward a society in which women and men enjoy equal rights and opportunities.

SUMMARY

1. Gender refers to the meaning a culture attaches to being female and male. Because society gives men more power and resources than women, gender is an important dimension of social stratification.

2. Although some degree of patriarchy exists everywhere, gender varies throughout history and across cultures.

3. Through the socialization process, people incorporate gender into their personalities (gender identity) as well as their actions (gender roles). The major agents of socialization—family, peer groups, schools, and the mass media—reinforce cultural definitions of what is feminine and masculine.

4. Gender stratification shapes the workplace. Although a majority of women are now in the paid labor force, most hold clerical or service jobs. Unpaid housework remains a task performed mostly by women, whether or not they hold jobs outside the home.

5. On average, women earn 72 percent as much as men. This disparity stems from differences in jobs and family responsibilities, as well as discrimination.

6. Women now earn a slight majority of all bachelor's and master's degrees. Men still earn a majority of doctorates and professional degrees.

7. The number of women in politics has increased sharply in recent decades. Still, the vast majority of elected officials, especially at the national level, are men. Moreover, women make up only 15 percent of U.S. military personnel.

8. Because women have a distinctive identity and are disadvantaged, they are a minority, although most do not think of themselves that way. Minority women encounter greater social disadvantages than white women. Overall, minority women earn about 58 percent as much as white men.

9. Violence against women is a widespread problem in the United States. Our society is also grappling with issues of sexual harassment and pornography.

10. Structural-functional analysis suggests that in preindustrial societies distinct roles for females and males reflect biological differences between the sexes. In industrial societies, marked gender inequality becomes dysfunctional and gradually decreases. Talcott Parsons claimed that complementary gender roles promote the social integration of families and society as a whole.

11. Social-conflict analysis views gender as a dimension of social inequality and conflict. Friedrich Engels tied gender stratification to the development of private property.

12. Feminism endorses the social equality of the sexes and opposes patriarchy and sexism. Feminism also seeks to eliminate violence against women and give women control over their sexuality and reproduction.

13. There are three variants of feminist thinking. Liberal feminism seeks equal opportunity for both sexes within current social arrangements; socialist feminism advocates abolishing private property as the means to social equality; radical feminism seeks to create a gender-free society.

14. Although two-thirds of U.S. adults support the Equal Rights Amendment, this legislation— first proposed in Congress in 1923—has yet to become part of the U.S. Constitution.

KEY CONCEPTS

gender (p. 247) the personal traits and social positions that members of a society attach to being female and male

gender stratification (p. 247) unequal distribution of wealth, power, and privilege between men and women

patriarchy (p. 249) a form of social organization in which males dominate females

matriarchy (p. 249) a form of social organization in which females dominate males

sexism (p. 250) the belief that one sex is innately superior to the other

gender roles (sex roles) (p. 252) attitudes and activities that a society links to each sex

minority (p. 259) any category of people, characterized by physical or cultural difference, that a society sets apart and subordinates

sexual harassment (p. 261) comments, gestures, or physical contact of a sexual nature that are deliberate, repeated, and unwelcome

feminism (p. 264) the advocacy of social equality for men and women, in opposition to patriarchy and sexism

CRITICAL-THINKING QUESTIONS

1. How do we know that the different and unequal social standing of women and men is not natural and inevitable?

2. What techniques do the mass media use to "sell" conventional ideas about gender to women and men?

3. Why is gender a dimension of social stratification? How does gender overlap with inequality based on class, race, and ethnicity?

4. What are the key assertions of feminism? How do liberal, socialist, and radical feminism differ from one another?

5. A number of European nations, including Great Britain, Norway, Denmark, and Finland, require that at least 25 percent of candidates for national offices be women. Since just 14 percent of the people in Congress are women, should the United States do likewise?

APPLICATIONS AND EXERCISES

1. Take a walk through a business area of your local community. Which businesses are frequented almost entirely by women? By men? By both men and women? Try to explain the patterns you find.

2. Watch several hours of children's television programming on a Saturday morning. Notice the advertising, which mostly sells toys and breakfast cereal. Keep track of what share of toys is "gendered," that is, aimed at one sex or the other. What traits do you associate with toys intended for boys and those intended for girls?

3. Do some research on the history of women's issues in your state. When was the first woman sent to Congress? What laws have existed restricting the work women could do? Are there any such laws today? Did your state support the passage of the Equal Rights Amendment or not? What share of political officials today is women?

4. Install the CD-ROM packaged in the back of this new textbook to access a variety of study, review, and applications exercises designed to help you better understand the material covered in this chapter. The CD includes an author's tip video, as well as interactive maps, video application exercises, Web links, and study questions.

 SITES TO SEE

http://www.prenhall.com/macionis
Visit the interactive Web site that accompanies this text. Begin by clicking on the cover of your book. You will find a chapter-by-chapter study guide, practice tests, chat room, and many suggested Web links.

http://www.macionis.com
(or http://www.thesociologypage.com)
The author's Web site contains a Links Library that includes dozens of sites providing information about women's lives and women's issues.

http://www.wwwomen.com/
This site provides a search engine to locate all sorts of information concerning women.

http://www.educationindex.com/women/
This site provides numerous and widely varied links to sites concerned with women's issues.

http://www.feminist.org
The Feminist Majority Foundation Online offers news and information about the women's movement.

http://www.catalystwomen.org
This site includes research and information on the social standing of women in business.

http://www.now.org
Visit the Web site for the National Organization of Women to discover the goals and strategies of this organization.

http://www.iwpr.org
Another informative site is run by the Institute for Women's Policy Research. Identify the issues this organization finds most important. Would you characterize this site as feminist? Why or why not?

CHAPTER 11

RACE AND ETHNICITY

On a bright, early fall day almost fifty years ago, in the city of Topeka, Kansas, a minister walked hand in hand with his daughter to the elementary school four blocks from their home. But school officials refused to enroll Linda Brown; they informed her father that she must attend another school, two miles away. This meant a daily six-block walk to a bus stop where Linda sometimes had to wait half an hour for the bus. In bad weather, she could be soaking wet by the time the bus came; one day she became so cold at the bus stop that she walked back home. Why, Linda asked her parents, could she not attend the school that was close by?

The answer—difficult for loving parents to give their child—was Linda Brown's introduction to a harsh fact: Skin color made her a second-class citizen in the United States. The injustice of separate schools for black and white children led the Browns and others to file a lawsuit on behalf of Linda Brown and other children, and, in 1954, Linda's question was put to the Supreme Court of the United States. In Brown v. the Board of Education of Topeka, the Supreme Court ruled unanimously that racially segregated schools provide African Americans with inferior schooling, thus striking down the earlier policy of "separate but equal" education for the two races.

Many greeted the Supreme Court's decision as a turning point in U.S. education. Yet, at the end of the twentieth century, most U.S. children still attended racially imbalanced schools. Although this nation is officially committed to the notion that all people are created equal, race and ethnicity continue to guide the lives of men, women, and children in all sorts of ways.

Around the world, the pattern of inequality and conflict based on color and culture is even more striking.

Since the fall of the former Soviet Union, Ukrainians, Moldavians, Azerbaijanis, and a host of other ethnic peoples in Eastern Europe have struggled to recover their cultural identity. In the Middle East, Arabs and Jews are trying to overcome deep-rooted tensions, as are Protestants and Catholics in Northern Ireland. In dozens of the world's nations, color and culture often flare up in violent confrontation.

An irony of the human condition is that color and culture—a source of great pride—also cause people to degrade themselves with hatred and violence. This chapter examines the meaning of race and ethnicity, explains how these social constructs have shaped our history, and suggests why they continue to play such a central part, for better or worse, in the world today.

THE SOCIAL MEANING OF RACE AND ETHNICITY

People frequently confuse the terms *race* and *ethnicity*. For this reason, we begin with important definitions.

RACE

A **race** is *a socially constructed category composed of people who share biologically transmitted traits that members of a society consider important*. People classify each other racially based on physical characteristics such as skin color, facial features, hair texture, and body shape.

Physical diversity appeared among our human ancestors as the result of living in different regions of

The range of biological variation in human beings is far greater than any system of racial classification allows. This fact is made obvious by trying to place all of the people pictured here into simple racial categories.

the world. In regions of intense heat, for example, people developed darker skin (from the natural pigment melanin) as protection from the sun; in moderate climates, people developed lighter skin. Such traits are—literally—only skin deep because *every* human being the world over is a member of one biological species.

The striking variety of racial traits found today is also the product of migration, so that genetic characteristics once common to a single place are now found in many lands. Especially pronounced is the racial mix in the Middle East (that is, western Asia), historically a crossroads of migration. Greater racial uniformity, by contrast, characterizes more isolated peoples, such as the island-dwelling Japanese. But every population has some genetic mixture, and increasing contact among the world's people ensures even more racial blending in the future.

Although racial categories point to some biological elements, race is a socially constructed concept. This means that racial categories only come into being because a society considers some physical traits important. Around the world, societies show considerable variation in this regard: Typically, people in the

United States attach more meaning to skin color than, say, people in Brazil. In addition, definitions and meanings concerning race change over time. In 2000, for the first time, the U.S. Census Bureau allowed people to describe themselves by using more than one racial category, thus recognizing people as multiracial.

Racial types. Race came into being as a social category when nineteenth-century biologists tried to organize human physical diversity by constructing three racial types. They called people with light skin and fine hair *Caucasoid;* people with dark skin and coarse hair, *Negroid;* and people with yellow or brown skin and distinctive folds on the eyelids, *Mongoloid.*

Sociologists consider such terms misleading at best, and harmful at worst. For one thing, no society contains biologically "pure" people. The skin color of people we might call "Caucasoid" (or "Indo-European," "Caucasian," or, more commonly, "white") ranges from very light (typical in Scandinavia) to very dark (in southern India). The same variation exists among so-called "Negroids" ("Africans," or, more commonly, "black" people) and "Mongoloids" (that is, "Asians"). In fact, many "white" people (say, in southern India) actually have darker skin than many "black" people (like the Negroid Aborigines of Australia).

The population of the United States is racially mixed to a greater degree than most people realize. Over many generations and throughout the Americas, the genetic traits of Negroid Africans, Caucasoid Europeans, and Mongoloid Native Americans (whose ancestors came from Asia) have intermingled. Many "black" people, therefore, have a significant Caucasoid ancestry, and many "white" people have some Negroid genes. In short, whatever people may think, race is no black-and-white issue.

Why, then, do people construct these racial categories in the first place? The reason is that such categories allow societies to rank people in a racial hierarchy, claiming some are inherently "better" than others, although no sound scientific evidence supports such beliefs. But because so much is at stake, societies may construct racial categories in ways that may seem extreme. Throughout much of the twentieth century, for example, many southern states labeled as "colored" anyone with as little as one-thirty-second African ancestry (that is, one African American great-great-great-grandparent). Today, the law allows parents to declare the race of a child however they wish. Even so, most people in the United States are still very sensitive to people's racial background.

A trend toward mixture. The number of officially recorded interracial births has doubled in the last two decades to 159,000, annually about 5 percent of all births. Moreover, when completing their 2000 census forms, almost 7 million people (2.4 percent of the U.S. population) described themselves by checking more than one racial category. Although members of U.S. society attach considerable importance to race, biologically speaking, race has less and less meaning in the United States.

ETHNICITY

Ethnicity is *a shared cultural heritage.* People define themselves—or others—as members of an *ethnic category* based on having common ancestors, language, and religion that confer a distinctive social identity. The United States is a multiethnic society, as shown in Table 11–1. Although English is the favored language, some 30 million people across the country speak Spanish, Italian, German, French, or some other tongue in their homes. Similarly, the United States is a predominantly Protestant nation, but most people of

TABLE 11–1 Racial and Ethnic Categories in the United States, 2000		
Racial or Ethnic Classification*	Approximate U.S. Population	Percent of Total Population
Hispanic descent	**35,305,818**	**12.5%**
Mexican		
Puerto Rican		
Cuban		
Other Hispanic		
African descent	**34,658,190**	**12.3%**
Native American descent	**2,475,956**	**0.9%**
American Indian		
Eskimo		
Aleut		
Asian or Pacific Islander descent	**10,242,998**	**3.6%**
Chinese		
Filipino		
Japanese		
Asian Indian		
Korean		
Vietnamese		
Hawaiian		
Samoan		
Guamanian		
Other Asian or Pacific Islander		
European descent	**211,460,626**	**75.1%**
German		
Irish		
English		
Italian		
French		
Polish		
Dutch		
Scotch-Irish		
Scottish		
Swedish		
Norwegian		
Russian		
Welsh		
Danish		
Hungarian		
Two or more races	**6,826,228**	**2.4%**

*People of Hispanic descent may be of any race. Subcategories are listed according to size in 1990.

Source: U.S. Census Bureau (2001).

Spanish, Italian, and Polish ancestry are Roman Catholic, while many others of Greek, Ukrainian, and Russian descent belong to the Eastern Orthodox Church. More than 6 million Jewish Americans (with ancestral ties to various nations) share a religious

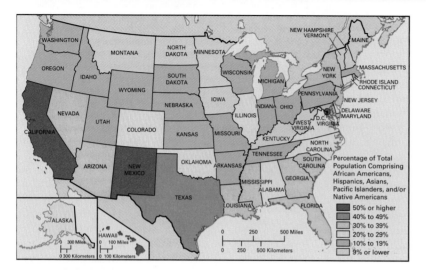

NATIONAL MAP 11–1
Where the Minority-Majority Already Exists

In 2000, minorities had become a majority in three states—Hawaii, California, and New Mexico—as well as the nation's capital, the District of Columbia. With a 45 percent minority population, Texas is approaching a minority-majority. At the other extreme, Vermont and Maine have the lowest share of racial and ethnic minorities (about 2 percent). Why are states with high minority populations in the South and Southwest?

Source: "America 2000: A Map of the Mix," *Newsweek*, September 18, 2000, p. 48.

history. Similarly, at least 7 million men and women are Muslim, and they now outnumber Episcopalians (Blank, 1998).

Race and ethnicity, then, are quite different: One involves biological traits; the other involves culture. But the two may go hand in hand. Japanese Americans, for example, have distinctive physical traits and, for those who maintain a traditional way of life, a distinctive culture as well.

People can fairly easily modify their ethnicity: Immigrants may discard their cultural traditions over time or, like many people of Native American descent, try to revive their heritage (Nagel, 1994; Spencer, 1994). Assuming people mate with others like themselves, however, racial distinctiveness persists over generations.

Finally, ethnicity involves even more variability and mixture than race does, for most people identify with more than one ethnic background. Golf star Tiger Woods, for example, describes himself as one-eighth white, one-eighth American Indian, one-fourth black, one-fourth Thai, and one-fourth Chinese (White, 1997).

MINORITIES

As Chapter 10 ("Gender Stratification") described, a *minority* is a category of people, distinguished by physical or cultural traits and socially disadvantaged.

Distinct from the dominant majority, in other words, societies set apart minorities and subordinate them.

Both race and ethnicity are the basis for minority standing. As shown in Table 11–1, white people of non-Hispanic background (75.1 percent of the total) continue to predominate numerically. But the absolute numbers and share of population for virtually every minority are growing rapidly, so that, within a century, minorities, taken together, will likely become a majority of the U.S. population. National Map 11–1 shows where a minority-majority already exists.

Minorities have two major characteristics. First, they share a *distinctive identity*. Because societies attach importance to race, and these physical traits are virtually impossible for a person to change, most minority men and women are keenly aware of their physical appearance. The significance of ethnicity (which people *can* change) is more variable. Throughout U.S. history, some people (such as Reform Jews) have downplayed their historic ethnicity, while others (including many Orthodox Jews) have maintained distinctive cultural traditions and even formed their own neighborhoods.

A second characteristic of minorities is *subordination*. As the remainder of this chapter shows, U.S. minorities typically have lower income, lower occupational prestige, and limited schooling. This means that class, race, and ethnicity, as well as gender, are overlapping and reinforcing dimensions of social stratification.

Hard Work:
The Immigrant Life in the United States

Early in the morning, it is already hot in Houston as a line of pickup trucks snakes slowly into a dusty yard, where 200 laborers have been gathering since dawn, hoping for a day's work. The driver of the first truck opens his window and tells the foreman that he is looking for a crew to spread boiling tar on a roof. The foreman turns to the crowd and, after a few minutes, three workers step forward and climb into the back of the truck. The next driver is looking for two experienced house painters. The scene is repeated over and over, as men and a few women leave to dig ditches, spread cement, hang drywall, open clogged septic tanks, and even crawl under houses to poison rats.

To each driver who enters, Abdonel Cespedes, the foreman, asks, "How much?" Most of the people in the trucks offer five dollars an hour. Cespedes automatically responds, "Six-fifty; the going rate is $6.50 for a hour's hard work." Sometimes he convinces people to pay that much, but usually not. The workers, who come from Mexico, El Salvador, and Guatemala, know that dozens of them will end up with no work at all this day. Most jump at the offer of five dollars an hour because they know, when the day is over, they will have fifty dollars in their pocket.

Labor markets like this one are common in large cities, especially across the southwestern United States. The surge in immigration in recent years has brought millions of people in search of work, and most have little schooling and speak little English.

Manuel Barrera has taken a day's work moving the entire contents of a store to a storage site as part of a repossession. He arrives at the boarded-up store and gazes at the mountains of heavy furniture that he must carry out to a moving van, drive across town, and then carry

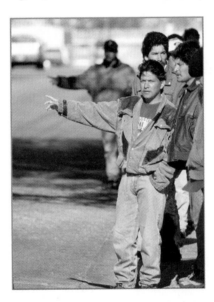

again. He sighs when he realizes that the store has no air conditioning. There is no break for lunch. No one says anything about toilets. Barrera shakes his head, "I will do this kind of work because it puts food on the table. But I did not foresee it would turn out like this."

The hard truth is that immigrants to the United States do the jobs that no one else wants. Indeed, immigrants represent the bottom level of the national economy, working in restaurants and hotels, on construction crews, and in private homes cooking, cleaning, and caring for children. Many well-off families take the labor of immigrants as much for granted as their sport utility vehicles and cell phones. Few immigrants make much more than the minimum wage ($5.15 per hour), and it is rare that an immigrant worker receives any health or pension benefits. Across the United States, about half of all housekeepers, household cooks, tailors, and restaurant waiters are men or women born abroad. In sum, much low-paying service work is performed by immigrants who are, literally, "at your service."

Source: Based on Booth (1998).

The box profiles the struggles of Latin Americans who are recent immigrants to the United States.

Of course, not all members of any minority category are disadvantaged. Some Latinos, for example, are quite wealthy; certain Chinese Americans are celebrated business leaders; and African Americans are included among our nation's leading scholars. But even

the greatest achievement rarely allows individuals to transcend their minority standing (Benjamin, 1991). That is, race or ethnicity often serves as a *master status* (described in Chapter 4, "Social Interaction in Everyday Life") that overshadows personal accomplishments.

Finally, minorities are usually a small proportion of a society's population, but this is not always the

Racial and ethnic stereotypes are deeply embedded in our culture and language. Many people speak of someone "gypping" another without realizing that this word insults European Gypsies, a category of people long pushed to the margins of European societies. What about terms such as "Dutch treat," "French kiss," or "Indian giver"?

case. For example, black South Africans are disadvantaged even though they are a numerical majority in their country. In the United States, women represent slightly more than half the population but are still struggling for the opportunities and privileges enjoyed by men.

PREJUDICE AND STEREOTYPES

November 19, 1994, Jerusalem, Israel. We are driving along the outskirts of this historic city—a holy place to Jews, Christians, and Muslims—when Razi, our taxi driver, spots a small group of Ethiopian Jews at a street corner. "Those people over there," he begins, "they are different. They don't drive cars. They don't want to improve themselves. Even when our country offers them schooling, they don't take it." He shakes his head and pronounces the Ethiopians "socially incorrigible."

Prejudice is *a rigid and irrational generalization about an entire category of people.* Prejudice is irrational insofar as people hold inflexible attitudes supported by little or no direct evidence. Prejudice may target people of a particular social class, sex, sexual orientation, age, political affiliation, race, or ethnicity.

Prejudices are *prejudgments* that can be positive or negative. Our positive prejudices exaggerate the virtues of people like ourselves, while our negative prejudices condemn those who differ from us. Negative prejudice runs along a continuum from mild aversion to outright hostility. Because such attitudes are embedded in culture, everyone has at least some measure of prejudice.

Prejudice often takes the form of *stereotypes* (*stereo* is derived from the Greek, meaning "hard" or "solid"), which are exaggerated descriptions applied to every person in some category. Many white people hold stereotypical views of minorities. But minorities, too, use stereotypes, sometimes of whites and sometimes of other minorities, including themselves. Some Koreans, for example, portray African Americans as dishonest. Some African Americans, in turn, express the same attitude toward Jewish people (Smith, 1996; Cummings & Lambert, 1997).

RACISM

A powerful and destructive form of prejudice, **racism** refers to *the belief that one racial category is innately superior or inferior to another.* Racism has pervaded world history. The ancient Greeks, the peoples of India, and the Chinese—despite their many notable achievements—were all quick to consider people unlike themselves as inferior.

Racism has also been widespread in the United States, where, for centuries, ideas about racial inferiority supported slavery. Today, overt racism in this country has subsided to some extent because our more egalitarian culture urges us to evaluate people, in the Reverend Martin Luther King, Jr.'s, words,

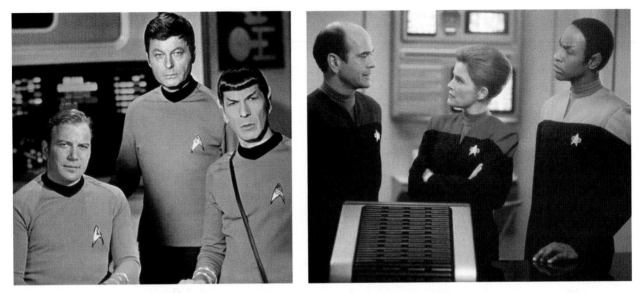

Historically, minorities have been absent from public life, but this situation is changing. "Star Trek" has been a television favorite for more than thirty years. Compare the cast of the original show, which first aired in 1966, to the crew of the most recent "Star Trek: Voyager." What does the difference in casting suggest about our society's changing view of racial and ethnic minorities?

"not by the color of their skin but by the content of their character."

Even so, racism—in thought and deed—remains a serious social problem everywhere as people still contend that some racial and ethnic categories are "better" than others. Indeed, some people wonder if members of one race are smarter than those of another. As the box on pages 278–79 explains, however, measures of intelligence are affected by environment, not by biology.

THEORIES OF PREJUDICE

What are the origins of prejudice? Social scientists provide various answers to this vexing question, focusing on frustration, personality, culture, and social conflict.

Scapegoat theory. *Scapegoat theory* holds that prejudice springs from frustration among people who are themselves disadvantaged (Dollard, 1939). Take the case of a white woman unhappy with the low wages she earns at a textile factory. Directing hostility at the powerful people who employ her carries obvious risk; therefore, she may instead blame her low pay on the presence of minority co-workers. Her prejudice does not improve her situation, but it serves as a relatively safe way to vent anger, and it may give her the comforting sense that at least she is superior to someone.

A **scapegoat**, then, is *a person or category of people, typically with little power, whom people unfairly blame for their own troubles.* Because they are "safe targets," minorities are often scapegoats.

Authoritarian personality theory. According to T. W. Adorno (1950), extreme prejudice is a personality trait in certain individuals. This conclusion is supported by research showing that people who display strong prejudice toward one minority are usually intolerant of all minorities. These *authoritarian personalities* rigidly conform to conventional cultural values, see moral issues as clear-cut matters of right and wrong, and look upon society as naturally competitive, with "better" people (like themselves) inevitably dominating those who are weaker. Adorno also found that people tolerant toward one minority are likely to be accepting of all; they tend to be more flexible in their moral judgments and treat all people as equals.

Adorno thought that people with little education and those raised by cold and demanding parents tend to develop authoritarian personalities. Filled with anger and anxiety as children, they grow into hostile

CRITICAL THINKING

Does Race Affect Intelligence?

Are Asian Americans smarter than white people? Is the typical white person more intelligent than the average African American? Throughout the history of the United States, we have painted one category of people as intellectually more gifted than another. Moreover, people have used such thinking to justify the privileges of the allegedly superior category and even to bar supposedly inferior people from entering this country.

Scientists know that the distribution of the intelligence of individuals forms a "bell curve," as shown in the figure at the right. By convention, average performance is defined as an intelligence quotient (IQ) score of 100 (technically, an IQ score is mental age as measured by a test divided by age in years with the result multiplied by 100; thus, an eight-year-old who performs like a ten-year-old has an IQ of $10/8 = 1.25 \times 100 = 125$).

In a controversial study of intelligence and social inequality, Richard Herrnstein and Charles Murray (1994) claimed that overwhelming evidence shows that

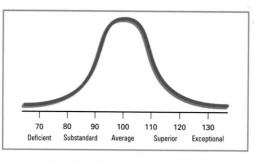

70	80	90	100	110	120	130
Deficient	Substandard		Average		Superior	Exceptional

IQ: The Distribution of Intelligence

race is related to measures of intelligence. More specifically, they say the average IQ of people with European ancestry is 100; the average for people of East Asian ancestry is 103; and for people of African descent, the average is 90.

Of course, assertions of this kind are explosive because they fly in the face of our democratic and egalitarian sentiments, which hold that no racial type is inherently "better" than another. Such assertions have led some critics to charge that intelligence tests are not valid, and even that the concept of intelligence has little real meaning.

Most social scientists acknowledge that IQ tests do measure something important that we think of as "intelligence," and they agree that *individuals* vary in intellectual

and aggressive adults, seeking scapegoats whom they consider inferior.

Culture theory. A third theory contends that while extreme prejudice is found in certain people, some prejudice is found in everyone because it is embedded in culture. Emory Bogardus (1968) studied the effects of culturally rooted prejudices for more than forty years. He developed the concept of *social distance* to gauge how close or distant people feel toward various racial and ethnic categories. Bogardus found that most people in the United States feel closest to individuals with English, Canadian, and Scottish backgrounds, even welcoming marriage with them. Attitudes are less favorable toward the French, Germans, Swedes, and Dutch, and most negative toward people of Asian and African descent.

According to Bogardus, prejudice is so widespread that we cannot explain it as merely a trait of a handful of people with authoritarian personalities, as Adorno suggested. Rather, Bogardus believed, everyone in U.S. society expresses some bigotry because we live in

a "culture of prejudice" that has taught us to view certain categories of people as inferior to others.

Conflict theory. A fourth explanation is that powerful people use prejudice to justify oppressing others. To the extent that Anglos look down on Latino immigrants in the Southwest, for example, the well-off among them can get away with paying immigrants low wages for hard work. Similarly, all elites benefit when prejudice divides workers along racial and ethnic lines and discourages them from working together to advance their common interests (Geschwender, 1978; Olzak, 1989).

Another conflict-based argument, advanced by Shelby Steele (1990), is that minorities themselves cultivate a climate of *race consciousness* in order to win greater power and privileges. Because of their historic disadvantage, minorities claim that they are now victims entitled to special consideration based on their race. While this strategy can yield short-term gains, Steele cautions that such thinking can spark a backlash from whites or others who oppose "special treatment" for anyone on the basis of race or ethnicity.

aptitude. But they reject the notion that any *category* of people, on average, is smarter than any other. Research does show that categories of people display small differences in measured intelligence; but the crucial question is *why*.

Thomas Sowell explains that most of the documented differences in intelligence are not due to biology but to environment. In some skillful sociological detective work, Sowell traced IQ scores for various racial and ethnic categories throughout the twentieth century. He found that, on average, immigrants from European nations such as Poland, Lithuania, Italy, and Greece, as well as Asian countries including China and Japan, scored ten to fifteen points below the U.S. average. But, *today*, people in these same categories have IQ scores that are average or above average. Among Italian Americans, for example, average IQ jumped almost ten points in fifty years; among Polish and Chinese Americans, the jump was almost twenty points.

Because genetic changes occur over thousands of years and most people in the various categories married others like themselves, biological factors cannot explain such a rapid rise in IQ scores. The only plausible explanation is cultural: The descendants of early immigrants improved their intellectual performance as their living conditions improved and opportunities for schooling increased.

Sowell found a similar pattern for African Americans. Historically, the average IQ score of African Americans living in the North is about ten points higher than the average score of those living in the South. Further, among the descendants of African Americans who migrated from the South to the North after 1940, IQ scores went up just as they did with descendants of earlier immigrants. Thus, if environmental factors are the same for various categories of people, racial IQ differences largely disappear.

What these test score differences do tell, Sowell continues, is that *cultural patterns* matter. If Asians score high on tests, it is not because all Asians are smart, but because they have been raised to value learning and pursue excellence. For their part, African Americans are no less intelligent than anyone else, but they carry a legacy of disadvantage that can undermine self-confidence and discourage achievement.

What do you think?

1. *Do measures of intelligence always reflect people's environment? To what extent are IQ scores valid measures?*

2. *Why, according to Thomas Sowell, do some racial and ethnic categories show dramatic, short-term changes in average IQ scores?*

3. *What could schools do to raise the IQ scores of children, especially those from disadvantaged backgrounds?*

Sources: Herrnstein & Murray (1994) and Sowell (1994, 1995).

DISCRIMINATION

Closely related to prejudice is **discrimination**, *treating various categories of people unequally*. While prejudice refers to attitudes, discrimination is a matter of actions. Like prejudice, discrimination can be either positive (providing special advantages) or negative (creating obstacles). Discrimination also ranges from subtle to blatant.

Prejudice and discrimination often occur together: A prejudiced personnel manager, for example, may refuse to hire minorities. Robert Merton (1976) describes such a person as an *active bigot* (see Figure 11–1a on page 280). But prejudice and discrimination may not occur together, as in the case of the prejudiced personnel manager who, out of fear of lawsuits, *does* hire minorities. Merton calls this person a *timid bigot*. People who are generally tolerant of minorities yet discriminate when it is to their advantage to do so are *fair-weather liberals*. Finally, Merton's *all-weather liberal* is free of both prejudice and discrimination.

INSTITUTIONAL PREJUDICE AND DISCRIMINATION

We typically think of prejudice and discrimination as the hateful ideas or actions of specific people. But more than thirty years ago, Stokely Carmichael and Charles Hamilton (1967) pointed out that far greater harm results from **institutional prejudice and discrimination**, which refers to *bias inherent in the operation of society's institutions*, including schools, hospitals, the police, and the workplace. For example, researchers have shown that banks reject home mortgage applications from minorities at a higher rate than those from white people, even when income and quality of neighborhood are held constant (Gotham, 1998).

According to Carmichael and Hamilton, people are slow to condemn or even recognize institutional prejudice and discrimination because it often involves respected public officials and long-established traditions. A case in point is the Supreme Court's 1954 *Brown* decision, described in the opening to this chapter.

FIGURE 11–1 Patterns of Prejudice and Discrimination

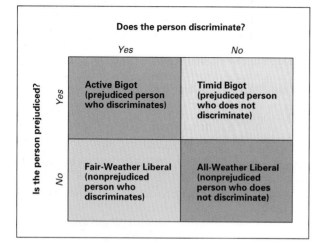

Does the person discriminate?

	Yes	No
Is the person prejudiced? — Yes	**Active Bigot** (prejudiced person who discriminates)	**Timid Bigot** (prejudiced person who does not discriminate)
Is the person prejudiced? — No	**Fair-Weather Liberal** (nonprejudiced person who discriminates)	**All-Weather Liberal** (nonprejudiced person who does not discriminate)

(a) Prejudice and Discrimination: Various Combinations

Source: Merton (1976).

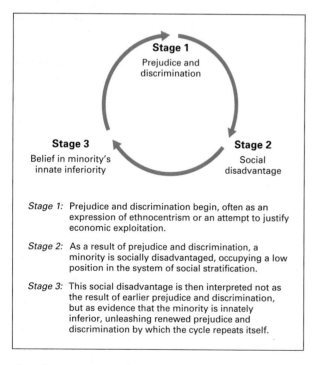

Stage 1
Prejudice and discrimination

Stage 3
Belief in minority's innate inferiority

Stage 2
Social disadvantage

Stage 1: Prejudice and discrimination begin, often as an expression of ethnocentrism or an attempt to justify economic exploitation.

Stage 2: As a result of prejudice and discrimination, a minority is socially disadvantaged, occupying a low position in the system of social stratification.

Stage 3: This social disadvantage is then interpreted not as the result of earlier prejudice and discrimination, but as evidence that the minority is innately inferior, unleashing renewed prejudice and discrimination by which the cycle repeats itself.

(b) The Vicious Cycle

Prejudice and discrimination can form a vicious cycle, perpetuating themselves.

Before this, the principle of "separate but equal" was the law of the land, upholding institutional racism in the form of an educational caste system. Today, decades later, the law may have changed but most U.S. students still attend schools that are overwhelmingly one race or the other. Indeed, in 1991, the courts declared that neighborhood schools will never provide equal education as long as our population is segregated with most African Americans living in central cities and most white people (and Asian Americans) living beyond the city limits in suburbs.

PREJUDICE AND DISCRIMINATION: THE VICIOUS CYCLE

Prejudice and discrimination reinforce each other. The Thomas theorem, discussed in Chapter 4 ("Social Interaction in Everyday Life"), offers a simple explanation of this fact: *Situations that are defined as real become real in their consequences* (Thomas, 1966:301; orig. 1931).

As W. I. Thomas recognized, stereotypes become real to people who believe them, sometimes even to those victimized by them. Prejudice on the part of white people toward African Americans, for example, does not produce *innate* inferiority, but it can produce *social* inferiority, pushing minorities into low-paying jobs. Then, if white people interpret social disadvantage as evidence that minorities do not measure up to their standards, they unleash a new round of prejudice and discrimination, giving rise to a vicious cycle whereby each perpetuates the other, as shown in Figure 11–1b.

MAJORITY AND MINORITY: PATTERNS OF INTERACTION

Social scientists describe interaction between majority and minority members of a society in terms of four models: pluralism, assimilation, segregation, and genocide.

PLURALISM

Pluralism is *a state in which racial and ethnic minorities are distinct but have social parity.* In other words, people who differ in appearance or cultural heritage all share resources more or less equally.

The United States is pluralistic to the extent that all people have equal standing under the law. Moreover, large cities contain countless "ethnic villages" where people proudly display the traditions of their immigrant ancestors. These include New York's Spanish Harlem, Little Italy, and Chinatown; Philadelphia's

In the years following the founding of the National League in 1876, a handful of talented African American players joined a number of professional baseball teams. By the 1890s, however, a "color line" had been drawn, racially segregating professional baseball and giving rise to the "Negro leagues," which reached their greatest popularity in the 1930s and 1940s. After professional baseball was once again integrated in 1947 (first by Jackie Robinson of the New York Giants and, months later, by Larry Dobie of the Cleveland Indians), the "Negro leagues" faded away in the 1950s.

Italian "South Philly"; Chicago's "Little Saigon"; and Latino East Los Angeles.

But the United States is not really pluralistic for three reasons. First, while many people appreciate their cultural heritage, only a small proportion want to live with only their "own kind" (NORC, 1999). Second, our tolerance for social diversity is limited. One reaction to the growing proportion of minorities in the United States, for example, is a social movement to make English this nation's official language. Third, as we shall see later in this chapter, it is simply a fact that people of various colors and cultures have unequal social standing.

ASSIMILATION

Many people think of the United States as a "melting pot" in which different nationalities blend together. In truth, however, rather than everyone "melting" into some new cultural pattern, most minorities have adopted the dominant culture established by the earliest settlers. Why? Because doing so is both the avenue to upward social mobility and a way to escape the prejudice and discrimination directed against more visible foreigners (Newman, 1973). Sociologists use the term **assimilation** to describe *the process by which minorities gradually adopt patterns of the dominant category.* Assimilation involves changing styles of dress, values, religion, language, and friends.

The degree of assimilation in the United States varies by category. For example, Germans and Irish have "melted" more than Italians, and the Japanese more than the Chinese or Koreans. Multiculturalists,

however, oppose assimilation because it suggests that minorities are "the problem" and defines them (rather than majority people) as the ones who need to do all the changing.

Note, too, that assimilation involves changes in ethnicity but not in race. For example, many descendants of Japanese immigrants have discarded their traditions although they retain their racial identity. For racial traits to diminish over generations requires **miscegenation,** *biological reproduction by partners of different racial categories.* Although the rate of interracial marriage is rising, it is still low; thus, only 5 in 100 births are to parents of different races.

SEGREGATION

Segregation is *the physical and social separation of categories of people.* Sometimes minorities, especially religious orders like the Amish, voluntarily segregate themselves. Usually, however, majorities segregate minorities by excluding them. Neighborhoods, schools, occupations, hospitals, and even cemeteries can be segregated. While pluralism fosters distinctiveness without disadvantage, segregation enforces separation to the detriment of a minority.

Racial segregation has a long history in the United States, beginning with slavery and evolving into racially separate lodging, schooling, buses, and trains. Decisions such as the 1954 *Brown* case have reduced *de jure* (Latin, meaning "by law") discrimination in the United States. However, *de facto* ("in fact") segregation continues in the form of countless neighborhoods that are home to people of a single race.

A resurgence of Native American pride is evident in this celebration held in Window Rock, Arizona, in 1991 to honor Navajo soldiers returning from the Persian Gulf War. The older men shown here are World War II veterans—famous Navajo "code talkers"—who fought in the Pacific and devised a code from their native language that the opposing Japanese army was never able to understand.

Segregation in the United States has declined somewhat in recent decades (Farley, 1997). Yet Douglas Massey and Nancy Denton (1989) have documented the *hypersegregation* of African Americans in some inner cities. These people have little contact of any kind with people in the larger society. Hypersegregation affects about one-fifth of all African Americans but only a few percent of comparably poor whites (Jagarowsky & Bane, 1990; Krivo et al., 1998).

Segregated minorities understandably resent their second-class citizenship, and sometimes the actions of even a single person can bring about change. On December 1, 1955, Rosa Parks boarded a bus in Montgomery, Alabama, and sat in a section designated by law for African Americans. When a crowd of white passengers boarded the bus, the driver asked four black people to give up their seats to white people. Three did so, but Rosa Parks refused. The driver left the bus and returned with police, who arrested her for violating the racial segregation laws. She was later convicted in court and fined $14. Her stand (or sitting) for justice rallied the African American community of Montgomery to boycott city buses and ultimately ended this form of segregation (King, 1969).

GENOCIDE

Genocide is *the systematic killing of one category of people by another.* Although this deadly form of racism and ethnocentrism violates nearly every recognized moral standard, it has occurred time and again in human history.

Genocide figured prominently in contact between Europeans and the original inhabitants of the Americas. From the sixteenth century on, as the Spanish, Portuguese, English, French, and Dutch forcibly colonized vast empires, they decimated native populations. Some native peoples fell victim to calculated killing, but most succumbed to diseases brought by Europeans, to which they had no natural defenses (Matthiessen, 1984; Sale, 1990).

Genocide also occurred in the twentieth century. Unimaginable horror befell European Jews in the 1930s and 1940s during Adolf Hitler's reign of terror known as the Holocaust. The Nazis murdered more than 6 million Jewish men, women, and children. The Soviet dictator Josef Stalin murdered on an even greater scale, killing some 30 million real and imagined enemies during his violent rule. Between 1975 and 1980, Pol Pot's Communist regime in Cambodia butchered all "capitalists," which included anyone able to speak a Western language. In all, some 2 million people (one-fourth of the population) perished in the Cambodian "killing fields" (Shawcross, 1979).

Tragically, genocide continues. Recent examples include Hutus killing Tutsis in the African nation of Rwanda and Serbs killing Bosnians in the Balkans of Eastern Europe.

These four patterns of minority-majority contact have all been played out in the United States. While many people proudly point to patterns of pluralism and assimilation, it is also important to recognize the degree to which U.S. society has been built on segregation (of African Americans) and genocide (of Native Americans). The remainder of this chapter examines how these four patterns have shaped the past and present social standing of major racial and ethnic categories in the United States.

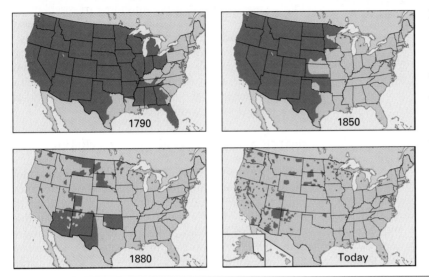

NATIONAL MAP 11–2
Land Controlled
by Native Americans,
1790–1998

Two hundred years ago, Native Americans controlled three-fourths of the land that would eventually become today's United States. Today, Native Americans control 314 reservations—scattered across the United States—that, together, account for just 2 percent of the country's land area. How would you characterize these locations?

Source: Copyright © 1998 by The New York Times Co. Reprinted by permission.

RACE AND ETHNICITY IN THE UNITED STATES

> Give me your tired, your poor,
> Your huddled masses yearning to breathe free,
> The wretched refuse of your teeming shore,
> Send these, the homeless, tempest-tossed to me:
> I lift my lamp beside the golden door.

These words by Emma Lazarus, inscribed on the Statue of Liberty, express cultural ideals of human dignity, personal freedom, and opportunity. Indeed, the United States has provided more of the "good life" to more immigrants than any other nation. But as the history of this country's minorities reveals, our golden door has opened more widely for some than for others.

NATIVE AMERICANS

The term *Native Americans* refers to the hundreds of societies—including Aleuts, Cherokee, Zuni, Sioux, Mohawk, Aztec, and Inca—who first settled the Western Hemisphere. Some 30,000 years before Columbus stumbled on the Americas, migrating peoples crossed a land bridge from Asia to North America where the Bering Strait (off the coast of Alaska) lies today. Gradually, they spread throughout North and South America.

When the first Europeans arrived, late in the fifteenth century, the Native American population was in the millions. But by the beginning of the twentieth century, after relentless subjugation and acts of genocide, the "vanishing Americans" numbered a mere 250,000 (Dobyns, 1966; Tyler, 1973); the lands they controlled had also shrunk dramatically, as shown in National Map 11–2.

It was Christopher Columbus (1446–1506) who first referred to Native Americans as *Indians*, because he thought he had reached India; actually, he had landed in the Bahama Islands in the Caribbean. Columbus found the indigenous people passive and peaceful, a stark contrast to materialistic and competitive Europeans (Matthiessen, 1984; Sale, 1990). Yet, even as Europeans seized the lands of Native Americans, they justified their actions by calling their victims thieves and murderers (Unruh, 1979; Josephy, 1982).

After the Revolutionary War, the new United States government adopted a pluralist approach to Native American societies and sought to gain more land from them through treaties. Payment for land was far from fair, however, and when Native Americans resisted surrender of their homelands, the U.S. government simply used superior military power to evict them. By the early 1800s, few Native Americans remained east of the Mississippi River.

In 1871, the United States declared Native Americans wards of the government and adopted a strategy of forced assimilation. Now Native Americans continued to lose their land, and they were well on their way

TABLE 11–2 The Social Standing of Native Americans, 1990		
	Native Americans	Entire United States
Median family income	$21,750	$35,225
Percent in poverty	30.9%	13.1%
Completion of four or more years of college (age 25 and over)	9.3%	20.3%

Source: U.S. Census Bureau (2000).

to losing their culture as well. Reservation life fostered dependency, replacing ancestral languages with English and traditional religions with Christianity. Officials took many children from their parents and handed them over to boarding schools, where they were resocialized as "Americans." Authorities gave local control of reservations to the few Native Americans who supported government policies, and distributed reservation land—traditionally held collectively—as private property to individual families (Tyler, 1973).

Not until 1924 were Native Americans entitled to U.S. citizenship. After that, many migrated from reservations, adopting mainstream cultural patterns and marrying non–Native Americans. Today, Native Americans control just a small share of land in this country; their median family income is far below the U.S. average, as shown in Table 11–2; and relatively few Native Americans earn a college degree.[1]

From in-depth interviews with Native Americans in a western city, Joan Albon (1971) concluded that their low social standing reflects cultural factors, including a noncompetitive view of life and reluctance to pursue higher education. In addition, she noted, many Native Americans have dark skin, which makes them targets of prejudice and discrimination.

Like other racial and ethnic minorities in the United States, Native Americans have reasserted pride in their cultural heritage. Native American organizations report a surge in new membership applications,

and many children can speak native tongues better than their parents (Fost, 1991; Johnson, 1991; Nagel, 1996). Moreover, the legal autonomy of reservations has turned out to be an ace-up-the-sleeve for many Native American tribes, who have built gaming casinos and now control 20 percent of all U.S. gambling. But such financial windfalls benefit relatively few native people; most endure their disadvantages with a profound sense of the injustice they have suffered at the hands of white people.

WHITE ANGLO-SAXON PROTESTANTS

White Anglo-Saxon Protestants (WASPs) were not the first people to inhabit the United States, but they came to dominate this nation once English settlement began. Most WASPs are of English ancestry, but this category also includes Scots and Welsh. With more than 50 million people of English ancestry, one in five members of our society claims some WASP background. National Map 11–3 shows where the highest concentrations of WASPs are found.

Historically, WASP immigrants were highly skilled and motivated toward achievement by what we now call the Protestant work ethic. Because of their numbers and power, WASPs were not subject to the prejudice and discrimination experienced by other categories of immigrants. In fact, the historical dominance of WASPs has led others to want to become more like them.

WASPs were never one single group; especially during colonial times, considerable hostility separated English Anglicans, for example, from Scot-Irish Presbyterians (Parrillo, 1994). But during the nineteenth century, most WASPs joined together to oppose the arrival of "undesirable foreigners"—Germans in the 1840s and Italians in the 1880s. Political movements managed to legally limit the flow of immigrants. Those WASPs who could afford it sheltered themselves in exclusive suburbs and restrictive clubs. Thus the 1880s—the decade that saw the Statue of Liberty welcome immigrants to the United States—also saw the founding of the first country club with only WASP members (Baltzell, 1964).

By the mid-twentieth century, however, WASP wealth and power had peaked, as indicated by the 1960 election of John Fitzgerald Kennedy as the first Irish-Catholic president. But the majority of people in the upper-upper class are still WASPs (Baltzell, 1964, 1976, 1979b, 1988), and the WASP cultural legacy remains. English is this country's dominant language and Protestantism, the majority religion. Our legal

---

[1]In making comparisons of education and income, keep in mind that categories of the U.S. population have different median ages. The 1999 median age for all U.S. people was 37.0 years. White people have a median age of 36.7 years; for Native Americans, the figure is 27.7 years. Because people's income and schooling increase over time, this age different accounts for some of the disparities shown in Table 11–2.

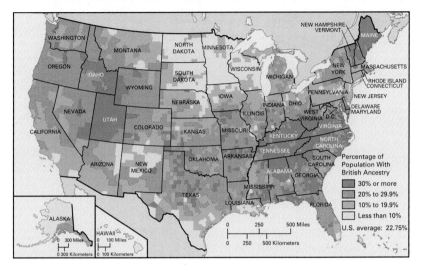

NATIONAL MAP 11–3
The Concentration of People of WASP Ancestry across the United States

Many people associate white Anglo-Saxon Protestants with elite communities along the eastern and western seaboards of the United States. But the highest concentrations of WASPs are in Utah (due to migrations of Mormons with English ancestry) and Appalachia and northern New England (due to historic immigration). Overall, however, WASPs form a large share of the U.S. population almost everywhere except Alaska, South Texas, and the upper Great Plains. Do you know why?

Source: From Rodger Doyle, *Atlas of Contemporary America*. Copyright © 1994 by Rodger Doyle. Reprinted with permission of Facts on File, Inc., New York, N.Y.

system, too, reflects its English origins. But the historical dominance of WASPs is most evident in the widespread use of the terms "race" and "ethnicity" to describe everyone but them.

AFRICAN AMERICANS

Although African Americans accompanied Spanish explorers to the New World in the fifteenth century, most accounts mark the beginning of black history in the United States as 1619, when a Dutch trading ship brought twenty Africans to Jamestown, Virginia. Whether these people arrived as slaves or as indentured servants who paid their passage by performing labor for a specified period, being of African descent on these shores soon became virtually synonymous with being a slave. In 1661, Virginia enacted the first law recognizing slavery (Sowell, 1981).

Slavery was the foundation of the southern colonies' plantation system. White people ran plantations using slave labor and, until 1808, some were slave traders as well. Traders—including North Americans, Africans, and Europeans—forcibly transported some 10 million Africans to various countries in the Americas, including 400,000 to the United States. On board small sailing ships, hundreds of slaves were chained for the several weeks it took to cross the Atlantic Ocean.

Filth and disease killed many and drove others to suicide. Overall, perhaps half died en route (Tannenbaum, 1946; Franklin, 1967; Sowell, 1981).

Surviving the journey was a mixed blessing, in that it inevitably ended in a life of servitude. Although some slaves worked in cities at various trades, most labored in the fields, often from daybreak until sunset and even longer during harvest season. The law allowed owners to use whatever disciplinary measures they deemed necessary to ensure that slaves were obedient and productive; even killing a slave rarely prompted legal action. Owners often split up slave families at public auctions, where human beings were bought and sold as pieces of property. Unschooled and dependent on their owners for all their basic needs, slaves had little control over their destinies (Franklin, 1967; Sowell, 1981).

Despite the fact that some free persons of color lived in both the North and the South, where they labored as small-scale farmers, skilled workers, and small business owners, the lives of most African Americans stood in glaring contradiction to the principles of freedom on which the United States was founded. The Declaration of Independence states:

> We hold these Truths to be self-evident, that all
> Men are created equal, that they are endowed by
> their Creator with certain unalienable Rights, that

CHAPTER 11 Race and Ethnicity **285**

The efforts of these four women greatly advanced the social standing of African Americans in the United States. Pictured above, from left to right: Sojourner Truth (1797–1883), born a slave, became an influential preacher and outspoken abolitionist who was honored by President Lincoln at the White House. Harriet Tubman (1820–1913), after escaping from slavery herself, masterminded the flight from bondage of hundreds of African American men and women via the "Underground Railroad." Ida Wells-Barnett (1862–1931), born to slave parents, became a partner in a Memphis newspaper and served as a tireless crusader against the terror of lynching. Marian Anderson (1902–1993), an exceptional singer whose early career was restrained by racial prejudice, broke symbolic "color lines" by singing in the White House (1936) and on the steps of the Lincoln Memorial to a crowd of almost 100,000 people (1939).

among these are Life, Liberty, and the Pursuit of Happiness.

Most white people, however, did not apply these ideals to African Americans. In the Dred Scott case in 1857, the U.S. Supreme Court addressed the question, "Are blacks citizens?" by writing, "We think they are not, and that they are not included, and were not intended to be included, under the word 'citizens' in the Constitution, and can therefore claim none of the rights and privileges which that instrument provides for and secures for citizens of the United States" (quoted in Blaustein & Zangrando, 1968:160). Thus arose what Swedish sociologist Gunnar Myrdal (1944) termed the "American dilemma": a democratic society's denial of basic rights and freedoms to an entire category of people. To ease this dilemma, many white people simply defined African Americans as innately inferior.

In 1865, the Thirteenth Amendment to the Constitution outlawed slavery. Three years later, the Fourteenth Amendment reversed the Dred Scott ruling, granting citizenship to all people born in the United States. The Fifteenth Amendment, ratified in 1870, stated that neither race nor previous condition of servitude should deprive anyone of the right to vote. However, so-called "Jim Crow" laws—classic cases of institutionalized discrimination—segregated U.S. society into two racial castes. Especially in the South, white people beat and lynched black people (and some white people) who challenged the racial hierarchy.

The twentieth century brought dramatic changes to African Americans. After World War I, tens of thousands of women and men fled the rural South for jobs in northern factories. While some did find more economic opportunity, few escaped racial prejudice and discrimination, which placed them lower in the social hierarchy than white immigrants arriving from Europe.

In the 1950s and 1960s, a national civil rights movement grew out of landmark judicial decisions that outlawed segregated schools and overt discrimination in employment and public accommodations. In addition, the "black power" movement gave African Americans a renewed sense of pride and purpose.

Gains notwithstanding, people of African descent continue to occupy a subordinate position in the United States, as shown in Table 11–3. The median income of African American families in 1999 ($33,805) was only 65 percent of white family income

($51,912), a ratio that has changed little in thirty years.[2] Black families remain three times as likely as white families to be poor.

The number of African American families securely in the middle class rose by more than half between 1980 and 2000; 47 percent earned more than $35,000 a year and 31 percent earned $50,000 or more. But, for some African Americans, earnings have slipped during the last fifteen years as factory jobs—vital to residents of inner cities—have been lost to other countries where labor costs are lower. Thus, black unemployment is more than twice as high as white unemployment; among African American teenagers in many cities, the figure exceeds 40 percent (Jacob, 1986; Lichter, 1989; U.S. Department of Labor, 2001).

Since 1980, African Americans have made remarkable educational strides. The share of adults completing high school rose from half to more than three-fourths, nearly closing the gap between whites and blacks. Between 1980 and 1999, the share of African American adults with at least a college degree rose from 8 to more than 15 percent. But, as Table 11–3 shows, African Americans are still at little more than half the national standard when it comes to completing four years of college.

The political clout of African Americans has also increased. Half of this country's ten largest cities have elected African American mayors, a reflection of both black migration to the cities and white flight to the suburbs. At the national level, however, only 2 percent of elected leaders are African Americans. After the 2000 congressional elections, 36 black men and women (of 435) were in the House of Representatives and not one black person (of 100) was in the Senate.

In sum, for more than 350 years, people of African ancestry in the United States have struggled for social equality. As a nation, the United States has come far in this pursuit. Overt discrimination is now illegal, and research documents a long-term decline in prejudice against African Americans (Firebaugh & Davis, 1988; J. Q. Wilson, 1992; NORC, 1999).

In 1913—fifty years after the abolition of slavery—W. E. B. Du Bois proudly noted the extent of black achievement. But Du Bois also cautioned that racial

[2]Here, again, a median age difference (white people, 37.0; black people, 30.4) accounts for a small part of the income and educational disparities shown here. More important is a higher proportion of one-parent families among blacks than whites. Comparing only married-couple families, African Americans (median income $50,758 in 1999) earned 89 percent as much as whites ($57,242).

TABLE 11–3 The Social Standing of African Americans, 1999*		
	African Americans	Entire United States
Median family income	$33,805	$49,940
Percent in poverty	23.6%	11.8%
Completion of four or more years of college (age 25 and over)	15.4%	25.2%

*For purposes of comparison with other tables in this chapter, 1990 data are as follows: median family income, $21,423; percent in poverty, 31.9%; completion of four or more years of college, 11.3%.

Source: U.S. Census Bureau (2000).

caste remained strong in the United States, and, in the twenty-first century, the racial hierarchy persists.

ASIAN AMERICANS

Although all Asian Americans share some racial traits, enormous cultural diversity marks this category of people. In 2000, the total number of Asian Americans exceeded 10 million, approaching 4 percent of the U.S. population. The largest category of Asian Americans is people of Chinese ancestry (2.2 million), followed by those of Filipino (2.0 million), Asian Indian (1.2 million), Korean (980,000), and Japanese (925,000) descent. More than one-third of Asian Americans live in California.

Young Asian Americans have commanded attention and respect as high achievers and are disproportionately represented at our country's best colleges and universities. Many of their elders, too, have made economic and social gains; most Asian Americans now live in middle-class suburbs (O'Hare, Frey, & Fost, 1994). Yet, despite (and sometimes because of) their record of achievement, Asian Americans sometimes find others aloof or outright hostile toward them.

At the same time, the "model minority" image of Asian Americans obscures the poverty found among their ranks. We will focus on the history and current standing of Chinese Americans and Japanese Americans—the longest-established Asian American minorities—and conclude with a brief look at the most recent arrivals.

Chinese Americans. Chinese immigration to the United States began in 1849 with the economic boom of California's Gold Rush. New towns and businesses

TABLE 11–4 The Social Standing of Asian Americans, 1990

	All Asian Americans	Chinese Americans	Japanese Americans	Korean Americans	Filipino Americans	Entire United States
Median family income	$42,240	$41,316	$51,550	$33,909	$46,698	$35,225
Percent in poverty	14.0%	14.0%	7.0%	13.7%	6.4%	13.1%
Completion of four or more years of college (age 25 and over)	37.7%	40.7%	34.5%	34.5%	39.3%	20.3%

Source: U.S. Census Bureau (2000).

sprang up overnight, and the demand for cheap labor attracted some 100,000 Chinese immigrants. Most Chinese workers were young, hardworking men willing to take lower-status jobs shunned by whites. But the economy soured in the 1870s, and desperate whites began to compete with the Chinese for whatever jobs could be found. Suddenly the industriousness of the Chinese posed a threat. In short, economic hard times led to prejudice and discrimination (Ling, 1971; Boswell, 1986).

Soon, whites acted to bar the Chinese from many occupations. Courts also withdrew legal protections, unleashing vicious campaigns against the "Yellow Peril." Everyone seemed to line up against the Chinese, as expressed in the popular phrase of the time, that someone up against great odds "didn't have a Chinaman's chance" (Sung, 1967; Sowell, 1981).

In 1882, the U.S. government passed the first of several laws curtailing Chinese immigration. This action created domestic hardship because, in the United States, Chinese men outnumbered women by twenty to one. This sex imbalance sent the Chinese population plummeting to only 60,000 by 1920. Chinese women already in the United States, however, were in high demand, and they soon shed their traditional submissiveness toward men (Hsu, 1971; Lai, 1980; Sowell, 1981).

Responding to racial hostility, some Chinese moved eastward; many more sought the relative safety of urban Chinatowns. There, Chinese traditions flourished, and kinship networks, called clans, offered financial assistance to individuals and represented the interests of all. At the same time, however, living in Chinatown discouraged people from learning English, which limited their job opportunities (Wong, 1971).

A renewed need for labor during World War II prompted President Franklin Roosevelt to end the ban on Chinese immigration in 1943 and to extend the rights of citizenship to Chinese Americans born

abroad. Many responded by moving out of Chinatowns and pursuing cultural assimilation. In turn-of-the-century Honolulu, for example, 70 percent of the Chinese people lived in Chinatown; today, the figure is below 20 percent.

By 1950, many Chinese Americans had experienced upward social mobility. Today, people of Chinese ancestry are no longer restricted to self-employment in laundries and restaurants; many hold high-prestige positions, especially in fields related to science and new information technology.

As shown in Table 11–4, the median family income of Chinese Americans in 1990 ($41,316) stood above the national average ($35,225). Note, however, that the higher income of all Asian Americans reflects a larger number of family members in the labor force.[3] Chinese Americans also have an enviable record of educational achievement, with twice the national average of college graduates.

Despite their success, many Chinese Americans still grapple with subtle (and sometimes overt) prejudice and discrimination. Such hostility is one reason that poverty among Chinese Americans stands above the national average. Poverty is higher still among those who remain in the restrictive circle of Chinatowns, working in restaurants or other low-paying jobs. Thus, sociologists debate whether racial and ethnic enclaves help their residents or exploit them (Portes & Jensen, 1989; Zhou & Logan, 1989; Kinkead, 1992; Gilbertson & Gurak, 1993).

---

[3]Data for 1994 place median family income of Chinese Americans at $44,456, above the national figure of $36,782. Median age for all Asian Americans in 2000 was 32.1, somewhat below the national median of 35.9 and the white median of 37.0. But specific categories vary considerably in median age: Japanese, 36.1; Chinese, 32.1; Filipino, 31.1; Korean, 29.1; Asian Indian, 28.9; Cambodian, 19.4; Hmong, 12.5 (U.S. Census Bureau, 1995, 2000).

Japanese Americans. Japanese immigration to the United States began slowly in the 1860s, reaching only 3,000 by 1890. Most of these immigrants came to the Hawaiian Islands (annexed by the United States in 1898 and made a state in 1959) as a source of cheap labor. Early in the twentieth century, however, as the number of Japanese immigrants to California rose and they demanded better pay, white people responded by seeking limits to immigration (Daniels, 1971). In 1907, the United States signed an agreement with Japan curbing the entry of men—the chief economic threat—while allowing Japanese women to immigrate to ease the sex ratio imbalance. In the 1920s, laws in California and dozens of other states mandated segregation and prohibited interracial marriage, virtually ending further Japanese immigration. Not until 1952 did the United States extend citizenship to foreign-born Japanese.

Japanese and Chinese immigrants differed in three ways. First, there were fewer Japanese immigrants, so they escaped some of the hostility directed at the more numerous Chinese. Second, the Japanese knew much more about the United States than the Chinese did, which helped them assimilate (Sowell, 1981). Third, Japanese immigrants favored rural farming to clustering together in cities. But many white people objected to Japanese ownership of farmland, so, in 1913, the California legislature barred further land purchases by immigrants. Many foreign-born Japanese (called *Issei*) subsequently operated farms legally owned by their U.S.–born children (*Nisei*), who were constitutionally entitled to citizenship.

Japanese Americans faced their greatest crisis after Japan bombed the U.S. naval fleet at Hawaii's Pearl Harbor on December 7, 1941. Rage toward Japan was directed at the Japanese living in the United States. Some feared that the Japanese here would spy for Japan or commit acts of sabotage. Within a year, President Franklin Roosevelt signed Executive Order 9066, an unprecedented action intended to protect national security by detaining people of Japanese descent in military camps. Authorities soon relocated 110,000 people (90 percent of all U.S. Japanese) to remote inland reservations (Sun, 1998).

While concern about national security always heightens in times of war, Japanese internment was sharply criticized. First, it targeted an entire category of people, not one of whom was ever known to have committed a disloyal act. Second, roughly two-thirds of those imprisoned were *Nisei*—U.S. citizens by birth. Third, although the United States was also at

Between 1942 and 1944, more than 100,000 men, women, and children of Japanese ancestry were forcibly removed from their homes and businesses and taken to detention camps. Here, a mother fights back tears as the army prepares to move her and her three small children (note the identification tags) from Bainbridge Island (off the coast of Washington state) to the mainland.

war with Germany and Italy, no such action was taken against people of German or Italian ancestry.

Relocation meant selling homes, furnishings, and businesses on short notice for pennies on the dollar. As a result, almost the entire Japanese American population was economically devastated. In military prisons—surrounded by barbed wire and guarded by armed soldiers—families crowded into single rooms, often in buildings that had previously sheltered livestock (Fujimoto, 1971; Bloom, 1980). The internment ended in 1944, when the Supreme Court declared the policy unconstitutional. In 1988, Congress awarded $20,000 as token compensation to each victim.

After World War II, Japanese Americans staged a dramatic recovery. Having lost their traditional

Although sometimes portrayed as a successful "model minority," Asian Americans are highly diverse and, like other categories of people, include both rich and poor. These young people contend with many of the same patterns of prejudice and discrimination familiar to members of other minorities.

businesses, many entered new occupations, and because their culture values education and hard work, Japanese Americans have enjoyed remarkable success. In 1990, the median income of Japanese American households was almost 50 percent above the national average, and their poverty rate was only half the national figure.

Upward social mobility has encouraged cultural assimilation and interracial marriage. The third and fourth generations of Japanese Americans (the *Sansei* and *Yonsei*) rarely live in residential enclaves, as many Chinese Americans still do, and a majority marry non-Japanese partners. In the process, many have abandoned their traditions and lost the ability to speak Japanese. A high proportion of Japanese Americans belong to ethnic associations as a way of maintaining their ethnic identity (Fugita & O'Brien, 1985). Still, some appear to be caught between two worlds, no longer culturally Japanese yet not completely accepted in the larger society because of racial differences.

Recent Asian immigrants. More recent immigrants from Asia include Koreans, Filipinos, Indians, Vietnamese, Samoans, and Guamanians. When added to the existing population of Chinese and Japanese

descent, Asian Americans are this country's fastest-growing minority, accounting for one-third of all immigration to the United States (U.S. Immigration and Naturalization Service, 1999). National Map 11–4 locates the Asian American, African American, and Hispanic populations across the United States.

Generally speaking, the entrepreneurial spirit remains strong among Asian immigrants. Asians are slightly more likely than white people, three times more likely than Latinos, and four times more likely than African Americans and Native Americans, to own and operate small businesses (U.S. Census Bureau, 1995). Among all Asian Americans, moreover, Koreans are the most likely to own small businesses. Residents of New York City, for example, know that most small grocery stores there are Korean-owned; Los Angeles residents know that Koreans operate a large share of liquor stores. Many Koreans work long hours; even so, Korean American families earn slightly lower than average incomes, as shown in Table 11–4. Moreover, Korean Americans face limited social acceptance, even among other categories of Asian Americans.

The data in Table 11–4 show that Filipinos generally have fared well. But a closer look reveals a mixed pattern, with some Filipinos highly successful in the professions (especially in medicine), while others hold low-skill jobs (Parrillo, 1994). For many Filipino families, the key to high income is working women. Almost three-fourths of Filipino American women are in the labor force, compared to just half of Korean American women. Moreover, many of these women are professionals, reflecting the fact that 42 percent of Filipino American women have a four-year college degree compared to 26 percent of Korean American women.

In sum, a survey of Asian Americans presents a complex picture. The Japanese come closest to having achieved social acceptance; but, especially for Korean and Chinese Americans, economic success has not toppled historical prejudice and discrimination. Although many Asian Americans have prospered, others remain poor. One clear trend is that their exceptionally high immigration rate means that people of Asian ancestry will play a central role in U.S. society in the twenty-first century (Lee, 1994).

HISPANIC AMERICANS

In 2000, Hispanics numbered more than 35 million, 12.5 percent of the U.S. population. Yet few actually describe themselves as "Hispanic" or "Latino." Like

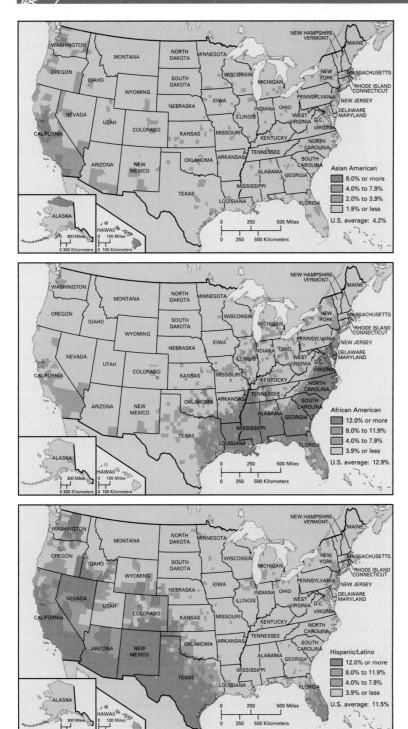

NATIONAL MAP 11–4
The Concentration of Asian Americans, African Americans, and Hispanics/Latinos, by County, Projections for 2001

In 1990, Asian Americans represented 3 percent of the U.S. population, compared with 12 percent African Americans and 9 percent people of Hispanic/Latino descent. These three maps show the geographic distribution of these categories of people as projected for 2001. Comparing them, we see that the southern half of the United States is and will be home to far more minorities than the northern half. But do the three concentrate in the same areas? What patterns do the maps reveal?

Source: From *American Demographics* (November 1996, January 1997, and February 1997). Copyright © 1996, 1997 by *American Demographics*. Reprinted with permission.

Asian American
- 8.0% or more
- 4.0% to 7.9%
- 2.0% to 3.9%
- 1.9% or less

U.S. average: 4.2%

African American
- 12.0% or more
- 8.0% to 11.9%
- 4.0% to 7.9%
- 3.9% or less

U.S. average: 12.9%

Hispanic/Latino
- 12.0% or more
- 8.0% to 11.9%
- 4.0% to 7.9%
- 3.9% or less

U.S. average: 11.5%

The strength of family bonds and neighborhood ties is evident in this painting of street life in old San Juan, La Vida en Broma, *by Puerto Rican artist Nick Quijano.*

© Nick Quijano 1997. *La Vida en Broma, 1988: Streetlife in Old San Juan.*

Asian Americans, Hispanics are really a cluster of distinct populations, each of which identifies with a particular ancestral nation (Marín & Marín, 1991).

About two out of three Hispanics (more than 20 million) are Mexican Americans, or "Chicanos." Puerto Ricans are next in population size (3 million), followed by Cuban Americans (1.4 million). Many other societies of Latin America are represented by smaller numbers. Due to a high birth rate and heavy immigration, Hispanics have now surpassed African Americans to become this nation's largest racial or ethnic minority, as documented by the 2000 census (U.S. Census Bureau, 2001).

Much of the U.S. Hispanic population lives in the Southwest. One of four Californians is Latino (in greater Los Angeles, almost half the people are Latino). Median family income for all Hispanics—$33,077 in 1999—stands well below the national average.[4] As the following sections reveal, however, some categories of Hispanics have fared better than others.

Mexican Americans. Some Chicanos are descendants of people who lived in a part of Mexico annexed by the United States after the Mexican War (1846–1848). Most Mexican Americans, however, are recent immigrants. In recent decades, more immigrants have come

[4]The 2000 median age of the U.S. Hispanic population was 26.6 years, well below the national median of 35.9 years. This differential accounts for some of the disparity in income and education.

to the United States from Mexico than from any other country.

Like many other immigrants, many Mexican Americans have worked as low-wage laborers, on farms or elsewhere. Table 11–5 shows the 1990 median family income for Mexican Americans was $23,240, about two-thirds the national standard. One-fourth of Chicano families are poor—almost twice the national average. Finally, despite gains since 1980, Mexican Americans still have a high dropout rate and, on average, receive less schooling than U.S. adults on the whole.

Puerto Ricans. Puerto Rico (like the Philippines) became a possession of the United States when the Spanish-American War ended in 1898. In 1917, Puerto Ricans (but not Filipinos) became U.S. citizens.

New York City is the center of Puerto Rican life in the continental United States and is home to about 1 million Puerto Ricans. However, one-third of this community is severely disadvantaged. Adjusting to cultural patterns on the mainland—including, for many, learning English—is one major challenge; also, Puerto Ricans with darker skin encounter prejudice and discrimination. As a result, about as many people return to Puerto Rico each year as arrive.

This "revolving door" pattern hampers assimilation. About three-fourths of Puerto Rican families in the United States speak Spanish at home, compared with about half of Mexican American families (Sowell, 1981; Stevens & Swicegood, 1987). Speaking only

TABLE 11–5 The Social Standing of Hispanic Americans, 1990

	All Hispanics	Mexican Americans	Puerto Ricans	Cuban Americans	Entire United States
Median family income	$23,431	$23,240	$18,008	$31,439	$35,225
Percent in poverty	25.0%	25.0%	37.5%	13.8%	13.1%
Completion of four or more years of college (age 25 and over)	9.2%	6.2%	10.1%	18.5%	20.3%

Source: U.S. Census Bureau (2000).

Spanish maintains a strong ethnic identity but it also limits economic opportunity. Puerto Ricans also have a higher incidence of female-headed households than other Hispanics, a pattern that raises a family's risk of poverty. Table 11–5 shows that in 1990 the median household income for Puerto Ricans was $18,008, about half the national average. Although long-term mainland residents have made economic gains, more recent immigrants from Puerto Rico continue to struggle to find work. Averaging out the differences, Puerto Ricans remain the most disadvantaged Hispanic minority (Rivera-Batiz & Santiago, 1994; Holmes, 1996b).

Cuban Americans. Within little more than a decade after the 1959 Marxist revolution led by Fidel Castro, 400,000 Cubans had fled to the United States. Most settled in Miami, and many were highly educated business and professional people who wasted little time becoming as successful in the United States as in their homeland (Fallows, 1983; Krafft, 1993).

Table 11–5 shows that the median household income for Cuban Americans in 1990 was $31,439—above that of other Hispanics yet still below the national average. The 1 million Cuban Americans living in the United States today have managed a delicate balancing act—achieving success in the larger society while retaining much of their traditional culture. Of all Hispanics, Cubans are the most likely to speak Spanish in their homes; eight out of ten families do (Sowell, 1981). However, their cultural distinctiveness and their highly visible communities, like Miami's Little Havana, provoke hostility from some people.

WHITE ETHNIC AMERICANS

The term *white ethnics* recognizes the ethnic heritage—and social disadvantages—of many white people. White ethnics are non-WASP people whose

ancestors lived in Ireland, Poland, Germany, Italy, or other European countries. More than half of the U.S. population falls into one or another white ethnic category (Alba, 1990).

Unprecedented emigration from Europe during the nineteenth century first brought Germans and Irish and then Italians and Jews to our shores. Despite cultural differences, all shared the hope that the United States would offer greater political freedom and economic opportunity than their homelands. Most did live better in this country, but the belief that "the streets of America are paved with gold" turned out to be a far cry from reality. Many immigrants found only hard labor for low wages.

White ethnics also endured their share of prejudice and discrimination. Nativist organizations opposed the entry of non-WASP Europeans to the United States and many newspaper ads seeking workers warned new arrivals: "None need apply but Americans" (Handlin, 1941:67).

In 1921, the nativists declared victory when Congress passed legislation that imposed a quota on immigration; not until 1968 were these restrictions lifted. The most severe quotas targeted southern and eastern Europeans—people likely to have darker skin and to differ culturally from the dominant WASPs (Fallows, 1983).

In response to bigotry, many white ethnics formed supportive residential enclaves. Some also gained footholds in certain businesses and trades: Italian Americans entered the construction industry; Irish Americans worked in construction and took civil service jobs; Jews predominated in the garment industry; many Greeks (like the Chinese) worked in the retail food business (Newman, 1973).

Many working-class people still live in traditional neighborhoods, although those who prospered gradually assimilated. Most descendants of the immigrants who labored in sweatshops and lived in crowded tenements

CONTROVERSY & DEBATE

Affirmative Action: Solution or Problem?

Adarand Constructors, a white-owned Colorado company, submitted the low bid for a federal highway project erecting guard rails. But Adarand did not get the job. Despite having to pay a higher price, the government selected Gonzales Construction, a minority-owned firm. The management of Adarand was bitterly angry. Company manager Randy Perch put it this way: "What is prejudice? It's when government makes a decision based on something that doesn't matter, like race or gender."

Should race or ethnicity or gender matter in how we treat people? This question lies at the heart of the affirmative action debate. To begin, what, exactly, is this controversial policy and how did it start?

After World War II, the U.S. government funded higher education for veterans of all races. The G.I. Bill held special promise for African Americans, most of whom needed financial assistance to enroll in

college. The program was so successful that, by 1960, some 350,000 black men and women were on college campuses with government funding.

But a problem remained: These individuals were not finding the kinds of jobs for which they were qualified. In short, *educational* opportunity was not producing *economic* opportunity.

Supporters argue that affirmative action in college admissions is needed to ensure a socially diverse campus.

Thus, in the early 1960s, the Kennedy administration devised a program of "affirmative action" to provide a broader "net of opportunity" for qualified minorities. Employers and educators were instructed to carefully monitor hiring, promotion, and admissions policies to eliminate discrimination—even if unintended—against minorities.

Defenders of affirmative action see the policy, first, as a sensible response to our nation's racial and ethnic history, especially for African Americans, who suffered through two centuries of slavery and a century of segregation under Jim Crow laws. Throughout our history, they claim, being white gave people a big advantage. Thus, minority preference today is a fair step toward just compensation for unfair majority preference in the past.

Second, given our racial history, the promise of a color-blind society strikes many analysts as hollow. Prejudice and discrimination are deep in the fabric of U.S.

now lead comfortable lives with decent incomes. As a result, their ethnic heritage is a source of pride.

RACE AND ETHNICITY: LOOKING AHEAD

The United States has been, and will probably remain, a land of immigrants. Immigration has brought striking cultural diversity and tales of success, hope, and struggle told in hundreds of tongues.

Most immigrants arrived in a great wave that peaked about 1910. The next two generations brought gradual economic gain and at least some cultural assimilation. The government also extended citizenship to

Native Americans (1924), foreign-born Filipinos (1942), Chinese Americans (1943), and Japanese Americans (1952).

A second wave of immigration began after World War II, and swelled as the government relaxed immigration laws in the 1960s. During the 1990s, about 1 million people came to the United States each year, more than twice the number that arrived during the "Great Immigration" a century ago (although newcomers now enter a country that has five times as many people). Today's immigrants, however, come not from Europe but from Latin America and Asia, with Mexicans, Filipinos, and South Koreans arriving in the largest numbers.

society; thus, simply endorsing the principle of color-blindness does not mean everyone will compete fairly.

Third, proponents maintain that affirmative action has worked. Where would minorities be if our government had not enacted this policy three decades ago? Indeed, major employers, such as fire and police departments in large cities, began hiring minorities and women only because of affirmative action. Affirmative action has played an important part in the expansion of the African American middle class. Further, affirmative action has increased interracial interaction on the campus and advanced the careers of a generation of black students (Bowen & Bok, 1999).

But affirmative action has always drawn criticism, and, by the mid-1990s, courts began cutbacks in such programs. Critics argue that affirmative action started out as a temporary remedy to ensure fair competition but became a system of "group preferences" and quotas. In other words, the policy did not remain true to the goal of promoting color-blindness as set out in the 1964 Civil Rights Act. Within a decade, it had become "reverse discrimination," favoring people not because of their qualifications or performance but on the basis of their race, ethnicity, or sex.

Second, critics contend that affirmative action is polarizing. If racial preferences were wrong in the past, they are wrong now. Moreover, why should whites or men today—many of whom are far from privileged—be penalized for past discrimination that was in no way their fault? Our society has undone most of the institutionalized prejudice and discrimination of earlier times, opponents continue, so that minorities can and do enjoy success when they have the talent and make the effort. Giving entire categories of people special treatment inevitably compromises standards, calls into question the real accomplishments of minorities, and provokes a hostile response from white people.

A third argument is that affirmative action benefits those who need it least. Favoring minority-owned corporations or allocating places in law school for minorities helps already-privileged people. Affirmative action has done little for the African American underclass, which most needs a leg up.

In sum, there are good reasons to argue for or against affirmative action. Indeed, people who believe the ultimate goal is a society where no racial or ethnic category dominates fall on both sides of this debate. The disagreement is not over whether people of all colors should have equal opportunity but whether a particular policy—affirmative action—is part of the solution or part of the problem.

Continue the debate . . .

1. *Since, historically, society has favored males over females and whites over people of color, would you agree that white males have received more "affirmative action" than anyone? Why or why not?*

2. *Should affirmative action include only disadvantaged categories of minorities (say, African Americans and Native Americans) and exclude more affluent categories (such as Japanese Americans)? Why or why not?*

3. *What about replacing race-based affirmative action with a class-based policy? Would this help those who need it most?*

Sources: Carr (1995), Cohen (1995), Curry (1996), Bowen & Bok (1999), and NORC (1999).

Many new arrivals face much the same prejudice and discrimination as those who came before them. Indeed, recent years have witnessed rising hostility toward foreigners (sometimes called *xenophobia*, with Greek roots meaning "fear of what is strange"). In 1994, California voters passed Proposition 187, cutting social services (including schooling) to illegal immigrants. More recently, voters there mandated that all children learn English in school. In 2000, some landowners along the southwestern border of the United States took up arms and formed vigilante groups to discourage the large numbers of illegal immigrants crossing the border from Mexico, and some political candidates have called for drastic action to cut off further immigration. More broadly, as the final box explains, U.S. society still debates the pros and cons of affirmative action, a policy intended to help minorities overcome historical prejudice and discrimination.

Like their predecessors, most immigrants today try to blend into U.S. society without completely giving up their traditional culture. Some still build racial and ethnic enclaves, so that the Little Havanas and Koreatowns of today stand alongside the Little Italys and Germantowns of the past. In addition, new arrivals still carry the traditional hope that their racial and ethnic diversity can be a source of pride and not a badge of inferiority.

SUMMARY

1. Races are socially constructed categories by which societies set apart people according to various physical traits. Although a century ago scientists identified three broad categories—Caucasoids, Negroids, and Mongoloids—there are no pure races.

2. Ethnicity is based not on biology but on shared cultural heritage.

3. Minorities—including people of certain races and ethnicities—are categories of people society sets apart, making them both distinct and disadvantaged.

4. Prejudice is a rigid and biased generalization about a category of people. Racism, a destructive type of prejudice, asserts that one race is innately superior or inferior to another.

5. Discrimination is a pattern of action by which a person treats various categories of people unequally.

6. Pluralism means that racial and ethnic categories, although distinct, have equal social standing. Assimilation is a process by which minorities gradually adopt the patterns of the dominant category. Segregation is the physical and social separation of categories of people. Genocide is the extermination of a category of people.

7. Native Americans—the earliest human inhabitants of the Americas—have endured genocide, segregation, and forced assimilation. Today, Native American social standing is well below the national average.

8. WASPs predominated among the original European settlers of the United States, and many continue to enjoy high social standing today.

9. African Americans experienced two centuries of slavery. Emancipation in 1865 gave way to segregation by law. Today, despite legal equality, African Americans are still relatively disadvantaged.

10. Chinese Americans and Japanese Americans have suffered both racial and ethnic hostility. Although some prejudice and discrimination continues, both categories now have above-average income and schooling. Recent Asian immigration—especially of Koreans and Filipinos—makes Asian Americans the fastest-growing racial category of the U.S. population.

11. Hispanics include many ethnicities sharing a Spanish heritage. Mexican Americans, the largest Hispanic minority, are concentrated in the Southwest. Puerto Ricans, most of whom live in New York, are the poorest Hispanics. Cubans, concentrated in Miami, are the most affluent.

12. White ethnics are non-WASPs of European ancestry. While making gains during the last century, many white ethnics still struggle for economic security.

13. Immigration has increased in recent years. No longer primarily from Europe, most immigrants now arrive from Latin America and Asia.

KEY CONCEPTS

race (p. 271) a socially constructed category composed of people who share biologically transmitted traits that members of a society consider important

ethnicity (p. 273) a shared cultural heritage

prejudice (p. 276) a rigid and irrational generalization about an entire category of people

racism (p. 276) the belief that one racial category is innately superior or inferior to another

scapegoat (p. 277) a person or category of people, typically with little power, whom people unfairly blame for their own troubles

discrimination (p. 279) any action that involves treating various categories of people unequally

institutional prejudice and discrimination (p. 279) bias inherent in the operation of society's institutions

pluralism (p. 280) a state in which racial and ethnic minorities are distinct but have social parity

assimilation (p. 281) the process by which minorities gradually adopt patterns of the dominant category

miscegenation (p. 281) biological reproduction by partners of different racial categories

segregation (p. 281) the physical and social separation of categories of people

genocide (p. 282) the systematic killing of one category of people by another

CRITICAL-THINKING QUESTIONS

1. Differentiate between race and ethnicity. Do you think all nonwhite people should be considered minorities, even if they have above-average incomes? Why or why not?

2. In what ways do prejudice and discrimination reinforce each other?

3. What does the growing popularity of Latin music by performers such as Gloria and Emilio Estefan and Ricky Martin suggest about ethnicity in the United States?

4. Do you think U.S. society is becoming more, or less, color-blind? Is color-blindness a goal worth striving for? Why or why not?

APPLICATIONS AND EXERCISES

1. Does your college or university take account of race and ethnicity in its admissions policies? Ask to speak with an admissions officer, and see what you can learn about your school's policies and the reasons for them. Ask, too, if there is a "legacy" policy that favors children of those who attended the school.

2. Give several of your friends or family members a quick quiz, asking them what share of the U.S. population is white, Hispanic, African American, and Asian (see Table 11–1). If they are like most people, they will exaggerate the share of all minorities and understate the white proportion (Labovitz, 1996). What do you make of the results?

3. There are probably immigrants on your campus or in your local community. Have you ever thought about asking them to tell you about their homeland and their experiences since arriving in the United States? Most immigrants would be pleased to be asked, and you can learn a great deal.

4. Install the CD-ROM packaged in the back of this new textbook to access a variety of study, review, and applications exercises designed to help you better understand the material covered in this chapter. The CD includes an author's tip video, as well as interactive maps, video application exercises, Web links, and study questions.

SITES TO SEE

http://www.prenhall.com/macionis

Visit the interactive Web site that accompanies this text. Begin by clicking on the cover of your book. You will find a chapter-by-chapter study guide, practice tests, chat room, and many suggested Web links.

http://www.macionis.com
(or http://www.thesociologypage.com)

At the author's home page, you can find additional links to organizations concerned with racial and ethnic inequality.

http:www.naacp.org
http://www.jdl.org

These two organizations—the National Association for the Advancement of Colored People and the Jewish Defense League—are concerned with combating prejudice and discrimination and advancing the social standing of minorities in the United States. Determine each organization's strategies and goals.

http://www.access.gpo.gov/eop/ca/index.html

This worthwhile data site, operated by the Council of Economic Advisors, provides an assessment of social and economic well-being of various racial and ethnic categories of this country's population.

http://www.collegeboard.org/press/html9900/html/991017.html

Read the report of the College Board's National Task Force on Minority High Achievement, which analyzes racial and ethnic differences in higher education.

NEW INFORMATION TECHNOLOGY AND SOCIAL STRATIFICATION

Change in technology transforms the nature of work. Just as important, such shifts alter the reward structure, reshaping patterns of social inequality. This third cyber.scope considers several ways in which the spread of computer technology is linked to social stratification.

The Information Revolution and U.S. Stratification

Most analysts agree that recent decades have witnessed economic polarization in the United States, with economic growth primarily enriching families that already had high incomes (Keister, 2000; U.S. Census Bureau, 2000). At the outset, at least, technological revolution typically concentrates income and wealth as a small number of people make key discoveries, establishing and expanding new markets. Just as John D. Rockefeller and Andrew Carnegie amassed great fortunes a century ago as captains of the Industrial Revolution, the Information Revolution has created a new elite today. For several years, the richest person in the country has been Bill Gates, a founder of Microsoft Corporation that produces, not oil or steel, but the operating systems found in most of today's personal computers. More broadly, it is those with money to invest (many of whom make up what Karl Marx called the capitalist class) who reap most of the profits from successful new industries. During the 1990s, as the Information Revolution rolled ahead, key stock market indicators leaped fivefold, with new technology companies such as

Microsoft (software), Intel (computer chips), Dell (personal computers), and Cisco Systems (computer networking) making even more spectacular gains (despite a downturn in 2000).

But the wave of technological change does not benefit everyone. As companies adopt new technology in their efforts to become more efficient and profitable, some people lose out. In recent decades, for example, tens of millions of jobs in the United States have simply disappeared. For

Both blind and deaf, Georgia Griffith was able to communicate only through conversations traced out on her palms, until specially equipped computers opened up her life. Do you think that, in general, advances in information technology will improve the lives of all persons with disabilities? Or will these people be left behind by the Information Revolution?

each job lost, a worker—and usually an entire family—suffers.

Another key link between new information technology and social inequality concerns the unequal spread of computing skills. In 2000, more than 50 percent of the U.S. population aged sixteen or older were users of the Internet. Yet these users are not average people; they represent an information elite, privileged in more ways than one. About 95 percent are white (compared to 85 percent of the population), 60 percent are men (versus half the population), and 40 percent are professionals or managers (versus 18 percent of the population). Computer users are, in short, people with above-average incomes. College students stand out among computer users but, even among them, differences emerge. Figure Cyber III–1 shows that students attending private (and more expensive) universities and colleges are more likely to use e-mail frequently than those at public institutions. Similarly, students at two-year colleges and at historically black colleges also make less use of computers.

It is likely that, over time, computer users will come to mirror more closely the population as a whole. But there can be little doubt that, at least for now, new information technology plays a role in rising levels of economic inequality as it creates a cyber-elite and generates a new underclass made up of those without crucial symbolic skills (Wynter, 1995; Edmondson, 1997b).

The Information Revolution: Gender, Race, and Age

The Industrial Revolution ushered in a trend by which women and men are becoming more socially equal. Machinery eroded the link between physical strength and ability to work, and more women entered the labor force as birth control technology helped lower the birth rate by making motherhood a matter of individual choice. The Information Revolution promises to continue this trend. Work in the computer age involves not making or moving *things* but manipulating *ideas*—activity that favors neither men nor women.

Note, too, that communication via computers obscures a person's sex—obvious in face-to-face interaction—placing men and women on more equal footing. The same holds for race and ethnicity, so that the coming cyber-society may well be marked by greater contact among people of all races and cultural backgrounds.

But an important counterpoint involves *access* to computer technology. To date, cultural biases within the new cyber-society have favored males: Most games that introduce children to computers are designed for boys, just as computer science courses in colleges enroll mostly men. Similarly, to the extent that racial and ethnic minorities are economically disadvantaged and have access to inferior schools, this segment of our population will be cut off from owning and operating computers—the key to success in the labor force in this new century.

Finally, the effects of computing on age stratification are likely to be mixed. On the one hand, the fact that computing demands mental more than physical vitality—and allows work to be performed almost anywhere—should expand opportunities for

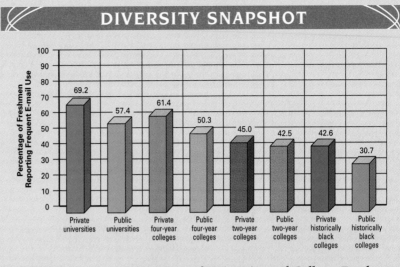

DIVERSITY SNAPSHOT

FIGURE Cyber III–1 Percentage of University and College Freshmen Reporting Frequent E-mail Use during the Past Year, 1999

Source: Sax et al. (1999).

people to continue to work well past the standard of "retirement" that emerged during the industrial era. On the other hand, new technology is almost always age-biased, in that it is readily adopted by the young, but regarded more cautiously by the old whose life experiences have been shaped by earlier ways. Unless our society expands programs of adult education, then, younger people are likely to predominate in, and benefit from, work and other activities that rely heavily on new information technology.

The Information Revolution and Global Stratification

Worldwide, the elite pattern we have described holds even more. The Information Revolution directly involves only a tiny share of the planet's people. A look back at Global Map 5–1, on page 116, shows that it is the rich regions of the world where personal computers

are most widely available, at least to those who can afford it. In most of Africa, by contrast, people are far less likely to have a computer, and, in some countries, there are few computers and almost no Internet access. Moreover, the large number of African languages and alphabets will slow the spread of computing there.

While Internet access is found in most of Asia, at present, a cultural and technical problem limits the spread of computing there: Almost all computer keyboards use the Latin alphabet. In China and other Asian nations, while members of the technical elite are likely to speak and write English, most people utilize complex character sets that have yet to be incorporated into computer technology. Overall, then, the Information Revolution has come to that part of the world already benefiting from industrial technology—yet another case of the rich getting richer.

New Information Technology and Social Stratification **299**

ECONOMICS AND POLITICS

*S*ome years back, you could spot the office temps in a minute. They were the ones with the bewildered faces and the questions about where everything was. Just about the time they figured it all out, off they went to another company to begin the process all over again.

But in the 1980s, things began to change. Big companies were merging and laying off workers—a process executives called "restructuring" and "downsizing." Cautious about adding full-time employees, companies began meeting their needs by hiring more and more temporary workers until economic trends became clear. By the 1990s, temps were becoming permanent fixtures in the office, and their numbers soared from 1.2 million in 1990 to 3 million in 2000. Why? Companies discovered that using temps lowered health care and pension costs (since temps do not usually receive such benefits) as well as salary costs. It also gave businesses the option to let people go at any time (Eisenberg, 1999).

The college campus, too, is now awash with temporary instructors. By one count, 25 percent of faculty at public institutions and up to 40 percent of faculty at private colleges and universities have temporary contracts (Will, 1999).

Whether in business or academia, some temporary workers are happy to keep their options open. But more have decided they deserve better and are fighting back. In 1999, for example, a court sided with 10,000 former Microsoft temps, saying that they should have been *allowed to take part in that company's employee stock-purchase plan. Across the country, the "nomads" of the labor force are seeking a return to the old idea that, just as companies expect loyalty from employees, companies should offer some security in return.*

This chapter explores the economy and the closely related institution of politics. As the chapter-opening story suggests, the economy does not always operate to everyone's advantage. Indeed, sociologists debate how both the economy and the political system ought to work and whose interests they ought to serve.

Economics and politics are each a major **social institution,** *an organized sphere of social life, or societal subsystem, designed to meet human needs.* The two chapters that follow consider other social institutions: Chapter 13 focuses on the family and religion, and Chapter 14 highlights education and medicine. These discussions show how social institutions have changed over the course of history, how they operate today, and what important controversies are likely to shape them tomorrow.

THE ECONOMY: HISTORICAL OVERVIEW

The **economy** is *the social institution that organizes a society's production, distribution, and consumption of goods and services.* As an institution, the economy operates—for better or worse—in a more or less predictable manner. *Goods* are commodities ranging from necessities (such as food, clothing, and shelter) to luxury items (such as automobiles, swimming pools, and yachts). *Services* refer to activities that benefit others (including the work of priests, physicians, professors, and parole officers).

THE AGRICULTURAL REVOLUTION

As Chapter 2 ("Culture") explained, the earliest societies were hunters and gatherers living off the land. In such societies, there was no distinct economy; producing and consuming were all part of family life.

When people harnessed animals to plows some 5,000 years ago, agriculture began, which was ten times as productive as hunting and gathering. The resulting surplus meant that not everyone had to produce food, so many people took on specialized work: making tools, raising animals, and building dwellings. Soon, towns sprang up, linked by networks of traders

(Jacobs, 1970). These four factors—agricultural technology, specialized work, permanent settlements, and trade—gave rise to the economy as a social institution.

THE INDUSTRIAL REVOLUTION

By the mid-eighteenth century, a second technological revolution began, first in England and then in North America. Industrialization brought even greater change than agriculture had, in five ways:

1. **New sources of energy.** Throughout history, "energy" had meant the muscle power of people or animals. Then, in 1765, the English inventor James Watt introduced the steam engine. A hundred times more powerful than muscle power, early steam engines soon drove heavy machinery.

2. **Centralization of work in factories.** Steam-powered machinery moved work from homes to factories—centralized workplaces housing the machines.

3. **Manufacturing and mass production.** Before the Industrial Revolution, most people grew or gathered raw materials (such as grain, wood, or wool). In an industrial economy, people working in factories turned raw materials into finished products (like furniture and clothing).

4. **Specialization.** Historically, artisans at home made products from beginning to end. In the factory, a laborer repeated a single task over and over, making only a small contribution to the finished product.

5. **Wage labor.** Instead of working for themselves in a household, factory workers became wage laborers who sold their labor to strangers, who often cared less for them than for the machines they operated.

The Industrial Revolution raised living standards as countless new products fueled an expanding economy. However, the benefits of industrial technology were shared very unequally, especially at the beginning. Some factory owners made vast fortunes, while the majority of workers lived close to poverty. Children, too, toiled in factories or deep in coal mines for pennies a day. With time, though, workers formed labor unions to collectively represent their interests to factory owners. During the twentieth century, new laws banned child labor, set minimum wage levels, improved workplace safety, and extended schooling and political rights to a larger segment of the population.

THE INFORMATION REVOLUTION
AND THE POSTINDUSTRIAL SOCIETY

By about 1950, the nature of production was changing once again. The United States was creating a **postindustrial economy,** *a productive system based on service work and high technology.* Automated machinery (and, more recently, robotics) reduced the role of human labor in production while simultaneously expanding the ranks of clerical workers and managers. Service industries—such as public relations, health care, advertising, banking, and sales—currently employ most working people in this country. The postindustrial era, then, is marked by a shift from industrial work to service work.

Driving this economic change is a third technological breakthrough: the computer. Just as factories did two centuries ago, the Information Revolution has introduced new kinds of products and new forms of communication, and has changed the character of work itself. In general, we see three changes:

1. **From tangible products to ideas.** The industrial era was defined by the production of goods; in the postindustrial era, work involves manipulating symbols. Computer programmers, writers, financial analysts, advertising executives, architects, editors, and all sorts of consultants make up the labor force of the information age.

2. **From mechanical skills to literacy skills.** The Industrial Revolution required mechanical skills, but the Information Revolution requires literacy skills—speaking and writing well and, of course, using computers. People able to communicate effectively enjoy new opportunities; people without these skills face declining prospects.

3. **From factories to almost anywhere.** Industrial technology drew workers to factories that were near power sources, but computer technology allows workers to be almost anywhere. Laptop computers, cell phones, and portable facsimile (fax) machines can turn the home, car, and even an airplane into a "virtual office." In short, new information technology blurs the line between work and home life.

SECTORS OF THE ECONOMY

The three revolutions just described reflect a shifting balance among the three sectors of the economy. The **primary sector** is *the part of the economy that draws raw materials from the natural environment.* The primary

The United States is now a postindustrial society: Industry employs just 26 percent of the labor force, while the service sector involves 72 percent of workers. How does this transformation change the nature as well as the location of work?

sector—agriculture, raising livestock, fishing, forestry, and mining—is largest in low-income, preindustrial nations. Figure 12–1 shows that 23 percent of the economic output of low-income countries is in the primary sector, compared to 9 percent of economic activity among middle-income nations and just 2 percent in high-income countries like the United States.

The **secondary sector** is *the part of the economy that transforms raw materials into manufactured goods.* This sector grows as societies industrialize and includes refining petroleum and turning metals into tools and automobiles.

The **tertiary sector** is *the part of the economy that involves services rather than goods.* Accounting for just 38 percent of economic output in low-income countries, the tertiary sector grows with industrialization, and accounts for 68 percent of production in high-income, postindustrial nations. Today, about 72 percent of the U.S. labor force does service work, including secretarial and clerical jobs and positions in food service, sales, law, health care, advertising, and teaching.

THE GLOBAL ECONOMY

New information technology is drawing nations of the world closer together, creating a **global economy—** *expanding economic activity with little regard for national*

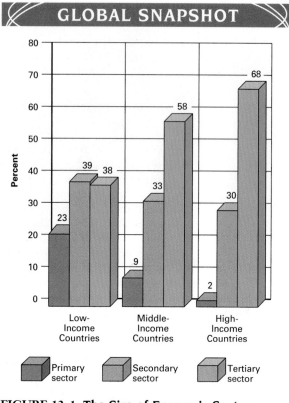

GLOBAL SNAPSHOT

**FIGURE 12–1 The Size of Economic Sectors
by Income Level of Country**

Source: Author estimates based on United Nations Development
Programme (2000) and The World Bank (2000).

borders. The development of a global economy has
four main consequences. First, we see a global division
of labor, so that different regions of the world specialize in one or another sector of economic activity. As
Global Map 12–1 shows, agriculture occupies more
than half of the work force in the world's poorest
countries. Global Map 12–2 indicates that service-
sector work dominates the economies of the world's
middle- and high-income countries.

Second, an increasing number of products pass
through more than one nation. Look no further than
your morning coffee, which may well have been grown
in Colombia and transported to New Orleans on a
freighter registered in Liberia, made in Japan using
steel from Korea, and fueled by oil from Venezuela.

A third consequence of the global economy is that
national governments no longer control the economic
activity that takes place within their borders. In fact,
governments cannot even regulate the value of their
national currencies, since dollars, pounds sterling,
yen, and other currencies are traded around the clock
in the financial centers of Tokyo, London, and New
York. Global markets depend on satellite communications that link the world's cities.

The fourth consequence of the global economy is
that a small number of businesses, operating interna-
tionally, now control a vast share of the world's economic activity. According to one estimate, the 600
largest multinational companies account for half the
world's entire economic output (Kidron & Segal, 1991).

The planet is still divided into 191 politically distinct nations. But increasing international economic
activity makes "nationhood" less significant than it
was even a decade ago.

ECONOMIC SYSTEMS: PATHS TO JUSTICE

October 20, 1995, Saigon, Vietnam. Sailing up the narrow Saigon River is an
unsettling experience for anyone who came
of age during the 1960s. We need to remember that Vietnam is a <u>country</u> not a <u>war</u>,
and that twenty years have passed since
the last U.S. helicopter lifted off the
rooftop of the U.S. embassy, ending our
country's presence there.

Saigon is on the brink of becoming a
boom town. Neon signs bathe the city's
waterfront in color; hotels, bankrolled
by Western corporations, push skyward
from a dozen construction sites; taxi
meters record fares in U.S. dollars, not
Vietnamese dong; Visa and American
Express stickers decorate the doors of
fashionable shops that cater to tourists
from Japan, France, and (since the U.S.
embargo on visiting Vietnam was lifted in
1994) the United States.

There is heavy irony here: After
decades of fighting, the loss of millions
of lives on both sides, and the victory
of Communist forces, the Vietnamese are
doing an about-face and turning toward
capitalism. What we see today is what
might well have happened had the U.S.
forces won the war.

304 CHAPTER 12 Economics and Politics

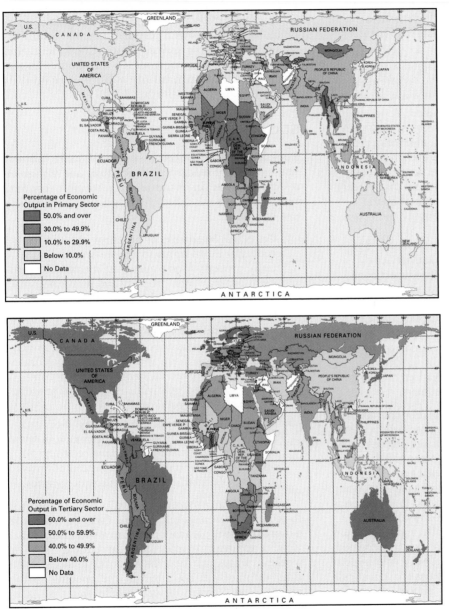

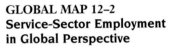

GLOBAL MAP 12–1
Agricultural Employment in Global Perspective

The primary sector of the economy is largest in societies that are least developed. Thus, in the poor countries of Africa and Asia, up to half of all workers are farmers. This picture is altogether different in the world's most economically developed countries—including the United States, Canada, Great Britain, and Australia—which have 2 percent of their work force in agriculture.

GLOBAL MAP 12–2
Service-Sector Employment in Global Perspective

The tertiary sector of the economy becomes ever larger as a nation's income level rises. In the United States, Canada, the countries of Western Europe, Australia, and Japan, about two-thirds of the labor force performs service work.

Sources: By the author, using data from United Nations Development Programme (2000) and The World Bank (2000, 2001); map projection from *Peters Atlas of the World* (1990).

Every society's economy makes a statement about justice, since it determines who gets what. Two general economic models are capitalism and socialism. No nation has an economy that is completely one or the other; capitalism and socialism represent two ends of a spectrum along which actual economies can be located.

CAPITALISM

Capitalism refers to *an economic system in which natural resources and the means of producing goods and services are privately owned.* An ideal capitalist economy has three distinctive features:

1. **Private ownership of property.** In a capitalist economy, individuals can own almost anything. The more capitalist an economy, the more private ownership there is of wealth-producing property like factories, real estate, and natural resources.

2. **Pursuit of personal profit.** A capitalist society promotes profit and wealth. The "profit motive" is considered the natural way of "doing business."

3. **Competition and consumer choice.** A purely capitalist economy is a free-market system with no government interference (sometimes called a *laissez-faire* economy, from the French words meaning "to leave alone"). The Scottish economist Adam Smith (1723–1790) held that a freely competitive economy regulates itself by the "invisible hand" of the law of supply and demand (1937; orig. 1776).

   Consumers guide a market economy, Smith continued, by selecting goods and services offering the greatest value. As producers compete for the customer's business, they provide the highest-quality goods at the lowest prices. In Smith's time-honored phrase, from narrow self-interest comes "the greatest good for the greatest number of people." Government control of an economy, on the other hand, distorts market forces, reduces producer motivation, diminishes quality, and shortchanges consumers.

"Justice" in a capitalist context amounts to freedom of the marketplace, where one can produce, buy, and invest according to individual self-interest. The worth of products and labor is determined by the dynamic process of supply and demand. Replacing much of the work force with lower-paid temporary workers, as described in the opening to this chapter, is "just" if it is profitable to the company's owners.

The United States is a capitalist nation because the vast majority of businesses are privately owned. Even so, government plays an extensive role in economic affairs. Government itself owns and operates a number of businesses, including almost all of this country's schools, roads, parks and museums, the U.S. Postal Service, the Amtrak railroad system, and the entire U.S. military. The U.S. government also had a major hand in building the Internet. In addition, governments use taxation and other forms of regulation to influence what companies produce, to control the quality and cost of merchandise, to regulate what businesses import and export, and to motivate consumers to conserve natural resources.

Further, government sets minimum wage levels, enforces workplace safety standards, regulates corporate mergers, provides farm price supports, and gives income in the form of Social Security, public assistance, student loans, and veterans' benefits to a majority of people in the United States. Local, state, and federal governments together are the nation's biggest employer, with 14 percent of the labor force on their payrolls (U.S. Census Bureau, 2000).

SOCIALISM

Socialism is *an economic system in which natural resources and the means of producing goods and services are collectively owned.* In its ideal form, a socialist economy rejects each of the three characteristics of capitalism just described.

1. **Collective ownership of property.** A socialist economy limits rights to private property, especially property used to generate income. Government controls such property and makes housing and other goods available to all, not just the people with the most money.

2. **Pursuit of collective goals.** The individualistic pursuit of profit is at odds with the collective orientation of socialism. What capitalism celebrates as the "entrepreneurial spirit," socialism condemns as "greed"; individuals are urged to work for the common good of all.

3. **Government control of the economy.** Socialism rejects capitalism's laissez-faire approach in favor of a *centrally controlled* or *command* economy operated by government. Commercial advertising thus plays little role in socialist economies.

"Justice" in a socialist context is not competition to accumulate wealth, but meeting everyone's needs in a more or less equal manner. From a socialist point of view, a capitalist practice such as cutting back on workers' wages and benefits in order to boost company earnings—as described in the opening to this chapter—puts profits before people and thus is an injustice.

The People's Republic of China and some two dozen other nations in Asia, Africa, and Latin America have socialist economies, with almost all wealth-generating property under state control (McColm et al., 1991). The extent of world socialism has declined in recent years as countries in Eastern Europe and the former Soviet Union have geared their economies toward a market system.

Capitalism still thrives in Hong Kong (left), evident in streets choked with advertising and shoppers. Socialism is more the rule in China's capital of Beijing (right), a city dominated by government buildings rather than a downtown business district.

WELFARE CAPITALISM AND STATE CAPITALISM

Some nations in Western Europe, including Sweden and Italy, have a market-based economy but also offer broad social welfare programs. Analysts call this "third way" **welfare capitalism,** *an economic and political system that combines a mostly market-based economy with extensive social welfare programs.*

Under welfare capitalism, the government owns some of the largest industries and services, such as transportation, the mass media, and health care. In Sweden and Italy, about 12 percent of economic production is "nationalized," or state controlled. That leaves most industry in private hands, although subject to extensive government regulation. High taxation (aimed especially at the rich) funds a wide range of social welfare programs, including universal health care and child care (Olsen, 1996).

Yet another alternative is **state capitalism,** *an economic and political system in which companies are privately owned but cooperate closely with the government.* State capitalism is the rule in the nations along the Pacific Rim. Japan, South Korea, and Singapore, for example, are all capitalist countries, but their governments work in partnership with large companies, supplying financial assistance and controlling foreign imports to help their businesses compete in world markets (Gerlach, 1992).

RELATIVE ADVANTAGES OF CAPITALISM AND SOCIALISM

In practice, which economic system works best? Comparing economic models is difficult because all countries mix capitalism and socialism to varying degrees. Moreover, nations differ in cultural attitudes toward work, natural resources, technological development, and patterns of trade (Gregory & Stuart, 1985). Despite such complicating factors, some crude comparisons are revealing.

Economic productivity. One key dimension of economic performance is productivity. A commonly used measure of output is gross domestic product (GDP), the total value of all goods and services produced annually. "Per capita" (per person) GDP allows us to compare the economic performance of nations of different population sizes.

While the output of mostly capitalist countries at the end of the 1980s varied somewhat, averaging the figures for the United States, Canada, and the nations of Western Europe yields a per capita GDP of about $13,500. The comparable figure for the former Soviet Union and the nations of Eastern Europe is about $5,000. This means that the capitalist countries outproduced the socialist nations by a ratio of 2.7 to 1 (United Nations Development Programme, 1990).

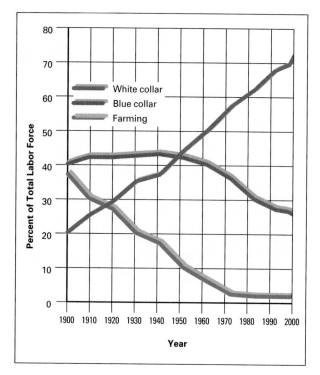

**FIGURE 12–2 The Changing Pattern of Work
in the United States, 1900–2000**

Sources: Author estimates based on United Nations Development
Programme (2000) and The World Bank (2000).

Economic equality. How resources are distributed within the population is another important measure. A comparative study in the mid-1970s looked at income ratios based on the earnings of the richest 5 percent of the population and the poorest 5 percent (Wiles, 1977). The result was that societies with mostly capitalist economies had an income ratio of about 10 to 1; the figure for socialist countries was 5 to 1. In other words, *capitalist economies support a higher overall standard of living but with greater income disparity.* Or, put otherwise, *socialist economies create more economic equality but with a lower overall living standard.*

Personal freedom. One additional consideration in evaluating capitalism and socialism is the personal freedom each system affords its people. Capitalism emphasizes *freedom to* pursue one's own self-interest. Capitalism, after all, depends on the freedom of producers and consumers to interact with little interference from the state. On the other hand, socialism emphasizes *freedom from* basic want. Equality is the

goal, which requires state intervention in the economy, which in turn limits personal choices for citizens.

No system has yet been able to offer both political freedom and economic equality. In the capitalist United States, our political system offers many personal freedoms, but are they worth as much to a poor person as a rich one? On the other side of the coin, China has more economic equality but people cannot freely speak out or travel inside and outside the country.

CHANGES IN SOCIALIST COUNTRIES

In 1989 and 1990, the nations of Eastern Europe, which had been seized by the former Soviet Union at the end of World War II, shook off their socialist regimes. These nations—including the former German Democratic Republic, the Czech Republic, Slovakia, Hungary, Romania, and Bulgaria—are moving toward market systems after decades of state-controlled economies. In 1992, the Soviet Union itself formally dissolved and has introduced some free-market principles.

There were many reasons for these sweeping changes. First, the mostly socialist economies underproduced their capitalist counterparts. They were successful in achieving economic equality, but living standards were low compared to those of Western Europe. Second, Soviet socialism was heavy-handed, rigidly controlling the media and restricting individual freedoms. In short, socialism did away with *economic* elites, as Karl Marx predicted. But, as Max Weber foresaw, socialism increased the clout of *political* elites.

So far, the market reforms in Eastern Europe are proceeding unevenly. Some nations (Czech Republic, Slovakia, Poland, and the Baltic states of Latvia, Estonia, and Lithuania) are faring pretty well. But other countries (Romania, Bulgaria, and the Russian Federation) are buffeted by price increases and falling living standards. Officials hope that expanding production eventually will bring a turnaround. There is already evidence, though, that a rising standard of living will be accompanied by increasing economic inequality (Pohl, 1996; Buraway, 1997; Specter, 1997a).

WORK IN THE POSTINDUSTRIAL ECONOMY

Economic change is occurring not just in the socialist world but also in the United States. In 2000, the U.S. government reports, 141 million people were in the labor force, representing two-thirds of those aged

Teaching is one of the most personally rewarding occupations anyone can have. But do all teachers have equal claim to being professionals? Primary school teachers (such as the woman on the left) usually teach a curriculum controlled by the school and state officials. College teachers (such as the man on the right) typically have far more autonomy in deciding what, how, when, and where they teach. What factors account for this difference?

sixteen and over. A larger share of men (74.7 percent) than women (60.2 percent) had income-producing jobs, although the gap is closing. Among men, 69.0 percent of African Americans are in the labor force, compared to 75.4 percent of white people and 80.6 percent of Hispanics. Among women, 63.2 percent of African Americans are employed, compared to 59.8 percent of white people and 56.9 percent of Hispanics.

THE CHANGING WORKPLACE

In 1900, 40 percent of U.S. workers were farmers. In 2000, just 2 percent were in agriculture. Figure 12–2 illustrates the shrinking role of the primary sector in the U.S. economy.

Similarly, a century ago, industrialization swelled the ranks of blue-collar workers. By 1950, however, a white-collar revolution had moved most workers into service occupations. By 2000, 90 percent of new jobs were in the service sector, and 72 percent of the labor force performed service work.

As Chapter 8 ("Social Stratification") explained, much service work—including sales, clerical positions, and work in hospitals and restaurants—yields little of the income and prestige of white-collar professions, and, at the same time, it offers fewer financial rewards

than factory work. In sum, many jobs in this postindustrial era provide only a modest standard of living.

LABOR UNIONS

The changing U.S. economy has seen a decline in *labor unions*, organizations that seek to improve wages and working conditions. Union membership increased rapidly after 1935, to more than one-third of nonfarm workers by 1950. By 1970, membership peaked at almost 25 million people. Since then, union rolls have declined to about 14 percent of the non-farm workers, or some 16.3 million men and women.

The pattern of union decline holds in other high-income countries as well. Yet, unions claim a far smaller share of workers in the United States than elsewhere. In Canada and Japan, about 33 percent of workers belong to unions; across Europe, about 40 percent belong; in the Scandinavian countries, the share is 80 percent (Western, 1993, 1995).

The global decline in union membership follows the shrinking industrial sector; newer service jobs are less likely to be unionized. But, as some analysts see it, decreased job security may well make unions more popular in years to come. If so, unions will have to adapt to the new global economy. Union members in the United

Jose Clemente Orozco's painting The Unemployed *is a powerful statement of the personal collapse and private despair that afflict men and women who are out of work. How does a sociological perspective help us to understand being out of work as more than a personal problem?*

Jose Clemente Orozco, *The Unemployed.* Photograph © Christie's Images. © Orozco Valladares Family. Reproduction authorized by the Instituto Nacional de Bellas Artes y Literatura.

States, used to seeing foreign workers as "the enemy," will have to build new international alliances (Mabry, 1992; Church, 1994; Greenhouse, 2000).

PROFESSIONS

All kinds of work today are called *professional;* we hear of professional tennis players, professional house cleaners, and even professional exterminators. As distinct from an *amateur* (from the Latin for "lover," meaning one who acts out of love for the activity itself), a professional does some task for a living. But what exactly is a *profession?*

A **profession** is *a prestigious, white-collar occupation that requires extensive formal education.* Those performing this kind of work make a profession, or public

declaration, of willingness to abide by certain principles. Professions include the ministry, medicine, law, academia, and, more recently, architecture, accountancy, and social work. Occupations are professional to the extent that they demonstrate the following four characteristics (Goode, 1960; Ritzer & Walczak, 1990):

1. **Theoretical knowledge.** Professionals have theoretical knowledge of their field rather than mere technical training. Anyone can learn first-aid skills, for example, but physicians have a theoretical understanding of human health.

2. **Self-regulating practice.** The typical professional is self-employed, "in practice" rather than working for a company. Professionals oversee their own work and observe a code of ethics.

3. **Authority over clients.** Based on extensive training, professionals advise clients and expect them to follow their direction.

4. **Community orientation rather than self-interest.** The traditional "professing" of duty states an intention to serve the community rather than merely seek income.

Many new occupations in the postindustrial economy seek to *professionalize* their services. Claiming professional standing usually begins by renaming the work to imply special, theoretical knowledge, thereby distancing the field from its previously less distinguished reputation. Stockroom workers, for example, become "inventory supply managers," and exterminators are reborn as "insect-control specialists."

Interested parties may also form a professional association to formally attest to their skills. The organization licenses people who perform the work and writes a code of ethics emphasizing the occupation's role in the community. To win public acceptance, a professional association may also establish schools or other training facilities and perhaps start a professional journal (Abbott, 1988). Not all occupations try to claim professional status. Some *paraprofessionals,* including paralegals and medical technicians, possess specialized skills but lack the extensive theoretical education required of full professionals.

SELF-EMPLOYMENT

Self-employment—earning a living without working for a large organization—was once common in the United States. About 80 percent of the labor force was self-employed in 1800, compared to just 7.0 percent of workers today (8.2 percent of men and 5.7 percent of women) (U.S. Department of Labor, 2001).

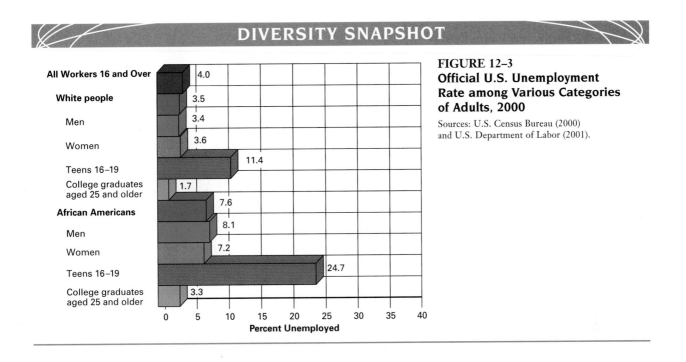

All Workers 16 and Over — 4.0

White people — 3.5

Men — 3.4

Women — 3.6

Teens 16–19 — 11.4

College graduates aged 25 and older — 1.7

African Americans — 7.6

Men — 8.1

Women — 7.2

Teens 16–19 — 24.7

College graduates aged 25 and older — 3.3

Percent Unemployed

FIGURE 12–3
Official U.S. Unemployment Rate among Various Categories of Adults, 2000

Sources: U.S. Census Bureau (2000) and U.S. Department of Labor (2001).

Lawyers, physicians, and other professionals are well represented among the ranks of the self-employed. But most self-employed workers are small business owners (an increasing share of whom are using the Internet to run their businesses), farmers, plumbers, carpenters, freelance writers and editors, artists, and long-distance truck drivers. Overall, the self-employed are more likely to have blue-collar than white-collar jobs.

Finally, a notable trend is that women own nearly 40 percent of this nation's small businesses, and the share is rising. Moreover, the 9.1 million firms owned by U.S. women now employ almost 30 million people and generate close to $4 trillion in annual sales (Small Business Administration, 2001).

UNEMPLOYMENT

Every society has some unemployment. Few young people entering the labor force find a job right away; workers may temporarily leave their jobs to seek new work or have children; some may be on strike; others suffer from long-term illnesses; and still others are illiterate or without the skills to perform useful work.

But unemployment is also caused by the economy itself. Jobs disappear as occupations become obsolete, businesses close in the face of foreign competition or economic recession, and companies "downsize" to become more profitable. Since 1980, the 500 largest U.S. businesses have eliminated some 5 million jobs—one-fourth of the total.

In 2000, 5.7 million people over the age of sixteen were unemployed—about 4.0 percent of the labor force. Even so, some regions of the country, including parts of West Virginia and New Mexico, have high unemployment—in some cases, twice the national rate.

Figure 12–3 shows that unemployment among African Americans (7.6 percent) is more than twice the rate among white people (3.5 percent). For both races, men and women have about the same rates of unemployment.

WORKPLACE DIVERSITY: RACE AND GENDER

Traditionally, white men have been the mainstay of the U.S. labor force. As explained in Chapter 11 ("Race and Ethnicity"), however, the proportion of minorities is rising rapidly. Between 1990 and 2000, the African American population increased by 16.2 percent, more than three times the 4.6 percent increase for white people. The jump in the Hispanic population was even greater, at 46.7 percent, and, among Asian Americans, 51.6 percent. The box on page 312 takes a look at how increasing social diversity will affect the workplace.

SOCIAL DIVERSITY

Diversity in the New Century: Changes in the Workplace

An upward trend in the U.S. minority population is changing the face of the workplace. As the figure shows, the number of white men in the U.S. labor force will rise by a modest 7 percent between 1998 and 2008, but the increase among African American men will be 18 percent, and among Hispanic men, a much greater 29 percent. Among white women, the projected rise is 13 percent, and among African American women, 21 percent. Hispanic women will show the greatest gains, estimated at 49 percent.

The overall result is that, within a decade, non-Hispanic white men will represent 38 percent of all workers, and that figure will continue to drop. Therefore, companies that welcome social diversity will tap the largest talent pool and enjoy a competitive advantage.

Welcoming social diversity means, first, recruiting talented workers of both sexes as well as of all colors and cultural backgrounds. But developing the potential of all employees requires meeting the special needs of women and other minorities, which may

not be the same as those of white men. For example, in the twenty-first century, corporations will be pressed to provide child care at the workplace.

Second, businesses need to develop effective ways to defuse tension that arises from social differences. They will have to work harder at treating workers

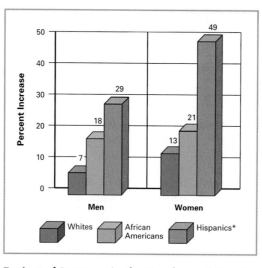

Projected Increase in the Numbers of People in the U.S. Labor Force, 1998–2008

*Hispanics can be of any race.

Source: U.S. Department of Labor (1999).

equally and respectfully; also, no corporate culture can tolerate racial or sexual harassment.

Third, companies will have to rethink current promotion practices. At present, only 4 percent of Fortune 500 top executives are women, and just 1 percent are other minorities. In a broad survey of U.S. companies, the U.S. Equal Employment Opportunity Commission confirmed that white men (42 percent of adults aged twenty to sixty-four) hold 59 percent of management jobs; the comparable figures for white women are 42 and 28 percent; for African Americans, 12 and 6 percent; and, for Hispanics, 10 and 4 percent.

In sum, "glass ceilings" that limit the advancement of skilled workers not only discourage effort but deprive companies of their largest source of talent—women and other minorities.

Sources: U.S. Department of Labor (1999), U.S. Equal Employment Opportunity Commission (2000), and Catalyst (2001).

NEW INFORMATION TECHNOLOGY AND WORK

Another workplace issue of this new century is the central role of computers and new information technology. The Information Revolution is changing what people do in some basic ways (Zuboff, 1982; Rule & Brantley, 1992; Vallas & Beck, 1996):

1. **Computers are "deskilling" labor.** Just as industrial machines replaced the master craftsworkers

of an earlier era, so computers now threaten the skills of managers. More business operations are based not on executive decisions but on computer modeling. In other words, a machine decides whether to place an order, resupply a client, or approve a loan application.

2. **Computers are making work more abstract.** Most industrial workers have a "hands on" relationship with their product. Postindustrial workers manipulate symbols in pursuit of

Although the Information Revolution is centered in high-income countries such as the United States, the effects of high technology are becoming evident even in low-income nations. Do you think the expansion of information technology will change the lives of rural people such as these peasants in Vietnam? If so, how?

abstract goals, such as making a company more profitable or software more "user friendly."

3. **Computers limit workplace interaction.** As workers spend more time at computer terminals, they become isolated from one another.

4. **Computers increase employers' control of workers.** Computers allow supervisors to check employees' output continuously, whether they work at keyboards or on assembly lines.

Such changes remind us that technology is not socially neutral. Computers alter not only the way we work but also the balance of power between employer and employees. Understandably, then, people may welcome some aspects of the Information Revolution and oppose others.

CORPORATIONS

At the core of today's capitalist economy is the **corporation**, *an organization with a legal existence, including rights and liabilities, apart from those of its members.* Incorporating makes an organization a legal entity unto itself, able to enter into contracts and own property. Of the 24 million businesses in the United States, 5 million are incorporated (U.S. Census Bureau, 2000). Incorporating protects the wealth of owners from lawsuits that arise as a result of business debts or harm to consumers; often, it also means a lower tax rate on the company's profits.

ECONOMIC CONCENTRATION

About half of U.S. corporations are small, with assets of less than $100,000. The largest corporations, however, dominate our nation's economy. In 1997, 549 corporations had assets exceeding $1 billion, representing three-fourths of all corporate assets and profits (U.S. Census Bureau, 2000).

The largest U.S. corporation in terms of sales is General Motors, with $274 billion in total assets. GM employs more people than the state governments of California, Oregon, Washington, Alaska, and Hawaii combined. Its sales ($161 billion in 1999) equal the tax revenues of half the states.

CORPORATE LINKAGES

Economic concentration creates *conglomerates*, giant corporations composed of many smaller corporations. Conglomerates form as corporations enter new markets, spin off new companies, or merge with other companies. For example, RJR-Nabisco is a conglomerate that sells not only cigarettes but dozens of familiar household products.

Yet another type of corporate linkage is the *interlocking directorate*, a social network of people who serve as directors of many corporations (Herman, 1981; Scott & Griff, 1985; Weidenbaum, 1995; Kono et al., 1998). These boardroom connections provide access to valuable information about other companies' products and marketing strategies. Beth Mintz and

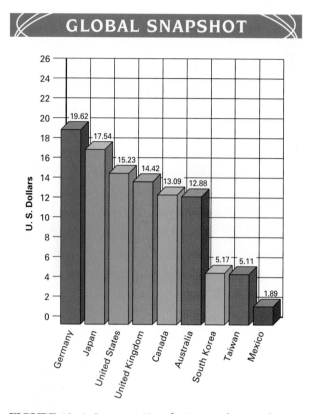

FIGURE 12–4 Average Hourly Wages for Workers in Manufacturing, 1999

Source: Calculations by the author based on U.S. Department of Labor (2000).

Michael Schwartz (1981) found that General Motors is linked through its board members to 700 other companies. Such linkages do not necessarily oppose the public interest, but they may encourage illegal activity such as price-fixing, and they certainly concentrate wealth and power.

CORPORATIONS: ARE THEY COMPETITIVE?

According to the capitalist model, businesses operate independently in a competitive market. But large corporations have extensive linkages, which means that, in reality, they do not operate independently. Second, a small number of corporations dominate many large markets. Large corporations are not, therefore, truly competitive.

Law forbids a large company from establishing a **monopoly,** *domination of a market by a single producer,* because a monopoly could simply dictate prices. But a common practice is **oligopoly,** *domination of a market by a few producers.* Oligopoly arises because the vast investment needed to enter a major market, like the auto industry, is beyond the reach of all but the biggest companies. Moreover, true competition means risk, which big business tries to avoid.

CORPORATIONS AND THE GLOBAL ECONOMY

Corporations have grown so large that they now account for most of the world's economic output. The biggest corporations are based in the United States, Japan, and Western Europe, but they consider the entire world one huge marketplace.

Poor nations attract the attention of global corporations because most of the world's people and resources are found within their borders. In addition, as shown in Figure 12–4, labor costs there are attractively low: A manufacturing worker in Mexico labors for two weeks to earn about what a German worker earns in a single day.

The impact of multinationals on low-income countries is controversial, as Chapter 9 ("Global Stratification") explained. On one side of the argument, modernization theorists claim that multinationals, by unleashing the great productivity of capitalism, raise living standards in poor nations. Specifically, corporations offer poor nations tax revenues, capital investment, new jobs, and advanced technology that, together, accelerate economic growth (Rostow, 1978; Madsen, 1980; Berger, 1986; Firebaugh & Beck, 1994).

Dependency theorists, on the other hand, respond that multinationals intensify global inequality. Multinationals, they contend, fail to improve the job market because they block the development of local industries and push poor countries to make goods for export rather than food and other products for local consumption. From this standpoint, multinationals make poor nations poorer and increasingly dependent on rich nations (Vaughan, 1978; Wallerstein, 1979; Delacroix & Ragin, 1981; Bergesen, 1983; Walton & Ragin, 1990).

LOOKING AHEAD: THE ECONOMY OF THE TWENTY-FIRST CENTURY

Social institutions are a society's ways of meeting people's needs. But, as we have seen, the U.S. economy only partly succeeds in this respect. Although highly productive, our economy provides for some much better than for others. Moreover, as we begin the

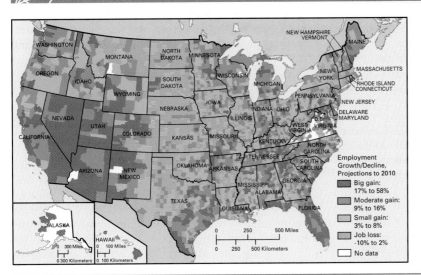

NATIONAL MAP 12–1
Where the Jobs Will Be: Projections to 2010

The economic prospects of counties across the United States are not the same. Much of the mid-section of the country is projected to lose jobs. By contrast, the coastal regions—and most of the West—are rapidly gaining jobs. What factors might account for this pattern?

Source: Used with permission of Woods & Poole Economics, Washington, D.C.

twenty-first century, the Information Revolution continues to change our economy. First, the share of the U.S. labor force engaged in manufacturing is now half of what it was in 1960; service work—especially computer-related jobs—makes up the difference. For industrial workers, then, the postindustrial economy has brought unemployment and declining wages. Our society must face up to the challenge of providing millions of men and women with the language and computer skills needed in the new economy. We must also take into account that some regions of the country are experiencing an economic boom, as shown in National Map 12–1, while other regions are projected to lose jobs in the next decade.

A second transformation that will mark the new century is the expansion of the global economy. Two centuries ago, the ups and downs of a local economy reflected events and trends in a single town. One century ago, communities across the country became economically linked so that one town's prosperity depended on producing goods demanded by people elsewhere in the country. Today, it makes less sense to speak of a national economy since what people in a Kansas farm town produce and consume may be affected more by what happens in the wheat-growing region of Russia than by events in their own state capital. In short, U.S. workers are not only creating new products and services but are working in response to factors and forces that are distant and unseen.

Finally, analysts around the world are rethinking conventional economic models. The global economy shows that socialism is less productive than capitalism, one reason for the collapse of socialist regimes in Eastern Europe and the former Soviet Union. But capitalism, too, is changing and now operates with significant government regulation, partly to address the economic inequality generated by market systems.

What are the long-term effects of these changes? Two conclusions seem inescapable. First, the economic future of the United States and other nations will be played out in a global arena. The new postindustrial economy in the United States is, after all, inseparable from the increasing industrial production of other nations. Second, we must address the pressing challenges of global inequality and population increase (Firebaugh, 1999). Whether the world economy reduces or deepens the disparity between rich and poor societies may end up steering our planet toward peace or war.

POLITICS: HISTORICAL OVERVIEW

Closely related to economics is **politics** (or "the polity"), *the social institution that distributes power, sets a society's agenda, and makes decisions.* Early in the twentieth century, Max Weber (1978; orig. 1921) defined **power** as *the ability to achieve desired ends despite resistance from others.*

Brute force is the most basic form of power. But no society that derives power *only* from sheer force lasts long, and life in such a society would be a nightmare of terror. On the contrary, social organization depends on creating agreement about goals and how to attain them. This brings us to the concept of **authority,** *power that people perceive as legitimate rather than coercive.*

A society's source of authority depends, in turn, on its economy. According to Max Weber, preindustrial societies rely on *traditional authority,* power legitimized through respect for long-established cultural patterns. Woven into a society's collective memory, traditional authority may seem almost sacred. Chinese emperors in antiquity were legitimized by tradition, as were the nobles in medieval Europe.

But traditional authority declines as societies industrialize. Royal families still exist in ten European nations, for example, but their democratic cultures have shifted power to commoners elected to office. Thus, Weber continued, the expansion of rational bureaucracy provides a distinctly modern path to authority. *Rational-legal authority* (sometimes called *bureaucratic authority*), said Weber, is power legitimized by rationally enacted law.

Just as traditional authority is tied to family, rational-legal authority flows from offices in governments. In other words, while a traditional monarch passes power on to heirs, a modern president takes and gives up power according to law.

Weber described one additional type of authority that has surfaced throughout history. *Charismatic authority* is power legitimized by the extraordinary personal abilities—charisma—of a leader. Unlike its traditional and rational-legal counterparts, charismatic authority depends less on a person's ancestry or office and more on individual personality. Followers see in charismatic leaders some special, perhaps even divine, power. Examples of charismatic leaders include Jesus of Nazareth, Nazi Germany's Adolf Hitler, and the liberator of India, Mahatma Gandhi. All charismatics share a goal of radically transforming society, which makes them highly controversial (and explains why few charismatics die of old age).

Because charismatic authority flows from a single individual, the leader's death creates a crisis. The survival of a charismatic movement, Max Weber explained, requires the **routinization of charisma**—*the transformation of charismatic authority into some combination of traditional and bureaucratic authority.* After the death of Jesus, for example, followers institutionalized his teachings in a church, built on tradition and bureaucracy, that flourishes today, 2,000 years later.

GLOBAL POLITICAL SYSTEMS

The world's political systems differ in countless ways. Generally, however, they fall into four categories: monarchy, democracy, authoritarianism, and totalitarianism.

MONARCHY

Monarchy (with Latin and Greek roots, meaning "one ruler") is *a type of political system in which a single family rules from generation to generation.* Monarchy is commonly found in agrarian societies; the Bible, for example, tells of great kings such as David and Solomon. In the world today, twenty-eight nations have royal families;[1] most trace their ancestry back for centuries. In Weber's analysis, then, monarchy is legitimized by tradition.

During the Middle Ages, *absolute monarchs* in much of the world claimed a virtual monopoly of power based on divine right. In some nations—including Kuwait, Saudi Arabia, and Brunei—monarchs still exercise virtually absolute control over their people.

With industrialization, however, monarchs gradually pass from the scene in favor of elected officials. All the European societies where royal families remain are *constitutional monarchies,* in that their monarchs are little more than symbolic heads of state; actual governing is the responsibility of elected officials, led by a prime minister and guided by a constitution. In these countries, nobility formally reigns, but elected officials actually rule.

DEMOCRACY

The historical trend in the world has favored **democracy,** *a type of political system which gives power to the people as a whole.* More correctly, a system of *representative democracy* puts authority in the hands of leaders who, from time to time, compete for office in elections.

Most rich countries in the world claim to be democratic (including those that still have royal families). Industrialization and democracy go together

---

[1]In Europe, these include Sweden, Norway, Denmark, Great Britain, the Netherlands, Liechtenstein, Luxembourg, Belgium, Spain, and Monaco; in the Middle East, Jordan, Saudi Arabia, Oman, Qatar, Bahrain, and Kuwait; in Africa, Lesotho, Swaziland, and Morocco; in Asia, Brunei, Samoa, Tonga, Thailand, Malaysia, Cambodia, Nepal, Bhutan, and Japan.

because both require a literate populace. Moreover, the traditional legitimization of power in a monarchy gives way, with industrialization, to rational-legal authority. Thus, democracy and rational-legal authority are linked just as monarchy and traditional authority are.

But high-income countries such as the United States are not truly democratic for two reasons. First, there is the problem of bureaucracy. The U.S. federal government employs nearly 3 million people (excluding the armed forces), and another 17 million people work in some 87,000 state and local governments. Many of these employees serve in an "official" capacity; thus, the vast majority of officials are never elected by anyone and are not directly accountable to the people (Scaff, 1981; Edwards, 1985; Etzioni-Halevy, 1985).

The second problem involves economic inequality, since rich people have far more political clout than poor people. One reason George W. Bush got off to such a fast start in the 2000 presidential campaign was that, as a rich man with many rich friends, he was able to raise more than $50 million in a short time. Magazine magnate Steve Forbes financed his own run for the White House, spending $50 million of his own fortune in 1996 and 2000 (although he did not get very far in the primaries). Moreover, given the even greater resources of multibillion-dollar corporations, how can we think that our "democratic" system responds to—or even hears—the voices of "average people"?

Still, democratic nations provide many rights and freedoms. Global Map 12–3 on page 318 shows one assessment of the extent of political freedom around the world. According to Freedom House, an organization that tracks political trends, by 2000, eighty-five of the world's nations (with 40 percent of the global population) were "free," with considerable respect for civil liberties. This represents a strong gain for democracy: Just sixty-one nations were free a decade earlier (Freedom House, 2000).

AUTHORITARIANISM

Not all governments try to involve their people in politics. **Authoritarianism** refers to *a political system that denies popular participation in government.* An authoritarian government is both indifferent to people's needs and offers them no voice in selecting leaders. The absolute monarchies in Saudi Arabia and Kuwait are authoritarian, as are the military juntas in Iraq and Ethiopia.

In 2000, just 28 of the world's 191 nations were political monarchies where single families pass power from generation to generation. The African nation of Swaziland recently celebrated the coronation of a young king.

TOTALITARIANISM

October 22, 1994, near Saigon, Vietnam. Six U.S. students have been arrested, allegedly for talking to Vietnamese students and also taking pictures at the university. The Vietnamese Minister of Education has canceled the reception tonight, claiming that our students meeting with their students threatens Vietnam's security.

The most intensely controlled political form is **totalitarianism,** *a highly centralized political system that extensively regulates people's lives.* Totalitarian systems emerged during the twentieth century, as governments gained the ability to rigidly regulate a population. The Vietnamese government closely monitors the activities not just of visitors but of all its citizens. Similarly, the government of North Korea uses surveillance equipment and powerful computers to collect and store information and thereby control the entire population.

Some totalitarian governments claim to represent the will of the people, but most seek to bend people to the will of the government. Such governments are *total*

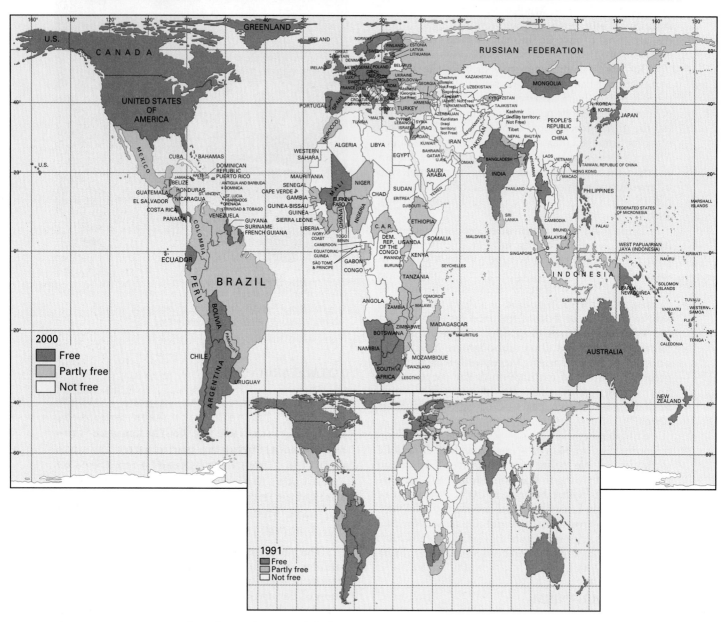

GLOBAL MAP 12–3 Political Freedom in Global Perspective

In 2000, 85 of the world's nations, containing 40 percent of all people, were politically "free"—that is, they offered their citizens extensive political rights and civil liberties. Another 59 countries, which included 25 percent of the world's people, were "partly free," with more limited rights and liberties. The remaining 47 nations, home to 35 percent of humanity, fall into the category of "not free." In these countries, government sharply restricts individual initiative. Between 1980 and 2000, democracy made significant gains, largely in Latin America and Eastern Europe. In Asia, moreover, India (containing 1 billion people) returned to the "free" category in 1999.

Source: Freedom House (2000).

Throughout our nation's history, company leaders have been able to enlist the help of the state to defend their interests. In 1936, police attacked strikers at Chicago's Republic Steel Mill, leaving ten workers dead. Philip Evergood commemorates the event in his painting American Tragedy.

Philip Evergood, *American Tragedy*, 1936, oil on canvas, 29½ x 39½", Terry Dintenfass Gallery, New York.

concentrations of power, allowing no organized opposition. Denying people the right to assemble and controlling access to information, these governments create an atmosphere of isolation and fear. In the former Soviet Union, for example, most citizens could not own telephone directories, copying equipment, fax machines, or even accurate city maps.

Socialization in totalitarian societies is highly political, seeking not just obedience but commitment to the system. In North Korea, one of the most totalitarian states in the world, pictures of leaders and political messages are everywhere, reminding citizens that they owe total allegiance to the state. Government-controlled schools and mass media present only official versions of events.

Totalitarian governments span the political spectrum from fascist (including Nazi Germany) to communist (such as North Korea). In some totalitarian states, businesses are privately owned (as in Nazi Germany and, more recently, Chile); in others, businesses are government owned (as in North Korea, Cuba, and the former Soviet Union). In all cases, however, one party claims total control of the society and permits no opposition.

A GLOBAL POLITICAL SYSTEM?

We have already noted the emergence of a global economy. Is there a parallel development of a global political system? On one level, the answer is no. Although most of today's economic activity is international, the world remains divided into nation-states just as it has been for centuries. The United Nations (founded in 1945) was a small step toward global government, but, to date, its political role in world affairs has been limited.

On another level, however, politics has become a global process. For some analysts, multinational corporations represent a new political order since they have enormous power to shape events throughout the world. In other words, politics is dissolving into business as corporations grow larger than governments.

Then, too, the Information Revolution has moved national politics onto the world stage. Electronic mail over the Internet, cellular phones, satellite transmission systems, and fax machines mean that few countries can conduct their political affairs in complete privacy.

Finally, several thousand *nongovernmental organizations (NGOs)* seek to advance global issues, such as human rights (Amnesty International) and protection of the environment (Greenpeace). In the new century, NGOs will almost certainly play a key role in expanding the global political culture (Boli & Thomas, 1997).

In sum, just as individual nations are losing control of their own economies, neither can governments fully manage the political events that occur within their borders.

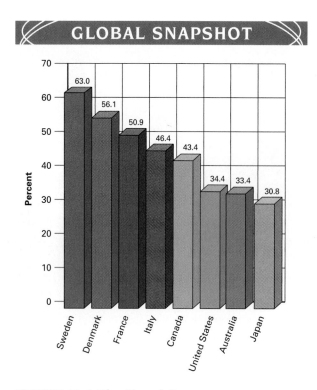

FIGURE 12–5 The Size of Government: Tax Revenues as Share of Gross Domestic Product, 1998

Source: U.S. Census Bureau (1999).

POLITICS IN THE UNITED STATES

After fighting a revolutionary war against Great Britain to gain political independence, the United States replaced the British monarchy with a democratic political system. Our nation's political development reflects its distinctive history, capitalist economy, and cultural heritage.

U.S. CULTURE AND THE RISE OF THE WELFARE STATE

The political culture of the United States can be summed up in a word: individualism. This emphasis is found in the Bill of Rights, which guarantees freedom from undue government interference. It was this individualism that nineteenth-century poet and philosopher Ralph Waldo Emerson had in mind when he said, "The government that governs best is the government that governs least."

But taking Emerson literally would find little support among the majority of this nation's people, who recognize that government is necessary to maintain national defense, highway systems, schools, and law and order. Moreover, government has grown into a vast and complex **welfare state,** *a range of government agencies and programs that provides benefits to the population.* Government benefits begin even before birth (through prenatal nutrition programs) and continue into old age (through Social Security and Medicare). Some programs are especially important to the poor, who are not well served by our capitalist economic system; nevertheless, students, farmers, homeowners, small business operators, veterans, performing artists, and even giant corporations also get various subsidies and supports. In fact, a majority of U.S. adults look to government for at least part of their income (Caplow et al., 1982; Devine, 1985; Bartlett & Steele, 1998).

Today's welfare state is the result of a gradual increase in the size and scope of government. Back in 1789, when the presence of the federal government amounted to little more than a flag in most communities, the entire federal budget was a mere $4.5 million ($1.50 for every person in the nation). Since then, it has steadily risen, reaching $1.8 trillion in 2000 (a per capita figure of $6,500).

Similarly, in 1789, one government employee served every 1,800 citizens. Today, there is one official to serve every fourteen citizens, for a total of 20 million government employees, more than are engaged in manufacturing (U.S. Census Bureau, 2000).

As much as government has expanded in this country, the U.S. welfare state is still smaller than in many other industrial nations. Figure 12–5 shows that government is larger in most of Europe, and especially in Scandinavian countries like Denmark and Sweden.

THE POLITICAL SPECTRUM

Who supports the welfare state? Who would want to see it grow? Or be cut way back? Such questions tap attitudes that form the *political spectrum,* which ranges from the extremely liberal on the left to the extremely conservative on the right.

One cluster of attitudes concerns *economic issues.* Economic liberals support extensive government regulation of the economy in order to reduce disparities in income. Economic conservatives want to limit the hand of government in the economy and allow market forces freer rein.

Social issues are moral questions ranging from abortion and the death penalty to gay rights and treatment

Lower-income people have more pressing financial needs and so they tend to focus on economic issues, such as the level of the minimum wage. Higher-income people, by contrast, provide support for many social issues, such as animal rights.

of minorities. Social liberals endorse equal rights and opportunities for all categories of people, view abortion as a matter of individual choice, and oppose the death penalty because it has been unfairly applied to minorities. The "family values" agenda of social conservatives supports traditional gender roles and opposes gay families, affirmative action, and other "special programs" for minorities. Social conservatives condemn abortion as morally wrong and support the death penalty.

Of the two major political parties in the United States, the Republican party is more conservative on both economic and social issues while the Democratic party is more liberal. But most people are not consistently either conservative or liberal. With wealth to protect, most higher-income people hold conservative views on economic issues. Yet their extensive schooling and secure social standing lead them to be social liberals. Lower-income people show the opposite pattern, being liberal on economic issues but supporting a socially conservative agenda (Nunn, Crockett, & Williams, 1978; Erikson, Luttbeg, & Tedin, 1980; McBroom & Reed, 1990). African Americans, both rich and poor, tend to be liberal (especially on economic issues) and, for half a century, have voted Democratic. Historically, Latinos and Jews have also supported the Democratic party. Asian Americans were the only minority to vote Republican in the 1996 presidential election.

PARTY IDENTIFICATION

Because many people hold mixed political attitudes—with liberal views on some issues and conservative stands on others—party identification in the United States is weak. According to a recent national survey, about 47 percent of U.S. adults identified themselves, to some degree, as Democrats and about 34 percent as Republicans. Seventeen percent claimed to be independents, voicing no preference for either major party (NORC, 1999). Even though a large majority declare a party preference, their allegiance is weak. Republicans scored a landslide victory in the 1994 congressional elections, for example, while the Democrats held the White House in 1996 and gained ground in Congress in 1996, 1998, and 2000. National Map 12–2 on page 322 shows the results of the 2000 presidential election—the closest in more than a century—in which Republican George W. Bush finally claimed victory.

SPECIAL-INTEREST GROUPS

In the wake of recent shootings in public schools, public support for gun control has been rising. The National Rifle Association, representing several million people who are active hunters as well as millions more social conservatives, has steadily worked in opposition to this goal.

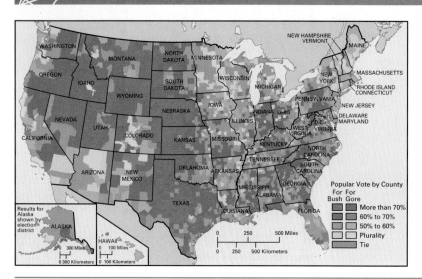

NATIONAL MAP 12–2
The Presidential Election, 2000:
Popular Vote by County

The 2000 presidential election was the closest in more than a century. The vast majority of the nation's counties went for President Bush, but densely populated areas—especially along both coasts—provided strong support for Al Gore. What social differences do you think distinguish the areas that voted Republican and Democratic? How important do you consider these differences to be?

Source: Copyright ©2000 The New York Times Co. Reprinted by permission.

The "gun lobby," which has been successful so far in fending off change, is an example of a *special-interest group*, people with an interest in some economic or social issue. Special-interest groups, which include associations of senior citizens, farmers, fireworks producers, and environmentalists, flourish in nations such as the United States, where loyalty to political parties tends to be low. Many special-interest groups employ *lobbyists* (Washington, D.C., is home to some 75,000 of them) to work on their behalf.

Political action committees (PACs) are formed by special-interest groups to raise and spend money in support of political aims. PACs channel most of their funds directly to candidates likely to support their interests. Since the 1970s, the number of PACs has grown rapidly to 4,400 (U.S. Federal Election Commission, 2000).

Because of the rising costs of campaigns, most candidates eagerly accept financial support from political action committees. In the 1998 congressional elections, 40 percent of all funding came from PACs and two-thirds of all senators seeking reelection received at least $1 million each in PAC contributions. Supporters maintain that PACs represent the interests of a vast array of businesses, unions, and church groups, thereby increasing political participation. Critics counter that organizations supplying cash to politicians expect to be treated favorably in return so that, in effect, PACs try to buy political influence (Allen & Broyles, 1991; Cook, 1993; Center for Responsive Politics, 1998).

The 2000 presidential campaign highlighted the importance of money in our political system. The rising costs of campaigns are a concern for all candidates, but incumbents have an edge because they have better access to PACs. For example, in the 1996 congressional elections, 66 percent of PAC funds went to those already in office, 94 percent of whom won reelection. No wonder members of Congress are reluctant to bring about campaign finance reform.

VOTER APATHY

It is a disturbing fact of U.S. political life that many people are indifferent about voting. In fact, U.S. citizens are less likely to vote today than they were a century ago. In the 2000 presidential election—an election that turned on a few hundred votes—only half the registered voters actually went to the polls, below the comparable share in almost all other industrialized nations.

Who is and is not likely to vote? Women and men are equally likely to cast a ballot. People over sixty-five are three times as likely to vote as college-age adults. White people are more likely to vote (64 percent voted in 1996) than African Americans (58 percent) and Hispanics (30 percent). Generally speaking, people with a bigger stake in society—homeowners, parents with children at home, people with good jobs and extensive schooling—are most likely to vote. Income matters, too: People with incomes in the top 20 percent (73 percent) are twice as likely as people with incomes in the bottom 20 percent (39 percent) to vote (Bennett, 1991; Hackey, 1992; Lewis, McCracken, & Hunt, 1994; DeLuca, 1998; Fetto, 1999).

Some nonvoting, of course, is to be expected. At any given time, millions of people are sick or disabled; millions more are away from home, having made no arrangement to submit an absentee ballot. Many more people forget to reregister after moving to a new neighborhood. Moreover, registering and voting depend on the ability to read and write, which discourages the tens of millions of U.S. adults who have limited literacy skills.

Conservatives suggest that apathy amounts to *indifference* to politics because most people are, by and large, content with their lives. Liberals, and especially political radicals, counter that apathy reflects *alienation* from politics: People are so deeply dissatisfied with society that they doubt elections will make any real difference. Income is strongly related to whether or not people vote: Most high-income people *do* and most low-income people *don't*. The fact that it is the disadvantaged and powerless people who are least likely to vote suggests that the liberal explanation for apathy is probably closer to the truth.

THEORETICAL ANALYSIS OF POLITICS

Sociologists have long debated the distribution of power in the United States. Power is one of the most difficult topics to study because decision making is complex and takes place behind closed doors. Moreover, theories about power are hard to separate from the theorists' political leanings. Nevertheless, three competing models of power have emerged.

THE PLURALIST MODEL: THE PEOPLE RULE

The **pluralist model,** closely allied with structural-functional theory, is *an analysis of politics that sees power as dispersed among many competing interest groups.* Pluralists claim, first, that politics is an arena of negotiation. With limited resources, no organization can expect to achieve all of its goals. Organizations, therefore, operate as *veto groups,* realizing some objectives but mostly keeping opponents from achieving all of their ends. The political process, then, relies heavily on forging alliances and compromises among numerous interest groups so that policies gain wide support. In short, pluralists see power as widely dispersed throughout society, with all people having at least some voice in the political system (Dahl, 1961, 1982; Rothman & Black, 1998).

THE POWER-ELITE MODEL: A FEW PEOPLE RULE

The **power-elite model,** based on social-conflict theory, is *an analysis of politics that sees power as concentrated among the rich.* The term *power elite* was coined by C. Wright Mills (1956), a social-conflict theorist who argued that the upper class holds most of society's wealth, prestige, and power.

Mills claimed that members of the power elite head up the three major sectors of U.S. society: the economy, government, and the military. Thus, the power elite is made up of the "super rich" (corporate executives and major stockholders), top officials in Washington, D.C., and state capitals around the country, and the highest-ranking officers in the U.S. military (senior Pentagon officials).

Further, Mills explained, these elites move from one sector to another, building power as they go. Alexander Haig, for example, served as a top corporate executive, as a member of Ronald Reagan's cabinet (and 1988 presidential candidate), and as a general of the army. Haig is far from the exception. A majority of national political leaders enter government from top corporate positions—when President Clinton took office, ten of the thirteen members of his cabinet were reputed to be millionaires—and most return to the corporate world later on.

Power-elite theorists challenge the claim that the United States is a democracy; they say the concentration of wealth and power is simply too great for the average person's voice to be heard. They reject the pluralist idea that various centers of power serve as checks and balances on one another; according to the power-elite model, those at the top encounter no real opposition.

THE MARXIST MODEL: BIAS IN THE SYSTEM ITSELF

A third approach to understanding U.S. politics is the **Marxist political-economy model,** *an analysis that explains politics in terms of the operation of a society's economic system.* Like the power-elite model, the Marxist approach is a social-conflict model that rejects the idea that the United States is a political democracy. But while the power-elite model focuses on the disproportionate wealth and power of certain individuals,

TABLE 12–1 Three Models of U.S. Politics: A Summary

	Pluralist Model	Power-Elite Model	Marxist Model
How is power distributed in U.S. society?	Highly dispersed	Concentrated	Concentrated
Is the United States basically democratic?	Yes, because voting offers everyone a voice, and no one group or organization dominates society	No, because a small share of the people dominates the economy, government, and military	No, because the bias of the capitalist system is to concentrate both wealth and power
How should we understand voter apathy?	Apathy is indifference; after all, even poor people can organize for a greater voice if they wish	Apathy is understandable, given how difficult it is for ordinary people to oppose the rich and powerful	Apathy is alienation generated by a system that will always leave most people powerless

the Marxist model looks to the bias rooted in this nation's institutions, especially its economy. Karl Marx believed that a society's economic system (capitalist or socialist) shapes its political system. Power elites, therefore, do not simply appear on the scene; they are creations of capitalism itself.

From this point of view, reforming the political system—say, by limiting the amount of money that rich people can contribute to political candidates—is unlikely to bring about true democracy. The problem does not lie in the *people* who exercise great power or the *people* who don't vote; the problem is the *system* itself—what Marxists term the "political economy of capitalism." In other words, as long as the United States has a predominantly capitalist economy, just as the majority of people are exploited in the workplace, they will also be shut out of politics.

Critical evaluation. Which of the three different models of the U.S. political system is correct? Over the years, research has provided support for each, suggesting a case can be made for all three. In the end, of course, how one thinks our political system ought to work is as much a matter of political values as scientific fact.

Research by Nelson Polsby (1959) supports the pluralist model. Polsby studied the politics of New Haven, Connecticut, where he found that key decisions involving urban renewal, selecting political candidates, and running the city's schools were made by different groups. Polsby concluded that no one group—not even the New Haven upper class—rules all the others.

Supporting the power-elite position, Robert and Helen Lynd (1937) studied Muncie, Indiana (which they called "Middletown," to suggest it was a typical city), and documented the fortune amassed by a single family—the Balls—from their business producing glass canning jars. The Lynds showed how the Ball family dominated many dimensions of the city's life. If anyone doubted the Balls' prominence, one only had to note that the local bank, a university, a hospital, and a department store all had the family's name. In Muncie, according to the Lynds, the power elite more or less boiled down to a single family.

From the Marxist perspective, the point is not *which* individuals make decisions. Rather, as Alexander Liazos (1982:13) explains, "The basic tenets of capitalist society shape everyone's life: the inequalities of social classes and the importance of profits over people." As long as the basic institutions of society are organized to meet the needs of the few rather than the many, Liazos concludes, a truly democratic society is impossible.

Table 12–1 summarizes the three political models. Clearly, the U.S. political system gives almost everyone the right to participate in politics through elections. But, as the power-elite and Marxist models point out, at the very least the U.S. political system is far less democratic than most people think. Most citizens may have the right to vote, but the major political parties and their candidates typically support only those positions acceptable to the most powerful segments of society and consistent with the operation of our capitalist economy (Bachrach & Baratz, 1970).

Whatever the reasons, many people in the United States are losing confidence in their leaders. More than 80 percent of U.S. adults report having, at best, only "some confidence" that members of Congress and other government officials will do what is best for the country (NORC, 1999:778, 903).

POWER BEYOND THE RULES

Politics is always a matter of disagreement over a society's goals and the means to achieve them. A political system tries to resolve controversy within a system of

The first modern political revolution began in 1789 in France. This engraving, titled To Versailles, To Versailles, *depicts the march of women to the king's palace in Versailles, on the outskirts of Paris, on October 5th, 1789, where they demanded more bread. The day after, the people forcibly led the royal family to Paris. Eventually, in October, 1793, the royal family was executed by guillotine in a crowded public square.*

A Versailles, A Versailles (March of the Women on Versailles), Paris, October 5, 1789, engraving by French School (eighteenth century). Musée Carnavalet, Paris, France. Bulloz/The Bridgeman Art Library.

rules. But political activity sometimes breaks the rules, or tries to do away with the entire system.

REVOLUTION

Political revolution is *the overthrow of one political system in order to establish another.* Reform involves change *within* a system, modifying the law or, as an extreme case, a *coup d'état* (in French, literally "stroke of the state"), by which one leader topples another. Revolution, however, involves not just change at the top but a change *of the system itself.*

No type of political system is immune to revolution; nor does revolution produce any one kind of government. Our country's Revolutionary War changed colonial rule by the British monarchy into a democratic government. French revolutionaries in 1789 also overthrew a monarch, only to set the stage for the return of a monarchy in the person of Napoleon. In 1917, the Russian Revolution replaced a monarchy with a socialist government built on the ideas of Karl Marx. In 1992, the Soviet Union was reborn as the Russian Federation, moving toward a market system and a greater political voice for its people.

Despite their striking variety, revolutions share a number of traits (Tocqueville, 1955, orig. 1856; Davies, 1962; Brinton, 1965; Skocpol, 1979; Lewis, 1984; Tilly, 1986):

1. **Rising expectations.** Common sense would suggest that revolution is more likely when people are grossly deprived, but history shows that most revolutions occur when people's lives are improving. Rising expectations, rather than bitter resignation, fuel revolutionary fervor.

2. **Unresponsive government.** Revolution becomes likely to the extent that a government is unable or unwilling to reform, especially when demands for change are made by powerful segments of society.

3. **Radical leadership by intellectuals.** The English philosopher Thomas Hobbes (1588–1679) claimed intellectuals provide the justification for revolution, and universities frequently are at the center of political change. Students played a key role in China's pro-democracy movement and in the uprisings in Eastern Europe.

4. **Establishing a new legitimacy.** Overthrowing a political system is not easy, but more difficult still is ensuring a revolution's long-term success. Some revolutionary movements are unified merely by hatred of the past regime and fall apart once new leaders are installed. Revolutionaries must also guard against counter-revolutionary drives led by deposed leaders. This explains the speed and ruthlessness with which victorious revolutionaries typically dispose of former leaders.

Scientific research cannot declare that a revolution is good or bad. That judgment depends on one's values and, in any case, becomes evident only after

Not all terrorism is the work of individuals or groups. Since 1950, China has sought to maintain control of Tibet by force. This Tibetan refugee displays instruments of torture used against him by officials of the Chinese government.

many years. Ten years after its revolution, the future of the former Soviet Union remains unsettled.

TERRORISM

Terrorism refers to *acts of violence or the threat of such violence used by an individual or a group as a political strategy.* Like revolution, terrorism falls outside the rules of established political systems. Paul Johnson (1981) offers four insights into terrorism.

First, terrorists consider violence a legitimate political tactic, despite the fact that such acts are condemned by virtually every nation. Terrorists also bypass (or are excluded from) established channels of political negotiation. Terrorism is, therefore, a weak organization's strategy to harm a stronger foe. Attacks against the U.S. embassies in Tanzania and Kenya in 1998 and the U.S.S. *Cole* in 2000 may have been morally wrong for harming innocent people, but they did raise the profile of organizations with grievances against the United States.

Second, terrorism is employed not just by groups but also by governments against their own people.

State terrorism is the use of violence, usually beyond the rule of law, by government officials. State terrorism is common in some authoritarian and totalitarian states, which survive by inciting fear and intimidation. Saddam Hussein, for example, shores up his power in Iraq through state terrorism.

Third, democratic societies are especially vulnerable to terrorism because they afford extensive civil liberties to their people and have limited police networks. In contrast, while totalitarian regimes make widespread use of state terrorism, their extensive police power minimizes opportunities for individual terrorist acts.

Taking hostages and killing innocent people provoke widespread anger, but responding to terrorism is difficult. The immediate concern is identifying those responsible. Because terrorist groups are often shadowy organizations with no formal connection to any established state, targeting a reprisal may be all but impossible. Then, too, a forcible military reaction may broaden the scope of violence, increasing the risk of confrontation with other governments.

Fourth and finally, terrorism is always a matter of definitions. Governments claim the right to maintain order, even by force, and may brand opponents who use violence as "terrorists." Political differences help explain why one person's "terrorist" is another's "freedom fighter."

WAR AND PEACE

Perhaps the most critical political issue is **war,** *organized, armed conflict among the people of various societies, directed by their governments.* War is as old as humanity, of course, but understanding it is now an urgent matter since we possess the technological means to destroy ourselves.

For almost all of the twentieth century, nations somewhere were in violent conflict. In the short history of the United States, this country has participated in ten major wars that killed more than 1.3 million U.S. men and women, as shown in Figure 12–6, and injured many times that number. Thousands more died in "undeclared wars" and limited military actions in the Dominican Republic, Lebanon, Grenada, Panama, and elsewhere.

THE CAUSES OF WAR

Wars occur so often that we might think that there is something "natural" about armed conflict. But while many animals are naturally aggressive (Lorenz, 1966), research provides no evidence that human beings inevitably wage war under any particular circumstances. As Ashley Montagu (1976) observes, governments around the world usually have to force their people to mobilize for war.

Like other forms of social behavior, warfare is a product of *society* that varies in purpose and intensity from place to place. The Semai of Malaysia, among the most peace-loving of the world's peoples, rarely resort to violence. In contrast, the Yąnomamö, described in Chapter 2 ("Culture"), are quick to wage war.

If society holds the key to war or peace, under what circumstances *do* humans engage in warfare? Quincy Wright (1987) cites five factors that promote war:

1. **Perceived threats.** Societies mobilize in response to a perceived threat to their people, territory, or culture. The likelihood of armed conflict between the United States and the former Soviet Union, for example, has decreased as the two nations have become less fearful of each other.

2. **Social problems.** When internal problems cause widespread frustration at home, a nation's leaders may divert attention by attacking an external enemy as a form of scapegoating. Some analysts think the lack of economic development in the People's Republic of China, for example, led to hostility toward Vietnam, Tibet, and the former Soviet Union.

3. **Political objectives.** Poor nations, such as Vietnam, have used wars to end foreign domination. On the other hand, powerful countries such as the United States use a periodic "show of force" (such as the recent deployment of troops in Somalia, Haiti, and Bosnia) to enhance their global stature.

4. **Moral objectives.** Nations rarely claim to fight just to gain wealth and power. Instead, they infuse military campaigns with moral urgency, rallying their people around visions of "freedom" or "the fatherland." Although few doubt that the 1991 Persian Gulf War was largely about oil, U.S. leaders portrayed the mission as a drive to halt a Hitler-like Saddam Hussein.

5. **The absence of alternatives.** A fifth factor promoting war is the lack of alternatives. Although it is the United Nations' job to maintain international peace, the UN has had limited success in resolving tensions among nations.

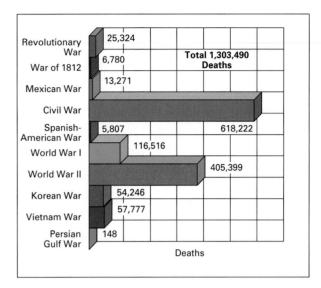

FIGURE 12–6 Deaths of Americans in Ten U.S. Wars

Sources: Compiled from various sources by Maris A. Vinovskis (1989) and the author.

THE COSTS AND CAUSES OF MILITARISM

The costs of war extend far beyond battlefield casualties. Together, the world's nations spend $1 trillion annually (about $160 for every person on the planet) for military purposes. Such expenditures, of course, divert resources from the desperate struggle for survival by millions of poor people.

For years, defense has been the U.S. government's single biggest expenditure, accounting for 16 percent of all federal spending, or $291 billion in 2000. Some of this huge sum is the result of the *arms race*, a military spending spree carried on for decades by the United States and the former Soviet Union.

Yet, even after the collapse of the Soviet Union, military spending remains high. Thus, some analysts (allied with power-elite theory) claim that the United States is dominated by a **military-industrial complex,** *the close association of the federal government, the military, and defense industries.* The roots of militarism, then, lie not just in external threats to our security but also in the institutional structures of U.S. society (Marullo, 1987).

Another reason for continuing militarism is regional conflict. During the 1990s, localized wars broke out in Bosnia, Chechnya, and Zambia, and tensions run high in a host of other countries, including

CRITICAL THINKING

Information Warfare:
Let Your Fingers Do the Fighting

For decades, scientists and military officials have studied how to use computers to defend against attacks by missiles and planes. Recently, however, the military has recognized that new information technology can fundamentally change the way war is waged. In place of rumbling tanks and screaming aircraft, electronic "smart bombs" can silently penetrate an enemy country's computer system and render it unable to transmit information.

In such "virtual wars," soldiers seated at workstation terminals would dispatch computer viruses to shut down the enemy's communication links, causing telephones to fall silent and air traffic control and railroad switching systems to fail. Computer systems would feed phony orders to field officers and televisions would broadcast "morphed" news bulletins urging people to turn against their leaders.

Like the venom of a poisonous snake, the weapons of "information warfare" could paralyze an enemy prior to a conventional military attack. Another, more hopeful possibility is that new information technology might not just set the stage for conventional fighting but might prevent it entirely. If the "victims" of computer warfare could be limited to a nation's communications links—rather than its cities and people—wouldn't we all be more secure?

Yet so-called "info-war" also poses new dangers, since, presumably, a few highly skilled operators with sophisticated electronic equipment could also wreak communications havoc on the United States. This country may be militarily without equal in the world, but, given our increasing reliance on high technology, we are also more vulnerable to cyber-attack than any nation on earth. As a result, in 1996, the Central

Intelligence Agency (CIA) began work on a defensive "cyber-war center" to prevent what one official termed an "electronic Pearl Harbor."

What do you think?

1. *Do you think it is realistic to imagine that virtual warfare might replace conventional battlefield fighting? Why or why not?*

2. *Can you see ways in which new information technology might increase the chances to resolve disputes peacefully?*

3. *What about ways in which computer technology might increase the dangers of war?*

Sources: Waller (1995) and Weiner (1996).

Ireland, Iraq, and a divided Korea. Even limited wars have the potential to escalate and involve other countries, including the United States. In 1998, for example, India and Pakistan exploded nuclear bombs, raising fears of atomic war in that region. As more nations acquire nuclear weapons, the risk that regional conflict will erupt into deadly wars goes up.

NUCLEAR WEAPONS

Despite the easing of superpower tensions, the world still contains almost 25,000 nuclear warheads, representing a destructive power equivalent to five tons of TNT for every person on the planet. Should even a small fraction of this arsenal be used in war, life as we know it would cease on much of the earth. Albert Einstein, whose genius contributed to the development of nuclear weapons, reflected: "The unleashed power

of the atom has changed everything *save our modes of thinking*, and we thus drift toward unparalleled catastrophe." In short, nuclear weapons make full-scale war unthinkable in a world not yet capable of peace.

Great Britain, France, the People's Republic of China, Israel, India, and Pakistan are current members of the "nuclear club," but the vast majority of nuclear weapons are held by the United States and the Russian Federation. These two nations have agreed to reduce their stockpiles of nuclear weapons by 75 percent by 2003. But even so, the danger of catastrophic war increases with *nuclear proliferation*, the acquisition of nuclear weapons by additional nations. Experts say Libya, Iran, Iraq, and North Korea have programs to develop nuclear weapons. While some nations have stopped the development of nuclear weapons—Argentina and Brazil halted work in 1990, and South Africa dismantled its arsenal in 1991—by

2010, as many as fifty countries could have the ability to fight a nuclear war. Such a trend makes any regional conflict far more dangerous (Thomas, Barry, & Liu, 1998).

PURSUING PEACE

How can the world reduce the dangers of war? Here are the most recent approaches to peace:

1. **Deterrence.** The logic of the arms race holds that security derives from a balance of terror between the superpowers. Thus, the principle of *mutually assured destruction (MAD)* demands that either side launching a first strike against the other sustain massive retaliation. This deterrence policy kept the peace for almost fifty years during the cold war. Yet, it encouraged a massive arms race, and it cannot control nuclear proliferation, which poses a growing threat to peace.

2. **High-technology defense.** If technology created the weapons, perhaps it can also protect us from them—such is the claim of the *strategic defense initiative (SDI)*. Under SDI, satellites and ground installations would destroy enemy missiles soon after they were launched. However, many analysts claim that "star wars" would be, at best, a leaky umbrella; others question the need for such an expensive scheme in light of the collapse of the Soviet Union.

   Worth noting, too, is that sophisticated technology raises not only new possibilities for defense but also new strategies for waging war. The box takes a closer look at the possibilities for "information warfare."

3. **Diplomacy and disarmament.** Some analysts believe that the best road to peace is diplomacy rather than technology (Dedrick & Yinger, 1990). Diplomacy can enhance security by reducing, rather than building, weapons stockpiles.

   But disarmament, too, has limitations. No nation wishes to become vulnerable by eliminating its defenses. Successful diplomacy, then, depends on everyone involved sharing responsibility for a common problem (Fisher & Ury, 1988). Furthermore, while the United States and the former Soviet Union have succeeded in negotiating arms reduction agreements, the threat from other nations like Libya, North Korea, and Iraq—all of which desire to build nuclear arsenals—remains large.

4. **Resolving underlying conflict.** In the end, reducing the dangers of war may depend on resolving the issues that have fueled the arms race. Even in the post–cold war era, regional conflicts remain in Latin America, Africa, Asia, and the Middle East. Is it sensible, some ask, for the world to spend thousands of times more money on militarism than on peacekeeping? (Sivard, 1988)

LOOKING AHEAD: POLITICS IN THE TWENTY-FIRST CENTURY

Just as economies are changing, so are political systems. As we enter the twenty-first century, several dilemmas and trends will likely command widespread attention.

One vexing problem in the United States is an inconsistency between our democratic ideals and our low turnout at the polls. Perhaps, as the pluralists contend, many people do not bother to vote because they are basically content with their lives. But perhaps the power-elite theorists are right in saying that people withdraw from a system that concentrates wealth and power in the hands of so few people. Or, as Marxist critics contend, perhaps people find that our political system offers little real choice, tied as it is to our capitalist economic system. (The final box, on pages 330–31, takes a look at one way money and power come together—the controversial practice of "corporate welfare.") In any case, it seems certain that we cannot endure a rising tide of apathy and falling confidence in government without moving toward real reform.

A second major trend is the global rethinking of political models. The cold war cast political debate in the form of two models, one based on capitalism, the other on socialism. But now analysts see a broader range of political systems, linking government to the economy in a variety of ways. "Welfare capitalism," as found in Sweden, or "state capitalism," as found in South Korea and Japan, are just two possibilities.

Third, we still face the danger of war in many parts of the world. Even as the United States and Russia dismantle some warheads, vast stockpiles of nuclear weapons remain, and nuclear technology continues to spread around the world. Moreover, new superpowers are likely to arise in the twenty-first century (the People's Republic of China and India are likely candidates), just as regional conflicts will surely continue to fester. One can only hope that our leaders will find nonviolent solutions to the age-old problems that provoke war.

CONTROVERSY & DEBATE

Them That's Got, Gets:
The Case of Corporate Welfare

What would you say if the government offered to slash your income taxes and abolish sales tax on your purchases? What if it offered you the chance to buy a new house at a below-market interest rate? Would you like the government to hook up all your utilities for free and pay your water and electric bills?

For an ordinary individual, such deals sound too good to be true. But our tax money is doing exactly this—not for individuals, but for big corporations. All a large company has to do is declare a willingness to relocate and then wait while the offers from state and local governments come pouring in.

Supporters call government aid to corporations "public-private partnerships." They point to the jobs companies create, sometimes in areas hard hit by earlier business closings. For a city or county with a high unemployment rate, the promise of a major corporation opening a new factory is simply too good to pass up. If some "incentives" in the form of tax relief or free utilities lure the company away from another possible site, it is considered money well spent.

Critics, however, call these arrangements "corporate welfare." They concede that companies do create some new jobs, but they also point out that the corporations get much more than they

give. In 1991, for example, the state of Indiana used $451 million in incentives to lure United Airlines to build an aircraft maintenance facility there. United Airlines built the facility and hired 6,300 people. But some simple math shows that the cost to Indiana came out to be a whopping $72,000 *per job*. Much the same happened in 1993, when Alabama offered $253 million in incentives to Mercedes-Benz to build an automobile assembly plant in Tuscaloosa. The plant opened and 1,500 people were hired, but at an average cost of $169,000 for each worker. In 1997, Pennsylvania gave $307 million in incentives to a Norwegian company to reopen part of

SUMMARY

ECONOMICS

1. The economy is the major social institution by which a society produces, distributes, and consumes goods and services.

2. The primary sector of the economy generates raw materials and is largest in low-income, preindustrial nations. The secondary, manufacturing sector is substantial in nations throughout the world. The tertiary, service sector dominates in postindustrial countries.

3. Capitalism is based on private ownership of productive property and the pursuit of profit in a competitive marketplace. Socialism is grounded in collective ownership of productive property through government control of the economy.

4. Capitalism's high productivity provides a high overall standard of living but with marked income inequality; socialism is less productive, generating lower living standards but with less economic inequality.

5. The emerging global economy links many nations, with little regard for national boundaries.

6. The United States is a postindustrial society where only a small percentage of workers hold agricultural jobs; just one-fourth have blue-collar, industrial jobs; 72 percent have white-collar, service jobs.

7. A profession is a special category of white-collar work based on theoretical knowledge, occupational autonomy, authority over clients, and emphasis on serving the community.

8. In 2000, 4.0 percent of U.S. workers were unemployed, with young people and minorities most likely to be jobless.

9. Women and other minorities represent an increasing share of the work force in the United States.

10. Corporations are the core of the U.S. economy. Most large conglomerates now operate in many countries.

Philadelphia's naval shipyard. Once the deal was signed, 950 people were hired, at a cost of $323,000 per job. Across the country, the pattern is much the same. Throughout the 1990s, in fact, government support to corporations exceeded $15 billion annually—far more than the "welfare" given to poor people.

In an uncertain economic climate, corporations willing to relocate their facilities can attract very generous offers from politicians eager to "create jobs." But, nationwide, while some jobs are created, more are simply moved elsewhere. Nor do many of the jobs pay well. And there is no guarantee that, once settled, a corporation will stay, since businesses are free to try to make a better deal to move elsewhere. In 1993, state and local governments in Kentucky granted General Electric $19 million in tax breaks so it would build a washing machine factory near Louisville. In 1999, GE announced that most of the 1,500 jobs in this plant would be lost because it was moving production to new factories in Georgia and Mexico, where wages are far lower.

Continue the debate . . .

1. *How do you think most people in towns that gain jobs feel about tax breaks for corporations that relocate?*

2. *On balance, do you think that so-called "corporate welfare" is a good or bad idea? Why?*

3. *Do you think corporations exert too much influence on the U.S. political system? Why or why not?*

Source: Adapted from Bartlett & Steele (1998).

POLITICS

1. Politics is the major social institution by which a society distributes power and organizes decision making. Max Weber claimed that power is legitimized by tradition, rationally enacted rules and regulations, or the personal charisma of a leader.

2. Monarchy is common to preindustrial societies; industrialization favors the development of democracy.

3. Authoritarian political systems deny popular participation in government. Totalitarian political systems go even further, controlling people's everyday lives.

4. The political spectrum—from the liberal left to the conservative right—involves attitudes on economic issues (such as the degree of government regulation of the economy) and social issues (including the rights and opportunities of various segments of the population).

5. Special-interest groups are typically strong in countries, such as the United States, that have relatively weak political parties. Only half of eligible U.S. voters cast ballots in national presidential elections.

6. The pluralist model of U.S. politics views power as widely dispersed; the power-elite model believes power is concentrated in a small, wealthy segment of our society; the Marxist political-economy model says the capitalist economy makes true democracy impossible.

7. Revolution radically transforms a political system. Terrorism employs violence in pursuit of a political goal.

8. War is armed conflict between governments. The development of nuclear weapons, and their proliferation, increase the threat of global catastrophe. World peace ultimately depends on resolving the tensions that underlie militarism.

9. New information technology is greatly expanding the flow of information across national boundaries as well as altering the nature of warfare.

KEY CONCEPTS

ECONOMICS

social institution (p. 302) an organized sphere of social life, or societal subsystem—such as the economy—designed to meet human needs

economy (p. 302) the social institution that organizes a society's production, distribution, and consumption of goods and services

postindustrial economy (p. 303) a productive system based on service work and high technology

primary sector (p. 303) the part of the economy that draws raw materials from the natural environment

secondary sector (p. 303) the part of the economy that transforms raw materials into manufactured goods

tertiary sector (p. 303) the part of the economy that involves services rather than goods

global economy (p. 303) expanding economic activity with little regard for national borders

capitalism (p. 305) an economic system in which natural resources and the means of producing goods and services are privately owned

socialism (p. 306) an economic system in which natural resources and the means of producing goods and services are collectively owned

welfare capitalism (p. 307) an economic and political system that combines a mostly market-based economy with extensive social welfare programs

state capitalism (p. 307) an economic and political system in which companies are privately owned but cooperate closely with the government

profession (p. 310) a prestigious, white-collar occupation that requires extensive formal education

corporation (p. 313) an organization with a legal existence, including rights and liabilities, apart from those of its members

monopoly (p. 314) domination of a market by a single producer

oligopoly (p. 314) domination of a market by a few producers

POLITICS

politics (p. 315) the social institution that distributes power, sets a society's agenda, and makes decisions

power (p. 315) the ability to achieve desired ends despite resistance from others

authority (p. 316) power that people perceive as legitimate rather than coercive

routinization of charisma (p. 316) the transformation of charismatic authority into some combination of traditional and bureaucratic authority

monarchy (p. 316) a type of political system in which a single family rules from generation to generation

democracy (p. 316) a type of political system which gives power to the people as a whole

authoritarianism (p. 317) a political system that denies popular participation in government

totalitarianism (p. 317) a highly centralized political system that extensively regulates people's lives

welfare state (p. 320) a range of government agencies and programs that provides benefits to the population

pluralist model (p. 323) an analysis of politics that sees power as dispersed among many competing interest groups

power-elite model (p. 323) an analysis of politics that sees power as concentrated among the rich

Marxist political-economy model (p. 323) an analysis that explains politics in terms of the operation of a society's economic system

political revolution (p. 325) the overthrow of one political system in order to establish another

terrorism (p. 326) acts of violence or the threat of such violence used by an individual or a group as a political strategy

war (p. 326) organized, armed conflict among the people of various societies, directed by their governments

military-industrial complex (p. 327) the close association of the federal government, the military, and defense industries

CRITICAL-THINKING QUESTIONS

1. As important social institutions, what are the economic and political systems supposed to do? How well, in your opinion, does each social institution do its job?

2. How did the Industrial Revolution alter the economy of the United States? How is today's Information Revolution changing the economy once again?

3. Identify different positions on the political spectrum. How do economic issues differ from social issues? How is class position linked to people's political opinions on each kind of issue?

4. How are both the economy and politics becoming global in scope? Imagine changes in both that may occur by the end of the twenty-first century.

APPLICATIONS AND EXERCISES

1. General data on the U.S. economy—72 percent of output in the service sector, 26 in the industrial sector, and 2 percent in the primary sector—obscures great variety within this country. Visit the library and locate data that profile your own city, county, or state.

2. Visit a discount store such as Wal-Mart or K-Mart and select an area of the store of interest to you. Do a little "fieldwork," inspecting products to see where they are made. Does your research support the existence of a global economy?

3. Do some research to trace the growth in the size of the federal government over the last fifty years. Then try to discover how organizations at different points along the political spectrum (from socialist organizations on the left through the Democratic and Republican parties to right-wing militia groups) assess the size of the current welfare state.

4. Freedom House, the organization that studies civil rights and political liberty around the world, publishes an annual report, *Freedom in the World.* Find a copy in the library (or write to the organization at 1319 Eighteenth Street, Washington, DC 20036), and examine the trends or political profiles of countries of interest to you.

5. Install the CD-ROM packaged in the back of this new textbook to access a variety of study, review, and applications exercises designed to help you better understand the material covered in this chapter. The CD includes an author's tip video, as well as interactive maps, video application exercises, Web links, and study questions.

 SITES TO SEE

http://www.prenhall.com/macionis
Visit the interactive Web site that accompanies this text. Begin by clicking on the cover of your book. You will find a chapter-by-chapter study guide, practice tests, chat room, and many suggested Web links.

http://stats.bls.gov/blshome.html
Visit the Web site operated by the Bureau of Labor Statistics, where you will find a wide range of interesting data and reports.

http://www.fao.org
The Food and Agriculture Organization is a part of the United Nations concerned with how well the global economy meets the needs of the world's people. From its home page, look for the FAO's annual report, titled *State of Food Insecurity in the World.*

http://www.nber.org
Another worthwhile site is run by the National Bureau of Economic Research, which explains the operation of the economy.

http://www.kenyon.edu/projects/famfarm/welcome/welcome.htm
Several years ago, students at Kenyon College in rural Ohio prepared this Web site to study family farms in the local, rural county.

http://www.amnesty.org
Amnesty International operates an informative Web site that offers information about the state of human rights around the world.

http://www.usis.usemb.se/terror/index.html
This Web site provides information on global terrorism.

http://www.coara.or.jp/~ryoji/abomb/e-index.html
Few of us have firsthand experience of the horrors of war. This Web site provides a survivor's personal account of the U.S. bombing of the Japanese city of Hiroshima, the first time the atomic bomb was used in warfare.

CHAPTER 13

FAMILY AND RELIGION

CHAPTER OUTLINE

A few minutes before midnight on June 30, 2000, Kathleen Peterson and Carolyn Conrad walked into Town Hall in Brattleboro, Vermont. The town clerk, Annette Cappy, had kept the office open late because she knew that, at midnight, a new Vermont law was to go into effect allowing gay and lesbian couples to form civil unions. She smiled as the two women approached and asked for the civil union form. Minutes later, the paperwork completed, the couple held hands as Cappy issued them the state's first civil union license. Vermont's civil union law legally recognizes same-sex couples and provides them with most of the same rights and benefits enjoyed by married partners (Trischitta, 2000).

Even so, civil unions are a step short of legal marriage. Indeed, same-sex marriages are not legal in any state, including Vermont. Moreover, a majority of states have either passed, or are considering, "man-woman" marriage laws that would explicitly bar gay men and lesbians from legal marriage. In 1996, the U.S. Congress also weighed in, passing the Defense of Marriage Act, which forbids gay couples from marrying. But same-sex marriage is now being discussed coast to coast. In fact, hundreds of cities and towns, as well as thousands of businesses (including many colleges and universities), have extended marital benefits (including family health insurance) to same-sex couples (Dunlap, 1996).

In high-income societies, members of extended families usually pursue their careers independently and live apart from one another. Periodically, however, they may gather for rituals such as weddings, funerals, and family reunions.

Should the law permit gay couples to marry? What exactly is a "family"? Are families disappearing? Such questions touch on many people's deeply held beliefs and are part of the current "family values" debate. To hear some tell it, the family is fast becoming an endangered species. Consider these statistics: The U.S. divorce rate has doubled over the past forty years, so that, if the trend holds, almost half of today's marriages will end in divorce. Marital breakdown, coupled with the fact that about one in three children is born to an unmarried woman, means that half of the U.S. children born today will live with a single parent at some time before reaching age eighteen. This trend is one reason that the share of U.S. children living in poverty has been rising steadily.

Together, these facts point to a basic truth: Families in the United States and in other industrial societies are changing, probably faster than any other social institution (Bianchi & Spain, 1996). Not long ago, the cultural ideal of the family consisted of a working husband, a homemaker wife, and their young children. Today, fewer people have such a singular vision of the family, and, at any given time, only about one in four U.S. households fits that description.

This chapter examines the family and religion, closely linked as society's prominent *symbolic institutions.* Both help establish morality, maintain traditions, and join people together. Moreover, along with change in families, we have seen change in religion, too, as membership in long-established churches is declining just as new sects are flourishing.

With an eye on the United States and making comparisons with other countries, we will examine why many people consider the family and religion bedrock foundations of social life, while others predict—and even encourage—the decline of both institutions.

THE FAMILY: BASIC CONCEPTS

The **family** is *a social institution found in all societies that unites people in cooperative groups to oversee the bearing and raising of children.* Family ties are also called **kinship,** *a social bond based on blood, marriage, or adoption.* All societies have families, but exactly who people call their kin has varied through history, and varies today from one culture to another. In the United States, most people regard a **family unit** as *a social group of two or more people, related by blood, marriage, or adoption, who usually live together.* Here, as elsewhere, families form around **marriage,** *a legally sanctioned relationship, usually involving economic cooperation as well as sexual activity and childbearing, that people expect to be enduring.*

Today, some people object to defining only married couples and children as "families" because doing so implies a single standard of moral conduct. Also, because some business and government programs still use this conventional definition, unmarried but committed partners—whether heterosexual or homosexual—are excluded from health care and other benefits. More and more, however, organizations are coming to recognize *families of affinity*—that is, people with or without legal or blood ties who feel they belong together and want to define themselves as a family.

The Census Bureau, too, uses the conventional definition of family. Thus, sociologists who use Census Bureau data describing "families" must accept this definition.[1] But the national trend is toward a more inclusive definition of family.

THE FAMILY: GLOBAL VARIATIONS

In preindustrial societies, people take a broad view of family ties, recognizing the **extended family,** *a family unit that includes parents and children, as well as other kin.* This group is also called the *consanguine family,* because it includes everyone with "shared blood." With industrialization, however, increasing social mobility and geographical migration give rise to the **nuclear family,** *a family unit composed of one or two parents and their children.* The nuclear family is also called the *conjugal family,* meaning "based on marriage." Although many members of our society live in extended families, the nuclear family is most common in the United States.

MARRIAGE PATTERNS

Cultural norms, and often laws, identify people as suitable or unsuitable marriage partners. Some norms promote **endogamy,** *marriage between people of the same social category.* Endogamy limits marriage prospects to others of the same age, village, race, religion, or social class. By contrast, **exogamy** refers to *marriage between people of different social categories.* In rural India, for example, a person is expected to marry someone from the same caste (endogamy) but from a different village (exogamy). The logic of endogamy is that people of similar position pass along their standing to their children, thereby maintaining the traditional social hierarchy. Exogamy, on the other hand, builds alliances and encourages cultural diffusion.

In higher-income nations, laws prescribe **monogamy** (from the Greek, meaning "one union"), *marriage uniting two partners.* Global Map 13–1 on page 338 shows that while monogamy is the rule throughout the Americas and Europe, many

lower-income countries—especially in Africa and southern Asia—permit **polygamy** (from the Greek, meaning "many unions"), *marriage that unites three or more people.* Polygamy has two forms. By far the more common is *polygyny* (from the Greek, meaning "many women"), a form of marriage that unites one male and two or more females. Islamic nations in the Middle East and Africa, for example, permit men up to four wives. Even so, most Islamic families are monogamous because few men can afford to support several wives and even more children. *Polyandry* (from the Greek, meaning "many men") unites one female and two or more males. One case of this rare pattern is in Tibet, a mountainous land where agriculture is difficult. There, polyandry discourages the division of land and allows several men to share the work.

Most of the world's societies have, at some time, permitted more than one marital pattern. Even so, as noted already, most marriages have been monogamous (Murdock, 1965). The historical preference for monogamy reflects two facts of life: Supporting several spouses is a heavy financial burden, and the number of men and women in most societies is roughly equal.

RESIDENTIAL PATTERNS

Just as societies regulate mate selection, so they designate where a couple lives. In lower-income nations, most newlyweds live with one set of parents who offer them protection, support, and assistance. Most often, married couples live with or near the husband's family, termed *patrilocality* (Greek for "place of the father"). But in some societies (such as the North American Iroquois) couples live with or near the wife's family, called *matrilocality* (meaning "place of the mother"). Societies that engage in frequent local warfare tend toward patrilocality, so sons are close to home to offer protection. Societies that engage in distant warfare may be patrilocal or matrilocal, depending on whether sons or daughters have greater economic value (Ember & Ember, 1971, 1991).

Higher-income countries show yet another pattern. Finances permitting, they favor *neolocality* (Greek, meaning "new place"), by which a married couple lives apart from both sets of parents.

PATTERNS OF DESCENT

Descent refers to *the system by which members of a society trace kinship over generations.* Most lower-income countries trace kinship through just the father's or the

---

[1]According to the Census Bureau, there were 103.9 million U.S. households in 1999, of which 71.5 million (69 percent) were family households. The remaining households contained single people or unrelated people living together. In 1960, 85 percent of all households were families.

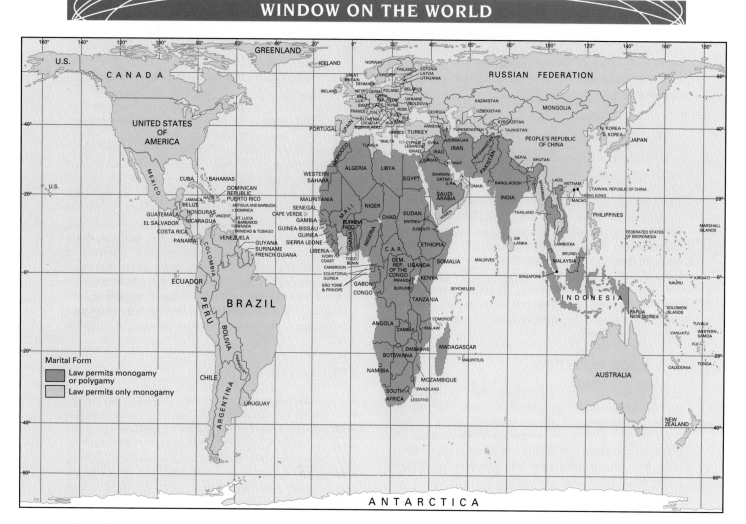

GLOBAL MAP 13–1 Marital Form in Global Perspective

Monogamy is the legally prescribed form of marriage throughout the Western Hemisphere and in much of the rest of the world. In most African nations and in southern Asia, however, polygamy is permitted by law. In many cases, this practice reflects the historic influence of Islam, a religion that allows a man to have up to four wives. Even so, most marriages in these traditional societies are monogamous, primarily for financial reasons.

Source: *Peters Atlas of the World* (1990).

mother's side of the family. *Patrilineal descent*, the more common, traces kinship through males, so that property flows from fathers to sons. Patrilineal descent characterizes most pastoral and agrarian societies, where men produce the most valued resources. *Matrilineal descent*, by which people define only the mother's side as kin, and property passes from mothers to

daughters, is found in horticultural societies where women are the primary food producers.

Higher-income nations, with their greater gender equality, recognize *bilateral descent* ("two-sided descent"). That is, children include as relatives people on both the father's side and the mother's side of the family.

PATTERNS OF AUTHORITY

The predominance of polygyny, patrilocality, and patrilineal descent reflects the global pattern of patriarchy. Indeed, as Chapter 10 ("Gender Stratification") explains, no truly matriarchal society has ever existed.

In industrial societies like the United States, more egalitarian families are evolving as the share of women in the labor force goes up. However, even here, men are typically heads of households, and most parents give children their father's last name.

THEORETICAL ANALYSIS OF THE FAMILY

As in earlier chapters, several theoretical approaches offer a range of insights about the family.

FUNCTIONS OF THE FAMILY: STRUCTURAL-FUNCTIONAL ANALYSIS

According to the structural-functional paradigm, the family performs many vital tasks. In fact, the family is "the backbone of society."

1. **Socialization.** As noted in Chapter 3 ("Socialization: From Infancy to Old Age"), the family is the first and most important setting for child rearing. Ideally, parents help children become well-integrated and contributing members of society (Parsons & Bales, 1955). Of course, family socialization continues throughout the life cycle. Adults change within marriage and, as any parent knows, mothers and fathers learn as much from their children as the children learn from them.

2. **Regulation of sexual activity.** Every culture regulates sexual activity in the interest of maintaining kinship organization and property rights. The incest taboo, discussed in Chapter 7 ("Sexuality"), is a norm forbidding sexual relations or marriage between close kin. Although the incest taboo exists everywhere, precisely where one draws the line in defining incest varies from one culture to another (Murdock, 1965).

   Reproduction between close relatives can mentally and physically impair offspring. Yet, only humans observe an incest taboo, suggesting that the key reason for controlling incest is social. Why? First, the incest taboo limits sexual competition in families by restricting sex to spouses. Second, since kinship defines people's rights and obligations toward each other, reproduction

among close relatives would hopelessly confuse kinship ties and threaten the social order. Third, forcing people to marry beyond their immediate families integrates the larger society.

3. **Social placement.** Families are not needed for people to reproduce, but they help maintain social organization. Parents confer their own social identity—in terms of race, ethnicity, religion, and social class—on children at birth.

4. **Material and emotional security.** The family can serve as a "haven in a heartless world," offering physical protection, emotional support, and financial assistance. Thus, people living in families tend to be healthier than people living alone.

Critical evaluation. Structural-functional analysis explains why society, at least as we know it, depends on families. But this approach glosses over the diversity of U.S. family life and also ignores how other social institutions (say, government) could meet at least some of the same human needs. Finally, structural-functionalism overlooks negative aspects of family life, including patriarchy and family violence.

INEQUALITY AND THE FAMILY: SOCIAL-CONFLICT ANALYSIS

The social-conflict paradigm also considers the family central to our way of life. But rather than focusing on ways that kinship benefits society, conflict theorists point out how the family perpetuates social inequality:

1. **Property and inheritance.** Friedrich Engels (1902; orig. 1884) traced the origin of the family to men's need (especially in the higher classes) to identify heirs so they could transmit property to their sons. Families thus concentrate wealth and reproduce the class structure in each succeeding generation (Mare, 1991).

2. **Patriarchy.** To know their heirs, men must control the sexuality of women. Families therefore transform women into the sexual and economic property of men. A century ago in the United States, most wives' earnings belonged to their husbands. Today, women still bear most responsibility for child rearing and housework (Fuchs, 1986; Hochschild, 1989; Presser, 1993; Keith & Schafer, 1994; Benokraitis & Feagin, 1995; Stapinski, 1998).

3. **Race and ethnicity.** Racial and ethnic categories persist over generations only to the degree that people marry others like themselves. Thus

Early to Wed: A Report from Rural India

Sumitra Jogi cries as her wedding is about to begin. Are they tears of joy? Not exactly. This "bride" is an eleven-month-old squirming in the arms of her mother. The groom? A boy of six.

In a remote village in India's western state of Rajasthan, the two families gather at midnight to celebrate a traditional wedding ritual. It is May 2nd, in Hindu tradition an especially good day to marry. Sumitra's father smiles as the ceremony begins; her mother cradles the infant, who has fallen asleep. The groom, wearing a special costume and a red and gold turban on his head, gently reaches up and grasps the baby's hand. Then, as the ceremony ends, the young boy leads the child and mother around the wedding fire three-and-one-half times, while the audience beams at the couple's first steps together as husband and wife.

Child weddings are illegal in India. But in rural regions, traditions are strong and marriage laws are hard to enforce. Thus, experts say, thousands of children marry each year. "In rural Rajasthan," explains one social worker, "all the girls are married by age fourteen. These are poor, illiterate families, and they don't want to keep girls past their first menstrual cycle."

For a time, Sumitra Jogi will remain with her parents. But in eight or ten years, a second ceremony will send her to live with her husband's family, and her married life will begin.

If the reality of marriage is years in the future, why do families push their children to marry so early? Parents of girls know that the younger the bride, the smaller the dowry offered to the groom's family. Then, too, when girls marry this young, there is no question about their virginity, which raises their value on the marriage market. Overall, arranged marriages are an alliance between families. No one thinks about love or the fact that the children are too young to understand what is taking place.

Source: Based on Anderson (1995).

endogamous marriage shores up racial and ethnic hierarchies.

Critical evaluation. Social-conflict analysis shows another side of family life: its role in social stratification. Engels criticized the family as part and parcel of capitalism. But noncapitalist societies have families (and family problems) all the same. The family may be linked to social inequality, as Engels argued, but the family carries out societal functions not easily accomplished by other means.

CONSTRUCTING FAMILY LIFE: MICRO-LEVEL ANALYSIS

Both structural-functional and social-conflict analyses view the family as a structural system. Micro-level approaches, by contrast, explore how individuals shape and experience family life.

Symbolic-interaction analysis. Ideally, family living offers an opportunity for *intimacy*, a word with Latin roots that mean "sharing fear." That is, as family members share many activities over time, they build emotional bonds. Of course, the fact that parents act as authority figures often limits their closeness with younger children. Only as young people reach adulthood do kinship ties "open up" to include sharing confidences as well as turning to one another for help with daily tasks and responsibilities (Macionis, 1978a).

Social-exchange analysis. Social-exchange analysis is another micro-level approach that depicts courtship and marriage as forms of negotiation (Blau, 1964). Dating allows each person to assess the advantages and disadvantages of taking another as a spouse, in light of what one has to offer in return. In essence, exchange analysts suggest, individuals "shop around" to make the best "deal" they can in a partner.

Physical attractiveness is one critical dimension of exchange. In patriarchal societies, men bring wealth and power to the marriage marketplace, and women are expected to bring beauty. The importance of beauty explains women's traditional concern with their appearance and sensitivity about revealing their age. But, as women have joined the labor force, they are less dependent on men to support them, which indicates that the terms of exchange are converging for men and women.

Critical evaluation. Micro-level analysis offers a useful balance to structural-functional and social-conflict visions of the family as an institutional system. Both the interaction and exchange viewpoints show the individual experience of family life and how people shape it for themselves. This approach, however, misses the bigger picture, that family life is similar for people in the same social and economic categories. U.S. families vary in some predictable ways according to social class and ethnicity, and, as the next section explains, they typically evolve through distinct stages linked to the life course.

STAGES OF FAMILY LIFE

Members of our society recognize several distinct stages of family life across the life course.

COURTSHIP AND ROMANTIC LOVE

November 2, 1994, Kandy, Sri Lanka. Winding through the rain forest of this beautiful island, our van driver, Harry, recounts how he met his wife. Actually, it was more of an arrangement: The two families were Buddhist and of the same caste. "We got along well, right from the start," recalls Harry. "We had the same background. I suppose she or I could have said 'no.' But 'love marriages' happen in the city, not in the village where I grew up."

In rural Sri Lanka, and in preindustrial societies throughout the world, most people consider courtship too important to be left to the young (Stone, 1977). *Arranged marriages* represent an alliance between two extended families of similar social standing and usually involve not just an exchange of children but also of wealth and favors. Romantic love has little to do with it, and parents may make such arrangements when

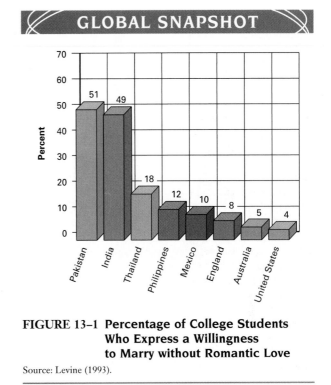

FIGURE 13–1 Percentage of College Students Who Express a Willingness to Marry without Romantic Love

Source: Levine (1993).

their children are very young. A century ago in Sri Lanka and India, half of all girls married before the age of fifteen (Mayo, 1927; Mace & Mace, 1960). As the box explains, in some parts of rural India, child marriage persists today.

Industrialization erodes the importance of extended families as it weakens traditions. Young people who choose their own mates delay marriage until they gain the experience needed to select a suitable partner. Dating sharpens courtship skills and allows sexual experimentation.

Our culture celebrates *romantic love*—affection and sexual passion toward another person—as the basis for marriage. We find it hard to imagine marriage without love, and our popular culture—from fairy tales like "Cinderella" to today's paperback romance novels—portrays love as the key to a successful marriage. However, as Figure 13–1 shows, in many countries romantic love plays a much smaller role in marriage.

Our society's emphasis on romantic love motivates young people to "leave the nest" to form families of their own; physical passion may also help a new couple through difficult adjustments in living together

People in every society recognize the reality of physical attraction. But the power of romantic love, captured in Christian Pierre's painting, I Do, *holds surprisingly little importance in traditional societies. In much of the world, it would be less correct to say that individuals marry individuals and more true to say that families marry families. In other words, parents arrange marriages for their children with an eye to the social position of the kin-groups involved.*

(Goode, 1959). On the other hand, because feelings wax and wane, romantic love is a less stable foundation for marriage than social and economic considerations—one reason that the divorce rate is much higher in the United States than in nations where culture limits choices in partners.

But even here, sociologists point out, society aims Cupid's arrow more than we like to think. Most people fall in love with others of the same race, of comparable age, and similar social class. Our society "arranges" marriages by encouraging **homogamy** (literally, "like marrying like"), *marriage between people with the same social characteristics.*

SETTLING IN: IDEAL AND REAL MARRIAGE

Our culture gives the young an idealized, "happily ever after" picture of marriage. Such optimism can lead to disappointment, especially for women, who are taught that marriage is the key to happiness. Then, too, romantic love involves a lot of fantasy. We fall in love with others, not always as they are but as we want them to be (Berscheid & Hatfield, 1983).

Sexuality, too, can be a source of disappointment. In the romantic haze of falling in love, people may see marriage as an endless sexual honeymoon only to realize that sex becomes less than an all-consuming passion. About two in three married people report that they are satisfied with the sexual dimension of their relationship, although frequency of marital sex does decline over time. In general, couples with the best sexual relationships experience the most satisfaction in their marriages. Sex may not be the key to marital bliss, but good sex and good relationships often go together (Blumstein & Schwartz, 1983; Laumann et al., 1994).

Infidelity—sexual activity outside marriage—is another area where the reality of marriage does not coincide with our cultural ideal. In a recent survey, 90 percent of U.S. adults said sex outside of marriage is "always wrong" or "almost always wrong." Even so, 21 percent of men and 13 percent of women admitted in a private, written questionnaire that they had, at least once, been sexually unfaithful to their partners (NORC, 1999:235, 996).

CHILD REARING

Despite the demands children make on us, adults in the United States overwhelmingly identify raising children as one of life's great joys (NORC, 1999:845). Today, however, few people want more than three children, as Table 13–1 documents. This is a change from two centuries ago, when *eight* children was the U.S. average.

Big families pay off in preindustrial societies because children supply needed labor. Thus, people regard having children as a wife's duty and, in the absence of effective birth control, childbearing is a regular event. Of course, a high death rate in preindustrial societies prevents many children from reaching adulthood; as late as 1900, one-third of children in the United States died by age ten (Wall, 1980).

Industrialization transforms children—economically speaking—from an asset to a liability. It now costs more than $200,000 to raise one child, including college tuition (Lino, 2000). No wonder the U.S. average steadily dropped during the twentieth century to one child per family.[2]

The trend toward smaller families holds for all higher-income nations. But in lower-income countries of Latin America, Asia, and especially Africa, where many women have few alternatives to bearing children, there has been less change. In such societies, four to six children is still the norm.

Parenting is not only expensive, it is a long-term commitment. As our society has given people greater choice about family life, more U.S. adults have opted to delay childbirth or to remain childless. In 1960, almost 90 percent of women between the ages of twenty-five and twenty-nine who had ever married had at least one child; by 1998, this proportion tumbled to 70 percent (U.S. Census Bureau, 2000).

About two-thirds of parents in the United States claim they would like to devote more of their time to child rearing (Snell, 1990). But, unless we accept a lower standard of living, economic realities demand that most parents pursue careers outside the home, even if that means giving less attention to their families.

Children of working parents spend most of the day at school. But after school, more than 2 million youngsters (roughly 13 percent of the total) are *latchkey kids* who fend for themselves (Capizano, Tout, & Adams, 2001). Traditionalists in the "family values" debate charge that many mothers work at the expense of their children, who receive less parenting. Progressives counter that such criticism targets women for wanting the same opportunities men have long enjoyed.

Congress took a step toward easing the conflict between family and job responsibilities by passing the Family and Medical Leave Act in 1993. This law allows up to ninety days' leave from work for a new child or serious family emergency. Still, most adults in this country have to juggle parental and occupational responsibilities. When mothers work, who cares for

---

[2]According to the Census Bureau, the median number of children per family was 0.99 in 1998. Among married couples with children, the medians were .89 for whites, 1.15 for African Americans, and 1.53 for Hispanics.

TABLE 13–1 The Ideal Number of Children for U.S. Adults, 1998	
Number of Children	Proportion of Respondents
0	1.3%
1	2.6
2	53.7
3	19.5
4	8.7
5	0.9
6 or more	1.0
As many as you want	8.4
No response	3.8

Source: *General Social Surveys, 1972–1998: Cumulative Codebook* (Chicago: National Opinion Research Center, 1999), p. 231.

the kids? One-third of the children of working mothers remain at home, usually with fathers or other relatives. Another one-third spend time in some other home, with relatives, neighbors, or friends. The remaining one-third go to an organized child-care facility, an option that has been gaining favor in recent decades (Capizano, Adams, & Sonenstein, 2001).

THE FAMILY IN LATER LIFE

Increasing life expectancy in the United States means that, barring divorce, couples stay married for a long time. By age sixty, most have completed the task of raising children. The remaining years of marriage bring a return to living with only one's spouse.

Like the birth of children, their departure—the "empty nest"—requires adjustments, although a marriage often becomes closer and more satisfying in midlife. Years of living together may have diminished a couple's sexual passion for each other, but understanding and commitment often increase.

Personal contact with children usually continues, since most older adults live a short distance from at least one of their children. Moreover, one-third of all U.S. adults (60 million) are grandparents, many of whom help with child care and other responsibilities. Among African Americans (who have a high rate of single parenting), grandmothers have a central position in family life (Cherlin & Furstenberg, 1986; Crispell, 1993; Jarrett, 1994).

The other side of the coin is that adults in midlife now provide more care for aging parents. The "empty nest" may not be filled by a parent coming to live in the home, but many adults find that caring for parents

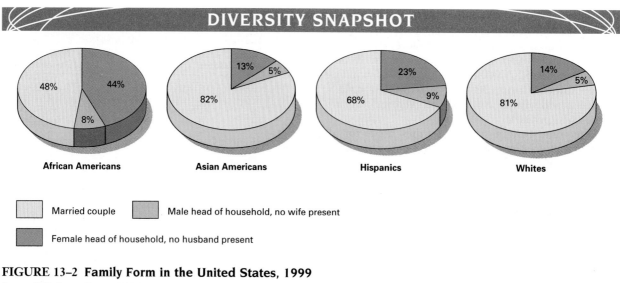

Married couple

Male head of household, no wife present

Female head of household, no husband present

FIGURE 13–2 Family Form in the United States, 1999
Source: U.S. Census Bureau (2000).

living to eighty and beyond can be more taxing than raising young children. The oldest of the "baby boomers"—now in their fifties—are called the "sandwich generation" because many (especially women) will spend as many years caring for their aging parents as they did caring for their children (Lund, 1993).

The final, and surely the most difficult, transition in married life comes with the death of a spouse. Wives typically outlive husbands because of women's greater life expectancy and the fact that women usually marry men several years older to begin with. Wives can thus expect to spend some years as widows. But the challenge of living alone following the death of a spouse is especially great for men, who usually have fewer friends than widows and may lack housekeeping skills.

U.S. FAMILIES: CLASS, RACE, AND GENDER

Dimensions of inequality—social class, ethnicity, race, and gender—are powerful forces that shape marriage and family life. This discussion addresses each factor in turn, but bear in mind that they overlap in our lives.

SOCIAL CLASS

Social class frames a family's financial security and range of opportunities. Interviewing working-class

women, Lillian Rubin (1976) found that wives thought a good husband was a man who held a steady job, did not drink too much, and was not violent. Rubin's middle-class informants, by contrast, never mentioned such things; these women simply *assumed* a husband would provide a safe and secure home. Their ideal husband was a man with whom they could communicate easily and share feelings and experiences. Clearly, what women (and men) feel they can hope for in marriage—and what they end up with—is linked to their social class. Much the same holds true for children: Boys and girls who are lucky enough to be born into more affluent families enjoy better mental and physical health, develop more self-confidence, and go on to greater achievement than children born to poor parents (Komarovsky, 1967; Bott, 1971; Rubin, 1976; McLeod & Shanahan, 1993; Duncan et al., 1998).

ETHNICITY AND RACE

Ethnicity and race, too, shape families. Even so, Latino and African American families (like white Anglo families) conform to no single stereotype (Allen, 1995).

Many Latinos enjoy the loyalty and support of extended families. Traditionally, too, Hispanic parents exercise greater control over children's courtship, considering marriage an alliance of families and not just a bond based on romantic love. Some Hispanic families also adhere to conventional gender roles with pro-nounced *machismo*—strength, daring, and sexual prowess—among men while women are both honored and closely supervised.

Assimilation into the larger society is changing these traditional patterns. Many Puerto Ricans who migrate to New York, for example, do not maintain the strong extended families they knew in Puerto Rico. Traditional male authority over women has also diminished, especially among affluent Latino families, whose number has tripled in the last twenty years (Moore & Pachon, 1985; Nielson, 1990; O'Hare, 1990; Lach, 1999).

African American families face economic disad-vantages. As explained in earlier chapters, the typical African American family earned $31,778 in 1999, or 64 percent of the national standard. People of African ancestry are also three times as likely as white people to be poor, and poverty means families experience unemployment, underemployment, and, in some cases, a physical environment plagued by crime and drug abuse.

Under these circumstances, maintaining stable family ties is difficult. For example, 25 percent of African American women in their forties have never married, compared with about 10 percent of white women of the same age (Bennett, Bloom, & Craig, 1989). This means that women of color—often with children—are more likely to be heads of households. Figure 13–2 shows that women headed 44 percent of African American families in 1999, compared with 23 percent of Hispanic families, 13 percent of Asian and Pacific Islander families, and 14 percent of white families (U.S. Census Bureau, 2000).

Regardless of race, single-mother families are always at high risk of poverty. Slightly less than one-fourth of families headed by white women are poor, and 41 percent of families headed by African Ameri-can women and Hispanic women are in poverty—good evidence of how class, race, and gender overlap to put women at a disadvantage. African American families with both wife and husband in the home, which represent half the total, are much stronger eco-nomically, earning 89 percent as much as comparable white families. But close to 70 percent of African American children are born to single women, and 33 percent of African American boys and girls are grow-ing up poor, meaning that these families carry much of the burden of child poverty in the United States (Hogan & Kitagawa, 1985; U.S. Census Bureau, 2000; U.S. National Center for Health Statistics, 2000).

Racially mixed couples are becoming more common, especially among the young. But do members of the white majority find people in all minority categories equally attractive? Why or why not? What patterns have you noticed on your campus?

Racially mixed marriages. Most spouses have simi-lar social backgrounds with regard to class, race, and ethnicity. But over the course of the twentieth cen-tury, ethnicity mattered less and less. Thus, a woman of German and French ancestry might readily marry a man of Irish and English background without invit-ing disapproval from their families or from society in general.

Race remains a more formidable consideration, however. Prior to a 1967 Supreme Court decision (*Loving* v. *Virginia*), interracial marriage was illegal in sixteen states. Today, African, Asian, and Native

During her long career conducting sociological research, Jessie Bernard provided evidence that marriage is something of a surprise for women. Taught to see marriage as a solution to life's problems, Bernard explained that many women who enter traditional marriages soon face problems they did not expect. Susan Pyzow's painting, Bridal Bouquet, *illustrates the idea.*

© Susan Pyzow, *Bridal Bouquet,* watercolor on paper, 10 × 13.5 in. Studio SPM Inc.

Americans represent 17 percent of the U.S. population, so we would expect about the same share of marriages to be "mixed" if people ignored race in choosing spouses. The actual proportion of mixed marriages is only 2.3 percent, however, which attests to the continuing importance of race in social relations. Even so, most U.S. teens now claim they have dated someone of another race, and the numbers of racially mixed marriages are rising steadily. Black-white marriages are most numerous, as the large

African American population (12 percent of the U.S. total) would lead us to expect. Proportionately, though, whites in racially mixed marriages are most likely to have partners of Asian ancestry (U.S. Census Bureau, 2000).

GENDER

Regardless of race, Jessie Bernard (1982) says that every marriage is actually *two* different relationships: a woman's marriage and a man's marriage. Today, few marriages are composed of two equal partners. Patriarchy has diminished, but we still expect husbands to be older and taller than their wives and to have more important careers (McRae, 1986).

Why, then, do many people think that marriage benefits women more than men? (Bernard, 1982) The positive stereotype of the carefree bachelor contrasts sharply with the negative image of the lonely spinster, suggesting that women are fulfilled only through being wives and mothers.

But, Bernard claims, married women have poorer mental health, less happiness, and more passive attitudes toward life than single women do. Married men, on the other hand, generally live longer, are mentally better off, and report being happier than single men. These differences suggests why, after divorce, men are more eager than women to find a new partner.

Bernard concludes that there is no better guarantor of long life, health, and happiness for a man than having a woman well socialized to devote her life to taking care of him and providing the security of a well-ordered home. She is quick to add that marriage *could* be healthful for women if husbands did not dominate wives and expect them to do almost all the housework. Indeed, research confirms that the wives and husbands with the best mental health are those who share responsibilities for earning income, raising children, and keeping the home (Ross, Mirowsky, & Huber, 1983; Mirowsky & Ross, 1984).

TRANSITIONS AND PROBLEMS IN FAMILY LIFE

Ann Landers (1984), a well-known observer of the U.S. scene, once said that one marriage in twenty is wonderful, five in twenty are good, ten in twenty are tolerable, and the remaining four are "pure hell." Families can be a source of joy, but the reality of family life often falls short of this ideal.

DIVORCE

U.S. society strongly supports marriage, and about nine out of ten people at some point "tie the knot." But many of today's marriages unravel. Figure 13–3 shows the tenfold increase in the U.S. divorce rate over the last century. By 1999, more than four in ten marriages were ending in divorce (for African Americans, the rate was about six in ten). Ours is the highest divorce rate in the world: twice as high as among Canadians, four times higher than in Japan, and ten times higher than in Italy (U.S. Census Bureau, 1998).

Causes of divorce. The high U.S. divorce rate has many causes (Thornton, 1985; Waite, Haggstrom, & Kanouse, 1985; Weitzman, 1985; Gerstel, 1987; Furstenberg & Cherlin, 1991; Etzioni, 1993):

1. **Individualism is on the rise.** Today's family members spend less time together. We have become more individualistic, more concerned with personal happiness than with the well-being of our families and children.

2. **Romantic love often subsides.** Because our culture bases marriage on romantic love, relationships may fail as sexual passion fades. Many people end a marriage in favor of a new relationship that promises renewed excitement and romance.

3. **Women are less dependent on men.** Women's increasing participation in the labor force has reduced wives' financial dependency on husbands. Thus, women find it easier to leave unhappy marriages.

4. **Many of today's marriages are stressful.** With both partners working outside the home in most cases, jobs leave less time and energy for family life. This makes raising children harder than ever. Children do stabilize some marriages, but divorce is most common during the early years of marriage when many couples have young children.

5. **Divorce is more socially acceptable.** Divorce no longer carries the powerful stigma it did a century ago. Family and friends are now less likely to discourage couples in conflict from divorcing.

6. **Legally, a divorce is easier to get.** In the past, courts required divorcing couples to demonstrate that one or both were guilty of behavior such as adultery or physical abuse. Today, all states allow divorce if a couple simply thinks their marriage

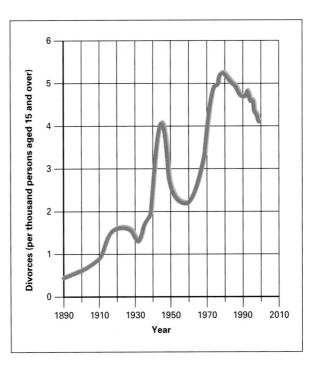

FIGURE 13–3 The Divorce Rate for the United States, 1890–1999

Source: U.S. Census Bureau (2000) and U.S. National Center for Health Statistics (2000).

has failed. Concern about easy divorce—voiced by more than half of U.S. adults—has led some states to consider rewriting their marriage laws. The box on page 348 takes a look at "covenant marriages."

Who divorces? At greatest risk of divorce are young couples—especially those who marry after a brief courtship—with little money, and who have yet to mature emotionally. The chance of divorce also rises if a couple marries after an unexpected pregnancy or if one or both partners have substance-abuse problems. People who are not religious are more likely to divorce than those who are.

Divorce also is more common if both partners have successful careers, perhaps due to the strains of a two-career marriage but also because financially secure people do not feel compelled to stay in an unhappy home. Finally, men and women who divorce once are more likely to divorce again, probably because problems follow them from one marriage to another (Booth & White, 1980; Yoder & Nichols,

CRITICAL THINKING

Which Will It Be:
Real Marriage or Marriage "Lite"?

"Til death us do part," we say in the marriage vows. In reality, however, divorce is as likely as death to end today's marriages. Part of the reason is the "no fault" divorce laws that were passed by all the states after the 1960s. Public opinion has now turned, with more than half of U.S. adults wanting to make divorces harder to get. Even so, no state has dropped the no-fault standard. But in 1997, Louisiana began offering not a new kind of divorce but a new kind of marriage (Walker, 1998).

The law in Louisiana, as well as in Arizona (twenty other states are considering it), allows couples to choose either a regular marriage or a *covenant* marriage. A covenant marriage requires both parties to agree that, before they ever seek a divorce, they will turn to marital counseling. They also agree that they will not divorce unless one partner commits adultery, abandons the other for at least a year, becomes a drug or alcohol abuser, assaults the partner or a child, or is sent to prison for a serious crime. What spouses who select a covenant marriage cannot do is walk away from each other simply because they no longer want to stay married (Nock, Wright, & Sanchez, 1999).

Some people defend the covenant marriage law in the belief that it will bring down the high U.S. divorce rate. Maybe, too, the law will make for better marriages: After all, if one partner balks at a covenant marriage, the other may well wonder why and reconsider the marriage.

Critics, however, claim that the new law will simply trap women and children in bad and, perhaps, abusive marriages.

Then, too, the courts may fill up with couples who are trying to escape their covenant bond. They point to early statistics showing that just a few percent of Louisiana's newlyweds are choosing covenant marriage as evidence that most people want to keep their options open—even in marriage (Whelan, 1998).

What do you think?

1. *Do you think it is too easy for married couples to divorce?*

2. *Do you support Louisiana's covenant marriage law? Why or why not?*

3. *Should society try to keep people married who may not want to be? Why or why not?*

STATE OF LOUISIANA

**DECLARATION OF INTENT
COVENANT MARRIAGE
(FOR USE BY COUPLES WHO ARE ALREADY MARRIED)**

A COVENANT MARRIAGE

We do solemnly declare that marriage is a covenant between a man and a woman who agree to live together as husband and wife for so long as they both may live. We understand the nature, purpose, and responsibilities of marriage. We have read the Covenant Marriage Act, and we understand that a Covenant Marriage is for life. If we experience marital difficulties, we commit ourselves to take all reasonable efforts to preserve our marriage, including marital counseling.

With full knowledge of what this commitment means, we do hereby declare that our marriage will be bound by Louisiana law on Covenant Marriage, and we renew our promise to love, honor, and care for one another as husband and wife for the rest of our lives.

_____
(Name of the Bride)

_____
(Name of the Groom)

_____
(Signature of the Bride)

_____
(Signature of the Groom)

_____
(Signature Date)

_____
(Signature Date)

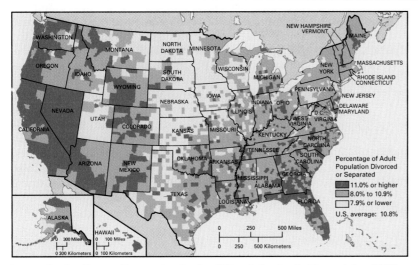

NATIONAL MAP 13–1
Divorced People across the United States

Overall, about 12 percent of the U.S. population aged fifteen and over are divorced or separated. Marriages are most vulnerable to breakup in the Pacific region of the country. Nevada has long been the U.S. divorce capital because of its exceedingly liberal divorce laws. But divorce is also pronounced where religious values are weaker and where people are more likely to move often, thus distancing themselves from a support network of family and friends. How would you characterize the West Coast with regard to these factors?

Source: *American Demographics* magazine, October 1992, p. 5. Reprinted with permission. ©1992, *American Demographics* magazine, Ithaca, New York. Data from the 1990 decennial census.

1980; Glenn & Shelton, 1985). National Map 13–1 takes a look at where in the United States the divorced population is greatest.

Because mothers usually secure custody of children but fathers typically earn more income, the well-being of many children depends on fathers making court-ordered child-support payments. Courts award child support in 54 percent of all divorces involving children. Yet, in any given year, nearly half of children legally entitled to support receive partial payments or no payments at all. Some 2.5 million "dead-beat dads" fail to support their youngsters. In response, federal legislation now requires employers to withhold money from the earnings of parents who fail to pay up, and in 1998, refusal to make child-support payments, or moving to another state to avoid making payments, became a felony (Waldman, 1992; Graham & Beller, 1996).

REMARRIAGE

Four out of five people who divorce remarry, most within five years. Nationwide, about half of all marriages are now remarriages for at least one partner. Men, who derive greater benefits from wedlock, are more likely than women to remarry.

Remarriage often creates *blended families*, composed of children and some combination of biological parents and stepparents. Members of blended families thus have to define precisely who is part of the child's nuclear family. Adjustments are necessary; an only child, for example, may suddenly find that she now has two older brothers. Nevertheless, blended families offer both young and old the chance to relax rigid family roles.

FAMILY VIOLENCE

The ideal family is a source of pleasure and support. The disturbing reality of many homes, however, is *family violence*, emotional, physical, or sexual abuse of one family member by another. Richard J. Gelles calls the family "the most violent group in society with the exception of the police and the military" (quoted in Roesch, 1984:75).

Violence against women. Family brutality often goes unreported to police, but the U.S. Bureau of Justice Statistics (1998) estimates that at least 840,000 women are victims of domestic violence each year. Twenty percent of women (but just 4 percent of men) who are victims of homicide are killed by spouses or, more often, ex-spouses. Nationwide, the death toll from family violence is 1,300 women each year. Overall, women are more likely to be injured by a family member than to be mugged or raped by a stranger or

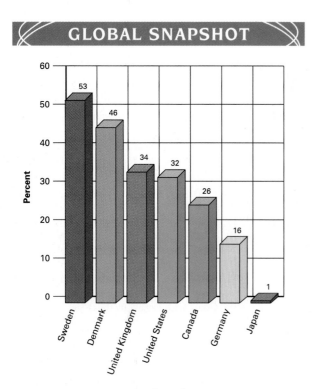

FIGURE 13–4 Percent of Births to Unmarried Women, 1995

Source: U.S. Census Bureau (1998).

hurt in an automobile accident (Straus & Gelles, 1986; Schwartz, 1987; Shupe, Stacey, & Hazlewood, 1987; Blankenhorn, 1995).

Historically, the law defined wives as the property of their husbands, so no man could be charged with raping his wife. Today, however, all states have enacted *marital rape laws.* The law no longer regards domestic violence as a private, family matter, and thus gives victims more options. Now, even without separation or divorce, a woman can obtain court protection from an abusive spouse. Half the states have "stalking laws" that prohibit an ex-partner from following or otherwise threatening someone. Finally, communities across North America have established shelters to provide counseling as well as temporary housing for women and children driven from their homes by domestic violence.

Violence against children. Family violence also victimizes children. In 1998, roughly 3 million reports of suspected child abuse or neglect were made; of these,

1 million turned out to involve serious harm to children, including 1,100 deaths. Child abuse entails more than physical injury; abusive adults can also misuse power and trust to damage a child's emotional well-being. Child abuse and neglect are most common among the youngest and most vulnerable children (Van Biema, 1994; Besharov & Laumann, 1996; U.S. National Clearinghouse on Child Abuse and Neglect, 2000).

Child abusers are as likely to be men as women, and they conform to no simple stereotype. But most abusers do share one trait: having been abused themselves as children. Researchers have found that violent behavior in close relationships is learned; in families, then, violence begets violence (Gwartney-Gibbs, Stockard, & Bohmer, 1987; Widom, 1996; Browning & Laumann, 1997).

ALTERNATIVE FAMILY FORMS

Most families in the United States are still composed of a married couple who raise children. But, in recent decades, our society has displayed greater diversity in family life.

ONE-PARENT FAMILIES

Twenty-eight percent of U.S. families with children under eighteen have only one parent in the household—a proportion that more than doubled during the last generation. Put another way, 29 percent of U.S. children now live with only one parent, and about half will do so before reaching eighteen. One-parent families—82 percent of which are headed by a single mother—result from divorce, death, or from an unmarried person's decision to have a child. Figure 13–4 compares the share of U.S. births out of wedlock to that of other industrial nations.

Single parenthood increases a woman's risk of poverty because it limits her ability to work and to further her education. The converse is also true: Poverty raises the odds that a woman will become a single mother (Trent, 1994). But single parenthood goes well beyond the poor, since one-third of women in the United States become pregnant as teenagers, and many decide to raise their children whether they marry or not. Looking back at Figure 13–2, note that 52 percent of African American families are headed by a single parent. Single parenthood is less common among Hispanics (32 percent), non-Hispanic whites (19 percent), and Asian Americans (18 percent). In many single-parent families, mothers turn to their own mothers for support. In the United States, then, the rise in single parenting is tied to a declining role for fathers and the growing importance of grandparenting.

Research indicates that growing up in a one-parent family usually disadvantages children. Some studies claim that because a father and a mother each makes a distinctive contribution to a child's social development, it is unrealistic to expect a single parent to do as good a job. But the most serious problem for one-parent families—especially if that parent is a woman—is poverty. On average, children growing up in a single-parent family start out poorer, get less schooling, and end up with lower incomes as adults. Such children are also more likely to be single parents themselves (Weisner & Eiduson, 1986; Wallerstein & Blakeslee, 1989; Astone & McLanahan, 1991; Li & Wojtkiewicz, 1992; Biblarz & Raftery, 1993; Popenoe, 1993a; Shapiro & Schrof, 1995; Webster, Orbuch, & House, 1995; Wu, 1996; Duncan et al., 1998).

COHABITATION

Cohabitation is *the sharing of a household by an unmarried couple.* The number of cohabiting couples in the United States has increased from about 500,000 in 1970 to about 5.9 million today (4.2 million heterosexual couples and 1.7 million homosexual couples), or about 10 percent of all couples (Miller, 1997b; U.S. Census Bureau, 1999).

In global perspective, cohabitation as a long-term form of family life, with or without children, is common in Sweden and other Scandinavian societies. But it is rare in more traditional (especially Roman Catholic) nations such as Italy. Cohabitation is gaining in popularity in the United States, with almost half of people between twenty-five and forty-four years of age having cohabited at some point. Cohabiting tends to appeal more to independent-minded individuals as well as those who favor gender equity (Brines & Joyner, 1999). In the end, most cohabiting couples split up, with just 40 percent eventually marrying. Indeed, mounting evidence suggests that living together actually discourages marriage, partly because partners become accustomed to low-commitment relationships (Macklin, 1983; Popenoe, 1988, 1991, 1992; Bumpass & Sweet, 1995; Raley, 1996; Popenoe & Whitehead, 1999).

GAY AND LESBIAN COUPLES

In 1989, Denmark became the first country to lift the legal ban on homosexual marriages. This change

While nowhere in the United States can gay couples legally marry, many cities, such as New York City, officially record domestic partnerships, which provide some of the legal and financial benefits of marriage.

extended social legitimacy to gay and lesbian couples and equalized advantages in inheritance, taxation, and joint property ownership. Norway (1993) and Sweden (1995) followed suit.

As noted in the chapter opening, however, in 1996, the U.S. Congress passed a law banning gay marriage. Homosexual marriage is not legal in any of the fifty states, although Vermont and Hawaii, as well as a number of major cities (including San Francisco and New York), confer limited marital benefits on gay and lesbian couples.

Most of the 1 million U.S. gay couples with children are raising the offspring of previous, heterosexual unions; some couples have adopted children. But many gay parents are quiet about their sexual orientation, not wishing to draw unwelcome attention to their children. Moreover, in several widely publicized cases, courts have removed children from homosexual couples, citing the best interests of the children.

Gay parenting challenges many traditional ideas. But it also indicates that many gay and lesbian couples want to form families just as heterosexuals do (Bell,

CONTROVERSY & DEBATE

Should We Save the Traditional Family?

What are "traditional families"? Are they vital to our way of life or a barrier to progress? To begin, people use the term *traditional family* to mean a married couple who, at some point in their lives, raises children. But the term is more than descriptive; it is also a moral statement. That is, support for the traditional family means placing a high value on becoming and remaining married, putting children ahead of one's own career, and favoring two-parent families over various "alternative lifestyles."

On one side of the debate, David Popenoe warns of the erosion of the traditional family since 1960. Back then, married couples with young children accounted for almost half of all households; today, the figure is 24 percent. Singlehood is up, from 10 percent forty years ago to 26 percent of households now. And the divorce rate has doubled, so that almost half of today's marriages end in permanent separation. Moreover, due to both divorce and children born out of wedlock, the share of youngsters who will live with a single parent before age eighteen has quadrupled since 1960 to 50 percent. In short, just one in four of today's children will grow up with two parents and go on to maintain a stable marriage as an adult.

In light of such data, Popenoe concludes, it may not be an exaggeration to say that the family is falling apart. He sees a fundamental shift from a "culture of marriage" to a "culture of divorce," where traditional vows of marital commitment—"'til death us do part"—now amount to little more than "as long as I am happy." Drawing on national survey data, Daniel Yankelovich (1994:20) sums it up this way:

> The quest for greater individual choice clashed directly with the obligations and social norms that

held families and communities together in earlier years. People came to feel that questions of how to live and with whom to live were a matter of individual choice not to be governed by restrictive norms. As a nation, we came to experience the bonds to marriage, family, children, job, community, and country as constraints that were no longer necessary. Commitments have loosened.

The negative consequences of the cultural trend toward weaker families, Popenoe continues, are obvious everywhere: As we pay less and less attention to children, the crime rate goes up along with a host of other problematic behaviors, including underage smoking and drinking and premarital sex.

As Popenoe sees it, then, we must work hard and quickly to reverse current trends. Government cannot be the

---

Weinberg, & Kiefer-Hammersmith, 1981; Gross, 1991; Pressley & Andrews, 1992; Henry, 1993).

SINGLEHOOD

Because nine out of ten people in the United States marry, we tend to see singlehood as a transitory stage of life. In recent decades, however, more people are deliberately choosing to live alone. In 1950, only one household in ten contained a single person. By 1999, this proportion had risen to one in four: a total of 26 million single adults.

Most striking is the number of single young women. In 1960, only 28 percent of women aged twenty to twenty-four were single; by 1999, the proportion had soared to 80 percent. Underlying this trend is women's greater participation in the labor force. Women who are economically secure view a

husband as a matter of choice rather than a financial necessity.

By midlife, however, unmarried women sense a lack of available men. Because we expect women to "marry up," the older a woman is, the more education she has, and the better her job, the more difficulty she will have finding a suitable husband (Leslie & Korman, 1989).

NEW REPRODUCTIVE TECHNOLOGY

Recent medical advances involving *new reproductive technology* are changing families, too. A generation ago, England's Louise Brown became the world's first "test-tube baby"; since then, tens of thousands of children have been conceived this way. Within a decade, 2 or 3 percent of births in industrial societies may result from new reproductive technologies.

solution, and may even be part of the problem: Since 1960, as families have weakened, government spending on social programs has soared fivefold. To save the traditional family, says Popenoe, we need a cultural turnaround, such as has happened with regard to cigarette smoking. In this case, we must replace our "me first" attitudes in favor of commitment to our spouse and children and publicly endorse the two-parent family as best for the well-being of children.

But Judith Stacey says "good riddance" to the traditional family and provides a counterpoint. To her, the traditional family is more problem than solution. Striking to the heart of the matter, Stacey writes (1990:269):

The family is not here to stay. Nor should we wish it were. On the contrary, I believe that all democratic people, whatever their kinship preferences, should work to hasten its demise.

The main reason for rejecting the traditional family, Stacey explains, is that it perpetuates social inequality. Families play a key role in maintaining the class hierarchy by transferring wealth as well as "cultural capital" from one generation to another. Moreover, feminists criticize the traditional family's patriarchal form, which subjects women to their husbands' authority and saddles them with most of the responsibility for housework and child care. From a gay rights perspective, Stacey adds, a society that values traditional families inevitably denies homosexual men and women equal participation in social life.

Stacey thus applauds the breakdown of the traditional family as a measure of social progress. She does not consider the family a basic social institution but a political construction that elevates one category of people—affluent white males—at the expense of women, homosexuals, and poor people.

Stacey also claims that the concept of "traditional family" is increasingly irrelevant in a diverse society where both men and women work for income. What our society needs, she concludes, is not a return to some golden age of the family but political and economic change, including income parity for women, universal health care, programs to reduce unemployment, and expanded sex education in the schools. Such measures not only help families but ensure that people in diverse family forms receive the respect and dignity everyone deserves.

Continue the debate . . .

1. *To strengthen families, Popenoe suggests that parents put children ahead of their own careers by limiting their joint work week to sixty hours. Do you agree? Why or why not?*

2. *Judith Stacey thinks that marriage is weaker today because women are rejecting patriarchal relationships. Do you agree? Why or why not?*

3. *Do you think we need to change family patterns for the well-being of our children? As you see it, what specific changes are called for?*

Sources: Popenoe (1993a), Stacey (1990, 1993), and Council on Families in America (1995).

Test-tube babies are the product of *in vitro fertilization*, whereby doctors unite a woman's egg and a man's sperm "in glass" rather than in a woman's body. When fertilization is successful, doctors can implant the resulting embryo in the womb of the woman who is to bear the child, or they can freeze it for use at a later time.

At present, new reproductive technologies help some couples who cannot conceive normally to have children. Looking ahead, these techniques may also help reduce the incidence of birth defects. Genetic screening of sperm and eggs would allow medical specialists to increase the odds for the birth of a healthy baby. But new reproductive technology raises fascinating questions: When one woman carries an embryo made from the egg of another, who is the mother? When a couple divorces, which spouse is entitled to use the frozen embryos? Can that partner have a child years later against the will of the other? Such questions remind us that technology changes faster than our capacity to understand the consequences of its use (Thompson, 1994; Cohen, 1998; Nock, Wright, & Sanchez, 1999).

LOOKING AHEAD: THE FAMILY IN THE TWENTY-FIRST CENTURY

Family life in the United States no doubt will continue to change in years to come, and change, of course, causes controversy. In the case of the family, advocates of "traditional family values" line up against those who support greater personal choice; the box sketches some of the issues. Sociologists cannot predict the outcome of this debate, but we can suggest five likely future trends.

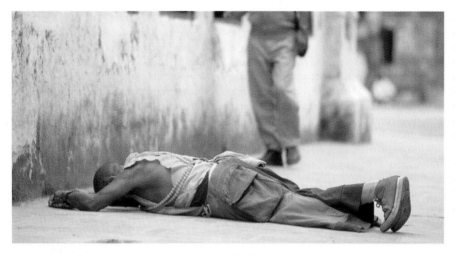

Religion is founded on the concept of the sacred: that which is set apart as extraordinary and which demands our submission. Bowing, kneeling, or prostrating oneself are all ways of symbolically surrendering to a higher power. This monk is performing an act of prostration circumambulation, a complicated way of saying that he falls flat on the ground every few steps as he moves around a holy shrine. In this way, he expresses his complete surrender to his faith.

First, the divorce rate is likely to remain high, even in the face of evidence that marital breakup harms children. Actually, today's marriages are about as durable as they were a century ago, when many were cut short by death (Kain, 1990); the difference is that now more couples *choose* to end marriages that fail to meet their expectations. Although the divorce rate declined slightly during the 1990s, it is unlikely that we will ever return to the low rates that marked the early decades of the twentieth century.

Second, family life in the twenty-first century will be more diverse than ever. Cohabiting couples, one-parent families, gay and lesbian families, and blended families are all on the increase. Most families are still based on marriage, and most married couples still have children. But, taken together, the diversity of family forms implies a trend toward more personal choice.

Third, men will play a limited role in child rearing. In the 1950s, a decade many people consider the "golden age" of families, men began to withdraw from active parenting (Snell, 1990; Stacey, 1990). A countertrend is now emerging as some men—older, on average, and more established in their careers—choose to devote more time to their children. But, on balance, the high U.S. divorce rate and the increase in single motherhood point to more children growing up with weaker ties to fathers. At the same time, evidence is building that the absence of fathers is detrimental to children, at the very least because such families are at high risk of being poor.

Fourth, we will continue to feel the effects of economic change in our families (Hochschild, 1989). In many homes, both household partners work, rendering marriage the interaction of weary men and women who try to squeeze in a little "quality time" for their children (Dizard & Gadlin, 1990). Two-career couples may advance the goal of gender equality, but the long-term effects on families as we have known them are likely to be mixed.

Fifth and finally, the importance of new reproductive technology will increase. Ethical concerns about whether what *can* be done *should* be done will surely slow these developments, but new forms of reproduction will continue to alter the traditional meaning of parenthood.

Despite the change and controversies that have buffeted the family in the United States, most people still report being happy as partners and parents. Marriage and family life will likely remain a foundation of our society for some time to come.

RELIGION: BASIC CONCEPTS

Like the family, religion has played a central part in the drama of human history. Families have long used religious rituals to celebrate birth, recognize adulthood, and mourn the dead.

French sociologist Emile Durkheim said religion involves "things that surpass the limits of our knowledge" (1965:62; orig. 1915). As human beings, we define most objects, events, and experiences as **profane** (from the Latin meaning "outside the temple"), *that which is an ordinary element of everyday life.* But we also consider some things **sacred**, *that which people set apart as extraordinary, inspiring a sense of awe and reverence.* Distinguishing the sacred from the profane is the essence of all religious belief. **Religion,** then, is *a social* *institution involving beliefs and practices based on a conception of the sacred.*

A global perspective reveals great variety in matters of faith, with no one thing sacred to everyone on earth. Although people regard most books as profane, Jews believe the Torah (the first five books of the Hebrew Bible or the Old Testament) is sacred, in the same way that Christians revere the Old and New Testaments of the Bible and Muslims exalt the Qur'an (Koran).

But no matter how a community of believers draws religious lines, Durkheim (1965:62) explained, people understand profane things in terms of everyday usefulness: We log onto the Internet with our computer or turn a key to start our car. What is sacred, however, we reverently set apart from daily life, giving it a "forbidden" aura. For example, Muslims remove their shoes before entering a mosque to avoid defiling a sacred place with soles that have touched the profane ground outside.

The sacred is embodied in *ritual*, or formal ceremonial behavior. Holy Communion is the central ritual of Christianity; to the Christian faithful, the wafer and wine consumed during Communion are never treated in a profane way as food but as the sacred symbols of the body and blood of Jesus Christ.

Since religion deals with ideas that transcend everyday experience, neither common sense nor sociology can verify or disprove religious doctrine. Religion is a matter of **faith**, *belief anchored in conviction rather than scientific evidence.* The New Testament of the Bible defines faith as "the conviction of things not seen" (Heb. 11:1) and exhorts Christians to "walk by faith, not by sight" (2 Cor. 5:7).

Some people with strong religious beliefs may be disturbed by the thought of sociologists turning a scientific eye on what they hold sacred. In truth, however, sociological study is no threat to anyone's faith. Sociologists study religion just as they study the family, to understand religious experiences around the world and how religion is tied to other social institutions. They make no judgments about whether a specific religion is right or wrong. Rather, sociological analysis takes a "worldly" approach by asking why religion takes a particular form in one society or another and how religious activity affects society as a whole.

THEORETICAL ANALYSIS OF RELIGION

Sociologists have applied various theoretical paradigms to the study of religion. Each provides distinctive insights about religious life.

Regularly taking part in religious rituals sharpens the distinction between the sacred and the profane. The wafer used in the Christian ritual of holy communion is never thought of in the everyday sense of food; rather, it is a sacred symbol of the body of Christ.

FUNCTIONS OF RELIGION: STRUCTURAL-FUNCTIONAL ANALYSIS

According to Emile Durkheim, society has an existence and power of its own beyond the life of any individual. In other words, society itself is godlike, surviving the ultimate deaths of its members, whose lives it shapes. Thus, in religion, people celebrate the awesome power of their society (1965; orig. 1915).

No wonder, then, that people around the world transform everyday objects into sacred symbols of their collective life. Members of technologically simple societies do this with a **totem**, *an object in the natural world collectively defined as sacred.* The totem—perhaps an animal or an elaborate work of art—becomes the centerpiece of ritual and symbolizes the power of collective life over any individual. In our society, the flag is a quasi-religious totem that is not to be used in a profane way (say, as clothing) or allowed to touch the ground.

Durkheim defined three major functions of religion that contribute to the operation of society:

1. **Social cohesion.** Religion unites people through shared symbolism, values, and norms. Religious thought and ritual establish morality and rules of fair play that make organized social life possible.

2. **Social control.** Society uses religious ideas to promote conformity. In medieval Europe, for

example, monarchs claimed to rule by divine right. Even today, our leaders publicly ask for God's blessing, implying to audiences that their efforts are right and just.

3. **Providing meaning and purpose.** Religious belief offers the comforting sense that our brief lives serve some greater purpose. Strengthened by such beliefs, people are less likely to despair when one of life's calamities strikes. For this reason, we mark major life transitions—including birth, marriage, and death—with religious observances.

Critical evaluation. In Durkheim's structural-functional analysis, religion represents the collective life of society. The major weakness of this approach is that it downplays religion's dysfunctions—especially the fact that strongly held beliefs can generate social conflict. Many nations have marched to war under the banner of their god; few people would dispute that religious beliefs have provoked more violence in the world than have differences of social class.

CONSTRUCTING THE SACRED: SYMBOLIC-INTERACTION ANALYSIS

From a symbolic-interaction point of view, religion (like all of society) is socially constructed (although perhaps with divine inspiration). Through various rituals—from daily prayer to annual events like Easter or Passover—people sharpen the distinction between sacred and profane. Further, says Peter Berger (1967:35–36), placing our fallible, brief lives within some "cosmic frame of reference" give us "the semblance of ultimate security and permanence."

Marriage is a good example. If two people look on marriage as simply a contract, they can end it whenever they want to. But defined as holy matrimony, their bond makes far stronger claims on them. This is surely why the divorce rate is lower among people who are religious. More generally, whenever humans face uncertainty or life-threatening situations—such as illness, war, and natural disaster—we embrace our sacred symbols.

Critical evaluation. In the symbolic-interaction approach, religion puts everyday life under a "sacred canopy" of meaning (Berger, 1967). Of course, Berger adds, the sacred's ability to give meaning and stabilize society depends on people ignoring its constructed character. After all, how much strength could we derive from sacred beliefs if we saw them as mere devices for coping with tragedy? Then, too, this micro-level view ignores religion's link to social inequality, to which we now turn.

INEQUALITY AND RELIGION: SOCIAL-CONFLICT ANALYSIS

The social-conflict paradigm highlights religion's support of social inequality. Religion, proclaimed Karl Marx, serves elites by legitimizing the status quo and diverting people's attention from social inequities.

Even today, the British monarch is the formal head of the Church of England, illustrating the close alliance between religious and political elites. In practical terms, working for political change may mean opposing the church—and, by implication, God. Religion also encourages people to endure without complaint the social problems of this world while they look hopefully to a "better world to come." In a well-known statement, Marx dismissed religion as "the sigh of the oppressed creature, the sentiment of a heartless world, and the soul of soulless conditions. It is the opium of the people" (1964b:27; orig 1848).

Religion and social inequality are also linked through gender: Virtually all the world's major religions are patriarchal. For example, the Qur'an (Koran)—the sacred text of Islam—gives men social dominance over women:

> Men are in charge of women. . . . Hence good women are obedient. . . . As for those whose rebelliousness you fear, admonish them, banish them from your bed, and scourge them. (quoted in Kaufman, 1976:163)

Christianity—the major religion in the Western Hemisphere—has also supported patriarchy. Although Christians revere Mary, the mother of Jesus, the New Testament instructs us:

> A man . . . is the image and glory of God; but woman is the glory of man. For man was not made from woman, but woman from man. Neither was man created for woman, but woman for man. (1 Cor. 11:7–9)

> As in all the churches of the saints, the women should keep silence in the churches. For they are not permitted to speak, but should be subordinate, as even the law says. If there is anything they desire to know, let them ask their husbands at home. For it is shameful for a woman to speak in church. (1 Cor. 14:33–35)

> Wives, be subject to your husbands, as to the Lord. For the husband is the head of the wife as Christ is the head of the church. . . .

As the church is subject to Christ, so let wives also be subject in everything to their husbands. (Eph. 5:22–24)

Judaism, too, has traditionally supported patriarchy. Male Orthodox Jews include the following daily prayer:

Blessed art thou, O Lord our God, King of the Universe, that I was not born a gentile. Blessed art thou, O Lord our God, King of the Universe, that I was not born a slave. Blessed art thou, O Lord our God, King of the Universe, that I was not born a woman.

Despite patriarchal traditions, most religions now have women in leadership roles, and many are introducing more gender-neutral language in hymnals and prayer books. Such changes involve not just organizational patterns but conceptions of God. Theologian Mary Daly puts the matter bluntly: "If God is male, then male is God" (cited in Woodward, 1989:58).

Critical evaluation. Social-conflict analysis emphasizes the power of religion to legitimize social inequality. Yet religion also promotes change toward equality. Nineteenth-century religious groups in the United States, for example, played an important role in the movement to abolish slavery. During the 1950s and 1960s, religious organizations and their leaders were at the core of the civil rights movement. During the 1960s and 1970s, many clergy actively opposed the Vietnam War, and, as explained presently, some support revolutionary change in Latin America and elsewhere.

RELIGION AND SOCIAL CHANGE

Religion is not just the conservative force portrayed by Karl Marx. In fact, at some points in history, as Max Weber (1958; orig. 1904–5) explained, religion has promoted dramatic social change.

MAX WEBER: PROTESTANTISM AND CAPITALISM

Weber contended that particular religious ideas set into motion a wave of change that brought about the industrialization of Western Europe. That is, industrial capitalism developed in the wake of Calvinism, a movement within the Protestant Reformation.

Central to the religious thought of John Calvin (1509–1564) is the doctrine of *predestination:* An all-knowing, all-powerful God has selected some people for salvation while condemning most to eternal damnation. Each individual's fate, sealed before birth

Sociologists debate whether religious organizations encourage or discourage change. But there is little doubt that these organizations are, themselves, changing. Most (but not all) U.S. religious denominations now ordain women, who make up about 10 percent of all U.S. clergy.

and known only to God, is either eternal glory or endless hellfire.

Driven by anxiety over their fate, Calvinists understandably sought signs of God's favor in *this* world, and came to regard prosperity as a sign of divine blessing. Religious conviction and a rigid devotion to duty thus led Calvinists to work diligently, and many amassed great wealth. But money was not for self-indulgent spending or for sharing with the poor, whose plight they saw as a mark of God's rejection. As agents for God's work on earth, Calvinists believed that they could best fulfill their "calling" by reinvesting profits and reaping ever-greater success in the process.

All the while, the Calvinists lived thrifty lives and embraced technological advances, thereby laying the groundwork for the rise of industrial capitalism. In time, the religious fervor that motivated early Calvinists weakened, leaving a profane "Protestant work ethic." To Max Weber, industrial capitalism itself was a "disenchanted" religion, further showing the power of religion to alter the shape of society.

LIBERATION THEOLOGY

Historically, Christianity has reached out to suffering and oppressed people, urging all to strengthen their faith in a better life to come. In recent decades, however, some church leaders and theologians have taken a decidedly political approach and endorsed **liberation**

theology, *a fusion of Christian principles with political activism, often Marxist in character.*

This social movement started in the late 1960s in Latin America's Roman Catholic church. Today, Christian activists continue to help people in poor nations liberate themselves from abysmal poverty. Their message is simple: Social oppression runs counter to Christian morality, so, as a matter of faith and justice, Christians must promote greater social equality.

Despite its Roman Catholic beginnings, Pope John Paul II condemns liberation theology for distorting church doctrine with left-wing politics. Nevertheless, the liberation theology movement has grown in Latin America, where many people find their Christian faith drives them to improve conditions for the world's poor (Boff, 1984; Neuhouser, 1989).

CHURCH, SECT, AND CULT

Sociologists categorize the hundreds of different religious organizations found in the United States along a continuum, with *churches* at one end and *sects* at the other. Drawing on the ideas of his teacher Max Weber, Ernst Troeltsch (1931) defined a **church** as *a type of religious organization well integrated into the larger society.* Churchlike organizations typically persist for centuries and include generations of the same families. Churches have well-established rules and regulations and expect leaders to be formally trained and ordained.

While concerned with the sacred, a church accepts the ways of the profane world. Church members conceive of God in intellectual terms (say, as a force for good) and favor abstract moral standards ("Do unto others as you would have them do unto you"). By teaching morality in safely abstract terms, church leaders can avoid social controversy. For example, many churches that celebrate the unity of all peoples have all-white memberships. Such duality minimizes conflict between the church and political life (Troeltsch, 1931).

December 11, 1994, Casablanca, Morocco.
The waves of the Atlantic crash along the walls of Casablanca's magnificent coastline mosque, reputedly the largest in the world. From the top of the towering structure, a green laser cuts through the sky pointing to Mecca, the holy city of Islam, toward which the faithful bow in prayer.

To pay for this monumental house of worship, King Hassam II, Morocco's head of state and religious leader, levied a tax on every citizen in his realm, all of whom are officially Muslim. This example of "government religion" contrasts sharply with our ideas about the separation of church and state.

A church may operate as an arm of the state. A **state church** is *a church formally allied with the state,* as illustrated by Islam in Morocco. State churches have existed throughout human history; for centuries Roman Catholicism was the official religion of the Roman Empire, as was Confucianism in China until early in the twentieth century. Today, the Anglican church is the official church of England, and Islam is the official religion of Pakistan and Iran. State churches count everyone in a society as a member, which sharply limits tolerance of religious differences.

A **denomination,** by contrast, is *a church, independent of the state, that recognizes religious pluralism.* Denominations exist in nations that formally separate church and state, such as ours. The United States has dozens of Christian denominations—including Catholics, Baptists, and Lutherans—as well as various categories of Judaism and other traditions. While members of any denomination hold to their own beliefs, they recognize the right of others to disagree.

Unlike a church, which tries to fit into the larger society, a **sect** is *a type of religious organization that stands apart from the larger society.* Sect members have rigid religious convictions and deny the beliefs of others. In extreme cases, members of a sect may withdraw completely from society to practice their faith without interference. The Amish are one example of a North American sect that isolates itself (Kraybill, 1994). Since U.S. culture generally holds religious tolerance as a virtue, members of sects are sometimes accused of being narrow-minded in insisting that they alone follow the true religion.

In organizational terms, sects are less formal than churches. Thus, sect members may be highly spontaneous and emotional in worship, while members of churches tend to listen passively to their leader. Sects also reject the intellectualized religion of churches, stressing instead the personal experience of divine power. Rodney Stark (1985:314) contrasts a church's vision of a distant God—"Our Father, who art in Heaven"—with a sect's more immediate God—"Lord, bless this poor sinner kneeling before you now."

A further distinction between church and sect turns on patterns of leadership. The more churchlike an organization, the more likely that its leaders are formally trained and ordained. Sectlike organizations, which celebrate the personal presence of God, expect their leaders to exude divine inspiration in the form of **charisma** (from the Greek, meaning "divine favor"), *extraordinary personal qualities that can turn an audience into followers,* infusing them with an emotional experience.

Sects generally form as breakaway groups from established religious organizations (Stark & Bainbridge, 1979). Their psychic intensity and informal structure render them less stable than churches, and many sects blossom only to disappear soon after. The sects that do endure typically become more like churches, losing fervor as they become more bureaucratic and established.

To sustain their membership, many sects actively recruit, or *proselytize,* new members. Sects value highly the experience of *conversion,* or religious rebirth. Jehovah's Witnesses, for example, visit door to door to share their faith with others in the hope of attracting new members.

Finally, churches and sects differ in their social composition. Because they are more closely tied to the world, well-established churches tend to include people of high social standing. Sects, by contrast, attract more disadvantaged people. A sect's openness to new members and promise of salvation and personal fulfillment appeal to people who perceive themselves as social outsiders.

A **cult** is *a religious organization that is largely outside a society's cultural traditions.* Whereas most sects spin off from a conventional religious organization, a cult typically forms around a highly charismatic leader who offers a compelling message of a new and very different way of life. As many as 5,000 cults now exist in the United States (Marquand & Wood, 1997).

Because some cult principles or practices are unconventional, many people view cults as deviant or even evil. The suicides of thirty-nine members of California's "Heaven's Gate" cult in 1997—people who claimed that dying was the doorway to a higher existence, perhaps in the company of aliens from outer space—confirmed the negative image the public holds of many cults. In short, say some scholars, calling a religious community a "cult" amounts to dismissing its members as crazy (Richardson, 1990; Shupe, 1995; Gleick, 1997).

This view of cults is unfortunate because there is nothing intrinsically wrong with this kind of religious

In global perspective, the range of religious activity is truly astonishing. Members of this Southeast Asian cult show their devotion to God by suspending themselves in the air using ropes and sharp hooks that pierce their skin.

organization. Many religions—Christianity, Islam, and Judaism included—began as cults. Of course, few cults exist for very long. One reason is that they are even more at odds with the larger society than sects. Many cults demand that members not only accept their doctrine but embrace a radically new lifestyle. This is why people sometimes accuse cults of brainwashing their members, although research suggests that most people who join cults experience no psychological harm (Barker, 1981; Kilbourne, 1983).

RELIGION IN HISTORY

Like the family, religion is a part of every known society. Also like the family, religion shows marked variation both historically and cross-culturally.

Early hunters and gatherers embraced **animism** (from the Latin, meaning "the breath of life"), *the belief that elements of the natural world are conscious life forms that affect humanity.* Animistic people view forests, oceans, mountains, and even the wind as

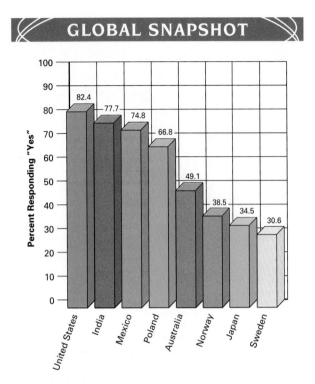

FIGURE 13–5 Religiosity in Global Perspective

Survey Question: "Do you gain comfort and strength from religion?"

Source: Inglehart et al. (2000).

spiritual forces. Many Native American societies are animistic, which accounts for their reverence for the natural environment.

Belief in a single divine power responsible for creating the world arose with pastoral and horticultural societies. Our conception of God as a "shepherd" should be no surprise since Christianity, Judaism, and Islam all had their beginnings among pastoral peoples.

In agrarian societies, religion becomes more important. The centrality of religion is evident in the huge cathedrals that dominated the towns of medieval Europe.

The Industrial Revolution ushered in a growing emphasis on science. More and more, people looked to physicians and scientists for the guidance and comfort they had sought from priests. Even so, religion persists because science is powerless to address issues of ultimate meaning in human life. In other words, *how* this world works is a matter for scientists; but *why* we and the rest of the universe exist at all is a question for religion to answer.

RELIGION IN THE UNITED STATES

Just as people debate the health of family life in the United States, so analysts disagree about the strength of religion in our society. Research shows that changes are underway, but also confirms the ongoing role of religion in social life (Collins, 1982; Greeley, 1989; Woodward, 1992a; Hadaway, Marler, & Chaves, 1993).

RELIGIOUS COMMITMENT

National surveys show that almost 90 percent of adults claim some religious preference (NORC, 1999:124). More than half of U.S. adults say they are Protestants, one-fourth Catholics, and 2 percent, Jews. Many more also adhere to dozens of other religions—from animism to Zen Buddhism—making our society as religiously diverse as any on earth. Furthermore, as Figure 13–5 shows, in few industrial societies do people claim to be as religious as in the United States.

The religious diversity of the United States stems from a constitutional ban on any government-sponsored religion and from our historically high numbers of immigrants from all over the world. National Map 13–2 shows the share of people who claim to belong to any church across the United States.

National Map 13–3 takes us one more step, showing that the religion most people identify with varies by region. New England and the Southwest are predominantly Catholic, for instance, the South is overwhelmingly Baptist, and in the northern Plains states Lutherans predominate. In and around Utah, there is a heavy concentration of members of the Church of Jesus Christ of Latter-day Saints (Mormons).

Religiosity is *the importance of religion in a person's life.* Exactly how religious we turn out to be, however, depends on precisely how we operationalize this concept. For example, 88 percent of U.S. adults claim to believe in a divine power, although just 60 percent claim that they "know that God exists and have no doubts about it" (NORC, 1999:367). Just half of adults say they pray at least once a day, and just 31 percent report attending religious services on a weekly or almost-weekly basis (NORC, 1999:128, 126, 133).

Clearly, the question "How religious are we?" yields no easy answers, and it is likely that many people claim to be more religious than they really are. Moreover, religiosity varies among denominations. Members of sects are the most religious of all, followed by Catholics and then "mainstream" Protestants (Stark & Glock, 1968; Hadaway, Marler, & Chaves, 1993).

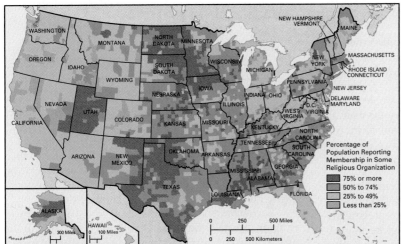

NATIONAL MAP 13–2
Religious Membership across the United States

In general, people in the United States are more religious than people in other high-income nations. Yet, membership in a religious organization is more common in some parts of the country than in others. What pattern do you see in the map? Can you explain the pattern?

Source: From Rodger Doyle, *Atlas of Contemporary America.* Copyright © 1994 by Rodger Doyle. Reprinted with the permission of Facts on File, Inc., New York, N.Y.

Percentage of Population Reporting Membership in Some Religious Organization
- 75% or more
- 50% to 74%
- 25% to 49%
- Less than 25%

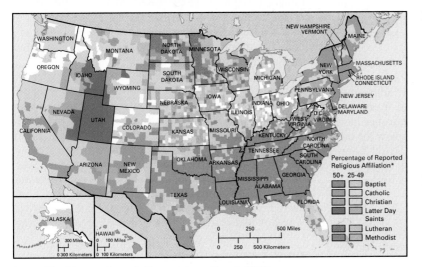

NATIONAL MAP 13–3
Religious Diversity across the United States

In the vast majority of counties, at least 25 percent of people who report having an affiliation are members of the same religious organization. Thus, although the United States is religiously diverse at the national level, most people live in communities where one denomination predominates. What historical facts might account for this pattern?

*When two or more churches have 25 to 49 percent of the membership in a county, the largest is shown. When no church has 25 percent of the membership that county is left blank. A few exceptions include Palm Beach County in southern Florida, which is primarily Jewish, and Holmes County in central Ohio, which is largely Amish.

Percentage of Reported Religious Affiliation*
50+ 25-49
- Baptist
- Catholic
- Christian
- Latter Day Saints
- Lutheran
- Methodist

Source: The Glenmary Research Center, Atlanta, Georgia (1990).

RELIGION: CLASS, ETHNICITY, AND RACE

Religious affiliation is related to a number of other factors. We shall consider three: social class, ethnicity, and race.

Social class. A study of *Who's Who in America*, which profiles U.S. high achievers, showed that 33 percent of the people who gave a religious affiliation were Episcopalians, Presbyterians, and United Church of Christ members, denominations that together account for less than 10 percent of the population. Jews, too, enjoy high social position, with this 2 percent of people accounting for 12 percent of listings in *Who's Who*. Research shows that, on average, members of other denominations—including Methodists and Catholics—have moderate social standing. Lower social standing is typical of Baptists, Lutherans, and members of sects. Within all denominations, of course, there is considerable variation (Roof, 1979; Davidson, Pyle, & Reyes, 1995; Waters, Heath, & Watson, 1995).

Ethnicity. Throughout the world, religion is tied to ethnicity, largely because one religion often predominates in a single nation or geographic region, such as Islam in the Middle East or Hinduism in India. Christianity and Judaism do not follow this pattern; while these religions are mostly Western, Christians and Jews are found all over the world.

Religion and national identity come together in the United States as well. We have, for example, *Anglo-Saxon* Protestants, *Irish* Catholics, and *Greek* Orthodox. This linking of nation and creed results from the influx of immigrants from nations with a single major religion. Still, nearly every ethnic category displays at least some religious diversity. People of English ancestry, for instance, may be Protestants, Roman Catholics, Jews, Hindus, or followers of other religions.

Race. Historically, the church has been central to the spiritual—and political—lives of African Americans. Transported to the Western Hemisphere, most Africans became Christians—the dominant religion in the Americas—but they blended Christian belief with elements of African religions. Guided by this religious mix, Christian people of color have developed rituals that are, by European standards, quite spontaneous and emotional (Frazier, 1965; Roberts, 1980).

When African Americans migrated from the rural South to the industrial cities of the North around 1940, the church played a major role in addressing problems of dislocation, poverty, and prejudice (Pattillo-McCoy, 1998). Further, black churches have provided an important avenue of achievement for talented men and women. The Reverends Ralph Abernathy, Martin Luther King, Jr., and Jesse Jackson have all achieved world recognition as religious leaders.

RELIGION IN A CHANGING SOCIETY

Just as we have seen change in family life, so we also see that religion continues to change in the United States. Sociologists focus on the process of secularization.

SECULARIZATION

Secularization refers to *the historical decline in the importance of the supernatural and the sacred.* Secularization (derived from the Latin, meaning "the present age") is commonly associated with modern, technologically advanced societies where science is the dominant mode of understanding.

Today, for example, we are more likely to experience the transitions of birth, illness, and death in the presence of physicians (with scientific knowledge) than church leaders (whose knowledge is based on faith).

This shift alone suggests that religion's relevance for our everyday lives has declined. Harvey Cox elaborates:

> The world looks less and less to religious rules and rituals for its morality or its meanings. For some, religion provides a hobby, for others a mark of national or ethnic identification, for still others an aesthetic delight. For fewer and fewer does it provide an inclusive and commanding system of personal and cosmic values and explanations. (1971:3; orig. 1965)

If Cox is right, should we expect religion to someday disappear? The consensus among U.S. sociologists is "no." The vast majority of people still profess a belief in God, and more people claim to pray each day than vote in national elections. Further, religious affiliation today is actually higher than it was in 1850 (Hammond, 1985; Hout & Greeley, 1987; McGuire, 1987).

Secularization does not, then, signal the death of religion. Some dimensions of religion (like belief in life after death) may have declined, but others (such as religious affiliation) have increased. Moreover, people are of two minds about whether secularization is good or bad. Conservatives see any weakening of religion as a mark of moral decline. Progressives, however, view secularization as liberation from the all-encompassing beliefs of the past, so people can choose what to believe. Secularization has also brought many religious practices (such as ordaining only men) into line with widespread social attitudes (including that of gender equality, exemplified by ordination of women and men).

Back in 1963, an important event in the secularization trend occurred when the U.S. Supreme Court banned prayer in school as violating the constitutional separation of church and state. In recent years, however, religion has returned to many public schools. The box takes a closer look at this controversial issue.

CIVIL RELIGION

One dimension of secularization is what Robert Bellah (1975) calls **civil religion,** *a quasi-religious loyalty based on citizenship.* Even in a mostly secular society, in other words, citizenship has religious qualities. Certainly, most people in the United States consider our way of life a force for moral good in the world. Many people also find religious qualities in political movements, whether liberal or conservative (Williams & Demerath, 1991).

Civil religion also involves a range of rituals, from standing to sing the national anthem at sporting events to waving the flag at public parades. At all such events, the U.S. flag serves as a sacred symbol of our national identity, and we expect people to treat it with respect.

Should Students Pray in School?

It is late afternoon on a cloudy, spring day in Minneapolis, and two dozen teenagers have come together to pray. They share warm smiles as they enter the room. As soon as everyone is seated, the prayers begin, with one voice following another. One girl prays for her brother, a boy prays for the success of an upcoming food drive, another asks God to comfort a favorite teacher who is having a hard time. Then they join their voices to pray for all the teachers at their school who are not Christians. Following the prayers, the young people sing Christian songs, discuss a Scripture lesson, and bring their meeting to a close with a group hug.

What is so unusual about this prayer meeting is that it is taking place in room 133 of Patrick Henry High School, a *public* institution. Indeed, in public schools from coast to coast, something of a religious revival is taking place as more and more students hold meetings like this one.

You would have to be at least in your mid-forties to remember when it was routine for public school students to begin the day with Bible reading and prayer. In 1963, the Supreme Court ruled that doing so violated the separation of church and state mandated by the U.S. Constitution, making any religious activity anywhere in public schools illegal. But, right from the outset, critics charged that, by supporting a wide range of other activities and clubs while banning religious activity, schools were really being *anti*religious. In 1990, the Supreme Court handed down a new ruling, stating that religious groups can meet on school property as long as group membership is voluntary, the meetings are held outside of regular class hours, and students rather than adults run them.

Today, student religious groups have formed in perhaps one-fourth of all public schools. Evangelical Christian organizations such as First Priority and National Network of Youth are using the Internet as well as word of mouth in an effort to expand the place of religion in every public school across the country. Opponents of school prayer, however, worry that religious zeal may lead some students to pressure others to join their groups, which ensures that the controversy over prayer in public schools will continue.

Continue the debate . . .

1. *Do you think that religious clubs should have the same freedom to operate on school grounds as other organizations? Why or why not?*

2. *The writers of our Constitution stated in the First Amendment that Congress should not establish any official religion and also pass no law that would interfere with the free practice of religion. How do you think this amendment applies to the issue of prayer in school?*

3. *In 1995, President Bill Clinton said, "Nothing in the First Amendment converts our public schools into religion-free zones." Do you think schools should support spiritual education and development, be neutral to religious activity, or oppose such activity? Why?*

Source: Based on Van Biema (1998, 1999).

RELIGIOUS REVIVAL

All things considered, religiosity in the United States has been stable in recent decades. But a great deal of change is going on within the world of organized religion. Membership in mainstream churches like the Episcopalian and Presbyterian denominations has plummeted by almost 50 percent since 1960. At the same time, affiliation with other religious organizations (including the Mormons, Seventh-day Adventists, and especially Christian sects) has risen just as dramatically.

Secularization itself may be self-limiting so that, as churchlike organizations become more worldly, many people leave them in favor of sectlike communities that offer a more intense religious experience (Stark & Bainbridge, 1981; Roof & McKinney, 1987; Jacquet & Jones, 1991; Warner, 1993; Iannaccone, 1994).

One striking religious trend today is the growth of **fundamentalism,** *a conservative religious doctrine that opposes intellectualism and worldly accommodation in favor of restoring traditional, otherworldly religion.* In the United States, fundamentalism has made the greatest

In this outstanding example of U.S. folk art, Anna Bell Lee Washington's Baptism 3 *(1924) depicts the life-changing experience by which many people enter the Christian faith.*

gains among Protestants. Southern Baptists, for example, are the largest religious community in the United States. But fundamentalist groups have also grown among Roman Catholics and Jews.

In response to what they see as the growing influence of science and the weakening of the conventional family, religious fundamentalists defend what they call "traditional values." As they see it, liberal churches are simply too open to change. Religious fundamentalism is distinctive in five ways (Hunter, 1983, 1985, 1987):

1. **Fundamentalists interpret sacred texts literally.** Fundamentalists literally interpret the Bible and other sacred texts to counter what they consider excessive intellectualism among liberal Christian organizations. Fundamentalist Christians, for example, believe God created the world in seven days precisely as described in Genesis.

2. **Fundamentalists reject religious pluralism.** Fundamentalists maintain that tolerance and relativism water down personal faith. They maintain, therefore, that their religious beliefs are true and other beliefs are not.

3. **Fundamentalists pursue the personal experience of God's presence.** In contrast to the worldliness and intellectualism of other religious organizations, fundamentalists seek to propagate "good old-time religion" and spiritual revival. Being "born again" and having a personal relationship with Jesus Christ should be evident in a person's everyday life.

4. **Fundamentalists oppose "secular humanism."** Fundamentalists think accommodation to the changing world undermines religious conviction. *Secular humanism* is a general term that refers to our society's tendency to look to scientific experts rather than God for guidance about how to live.

5. **Fundamentalists endorse conservative political goals.** Although fundamentalism tends to back away from worldly concerns, some fundamentalist leaders (such as Ralph Reed, Pat Robertson, and Gary Bauer) have entered politics to oppose the "liberal agenda" that includes feminism and gay rights. Fundamentalists oppose abortion, gay marriage, and liberal bias in the media; they support the traditional two-parent family and seek a return of prayer in schools (Hunter, 1983; Speer, 1984; Ellison & Sherkat, 1993; Green, 1993; Manza & Brooks, 1997; Thomma, 1997; Wilcox, Rozell, & Green, 1998).

Opponents find fundamentalism rigid and self-righteous. But many find in fundamentalism—with its greater religious certainty and emphasis on experiencing God's presence—an appealing alternative to the more intellectual, tolerant, and worldly mainstream denominations (Marquand, 1997).

Which religious organizations are "fundamentalist"? This term is most correctly applied to conservative organizations in the larger evangelical tradition, including Pentacostals, Southern Baptists, Seventh-day Adventists, and the Assemblies of God. Several national religious movements, including Promise Keepers for men and Chosen Women, have a fundamentalist orientation. In national surveys, 31 percent of U.S. adults describe their upbringing as "fundamentalist"; 39 percent claim a "moderate" religious upbringing; and 24 percent call their religious background "liberal" (NORC, 1999:143).

In contrast to local congregations of years past, some religious organizations—especially fundamentalist ones—have become *electronic churches* dominated by "prime-time preachers" (Hadden & Swain, 1981). Electronic religion is found only in the United States. It has propelled people like Oral Roberts, Pat Robertson, and Robert Schuller to greater prominence than all but a few clergy in the past. Perhaps 5 percent of the national television audience (about 10 million people) are regular viewers of religious television, while 20 percent (about 40 million) watch some religious programming every week (NORC, 1999).

LOOKING AHEAD: RELIGION IN THE TWENTY-FIRST CENTURY

The popularity of media ministries, the growth of religious fundamentalism, and the connection of millions more to mainstream churches show that religion will remain a major part of modern society. Moreover, high levels of immigration from many religious countries (in Latin America and elsewhere) should both intensify and diversify the religious character of U.S. society in this new century.

The world is becoming more complex, and rapid social change seems to outstrip our capacity to make sense of it all. But rather than undermining religion, this process fires the religious imagination. Moreover, new technology that can alter, sustain, and even create life confronts us with vexing moral dilemmas. Against this backdrop of uncertainty, it is little wonder that many people look to their faith for assurance and hope.

SUMMARY

FAMILY

1. Although found everywhere in the world, the family varies across cultures and over time.

2. In higher-income nations, marriage is monogamous. Many lower-income countries permit polygamy—either polygyny or polyandry.

3. Globally, patrilocality is more common than matrilocality. Higher-income nations favor neolocality, and descent is bilateral. Descent in most lower-income nations is either patrilineal or matrilineal.

4. Structural-functional analysis identifies major family functions: socializing the young, regulating sexual activity, and providing social placement and emotional support. Social-conflict theories highlight how the family perpetuates inequality based on class, ethnicity, race, and gender. Symbolic-interaction analysis highlights the dynamic and changeable experience of family life.

5. In the United States and elsewhere, family life evolves from courtship, through child rearing, to the eventual death of a spouse, usually in old age.

6. U.S. families are diverse, with certain patterns linked to class position, ethnicity, race, and gender.

7. The divorce rate today is ten times higher than a century ago; 40 percent of current marriages will end in divorce. Most people who divorce, especially men, remarry.

8. Family violence is an important public issue.

9. Our society's family life is becoming more varied. Singlehood, cohabitation, and one-parent families are on the rise. While homosexual men and women cannot legally marry, many form long-lasting relationships.

RELIGION

1. Religion is a major social institution based on setting the sacred apart from the profane. Religion is grounded in faith, not scientific evidence. Sociologists study how religion affects society, but make no claims as to the truth of any religious belief.

2. Through religion, said Durkheim, people celebrate the power of their society. His structural-functional analysis suggests that religion promotes social cohesion and conformity, and confers meaning and purpose on life.

3. Using the symbolic-interaction paradigm, Peter Berger explains that people socially construct religious beliefs as a response to life's uncertainties.

4. Social-conflict analyst Karl Marx claimed that religion supports inequality. On the other hand, Max Weber's analysis showed how religious ideas can trigger societal change.

5. Churches, which are religious organizations well integrated into their societies, fall into two

categories—state churches and denominations. Sects are marked by charismatic leadership and suspicion of the larger society. Cults represent new and unconventional religious beliefs and practices.

6. How religious our society is depends on how we operationalize the concept of religiosity. Most people say they believe in God, but only about one-third report attending religious services regularly.

7. The concept of secularization refers to the diminishing importance of religion. While some measures of U.S. religiosity (including membership in mainstream churches) have declined, others (such as membership in sects) are on the rise. It is unlikely, then, that religion will disappear.

8. Fundamentalism opposes religious accommodation to the world, advocates literal interpretation of sacred texts, and pursues the personal experience of God's presence. Some fundamentalist Christians have become a conservative force in politics.

KEY CONCEPTS

FAMILY

family (p. 336) a social institution found in all societies that unites people in cooperative groups to oversee the bearing and raising of children

kinship (p. 336) a social bond based on blood, marriage, or adoption

family unit (p. 336) a social group of two or more people, related by blood, marriage, or adoption, who usually live together

marriage (p. 336) a legally sanctioned relationship, usually involving economic cooperation as well as sexual activity and childbearing, that people expect to be enduring

extended family (consanguine family) (p. 337) a family unit that includes parents, children, other kin

nuclear family (conjugal family) (p. 337) a family unit composed of one or two parents and their children

endogamy (p. 337) marriage between people of the same social category

exogamy (p. 337) marriage between people of different social categories

monogamy (p. 337) marriage uniting two partners

polygamy (p. 337) marriage that unites three or more people

descent (p. 337) the system by which members of a society trace kinship over generations

homogamy (p. 342) marriage between people with the same social characteristics

cohabitation (p. 351) the sharing of a household by an unmarried couple

RELIGION

profane (p. 354) that which people define as an ordinary element of everyday life

sacred (p. 354) that which people set apart as extraordinary, inspiring a sense of awe and reverence

religion (p. 354) a social institution involving beliefs and practices based on a conception of the sacred

faith (p. 355) belief anchored in conviction rather than scientific evidence

totem (p. 355) an object in the natural world collectively defined as sacred

liberation theology (p. 357) a fusion of Christian principles with political activism, often Marxist in character

church (p. 358) a type of religious organization well integrated into the larger society

state church (p. 358) a church formally allied with the state

denomination (p. 358) a church, independent of the state, that recognizes religious pluralism

sect (p. 358) a type of religious organization that stands apart from the larger society

charisma (p. 359) extraordinary personal qualities that can turn an audience into followers

cult (p. 359) a religious organization that is largely outside a society's cultural traditions

animism (p. 359) the belief that elements of the natural world are conscious life forms that affect humanity

religiosity (p. 360) the importance of religion in a person's life

secularization (p. 362) the historical decline in the importance of the supernatural and the sacred

civil religion (p. 362) a quasi-religious loyalty based on citizenship

fundamentalism (p. 363) a conservative religious doctrine that opposes intellectualism and worldly accommodation in favor of restoring traditional, otherworldly religion

CRITICAL-THINKING QUESTIONS

1. Identify several changes in the family since 1960. What factors are responsible for these changes?

2. On balance, are families in the United States becoming weaker, or simply different? What evidence supports your contention?

3. Explain Karl Marx's contention that religion tends to support the status quo. Develop a counterargument, based on Max Weber's analysis of Calvinism, that religion is a major force for social change.

4. What evidence suggests that religion has declining importance in the United States? In what ways does religion seem to be getting stronger?

APPLICATIONS AND EXERCISES

1. Parents and grandparents can be a wonderful source of information about changes in marriage and the family. Spend an hour or two with married people of two different generations and ask about when they married, what their married lives have been like, and what changes in family life today stand out to them.

2. Relationships with various family members differ. With which family member—mother, father, brother, sister—do you most readily, and least readily, share secrets? Why? Which family member would you turn to first in a crisis? Why?

3. Some colleges are decidedly religious; others are passionately secular. Investigate the place of religion on your campus. Is your school affiliated with a religious organization? Was it ever? Is there a chaplain or other religious official? See if you can learn from sources on campus what share of students regularly attend any religious service.

4. Is religion getting weaker? To test the secularization thesis, go the library or local newspaper office and find an issue of your local newspaper published fifty years ago and, if possible, another from one hundred years ago. Compare attention to religious issues then and now.

5. Install the CD-ROM packaged in the back of this new textbook to access a variety of study, review, and applications exercises designed to help you better understand the material covered in this chapter. The CD includes an author's tip video, as well as interactive maps, video application exercises, Web links, and study questions.

 SITES TO SEE

http://www.prenhall.com/macionis
Visit the interactive Web site that accompanies this text. Begin by clicking on the cover of your book. You will find a chapter-by-chapter study guide, practice tests, chat room, and many suggested Web links.

http://www.frc.org
This is the Web address for the Family Research Council, a conservative organization supporting what it calls "traditional family values." What does the council consider a "traditional family"? What values does it defend? Why? Are there family problems that it ignores?

http://www.polyamorysociety.org
Survey the increasing diversity of family life at the Web site for the Polyamory Society. What do you make of the society's views of family life?

http://www.bwanet.org
http://www.churchworldservice.org
http://www.catholicrelief.org
http://www.jdc.org
A number of religious organizations are involved in addressing hunger and other social problems. These are the Web sites that describe the activities of the Baptist World Alliance, Church World Service, Catholic Relief Services, and the American Jewish Joint Distribution Committee.

http://www.parishioners.org/
Here is a site offering information on a variety of religious issues, including cults and toleration of religious differences.

http://www.trinityumc.net/youth/cool.htm
This Web site is just for fun. Check it out!

EDUCATION AND MEDICINE

"*This is class warfare!*" *The cry came from the back of the town hall in Dorset, a well-off town in the Vermont countryside. About a hundred of the townspeople had gathered on a warm June evening to discuss their state's new education funding law, and many of them were angry. The well-dressed man in the back continued: "This law attacks a system that works. What some people are saying is, 'You have no right to better schools than we have, even if you can afford them.' They want to spend* our *money to educate* their *kids."*

Stirring up the controversy is Vermont's Act 60, a new system of funding public schools. Before Act 60, communities taxed their own property owners to raise money to run the local schools. In practice, rich towns like Dorset could afford excellent schools. But hundreds of less prosperous towns could barely raise enough money to maintain any school, much less a good one. The Vermont Supreme Court declared that legislators had to find another way to provide for the poorer districts. The result was Act 60, which equalizes funding across the state, forcing rich towns to share their tax revenues with poorer ones. Supporters like to say that Act 60 "lets Vermonters take care of Vermonters." Opponents, however, are angry that their taxes are going up even as 60 or 70 cents of every tax dollar leave their communities to educate children elsewhere (Edwards, 1998; Shlaes, 1998).

The same kind of wrangling over school funding is taking place in cities and states across the country. The reason is simple: While many public schools do a good job of teaching children, many do not, and one reason for this pattern is striking differences in funding.

This chapter begins by exploring *education*, a vital social institution in industrial nations, including the United States. We shall explain *why* schooling is so important in modern societies, as well as *who* receives most educational benefits. The second half of the

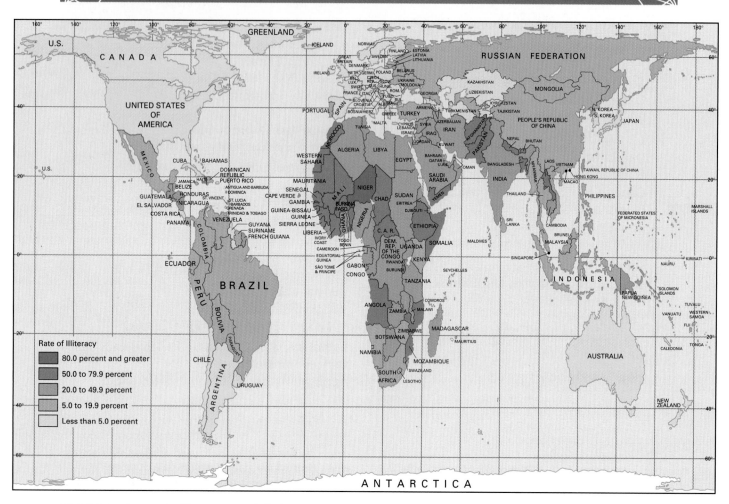

GLOBAL MAP 14–1 Illiteracy in Global Perspective

Reading and writing skills are widespread in high-income countries, with illiteracy rates generally below 5 percent. In much of Latin America, however, illiteracy is more commonplace—one consequence of limited economic development. In twenty-seven nations—twenty of them in Africa—illiteracy is the rule rather than the exception; there, people rely on "the oral tradition" of face-to-face communication rather than the written word.

Sources: United Nations Development Programme (2000); map projection from *Peters Atlas of the World* (1990).

chapter examines *medicine*, another social institution with great importance in the modern world. Good health, like quality schooling, is distributed unequally throughout our society's population. In addition, like education, medicine reveals striking variation from society to society.

EDUCATION: A GLOBAL SURVEY

Education is *the social institution through which society provides its members with important knowledge, including basic facts and job skills as well as cultural norms and values.* Education takes place in many ways, some as informal as a family discussion. In higher-income nations, education is largely a matter of **schooling**, *formal instruction under the direction of specially trained teachers.*

SCHOOLING IN LOW-INCOME COUNTRIES

In low-income countries, where most of the world's people live, families and local communities teach young people important knowledge and skills. Formal schooling, and especially learning that is not directly linked to work, is mostly available only to wealthy people. After all, the Greek root of the word "school" means "leisure." Thus, in ancient Greece, renowned teachers such as Plato, Socrates, and Aristotle taught aristocratic men; similarly, in ancient China, the famous philosopher K'ung Fu-tzu (Confucius) shared his wisdom with just a privileged few.

Schooling in low-income countries today is diverse because it reflects the local culture. In Iran, for example, schooling is closely tied to Islam. Similarly, schooling in Bangladesh (Asia), Zimbabwe (Africa), and Nicaragua (Latin America) has been molded by distinctive cultural traditions.

But all low-income countries have one trait in common when it comes to schooling—there is not very much of it. In the world as a whole, just half of all children reach the secondary grades; in the poorest nations (including several in central Africa), only half of all children ever get to school at all (Najafizadeh & Mennerick, 1992). As a result, 15 percent of Latin Americans, 30 percent of Asians, and 40 percent of Africans are illiterate. Global Map 14–1 shows the extent of illiteracy around the world.

A closer look: India. India is a low-income country where people earn about 7 percent of the income standard in the United States, and most poor families depend on the earnings of children. Thus, even though India has outlawed child labor, many children continue to work in factories—weaving rugs or making handicrafts—up to sixty hours per week, which greatly limits their chances for schooling.

Today, most people in India receive some primary education, typically in crowded schoolrooms where one teacher faces perhaps sixty children (twice as many as in U.S. classrooms). Yet less than half continue on to secondary education, and very few enter college. The result is that only half the people in this vast country are literate.

Patriarchy also shapes Indian education. Indian parents rejoice at the birth of a boy, since he and his future wife both will contribute income to the family.

Year	High School Graduates	College Graduates	Median Years of Schooling
1910	13.5%	2.7%	8.1
1920	16.4	3.3	8.2
1930	19.1	3.9	8.4
1940	24.1	4.6	8.6
1950	33.4	6.0	9.3
1960	41.1	7.7	10.5
1970	55.2	11.0	12.2
1980	68.7	17.0	12.5
1990	77.6	21.3	12.4
2000	84.1	25.6	12.7

TABLE 14–1 Educational Achievement in the United States, 1910–2000*

*For persons twenty-five years of age and over. Percentage for high school graduates includes those who go on to college. Percentage of high school dropouts can be calculated by subtracting percentage of high school graduates from 100 percent.

Source: U.S. Census Bureau (2000).

But a girl is a financial liability, first, because parents must provide a dowry at the time of her marriage, and second, because after her marriage a daughter's work then benefits her husband's family. Thus, many Indians see little reason to invest in the schooling of girls, which is why only 30 percent of girls reach the secondary grades compared to 45 percent of boys. The flip side of this pattern is that a large majority of the children working in Indian factories are girls—a family's way of benefiting from their daughters while they can (United Nations Development Programme, 1995).

SCHOOLING IN HIGH-INCOME COUNTRIES

Ideally, high-income countries offer schooling to everyone. Industrial production demands that workers learn at least the basic "three Rs"—reading, 'riting, and 'rithmetic. Also, literate citizens are able to participate actively in political life.

The United States was among the first countries to set a goal of mass public education. By 1850, half the U.S. population between the ages of five and nineteen was enrolled in school. By 1918, all states required children to attend school until age sixteen or completion of the eighth grade. Table 14–1 shows that a milestone was reached in the mid-1960s, when, for the first time, a majority of U.S. adults had high school diplomas. Today, more than four out of five adults have a high school education, and more than one in four has a four-year college degree.

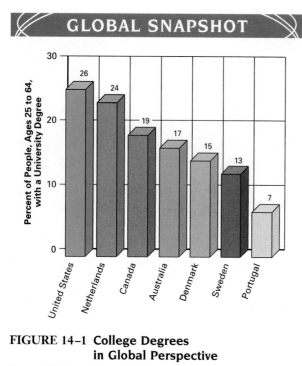

FIGURE 14–1 **College Degrees**
            in Global Perspective
Source: U.S. Census Bureau (2000).

A closer look: Japan. Before industrialization brought mandatory education to Japan in 1872, only a privileged few received schooling. Today, Japan's educational system is widely praised for producing some of the world's highest achievers.

The early grades concentrate on transmitting Japanese traditions, including obligation to family. Starting in their early teens, students take a series of rigorous and highly competitive examinations. These tests, similar to the Scholastic Aptitude Tests (SATs) in the United States, determine a Japanese student's future.

More men and women graduate from high school in Japan (90 percent) than in the United States (84 percent). But competitive examinations allow just 45 percent of high school graduates—compared to 63 percent in the United States—to enter college. Understandably, then, Japanese students take these examinations very seriously, and about half attend cram schools to prepare for them.

Japanese schooling produces impressive results. In a number of fields, notably mathematics and science, Japanese students outperform students in every other high-income country, including the United States (Benedict, 1974; Hayneman & Loxley, 1983; Rohlen, 1983; Brinton, 1988; Simons, 1989).

SCHOOLING IN THE UNITED STATES

Early in U.S. history, Thomas Jefferson declared that this nation could become democratic only if widespread schooling empowered people to "read and understand what is going on in the world" (quoted in Honeywell, 1931:13). As Figure 14–1 shows, no other country has as large a share of adults with university degrees (U.S. Census Bureau, 2000).

Schooling in the United States also tries to promote *equal opportunity.* Most U.S. adults think schooling is crucial to personal success, and a majority also believe that everyone has the chance to get an education consistent with personal talent and ability (NORC, 1999). But this view better expresses our aspirations than our achievement. Early in the twentieth century, for example, U.S. society all but barred women from higher education; and even today, most people who attend college come from families with above-average incomes.

In the United States, the educational system stresses the value of *practical* learning. Thus, today's college students select their majors with an eye toward future jobs. During the last decade, for example, growth areas of the economy (such as health sciences, environmental studies, and ethnic and cultural studies) have all attracted increasing numbers of students (U.S. National Center for Education Statistics, 2001).

THE FUNCTIONS OF SCHOOLING

Structural-functional analysis focuses on ways in which schooling enhances the operation and stability of society:

1. **Socialization.** Technologically simple societies look to families to transmit a way of life from one generation to another. As societies gain complex technology, they turn to trained teachers to convey specialized knowledge.

2. **Cultural innovation.** Schools create as well as transmit culture. Especially at centers of higher education, scholars conduct research that leads to discovery and changes our way of life.

3. **Social integration.** Schools mold a diverse population into a unified society sharing norms and values. This is one reason states enacted mandatory education laws a century ago when immigration turned upward. With minority students now constituting a majority in many urban areas, schooling continues to serve the same purpose today.

From a functionalist point of view, schooling provides children with the knowledge and skills they will need as adults. A conflict analysis adds that schooling differs according to the resources of the local community. When some schools offer children much more than others do, education perpetuates the class structure rather than increases equality of opportunity.

4. **Social placement.** Schools identify talent and see that students receive instruction to meet their needs. Thus, schooling enhances meritocracy by rewarding talent and hard work regardless of social background, and provides a path to upward social mobility.

5. **Latent functions of schooling.** Schooling serves several less widely recognized functions. It provides child care for the growing number of one-parent and two-career families. In addition, it occupies thousands of young people in their twenties who otherwise would be competing for limited opportunities in the job market. High schools, colleges, and universities also bring together people of marriageable age. Lastly, school networks can be a valuable career resource throughout life.

Critical evaluation. Structural-functional analysis stresses ways that formal education supports the operation of a modern society. However, functionalism overlooks the problems inherent in our educational system and ignores the ways in which schooling helps to reproduce the class structure in each generation. In the next section, social-conflict analysis examines precisely these issues.

SCHOOLING AND SOCIAL INEQUALITY

Social-conflict theory counters the functionalist idea that schooling develops everyone's talents and abilities. Rather, this approach studies how schooling causes and perpetuates social inequality:

1. **Social control.** As Samuel Bowles and Herbert Gintis (1976) see it, the clamor for public education in the late nineteenth century arose just as capitalists were demanding a docile and disciplined work force. Once in school, immigrants learned not only the English language but also the importance of discipline and punctuality.

2. **Testing and social inequality.** Critics claim that aptitude tests reflect our society's dominant culture, thereby placing minority students at a disadvantage. By defining majority students as smarter, standardized tests thus transform privilege into personal merit (Owen, 1985; Crouse & Trusheim, 1988; Putka, 1990).

3. **Tracking and social inequality.** Despite controversy over standardized tests, most U.S. schools use them for **tracking,** *assigning students to different types of educational programs,* such as college preparatory classes, general education, and

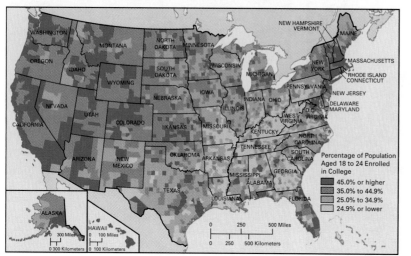

NATIONAL MAP 14-1
College Attendance across the United States

Generally speaking, college attendance is highest among adults along the Northeast and West coasts. By contrast, adults in the Midwest and the South (especially the Appalachian region) are the least likely members of our society to attend college. How would you explain this pattern? (Income is one obvious consideration. Would people's ideas about gender equality be another?)

Source: *American Demographics* magazine, April 1993, p. 60. Reprinted with permission. ©1993 *American Demographics* magazine, Ithaca, New York.

vocational and technical training. Tracking supposedly helps teachers meet a student's individual abilities and interests. Education critic Jonathan Kozol (1992), however, considers tracking one of the "savage inequalities" in our school system. Most students from privileged backgrounds get into higher tracks where they receive the best the school can offer. Students from disadvantaged backgrounds end up in lower tracks where teachers stress memorization and classroom drill (Bowles & Gintis, 1976; Persell, 1977; Davis & Haller, 1981; Oakes, 1982, 1985; Hallinan & Williams, 1989; Kilgore, 1991; Gamoran, 1992).

PUBLIC AND PRIVATE EDUCATION

In 1998, 90 percent of the 51 million primary and secondary school children in the United States attended state-funded public schools. The remainder went to private schools.

Most private school students attend one of the more than 8,000 *parochial* schools (from the Latin, meaning "of the parish") operated by the Roman Catholic church. The Catholic school system grew rapidly a century ago as cities swelled with immigrants. Today, after decades of flight from the inner city by white people, many parochial schools enroll non-Catholics, including a growing number of African Americans whose families seek an alternative to the neighborhood public school.

Protestants, too, have private schools, or Christian academies. These are favored by parents who want religious instruction for their children, as well as parents from all backgrounds who seek higher academic and disciplinary standards (James, 1989; Dent, 1996).

Some 6,000 nonreligious private schools enroll young people, mostly from well-to-do families. Many of these are prestigious and expensive preparatory schools—modeled on British boarding schools—that provide strong academic programs and also teach the mannerisms, attitudes, and social graces of the upper class. Many "preppies" maintain lifelong school-based networks that provide numerous social advantages.

Are private schools better than public schools? Research shows that, holding social background constant, students in private schools do outperform their public school counterparts. This advantage lies in private schools' smaller classes, more rigorous curricula, and greater discipline (Coleman, Hoffer, & Kilgore, 1981; Coleman & Hoffer, 1987).

But all public schools are not created equal. For example, Winnetka, Illinois, one of the richest suburbs in the country, spends more than $8,000 annually per student, compared to less than $3,000 in a poor area like Socorro, Texas (Carroll, 1990). Some states have enacted laws that equalize spending per student in all public school districts. Such measures, however, have met with considerable opposition, as in the case of Vermont, discussed in the opening to this chapter.

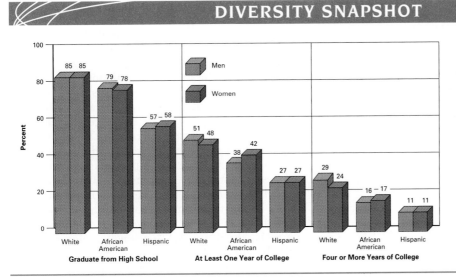

FIGURE 14–2
Educational Achievement for Various Categories of People, Aged 25 Years and Over, 2000

Source: U.S. Census Bureau (2000).

Schools in affluent neighborhoods offer better schooling than less well-funded schools in poor areas. This disparity, which benefits whites over minorities, led districts to institute *busing*—transporting students to achieve racial balance and equal opportunity in schools. Although only 5 percent of U.S. students are bused to schools outside their neighborhoods, this practice is controversial. Advocates claim that, given the reality of racial segregation, the only way governments will adequately fund schools in poor, minority neighborhoods is if white children from richer areas attend them. Critics respond that busing is expensive and undermines the concept of neighborhood schools. But both sides agree that, given the racial imbalance of most urban areas, an effective busing policy would have to join inner cities and suburbs—a plan that is almost never politically feasible.

A classic report by a research team headed by James Coleman (1966) confirmed that schools with predominantly minority enrollments suffer problems ranging from large class size to insufficient libraries and few science labs. But the Coleman report cautioned that more money by itself does not guarantee better schools. More important are the cooperative efforts of teachers, parents, and students. In other words, even if school funding were exactly the same everywhere, students whose families value and encourage learning would still perform better. Put differently, schools alone cannot overcome marked social inequality in the United States (Schneider et al., 1998).

ACCESS TO HIGHER EDUCATION

Schooling is the main path to good jobs. But only 63 percent of high school graduates enroll in college immediately after graduation (U.S. National Center for Education Statistics, 2001). Moreover, about 33 percent of young people aged eighteen to twenty-four are enrolled in college. National Map 14–1 shows where in the country college attendance is more or less likely.

The crucial factor affecting access to higher education is money. College is expensive: Even at state-supported colleges and universities, tuition averages about $3,000 annually, and tuition at the most expensive private colleges and universities exceeds $25,000. High cost is the reason that only one-fourth of families earning less than $20,000 send young people to college compared to two-thirds of affluent families earning $75,000 per year or more (U.S. Census Bureau, 1999).

The financial burden of higher education discourages many minorities, especially those with below-average incomes, from attending college. As Figure 14–2 shows, whites are more likely than African Americans and Latinos to complete high school, and this disparity remains at each step up the educational ladder. Schooling may be the path to social mobility, but it does not erase persistent racial inequality in the United States (Epps, 1995).

For those who complete college, rewards include not just intellectual growth but higher income. Over a lifetime, in fact, a college degree adds almost $500,000

TABLE 14–2 Median Income by Sex and Educational Attainment*		
Education	Men	Women
Professional degree	$96,275 (4.9)	$56,726 (3.9)
Doctorate	76,858 (3.9)	56,345 (3.9)
Master's	61,776 (3.1)	45,345 (3.2)
Bachelor's	51,005 (2.6)	36,340 (2.5)
1–3 years of college	37,245 (1.9)	26,456 (1.8)
4 years of high school	32,098 (1.6)	21,970 (1.5)
9–11 years of school	24,279 (1.2)	16,330 (1.1)
0–8 years of school	19,757 (1.0)	14,375 (1.0)

*Persons aged twenty-five years and over working full time, 1999. The earnings ratio, in parentheses, indicates how many times the lowest income level an individual with additional schooling earns.

Source: U.S. Census Bureau (2000).

to income (Speer, 1994). Table 14–2 shows why. In 1999, women with less than a ninth-grade education typically earned $14,375; high school graduates averaged $21,970, and college graduates, $36,340. The ratios in parentheses show that a woman with a bachelor's degree earns two-and-one-half times as much as a woman with eight or fewer years of schooling. Across the board, men earn considerably more than women; moreover, additional years of schooling boost income faster for men than for women. Finally, for both men and women, some of the greater earnings that come with more schooling have to do with social background, since the people with the most schooling are likely to come from relatively rich families to begin with.

CREDENTIALISM

Sociologist Randall Collins (1979) has dubbed the United States a *credential society* because people regard diplomas and degrees highly. In modern, technologically advanced societies, credentials say "who you are" as much as family background.

Credentialism, then, is *evaluating a person on the basis of educational degrees.* On the surface, credentialism is simply the way our modern society fills jobs with well-trained people. Collins, however, explains that credentials often bear little relation to the responsibilities of a specific job. In reality, advanced degrees often are an easy way to sort out people with the manners, attitudes, and even skin color favored by many employers. Credentialism is thus a gatekeeping strategy that restricts important occupations to a limited segment of the population.

PRIVILEGE AND PERSONAL MERIT

If, as social-conflict analysis suggests, attending college is a rite of passage for affluent men and women, then *schooling transforms social privilege into personal merit.* But, because of our cultural emphasis on individualism, we tend to see credentials as "badges of ability" rather than as symbols of family affluence (Sennett & Cobb, 1973). When we congratulate the new graduate, we rarely recognize the resources—both financial and cultural—that made this achievement possible. Yet, the fact is that young people from families with incomes exceeding $100,000 a year average 1,130 on college board exams—more than 200 points higher than young people from families with $15,000 income. In the same way, we are quick to label the high school dropout "personally deficient," with little thought to the social circumstances of that person's life. The box illustrates this process with the words of one bright but disillusioned child.

Critical evaluation. Social-conflict analysis links formal education to social inequality and shows how schooling transforms privilege into personal worthiness, and disadvantage into personal deficiency. However, critics say that the social-conflict approach minimizes the extent to which schooling provides upward mobility for talented women and men from all backgrounds. Further, despite claims that schooling supports the status quo, today's college curricula challenge social inequality on many fronts.

PROBLEMS IN THE SCHOOLS

An intense debate revolves around schooling in the United States. Because we expect schools to do so much—to equalize opportunity, instill discipline, and fire the individual imagination—few people think public schools are doing an excellent job; about half of adults give our schools a grade of "C" or below (Phi Delta Kappa International, 2000).

DISCIPLINE AND VIOLENCE

When many of today's older teachers think back to their own student days, school "problems" consisted of talking out of turn, chewing gum, breaking the dress code, or cutting class. But today's schools are also grappling with drug and alcohol abuse, teenage pregnancy, and outright violence. It is little wonder that, while almost everyone agrees schools should teach personal discipline, many think the job is no longer being done (NORC, 1999:758).

"Cooling Out" the Poor: Transforming Disadvantage into Deficiency

If schools paint disadvantaged students as "dumb," over time some of them come to believe it. This process of "cooling out" their ambitions sets into motion a self-fulfilling prophecy by which many poor students end up settling for no more than what society handed them when they were born. Eleven-year-old Ollie Taylor describes the experience in these words:

> The only thing that matters in my life is school and there they think I'm dumb and always will be. I'm starting to think they're right. Hell, I know they put all the black kids together in one group if they can, but that doesn't make any difference either. I'm still dumb. Even if I look

around and know that I'm the smartest in my group, all that means is that I'm the smartest of the dumbest, so I haven't got anywhere at all, have I? I'm right where I always was. Every word those teachers tell me, even the ones I like most, I can hear in their voice that what they're really saying is "All right you dumb kids. I'll make it as easy as I can, and if you don't get it then, you'll never get it. Ever." That's what I hear every day, man. From every one of them. Even the other kids talk that way to me too.

Source: Cottle (1974: 22–24.)

In recent years, violence has claimed the lives of students and teachers alike in schools across the United States. Moreover, in national surveys, about one-fourth of high school students and 11 percent of teachers report being victims of violence in and around schools in hundreds of thousands of cases that do not capture national headlines (Arnette & Walsleben, 1998).

Disorder spills into schools from the surrounding society. Nevertheless, schools do have the power to effect change for the better. The key to success appears to be firm disciplinary policies, supported by parents and, if necessary, police. Violence is a problem deep in society itself; however, schools can control violence by forging alliances with parents and community leaders (Gup, 1992).

BUREAUCRACY AND STUDENT PASSIVITY

If some schools are plagued by violence, many more are filled with passive, bored students. Some of the blame for passivity can be placed on television (which

now claims more of young people's time than school), on parents (who are not involved enough with their children), and on the students themselves. But schools, too, must share the blame (Coleman, Hoffer, & Kilgore, 1981).

The small, personal schools that served local communities a century ago have evolved into huge educational factories. In a study of high schools across the United States, Theodore Sizer (1984) identified five ways in which large, bureaucratic schools undermine education (1984:207–9):

1. **Rigid uniformity.** Bureaucratic schools run by outside specialists (such as state education officials) generally ignore the cultural character of local communities and the personal needs of their children.

2. **Numerical ratings**. School officials focus on attendance rates, dropout rates, and achievement test scores. They overlook dimensions of schooling that are difficult to quantify, such as creativity and enthusiasm.

3. **Rigid expectations**. Officials expect fifteen-year-olds to be in the tenth grade and eleventh graders to score at a certain level on a standardized verbal achievement test. Rarely are exceptionally bright and motivated students permitted to graduate early. Likewise, the system pushes poor performers on from grade to grade.

4. **Specialization**. High school students learn Spanish from one teacher, receive guidance from another, and are coached in sports by still others. No school official comes to know the complete student. Students experience this division of labor as a continual shuffling among fifty-minute periods throughout the school day.

5. **Little individual responsibility**. Highly bureaucratic schools do not empower students to learn on their own. Similarly, teachers have little say in what and how they teach; they dare not accelerate learning for fear of disrupting "the system."

Of course, with more than 50 million schoolchildren in the United States, schools have to be bureaucratic to get the job done. But Sizer recommends that we "humanize" schools by eliminating rigid scheduling, reducing class size, and training teachers more broadly to make them more involved in the lives of their students. Moreover, James Coleman (1993) suggests that schools should be less "administratively driven" and more "output-driven." Perhaps this transformation could begin by ensuring that graduation from high school depends on what students have learned rather than how many years they have spent in the building.

COLLEGE: THE SILENT CLASSROOM

Passivity is also common among college and university students (Gimenez, 1989). Sociologists rarely study the college classroom—a curious fact considering how much time they spend there. A fascinating exception is a study of a coeducational university where David Karp and William Yoels (1976) found that, even in small classes, only a few students speak up. Thus, passivity is a classroom norm, and students even become irritated if one of their number is especially talkative.

According to Karp and Yoels, most students think classroom passivity is their own fault. But as anyone who watches young people *outside* of class knows, they are usually active and vocal. Thus, it is schools that teach students to be passive, viewing instructors as "experts" who serve up "truth." Students see their proper role as quietly listening and taking notes. As a

result, the researchers estimate, just 10 percent of college class time is used for discussion.

DROPPING OUT

If many students are passive in class, others are not there at all. The problem of *dropping out*—quitting before earning even a high school diploma—leaves young people (many of whom are disadvantaged to begin with) ill-equipped for the world of work and at high risk for poverty.

The dropout rate has eased slightly in recent decades; currently about 12 percent of people between the ages of sixteen and twenty-four are high school dropouts, a total of some 3.6 million young women and men. Dropping out is least pronounced among non-Hispanic whites (8 percent), higher among non-Hispanic African Americans (14 percent), and most serious among Hispanics (30 percent) (U.S. National Center for Education Statistics, 2001).

Some students drop out because of problems with the English language or because of pregnancy; others must work to support families. The dropout rate (12.3 percent) among children growing up in the poorest 20 percent of all households is seven times higher than that (1.8 percent) for youngsters living in the richest 20 percent of households (U.S. National Center for Education Statistics, 1999). These data suggest that many dropouts are young people whose parents also have little schooling, revealing a multigenerational cycle of disadvantage (Pirog & Magee, 1997).

ACADEMIC STANDARDS

Perhaps the most serious educational issue confronting our society is the quality of schooling. *A Nation at Risk*, a 1983 study of the quality of U.S. schools by the National Commission on Excellence in Education, begins with this alarming statement:

> If an unfriendly foreign power had attempted to impose on America the mediocre educational performance that exists today, we might well have viewed it as an act of war. As it stands, we have allowed this to happen to ourselves. (1983:5)

The report notes that "nearly 40 percent of seventeen-year-olds cannot draw inferences from written material; only one-fifth can write a persuasive essay; and only one-third can solve mathematical problems requiring several steps" (1983:9). Furthermore, scores on the Scholastic Aptitude Test (SAT) have declined since the 1960s. In 1967, median scores were 516 in mathematics and 543 on the verbal test; by 1998, the averages had slipped to 512 and 505, respectively. Nationwide, about one-third of high school students—and more than half of those in urban schools—fail to master even the basics in reading, math, and science on the National Assessment of Education Progress examination (Sanchez, 1998).

A Nation at Risk also notes with alarm the extent of **functional illiteracy,** *a lack of reading and writing skills needed for everyday living.* Today, roughly one in eight U.S. children completes high school without learning basic reading and writing skills. For older people, the problem is even worse, so that about 40 million U.S. adults (about 21 percent of the total) read and write at an eighth-grade level or below. As Figure 14–3 shows, the extent of functional illiteracy in the United States is somewhat higher than in other rich countries such as Canada and Sweden.

A Nation at Risk recommends drastic reform. First, it calls for schools to require *all* students to complete several years of English, mathematics, social studies, general science, and computer science. Second, schools should not promote students from grade to grade until they meet achievement standards. Third, teacher training must improve and teachers' salaries be raised in order to draw talent into the profession. *A Nation at Risk* concludes that schools must meet public expectations and that citizens must be prepared to pay for a job well done.

In global perspective, U.S. students are lagging behind. Despite some recent improvement, our eighth graders place only seventeenth in the world in science achievement and twenty-eighth in mathematics (Bennett, 1997; Finn & Walberg, 1998). Cultural values play some part here. For example, U.S. students are less motivated than their Japanese counterparts and also do less homework. Moreover, Japanese young people spend sixty days more in school than U.S. students. Perhaps one approach to improving schools is simply to have students spend more time there.

RECENT ISSUES IN U.S. EDUCATION

Our society's schools continuously confront new challenges. Here we explore several recent and important educational issues.

SCHOOL CHOICE

Some analysts claim that our schools teach poorly because they have no competition. Thus, giving parents options about schooling their children might

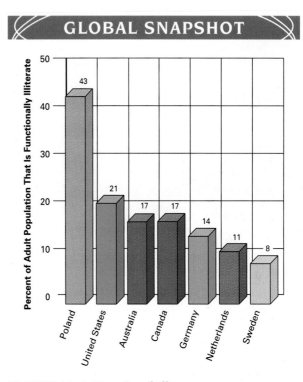

Percent of Adult Population That Is Functionally Illiterate

Poland 43
United States 21
Australia 17
Canada 17
Germany 14
Netherlands 11
Sweden 8

FIGURE 14–3 Functional Illiteracy in Global Perspective

Source: United Nations Development Programme (2000).

force all schools to do a better job. This is the essence of a policy called *school choice.*

Proponents of school choice want to create a market for education so parents and students can shop for the best value. According to one proposal, the government would provide vouchers to families with school-aged children and allow them to spend the money at public, private, or parochial schools. During the 1990s, Indianapolis, Minneapolis, Milwaukee, Cleveland, and the state of Florida experimented with choice plans designed at making public schools perform better to win the confidence of families. In addition, the Children's Scholarship Fund, a privately funded charity, has supported more than 40,000 children who wish to attend nonpublic schools, and has more than 1 million children on its waiting list.

Supporters of school choice claim that the policy does improve schools. But critics (including teachers' unions) charge that school choice amounts to giving up on our nation's commitment to public education and that it will do little to improve schools in the central

Educators have long debated the proper manner in which to school children with disabilities. On the one hand, such children may benefit from distinctive facilities and specially trained teachers. On the other hand, they are less likely to be stigmatized as "different" if included in regular classroom settings. What do you consider to be the ramifications of the "special education" versus "inclusive education" debate for the classroom experience of all *children, not only those who have disabilities?*

cities, where the need is greatest (Martinez et al., 1995; Godwin et al., 1998; Cohen, 1999; Forstmann, 1999).

Yet another recent development in the school choice movement is *schooling for profit*. Advocates say that private profit-making companies can operate schools more efficiently than local governments. Private schooling is nothing new; more than 10,000 schools are now operated by private organizations and religious groups. What is new, however, is the idea that business could carry out *mass* education in the United States.

Research confirms that many public school systems suffer from bureaucratic bloat, spending far too much and teaching far too little. Moreover, our society has long looked to competition to improve quality. But the results of schooling for profit appear mixed. Though companies claim they improve student learning, some cities disagree. In 1995, for example, Baltimore canceled the contract of the corporation that had taken over nine of its schools in 1992; school boards in Miami and Hartford, Connecticut, have also canceled contracts. In short, public school systems

perform poorly in many cities, but whether private business can improve on this record remains unclear.

Finally, *charter schools* are another recent innovation. These are public schools that operate with very little state regulation, so teachers and administrators can try out new teaching strategies. To obtain a "charter," a school must submit a plan for performing as well or better than other schools in the district. In 1998, some 700 charter schools were operating in about half the states (Putka & Stecklow, 1994; Kanamine, 1995; Ravitch & Viteritti, 1996; Bennett, 1997; Toch, 1998).

SCHOOLING PEOPLE WITH DISABILITIES

Bureaucratic school systems do meet the special needs of some children, including many of the 5 million U.S. children with physical impairments. Many children with disabilities have difficulty getting to and from school, and crutches or wheelchairs make it difficult to negotiate stairs and other obstacles in school buildings. Children with developmental disabilities like mental retardation require extensive personal attention from specially trained teachers. As a result, many children with mental and physical disabilities have received a public education only after persistent efforts by parents and other concerned citizens.

About one-fourth of children with disabilities are schooled in special facilities; the rest attend public schools, many joining regular classes. Including students with disabilities into the overall educational program is called *mainstreaming*. This form of *inclusive education* works best for physically impaired students who have no difficulty keeping up with the rest of the class. Moreover, putting children with and without disabilities in the same classroom allows everyone to learn to interact with people who differ from themselves.

ADULT EDUCATION

Most schooling involves young people. However, the share of U.S. students aged twenty-five and older is rising steadily and now accounts for 36 percent of people in the college classroom.

Beyond that, some 76 million U.S. adults (39 percent) enrolled in some educational activity in 1999. They range in age from the mid-twenties to beyond seventy. Adults in school are twice as likely to be women as men, and most have above-average incomes. Some are part-timers; others already have a college diploma or other advanced degrees (Speer, 1996; Miller, 1997a).

What draws adults back to school? The reasons are as varied as the students, but most return to enhance their careers, enrolling in business, health, and engineering courses. Many others, who study everything from astronomy to zen, simply enjoy learning.

LOOKING AHEAD: SCHOOLING IN THE TWENTY-FIRST CENTURY

Despite the fact that the United States leads the world in sending people to college, the public school system struggles with serious problems, many of which have their roots in the larger society. Thus, during the twenty-first century, we cannot expect schools *by themselves* to provide high-quality education. Schools will only improve to the extent that students, teachers, parents, and local communities commit to educational excellence. In short, educational problems are *social* problems, and there is no "quick fix."

For much of the twentieth century, there were just two models for education in the United States: public schools run by the government and private schools operated by nongovernmental organizations. In the last decade, however, many new ideas about schooling have come on the scene, including schooling for profit and a wide range of "choice" programs (Finn & Gau, 1998). In the decades ahead, we will likely see some significant changes in mass education guided, in part, by social science research pointing out the consequences of different strategies.

Another factor that will continue to shape schools is new information technology. Today, 97 percent of primary and secondary schools use computers for instruction. Computers prompt students to be more active and allow them to progress at their own pace. Even so, computers have their limitations; they can never replace the personal insight or imagination of a motivated human teacher. Nor will technology ever solve the problems, including violence and rigid bureaucracy, that plague our schools. What we need is a broad plan for social change that refires this country's early ambition to provide quality universal schooling—a goal that has so far eluded us.

HEALTH

Another institution that expands greatly in modern societies is **medicine,** *the social institution that focuses on combating disease and improving health*. In ideal terms, according to the World Health Organization (1946:3), **health** is *a state of complete physical, mental, and social well-being*. This definition underscores an important idea: *Health is as much a social as a biological issue.*

HEALTH AND SOCIETY

Society affects health in four basic ways:

1. **Cultural patterns define health.** Standards of health vary from culture to culture. Early in this century, yaws, a contagious skin disease, was so common in tropical Africa that people there considered it normal (Dubos, 1980; orig. 1965). "Health," therefore, is sometimes a matter of having the same diseases as one's neighbors (Pinhey, Rubenstein, & Colfax, 1997).

   What people see as healthful also reflects what they think is morally good. People (especially men) in the United States think a competitive way of life is "healthy" because it fits our cultural mores, but stress contributes to heart disease and many other illnesses. On the other hand, people who object to homosexuality on moral grounds often call it "sick," even though it is natural from a biological point of view. Thus, ideas about health amount to a form of social control that encourages conformity to cultural norms.

2. **Cultural standards of health change over time.** Early in the twentieth century, some physicians warned women not to go to college because higher education strained the female brain. Others denounced masturbation as a threat to health. Today, on both counts, we know differently. Fifty years ago, on the other hand, few physicians understood the dangers of cigarette smoking or too much sun exposure, practices that we now recognize as serious health risks.

3. **A society's technology affects people's health.** In poor nations, infectious diseases are rampant because of malnutrition and poor sanitation. As industrialization raises living standards, people become more healthy. But industrial technology also creates new threats to health. As Chapter 15 ("Population, Urbanization, and Environment") explains, rich societies endanger health by overtaxing the world's resources and creating pollution.

4. **Social inequality affects people's health.** All societies distribute resources unequally. Overall, the rich have far better physical, mental, and emotional health than the poor.

TABLE 14–3 The Leading Causes of Death in the United States, 1900 and 1999	
1900	**1999**
1. Influenza and pneumonia	1. Heart disease
2. Tuberculosis	2. Cancer
3. Stomach/ intestinal diseases	3. Stroke
4. Heart disease	4. Lung disease (noncancerous)
5. Cerebral hemorrhage	5. Accidents
6. Kidney disease	6. Pneumonia and influenza
7. Accidents	7. Diabetes
8. Cancer	8. Suicide
9. Diseases in early infancy	9. Kidney disease
10. Diphtheria	10. Chronic liver disease and cirrhosis

Sources: Information for 1900 is from William C. Cockerham, *Medical Sociology*, 2d ed. (Englewood Cliffs, N.J.: Prentice Hall, 1986), p. 24; information for 1999 is from U.S. National Center for Health Statistics, *National Vital Statistics Report* (Hyattsville, Md.: The Center, 2000), vol. 48, no. 11 (October 5, 2000).

HEALTH: A GLOBAL SURVEY

Because health is closely linked to social life, we find that human well-being has improved over the long course of history. For the same reason, we see striking differences in health around the world today.

HEALTH IN LOW-INCOME COUNTRIES

With only simple technology, our ancestors could do little to improve health. Hunters and gatherers faced frequent food shortages, which sometimes forced mothers to abandon their children. Those lucky enough to survive infancy were still vulnerable to injury and illness, so that half died by age twenty and few lived to forty (Lenski, Nolan, & Lenski, 1995).

As people developed agriculture, food became more plentiful. Yet, social inequality, too, increased, so that elites enjoyed better health than peasants and slaves, who lived in crowded, unsanitary shelters and often went hungry. In the growing cities of medieval Europe, human waste and refuse piled up in the streets, spreading infectious diseases, and plagues periodically wiped out entire towns (Mumford, 1961).

`November 1, 1988, central India.` Poverty is not just a matter of what you have; it shapes what you are. Most of the people we see in the villages here have never had

the benefit of a doctor or a dentist. The result is easy to see: People look old before their time.

In much of the world, poverty cuts decades off the life expectancy found in rich countries. A look back at Global Map 9–1 on page 228 shows that in the poorest countries of the world, most people die even before reaching their teens. To make matters worse, medical personnel are few and far between, so that many of the world's poorest people never see a physician.

The World Health Organization reports that 1 billion people around the world—one in six—suffer from serious illness due to poverty. Poor sanitation and malnutrition kill people of all ages. In a classic vicious cycle, poverty breeds disease, which, in turn, reduces people's ability to work. Moreover, when medical technology does control infectious disease, the populations of poor nations soar. But without resources to provide for the people they have now, poor societies can ill afford population growth. Thus, programs to lower death rates in poor countries must be coupled with programs to reduce birth rates as well.

HEALTH IN HIGH-INCOME COUNTRIES

Industrialization dramatically changed patterns of health in Europe, although, at first, not for the better. By 1800, as the Industrial Revolution took hold, factory jobs drew people from all over the countryside. Cities became overcrowded, creating serious sanitation problems. Soon after, factories fouled the air with smoke, and workplace accidents were common.

But industrialization gradually began to improve health in Western Europe and North America as rising living standards translated into better nutrition and safer housing for most people. After 1850, medical advances also improved health, primarily by controlling infectious diseases. In 1854, for example, researcher John Snow mapped the street addresses of London's cholera victims and found they had all drunk contaminated water from the same well (Rockett, 1994). Such discoveries led scientists to link cholera to specific bacteria and, eventually, to develop a vaccine against the deadly disease. Armed with scientific knowledge, early environmentalists campaigned against common practices such as discharging raw sewage into rivers used for drinking water. By the early twentieth century, death rates from infectious diseases had fallen sharply.

Thus, leading killers in 1900—influenza and pneumonia—account for just a few percent of deaths today in the United States. As Table 14–3 shows, it is

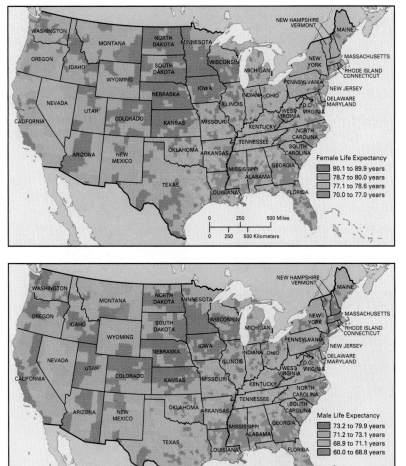

NATIONAL MAP 14–2
Life Expectancy across the United States

These two maps show that, on average, women live longer than men. Yet a gap of roughly twenty years separates people in the healthiest counties of the United States and those in the least healthy counties. Looking over the maps, in which regions of the country is health the best, and the worst? Compare these maps with the income distribution shown in National Map 8–1, on page 213, and the racial distribution shown in National Map 11–4, on page 291. Can you offer an explanation for the differences in health found here?

Source: C. J. L. Murray, C. M. Michand, M. McKenna, and J. Marks, "U.S. County Patterns of Mortality by Race, 1965–1994" (Boston: Harvard School of Public Health, 1997).

now chronic illnesses, such as heart disease, stroke, and cancer, that cause most deaths in the United States. Nothing alters the reality of death, but industrial societies at least manage to delay death until old age (Edmondson, 1997a).

HEALTH IN THE UNITED STATES

Because the United States is a rich nation, the health of its people is generally good by global standards. Still, some categories of people have much better health than others.

WHO IS HEALTHY?
AGE, GENDER, CLASS, AND RACE

Social epidemiology is *the study of how health and disease are distributed throughout a society's population.* Social epidemiologists examine the origin and spread of epidemic diseases and show how people's health is tied to their physical and social environments. National Map 14–2 presents life expectancy—one good measure of overall health—for women and men in different parts of the United States. Note that there is as much as a twenty-year difference in

Masculinity: A Threat to Health?

Doctors call it "coronary-prone behavior." Psychologists call it "Type A personality." Sociologists recognize it as our culture's conception of masculinity. It is a combination of attitudes and behavior, common among men in our society, that includes (1) chronic impatience ("C'mon! Go faster or get outta' my way!"), (2) uncontrolled ambition ("I've gotta' have it . . . I *need* that!"), and (3) free-floating hostility ("Why are so many people *such idiots*?").

This pattern, although normal from a cultural point of view, is one major reason that men who are driven to succeed are at high risk for heart disease. By acting out the Type A personality, we may get the job done, but we set in motion complex biochemical processes that are very hard on the human heart.

Here are a few questions to help you assess your own degree of risk (or that of someone important to you):

1. *Do you believe that a person has to be aggressive to succeed? For you, do "nice guys finish last"?* For your heart's sake, try to remove hostility from your life. One starting point: How about eliminating profanity from your speech? Try replacing aggression with compassion, which can be surprisingly effective in dealing with other people. Medically speaking, compassion and humor—rather than irritation and aggravation—will enhance your life.

2. *How well do you handle uncertainty and opposition?* Do you have moments when you fume, "Why won't the waiter take my order?" or

"Environmentalists are plain nuts!" We all like to know what's going on and we want others to agree with us. But the world often doesn't work this way. Accepting uncertainty and opposition makes us more mature and certainly healthier.

3. *Are you uneasy showing positive emotion?* Many men think giving and accepting love from women, from children, and from other men is a sign of weakness. But the medical truth is that love supports health and hate damages it.

As human beings, we have a great deal of choice about how we live. Think about the choices you make, and reflect on how our society's idea of masculinity often makes us hard on others (including those we love) and—just as important—hard on ourselves.

Sources: Based on Friedman & Rosenman (1974) and Levine (1990).

---

average life expectancy between the richest and poorest communities.

Age and gender. Death is now rare among young people. Still, young people do fall victim to accidents and, more recently, to acquired immune deficiency syndrome (AIDS).

Across the life course, women have better health than men. First, females are less likely than males to die before or immediately after birth. Then, as socialization begins, males develop more aggressive and individualistic personalities, which results in higher rates of accidents, violence, and suicide. As the box explains, the combination of chronic impatience, uncontrolled ambition, and frequent outbursts of hostility that doctors call "coronary-prone behavior" is a fairly close match with our culture's definition of masculinity.

Social class and race. *Infant mortality*—the death rate among children under one year of age—is twice as high for disadvantaged children in the United States as for children born to privilege. While the health of the richest children in this country is the best in the world, our poorest children are as vulnerable to disease as those in low-income nations such as Sudan and Vietnam.

Government researchers report that 74 percent of adults in families with incomes over $35,000 think their health is excellent or very good, but only 42 percent of adults in families earning less than $10,000 say the same. Conversely, only about 4 percent of higher-income people describe their health as fair or poor, compared to almost one-fourth of low-income people (U.S. National Center for Health Statistics, 1999).

Poverty among African Americans—which is about three times the white rate—helps to explain why black people are more likely to die in infancy and, as adults, suffer the effects of violence, drug abuse, and illness. Figure 14–4 shows that the life expectancy for white children born in 1999 is five years greater than for African American children (77.5 years compared to 72.2).

Sex is an even stronger predictor of health than race, since African American females outlive males of either race. From another angle, 79 percent of white men—but just 62 percent of African American men—will live to sixty-five. The comparable figures for women are 87 percent for whites and 77 percent for African Americans.

CIGARETTE SMOKING

Cigarette smoking tops the list of preventable health hazards. Only after World War I did smoking become popular in the United States, and despite growing evidence of its dangers, smoking remained fashionable even a generation ago. Today, however, most adults consider smoking a mild form of social deviance.

The popularity of cigarettes peaked in 1960, when 45 percent of U.S. adults smoked. By 1999, only 23 percent were lighting up (U.S. Centers for Disease Control and Prevention, 2000). Quitting is difficult because cigarette smoke contains nicotine, a physically addictive drug. And many people smoke to cope with stress: Divorced and separated people are likely to smoke, as are the unemployed and people in the armed forces.

Generally speaking, the less schooling people have, the greater their chances of smoking. Moreover, a slightly larger share of U.S. men (24 percent) than women (21 percent) smokes. But cigarettes—the only form of tobacco use popular among women—have taken a toll on women's health. By 1990, lung cancer surpassed breast cancer as a cause of death among U.S. women.

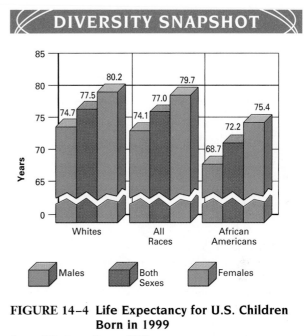

FIGURE 14–4 **Life Expectancy for U.S. Children Born in 1999**

Source: U.S. Census Bureau (2000).

Some 430,000 men and women die prematurely each year as a direct result of cigarette smoking, which exceeds the combined death toll from alcohol, cocaine, heroin, homicide, suicide, automobile accidents, and AIDS (Mosley & Cowley, 1991; U.S. Centers for Disease Control and Prevention, 2000). Smokers also suffer more frequently from minor illnesses such as flu, and pregnant women who smoke increase the likelihood of spontaneous abortion, prenatal death, and low birth-weight babies. Even nonsmokers exposed to cigarette smoke have a high risk of smoking-related diseases.

Tobacco is a $34-billion industry in the United States. In 1997, the tobacco industry conceded that cigarette smoking is harmful to health, and agreed to stop marketing cigarettes to young people. But, despite the antismoking trend in the United States, smoking among college students is on the rise, up from 22 percent in 1992 to 29 percent in 1997 (Neergaard, 1998). In addition, the use of chewing tobacco—also a threat to health—is increasing among the young.

Moreover, the tobacco industry has increased marketing abroad, where there is less government regulation of sales and advertising (Scherer, 1996; Pollack, 1997). Figure 14–5 shows that in many countries (especially in Asia) a large majority of men smoke.

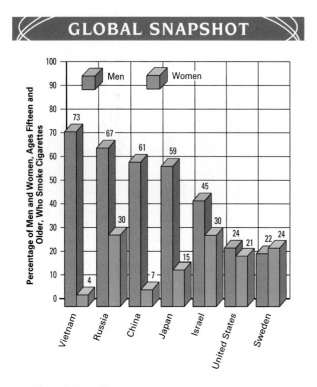

FIGURE 14–5 Cigarette Smoking in Selected Countries

Sources: U.S. Centers for Disease Control and Prevention (2000) and The World Bank (2000).

Worldwide, more than 1 billion adults (about 30 percent of the total) smoke, consuming some 6 trillion cigarettes annually, and smoking is on the rise. The good news is that about ten years after quitting, an ex-smoker's health is about as good as that of someone who never smoked at all.

EATING DISORDERS

An *eating disorder* is an intense form of dieting or other unhealthy method of weight control. One eating disorder, anorexia nervosa, is characterized by dieting to the point of starvation; another is bulimia, which involves binge-eating followed by induced vomiting to avoid weight gain.

One clue to the fact that eating disorders have a significant cultural component is that 95 percent of people who suffer from anorexia nervosa or bulimia are women, mostly from white, affluent families. For women, Michael Levine (1987) explains, U.S. culture equates slenderness with being successful and attractive to men. On the flip side, we tend to stereotype overweight women (and, to a lesser extent, men) as "lazy," "sloppy," and even "stupid."

Research shows that most college-age women believe (1) "guys like thin girls," (2) being thin is crucial to physical attractiveness, and (3) that they are not as thin as men would like. In fact, most college women want to be even thinner than most college men say women should be. For their part, most men display far less dissatisfaction with their own body shape (Fallon & Rozin, 1985).

Since few women approach our culture's unrealistic standards of beauty, many women develop a low self-image. Moreover, our idealized image of beauty leads many young women to diet to the point of risking their health.

SEXUALLY TRANSMITTED DISEASES

Sexual activity, while both pleasurable and vital to the continuation of our species, can transmit more than fifty kinds of infection, or *venereal disease* (from Venus, the Roman goddess of love). Since U.S. culture associates sex with sin, some people regard venereal diseases not only as illnesses but also as marks of immorality.

Sexually transmitted diseases (STDs) grabbed national attention during the "sexual revolution" of the 1960s when infection rates rose as people began sexual activity earlier and had a greater number of partners. As a result, STDs are an exception to the general decline in infectious diseases over the course of the last century. By the late 1980s, the rising danger of STDs, especially AIDS, generated a sexual counter-revolution against casual sex (Kain, 1987; Kain & Hart, 1987). The following sections briefly describe several common STDs.

Gonorrhea and syphilis. Gonorrhea and syphilis, among the oldest diseases, are caused by microscopic organisms that are almost always transmitted by sexual contact. Untreated, gonorrhea causes sterility, while syphilis can damage major organs and result in blindness, mental disorders, and death.

In 1999, about 360,000 cases of gonorrhea and 36,000 instances of syphilis were recorded in the United States, although the actual numbers may be several times higher. Most cases are contracted by non-Hispanic African Americans (77 percent), with lower numbers among non-Hispanic whites (15 percent), Latinos (6 percent), and Asian and Native

While the three wars noted on the billboard claimed 112,171 lives, the death toll from AIDS exceeds 439,000. As serious as this disease is here in the United States, in some world regions (especially sub-Saharan Africa) AIDS deaths are mounting so quickly that entire societies could collapse.

Americans (0.6 percent each) (Masters, Johnson, & Kolodny, 1988; Moran et al., 1989; U.S. Centers for Disease Control and Prevention, 2000). Both gonorrhea and syphilis can be easily cured with antibiotics such as penicillin. Thus, neither is currently a major health problem in the United States.

Genital herpes. Genital herpes is a virus that infects as many as 45 million adults in the United States (one in seven). Though far less serious than gonorrhea and syphilis, herpes is incurable. People with genital herpes may exhibit no symptoms or they may experience periodic, painful blisters on the genitals accompanied by fever and headache. Although not fatal to adults, women with active genital herpes can transmit the disease during a vaginal delivery, and it can be deadly to newborns. Such women, therefore, often give birth by Caesarean section.

AIDS. The most serious of all sexually transmitted diseases is acquired immune deficiency syndrome, or AIDS. Identified in 1981, it is incurable and almost always fatal. AIDS is caused by the human immunodeficiency virus (HIV), which attacks white blood cells, weakening the immune system. AIDS thus renders a person vulnerable to a wide range of other diseases that eventually cause death.

AIDS deaths in the United States dropped to 16,273 in 1999, the lowest number in a decade. But officials recorded some 54,000 new cases in the United States that year, raising the total number of

cases on record to more than 754,000. Of these, about 439,000 have died (U.S. Centers for Disease Control and Prevention, 2000).

Globally, HIV infects some 34 million people—half of them under age twenty-five—and the number is rising rapidly. Global Map 14–2 on page 388 shows that Africa (more specifically, countries south of the Sahara) has the highest HIV infection rate and accounts for two-thirds of all world cases. In the cities of African nations such as Zimbabwe, Botswana, Namibia, and Zambia, roughly one-fifth of all young adults are infected with HIV (Scommegna, 1996; United Nations Development Programme, 2000). It is in Asia, however, where this disease is spreading most quickly. North Americans account for less than 5 percent of global HIV cases.

Upon infection, people with HIV display no symptoms at all, so most are unaware of their condition. Not for a year or longer do symptoms of AIDS appear. Within five years, one-third of infected people develop full-blown AIDS; half develop AIDS within ten years, and almost all become sick within twenty years.

HIV is infectious but not contagious. That is, HIV is transmitted from person to person through blood, semen, or breast milk but *not* through casual contact such as shaking hands, hugging, sharing towels or dishes, swimming together, or even by coughing and sneezing. The risk of transmitting AIDS through saliva (as in kissing) is extremely low. Moreover, the risk of transmitting HIV through sexual activity is

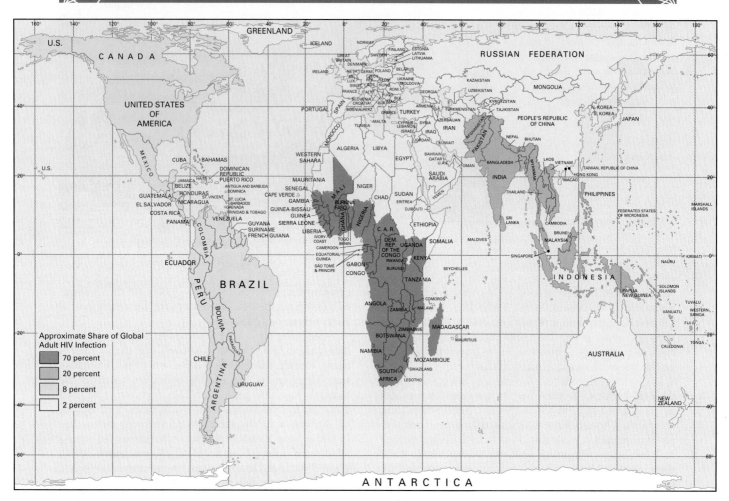

Approximate Share of Global Adult HIV Infection

- 70 percent
- 20 percent
- 8 percent
- 2 percent

GLOBAL MAP 14–2 HIV Infection of Adults in Global Perspective

Almost 70 percent of all global HIV cases are recorded in sub-Saharan Africa. This high infection rate reflects the prevalence of other sexually transmitted diseases and infrequent use of condoms, factors that promote heterosexual transmission of HIV. Southeast Asia, where HIV is spreading most rapidly, accounts for another 20 percent of infections. South and North America together account for 8 percent of all cases. The incidence of infection is still low in the remaining regions of the world.

Sources: Population Reference Bureau (2000); map projection from *Peters Atlas of the World* (1990).

greatly reduced by the use of latex condoms. But in the age of AIDS, abstinence or an exclusive relationship with an uninfected person is the only sure way to avoid infection.

Specific behaviors place people at high risk for HIV infection. The first is *anal sex*, which can cause rectal bleeding, allowing easy transmission of HIV from one person to another. The practice of anal sex explains why homosexual and bisexual men account for 46 percent of AIDS cases in the United States.

Sharing needles used to inject drugs is a second high-risk behavior. At present, intravenous drug users account for 25 percent of persons with AIDS. Sex with an intravenous drug user is also very risky. Because intravenous drug use is more common among poor people in the United States, AIDS is now becoming a disease of the socially disadvantaged. Although 43 percent of people with AIDS are non-Hispanic whites, African Americans (12 percent of the population) account for 38 percent of people with AIDS. More than half of all women with the disease and 59 percent of children with AIDS are African Americans. Similarly, Latinos (12 percent of the population) represent 18 percent of AIDS cases (and 20 percent of women with AIDS). Asian Americans and Native Americans, however, together account for only 1 percent of people with AIDS (Huber & Schneider, 1992; U.S. Centers for Disease Control and Prevention, 2000).

Using any drug, including alcohol, also increases the risk of being infected with HIV to the extent that it impairs judgment. In other words, even people who understand what places them at risk of infection may act less responsibly once they are under the influence of alcohol, marijuana, or some other drug.

As Figure 14–6 shows, only 10 percent of people with AIDS in the United States became infected through heterosexual contact (although heterosexuals, infected in various ways, account for more than 30 percent of AIDS cases). But heterosexual activity does transmit HIV, and the danger rises with the number of sexual partners, especially if they fall into high-risk categories. Worldwide, heterosexual relations are the primary means of HIV transmission, accounting for two-thirds of all infections.

Treating just one person with AIDS costs hundreds of thousands of dollars, and this figure may rise as new therapies appear. At present, government health programs, private insurance, and personal savings rarely cover more than a fraction of the cost of treatment. In addition, there is the mounting cost of caring for at least 75,000 U.S. children orphaned by AIDS. Overall, there is little doubt that AIDS represents both a medical and a social problem of monumental proportions.

The U.S. government responded slowly to the AIDS crisis, largely because gays and intravenous drug users are widely viewed as deviant. But funds allocated for AIDS research have increased (now totaling some $7 billion annually), and researchers have identified some drugs, including protease inhibitors, that suppress the symptoms of the disease. But educational programs remain the most effective weapon against AIDS, since prevention is the only way to stop a disease that has no cure.

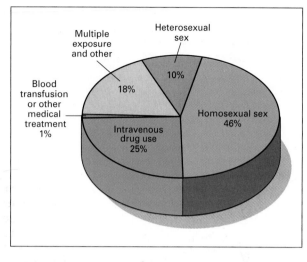

FIGURE 14–6 Types of Transmission for Reported U.S. AIDS Cases, as of 1999

Source: U.S. Centers for Disease Control and Prevention (2000).

ETHICAL ISSUES SURROUNDING DEATH

Another new dimension of health and illness involves medical ethics. Now that technological advances have given human beings the power to draw the line separating life and death, people must decide how and when to do so.

When does death occur? Common sense suggests that life ceases when breathing and heartbeat stop. But the ability to revive or replace a heart and artificially sustain respiration makes this definition of death obsolete. Thus, medical and legal experts in the United States define death as an *irreversible* state involving no response to stimulation, no movement or breathing, no reflexes, and no indication of brain activity (Ladd, 1979; Wall, 1980).

Do people have a right to die? Today, medical personnel, family members, and patients themselves bear the agonizing burden of deciding when a terminally ill person should die. Among the most difficult cases are the 10,000 people in the United States in a permanent vegetative state who cannot express their own desires about life and death. Generally speaking, the first duty of physicians and hospitals is to protect a patient's life. Even so, a mentally competent person in the process of dying can refuse medical treatment or even

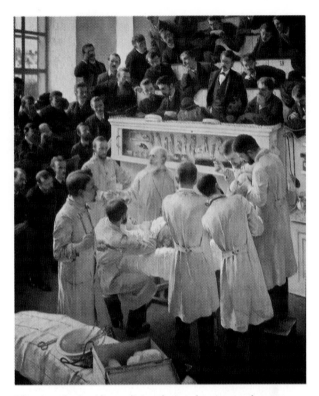

The rise of scientific medicine during the nineteenth century resulted in new skills and technology for treating many common ailments that had afflicted humanity for centuries. At the same time, however, scientific medicine pushed forms of health care involving women to the margins, and placed medicine under the control of men living in cities. We see this pattern in the A. F. Seligmann painting General Hospital, *showing an obviously all-male medical school class in Vienna in 1880.*

nutrition (either at the time or in advance, through a document called a "living will").

Mercy killing is the common term for **euthanasia,** *assisting in the death of a person suffering from an incurable disease.* Euthanasia (from the Greek, meaning "a good death") poses an ethical dilemma, being both an act of kindness and a form of killing.

Whether there is such a thing as a "right to die" is one of today's most difficult issues. All people with incurable diseases have a right to forgo treatment that might prolong their lives. But whether a doctor should be allowed to help bring about death is the heart of today's debate. In 1994, two states—Washington and California—asked voters if physicians should be able to help people who wanted to die; in both cases, voters said no. That same year, however, voters in Oregon approved such a measure. This law remained tied up in state courts until 1997, when voters again endorsed it. Since then, Oregon doctors have legally assisted in the death of terminally ill patients. In 1997, however, the U.S. Supreme Court decided that, under the U.S. Constitution, there is no "right to die," which has slowed the spread of such laws. Moreover, in 1999, Congress began debating a law that would prohibit states from adopting laws similar to the one in Oregon.

Supporters of *active* euthanasia—allowing a dying person to enlist the services of a physician to bring on a quick death—argue that there are circumstances (such as when a dying person suffers from great pain) that make death preferable to life. Critics, however, counter that permitting active euthanasia invites abuse. They fear that patients will feel pressure to end their lives to spare family members the burden of caring for them, as well as the high costs of hospitalization. Further, research in the Netherlands, where physician-assisted suicide is legal, indicates that about one-fifth of all such deaths have occurred without a patient explicitly requesting to die (Gillon, 1999).

In the United States, a majority of adults express support for giving dying people the right to choose to die with a doctor's help (Rosenbaum, 1997; NORC, 1999). Therefore, the "right to die" debate is sure to continue.

THE MEDICAL ESTABLISHMENT

Throughout most of human history, health care was the responsibility of individuals and their families. Medicine emerges as a social institution only as societies become more productive and people take on specialized work.

Members of agrarian societies today still turn to various traditional health practitioners, including acupuncturists and herbalists. In industrial societies, health care falls to specially trained and licensed professionals, from anesthesiologists to X-ray technicians. The medical establishment of modern, industrial societies took form over the last 150 years.

THE RISE OF SCIENTIFIC MEDICINE

In colonial times, herbalists, druggists, midwives, and ministers practiced the healing arts. But not all their methods were effective. Unsanitary instruments, no anesthesia, and simple ignorance made surgery a terrible ordeal, and doctors probably killed as many people as they saved.

But by studying human anatomy and physiology, doctors eventually established themselves as self-regulating professionals with medical degrees. The American Medical Association (AMA) was founded in 1847, and symbolized the growing acceptance of a scientific model of medicine.

Still, traditional approaches to health care had their defenders. The AMA opposed them by seeking control of the certification process. In the early 1900s, state licensing boards agreed to certify only physicians trained in the scientific programs approved by the AMA. As a result, schools teaching other healing skills began to close, which soon limited the practice of medicine to those holding an M.D. degree. Accordingly, the prestige and income of physicians rose dramatically; today, men and women with M.D. degrees earn, on average, almost $200,000 annually.

Practitioners of other approaches, such as osteopathic physicians, concluded that they had no choice but to fall in line and follow AMA standards. Thus osteopaths (with D.O. degrees), who were originally concerned with manipulating the skeleton and muscles, today treat illness with drugs in much the same way as medical doctors (who hold M.D. degrees). Chiropractors, herbalists, and midwives still practice but have been relegated to the fringes of the medical profession.

Scientific medicine, taught in expensive, urban medical schools, also changed the social profile of doctors, so that most physicians came from privileged backgrounds and practiced in cities. Furthermore, women, who had figured in many fields of healing, were scorned by the AMA. Some early medical schools did train women and African Americans, but, with few financial resources, most of these schools eventually closed. Only in recent decades has the social diversity of the medical profession increased, with women and African Americans representing 28 percent and 6 percent of physicians, respectively (Gordon, 1980; Starr, 1982; Huet-Cox, 1984; U.S. Department of Labor, 2001).

HOLISTIC MEDICINE

Recently, the scientific model of medicine has been tempered by the introduction of **holistic medicine,** *an approach to health care that emphasizes prevention of illness and takes into account a person's entire physical and social environment.* Holistic practitioners agree on the

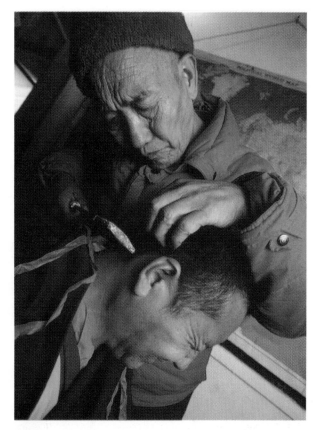

Traditional healers work to improve people's health throughout the world, especially in low-income nations. Here, a Chinese practitioner treats a patient by burning rolled herbs into his scalp.

need for drugs, surgery, artificial organs, and high technology, but they don't want high technology to turn medicine into narrow specialties concerned with symptoms rather than people, and with disease instead of health. Here are three foundations of holistic health care (Duhl, 1980; Ferguson, 1980; Gordon, 1980):

1. **Patients are people.** Holistic practitioners are concerned not only with symptoms but with how people's environment and lifestyle affect health. Holistic practitioners extend the bounds of conventional medicine, taking an active role in combating poverty, environmental pollution, and other dangers to public health.

2. **Responsibility, not dependency.** In the scientific model, patients are dependent on physicians. Holistic medicine tries to shift some responsibility for health from physicians to

GLOBAL SOCIOLOGY

When Health Fails: A Report from Russia

Night is falling in Pitkyaranta, a small town on the western edge of Russia, near the border with Finland. Andrei, a thirty-year-old man with a round face and a long ponytail, has spent much of the afternoon in a bar with friends, watching music videos while drinking vodka and smoking cigarettes. Andrei is a railroad worker, but, several months ago, he was laid off. "Now," he explains bitterly, "I have nothing to do but drink and smoke." Andrei shrugs off a question about his health. "The only thing I care about is finding a job. I am a grown man. I don't want to be supported by my mother and father." Andrei still thinks of himself as young; yet, according to current health patterns in Russia, for a man of thirty, life is half over.

After the collapse of the Soviet Union in 1991, living conditions began getting worse, year after year. One result, say doctors, is massive stress—especially on men who earn too little to support their families or are out of work entirely. Few people eat well any more, and Russian men now drink and smoke

as heavily as people anywhere in the world. The World Health Organization reports that alcohol abuse is Russia's number one killer, with cigarette smoking not far behind.

In towns like Pitkyaranta, the signs of poor health are everywhere: Women no longer breast-feed their babies; the

rate of accidents and illnesses among adults has soared; people look old before their time. Doctors are struggling to stop the health slide, but, with poorly equipped hospitals, they are simply overwhelmed. Statistically, while life expectancy dropped several years for women, men's went into free fall; only a recent recovery has raised men's life expectancy to sixty-one years, about where it was half a century ago. Just 100 miles to the west, in Finland, where economic trends are far better, the comparable figure is seventy-four years. In global context, life expectancy for Russian women has fallen below that in other European countries; for Russian men, life expectancy is only a little better than in some of the world's lowest-income nations.

A joke is making the rounds among young Russian men like Andrei. Their health may be failing, they say, but this cloud has a silver lining: At least they no longer have to worry about retirement.

Source: Adapted from Landsberg (1998).

---

people themselves by emphasizing health-promoting behavior. Holistic medicine favors an *active* approach to *health*, rather than a *reactive* approach to *illness*.

3. **Personal treatment.** Scientific medicine treats patients in impersonal offices and hospitals, both disease-centered settings. Holistic practitioners favor, as much as possible, a personal and relaxed environment such as the home.

In sum, holistic care does not oppose scientific medicine but shifts the emphasis from treating disease to achieving the greatest well-being for everyone. Considering that the AMA certifies more than fifty

medical specialties, there is a need for practitioners concerned with the whole patient.

PAYING FOR HEALTH: A GLOBAL SURVEY

As medicine has come to rely on high technology, the costs of health care in industrial societies have sky-rocketed. To meet these costs, countries have adopted various strategies.

The People's Republic of China. A poor, agrarian society in the process of industrializing, the People's Republic of China faces the daunting task of providing for the health of more than 1 billion people. China has experimented with private medicine, but the government controls most health care.

China's "barefoot doctors," roughly comparable to U.S. paramedics, bring some modern methods of medical care to peasants in rural villages. Traditional healing arts, involving acupuncture and medicinal herbs, are still widely practiced. In addition, the Chinese approach to health is based on a holistic concern with the interplay of mind and body (Sidel & Sidel, 1982b; Kaptchuk, 1985).

The Russian Federation. The Russian Federation is struggling to transform a state-dominated economy into more of a market system. For this reason, medical care is in transition. Nevertheless, the idea that everyone has a right to basic medical care remains widespread.

As in China, people in the Russian Federation do not choose a physician, but report to a local government health facility. Physicians have much lower income than their counterparts in the United States, earning about the same salary as skilled industrial workers (compared to roughly a five-to-one ratio in this country). Worth noting, too, is that about 70 percent of physicians are women, compared with 28 percent in the United States. As in this country, occupations dominated by women yield fewer financial rewards.

Funded by government taxes, health care in the Russian Federation has suffered setbacks in recent years, partly due to a falling standard of living, as the box explains. Moreover, a rising demand for medical care has strained a bureaucratic system that, at best, provides highly standardized and impersonal care. The optimistic view is that, as market reforms proceed, both living standards and the quality of medical service will improve. In any case, what does seem certain is that disparities in medical care among various segments of the population will increase (Specter, 1995; Landsberg, 1998).

Sweden. In 1891, Sweden began a compulsory, comprehensive system of government medical care. Citizens pay for this program with their taxes, which are among the highest in the world. Typically, physicians are government employees and most hospitals are government-managed. Sweden's system is called **socialized medicine,** *a medical care system in which the government owns and operates most medical facilities and employs most physicians.*

Great Britain. In 1948, Great Britain, too, established socialized medicine. The British did not do away with private care, however, but created a dual

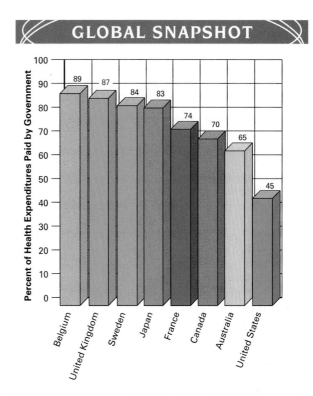

GLOBAL SNAPSHOT

FIGURE 14–7 Extent of Socialized Medicine in Selected Countries

Sources: U.S. Census Bureau (2000) and The World Bank (2000).

system of medical services. All British citizens are entitled to medical care provided by the National Health Service, but those who can afford it can also go to doctors and hospitals that operate privately.

Canada. Canada has a "single payer" model of health care. Like a vast insurance company, the Canadian government pays doctors and hospitals according to a set schedule of fees. But Canada also has a dual system similar to Great Britain's, with some physicians working privately and setting their own fees.

Canada boasts of providing care for everyone at a lower cost than the (nonuniversal) medical care system in the United States. At the same time, however, the Canadian system makes less use of state-of-the-art technology and responds slowly, so that some people wait months for major surgery (Grant, 1984; Vayda & Deber, 1984; Rosenthal, 1991).

Japan. Physicians in Japan operate privately, but a combination of government programs and private insurance pays medical costs. As shown in Figure 14–7, the Japanese approach health care much like the Europeans, with most medical expenses paid through the government.

MEDICINE IN THE UNITED STATES

With our primarily private system of medical care, the United States stands alone among industrialized societies in having no government-operated program of care for everyone. Called a **direct-fee system,** ours is *a medical care system in which patients pay directly for the services of physicians and hospitals.* Thus, while Europeans look to government to fund 80 percent of medical costs (paid for through taxation), the U.S. government pays less than half of this country's medical costs (Lohr, 1988; U.S. Census Bureau, 2000).

In the United States, rich people can purchase the best medical care in the world. Yet poor people fare worse than their counterparts in Europe. This disparity translates into relatively high death rates among both infants and adults in the United States compared to many European countries (United Nations Development Programme, 2000).

Why does the United States have no national health care program? First, our society historically has limited government in the interest of greater personal liberty. Second, political support for a national medical program has not been strong, even among labor unions, which have concentrated on winning health care benefits from employers. Third, the AMA and the insurance industry have strongly and consistently opposed national health care (Starr, 1982).

Medical expenditures in the United States have increased dramatically, from $12 billion in 1950 to more than $1 trillion in 1998. This amounts to more than $4,100 per person, more than any other industrial nation spends for medical care. Who pays the medical bills?

Private insurance programs. In 1999, 172 million people in the United States (63 percent) received medical care benefits from a family member's employer or labor union. Another 23 million people (8 percent) purchased some private coverage on their own. Seventy-one percent of our population, then, has private insurance (such as Blue Cross and Blue Shield), although few such programs pay all medical costs (U.S. Census Bureau, 2000).

Public insurance programs. In 1965, Congress created Medicare and Medicaid. Medicare pays some of the medical costs for people over age sixty-five; in 1999, it covered 36 million men and women, 13 percent of the population. In the same year, Medicaid, a medical insurance program for the poor, provided benefits to 28 million people, about 10 percent of the population. An additional 9 million veterans (3 percent) obtained free care in government-operated hospitals. In all, 24 percent of this country's people get medical benefits from the government, but most also have private insurance.

Health maintenance organizations. About 81 million people (30 percent) in the United States belong to a **health maintenance organization (HMO),** *an organization that provides comprehensive medical care to subscribers for a fixed fee.* HMOs vary in costs and benefits, but none provides full coverage. Their fixed-fee structure makes these organizations profitable if subscribers stay healthy; many, therefore, take a preventive approach to health.

In all, 84 percent of the U.S. population has some medical care coverage, either private or public. Yet most plans do not provide full coverage, so serious illness threatens even middle-class people with financial hardship. Most programs also exclude many medical services, such as dental care and treatment for mental health problems. Worse, 43 million people (about 16 percent of the population) have no medical insurance at all. Almost as many lose their coverage temporarily each year due to layoffs or job changes. Caught in the medical care bind are mostly low- to moderate-income people who cannot afford to become ill but cannot afford to pay for the medical care they need to stay healthy (Altman et al., 1989; Hersch & White-Means, 1993; Smith, 1993; U.S. Census Bureau, 2000).

THEORETICAL ANALYSIS OF MEDICINE

Each of the theoretical paradigms in sociology helps us organize and understand facts and issues concerning human health.

STRUCTURAL-FUNCTIONAL ANALYSIS

Talcott Parsons (1964; orig. 1951) viewed medicine as society's strategy to keep its members healthy. In this scheme, illness is dysfunctional because it reduces people's abilities to perform their roles.

The sick role. Society responds to illness, Parsons argued, not only by providing medical care but also

Our national view of medicine has changed during the last several decades. Television viewers in the 1970s watched doctors like Marcus Welby, M.D., confidently take charge of situations in a fatherly—and almost godlike—manner. By the 1990s, programs like "E.R." gave a more realistic view of the limitations of medicine to address illness, as well as the violence that wracks our society.

by affording people a **sick role,** *patterns of behavior defined as appropriate for those who are ill.* Insofar as people suffer from poor health, the sick role exempts them from everyday responsibilities. However, people cannot simply declare themselves ill; this assessment falls to a recognized medical expert. Furthermore, upon assuming the sick role, the patient must do whatever is needed to regain good health, including cooperating with health professionals.

The physicians' role. Physicians evaluate people's claims of sickness and help restore the sick to normal routines. The physicians' role follows from their specialized knowledge; they expect patients to follow "doctor's orders" in order to complete treatment.

Critical evaluation. Parsons places illness and medicine within the broader organization of society. Others have extended the concept of the sick role to other situations such as pregnancy (Myers & Grasmick, 1989).

One limitation of the sick role is that it applies to acute conditions (like the flu) better than to chronic illness (like heart disease), which may not be reversible. Moreover, a sick person's ability to take time off from work to regain health depends on the person's available resources.

SYMBOLIC-INTERACTION ANALYSIS

The symbolic-interaction paradigm sees society less as a grand system than as a series of complex and changing realities. Health and medical care, therefore, are socially constructed by people in everyday interaction.

Socially constructing illness. If we socially construct both health and illness, it follows that people in a poor society may view malnutrition as normal. Similarly, members of our own society give little thought to the harmful effects of a rich diet.

How we respond to illness, too, is based on social definitions that may or may not square with medical facts. For instance, people with AIDS may contend with prejudice that has no medical basis. Likewise, students may pay no attention to symptoms of illness on the eve of vacation, but dutifully report to the infirmary hours before a midterm examination. Health, in short, is less an objective fact than a negotiated outcome.

Indeed, how people define a medical situation may actually affect how they feel. Medical experts marvel at *psychosomatic* disorders (a fusion of the Greek words for "mind" and "body"), when state of mind guides physical sensations (Hamrick, Anspaugh, & Ezell, 1986). Applying sociologist W. I. Thomas's theorem (1966;

orig. 1931), we can say that when health or illness is defined as real, it becomes real in its consequences.

Socially constructing treatment. In Chapter 4, we used Erving Goffman's dramaturgical approach to explain how physicians tailor their physical surroundings (their office) and their behavior (the "presentation of self") so that others see them as competent and in charge. Sociologist Joan Emerson (1970) further illustrates this process of reality construction in her analysis of the gynecological examination carried out by a male doctor. The situation is vulnerable to serious misinterpretation since a man's touching a woman's genitals is conventionally viewed as a sexual act and possibly even an assault.

To ensure that the situation is defined as impersonal and professional, the staff wear uniforms, and the examination room is furnished with nothing but medical equipment. The doctor's manner is designed to make the patient feel that, to him, examining the genital area is no different from treating any other part of the body. A female nurse is usually present not only to assist the physician but to dispel any impression that a man and woman are "alone together."

Managing situational definitions is not taught in medical schools. This is unfortunate because, as Emerson's analysis shows, understanding how medical personnel construct reality in the examination room is as important as mastering the medical skills required for effective treatment.

Critical evaluation. The symbolic-interaction paradigm reveals that what people view as healthful or harmful may depend on factors that are not, strictly speaking, medical. This approach also shows that in any medical procedure both patient and medical staff engage in a subtle process of reality construction.

Critics fault this approach for implying that there are no objective standards of well-being. Certain physical conditions do indeed cause specific changes in people, regardless of how we may view those conditions. People who lack sufficient nutrition and safe water, for example, suffer from their unhealthy environment, whether they define their surroundings as normal or not.

SOCIAL-CONFLICT ANALYSIS

Social-conflict analysis points out the connection between health and social inequality and, taking a cue from Karl Marx, ties medicine to the operation of capitalism. Researchers have focused on three main issues: access to medical care, the effects of the profit motive, and the politics of medicine.

Access to care. Health is important to everyone. But by making health a commodity, capitalist societies allow health to follow wealth. The access problem is more serious in the United States than in most other high-income nations because our country has no universal medical care system.

Conflict theorists argue that capitalism provides excellent health care for the rich but not for the rest of the population. Most of the 43 million people in the United States who lack any medical care coverage at present have low incomes.

The profit motive. Some social-conflict analysts go further, arguing that the real problem is not access to medical care but the character of capitalist medicine itself. The profit motive turns physicians, hospitals, and the pharmaceutical industry into multibillion-dollar corporations. The quest for higher profits encourages unnecessary tests and surgery and an overreliance on drugs (Ehrenreich, 1978; Kaplan et al., 1985).

Of some 24 million surgical operations performed in the United States each year, three-fourths are "elective," meaning that they are intended to promote long-term health and are not prompted by a medical emergency. And, of course, any medical procedure or use of drugs is risky and harms between 5 and 10 percent of patients. Therefore, social-conflict theorists contend that most surgery reflects the financial interests of surgeons and hospitals as much as the medical needs of patients (Illich, 1976; Sidel & Sidel, 1982a; Cowley, 1995).

Finally, say conflict theorists, our society is all too tolerant of physicians having a direct financial interest in the tests and procedures they order for their patients (Pear & Eckholm, 1991). In short, health care should be motivated by a concern for people, not profits.

Medicine as politics. Although science declares itself to be politically neutral, scientific medicine frequently takes sides on significant social issues. For example, the medical establishment has always strongly opposed government health care programs. Moreover, the history of medicine shows that racial and sexual discrimination have been supported by "scientific" opinions (Leavitt, 1984). Consider the diagnosis of "hysteria," a term that has its origins in the Greek word *hyster*, meaning "uterus." In choosing this word to describe a wild, emotional state, the medical profession suggested that being a woman is somehow the same as being irrational.

Even today, according to conflict theory, scientific medicine explains illness in terms of bacteria and viruses, ignoring the damaging effects of social

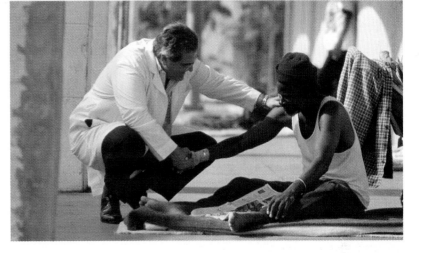

Despite the efforts of exemplary physicians such as Dr. Joe Greer, homeless people throughout the United States have a great need for medical support but receive little health care. In your opinion, what changes are needed to meet the needs of society's most vulnerable members?

inequality. In other words, scientific medicine depoliticizes health in the United States by reducing social issues to simple biology.

Critical evaluation. Social-conflict analysis provides still another view of the relationships among health, medicine, and society. According to this paradigm, social inequality is the reason some people have better health than others.

The most common objection to the conflict approach is that it minimizes the advances in U.S. health that can be credited to scientific medicine and higher living standards. Though there is plenty of room for improvement, health indicators for our population as a whole rose steadily over the course of the twentieth century, and we compare well with all other societies.

In sum, sociology's three major theoretical paradigms explain why health and medicine are social issues. Indeed, as the box on pages 398–99 explains, advancing technology is making this more true all the time. The famous French scientist Louis Pasteur (1822–1895), who spent much of his life studying how bacteria cause disease, said just before he died that health depends less on bacteria than on the social environment in which bacteria operate (Gordon, 1980:7). Explaining Pasteur's insight is sociology's contribution to human health.

LOOKING AHEAD: HEALTH IN THE TWENTY-FIRST CENTURY

At the beginning of the twentieth century, deaths from infectious diseases like diphtheria and measles were widespread, and scientists had yet to develop penicillin and other antibiotics. Even a simple infection from a minor wound, therefore, was sometimes life threatening. Today, a century later, most members of our society take good health and long life for granted. It seems reasonable to expect improvements in U.S. health to continue throughout this new century.

Another encouraging trend is that more people are taking responsibility for their own health (Caplow et al., 1991). Every one of us can live better and longer if we avoid tobacco, eat sensibly and in moderation, and exercise regularly.

Yet, health problems will continue to plague U.S. society in the decades to come. The biggest problem, discussed throughout this chapter, is this nation's double standard in health: well-being for the rich but higher rates of disease for the poor. International comparisons reveal that the United States lags in many measures of human health because we neglect those at the margins of our society. An important question for this new century, then, is, how can a rich society afford to let millions of people live without the security of medical care?

Finally, we find that health problems are far greater in low-income nations than in the United States. The good news is that life expectancy for the world as a whole has been rising—from forty-eight years in 1950 to sixty-six years today—and the biggest gains have been in poor countries (Population Reference Bureau, 2000). But in much of Latin America, Asia, and especially Africa, hundreds of millions of adults and children lack not only medical attention but adequate food and safe water. Improving the health of the world's poorest people is a critical challenge in the twenty-first century.

The Genetic Crystal Ball:
Do We Really Want to Look?

The liquid in the laboratory test tube seems ordinary enough, rather like a syrupy form of water. But this liquid is one of the greatest medical breakthroughs of all time; it may even hold the key to life itself. The liquid is deoxyribonucleic acid, or DNA, the spiraling molecule, found in every cell of the human body, that contains the blueprint for making each one of us human as well as different from every other person.

The human body is composed of some 100 trillion cells, most of which contain a nucleus of twenty-three pairs of chromosomes (one of each pair comes from each parent). Each chromosome is packed with DNA in segments called genes. Genes guide the production of protein, the building block of the human body.

If genetics sounds complicated (and it is), the social implications of genetic knowledge are even more complex. Scientists discovered the structure of the DNA molecule in 1952, and, in 2000, scientists reported that they were finally nearing the goal of "mapping" our genetic landscape. Doing this may lead to understanding how each bit of DNA shapes our being. But do we really want to turn the key, to understand life itself?

In the Human Genome Project, many scientists see the chance to stop illness before it begins. Research, they point out, already has identified genetic abnormalities that cause some forms of cancer, sickle cell anemia, muscular dystrophy, Huntington's disease, cystic fibrosis, and other crippling and deadly afflictions. In the twenty-first century, genetic screening—a scientific "crystal ball"—could tell people their medical destiny and allow doctors to manipulate segments of DNA to prevent diseases before they appear.

But many people urge caution in such research, warning that genetic information can easily be abused. At its worst, genetic mapping opens the door to Nazilike efforts to breed a "superrace." Indeed, in 1994, the People's Republic of China began to regulate

SUMMARY

EDUCATION

1. Education is a major social institution for transmitting knowledge and skills as well as passing on norms and values. In preindustrial societies, education occurs informally within the family; industrial societies develop formal systems of schooling.

2. The United States was among the first nations to institute compulsory mass public education, reflecting both democratic political ideals and the needs of an industrial-capitalist economy.

3. The structural-functional paradigm highlights the functions of schooling, including socialization, social placement, social integration, and innovation. Latent functions include child care and building social networks.

4. Social-conflict analysis links schooling to social hierarchies involving class, race, and gender. Formal education is seen as generating conformity in order to produce compliant adult workers.

5. The great majority of young people in the United States attend state-funded public schools. Most privately funded schools are affiliated with religious organizations.

6. More than one-fourth of U.S. adults over the age of twenty-five are college graduates, marking the emergence of a credential society.

7. National opinion is critical of public schools. Violence permeates many U.S. schools, and educational bureaucracy fosters high dropout rates and widespread student passivity. Declining achievement test scores point to a slide in academic standards.

8. The school choice movement seeks to make educational systems more responsive to the public they serve.

9. Children with mental or physical disabilities historically have been schooled in special classes or not at all. Mainstreaming is an attempt to afford them broader opportunities.

marriage and childbirth with the purpose of avoiding "new births of inferior quality."

It seems inevitable that some parents will want to use genetic testing in order to predict the health (or even the eye color) of their future child. What if they wish to abort a fetus because it falls short of their standards? Or, later, when genetic manipulations become possible, should parents be able to create "designer children"?

Then there is the issue of "genetic privacy." Can a prospective spouse request a genetic evaluation of her fiancé before agreeing to marry? Can life insurance companies demand genetic testing before issuing policies? Can an employer screen job applicants to weed out those whose future illnesses might drain their health care funds? Clearly, what is scientifically possible is not always morally desirable. Society is already grappling with

questions about the proper use of our expanding knowledge of human genetics. Such ethical dilemmas will only mount

Scientists are learning more and more about the genetic factors that prompt the eventual development of serious diseases. If offered the opportunity, would you want to undergo a genetic screening that would predict the long-term future of your own health?

as genetic research moves forward in years to come.

Continue the debate . . .

1. *Traditional wedding vows join couples "in sickness and in health." Do you think individuals have a right to know the future health of their potential partner before tying the knot?*

2. *What about the desire of some parents to genetically design their children?*

3. *Is it right that private companies doing genetic work are able to patent their discoveries so that they alone can profit from the results?*

Sources: Elmer-Dewitt (1994a), L. Thompson (1994), Nash (1995), Golden (1999a), and D. Thompson (1999).

MEDICINE

1. Health is a social issue because well-being depends on a society's technology and distribution of resources. Culture shapes definitions of health and patterns of health care.

2. Poor nations suffer from inadequate sanitation, hunger, and other problems linked to poverty. Life expectancy is about twenty years less than in rich countries such as the United States; in the poorest nations, half the children do not survive to adulthood.

3. Health improved dramatically in Western Europe and North America in the nineteenth century, first due to industrialization and later because of medical advances.

4. Infectious diseases were leading killers a century ago. Today, most people in the United States die in old age of chronic illnesses like heart disease, cancer, or stroke.

5. More than three-fourths of U.S. children born today can expect to reach age sixty-five. Throughout the life course, women have relatively better health than men, and people of high social position enjoy better health than others.

6. Cigarette smoking is the greatest preventable cause of death in the United States.

7. The incidence of sexually transmitted diseases has risen since 1960, an exception to the general decline in infectious disease.

8. Advancing medical technology presents ethical dilemmas concerning how and when death should occur.

9. Historically a family concern, health care is now the responsibility of trained specialists. The model of scientific medicine underlies the U.S. medical establishment. The holistic approach seeks to give people greater responsibility for their own health.

10. Socialist societies define medical care as a right that governments offer equally to everyone. Capitalist societies view medical care as a commodity to be purchased, although most capitalist governments (the United States being a significant exception) subsidize medical care through socialized medicine or national health insurance.

11. Central to the structural-functional analysis of health is the concept of the sick role, which releases sick people from routine responsibilities. The symbolic-interaction paradigm investigates the social construction of both health and medical treatment. Social-conflict analysis focuses on the unequal access to health care within the population and criticizes our medical system for its profit orientation.

KEY CONCEPTS

EDUCATION

education (p. 370) the social institution through which society provides its members with important knowledge, including basic facts and job skills as well as cultural norms and values

schooling (p. 371) formal instruction under the direction of specially trained teachers

tracking (p. 373) the assignment of students to different types of educational programs

credentialism (p. 376) evaluating a person on the basis of educational degrees

functional illiteracy (p. 379) a lack of reading and writing skills needed for everyday living

MEDICINE

medicine (p. 381) the social institution that focuses on combating disease and improving health

health (p. 381) a state of complete physical, mental, and social well-being

social epidemiology (p. 383) the study of how health and disease are distributed throughout a society's population

euthanasia (p. 390) (mercy killing) assisting in the death of a person suffering from an incurable illness

holistic medicine (p. 391) an approach to health care that emphasizes prevention of illness and takes into account a person's entire physical and social environment

socialized medicine (p. 393) a medical care system in which the government owns and operates most medical facilities and employs most physicians

direct-fee system (p. 394) a medical care system in which patients pay directly for the services of physicians and hospitals

health maintenance organization (HMO) (p. 394) an organization that provides comprehensive medical care to subscribers for a fixed fee

sick role (p. 395) patterns of behavior defined as appropriate for those who are ill

CRITICAL-THINKING QUESTIONS

1. Why does industrialization lead societies to expand their system of schooling?

2. Do you agree with research findings in this chapter that, by and large, college students are passive in class? How might colleges make students more active participants in learning?

3. Explain why health is as much a social as a biological issue.

4. Can you point to ways in which people can take responsibility for their own health? What traits of society as a whole shape patterns of health?

APPLICATIONS AND EXERCISES

1. Arrange to visit a secondary school near your college or home. Talk with an administrator to assess the extent of "tracking" the school uses. What seems to be the racial/economic/social background of most students in the higher-level, and lower-level, classes?

2. Most people agree that teaching our children is a vital task. Yet most teachers earn relatively low salaries. Check the prestige ranking for teachers back in Table 8–3 on page 203. What can you find out at the library (check with the government documents librarian) about the average salaries of teachers compared to other workers? Can you explain this pattern?

3. Since 1975, the federal government and every state have passed special education laws providing for children with physical disabilities. After the passage of the Americans with Disabilities Act in 1990, schools have sought to "accommodate" students with a broader range of physical and mental disabilities. Do some library research or contact officials on your campus to learn more about how these laws are changing education.

4. Arrange to speak with a midwife about her work helping women bear their babies. How do midwives differ in their approach from medical obstetricians?

5. In most communities, a trip to the local courthouse is all it takes to find public records showing people's cause of death. Take a look at such records for people who lived in your community a century ago, and for more recent residents. What patterns in life expectancy emerge? How do causes of death differ?

6. Install the CD-ROM packaged in the back of this new textbook to access a variety of study, review, and applications exercises designed to help you better understand the material covered in this chapter. The CD includes an author's tip video, as well as interactive maps, video application exercises, Web links, and study questions.

 SITES TO SEE

http://www.prenhall.com/macionis

Visit the interactive Web site that accompanies this text. Begin by clicking on the cover of your book. You will find a chapter-by-chapter study guide, practice tests, chat room, and many suggested Web links.

http://www.chronicle.com

This site provides general news and information about higher education.

http://www.kenyon.edu/projects/famfarm/welcome/welcome.htm

Visit the Family Farm Web site at Kenyon College. This site was created by students to share what they have learned about farming and rural life in a rural county in central Ohio.

http://www.acpe.asu.edu/VirtualU/

To explore how new information technology is reshaping education, read about the founding of Western Virtual University, this country's first "cyber-college." Think about the advantages and disadvantages of this type of schooling.

www.nces.ed.gov/pubs98/violence/index.html

School violence is the focus of this government Web site.

http://www.cdc.gov

The Web site for the Centers for Disease Control and Prevention provides health news, statistical data, and even traveler's health advisories.

http://www.who.int/

The World Health Organization provides health indicators for many of the world's nations, as well as data profiling the health of the U.S. population.

http://www.unaids.org

Up-to-date information about the global AIDS epidemic can be found at this site, operated by the United Nations.

http://www.doctorsoftheworld.org
http://www.imc-la.org
http://www.dwb.org

Here are Web sites for several organizations of physicians that are involved in improving health around the world. The first is operated by Doctors of the World; the second presents the International Medical Corps; and the third profiles Doctors without Borders.

NEW INFORMATION TECHNOLOGY AND SOCIAL INSTITUTIONS

Social institutions change over time for many reasons. One source of change is societal conflict over how social institutions ought to operate. In Chapters 12 through 14, we have highlighted debates about what kind of economy works best, how democratic our political system really is, the meaning of "the family," the role of religion in the modern world, the ways schools go about doing the job of teaching young people, and how nations provide health care to their people.

Another source of change is technology. In the information age, all social institutions are in transition as computers and other communications equipment play a greater role in our lives. This fourth cyber.scope briefly reviews ways in which computer technology is reshaping several of the major social institutions.

The Symbolic Economy

The computer is at the center of the postindustrial economy. As Chapter 12 ("Economics and Politics") noted, work in the postindustrial economy is less likely to involve making *things* and more likely to involve manipulating *symbols*. Thus, gaining literacy skills is as crucial to success in the new century as learning mechanical skills was to workers a century ago.

As the industrial age progressed, machines took over more and more of the manual skills performed by human workers. We might well wonder, then, if computers are destined to replace humans to perform many of the tasks that involve *thinking*. After all,

the human brain is capable of only 100 calculations per second; the most powerful computers process information a billion times faster.

Then, too, the expanding array of information available through the Internet to people with computer access may make many traditional jobs obsolete. Will we need as many librarians, when people can browse online catalogs of books? (Indeed, will we even need *libraries* as we have

A century ago, shopping meant walking down Main Street, the familiar business district at the center of countless cities and small towns. Fifty years ago, shopping took people to the suburban malls, larger and more impersonal retail centers. Today, commerce is moving to cyberspace, where people shop in a colorful but totally impersonal environment.

known them in the past?) Will there still be travel agents, when anyone can readily access flight schedules, shop for good fares, and purchase tickets, as well as reserve hotel rooms and rental cars on the 'Net? Even mall shopping is beginning to lose some of its popularity as consumers purchase more products from online vendors.

Finally, computer technology seems sure to accelerate the expansion of a global economy as the Internet draws together businesses and consumers into a worldwide market. Perhaps, in the computer-based economy of the twenty-first century, we will have to invent a new "virtual currency" to replace the outmoded idea of paper money.

Politics in the Information Age

Cyberspace, by its very nature, is both global and without centralized control. In the emerging information age, it is likely that the current system of dividing humanity into almost 200 distinct nation-states will evolve into a new form. In other words, because the flow of information is unaffected by national boundaries, it makes less and less sense to think of people—who may work, shop, and communicate with others all over the world—as citizens of one geographically bounded nation.

What effect will the global flow of information have on politics itself? By increasing the amount of available information and helping people to communicate more easily, cyber-technology undoubtedly will be a force for political democracy. As long as computer-based communication remains free of government control, at least, how can a totalitarian political order persist?

On the other hand, should governments gain control of computer-based communication, they will have a powerful new tool for spreading propaganda and manipulating their populations. Or, more modestly, governments bent on tyranny may not be able to control the global Internet, but they may try to control access to computer technology within their borders. Such regulation of information would be a blow to democracy, of course. At the same time, however, any nation would pay a high economic price for isolating itself from the expanding world of computer-based information and trade.

Families of the Future

Over the centuries, new technology has shaped and reshaped the family. The Industrial Revolution moved work from farm and home to factories, making "the job" and "the family" separate spheres of life.

More recently, the Information Revolution is creating the opposite effect as new communications technology allows people to work at home (or, with portable computers and telephones, to work anywhere). The trend toward *decentralizing* work means that, for more and more people, the line between "the office" and "the home" is disappearing.

In some respects, this trend should strengthen families, allowing parents, for example, to create more flexible work schedules and placing both fathers and mothers closer to children. Yet, in the cyber age, televisions

New information technology is spreading ideas and images around the world as never before. These young women live in Malaysia, a relatively traditional society. How do you think the spread of culture via the Internet from the United States and other high–income countries will affect the labor force, family patterns, and the desire for education in societies like this one? Will changes be for the better or worse? Why?

and computers are playing a larger role in socializing the young. In short, families may be able to spend more time together in this new century, but whether they will choose to do so is less certain.

Medicine and the Pursuit of Health

Just as computer technology is decentralizing work, so it is making medical care more readily available. In the years to come, many routine health checks (pulse rate, blood pressure, heart function) can be performed at home by people with computer access who transmit data via modem to specialists at medical centers.

Around the world, too, new information technology is making better health care available to more people. In the United States, hospitals now rely on Internet sites to match patients and available organs, with the result of saving lives. In villages throughout poor nations, practitioners in clinics now log on to computers to consult with specialists in

medical centers in the world's largest cities, gaining the information they need to provide more effective treatments. In recent years, for example, computer links have been vital in helping physicians in central Africa share news, skills, and equipment while fighting the outbreak of the deadly Ebola virus.

New information technology is also making an important contribution to the lives of people with mental and physical disabilities. On one level, new computer programs allow officials to determine whether or not plans for new public buildings and private homes will include access to people with disabilities. On another level, specialists at numerous universities and hospitals now use computer simulations to train children to operate wheelchairs and to teach mentally retarded adults to ride the train or bus. More broadly, computers now allow people with physical and mental limitations to enjoy and learn from virtual experiences, including travel, skiing, and even hang gliding, that seemed impossible a generation ago (Briggs, 1996).

Institutions and Technology: Each Shaping the Other

New technology is bringing changes to all aspects of our lives. But although technology is a powerful agent of change, it does not determine the shape of society. On the contrary, technology alters the boundaries of what is possible. Therefore, *how* and even *if* we employ new information technology is an important decision that societies must make. How we decide these questions comes back to our social institutions, which, after all, define *for whom* society should operate in the first place.

chapter 15

POPULATION, URBANIZATION, AND ENVIRONMENT

Millard Sheets, *Tenement Flats (Family Flats)*, ca. 1934.
National Museum of American Art, Washington, D.C./Art Resource, N.Y.

One hundred fifty years ago, the area was little more than wilderness. Today, the city of Atlanta stretches 110 miles across northern Georgia, and is pushing out in all directions as fast as any city in history. In the last twenty years, its physical size has doubled, and there is no end in sight. Atlanta is truly an urban explosion that is consuming 500 acres of fields and farmland every week (Lacayo, 1999).

Growth like this prompted experts to coin the term "urban sprawl." Such uncontrolled growth is the result of more and more people, all of whom want bigger houses as well as the conveniences offered by superhighways, schools, recreation facilities, and, of course, shopping malls. No doubt, many people in the United States see this kind of growth as good—a sign of economic prosperity.

But is it that simple? This chapter examines three closely related processes: population increase, urbanization, and the declining health of the natural environment. As we shall see, population has soared during the past two centuries—not just in the United States but around the world—and cities everywhere have grown rapidly. We shall consider how these changes have altered the shape of societies and what they mean for the future of the planet. We begin with population.

DEMOGRAPHY: THE STUDY OF POPULATION

From the time people first walked the earth some 250,000 years ago, up until just 250 years ago, the earth's entire population was about 500 million—about the number of people in Latin America and the Caribbean today. Life for our ancestors was often brutal and usually short. People fell victim to countless diseases, frequent injuries, and periodic natural disasters.

But about 1750, world population began to spike upward. We now add 77 million people to the planet each year so that, in 1999, the number of people living on the earth passed the 6 billion mark.

The causes and consequences of this drama are the focus of **demography,** *the study of human population.* Demography (from the Greek, meaning "description of people"), is a specialty within sociology that analyzes the size and composition of a population and studies how people move from place to place. Demographers

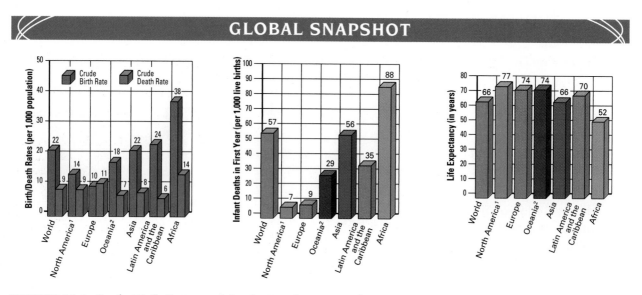

FIGURE 15–1 Crude Birth Rates and Crude Death Rates, Infant Mortality Rates, and Life Expectancy, 2000

[1]United States and Canada

[2]Australia, New Zealand, and South Pacific Islands

Source: Population Reference Bureau (2000).

not only collect statistics, they also pose important questions about the effects of population growth and how population might be controlled. The following sections present basic demographic concepts.

FERTILITY

The study of human population begins with how many people are born. **Fertility** is *the incidence of childbearing in a country's population.* During her childbearing years, from the onset of menstruation (typically in the early teens) to menopause (usually in the late forties), a woman is capable of bearing more than twenty children. But *fecundity,* or maximum possible childbearing, is sharply reduced by cultural norms, finances, and personal choice.

Demographers gauge fertility using the **crude birth rate,** *the number of live births in a given year for every thousand people in a population.* To calculate a crude birth rate, divide the number of live births in a year by the society's total population and multiply the result by 1,000. In the United States in 1998, there were 3.9 million live births in a population of 270 million (U.S. National Center for Health Statistics, 1998). That yields a crude birth rate of 14.4.

This birth rate is "crude" because it is based on the entire population, not just women in their childbearing years. Comparing crude birth rates for various countries can be misleading, then, if one society has a larger share of women of childbearing age than another. A crude birth rate also ignores differences among various racial and ethnic categories. But this measure is easy to calculate and gives a good measure of a society's overall fertility. Figure 15–1 shows that, in global perspective, the crude birth rate of North Americans is low.

MORTALITY

Population size also reflects **mortality,** *the incidence of death in a country's population.* To measure mortality, demographers use a **crude death rate,** *the number of deaths in a given year for every thousand people in a population.* This time, we take the number of deaths in a year, divide by the total population, and multiply the result by 1,000. In 1998, there were 2.4 million deaths in the U.S. population of 270 million, yielding a crude death rate of 8.8. As Figure 15–1 shows, in global context, this rate is about average.

A third useful demographic measure is the **infant mortality rate,** *the number of deaths among infants*

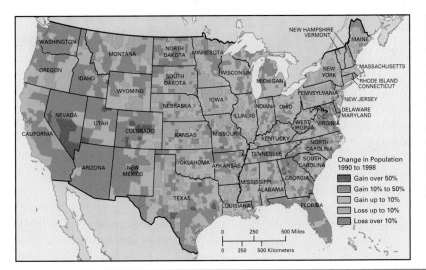

NATIONAL MAP 15–1
Population Change
across the United States

In general, population is moving from the heartland of the United States toward the coasts. What do you think is causing this internal migration? Can you offer a demographic profile of the people who remain in counties that are losing population?

Source: U.S. Census Bureau (2000). [Online] Available http://www.census.gov/population/www/estimates/countypop.html

under one year of age for each thousand live births in a given year. To compute infant mortality, divide the number of deaths of children under one year of age by the number of live births during the same year and multiply the result by 1,000. In 1998, there were 25,000 infant deaths and 3.9 million live births in the United States. Dividing the first number by the second and multiplying the result by 1,000 yields an infant mortality rate of 6.4. The second part of Figure 15–1 indicates that, by world standards, North American infant mortality is low.

But remember the differences among various categories of people. For example, African Americans, with nearly three times the burden of poverty as whites, have an infant mortality rate of 14—more than twice the white rate of 6.

Low infant mortality greatly raises **life expectancy,** *the average life span of a country's population.* U.S. males born in 1999 can expect to live seventy-four years, while females can look toward eighty years. As the third part of Figure 15–1 shows, life expectancy for North Americans is more than twenty years greater than that typical of low-income countries in Africa.

MIGRATION

Population size is also affected by **migration,** *the movement of people into and out of a specified territory.* Migration is sometimes involuntary, such as the forced transport of

10 million Africans to the Western Hemisphere as slaves. Voluntary migration, however, usually results from several "push-pull" factors. Dissatisfaction with life in a poor region may "push" people to move, while the opportunity for a better life may "pull" them to the city.

Movement into a territory—or *immigration*—is measured as an *in-migration rate,* calculated as the number of people entering an area for every thousand people in the population. Movement out of a territory—or *emigration*—is measured in terms of an *out-migration rate,* the number leaving for every thousand people. Both types of migration usually occur at once; the difference is the *net-migration rate.*

All nations also experience internal migration, that is, movement within their borders, from one region to another. National Map 15–1 shows where the U.S. population is moving, and the places being left behind.

POPULATION GROWTH

Fertility, mortality, and migration all affect the size of a society's population. In general, rich nations (like the United States) grow almost as much from immigration as natural increase; poorer nations (like India) grow almost entirely from natural increase.

To calculate a population's natural growth rate, demographers subtract the crude death rate from the crude birth rate. The natural growth rate of the U.S.

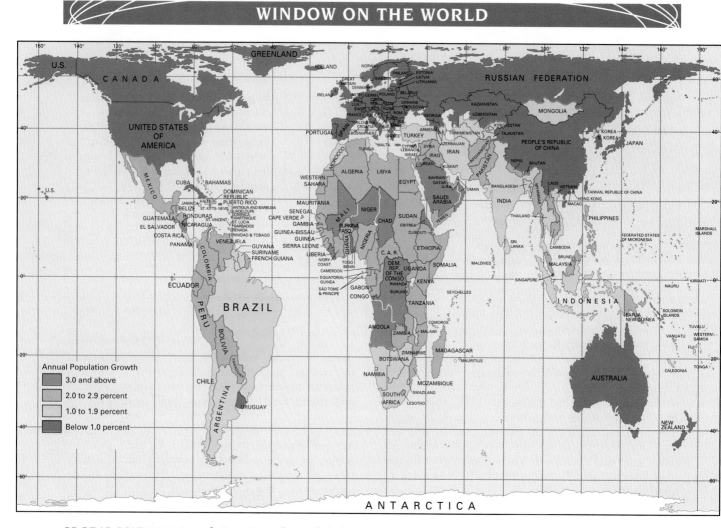

GLOBAL MAP 15–1 Population Growth in Global Perspective

The richest countries of the world—including the United States, Canada, and the nations of Europe—have growth rates below 1 percent. The nations of Latin America and Asia typically have growth rates around 1.6 percent, which double a population in forty-four years. Africa has an overall growth rate of 2.4 percent, which cuts the doubling time to twenty-nine years. In global perspective, we see that a society's standard of living is closely related to its rate of population growth: Population is rising fastest in the world regions that can least afford to support more people.

Source: Population Reference Bureau (2000); map projection from *Peters Atlas of the World* (1990).

population in 1998 was 5.6 per thousand (the crude birth rate of 14.4 minus the crude death rate of 8.8), or about 0.6 percent annual growth.

Global Map 15–1 shows that population growth in the United States and other high-income nations is well below the world average of 1.4 percent. The earth's low-growth continents are Europe (currently posting a slight decline, expressed as −0.1 percent annual growth), North America (0.6 percent), and Oceania (1.1 percent). Close to the global average are Asia (1.4

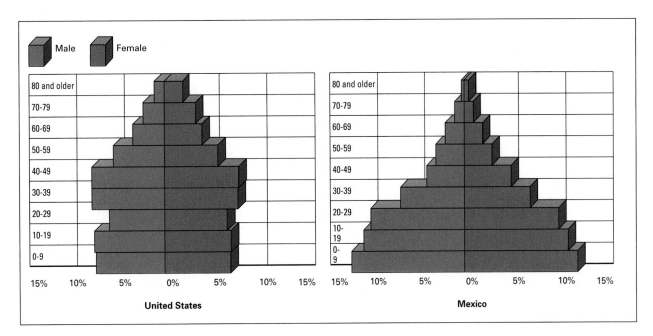

FIGURE 15–2 Age-Sex Population Pyramids for the United States and Mexico, 2000

Source: U.S. Census Bureau (2000).

percent) and Latin America (1.8 percent). The highest-growth region of the world is Africa (2.4 percent).

A handy rule of thumb for estimating population growth is to divide a society's population growth rate into the number 70 to calculate the *doubling time* in years. Thus, an annual growth rate of 2 percent (common in parts of Latin America) doubles a population in thirty-five years, and a 3 percent growth rate (found in some of Africa) drops the doubling time to just twenty-four years. The rapid population growth of the poorest countries is deeply troubling because they can barely support the populations they have now.

POPULATION COMPOSITION

Demographers also study the makeup of a society's population at a given point in time. One variable is the **sex ratio,** *the number of males for every hundred females in a nation's population.* In 2000, the sex ratio in the United States was 96, or 96 males for every 100 females. Sex ratios are usually below 100 because, on average, women outlive men. In India, however, the sex ratio is 107, because parents value sons more than daughters and may either abort a female fetus or, after birth, give more care to a male infant, raising the odds that a female child will die.

A more complex measure is the **age-sex pyramid,** *a graphic representation of the age and sex of a population.* Figure 15–2 presents the age-sex pyramids for the populations of the United States and Mexico. The higher mortality that occurs with advancing age gives these figures a roughly pyramid shape. In the U.S. pyramid, the bulge corresponding to ages thirty through the mid-fifties reflects high birth rates during the *baby boom* from the mid-1940s to 1970. The contraction we see just below the bulge—that is, people under thirty—reflects the subsequent *baby bust* as the birth rate dipped from 25.3 in 1957 to a low of 14.4 in 1998.

Comparing the U.S. and Mexican age-sex pyramids shows different demographic trends. The age-sex pyramid for Mexico, like that of other lower-income nations, is wide at the bottom (reflecting higher birth rates) and narrows quickly by what we would term middle age (due to higher mortality). Mexico, in short, is a much younger society, with a median age of twenty compared to thirty-five in the United States. With a larger share of females still in their childbearing years, therefore, Mexico's crude birth rate (24) is nearly twice our own (14), and its annual rate of population growth (2.0 percent) is almost four times the U.S. rate (0.6 percent).

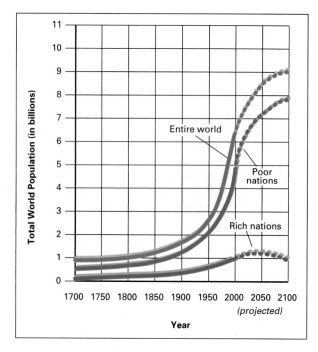

FIGURE 15–3 The Increase in World Population, 1700–2100

HISTORY AND THEORY OF POPULATION GROWTH

In the past, people favored large families, because human labor was the key to productivity. Moreover, until rubber condoms appeared 150 years ago, preventing pregnancy was an uncertain proposition at best. But high death rates from widespread infectious diseases put a constant brake on population growth.

A major demographic shift (shown in Figure 15–3) began about 1750 as the world's population turned upward, reaching the 1 billion mark by 1800. This milestone (requiring all of human history up to this point) was repeated by 1930—barely a century later—when a second billion people were added to the planet. In other words, not only was population increasing, but the *rate* of growth was accelerating. Global population reached 3 billion by 1962 (just thirty-two years later) and 4 billion by 1974 (a scant twelve years later). The rate of world population increase has slowed recently, but our planet passed the 5 billion mark in 1987 and the 6 billion mark late in 1999. In no previous century did the world's population even double. In the twentieth century, it increased *fourfold*.

Currently, the world is gaining 77 million people each year, with 96 percent of this increase in poor countries. Experts predict that the earth's population will reach between 8 and 9 billion by 2050 (Wattenberg, 1997; Thirunarayanapuram, 1998). Given the world's troubles feeding its present population, such an increase is a matter of urgent concern.

MALTHUSIAN THEORY

It was the sudden population growth 250 years ago that sparked the development of demography. Thomas Robert Malthus (1766–1834), an English economist and clergyman, warned that rapid population increase would lead to social chaos. Malthus (1926; orig. 1798) calculated that population would increase by what mathematicians call a *geometric progression*, illustrated by the series of numbers 2, 4, 8, 16, 32, and so on. At such a rate, Malthus concluded, world population would soon soar out of control.

Food production would also increase, Malthus explained, but only in *arithmetic progression* (as in the series 2, 3, 4, 5, 6, etc.) because, even with new agricultural technology, farmland is limited. Thus, Malthus presented a troubling vision of the future: people reproducing beyond what the planet could feed, leading ultimately to widespread starvation.

Malthus recognized that artificial birth control or abstinence might change the equation. But he found one morally wrong and the other quite impractical. Thus, famine and war stalked humanity in Malthus's scheme, and he was justly known as "the dismal parson."

Critical evaluation. Fortunately, Malthus's prediction was flawed. First, by 1850 the European birth rate began to drop, partly because children were becoming an economic liability rather than an asset, and partly because people began using artificial birth control. Second, Malthus underestimated human ingenuity: Irrigation, fertilizers, and pesticides have increased farm production far more than he imagined.

Some criticized Malthus for ignoring the role of social inequality in world abundance and famine. For example, Karl Marx (1967; orig. 1867) objected to his view of suffering as a "law of nature" rather than the curse of capitalism.

Still, Malthus offered an important lesson. Habitable land, clean water, and fresh air are limited resources and, as we explain presently, increased economic productivity has taken a heavy toll on the natural environment. In addition, medical advances have lowered death rates, pushing up world population. In

FIGURE 15–4
Demographic Transition Theory

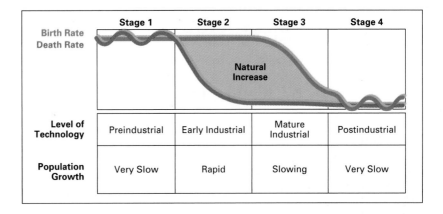

	Stage 1	Stage 2	Stage 3	Stage 4
Birth Rate Death Rate		Natural Increase		
Level of Technology	Preindustrial	Early Industrial	Mature Industrial	Postindustrial
Population Growth	Very Slow	Rapid	Slowing	Very Slow

principle, of course, no level of population growth can go on forever. Thus, people everywhere must become aware of the dangers of population increase.

DEMOGRAPHIC TRANSITION THEORY

A more complex analysis of population change is **demographic transition theory**, *the thesis that population patterns reflect a society's level of technological development.* Figure 15–4 shows the demographic consequences at four levels of technological development. Preindustrial, agrarian societies—those at Stage 1—have high birth rates because of the economic value of children and the absence of birth control. Death rates are also high due to low living standards and limited medical technology. Outbreaks of disease neutralize births, so population rises and falls with only a modest overall increase. This was the case for thousands of years in Europe before the Industrial Revolution.

Stage 2—the onset of industrialization—brings a demographic transition as death rates fall due to greater food supplies and scientific medicine. But birth rates remain high, resulting in rapid population growth. It was during Europe's Stage 2 that Malthus formulated his ideas, which accounts for his pessimistic view of the future. The world's poorest countries today are in this high-growth stage.

In Stage 3—a mature industrial economy—the birth rate drops, curbing population growth once again. Fertility falls, first, because most children survive to adulthood and, second, because high living standards make raising children expensive. Affluence, in short, transforms children from economic assets into economic liabilities. Smaller families, made possible by effective birth control, are also favored by women working outside the home. As birth rates follow death rates downward, population growth slows further.

Stage 4 corresponds to a postindustrial economy in which the demographic transition is complete. The birth rate keeps falling, partly because dual-income couples gradually become the norm and partly because the cost of raising children continues to rise. This trend, coupled with steady death rates, means that, at best, population grows only very slowly or even decreases. This is the case today in Japan, Europe, and the United States.

Critical evaluation. Demographic transition theory suggests that the key to population control lies in technology. Instead of the runaway population increase feared by Malthus, this theory sees technology reining in growth and spreading material plenty.

Demographic transition theory dovetails with modernization theory, one approach to global development discussed in Chapter 9 ("Global Stratification"). Modernization theorists are optimistic that poor countries will solve their population problems as they industrialize. But critics—notably dependency theorists—strongly disagree. Unless there is a significant redistribution of global resources, they maintain, our planet will become increasingly divided into high-income "haves," enjoying low population growth, and low-income "have-nots," struggling in vain to feed more and more people.

GLOBAL POPULATION TODAY: A BRIEF SURVEY

What can we say about population in today's world? Drawing on the discussion so far, we can identify important patterns and reach several conclusions.

The low-growth North. When the Industrial Revolution began in the Northern Hemisphere, population

Empowering Women:
The Key to Controlling Population Growth

Sohad Ahmad lives with her husband in a farming village fifty miles south of Cairo, Egypt's capital city. Ahmad lives a poor life, like hundreds of millions of other women in the world. Yet her situation differs in an important respect: She has had only two children and will have no more.

Why do Sohad and her husband reject the conventional wisdom that children are an economic asset? One part of the answer is that Egypt's growing population has already created such a demand for land that her family could not afford more even if they had the children to farm it. But the main reason is that Sohad Ahmad does not want her life defined only by childbearing.

Like Ahmad, more women in Egypt are taking control of their fertility and seeking educational and economic opportunities. Indeed, this country has made great progress in reducing its annual population growth from 3.0 percent just ten years ago to 2.0 percent today.

With its focus on raising the standing of women, the 1994 Cairo conference on global population broke new ground. Past population control programs have simply tried to make birth control technology available to women. This is vital, since only half of the

A simple truth: Women who have more opportunity for schooling and paid work have fewer children. As more women attend school in traditional societies, the fertility rate in these countries is falling.

world's married women use effective birth control. But even with available birth control, population continues to swell in societies that define women's primary responsibility as raising children.

Dr. Nafis Sadik, an Egyptian woman who heads the United Nations' efforts at population control, sums up the new approach to lowering birth rates this way: *Give women more life choices and they will have fewer children.* In other words, women with access to schooling and jobs, who can decide when and if they wish to marry, and who bear children as a matter of choice, will limit their own fertility. Schooling must be available to older women too, Sadik adds, because elders exercise great influence in local communities.

Evidence from countries around the world is that controlling population and raising the social standing of women are one and the same.

Sources: Linden (1994) and Ashford (1995).

---

growth in Western Europe and North America was a high 3 percent annually. But, in the centuries since, the growth rate steadily declined and, in 1970, fell below 1 percent. As our postindustrial society enters Stage 4, the U.S. birth rate is less than the replacement level of 2.1 children per woman, a point demographers term **zero population growth,** *the level of reproduction that maintains population at a steady state.* Some fifty nations, almost all of them rich, have passed the point of zero population growth (Wattenberg, 1997).

Factors holding down population in these postindustrial societies include a high proportion of men and women in the labor force, rising costs of raising children, trends toward later marriage and singlehood, and widespread use of contraceptives and abortion.

In postindustrial nations, therefore, population increase is not the pressing problem that it is in poor countries. Indeed, some analysts point to a future problem of *underpopulation* in countries such as Japan, Italy, and the United States, where the swelling ranks of the elderly have fewer and fewer young people to look to for support in old age (Chesnais, 1997).

The high-growth South. Population is a critical problem in poor nations of the Southern Hemisphere. No nation in the world lacks industrial technology entirely; demographic transition theory's Stage 1, therefore, applies just to remote rural areas of low-income nations. In Latin America, Africa, and Asia, many low-income nations are at Stage 2, with a mix of agrarian and industrial economies. Advanced medical technology, supplied by rich societies, has sharply reduced death rates, but birth rates remain high. This is why poor societies now account for two-thirds of the earth's people and 96 percent of global population increase.

In poor countries throughout the world, birth rates have fallen from an average of about six children per woman in 1950 to about four today. But fertility this high will only intensify global poverty. At a 1994 global population conference in Cairo, delegates from 180 nations agreed that a key element in controlling world population growth is to raise the status of women. The box takes a closer look.

In the last decade, the world has made significant progress in lowering fertility. Mortality, too, has come down. Although few would oppose medical programs that save lives—mostly children's—lower death rates mean rising population. In fact, population growth in most low-income regions of the world is due *mostly* to falling death rates. Around 1920, Europe and North America began taking steps to spread scientific medicine and better nutrition around the world. Since then, inoculations against infectious diseases and the use of antibiotics and insecticides have pushed down death rates with stunning effectiveness. For example, in Sri Lanka, malaria caused half of all deaths in the 1930s; a decade later, use of insecticides to kill malaria-carrying mosquitoes cut the death toll from this disease in half. Although this is a great medical achievement, Sri Lanka's population began to soar. Similarly, India's infant mortality rate slid from 130 in 1975 to 72 in 2000, boosting that nation's population over the 1 billion mark.

In short, in much of the world, fertility is falling. But mortality is falling even faster, especially among children. In order to limit population growth, the world—especially, poor countries—must control births as successfully as it has fended off death in the recent past.

URBANIZATION: GROWTH OF CITIES

October 8, 1994, Hong Kong. The cable train grinds to the top of Victoria Peak where we behold one of the world's most spectacular vistas: the city of Hong Kong at night! A million bright, colorful lights ring the harbor as ships, ferries, and traditional Chinese "junks" churn by. Few cities match Hong Kong for sheer energy: This small city is as economically productive as the state of Wisconsin or the nation of Finland. One could sit here for hours entranced by the spectacle of Hong Kong.

Throughout most of human history, the sights and sounds of great cities such as Hong Kong, New York, or Los Angeles were simply unimaginable. Our distant ancestors lived in small, nomadic groups, moving from place to place as they depleted vegetation or hunted migratory game. The small settlements that marked the emergence of civilization in the Middle East some 12,000 years ago held only a small fraction of the earth's people. Today, the largest three or four cities of the world hold as many people as the entire planet did back then.

Urbanization is *the concentration of humanity into cities.* Urbanization both redistributes population within a society and transforms many patterns of social life. We will trace these changes in terms of three urban revolutions—the emergence of cities beginning 10,000 years ago, the development of industrial cities after 1750, and the explosive growth of cities in poor countries today.

THE EVOLUTION OF CITIES

Cities are a relatively new development in human history. Only about 12,000 years ago did our ancestors begin founding permanent settlements, launching the *first urban revolution.*

The first cities. Hunting and gathering forced people to move all the time; once our ancestors discovered how to domesticate animals and cultivate crops, however, they were able to stay in one place (Lenski, Nolan, & Lenski, 1995). Raising their own food also created a material surplus, which freed some people from food production and allowed them to build shelters, make tools, weave cloth, and take part in religious rituals. The emergence of cities, then, led to specialization and higher living standards.

The first city—Jericho, which lies to the north of the Dead Sea and dates back 10,000 years—was home to only some 600 people. But, as the centuries passed, cities grew to tens of thousands of people, and became the centers of vast empires. By 3000 B.C.E., Egyptian cities flourished, as did cities in China about 2000 B.C.E., and in Latin America about 1500 B.C.E. In North America, however, only a few Native American societies formed settlements, so that widespread urbanization had to await the arrival of European settlers in the seventeenth century (Lamberg-Karlovsky, 1973; Change, 1977; Coe & Diehl, 1980).

Mont-St-Michel, a French town that rises against the Atlantic Ocean, is a wonderful example of a medieval settlement: small and walled, with narrow, irregular streets that, even today, make walking seem like a delightful stroll back in time.

Preindustrial European cities. European cities date back some 5,000 years to the Greeks and, later, the Romans, both of whom formed great empires and founded cities across Europe, including Vienna, Paris, and London. With the fall of the Roman Empire, the so-called Dark Ages began, as people withdrew within defensive walled settlements and warlords battled for territory. Only in the eleventh century did trade flourish once again, allowing cities to grow.

Medieval cities were quite different from those familiar to us today. Beneath towering cathedrals, the narrow, winding streets of London, Brussels, and Florence teemed with merchants, artisans, priests, peddlers, jugglers, nobles, and servants. Occupational groups such as bakers, carpenters, and metalworkers clustered in distinct sections or "quarters." Ethnicity also defined communities as people sought to keep out those who differed from themselves. The term "ghetto" (from the Italian word *borghetto*, meaning "outside the city walls") first described the segregation of Jews in Venice.

Industrial European cities. As the Middle Ages came to a close, steadily increasing commerce enriched a new urban middle class or *bourgeoisie* (French, meaning "of the town"). With more and more money, the bourgeoisie soon rivaled the hereditary nobility.

By about 1750, the Industrial Revolution triggered a *second urban revolution*, first in Europe and then in North America. Factories unleashed tremendous productive power, causing cities to grow to unprecedented size. London, the largest European city, reached 550,000 people by 1700 and exploded to 6.5 million by 1900 (A. Weber, 1963, orig. 1899; Chandler & Fox, 1974).

Cities not only grew but changed shape as well. Older winding streets gave way to broad, straight boulevards that held the flow of commercial traffic. Steam and electric trolleys, too, crisscrossed the expanding cities. Since land was now a commodity to be bought and sold, developers divided cities into regular-sized lots (Mumford, 1961). The center of the city was no longer the cathedral but a bustling central business district filled with banks, retail stores, and tall office buildings.

With a new focus on business, cities became ever more crowded and impersonal. Crime rates rose. Especially at the outset, a few industrialists lived in grand style, but most men, women, and children worked in factories for bare subsistence.

Organized efforts by workers to improve their lives eventually brought changes to the workplace, better housing, and the right to vote. Public services such as water, sewerage, and electricity further improved urban living. Today, some urbanites still live in poverty, but a rising standard of living has partly fulfilled the city's historical promise of a better life.

THE GROWTH OF U.S. CITIES

Most of the Native Americans who inhabited North America for thousands of years before the arrival of Europeans were migratory people who formed few permanent settlements. The spread of villages and towns, then, came after European colonization.

Colonial settlement: 1565–1800. In 1565, the Spanish built a settlement at St. Augustine, Florida, and, in 1607, the English founded Jamestown, Virginia. The first lasting settlement came in 1624 when the Dutch established New Amsterdam, later called New York.

New York and Boston (founded by the English in 1630) started out as tiny villages in a vast wilderness. They resembled medieval towns in Europe, with narrow, winding streets that still curve through lower Manhattan and downtown Boston.

But economic growth soon transformed these quiet villages into thriving towns with wide streets usually laid out in a grid pattern. Even so, when the first census was completed in 1790, as Table 15–1 shows, just 5 percent of the nation's people lived in cities.

Urban expansion: 1800–1860. Early in the nineteenth century, towns sprang up along the transportation routes that opened the American West. By 1860, Buffalo, Cleveland, Detroit, and Chicago were all changing the face of the Midwest, and about one-fifth of the U.S. population lived in cities.

Urban expansion was greatest in the northern states; New York City, for example, had ten times the population of Charleston, South Carolina. The division of the United States into the industrial-urban North and the agrarian-rural South was one major cause of the Civil War (Schlesinger, 1969).

The metropolitan era: 1860–1950. The Civil War (1861–65) gave an enormous boost to urbanization, as factories strained to produce weapons. Waves of people deserted the countryside for cities in hopes of finding better jobs. Joining them were tens of millions of immigrants—most from Europe—forming a culturally diverse urban mix.

In 1900, New York's population soared passed the 4 million mark, and Chicago—a city of scarcely 100,000 people in 1860—was closing in on 2 million. Such growth marked the era of the **metropolis** (from Greek words meaning "mother city"), *a large city that socially and economically dominates an urban area.* Metropolises became the economic centers of the United States. By 1920, cities were home to a majority of the U.S. population.

Industrial technology pushed cities ever higher. In the 1880s, steel girders and mechanical elevators raised structures over ten stories high. In 1930, New York's Empire State Building was hailed as an urban wonder, an early "skyscraper" stretching 102 stories into the clouds.

Urban decentralization: 1950–present. The industrial metropolis reached its peak about 1950. Since then, something of a turnaround—termed *urban decentralization*—has occurred as people have deserted downtown areas for outlying **suburbs,** *urban areas beyond the political boundaries of a city.* Thus, the old industrial cities of the Northeast and Midwest stopped growing, and some lost considerable population, in the decades after 1950. The urban landscape of densely packed central cities evolved into expanding suburban regions, as in the case of Atlanta, described in the opening to this chapter.

SUBURBS AND URBAN DECLINE

Imitating European nobility, some of the rich had always kept "town" houses as well as "country" homes

TABLE 15–1 The Urban Population of the United States, 1790–1998		
Year	Population (in millions)	Percent Urban
1790	3.9	5.1%
1800	5.3	6.1
1820	9.6	7.3
1840	17.1	10.5
1860	31.4	19.7
1880	50.2	28.1
1900	76.0	39.7
1920	105.7	51.3
1940	131.7	56.5
1960	179.3	69.9
1980	226.5	73.7
1990	253.0	75.2
1998	270.3	80.1

Source: U.S. Census Bureau (2000).

beyond the city limits (Baltzell, 1979a). But it was not until after World War II that ordinary people found a suburban home within their reach. With more and more cars, new four-lane beltways, government-backed mortgages, and inexpensive tract homes, suburbs grew as never before. By 1999, most of the U.S. population lived in suburbs, where they frequented nearby shopping malls rather than the older "downtown" shopping districts (Geist, 1985; Palen, 1995; Petersen, 1999).

Suburban growth threw many older cities of the Snowbelt—the Northeast and Midwest—into financial crisis. Cities lost affluent taxpayers to the suburbs and were left with the burden of funding expensive social programs for the poor who stayed behind. As a result, inner-city decay began to scar cities throughout the Northeast and Midwest. Especially to white people, the inner cities became synonymous with slum housing, crime, drugs, unemployment, the poor, and minorities (Sternlieb & Hughes, 1983; Logan & Schneider, 1984; Stahura, 1986; Galster, 1991).

POSTINDUSTRIAL SUNBELT CITIES

The picture has been different in the Sunbelt—the South and West. Population has been shifting to the Sunbelt, and 60 percent of the country's people now live there. In 1950, nine of the ten largest U.S. cities were in the Snowbelt; by 1998, six of the top ten were in the Sunbelt (U.S. Census Bureau, 2000).

Why are Sunbelt cities growing so quickly? Unlike their colder counterparts, these cities came of age *after* urban decentralization began. So while Snowbelt cities have long been enclosed by a ring of politically independent suburbs, Sunbelt cities have pushed their boundaries outward with the population flow. Compare Houston's 540 square miles to Chicago's 227.

The great sprawl of Sunbelt cities does have drawbacks, however. Many people in cities like Atlanta, Dallas, Phoenix, or Los Angeles argue that the growth follows no plan and only ends up with clogged roads leading to slapdash developments. A sign of the times: In the 1998 elections, no fewer than 240 anti-sprawl initiatives were on the ballot across the United States—and voters passed most of them (Lacayo, 1999).

MEGALOPOLIS: REGIONAL CITIES

Another result of urban decentralization is urban regions, or regional cities. The U.S. Census Bureau (2000) recognized 275 urban regions, which the Bureau calls *metropolitan statistical areas* (MSAs). Each MSA includes at least one city with 50,000 or more people plus densely populated surrounding counties. Almost all of the fifty fastest-growing MSAs are in the Sunbelt.

The biggest MSAs, containing more than 1 million people, are called *consolidated metropolitan statistical areas* (CMSAs). In 1999, there were eighteen CMSAs. Heading the list is New York and its adjacent urban areas in Long Island, western Connecticut, and northern New Jersey, with a total population of more than 20 million. Next in size is the CMSA in southern California that includes Los Angeles, Riverside, and Anaheim, with a population of almost 16 million.

As regional cities grow, they begin to overlap each other. For example, along the East Coast a 400-mile supercity stretches all the way from New England to Virginia. In the early 1960s, French geographer Jean Gottmann (1961) coined the term **megalopolis** to designate *a vast urban region containing a number of cities and their surrounding suburbs.* Other supercities cover the eastern coast of Florida and stretch from Cleveland west to Chicago. More megalopolises will undoubtedly emerge, especially in the fast-growing Sunbelt.

EDGE CITIES

Urban decentralization has also created *edge cities*, business centers some distance from the old downtowns. Edge cities—a mix of corporate office buildings, shopping malls, hotels, and entertainment complexes—differ from suburbs, which contain mostly homes. Thus, while the population of suburbs peaks at night, the population of edge cities peaks during the workday.

As part of expanding urban regions, most edge cities have no clear physical boundaries. Some do have

names, including Los Colinas (near the Dallas-Fort Worth airport), Tyson's Corner (in Virginia, near Washington, D.C.), and King of Prussia (northwest of Philadelphia). Other edge cities are known only by the major highways that flow through them, including Route 1 in Princeton, New Jersey, and Route 128 near Boston (Garreau, 1991; Macionis & Parrillo, 2001).

URBANISM AS A WAY OF LIFE

Early sociologists in Europe and the United States focused their attention on the rise of cities. We briefly present their accounts of urbanism as a way of life.

FERDINAND TÖNNIES: *GEMEINSCHAFT* AND *GESELLSCHAFT*

In the late nineteenth century, the German sociologist Ferdinand Tönnies (1855–1936) studied how life in the new industrial metropolis differed from life in rural villages. He developed two concepts that have become a lasting part of sociology's terminology.

Tönnies (1963; orig. 1887) used the German word **Gemeinschaft** (meaning roughly "community") to refer to *a type of social organization by which people are closely tied by kinship and tradition.* The *Gemeinschaft* of the rural village, Tönnies explained, joins people in what amounts to a single primary group.

By and large, argued Tönnies, *Gemeinschaft* is absent in the modern city. On the contrary, urbanization fosters **Gesellschaft** (a German word, meaning roughly "association"), *a type of social organization by which people come together only on the basis of individual self-interest.* In the *Gesellschaft* way of life, individuals are motivated by their own needs rather than by a desire to enhance the well-being of everyone. By and large, city dwellers display little sense of community or common identity and look to others mostly as a means of advancing their individual goals. Thus, Tönnies saw in urbanization the erosion of close, enduring social relations in favor of the fleeting and impersonal ties typical of business.

EMILE DURKHEIM: MECHANICAL AND ORGANIC SOLIDARITY

French sociologist Emile Durkheim agreed with much of Tönnies's thinking about cities. Yet, Durkheim countered, urbanites do not lack social bonds; they simply organize social life differently than rural people.

Durkheim described traditional, rural life as *mechanical solidarity*, social bonds based on common sentiments and shared moral values. With its emphasis on tradition, Durkheim's concept of mechanical solidarity bears a striking similarity to Tönnies's *Gemeinschaft*. Urbanization erodes mechanical solidarity, Durkheim explained, but it also generates a new type of bonding, which he termed *organic solidarity*, social bonds based on specialization and interdependence. This concept, which parallels Tönnies's *Gesellschaft*, reveals an important difference between the two thinkers. Both thought the growth of industrial cities undermined tradition, but Durkheim optimistically pointed to a new kind of solidarity. Where societies had been built on *likeness*, Durkheim now saw social life based on *difference*.

For Durkheim, urban society offers more individual choice, moral tolerance, and personal privacy than people find in rural villages. In sum, Durkheim thought, something is lost in the process of urbanization, but much is gained.

GEORG SIMMEL: THE BLASÉ URBANITE

German sociologist Georg Simmel (1858–1918) offered a micro-analysis of cities, studying how urban life shapes individual experience. According to Simmel, individuals perceive the city as a crush of people, objects, and events. To prevent being overwhelmed by all this stimulation, urbanites develop a *blasé attitude*, tuning out much of what goes on around them. Such detachment does not mean that city dwellers lack compassion for others; they simply keep their distance as a survival strategy so they can focus their time and energy on those who really matter to them.

THE CHICAGO SCHOOL: ROBERT PARK AND LOUIS WIRTH

Sociologists in the United States soon joined the study of rapidly growing cities. Robert Park, a leader of the first U.S. sociology program at the University of Chicago, sought to add a street-level perspective by getting out and studying real cities. As he said of himself:

> I suspect that I have actually covered more
> ground, tramping about in cities in different parts
> of the world, than any other living man. (1950:viii)

Walking the streets, Park found the city to be an organized mosaic of distinctive ethnic communities, commercial centers, and industrial districts. Over time, he observed, these "natural areas" develop and change in relation to one another. To Park, then, the city was a living organism—a human kaleidoscope.

Another major figure in the Chicago School of urban sociology was Louis Wirth (1897–1952). Wirth

The painting Nocturne *by Ernest Fiene conveys the impersonality that lies at the heart of Tönnies's concept of* Gesellschaft. *In modern, urban living, he maintained, we remain aloof from those around us. But do we owe others anything? Do we expect anything from them? In your opinion, what?*

Ernest Fiene (1894–1965), *Nocturne*. Photograph © Christie's Images.

(1938) is best-known for blending the ideas of Tönnies, Durkheim, Simmel, and Park into a comprehensive theory of urban life.

Wirth began by defining the city as a setting with a large, dense, and socially diverse population. These traits result in an impersonal, superficial, and transitory way of life. Living among millions of others, urbanites come into contact with many more people than rural residents do. Thus, when city people notice others at all, they usually know them not in terms of *who they are* but *what they do*—as, for instance, the bus driver, florist, or grocery store clerk. Specialized, urban relationships are sometimes pleasant for all concerned. But, we should remember that self-interest rather than friendship is the main reason for the interaction.

Finally, limited social involvement coupled with great social diversity make city dwellers more tolerant than rural villagers. Rural communities often jealously enforce their narrow traditions, but the heterogeneous population of a city rarely shares any single code of moral conduct (T. Wilson, 1985; Wilson, 1995).

Critical evaluation. Both in Europe and the United States, early sociologists presented a mixed view of urban living. On the one hand, rapid urbanization was troubling. Tönnies and Wirth saw personal ties and traditional morality lost in the anonymous rush of the city. On the other hand, Durkheim and Park emphasized urbanism's positive face, pointing to greater personal autonomy and greater personal choice.

One problem is that Wirth and others painted urbanism in broad strokes that overlook the effects of class, race, and gender. There are many kinds of urbanites—rich and poor, black and white, Anglo and Latino, women and men—all leading distinctive lives (Gans, 1968). In fact, cities can intensify these social differences. That is, we see the extent of social diversity most clearly in cities, where various categories can form "critical masses" (Macionis & Parrillo, 2001).

URBAN ECOLOGY

Sociologists (especially members of the Chicago School) also developed **urban ecology,** *the study of the link between the physical and social dimensions of cities.* Consider, for example, why cities are located where they are. The first cities emerged in fertile regions where the ecology favored raising crops. Preindustrial people, concerned with defense, built their cities on mountains (ancient Athens was perched on an outcropping of rock) or surrounded by water (Paris and Mexico City were founded on islands). With the Industrial Revolution, economic considerations situated all the major U.S. cities near rivers and natural harbors that facilitated trade.

Urban ecologists also study the physical design of cities. In 1925, Ernest W. Burgess, a student and colleague of Robert Park, described land use in Chicago in terms of *concentric zones.* City centers, Burgess observed, are business districts bordered by a ring of factories, followed by residential rings with housing that becomes more expensive the farther it is from the noise and pollution of the city's center.

Homer Hoyt (1939) refined Burgess's observations, noting that distinctive districts sometimes form *wedge-shaped sectors.* For example, one fashionable area

may develop next to another, or an industrial district may extend outward from a city's center along a train or trolley line.

Chauncy Harris and Edward Ullman (1945) added yet another insight: As cities decentralize, they lose their single-center form in favor of a *multicentered model.* As cities grow, residential, shopping, and industrial areas typically push away from one another. Few people wish to live close to industrial parks, for example, so the city becomes a mosaic of distinct districts.

Social area analysis investigates what people in particular neighborhoods have in common. Three factors seem to explain most of the variation—namely, family patterns, social class, and race and ethnicity (Shevky & Bell, 1955; Johnston, 1976). Families with children gravitate toward areas with large apartments or single-family homes and good schools. The rich seek high-prestige neighborhoods, often in the central city near cultural attractions. People with a common social heritage cluster in distinctive communities.

Finally, Brian Berry and Philip Rees (1969) tied together many of these insights. They explained that distinct family types tend to settle in the concentric zones described by Ernest Burgess. Specifically, households with few children tend to cluster toward the city's center, while those with more children live farther away. Social class differences are primarily responsible for the sector-shaped districts described by Homer Hoyt as, for instance, the rich occupy one "side of the tracks" and the poor, the other. And racial and ethnic neighborhoods are found at various points throughout the city, consistent with Harris and Ullman's multicentered model.

URBAN POLITICAL ECONOMY

In the late 1960s, many large U.S. cities were rocked by rioting. In the wake of this unrest, some analysts turned away from the ecological approach to a social-conflict understanding of city life. The *urban political-economy* model applies Karl Marx's analysis of conflict in the workplace to conflict in the city (Lindstrom, 1995).

The ecological approach sees the city as a natural organism, with particular districts developing according to an internal logic. Political economists disagree. They claim that city life is defined by powerful people: corporate leaders and political officials. Capitalism, which transforms the city into "real estate" traded for profit and concentrates wealth in the hands of the few, is the key to understanding city life. From this point of view, the decline in industrial Snowbelt cities after 1950 was the result of deliberate decisions by the corporate elite to move their production facilities to the Sunbelt (where labor is cheaper and less likely to be unionized) or move them out of the country entirely to low-income nations (Harvey, 1976; Molotch, 1976; Castells, 1977, 1983; Feagin, 1983; Lefebvre, 1991).

Critical evaluation. Compared to the older, urban ecology approach, the political-economy view seems better able to address the fact that many U.S. cities are in *crisis*, with widespread poverty, high crime, and barely functioning schools. But one criticism applies to both approaches: They focus on U.S. cities during a limited period of history. Much of what we know about industrial cities does not apply to preindustrial towns in our own past or the rapidly growing cities in many poor nations today. Therefore, it is unlikely that any single model of cities can account for the full range of urban diversity that we find in the world today.

URBANIZATION IN POOR SOCIETIES

`November 16, 1988, Cairo, Egypt.` People call the vast Muslim cemetery in Old Cairo "The City of the Dead." In truth, it is very much alive: Tens of thousands of squatters have moved into the mausoleums, making this place an eerie mix of life and death. Children run across the stone floors, clotheslines stretch between the monuments, and an occasional television antenna protrudes from a tomb roof. With Cairo gaining 1,000 people a day, families live where they can.

Twice in human history the world has experienced a revolutionary expansion of cities. The first urban revolution began about 8000 B.C.E. with the first urban settlements and continued until permanent settlements were in place on several continents. Then, about 1750, the second urban revolution took off and lasted for two centuries as the Industrial Revolution touched off rapid growth of cities in Europe and North America.

A third urban revolution is now underway. Today, 75 percent of people in high-income countries are already city dwellers. But extraordinary urban growth is occurring in poor nations. In 1950, about 25 percent of the people in low-income countries lived in cities; by 2005, the figure will exceed 50 percent. Moreover, in 1950, only seven cities in the world had populations over 5 million, and only two of these were in low-

In low-income countries throughout the world, people are migrating from rural areas to cities in hopes of a better life. The result is that many cities are overwhelmed with newcomers, who are forced to live wherever they can. Shanty settlements, such as this one in Manila, Philippines, pose obvious dangers to residents (and, especially, children) in terms of accidents and disease. What do you think would happen if heavy rains flooded this neighborhood?

income countries. By 2000, forty-eight cities had passed this mark, and thirty-two of them were in less developed nations (*Time Almanac 2001*, 2000).

This third urban revolution is taking place because many poor nations have entered the high-growth Stage 2 of demographic transition theory. Falling death rates have fueled population increase in Latin America, Asia, and especially Africa. For urban areas, the rate of increase is *twice* as high because, in addition to natural increase, millions of people leave the countryside each year in search of jobs, health care, education, and conveniences like running water and electricity.

Cities do offer more opportunities than rural areas, but they provide no quick fix for the massive problems of escalating population and grinding poverty. Many cities in less developed nations—including Mexico City, Egypt's Cairo, India's Calcutta, and Manila in the Philippines—are simply unable to meet the basic needs of much of their population. All these cities are surrounded by wretched shantytowns—settlements of makeshift homes built from discarded materials. As noted in Chapter 9 ("Global Stratification"), even city dumps are home to thousands of poor people, who pick through the waste hoping to find enough to survive for another day.

ENVIRONMENT AND SOCIETY

Our species has prospered, rapidly increasing the population of the planet. Moreover, an increasing share of humanity now lives in large, complex settlements that offer the promise of a better life than that found in rural villages.

But these advances have come at a high price. Never before in history have human beings placed such demands on the earth. This disturbing development brings us to the final section of this chapter: a look at the interplay of the natural environment and society. Like demography, **ecology** is another cousin of sociology, formally defined as *the study of the interaction between living organisms and the natural environment.* Ecology rests on the research of not only social scientists but natural scientists as well. Here, however, we focus on those aspects of ecology that involve familiar sociological concepts and issues.

The **natural environment** refers to *the earth's surface and atmosphere, including living organisms, air, water, soil, and other resources necessary to sustain life.* Like every other species, humans depend on the natural environment to live. Yet, with our capacity for culture, humans stand apart from other species, as we alone take deliberate action to remake the world according to our own interests and desires. Thus, human beings are unique in our capacity to transform the world, for better and worse.

Why is the environment of interest to sociologists? Simply because environmental problems—from pollution to acid rain to global warming—do not arise from the natural world operating on its own. Rather, as we shall explain, they result from the specific actions of human beings, making them *social* issues (Marx, 1994).

THE GLOBAL DIMENSION

The study of the natural environment must be approached from a global perspective. The reason is that, regardless of political divisions among nations, the planet is a single **ecosystem,** a *system composed of the interaction of all living organisms and their natural environment.*

The Greek meaning of *eco* is "house," reminding us that this planet is our home and that all living things and their natural environment are *interrelated.* In practice, any change in part of the natural environment ripples throughout the entire global ecosystem.

Consider, from an ecological point of view, our national love of eating hamburgers. People in North America (and, increasingly, around the world) have created a huge demand for beef, which has greatly expanded ranching in Brazil, Costa Rica, and other Latin American nations. To produce the lean meat sought by fast-food corporations, cattle in Latin America feed on grass, which uses a great deal of land. Latin American ranchers clear the land for grazing by destroying thousands of square miles of forests each year. These tropical forests, as we shall explain presently, are vital to maintaining the earth's atmosphere. Deforestation ends up threatening everyone, including people back in the United States who enjoy hamburgers without a thought to the environment (Myers, 1984a).

TECHNOLOGY AND THE ENVIRONMENTAL DEFICIT

Our capacity for culture gives humans the power to alter the natural environment, making and remaking the world as we choose. Members of societies with simple hunting and gathering technology have scarcely any ability to affect the environment. On the contrary, members of such societies are keenly dependent on nature, so that their lives are defined by the migration of game and the rhythm of the seasons. They are especially vulnerable to natural catastrophes, such as fires, floods, droughts, and storms.

Societies at intermediate stages of sociocultural evolution have a somewhat greater capacity to affect the environment. But the environmental impact of horticulture (small-scale farming), pastoralism (the herding of animals), and even agriculture (the use of animal-drawn plows) is limited because people still rely on muscle power for producing food and other goods.

Human control of the natural environment increased dramatically with the Industrial Revolution. Muscle power gave way to engines that burn fossil fuels: coal, at first, and then oil. Such machinery affects the environment in two ways: by consuming natural resources and by releasing pollutants into the atmosphere. Even more important, humans armed with industrial technology are able to bend nature to their will, tunneling through mountains, damming rivers,

The earth's rain forests—vital to the planet's ecology—are now half their original size and become smaller every year. Once the lush vegetation of such forests is lost, the soil is at risk of drying out and turning into a desert. Thus, environmental damage is often irreversible.

irrigating deserts, and drilling for oil on the ocean floor. This explains how people in rich nations, who represent just 18 percent of humanity, use 80 percent of the world's energy (Connett, 1991; Miller, 1992).

The environmental impact of industrial technology goes beyond energy consumption. Just as important is the fact that members of industrial societies produce 100 times more goods than people in agrarian societies. Higher living standards, in turn, increase the problems of solid waste (because people ultimately throw away most of what they produce) and pollution (industrial production generates smoke and other toxic substances).

Right from the start, people recognized the material benefits of industrial technology. But only a century later did they begin to see its long-term effects on the natural environment. Indeed, one trait of the recent postindustrial era is a growing concern for environmental quality (Abrahamson, 1997; Kidd & Lee, 1997). Today, we realize that the technological power to make our lives better can also put the lives of future generations in jeopardy (Voight, cited in Bormann & Kellert, 1991:ix–x).

Evidence is mounting that we are running up an **environmental deficit,** *profound and negative long-term harm to the natural environment caused by humanity's focus on short-term material affluence* (Bormann, 1990). The concept of environmental deficit is important for three reasons. First, it reminds us that the state of the environment is a *social issue*, reflecting choices people make about how to live. Second, it suggests that much

environmental damage—to the air, land, or water—is *unintended*. By focusing on the short-term benefits of, say, cutting down forests, strip mining, or using throwaway packaging, we fail to see their long-term environmental effects. Third, in some respects, the environmental deficit is *reversible*. Inasmuch as societies have created environmental problems, in other words, societies can undo many of them.

CULTURE: GROWTH AND LIMITS

Whether we recognize environmental dangers and decide to do something about them is a cultural matter. Thus, along with technology, culture has powerful environmental consequences.

The logic of growth. When this country sets aside specific areas as parks and game preserves, we seem to be saying that, except for these special areas, people can use, and abuse, natural resources freely for their own purposes (Myers, 1991). This aggressive approach to the natural environment has long been central to our way of life.

Chapter 2 ("Culture") described the core values that underlie social life in the United States. One of these is *material comfort*, the belief that money and the things it buys enrich our lives. We also believe in the idea of *progress*, thinking that the future will be better than the present. Moreover, we look to *science* to make our lives easier and more rewarding. Taken together, such cultural values form *the logic of growth.*

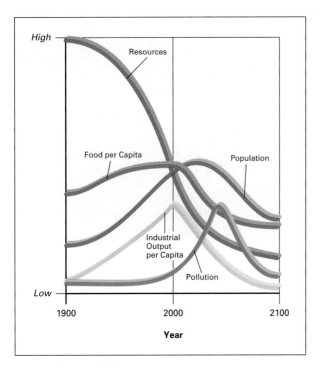

High ─

Resources

Food per Capita

Population

Industrial
Output
per Capita

Pollution

Low ─

1900　　　　　2000　　　　　2100

Year

FIGURE 15–5 The Limits to Growth: Projections
Source: Based on Meadows et al. (1972).

The logic of growth is an optimistic view of the world. It holds that more powerful technology has improved our lives and that new discoveries will continue to do so into the future. In simple terms, the logic of growth asserts that "people are clever," "having things is good," and "life gets better." A powerful force throughout the history of the United States and other high-income nations, the logic of growth is the driving force behind settling the wilderness, building towns and roads, and pursuing material affluence.

Even so, "progress" can lead to unexpected problems, including strain on the environment. The logic of growth responds by arguing that people (especially scientists and other technology experts) will find a way out of any problem that growth places in our path. If, say, the world runs short of oil, scientists will come up with electric, solar, or nuclear engines or some as-yet-unknown technology to meet the world's energy needs.

But environmentalists counter that the logic of growth is flawed in assuming that natural resources such as oil, clean air, fresh water, and the earth's topsoil will always be plentiful. On the contrary, they claim, these are *finite* resources that we can and will

exhaust if we continue to pursue growth at any cost. Echoing Malthus, environmentalists warn that if we call on the earth to support increasing numbers of people, we will surely deplete finite resources, destroying the environment—and ourselves—in the process (Milbrath, 1989; Livernash & Rodenburg, 1998).

The limits to growth. If we cannot invent our way out of the problems created by the logic of growth, perhaps we need another way of thinking about the world. Environmentalists, therefore, counter that growth must have limits. Stated simply, the *limits to growth thesis* is that humanity must implement policies to control the growth of population, production, and use of resources in order to avoid environmental collapse.

In *The Limits to Growth*, a controversial book that had a large hand in launching the environmental movement, Donella Meadows and her colleagues (1972) used a computer model to calculate the planet's available resources, rates of population growth, amount of land available for cultivation, levels of industrial and food production, and amount of pollutants released into the atmosphere. The model reflects changes that have occurred since 1900, and projects forward to the end of the twenty-first century. The authors concede that such long-range predictions are speculative, and some critics think they are plain wrong (Simon, 1981). But, right or wrong, the general conclusions of the study, shown in Figure 15–5, call for serious consideration.

According to the limits to growth thesis, we are quickly consuming the earth's finite resources. Supplies of oil, natural gas, and other energy sources are already falling sharply and will continue to drop, a little faster or slower depending on conservation policies in rich nations and how fast other nations industrialize. While food production per person will continue to rise during this century, world hunger will persist because existing food supplies are distributed so unequally. By 2050, the model predicts that hunger will reach a crisis level, first stabilizing population and then sending it back downward. Eventually, depletion of resources will cripple industrial output as well. Only then will pollution rates fall.

Limits to growth theorists are also known as neo-Malthusians because they share Malthus's pessimism about the future. They doubt that current patterns of life are sustainable for even another century. If so, we face a fundamental choice: Either we make deliberate changes in how we live, or widespread calamity will force change upon us.

SOLID WASTE: THE DISPOSABLE SOCIETY

As an interesting exercise, carry a trash bag around for a single day and collect everything you throw away. Most people are surprised to find that the average person in the United States discards close to five pounds of paper, metal, plastic, and other materials daily (over a lifetime, that's about fifty tons!). For the country as a whole, this amounts to about 1 billion pounds of solid waste *each and every day*. Figure 15–6 shows the composition of a normal household's trash.

As a rich nation containing people who value convenience, the United States has become a *disposable society*. We consume more products than virtually any nation on earth, and much of them have throwaway packaging. The most familiar case is fast food, served with cardboard, plastic, and Styrofoam containers that we throw away within minutes. But countless other products—from film to fishhooks—are elaborately packaged to make the product more attractive to the customer and to discourage tampering and theft.

Consider, too, that manufacturers market soft drinks, beer, and fruit juices in aluminum cans, glass jars, and plastic containers, which not only consume finite resources but also generate mountains of solid waste. Then there are countless items intentionally designed to be disposable: pens, razors, flashlights, batteries, even cameras. Other goods—from light bulbs to automobiles—are designed to have a limited useful life and then become unwanted junk. As Paul H. Connett (1991) points out, even the words we use to describe what we throw away—*waste, litter, trash, refuse, garbage, rubbish*—show how little we value what we cannot immediately use. But this was not always the case, as the box on page 424 explains.

Living in a rich society, the average person in the United States consumes 50 times more steel, 170 times more newspaper, 250 times more gasoline, and 300 times more plastic each year than the typical individual in India (Miller, 1992). This high level of consumption means that we in the United States not only use a disproportionate share of the planet's natural resources, but also generate most of the world's refuse.

We like to say that we "throw things away." But 80 percent of our solid waste is not burned or recycled and never "goes away." Rather, it ends up in landfills, which are, literally, filling up. Material in landfills also can pollute ground water. Although, in most places, laws now regulate what can be discarded in a landfill, the Environmental Protection Agency has identified 30,000 dump sites across the United States containing hazardous materials that are polluting water both

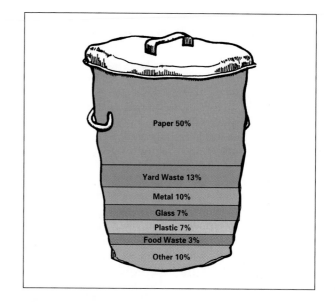

FIGURE 15–6 Composition of Household Trash
Sources: Based on Franklin Associates (1986) and Corley et al. (1993).

above and below the ground. In addition, what goes into landfills all too often stays there—sometimes for centuries. Tens of millions of tires, diapers, and other items that we bury in landfills each year do not decompose and will be an unwelcome legacy for future generations.

Environmentalists argue that we should address the problem of solid waste by doing what many of our grandparents did: Turn "waste" into a resource. One way to do this is through *recycling*, reusing resources we would otherwise discard. Recycling is an accepted practice in Japan and many other nations, and it is becoming more common in the United States, where we now reuse about 30 percent of waste materials. The share is increasing as laws mandate reuse of certain materials such as glass bottles and aluminum cans. In addition, because our nation has a market-based economy, recycling is bound to increase as it becomes more profitable.

WATER AND AIR

Oceans, lakes, and streams are the lifeblood of the global ecosystem. Humans depend on water for drinking, bathing, cooling, and cooking, for recreation, and for a host of other activities.

According to what scientists call the *hydrological cycle*, the earth naturally recycles water and refreshes the land. The process begins as heat from the sun

Why Grandmother Had No Trash

Grandma Macionis, we always used to say, never threw away anything. She was born and raised in Lithuania—the "old country"—where life in a poor village shaped her in ways that never changed, even after she immigrated to the United States as a young woman.

After opening a birthday present, she would carefully save the box, wrapping paper, and ribbon, which meant as much to her as the gift they contained. Grandma never wore new clothes, her kitchen knives were worn thin from decades of sharpening, and all her garbage was "recycled" as compost for her vegetable garden.

As strange as Grandma seemed to her grandchildren, she was a product of her culture. A century ago, there was little "trash." If a pair of socks wore thin, Grandma mended them, probably more

than once. When they were beyond repair, she used them as a rag for cleaning, or sewed them (with other old clothing) into a quilt. For her, everything had value, one way or another.

During this century, as women joined men working outside of the

home, income went up and families began buying more and more "time-saving" products. Before long, few people cared about the home recycling that Grandma practiced. Soon, cities sent crews from block to block to pick up truckloads of discarded material. The era of "trash" had begun.

What do you think?

1. *Just as Grandma Macionis was a product of her culture, so are we. What cultural values make people today demand "time-saving" products and "convenience" packaging?*

2. *What do you think are the prospects for expanding recycling of materials in the near future?*

3. *Would you support laws that limited people's trash? Why or why not?*

---

causes the earth's water, 97 percent of which is in the oceans, to evaporate and form clouds. Because water evaporates at lower temperatures than most pollutants, the water vapor that rises from the seas is relatively pure, leaving various contaminants behind. Water then falls to the earth as rain, which drains into streams and rivers and, finally, returns to the sea. Two major concerns about water, then, are supply and pollution.

Water supply. For thousands of years, since the time of the ancient civilizations of China, Egypt, and Rome, water rights have figured prominently in codes of law. Today, as Global Map 15–2 shows, some regions of the world, especially the tropics, enjoy a plentiful supply of water. High demand, coupled with modest reserves, makes water supply a matter of concern in much of North America and Asia, where people look to rivers, rather than rainfall, for their water. In the Middle East, water supply has already reached a critical level. In Egypt, for instance, an arid region of the world, people depend on the Nile River for most

of their water. But, as the Egyptian population increases, shortages are becoming frequent. Egyptians today must make do with one-sixth the amount of water per person from the Nile compared to 1900. Across much of northern Africa and the Middle East, experts predict, as many as 1 billion people may lack the water they need for irrigation and drinking within thirty years (Myers, 1984c; Postel, 1993).

But, the world over, soaring population and complex technology have greatly increased societies' appetite for water. The global consumption of water (now more than 6 billion cubic feet per year) has tripled since 1950 and is expanding even faster than the world's population. As a result, even in parts of the world that receive plenty of rainfall, people are using groundwater faster than it can be naturally replenished. In the Tamil Nadu region of southern India, for example, people are drawing so much groundwater that the local water table has fallen 100 feet over the last several decades. Mexico City—which has sprawled to some 1,400 square miles—has pumped so much

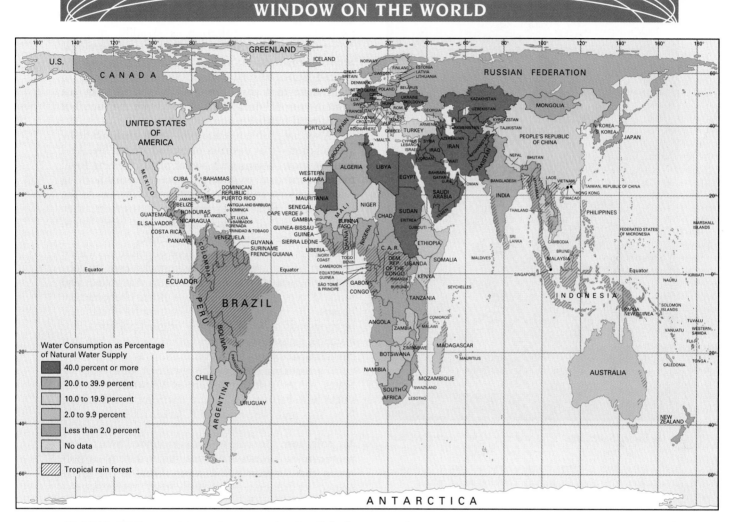

GLOBAL MAP 15–2 Water Consumption in Global Perspective

This map shows water consumption as a percentage of each country's renewable water resources. Nations near the equator consume only a tiny share of their available resources; indeed, much of this region is covered with rain forest. Northern Africa and the Middle East are a different story, however, with dense populations drawing on very limited water resources. As a result, in countries like Libya, Egypt, and Saudi Arabia, people (especially the poor) do not have as much water as they would like or, often, as they need.

Source: United Nations Development Programme (2000).

water from its underground aquifer that the city has sunk thirty feet during the last century and is dropping about two more inches per year. Farther north in the United States, the Ogallala aquifer, which lies below seven states from South Dakota to Texas, is now being pumped so rapidly that some experts fear it could run dry within several decades.

In light of such developments, we must face the reality that water is a valuable, finite resource. Greater conservation of water by individuals (the average person consumes 10 million gallons in a lifetime) is part of the answer. However, households around the world account for just 10 percent of water use. We need to curb water consumption by industry, which uses

In the United States, most of us take safe water for granted. But people, and especially children, in poor countries around the world are at high risk from infectious diseases that are spread by unclean water used for bathing, cooking, and drinking.

25 percent of the global total, and farming, which consumes two-thirds of the total for irrigation.

New irrigation technology may reduce the demand for water in the future. But, here again, we see how population increase, as well as economic growth, strains our ecosystem (Myers, 1984a; Goldfarb, 1991; Falkenmark & Widstrand, 1992; Postel, 1993).

Water pollution. In large cities—from Mexico City to Cairo to Shanghai—many people have no choice but to drink contaminated water. Infectious diseases like typhoid, cholera, and dysentery, all caused by water-borne micro-organisms, spread rapidly through these populations (Clarke, 1984b; Falkenmark & Widstrand, 1992). Besides ensuring ample *supplies* of water, then, we must protect the *quality* of water.

Water quality in the United States is generally good by global standards. However, even here the problem of water pollution is steadily growing. According to the Sierra Club, an environmental activist organization, rivers and streams across the United States absorb some 500 million pounds of toxic waste each year. This pollution results not just from intentional dumping, but also from the runoff of agricultural fertilizers and lawn chemicals.

A special problem is *acid rain*—rain made acidic by air pollution—that destroys plant and animal life. Acid rain (or snow) begins with power plants burning fossil fuels (oil and coal) to generate electricity; this burning releases sulfuric and nitrous oxides into the air. As the wind sweeps these gases into the atmosphere, they react with the air to form sulfuric and nitric acids, which turn atmospheric moisture acidic.

This is a clear case of one type of pollution causing another: air pollution (from smokestacks) ends up contaminating water (in lakes and streams that collect acid rain). Moreover, acid rain is truly a global phenomenon, because the regions that suffer the harmful effects may be thousands of miles from the original pollution. For instance, British power plants have caused acid rain that has devastated forests and fish in Norway and Sweden, up to a thousand miles to the northeast. In the United States, we see a similar pattern as Midwestern smokestacks have harmed the natural environment of upstate New York and New England (Clarke, 1984a).

Air pollution. Because we are surrounded by air, most people in the United States are more aware of air pollution than contaminated water. One of the unexpected consequences of industrial technology—especially the factory and the motor vehicle—has been a decline in air quality. In 1950, exhaust fumes from automobiles shrouded cities like Los Angeles. In London, factory smokestacks, automobiles, and coal fires used to heat households all added to what was probably the worst urban air quality of the last century. What some British jokingly called "pea soup" was, in reality, a deadly mix of pollution: During five days in 1952, an especially thick haze that hung over London killed 4,000 people (Clarke, 1984a).

Air quality improved in the final decades of the last century. Rich nations passed laws that banned high-pollution heating, including the coal fires that choked London fifty years ago. In addition, scientists devised ways to reduce the noxious output of factories and the growing numbers of automobiles and trucks.

If high-income countries can breathe a bit more easily than they once did, the problem of air pollution in poor societies is becoming more serious. One reason is that people in low-income countries still rely on wood, coal, peat, or other "dirty" fuels for cooking fires and to heat their homes. Moreover, nations eager to encourage short-term industrial development may pay little heed to the longer-term dangers of air pollution. As a result, many cities in Latin America, Eastern Europe, and Asia are plagued by air pollution as bad as London's fifty years ago.

THE RAIN FORESTS

Rain forests are *regions of dense forestation, most of which circle the globe close to the equator.* A glance back at Global Map 15–2, on page 425, shows that the largest tropical rain forests are in South America (notably Brazil), west-central Africa, and Southeast Asia. In all, the world's rain forests cover some 2 billion acres, or 7 percent of the earth's total land surface.

Like other global resources, rain forests are falling victim to the needs and appetites of the surging world population. As noted earlier, to meet the demand for beef, ranchers in Latin America burn forested areas to increase their supply of grazing land. We are also losing rain forests to the hardwood trade. People in rich nations pay high prices for mahogany and other woods because, as environmentalist Norman Myers (1984b:88) puts it, they have "a penchant for parquet floors, fine furniture, fancy paneling, weekend yachts, and high-grade coffins." Under such economic pressure, the world's rain forests are now just half their original size, and they continue to shrink by about 1 percent (65,000 square miles) annually. Unless we stop this loss, the rain forests will vanish before the end of the twenty-first century, and, with them, protection for the earth's biodiversity and climate.

Global warming. Why are rain forests so important? One reason is that they cleanse the atmosphere of carbon dioxide (CO_2). Since the beginning of the Industrial Revolution, the amount of carbon dioxide produced by humans (mostly from factories and automobiles) has risen sharply. Much of this CO_2 is absorbed by the oceans. But plants take in carbon dioxide and expel oxygen. This is why the rain forests are vital to maintaining the chemical balance of the atmosphere.

The problem, then, is that production of carbon dioxide is rising while the amount of plant life on the earth is shrinking. To make matters worse, rain forests are being destroyed mostly by burning, which releases even more carbon dioxide into the atmosphere.

Experts estimate the atmospheric concentration of carbon dioxide is now 20 to 30 percent higher than it was 150 years ago.

High above the earth, carbon dioxide acts like the glass roof of a greenhouse, letting heat from the sun pass through to the earth while preventing much of it from radiating back away from the planet. The result, say ecologists, is a **greenhouse effect,** *a rise in the earth's average temperature (global warming) due to an increasing concentration of carbon dioxide in the atmosphere.* Over the last century, the global temperature has risen about 1.0° Fahrenheit (to an average of 58° F). Scientists warn that it could rise by 5° to 10° during this century, which would melt vast areas of the polar ice caps and raise the sea level to cover low-lying land around the world. Were this to happen, water would cover all of Bangladesh, for example, and much of the coastal United States, including Washington, D.C., right up to the steps of the White House. On the other hand, the U.S. Midwest—currently one of the most productive agricultural regions in the world—would likely become arid.

Not all scientists share this vision of future global warming. Some point out that global temperature changes have been taking place throughout history, apparently with little or nothing to do with rain forests. Moreover, higher concentrations of carbon dioxide in the atmosphere might speed up plant growth (since plants thrive on this gas), which would correct the imbalance and nudge the earth's temperature downward once again. Still other scientists think global warming might even have benefits, including longer growing seasons and lower food prices (Silverberg, 1991; Moore, 1995; Begley, 1997; McDonald, 1999).

Declining biodiversity. Clearing rain forests also reduces the earth's *biodiversity.* This is because rain forests are home to almost half of this planet's living species.

On earth, there are as many as 30 million species of animals, plants, and micro-organisms. Several dozen unique species of plants and animals cease to exist each day; but, given the vast number of living species, why should we be concerned? Environmentalists give three reasons. First, our planet's biodiversity provides a varied source of human food. Using agricultural high technology, scientists can "splice" familiar crops with more exotic plant life, making food more bountiful as well as more resistant to insects and disease. Thus, biodiversity is needed to feed our planet's rapidly increasing population.

Members of small, simple societies, such as the Tan't Batu, who thrive in the Philippines, live in harmony with nature; such people do not have the technological means to greatly affect the natural world. Although we in complex societies like to think of ourselves as superior to such people, the truth is that there is much we can—and must—learn from them.

Second, animal and plant biodiversity is a vital genetic resource. Medical and pharmaceutical researchers rely on it to provide hundreds of new compounds each year that cure disease and improve our lives. Children in the United States, for example, now have a good chance of surviving leukemia, a disease that was almost a sure killer two generations ago, because of a compound derived from a pretty tropical flower called the rosy periwinkle. The oral birth control pill, used by tens of millions of women in this country, is another product of plant research, this time involving the Mexican forest yam.

Third, with the loss of any species of life—whether it is the magnificent California condor, the famed Chinese panda, the spotted owl, or even one variety of ant—the beauty and complexity of our natural environment are diminished. And there are clear warning signs: Three-fourths of the world's 9,000 species of birds are declining in number.

Finally, note that, unlike pollution, the extinction of any species is irreversible and final. An important ethical question, then, is whether we who live today

have the right to impoverish the world for those who live tomorrow (Myers, 1984b; Myers, 1991; Wilson, 1991; Brown et al., 1993).

ENVIRONMENTAL RACISM

Conflict theory has given birth to the concept of **environmental racism,** *the pattern by which environmental hazards are greatest for poor people, especially minorities.* Historically, factories that spew pollution have stood near neighborhoods of the poor and people of color. Why? In part, because the poor themselves were drawn to factories in search of work and, once hired, their low incomes often meant they could afford housing only in undesirable neighborhoods. Sometimes the only housing that fit their budgets stood in the very shadow of the plants and mills where they worked.

Nobody wants a factory or dump nearby, of course, but the poor have little power to resist. Through the years, then, the most serious environmental hazards have been placed near Newark, New Jersey (not in upscale Bergen County), in southside Chicago (not wealthy Lake Forest), or on Native American reservations in the West (not in affluent suburbs of Denver or Phoenix) (Perrolle, 1993; Commission for Racial Justice, United Church of Christ, 1994; Szasz, 1994; Pollock & Vittas, 1995).

LOOKING AHEAD: TOWARD A SUSTAINABLE SOCIETY AND WORLD

The demographic analysis presented in this chapter points to some disturbing trends. We see, first, that the earth's population has reached record levels because birth rates remain high in poor nations and death rates have fallen just about everywhere. Reducing fertility will remain a pressing issue throughout this century. Even with some recent decline in population increase, the nightmare of Thomas Malthus is still a real possibility, as the final box on page 430 explains.

Further, population growth remains greatest in the poorest countries of the world, those without the means to support their present populations, much less their future ones. Supporting 77 million additional people on our planet each year—almost 74 million of whom are in poor societies—will require a global commitment to provide not only food but housing, schools, and employment. The well-being of the entire world may ultimately depend on resolving the economic and social problems of poor, overly populated countries and bridging the widening gulf between "have" and "have-not" societies.

Urbanization, too, is continuing, especially in poor countries. People have always sought out cities in the hope of finding a better life. But the sheer numbers of people who now live in the emerging global super-cities, including Mexico City, São Paulo (Brazil), Kinshasa (Democratic Republic of the Congo), Bombay (India), and Manila (the Philippines), have created urban problems on a massive scale.

Throughout the entire world, humanity is facing a serious environmental challenge. Part of this problem is population increase, which is greatest in poor societies. But part of the problem is also high levels of consumption, which mark rich nations such as our own. By increasing the planet's environmental deficit, our present way of life is borrowing against the well-being of our children and their children. Globally, members of rich societies, who currently consume so much of the earth's resources, are mortgaging the future security of the poor countries of the world.

The answer, in principle, is to form an **ecologically sustainable culture,** *a way of life that meets the needs of the present generation without threatening the environmental legacy of future generations.* Sustainable living depends on three strategies.

First, the world needs to bring population growth under control. The current population of more than 6 billion is already straining the natural environment. Clearly, the higher world population climbs, the more difficult environmental problems will become. Even if the recent slowing of population growth continues, the world will have 8 billion people by 2050. Few analysts think that the earth can support this many people; most argue that we must hold the line at about 7 billion and some argue that we must *decrease* population in the coming decades (Smail, 2001).

A second strategy is *conservation of finite resources.* This means meeting our needs with a responsible eye toward the future by using resources efficiently, seeking alternative sources of energy, and, in some cases, learning to live with less.

A third strategy is *reducing waste.* Whenever possible, simply using less is the best way to do this. But recycling programs, too, are part of the answer.

In the end, making all these strategies work depends on a more basic change in the way we think about ourselves and our world. Our *egocentric* outlook sets our own interests as standards for how to live; a sustainable environment demands an *ecocentric* outlook that helps us to see that the present is tied to the future and that everyone must work together. Most nations in the

No one wants to live or work in a dangerous environment. But, in a world of political competition, it is the poor who often end up with the hazards in their backyards. Here, residents of this urban neighborhood protest plans to construct a power plant in the area.

southern half of the world are *underdeveloped,* unable to meet the basic needs of their people. At the same time, most countries in the northern half of the world are *overdeveloped,* using more resources than the earth can sustain over time. Changes needed to create a sustainable ecosystem will not come easily. But the price of not responding to the growing environmental deficit will certainly be greater (Humphrey & Buttel, 1982; Burke, 1984; Kellert & Bormann, 1991; Brown et al., 1993).

In closing, consider that the great dinosaurs dominated this planet for some 160 million years and then perished forever. Humanity is far younger, having existed for a mere 250,000 years. Compared to the rather dim-witted dinosaurs, our species has the gift of great intelligence. But how will we use this ability? What are the chances that humans will continue to flourish 160 million years—or even 1,000 years—from now? The shape of tomorrow's world depends on choices we make today.

CONTROVERSY & DEBATE

Apocalypse: Will People Overwhelm the Earth?

Are you worried about the world's increasing population? Think about this: By the time you finish reading this box, more than 1,000 people will be added to our planet. By this time tomorrow, global population will rise by 210,000. Currently, as the table below shows, there are about four births for every two deaths on the planet, pushing the world's population upward by 77 million annually. Put another way, global population growth amounts to adding another Germany to the world every year.

It is no wonder that many demographers and environmentalists are deeply concerned about the future. The earth has an unprecedented population: The 2 billion people we have *added* since 1974 alone exceeds the planet's total in 1900. Might Thomas Robert Malthus—who predicted that population would outstrip the earth's resources and plunge humanity into war and suffering—be right after all?

genetics) could boost the planet's agricultural output. But he maintains that the earth's rising population is nevertheless rapidly outstripping its finite resources. Families in many poor countries can find little firewood; members of rich societies are depleting the oil reserves; everyone is draining our supply of clean water.

Moreover, according to the neo-Malthusians, we are steadily poisoning the planet with waste. There is a limit to the earth's capacity to absorb pollution, they warn, and as the number of people continues to increase, the quality of life will decline. Some analysts, in fact, argue that we have already exceeded the earth's "carrying capacity" for population. Holding the line on growth will not be enough; as they see it, we need to *reduce* global population to perhaps half of what it is today (Smail, 2001).

But another camp of analysts—the *anti-Malthusians*—sharply disagrees.

current state of the planet is cause for celebration.

The mistake of the neo-Malthusians, Simon argues, is assuming the world has finite resources that are spread thinner and thinner as population increases. Rather, people have the capacity to control population growth and to improve their lives in many ways. Furthermore, we do not know what number of people the earth can support because humans keep rewriting the rules, in effect, by developing new fertilizers, new crops, and new forms of energy. Simon notes that today's global economy makes available more resources than ever (including energy and consumer goods) at increasingly low prices. He looks optimistically to the future because technology, economic investment, and, above all, human ingenuity, have consistently proven the doomsayers wrong. And he is betting they will continue to do so.

Continue the debate . . .

1. *Where do you place your bet? Do you think the earth can support 4, 6, 8, or 10 billion people? Why?*

2. *Ninety-six percent of current population growth is in poor countries. What does this mean for the future of rich nations? For the future of poor ones?*

3. *What should people in rich countries do to ensure the future of children everywhere?*

Global Population Increase

	Births	Deaths	Net Increase
Per Year	131,571,719	55,001,289	76,570,430
Per Month	10,964,310	4,583,441	6,380,869
Per Day	360,470	150,688	209,782
Per Hour	15,020	6,279	8,741
Per Minute	250	105	146
Per Second	4.2	1.7	2.4

Lester Brown, a population and environmental activist, represents the *neo-Malthusians*, who foresee a coming apocalypse if we do not change our ways. Brown concedes that Malthus failed to imagine how much technology (especially fertilizers and altering plant

Asks economist Julian Simon, "Why the doom and gloom?" Two centuries ago, he points out, Malthus predicted catastrophe. But today the earth supports almost six times as many people who, on average, live longer, healthier lives than ever before. As Simon sees it, the

Sources: Based, in part, on Brown et al. (1993), Brown (1995), Simon (1995), and Smail (2001).

SUMMARY

POPULATION

1. Fertility and mortality, measured as crude birth rates and crude death rates, are major factors affecting population size.

2. Migration, another key demographic concept, has special importance to the historical growth of the United States and to cities everywhere.

3. Demographers use age-sex pyramids to graphically show the composition of a population and to project population trends. Sex ratio refers to a society's balance of females and males.

4. Historically, world population grew slowly because high birth rates were largely offset by high death rates. About 1750, a demographic transition began as world population rose sharply, mostly due to falling death rates.

5. Thomas Robert Malthus warned that population growth would outpace food production, resulting in social calamity. Demographic transition theory, however, contends that technological advances gradually slow population increase.

6. World population is expected to reach between 8 and 9 billion by 2050. Such an increase will likely overwhelm many poor societies, where most of the increase will take place.

URBANIZATION

1. The first urban revolution began with the appearance of cities about 8000 B.C.E. By the start of the common era, cities had emerged in most regions of the world except for North America.

2. Preindustrial cities are characterized by low-rise buildings, narrow, winding streets, and personal social ties.

3. A second urban revolution began about 1750 as the Industrial Revolution propelled rapid urban growth in Europe. The physical form of cities changed, as planners created wide, regular streets to facilitate trade. The emphasis on commerce, as well as the increasing size of cities, made urban life more anonymous.

4. Urbanism came to North America with Europeans, who settled in a string of colonial towns dotting the Atlantic coastline. By 1850, hundreds of new cities were founded from coast to coast.

5. By 1920, a majority of the U.S. population lived in urban areas, and the largest metropolises were home to millions of people.

6. About 1950, cities began to decentralize with the growth of suburbs and edge cities. Nationally, Sunbelt cities—but not most older, Snowbelt cities—are increasing in size and population.

7. Rapid urbanization in Europe during the nineteenth century led early sociologists to contrast rural and urban life. Ferdinand Tönnies built his analysis on the concepts of *Gemeinshaft* and *Gesellschaft*, and Emile Durkheim devised parallel concepts of mechanical solidarity and organic solidarity. Georg Simmel claimed that the overstimulation of city life produced a blasé attitude in urbanites.

8. At the University of Chicago, Robert Park believed cities permit greater social freedom. Louis Wirth saw large, dense, heterogeneous populations creating an impersonal and self-interested—thought tolerant—way of life. Other researchers have explored urban ecology and urban political economy.

9. A third urban revolution is now occurring in poor countries, where most brought on by the world's largest cities will soon be found.

ENVIRONMENT

1. A key factor affecting the natural environment is how human beings organize social life. Thus, ecologists study how living organisms interact with their environment.

2. Societies increase the environmental deficit by focusing on short-term benefits and ignoring the long-term consequences brought on by their way of life.

3. Our ability to alter the natural world lies in our capacity for culture. Humanity's effect on the environment has increased along with the development of complex technology.

4. The "logic of growth" supports economic development, claiming that people can solve environmental problems as they arise. The opposing "limits to growth" thesis states that societies must curb development to prevent eventual environmental collapse.

5. Environmental issues include disposing of solid waste as well as protecting the quality of air and water. The supply of clean water is already low in some parts of the world.

6. Rain forests help remove carbon dioxide from the atmosphere and are home to a large share of this planet's living species. Under pressure from commercial interests, the world's rain forests are now half their original size and are shrinking by about 1 percent annually.

7. Environmental racism refers to the pattern by which the poor—especially minorities—suffer most from environmental hazards.

8. A sustainable environment does not threaten the well-being of future generations. Achieving this goal requires controlling world population, conserving finite resources, and reducing waste and pollution.

KEY CONCEPTS

POPULATION

demography (p. 405) the study of human population

fertility (p. 406) the incidence of childbearing in a country's population

crude birth rate (p. 406) the number of live births in a given year for every thousand people in a population

mortality (p. 406) the incidence of death in a country's population

crude death rate (p. 406) the number of deaths in a given year for every thousand people in a population

infant mortality rate (p. 406) the number of deaths among infants under one year of age for each thousand live births in a given year

life expectancy (p. 407) the average life span of a country's population

migration (p. 407) the movement of people into and out of a specified territory

sex ratio (p. 409) the number of males for every hundred females in a nation's population

age-sex pyramid (p. 409) a graphic representation of the age and sex of a population

demographic transition theory (p. 411) the thesis that population patterns reflect a society's level of technological development

zero population growth (p. 412) the level of reproduction that maintains population at a steady state

URBANIZATION

urbanization (p. 413) the concentration of humanity into cities

metropolis (p. 415) a large city that socially and economically dominates an urban area

suburbs (p. 415) urban areas beyond the political boundaries of a city

megalopolis (p. 416) a vast urban region containing a number of cities and their surrounding suburbs

Gemeinschaft (p. 416) a type of social organization by which people are closely tied by kinship and tradition

Gesellschaft (p. 416) a type of social organization by which people come together only on the basis of individual self-interest

urban ecology (p. 418) the study of the link between the physical and social dimensions of cities

ENVIRONMENT

ecology (p. 420) the study of the interaction between living organisms and the natural environment

natural environment (p. 420) the earth's surface and atmosphere, including living organisms, air, water, soil, and other resources necessary to sustain life

ecosystem (p. 420) a system composed of the interaction of all living organisms and their natural environment

environmental deficit (p. 421) profound and negative long-term harm to the natural environment caused by humanity's focus on short-term material affluence

rain forests (p. 427) regions of dense forestation, most of which circle the globe close to the equator

greenhouse effect (p. 427) a rise in the earth's average temperature (global warming) due to an increasing concentration of carbon dioxide in the atmosphere

environmental racism (p. 428) the pattern by which environmental hazards are greatest for poor people, especially minorities

ecologically sustainable culture (p. 429) a way of life that meets the needs of the present generation without threatening the environmental legacy of future generations

CRITICAL-THINKING QUESTIONS

1. What are fertility and mortality rates? Which one has been more important in increasing global population?

2. How does demographic transition theory explain population patterns in terms of technological development?

3. According to Ferdinand Tönnies, Emile Durkheim, Georg Simmel, and Louis Wirth, what characterizes urbanism as a way of life? Note several differences in the ideas of these thinkers.

4. Evaluate the environmental prediction of Thomas Robert Malthus. On balance, do you think he was more wrong or more right? Why?

APPLICATIONS AND EXERCISES

1. Here is an illustration of the problem of runaway growth (Milbrath, 1989:10): *A pond has a single water lily growing on it. The lily doubles in size each day. In thirty days, it covers the entire pond. On which day does it cover half the pond?* When you realize the answer, discuss the implications of this example for population increase.

2. Draw a "mental map" of a city familiar to you, with as much detail of specific places, districts, roads, and transportation facilities as you can. Compare your map to a "real" one, or, better yet, a map drawn by someone else. Try to account for the differences.

3. Carry a plastic trash bag around with you for one full day. Put everything you throw away in the bag.

Afterward, weigh what you have; multiply this amount by 365 to estimate your yearly "trash factor." Multiply this amount by 275 million to estimate the annual waste of the entire U.S. population.

4. In the Bible, read Genesis, chapter 1, especially verses 28–31. According to this account of creation, are humans empowered to do what we wish to the earth? Or are we charged to care for the earth? For more on this idea, see Wolkomir et al. (1997).

5. Install the CD-ROM packaged in the back of this new textbook to access a variety of study, review, and applications exercises. The CD includes an author's tip video, interactive maps, video application exercises, Web links, and study questions.

 SITES TO SEE

http://www.prenhall.com/macionis

Visit the interactive Web site that accompanies this text. Begin by clicking on the cover of your book. You will find a chapter-by-chapter study guide, practice tests, chat room, and many suggested Web links.

http://www.eclac.org

This site, created by the Latin American and Caribbean Demographic Center (part of the United Nations), provides statistics on population patterns for this region of the world. Most of the site is available in both English and Spanish.

http://www.urban.nyu.edu

New York University's Taub Urban Research Center is on the Internet. Visit this site to survey recent research on urban issues.

http://www.mte.com/webcam/

Watch big-city life from the comfort of your own home: This site uses a cyber-view camera showing the action on New York City's Fifth Avenue and Forty-fifth Street. What can you learn from "people watching" in this way? What does this observation *not* tell you about urban life?

http://www.sierraclub.org
http://www.greenpeace.org

Here are two environmental sites maintained by the Sierra Club and Greenpeace. Visit the sites and see how these two organizations are similar to one another as well as how they differ.

http://www.kenyon.edu/projects/agri/

This site, constructed by college students, investigates how the way we live affects the planet and how the state of our planet affects our lives.

CHAPTER
16

SOCIAL CHANGE:
MODERN AND POSTMODERN
SOCIETIES

CHAPTER OUTLINE

What Is Social Change?

Causes of Social Change

Culture and Change
Conflict and Change
Ideas and Change
Demographic Change
Social Movements and Change

Modernity

Ferdinand Tönnies: The Loss of Community
Emile Durkheim: The Division of Labor
Max Weber: Rationalization
Karl Marx: Capitalism

**Structural-Functional Analysis:
The Theory of Mass Society**

The Mass Scale of Modern Life
The Ever-Expanding State

**Social-Conflict Analysis:
The Theory of Class Society**

Capitalism
Persistent Inequality

Modernity and the Individual

Mass Society: Problems of Identity
Class Society: Problems of Powerlessness

Modernity and Progress

Modernity: Global Variation

Postmodernity

**Looking Ahead:
Modernization and Our Global Future**

• Summary • Key Concepts
• Critical-Thinking Questions
• Applications and Exercises • Sites to See

In 1900, people lined up at the Paris Exposition to catch a glimpse of some of the world's latest inventions, including something called a "voice recorder" and the Kodak company's first small camera, the "Brownie." The same year, not far away in Germany, a physicist named Max Planck had just discovered atomic radiation, although he was not sure exactly what it was and had little idea of what people might do with it. Another German, a doctor named Sigmund Freud, published a book on the interpretation of dreams, which few people found very convincing. Farther east in Russia, a young man named Vladimir Lenin published his first newspaper article calling for a people's revolution to overthrow the government. In China, a rebellion against exploitation by foreign powers started the world thinking about the evils of colonialism.

Across the Atlantic Ocean in the United States, 1900 saw the Wright brothers arrive in Kitty Hawk, North Carolina, with the idea of building a machine that would allow people to fly. Meanwhile, in New York City, J. P. Morgan was already flying high, having just signed a deal to create U.S. Steel, the world's first billion-dollar corporation (Issacson, 1998).

It is scarcely possible for people today to imagine how different life was a century ago. Most people in the United States still lived in small towns and on farms. They had no computers, televisions, or even radios. Most homes did not even have electricity. There were no super-highways—only a few people had ever seen an automobile (known back then as a "horseless carriage"). Most people traveled around their communities by foot or on horseback, and a few went greater distances by railroad, in passenger cars pulled by steam-powered locomotives. Almost all women worked only in the home; none was permitted by law to vote. For both women and men, life was also much shorter: On average, people lived only about fifty years.

It is easy to find ways in which life today seems better than a century ago. We now enjoy countless conveniences, travel farther and faster, and live longer than ever before. Yet, as this chapter explains, social change is a process with negative as well as positive consequences. Indeed, as we shall see, the founding thinkers of sociology were mixed in their assessment of *modernity*, changes brought about by the Industrial Revolution. Likewise, today's sociologists point to both good and bad qualities of *postmodernity*, the recent transformations caused by the Information Revolution and the postindustrial economy. What is clear—for better and worse—is that the rate of change has never been faster than it is now.

WHAT IS SOCIAL CHANGE?

In earlier chapters, we examined relatively *static* social patterns, including status and role, social stratification, and social institutions. We also looked at the *dynamic* forces that have shaped our way of life, ranging from innovations in technology to the growth of bureaucracy and the expansion of cities. These are all dimensions of

CHAPTER 16 Social Change: Modern and Postmodern Societies   **435**

Because change in modern societies is so rapid, we can see differences in personal appearance—one important kind of fashion—over short periods of time. The five photographs (beginning with the top left) show hair styles commonly worn by women in the 1950s, 1960s, 1970s, 1980s, and 1990s.

social change, *the transformation of culture and social institutions over time.* This complex process has four major characteristics:

1. **Social change happens all the time.** "Nothing is certain except death and taxes," goes the old saying. Yet our thoughts about death have changed dramatically as life expectancy in the United States has doubled since 1850. Taxes, meanwhile, were unknown through most of human history, beginning only as societies grew in size several thousand years ago. In short, virtually everything is subject to the twists and turns of change.

   Still, some societies change faster than others. As Chapter 2 ("Culture") explained, hunting

and gathering societies change quite slowly; members of technologically complex societies, on the other hand, can witness significant change within a single lifetime.

   Moreover, in a given society, some cultural elements change faster than others. William Ogburn's (1964) theory of *cultural lag* (see Chapter 2) asserts that material culture (that is, things) usually changes faster than nonmaterial culture (ideas and attitudes). For example, medical technology that prolongs life has developed more rapidly than have ethical standards for deciding when and how to use it.

2. **Social change is sometimes intentional but often unplanned.** Industrial societies actively promote many kinds of change. For example,

scientists seek more efficient forms of energy, and advertisers try to convince us that life is incomplete without this or that new gadget. Yet rarely can anyone envision all the consequences of the changes that are set in motion.

Early automobile manufacturers understood that cars would allow people to travel in a single day distances that had required weeks or months a century before. But no one could see how much the mobility provided by automobiles would alter life in the United States, scattering family members, threatening the environment, and reshaping cities and suburbs. Neither could automotive pioneers have predicted the more than 43,000 deaths each year in car accidents in the United States alone.

3. **Social change is controversial.** As the history of the automobile demonstrates, social change has both good and bad consequences. Capitalists welcomed the Industrial Revolution because advancing technology increased productivity and swelled profits. Many workers, however, feared that machines would make their skills obsolete and resisted the push towards "progress."

In the United States, changing patterns of social interaction between black people and white people, women and men, and gays and heterosexuals, give rise to both celebration and backlash as people disagree about how we ought to live.

4. **Some changes matter more than others.** Some changes (such as clothing fads) have only passing significance, whereas other innovations (like computers) last a long time and may change the entire world. Looking ahead, will the Information Revolution turn out to be as pivotal as the Industrial Revolution? Like the automobile and television, computers will continue to have both positive and negative effects, providing new kinds of jobs while eliminating old ones, isolating people in offices while linking people in global electronic networks, offering vast amounts of information while threatening personal privacy.

CAUSES OF SOCIAL CHANGE

Social change has many causes. And, in a world linked by sophisticated communication and transportation technology, change in one place often begets change elsewhere.

Today, most of the people with access to computers live in rich countries such as the United States. But the number of people in low-income nations going "online" is on the rise. How do you think the introduction of new information technology will change more traditional societies? Are all the changes likely to be for the good?

CULTURE AND CHANGE

Chapter 2 ("Culture") identified three important sources of cultural change. First, *invention* produces new objects, ideas, and social patterns. Rocket propulsion research, which began in the 1940s, has produced sophisticated spacecraft that can reach toward the stars. Today we take such technology for granted; during the twenty-first century, a significant number of people may well travel in space.

Second, *discovery* occurs as people take notice of existing elements of the world. Medical advances, for example, offer a growing understanding of the human body. Beyond their direct effects on human health, medical discoveries have stretched life expectancy, setting in motion the "graying" of U.S. society (see Chapter 3, "Socialization: From Infancy to Old Age").

Third, *diffusion* creates change as products, people, and information spread from one society to another. Ralph Linton (1937a) recognized that many familiar aspects of our culture came from other lands. For example, cloth (developed in Asia), clocks (invented in

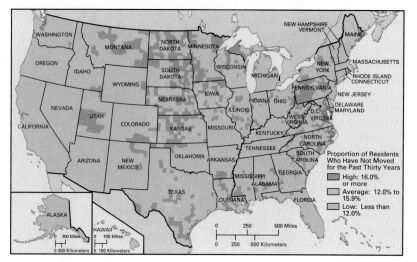

Overall, only about 9 percent of U.S. residents have not moved during the last thirty years. Counties with a higher proportion of "long-termers" typically have experienced less change over recent decades: Many neighborhoods have been in place since before World War II, and many of the same families live in them. Looking at the map, what can you say about these relatively stable areas? Why are most of these counties rural and some distance from the coasts?

Source: U.S. Census Bureau (1996).

Europe), and coins (devised in Turkey) have all become part of our way of life. In general, material things diffuse more easily than cultural ideas. In addition, new breakthroughs (such as the science of cloning) occur faster than our understanding of when—and even if—they are morally desirable.

CONFLICT AND CHANGE

Tension and conflict within a society also produce change. Karl Marx saw class conflict as the engine that drives societies from one historical era to another. In industrial-capitalist societies, he maintained, the struggle between capitalists and workers propels society toward a socialist system of production.

In more than a century since Marx's death, this model has proven simplistic. Yet, Marx correctly foresaw that social conflict arising from inequality (involving not just class but race and gender) would force changes in every society, including our own.

IDEAS AND CHANGE

Max Weber also contributed to our understanding of social change. While Weber acknowledged that conflict could bring about change, he traced the roots of most social changes to ideas. For example, people with charisma can carry a message that sometimes changes the world.

Weber highlighted the importance of ideas by revealing how the religious beliefs of early Protestants set the stage for the spread of industrial capitalism (see Chapter 13, "Family and Religion"). The fact that industrial capitalism developed primarily in areas of Western Europe where the Protestant work ethic was strong proved to Weber (1958; orig. 1904–5) the power of ideas to bring about change.

DEMOGRAPHIC CHANGE

Population patterns can also transform a society. Profound change is taking place as our population, collectively speaking, grows older. As Chapter 3 ("Socialization: From Infancy to Old Age") explained, 13 percent of the U.S. population was over age sixty-five in 2000, triple the proportion in 1900. By the year 2030, seniors will account for 20 percent of the total (U.S. Census Bureau, 2000). Medical research and health care services already focus extensively on the elderly, and life will change in countless additional ways as homes and household products are redesigned to meet the needs of growing ranks of older consumers.

Migration within and among societies is another demographic factor that promotes change. Between 1870 and 1930, tens of millions of immigrants entered the industrial cities in the United States. Millions more from rural areas joined the rush. As a result, farm communities declined, metropolises expanded, and the United States for the first time became a predominantly urban nation. Similar changes are taking place today as people moving from the Snowbelt to the Sunbelt mix with new immigrants from Latin America and Asia.

Where in the United States have demographic changes been greatest? National Map 16–1 provides one answer, showing where the largest share of people do—and do not—move.

SOCIAL MOVEMENTS AND CHANGE

A final cause of social change lies in our own efforts. People commonly band together to form **social movements,** *organized activity that encourages or discourages social change.* Our nation's history is the story of all kinds of social movements, from the colonial drive for independence to today's organizations supporting or opposing abortion, gay rights, and the death penalty.

Types of social movements. Researchers classify social movements according to the kind of change they seek (Aberle, 1966; Cameron, 1966; Blumer, 1969). One variable asks, *Who is changed?* Some movements target selected people while others try to change everyone. A second variable asks, *How much change?* Some movements attempt only superficial change, while others pursue a radical transformation of society. Combining these variables results in four types of social movements, shown in Figure 16–1.

Alternative social movements are the least threatening to the status quo because they seek limited change in only some part of the population. Promise Keepers, one example of an alternative social movement, encourages Christian men to be more spiritual and supportive of their families.

Redemptive social movements also have a selective focus, seeking radical change in some individuals. For example, Alcoholics Anonymous is an organization that helps people with an alcohol addiction achieve a sober life.

Reformative social movements aim for only limited change, but target everyone. The environmental movement seeks to interest everyone in protecting the natural environment.

Revolutionary social movements are the most extreme of all, striving for major transformation of an entire society. Sometimes pursuing specific goals, sometimes spinning utopian dreams, these social movements (including both the left-wing Communist Party and right-wing militia organizations) seek to radically alter our social institutions.

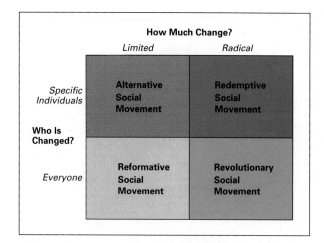

FIGURE 16–1 Four Types of Social Movements
Source: Based on Aberle (1966).

Explaining social movements. Sociologists have devised several ways of looking at social movements. One approach, *deprivation theory,* holds that social movements arise among people who feel deprived of something, say, income, safe working conditions, or political rights. Whether one feels deprived or not, of course, depends on one's expectations. Thus, people mobilize in response to **relative deprivation,** *a perceived disadvantage arising from some specific comparison.* This concept helps explain why movements for change surface in both good and bad times: It is not people's absolute standing that counts but how they subjectively perceive their own situation (Tocqueville, 1955, orig. 1856; Davies, 1962; Merton, 1968).

Mass-society theory, a second approach, argues that social movements attract socially isolated people who seek, through their membership, a sense of identity and purpose. From this point of view, social movements have a personal as well as a political agenda (Kornhauser, 1959; Melucci, 1989).

Resource-mobilization theory, a third theoretical scheme, links the success of any social movement to available resources—including money, human labor, and access to the mass media. Since most social movements begin small, they must look beyond themselves to mobilize the resources needed to increase their chances for success (Killian, 1984; Snow et al., 1986; Baron, Mittman, & Newman, 1991; Burstein, 1991; Meyer & Whittier, 1994; Zhao, 1998).

Fourth, *culture theory* points out that social movements depend not only on material resources but also

One example of a new social movement is the worldwide effort to eliminate land mines. Years after hostilities cease, these mines remain in place and take a staggering toll in civilian lives. At a protest in Berlin, Germany, a mountain of shoes stands as a memorial to the tens of thousands who have been crippled or died as a result of stepping on underground mines.

on cultural symbols. People must have a shared understanding of injustice in the world before they can mobilize to bring about change. In addition, specific symbols (such as mass media images of starving children around the world) can generate powerful feelings that motivate people to act (Morris & Mueller, 1992; Giugni, 1998; Staggenborg, 1998).

Fifth, and finally, *new social movements theory* points out the distinctive character of recent social movements in postindustrial societies. Not only are these movements typically national or international in scope, but most focus on quality-of-life issues—including the natural environment, world peace, or animal rights—rather than the traditional concern with economic issues. This broader scope of contemporary social movements results from closer ties among governments and among ordinary people around the world, who are now linked by the mass media and new information technology (Melucci, 1980; McAdam, McCarthy, & Zald, 1988; Kriesi, 1989; Pakulski, 1993; Jenkins & Wallace, 1996).

Stages in social movements. Social movements typically unfold in stages. The *emergence* of social movements occurs when a small group believes society is flawed. Both the women's movement and the response to the AIDS crisis began with a small vanguard who tried to mobilize the public.

The *coalescence* of a social movement depends on available resources. A newly formed movement must clearly state its goal, recruit new members, and devise policies and tactics. Leaders must also gain access to the mass media and forge alliances with other organizations.

As it accumulates resources, a social movement may undergo *bureaucratization*. This means that a movement becomes established, depending less on the charisma and talents of a few leaders and more on a professional staff, which increases the chances for the movement's long-term survival.

Finally, social movements *decline* as resources dry up, the group faces overwhelming opposition, or members achieve their goals and lose interest. Some well-established organizations outlive their original causes and move on to new crusades; others lose touch with the idea of changing society and choose, instead, to become part of the "system" (Piven & Cloward, 1977; Miller, 1983).

MODERNITY

A central concept in the study of social change is **modernity,** *social patterns resulting from industrialization.* In everyday terms, modernity (its Latin root means "lately") refers to the present in relation to the past. Sociologists use this catch-all concept to describe the many social patterns set in motion by the Industrial Revolution beginning in Western Europe in the mid-eighteenth century. **Modernization,** then, is *the process of social change begun by industrialization.* Peter Berger (1977) identified four major characteristics of modernization:

1. **The decline of small, traditional communities.** Modernity involves "the progressive weakening, if not destruction, of the . . . relatively cohesive communities in which human beings have found solidarity and meaning throughout most of history" (Berger, 1977:72). For thousands of years, in the camps of hunters and gatherers and in the rural villages of Europe and North America, people lived in small-scale communities where life revolved around family and neighborhood. Such traditional worlds give each person a

George Tooker's 1950 painting The Subway *depicts a common problem of modern life: Weakening social ties and eroding traditions create a generic humanity in which everyone is alike yet each person is an anxious stranger in the midst of others.*

George Tooker, *The Subway*, 1950, egg tempera on gesso panel, 18⅛ x 36⅛", Whitney Museum of American Art, New York. Purchased with funds from the Julianna Force Purchase Award, 50.23. Photograph ©2000 Whitney Museum of American Art.

well-defined place that, while limiting range of choice, offers a strong sense of identity, belonging, and purpose.

Small, isolated communities still exist in the United States, of course, but they are now home to only a small percentage of our nation's people. These days, their isolation is only geographic: Cars, telephones, television, and, increasingly, computers, give most rural families the pulse of the larger society and connect them to the entire world.

2. **The expansion of personal choice.** People in traditional, preindustrial societies view their lives as shaped by forces—gods, spirits, or, simply, fate—beyond human control. As the power of tradition erodes, people come to see their lives as an unending series of options, a process Berger calls *individualization*. Many people in the United States, for instance, adopt one "lifestyle" and discard another, showing an openness to change. Indeed, a common belief is that people *should* take control of their lives.

3. **Increasing social diversity.** In preindustrial societies, strong family ties and powerful religious beliefs enforce conformity and discourage diversity and change. Modernization promotes a more rational, scientific worldview, as tradition loses its hold and people gain more and more individual choice. The growth of cities, expansion of impersonal bureaucracy, and the social mix of people from various backgrounds combine to foster diverse beliefs and behavior.

4. **Future orientation and growing awareness of time.** While premodern people focus on the past, people in modern societies think more about the future. Modern people are not only forward-looking but optimistic that new inventions and discoveries will improve their lives.

Modern people also organize daily routines down to the very minute. With the invention of clocks in the late Middle Ages, Europeans began to think not in terms of sunlight and seasons but in terms of hours and minutes. Preoccupied with personal gain, modern people demand precise measurement of time and are likely to agree that "Time is money." Berger points out that one indicator of a society's degree of industrialization is the proportion of people wearing wristwatches.

Finally, recall that modernization touched off the development of sociology itself. As Chapter 1 ("Sociology: Perspective, Theory, and Method") explained, the discipline originated in the wake of the Industrial Revolution in Western Europe, a time and place where social change was proceeding most intensely. Early European and U.S. sociologists tried to analyze the rise of modern society and its consequences—both good and bad—for human beings.

FERDINAND TÖNNIES: THE LOSS OF COMMUNITY

The German sociologist Ferdinand Tönnies (1855–1937) produced a lasting account of modernization in his theory of *Gemeinschaft* and *Gesellschaft* (see Chapter 15. "Population, Urbanization, and Environment"). Like Peter Berger, whose work he influenced, Tönnies (1963; orig. 1887) viewed modernization as the progressive loss of *Gemeinschaft*, or human community. As Tönnies saw it, the Industrial Revolution weakened the social fabric of family and tradition by introducing a businesslike emphasis on facts, efficiency, and money. European and North American societies gradually became rootless and impersonal as people came to associate with one another mostly on the basis of self-interest—the state Tönnies termed *Gesellschaft*.

Early in the twentieth century, at least some of the United States approximated Tönnies's concept of *Gemeinschaft*. Families that had lived for many generations in small villages and towns were bound together into a hard-working, slow-moving way of life. Telephones (invented in 1876) were rare; it wasn't until 1915 that someone placed the first coast-to-coast call (see the time line inside the front cover of this book). Living without television (introduced in 1939 and widespread after 1950), families entertained themselves, often gathering with friends in the evening to share stories, sorrows, or song. Without rapid transportation (Henry Ford's assembly line began in 1908, but cars became common only after World War II), many people's own town was their entire world.

Inevitable tensions and conflicts divided these communities of the past. But, according to Tönnies, the traditional spirit of *Gemeinschaft* meant that people were "essentially united in spite of all separating factors" (1963:65; orig. 1887).

Modernity turns society inside out so that, as Tönnies put it, people are "essentially separated in spite of uniting factors" (1963:65; orig. 1887). This is the world of *Gesellschaft* where, especially in large cities, most people live among strangers and ignore those they pass on the street. Trust is hard to come by in a mobile and anonymous society in which, according to researchers, people tend to put their personal needs ahead of group loyalty and a majority of adults believe "you can't be too careful" in dealing with people (NORC, 1999:173). No wonder that millions of men and women attend weekly support groups (also made up of strangers) where they establish temporary emotional ties and find someone who is willing simply to *listen* (Leerhsen, 1990).

Critical evaluation. Tönnies's theory of *Gemeinschaft* and *Gesellschaft* is widely used to describe modernization. The theory's strength lies in its synthesis of various dimensions of change—growing population, the

rise of cities, increasing impersonality in interaction. But modern life, while often impersonal, is not devoid of *Gemeinschaft*. Even in a world of strangers, modern friendships can be strong and lasting. Moreover, some analysts think that Tönnies favored—perhaps even romanticized—traditional societies while overlooking bonds of family and friendship that continue to flourish in modern societies.

EMILE DURKHEIM: THE DIVISION OF LABOR

The French sociologist Emile Durkheim shared Tönnies's interest in the profound social changes wrought by the Industrial Revolution. For Durkheim, modernization was marked by increasing **division of labor,** or *specialized economic activity* (1964b; orig. 1893). Whereas every member of a traditional society performs more or less the same daily round of activities, modern societies function by having people perform highly specialized roles.

Durkheim explained that preindustrial societies are held together by *mechanical solidarity*, or shared moral sentiments (see Chapter 15, "Population, Urbanization, and Environment"). Thus members of such societies view everyone as basically alike, doing the same work and belonging together. Durkheim's concept of mechanical solidarity is virtually the same as Tönnies's *Gemeinschaft*.

With modernization, the division of labor becomes more and more pronounced. To Durkheim, this change meant less mechanical solidarity, but *more* of another kind of tie: *organic solidarity*, or the mutual dependency among people engaged in specialized work. Put simply, modern societies are held together not by likeness but by difference: All of us must depend on others to meet most of our needs. Organic solidarity corresponds to Tönnies's concept of *Gesellschaft*.

Despite obvious similarities in their thinking, Durkheim and Tönnies viewed modernity somewhat differently. To Tönnies, modern *Gesellschaft* amounted to the loss of social solidarity because people lose the "natural" and "organic" bonds of the rural village, leaving only the "artificial" and "mechanical" ties of the big city. Durkheim had a different take on modernity, even reversing Tönnies's language to bring home the point. Durkheim labeled modern society "organic," arguing that modern society is no less natural than any other, and he described traditional societies as "mechanical" because they are so regimented. Thus, Durkheim viewed modernization not so much as a loss of community as a change from community

Max Weber maintained that the distinctive character of modern society was its rational worldview. Virtually all of Weber's work on modernity centered on types of people he considered typical of their age: the scientist, the capitalist, and the bureaucrat. Each is rational to the core: The scientist is committed to the orderly discovery of truth, the capitalist to the orderly pursuit of profit, and the bureaucrat to orderly conformity to a system of rules.

based on bonds of likeness (kinship and neighborhood) to community based on economic interdependence (the division of labor). Durkheim's view of modernity is thus both more complex and more positive than Tönnies's view.

Critical evaluation. Durkheim's work stands alongside that of Tönnies, which it closely resembles, as a highly influential analysis of modernity. Of the two, Durkheim was the more optimistic; still, he feared that modern societies might become so diverse that they would collapse into **anomie,** *a condition in which society provides little moral guidance to individuals.* Living with weak moral norms, modern people can become egocentric, placing their own needs above those of others and finding little purpose in life.

The suicide rate—which Durkheim considered a good index of anomie—did, in fact, increase in the United States over the course of the twentieth century. Moreover, the vast majority of U.S. adults report that they see moral questions not in clear terms of right and wrong but as confusing "shades of gray" (NORC, 1999:369). Yet, shared norms and values seem strong enough to give most people a sense of meaning and purpose. Moreover, whatever the hazards of anomie, most people value the personal freedom modern society affords.

MAX WEBER: RATIONALIZATION

For Max Weber, modernity meant replacing a traditional worldview with a rational way of thinking. In preindustrial societies, tradition acts as a constant brake to change. To traditional people, "truth" is roughly the same as "what has always been" (1978:36; orig. 1921). To modern people, by contrast, truth is the result of rational calculation. Because they value efficiency and have little reverence for the past, modern people will adopt whatever social patterns allow them to achieve their goals.

Echoing Tönnies's and Durkheim's assertion that industrialization weakens tradition, Weber declared modern society to be "disenchanted." The unquestioned truths of an earlier time have been challenged by rational thinking: In short, modern society turns away from the gods. Throughout his life, then, Weber studied various modern "types"—the scientist, the capitalist, the bureaucrat—all of whom share the detached worldview that he believed was coming to dominate humanity.

Critical evaluation. Compared with Tönnies, and especially Durkheim, Weber was critical of modern society. He knew that science could produce technological and organizational wonders, yet he worried that science was carrying us away from more basic questions about the meaning and purpose of human existence. Weber feared that rationalization, especially in bureaucracies, would erode the human spirit with endless rules and regulations.

Finally, some of Weber's critics think that the alienation Weber attributed to bureaucracy actually stemmed from social inequality. This criticism leads us to the ideas of Karl Marx.

KARL MARX: CAPITALISM

For Karl Marx, modern society was synonymous with capitalism; he saw the Industrial Revolution primarily as a *capitalist revolution*. Marx traced the emergence of the bourgeoisie in medieval Europe to the expansion of commerce. The bourgeoisie gradually displaced a feudal aristocracy as the Industrial Revolution placed a powerful new productive system under its control.

Marx agreed that modernity weakened small-scale communities (as described by Tönnies), increased the division of labor (as noted by Durkheim), and fostered a rational worldview (as Weber claimed). But he saw these simply as conditions necessary for capitalism to flourish. Capitalism, according to Marx, draws population from farms and small towns into an ever-expanding market system centered in the cities; specialization is needed for efficient factories; and rationality is exemplified by the capitalists' relentless pursuit of profit.

Earlier chapters have painted Marx as a spirited critic of capitalist society, but his vision of modernity also incorporates a considerable measure of optimism. Unlike Weber, who viewed modern society as an "iron cage" of bureaucracy, Marx believed that social conflict in capitalist societies would sow the seeds of revolutionary change, leading to an egalitarian socialism. Such a society, as he saw it, would harness the wonders of industrial technology to enrich people's lives and also rid the world of classes, the source of social conflict and so much suffering. While Marx's evaluation of modern capitalist society was highly negative, then, he imagined a future of human freedom, creativity, and community.

Critical evaluation. Marx's theory of modernization is a complex theory of capitalism. But he underestimated the dominance of bureaucracy in shaping modern societies. In socialist societies, in particular, the stifling effects of bureaucracy turned out to be as bad as, or even worse than, the dehumanizing aspects of capitalism. The upheavals in Eastern Europe and the former Soviet Union reveal the depth of popular opposition to oppressive state bureaucracies.

STRUCTURAL-FUNCTIONAL ANALYSIS: THE THEORY OF MASS SOCIETY

The rise of modernity is a complex process involving many dimensions of change, described in previous chapters and summarized in Table 16–1. How can we make sense of so many changes going on at once? Sociologists have devised two broad explanations of modern society, one guided by the structural-functional paradigm and the other based on social-conflict theory.

The first approach—guided by the structural-functional paradigm and drawing on the ideas of Tönnies, Durkheim, and Weber—understands modernity as the emergence of *mass society* (Dahrendorf, 1959; Kornhauser, 1959; Nisbet, 1966, 1969; Baltzell, 1968; Stein, 1972; Berger, Berger, & Kellner, 1974; Pearson, 1993). A **mass society** is *a society in which industry and bureaucracy have eroded traditional social ties*. A mass society is marked by weak kinship and impersonal neighborhoods, so individuals are socially isolated. This isolation, in turn, leaves members of mass societies morally uncertain and personally powerlessness.

THE MASS SCALE OF MODERN LIFE

Mass-society theory argues, first, that the scale of modern life has greatly increased. Before the Industrial Revolution, Europe and North America formed a mosaic of countless rural villages and small towns. In these local communities, which inspired Tönnies's concept of *Gemeinschaft*, people lived out their lives surrounded by kin and guided by a shared heritage. Gossip was an informal, yet highly effective, way of ensuring conformity to community standards. Such small communities tolerated little social diversity—the state of mechanical solidarity described by Durkheim.

For example, before 1690, English law demanded that everyone regularly participate in the Christian ritual of Holy Communion (Laslett, 1984). On this continent, only Rhode Island among the New England colonies tolerated any religious dissent. Because social differences were repressed, subcultures and countercultures were few, and change proceeded slowly.

Increasing population, the growth of cities, and specialized economic activity driven by the Industrial Revolution gradually altered this pattern. People came to know one another by their jobs (for example, as "the

TABLE 16–1 Traditional and Modern Societies: The Big Picture

Elements of Society	Traditional Societies	Modern Societies
Cultural Patterns		
Values	Homogeneous; sacred character; few subcultures and countercultures	Heterogeneous; secular character; many subcultures and countercultures
Norms	High moral significance; little tolerance of diversity	Variable moral significance; high tolerance of diversity
Time orientation	Present linked to past	Present linked to future
Technology	Preindustrial; human and animal energy	Industrial; advanced energy sources
Social Structure		
Status and role	Few statuses, most ascribed; few specialized roles	Many statuses, some ascribed and some achieved; many specialized roles
Relationships	Typically primary; little anonymity or privacy	Typically secondary; considerable anonymity and privacy
Communication	Face to face	Face-to-face communication supplemented by mass media
Social control	Informal gossip	Formal police and legal system
Social stratification	Rigid patterns of social inequality; little mobility	Fluid patterns of social inequality; considerable mobility
Gender patterns	Pronounced patriarchy; women's lives centered on the home	Declining patriarchy; increasing number of women in the paid labor force
Settlement patterns	Small scale; population typically small and widely dispersed in rural villages and small towns	Large scale; population typically large and concentrated in cities
Social Institutions		
Economy	Based on agriculture; much manufacturing in the home; little white-collar work	Based on industrial mass production; factories become centers of production; increasing white-collar work
State	Small-scale government; little state intervention in society	Large-scale government; considerable state intervention in society
Family	Extended family as the primary means of socialization and economic production	Nuclear family retains some socialization functions but is more a unit of consumption than of production
Religion	Religion guides worldview; little religious pluralism	Religion weakens with the rise of science; extensive religious pluralism
Education	Formal schooling limited to elites	Basic schooling becomes universal, with growing proportion receiving advanced education
Health	High birth and death rates; short life expectancy because of low standard of living and simple medical technology	Low birth and death rates; longer life expectancy because of higher standard of living and sophisticated medical technology
Social Change	Slow; change evident over many generations	Rapid; change evident within a single generation

doctor" or "the bank clerk") rather than by their kinship group or hometown. People looked on most others simply as strangers. The face-to-face communication of the village was eventually replaced by the impersonal mass media—newspapers, radio, television, and, more recently, computer networks. Large organizations steadily assumed more and more responsibility for the daily needs that had once been fulfilled by family, friends, and neighbors; public education drew more and more people to schools; police, lawyers, and courts

supervised a formal criminal justice system. Even charity became the work of faceless bureaucrats working for various social welfare agencies.

Geographic mobility, mass communications, and exposure to diverse ways of life all erode traditional values. People become more tolerant of social diversity, defending individual rights and freedom of choice. Subcultures and countercultures multiply. Treating people differently according to their race, sex, or religion comes to be defined as backward and unjust. In the process, minorities at the margins of society gain greater power and broader participation in public life. Yet, mass society theorists fear that transforming people of various backgrounds into a generic mass may end up dehumanizing everyone.

THE EVER-EXPANDING STATE

In the small-scale, preindustrial societies of Europe, government amounted to little more than a local noble. A royal family formally reigned over an entire nation, but in the absence of swift transportation and efficient communication, the power of even absolute monarchs fell far short of that wielded by today's political leaders.

As technological innovation allowed government to expand, the centralized state grew in size and importance. At the time the United States gained independence from Great Britain, the federal government was a tiny organization whose prime function was national defense. Since then, government has assumed responsibility for more and more areas of social life—schooling the population, regulating wages and working conditions, establishing standards for products of all sorts, and offering financial assistance to the ill and the unemployed. To pay for such programs, taxes have soared: Today's average worker labors more than four months a year just to pay for the broad array of services the government provides.

In a mass society, power resides in large bureaucracies, leaving people in local communities little control over their lives. For example, state officials mandate that local schools must meet educational standards, local products must be government certified, and every citizen must maintain extensive tax records. While such regulations may protect people and enhance social equality, they also force us to deal more and more with nameless officials in distant and often unresponsive bureaucracies, and they undermine the autonomy of families and local communities.

The growing scale of modern life may have positive aspects, but only at the cost of our losing our cultural heritage. Modern societies increase individual rights, tolerate social differences, and raise living standards. But they are prone to what Weber feared most—excessive bureaucracy—as well as to Tönnies's self-centeredness and Durkheim's anomie. Their size, complexity, and tolerance of diversity in modern societies all but doom traditional values and family patterns, leaving individuals isolated, powerless, and materialistic. As Chapter 12 ("Economics and Politics") noted, voter apathy is a serious problem in the United States. But should we be surprised that

individuals in vast, impersonal societies end up thinking that no one person can make a difference?

Critical evaluation. Critics contend that mass-society theory romanticizes the past. They remind us that many people in the small towns of our past were eager to set out for a better standard of living in cities. Moreover, this approach ignores problems of social inequality. Critics say mass-society theory attracts social and economic conservatives who defend conventional morality and are indifferent to the historical plight of women and other minorities.

SOCIAL-CONFLICT ANALYSIS: THE THEORY OF CLASS SOCIETY

The second interpretation of modernity derives mostly from the ideas of Karl Marx. From a social-conflict perspective, modernity takes the form of a **class society,** *a capitalist society with pronounced social stratification.* That is, while agreeing that modern societies have expanded to a mass scale, this approach views the heart of modernization as an expanding capitalist economy, rife with inequality (Miliband, 1969; Habermas, 1970; Polenberg, 1980; Blumberg, 1981; Harrington, 1984).

CAPITALISM

Class-society theory follows Marx in claiming that the increasing scale of social life in modern times has resulted from the insatiable appetite of capitalism. Because a capitalist economy pursues ever-increasing profits, both production and consumption steadily increase.

According to Marx, capitalism rests on "naked self-interest" (1972:337; orig. 1848). This self-centeredness erodes the social ties that once cemented small-scale communities. Capitalism also treats people as commodities: as a source of labor and a market for capitalist products.

Capitalism supports science, not just as the key to greater productivity, but as an ideology that justifies the status quo. That is, modern societies encourage people to view human well-being as a *technical* puzzle to be solved by engineers and other experts rather than through the pursuit of *social* justice (Habermas, 1970). A capitalist culture, for example, seeks to improve health through scientific medicine rather than by eliminating poverty, which threatens many people's health in the first place.

Many people marveled at the industrial technology that was changing the world a century ago. But some critics pointed out that the social consequences of the Industrial Revolution were not all positive. The painting Trabajadores (Workers) *by Mirta Cerra portrays the exhausting and mind-numbing routines of manual workers.*

Mirta Cerra (1904–1986), *Trabajadores*, oil on canvas laid down on panel, 46 × 62 in. (107.3 × 157.5 cm). © Christie's Images.

Businesses also raise the banner of scientific logic, trying to increase profits through greater efficiency. As Chapter 12 ("Economics and Politics") explained, capitalist corporations have reached enormous size and control unimaginable wealth by "going global" as multinationals. From the class-society point of view, then, the expanding scale of life is less a function of *Gesellschaft* than the inevitable and destructive consequence of capitalism.

PERSISTENT INEQUALITY

Modernity has gradually worn away some of the rigid categorical distinctions that divided preindustrial societies. But class-society theory maintains that elites persist—albeit now as capitalist millionaires rather than nobles born to wealth and power. In the United States, we may have no hereditary monarchy, but the richest 5 percent of the population nevertheless controls more than half of all property.

What of the state? Mass-society theorists contend that the state works to increase equality and combat social problems. Marx was skeptical that the state could accomplish more than minor reforms because, as he saw it, real power lies mostly in the hands of capitalists who control the economy. Class-society theorists add that, to the extent that working people

and minorities do have greater political rights and enjoy a higher standard of living today, these changes are the fruits of political struggle, not expressions of government goodwill. In short, they conclude, despite our pretensions of democracy, most people are still powerless in the face of wealthy elites.

Class-society theory also dismisses Durkheim's argument that people in modern societies suffer from anomie, claiming instead that people contend with alienation and powerlessness. Not surprisingly, then, the class-society interpretation of modernity enjoys widespread support among liberals (and radicals) who favor greater equality and seek extensive regulation (or abolition) of the capitalist marketplace.

Critical evaluation. A basic criticism of class-society theory is that it overlooks the increasing prosperity of modern societies, as well as the fact that discrimination based on race, ethnicity, religion, and gender is now illegal and is widely regarded as a social problem. Further, most people in the United States do not want an egalitarian society—they prefer a system of unequal rewards that reflects personal differences in talent and effort.

Moreover, few observers think that a centralized economy would cure the ills of modernity in light of socialism's failure to generate a high overall standard

TABLE 16–2	Two Interpretations of Modernity: A Summary	
	Process of Modernization	**Effects of Modernization**
Mass-Society Theory	Industrialization; growth of bureaucracy	Increasing scale of life; rise of the state and other formal organizations
Class-Society Theory	Rise of capitalism	Expansion of the capitalist economy; persistence of social inequality

of living. Many other problems in the United States—from unemployment, homelessness, and industrial pollution to unresponsive government—have also been commonplace in socialist nations such as the former Soviet Union.

Table 16–2 summarizes the views of modern society offered by mass-society theory and class-society theory. While the former focuses on the increasing scale of social life and growth of government, the latter stresses the expansion of capitalism and the persistence of inequality.

MODERNITY AND THE INDIVIDUAL

Both mass- and class-society theories focus on broad patterns of change since the Industrial Revolution. But from these macro-level approaches, we can also draw micro-level insights into how modernity shapes individual lives.

MASS SOCIETY: PROBLEMS OF IDENTITY

Modernity liberated individuals from small, tightly knit communities of the past. Most members of modern societies have privacy and freedom to express their individuality. Mass-society theory suggests, however, that extensive social diversity, isolation, and rapid social change make it difficult for many people to establish any coherent identity at all (Wheelis, 1958; Riesman, 1970; Berger, Berger, & Kellner, 1974).

Chapter 3 ("Socialization: From Infancy to Old Age") explained that people's personalities are mostly a product of their social experiences. The small, homogeneous, and slowly changing societies of the past provided a firm (if narrow) foundation for building a personal identity. Even today, Amish communities that flourish in the United States teach young men

and women "correct" ways to think and behave. Not everyone born into an Amish community can tolerate such rigid demands for conformity, but most members establish a well-integrated and satisfying personal identity (Hostetler, 1980; Kraybill & Olshan, 1994).

Because mass societies are socially diverse and rapidly changing, they offer only shifting sands on which to build a personal identity. Left to make many life decisions on their own, people—especially those with greater affluence—face a bewildering range of options. The freedom to choose has little value without standards to guide the selection process, however, and in a tolerant mass society, people may find one path no more compelling than the next. Not surprisingly, many people shuttle from one identity to another, changing their lifestyle, relationships, and even religion in search of an elusive "true self." Beset by the widespread relativism of modern societies, people without a moral compass suffer a loss of civility and find little of the virtue, security, and certainty once provided by tradition.

To David Riesman (1970; orig. 1950), modernization brings changes in **social character,** *personality patterns common to members of a particular society.* Preindustrial societies promote what Riesman calls **tradition-directedness,** *rigid conformity to time-honored ways of living.* Members of such societies model their lives on those of their ancestors, so that "living the good life" amounts to "doing what people have always done."

Tradition-directedness corresponds to Tönnies's *Gemeinschaft* and Durkheim's mechanical solidarity. Culturally conservative, tradition-directed people think and act alike. Unlike the conformity often found in modern societies, the uniformity of tradition-directedness is not an effort to mimic one another. Instead, people are alike because they all draw on the same solid cultural foundation. Amish women and men exemplify tradition-directedness; in the Amish culture, tradition ties everyone to ancestors and descendants in an unbroken chain of righteous living.

Members of diverse and rapidly changing societies define a tradition-directed personality as deviant because it seems so rigid. Modern people, by and large, prize personal flexibility, the capacity to adapt, and sensitivity to others. Riesman calls this type of social character **other-directedness,** *a receptiveness to the latest trends and fashions, often expressed by imitating others.* Because their socialization occurs within societies that are continuously in flux, other-directed people develop fluid identities marked by superficiality, inconsistency, and change. They try on different

Mass-society theory attributes feelings of anxiety, isolation, and lack of meaning in the modern world to rapid social change that washes away tradition. Edvard Munch captured this vision of modern emptiness in his painting The Scream *(left). Class-society theory, by contrast, ties such feelings to social inequality, by which some categories of people are made into second-class citizens (or not made citizens at all). Paul Marcus portrays modern injustice in the painting* Crossing the Rio Grande *(right).*

Edvard Munch, *The Scream*, Oslo, National Gallery. Scala/Art Resource, NY. © 1998 Artists Rights Society (ARS), NY/ADAGP, Paris. © Paul Marcus, *Crossing the Rio Grande*, 1999, oil painting on canvas, 63 × 72 in. Studio SPM Inc.

"selves," almost like so many pieces of new clothing, seek out "role models," and engage in varied "performances" as they move from setting to setting (Goffman, 1959). In a traditional society, such "shiftiness" marks a person as untrustworthy; but in a changing, modern society, the chameleonlike ability to fit in virtually anywhere is very useful.

In societies that value the up-to-date rather than the traditional, people anxiously look to others for approval, using members of their own generation rather than elders as role models. "Peer pressure" can be irresistible to people without strong, enduring standards to guide them. Our society urges people to be true to themselves; but when social surroundings change so rapidly, how can people develop the self to which they should be true? This problem lies at the root of the identity crisis so widespread in high-income countries today. "Who am I?" and "What is right?" are nagging questions that many of us struggle to answer. In truth, this problem is not so much psychological as sociological, reflecting the cultural instability of modern mass society.

CLASS SOCIETY: PROBLEMS OF POWERLESSNESS

Class-society theory paints a different picture of modernity's effects on individuals. This approach maintains that persistent inequality undermines modern society's promise of individual freedom. For some, modernity serves up great privilege, but, for many, everyday life means coping with economic uncertainty and a gnawing sense of powerlessness (Newman, 1993).

For racial and ethnic minorities, the problem of relative disadvantage looms even larger. Similarly, although women participate more broadly in modern societies, they continue to run up against traditional barriers of sexism. In short, this approach rejects mass-society theory's claim that people suffer from too much freedom. Instead, class-society theory holds that our society still denies a majority of people full participation in social life.

On a global scale, as Chapter 9 ("Global Stratification") explained, the expanding scope of world

Does "Modern" Mean "Progress"?
The Case of Brazil's Kaiapo

The firelight flickers in the gathering darkness as Chief Kanhonk sits, as he has done at the end of the day for many years, ready to begin an evening of animated talk and storytelling. This is the hour when the Kaiapo, a small society in Brazil's lush Amazon region, celebrate their heritage. Because the Kaiapo are a traditional people with no written language, the elders rely on evenings by the fire to pass along their culture to their children and grandchildren. In the past, evenings like this have been filled with tales of brave Kaiapo warriors fighting off Portuguese traders in pursuit of slaves and gold.

But as the minutes pass, only a few older villagers assemble for the evening ritual. "It is the Big Ghost," one man grumbles, explaining the poor turnout. The "Big Ghost" has indeed descended upon them; its bluish glow spills from windows throughout the village. The Kaiapo children—and many adults as well—are watching sitcoms on television. Installing a satellite dish in the village several years ago has had consequences greater than anyone imagined. In the end, what their enemies failed to do with guns, the Kaiapo

may well do to themselves with prime-time programming.

The Kaiapo are among the 230,000 native peoples who inhabit the country we call Brazil. They stand out because of their striking body paint and ornate ceremonial dress. Beginning in the 1980s, they became rich from gold mining and harvesting mahogany trees. Now they must decide if their new-found fortune is a blessing or a curse.

To some, affluence means the opportunity to learn about the outside world through travel and television. Others, like Chief Kanhonk, are not so sure. Sitting by the fire, he thinks aloud, "I have been saying that people must buy useful

things like knives and fishing hooks. Television does not fill the stomach. It only shows our children and grandchildren white people's things." Bebtopup, the oldest priest, nods in agreement: "The night is the time the old people teach the young people. Television has stolen the night" (Simons, 2001:497).

The Kaiapo story shows us that change is not a simple path toward "progress." The Kaiapo are moving toward modernity, and this process will have both positive and negative consequences. On the one hand, they now enjoy a higher standard of living, with better shelters, more clothing, and new technology like television to connect them to the larger world. On the other hand, this new affluence has greatly weakened Kaiapo traditions, so that many of their number now wonder—with good reason—who or what they have become. The drama of the Kaiapo is being played out around the world as more and more traditional cultures are being lured away from their heritage by the affluence and materialism of rich societies.

Source: Based on Simons (2001).

capitalism has placed more of the earth's population under the influence of multinational corporations. As a result, more than half the world's income is concentrated in the rich industrial nations, where just 18 percent of its people live. It is any wonder, class-society theorists ask, that people in poor nations seek greater power to shape their own lives?

The problem of widespread powerlessness led Herbert Marcuse (1964) to challenge Max Weber's contention that modern society is rational. Marcuse condemned modern society as irrational for failing to meet the needs of so many people. While modern capitalist societies produce unparalleled wealth, poverty remains the daily plight of more than 1 billion people.

Moreover, Marcuse argued, technological advances further reduce people's control over their own lives. The advent of high technology generally has conferred a great deal of power on a core of specialists—not the majority of people—who now dominate discussion of events such as computing, energy production, and health care. Countering the popular view that technology *solves* the world's problems, Marcuse suggested that it is more accurate to say that science *causes* them. In sum, class-society theory asserts that people suffer because modern societies have concentrated both wealth and power in the hands of a privileged few.

MODERNITY AND PROGRESS

In modern societies, most people expect—and applaud—social change. We link modernity to the idea of *progress* (from the Latin, meaning "moving forward"), a state of continual improvement. By contrast, we see stability as stagnation.

Given our bias in favor of change, members of our society tend to look upon traditional cultures as backward. But change, particularly toward material affluence, is a mixed blessing. As the box shows, social change is too complex to equate with progress.

Even getting rich has its advantages and disadvantages, as the case of the Kaiapo shows. Historically, among people in the United States, a rising standard of living made lives longer and, in a material sense, more comfortable. At the same time, many people wonder if today's routines are too stressful, with families often having little time for relaxation or simply spending time together.

Science, too, has its pluses and minuses. As Figure 16–2 shows, people in the United States have considerable confidence—more than those in most other societies—that science improves our lives. But surveys also show that many adults in the United States feel that science "makes our way of life change too fast" (NORC, 1999:356).

New technology has always sparked controversy. A century ago, the introduction of automobiles and telephones allowed more rapid transportation and more efficient communication. But, at the same time, such technology also weakened traditional attachments to hometowns and even to families. Today, people might well wonder if computer technology will do the same thing: giving us access to people around the world, but shielding us from the community right outside our doors; providing more information than ever before but, in the process, threatening personal privacy. In

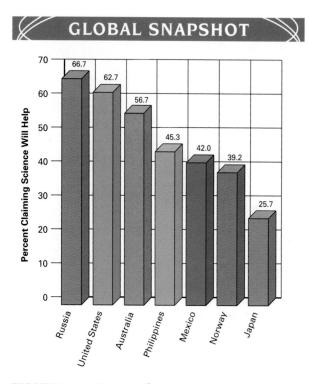

GLOBAL SNAPSHOT

FIGURE 16–2 Support for Science: A Global Survey

Survey Question: "In the long run, do you think the scientific advances we are making will help or harm humankind?"

Source: Inglehart et al. (2000).

short, we all realize that social change comes faster all the time, but we may disagree about whether a particular change is progress or a step backwards.

MODERNITY: GLOBAL VARIATION

October 1, 1994, Kobe, Japan. Riding the computer-controlled monorail high above the streets of Kobe or the 200-mile-per-hour bullet train to Tokyo, we see Japan as the society of the future, in love with high technology. Yet the Japanese remain strikingly traditional in other respects: Few corporate executives and almost no politicians are women; young people still accord seniors considerable respect; and

Does advancing technology make society better? In some ways, perhaps. However, many films—including Frankenstein *(1931) and* Jurassic Park *(1993)—have expressed the concern that new technology not only solves old problems but creates new ones. All the sociological theorists discussed in this chapter shared this ambivalent view of the modern world.*

public orderliness contrasts with the turmoil of U.S. cities.

Japan is a nation at once traditional and modern. This contradiction reminds us that, while it is useful to contrast traditional and modern social patterns, the old and the new often coexist in unexpected ways. In the People's Republic of China, ancient Confucian principles are mixed with contemporary socialist thinking. Similarly, in Mexico and much of Latin America, people observe centuries-old Christian rituals even as they struggle to move ahead economically. In short, combinations of traditional and modern are far from unusual—indeed, they are found throughout the world.

POSTMODERNITY

If modernity was the product of the Industrial Revolution, is the Information Revolution creating a postmodern era? A number of scholars think so, and use the term **postmodernity** to refer to *social patterns characteristic of postindustrial societies.*

Precisely what postmodernism is remains a matter of debate. This term has been used for decades in literary, philosophical, and even architectural circles. It has moved into sociology on a wave of social criticism that has been building since the spread of left-leaning politics in the 1960s. Although there are many variants of postmodern thinking, all share the following five themes (Bernstein, 1992; Borgmann, 1992; Crook, Pakulski, and Waters, 1992; Hall & Neitz, 1993; Inglehart, 1997; Rudel & Gerson, 1999):

1. **In important respects, modernity has failed.** The promise of modernity was a life free from want. As many postmodernist critics see it, however, the twentieth century was unsuccessful in solving social problems like poverty, since many people still lack financial security.

2. **The bright light of "progress" is fading.** Modern people look to the future expecting that their lives will improve in significant ways. Members (even leaders) of a postmodern society, however, have less confidence about what the future holds. Furthermore, the buoyant optimism that carried society into the modern era more than a century ago has given way to stark pessimism: Most U.S. adults believe that life is getting worse (NORC, 1999:204).

3. **Science no longer holds the answers.** The defining trait of the modern era was a

scientific outlook and a confident belief that technology would make life better. But postmodern critics contend that science has failed to solve many old problems (like poor health) and has even created new problems (such as degrading the environment).

More generally, postmodernist thinkers discredit science as a "metanarrative" that implies a singular truth. On the contrary, they maintain, objective reality and truth do not exist at all. Reality amounts to so much "social construction," they say; moreover, we can "deconstruct" science to see how it has been widely used for political purposes, especially by powerful segments of society.

4. **Cultural debates are intensifying.** As we have already explained, modernity represented an era of enhanced individuality and expanding tolerance. But feminists point out that patriarchy continues to limit the lives of women, and multiculturalists remind us that racial and ethnic minorities still live at the margins of society.

Moreover, now that more people have all the material things they really need, ideas are taking on more importance. Thus, postmodernity is also a postmaterialist era, in which issues like social justice, as well as the environment and animal rights, command more and more public attention.

5. **Social institutions are changing.** Just as industrialization brought sweeping transformation to social institutions, the rise of a postindustrial society is remaking society all over again. For example, the Industrial Revolution placed *material things* at the center of productive life; now, the Information Revolution emphasizes *ideas*. Similarly, the postmodern family no longer conforms to any one pattern; on the contrary, individuals are choosing among many family forms.

Critical evaluation. Analysts who claim that the United States and other high-income nations are entering a postmodern era criticize modernity for failing to meet human needs. Yet, in defense of modernity, we might note the marked increases in longevity and living standards over the course of the last century. Moreover, even if we were to accept postmodernist views that science is bankrupt and progress is a sham, what are the alternatives?

Finally, many voices offer different understandings of recent social trends. The box on pages 454–55 provides one case in point.

We tend to view tradition and modernity as opposites—the more of one found in a society, the less there is of the other. In reality, these concepts can operate independently, as we see in Japan, where traditional and modern aspects of life are often seen side by side.

LOOKING AHEAD: MODERNIZATION AND OUR GLOBAL FUTURE

Imagine the entire world's population reduced to a single village of 1,000 people. The 200 richest people in the village earn 80 percent of all income. By contrast, the 200 poorest people (who, together, earn less than the village's richest person) lack secure housing and safe drinking water so that their lives are at risk.

The tragic plight of the world's poor shows that some desperately needed change has not yet occurred. Chapter 9 ("Global Stratification") presented two competing views of why 1 billion people the world over are poor. *Modernization theory* claims that in the past the entire world was poor and that technological change, especially the Industrial Revolution, enhanced human productivity and raised living standards in

Tracking Change: Is Life in the United States Getting Better or Worse?

We began this chapter with a look at what life was like in 1900—more than a century ago. It is easy to see that, in many ways, life is far better today than it was for our great-grandparents. But, especially in recent decades, the indicators are not so clear-cut: Life may be improving in some respects, but, in others it is getting worse.

Here is a look at some trends shaping the United States since 1970.

First, the good news: By some measures—shown in the first set of figures—life in this country is clearly improving. Infant mortality has fallen steadily, meaning that fewer and fewer children die soon after birth. In addition, an increasing share of people are reaching old age and, after reaching sixty-five, they are living longer than ever. More good news: The poverty rate among the elderly is well below what it was in 1970. Schooling is another area of improvement: The share of people dropping out of high school is down, while the share completing college is up, compared to a generation ago.

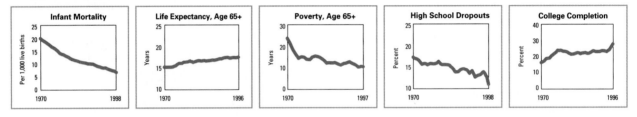

Second, some "no-news" results: A number of indicators show that life is about the same as it was in 1970. Teenage drug use, for example, was about the same in 1996 as a generation before. Likewise, alcohol-related traffic deaths show only a slight decline. Unemployment has had its ups and downs, but the overall level has stayed about the same. Finally, there was about the same amount of affordable housing in the United States in 1996 as in 1970.

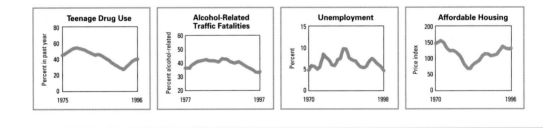

many nations. From this point of view, the solution to global poverty is to promote technological development around the world.

For reasons suggested earlier, however, global modernization may be difficult to achieve. Recall that David Riesman portrayed preindustrial people as *tradition-directed* and likely to resist change. So modernization theorists urge the world's rich societies to help poor countries grow economically. High-income nations can speed development by exporting technology to poor regions, welcoming students from these countries, and providing foreign aid to stimulate economic growth.

The review of modernization theory in Chapter 9 points to some success for these policies in Latin America and, especially, in the small Asian countries of Taiwan, South Korea, Singapore, and Hong Kong. But jump-starting development in the poorest countries of the world poses greater challenges. Moreover, even where dramatic change has occurred, modernization

Third, the bad news: By some measures—several having to do with children—the quality of life in the United States has actually fallen. The official rate of child abuse is up, as is the level of child poverty and the rate of suicide among youths. Although the level of violent crime fell through most of the 1990s, it is still above the 1970 level. Average hourly wages—one measure of basic economic security—show a downward trend, so that families have had to rely on two or more wage-earners to maintain family income. The number of people without health insurance is also on the rise. Finally, economic inequality in this country has been increasing.

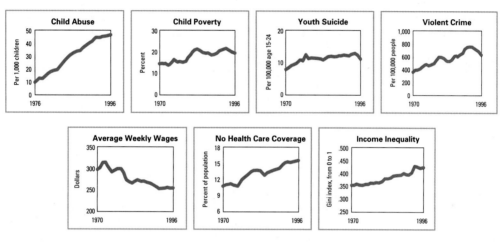

Overall, then, the evidence does not support any simple ideas about "progress over time." Social change has been—and probably will continue to be—a complex process that reflects the kinds of priorities we set for this nation as well as our will to achieve them.

What do you think?

1. *Based on material from earlier chapters, can you explain any of the trends shown here? Which ones?*

2. *Which of the trends above do you find most important? Why?*

3. *On balance, do you think the quality of life in the United States is improving or not? Why?*

Source: Miringoff & Miringoff (1999).

entails a trade-off. Traditional people, such as Brazil's Kaiapo, may acquire wealth through economic development, but only at the cost of losing their traditional identity and values as they are drawn into a global "McCulture" based on Western materialism, pop music, trendy clothes, and fast food. One Brazilian anthropologist expressed hope about the future of the Kaiapo: "At least they quickly understood the consequences of watching television. . . . Now [they] can make a choice" (Simons, 2001:497).

Not everyone even thinks that modernization is really an option. According to a second approach to global stratification, *dependency theory*, today's poor societies have little ability to modernize, even if they want to. From this point of view, the major barrier to economic development is not traditionalism but global domination by rich capitalist societies. Initially, as Chapter 9 explains, this system took the form of colonialism whereby European nations seized much of Latin America, Africa, and Asia. Trading relationships

CONTROVERSY & DEBATE

Personal Freedom and Social Responsibility: Can We Have It Both Ways?

Shortly after midnight on a crisp March evening in 1964, a car pulled into the parking lot of a New York apartment complex. Kitty Genovese turned off the headlights, locked the doors of her vehicle, and headed across the blacktop toward the entrance to her building. Seconds later, a man wielding a knife lunged at her, and, as she shrieked in terror, he stabbed her repeatedly. Windows opened above as curious neighbors searched for the cause of the commotion. But the attack continued—for more than thirty minutes—until Genovese lay dead in the doorway. Subsequent investigation failed to identify the assailant but did confirm a stunning fact: *Not one of dozens of neighbors who witnessed the attack on Kitty Genovese went to her aid or even called the police.*

Decades later, people still recall the Genovese tragedy in discussions of what we owe others. As members of modern societies, we prize our individual rights and personal privacy, but we sometimes withdraw from public responsibility and turn a cold shoulder to people in need. When a cry for help is met by indifference, have we pushed our modern idea of personal autonomy too

far? In a cultural climate of ever more individual rights, can we keep a sense of human community?

These questions point up the tension between traditional and modern social

systems, which is evident in the writings of all the sociologists discussed in this chapter. Tönnies, Durkheim, and others concluded that, in some respects, traditional community and modern

In today's world, people can find new ways to express age-old virtues such as concern for their neighbors. Habitat for Humanity, an organization with chapters in cities and towns across the United States, is made up of people who want to lend a helping hand to those in need. This Washington, D.C., chapter is helping local families realize their dream of owning a home.

soon enriched England, Spain, and other colonial powers, while their colonies became poorer and poorer. Almost all societies subjected to this form of domination are now politically independent, but colonial-style ties continue in the form of multinational corporations operating around the world.

In effect, dependency theory asserts, rich nations achieved their modernization at the expense of poor ones, which provided them with valuable natural resources and human labor. Even today, the world's

poorest countries remain locked in a disadvantageous economic relationship with rich nations, dependent on wealthy countries to buy their raw materials and in return provide them with whatever manufactured products they can afford. Overall, dependency theorists conclude, continuing ties with rich societies will only perpetuate current patterns of global inequality.

Whichever approach one finds more convincing, we can no longer isolate the study of the United States from the rest of the world. At the beginning of the

individualism don't go together. That is, society can unite its members in a moral community only to the extent that it limits their range of personal choices about how to live. In short, while we value both community and autonomy, we can't have it both ways.

Sociologist Amitai Etzioni (1993) has tried to strike a middle ground. The communitarian movement, for which he is the major spokesperson, rests on the simple premise that "strong rights presume strong responsibilities." Or, put otherwise, an individual's pursuit of self-interest must be balanced by a commitment to the larger community.

Etzioni claims modern people have become too focused on individual rights. That is, people expect the system to provide for them, but they are reluctant to give of themselves to support the system. For example, while we believe in the principle of trial by a jury of one's peers, fewer and fewer people today are willing to perform jury duty; similarly, the public is quick to accept government services, but increasingly reluctant to pay the taxes that subsidize these services.

Communitarians advance four proposals toward balancing individual rights with public responsibilities. First, our society should halt the expanding "culture of rights" by which people have placed their own interests ahead of social involvement (after all, nothing in the Constitution allows us to do whatever we want to). Second, communitarians remind us, all rights involve responsibilities (we cannot simply take from society without giving something back). Third, some responsibilities, such as upholding the law or protecting the natural environment, are too important for anyone to ignore. Fourth, defending legitimate community interests may mean limiting individual rights (protecting public safety, for example, might mean subjecting workers to drug tests).

The communitarian movement appeals to many people who, along with Etzioni, seek to balance personal freedom with social responsibility. But critics have attacked this initiative from both sides of the political spectrum. To those on the left, problems ranging from voter apathy to street crime cannot be solved by some vague notion of "social reintegration." Instead, we need expanded government programs to increase social equality. Specifically, these critics say, we must curb the political influence of the rich and actively combat racism and sexism.

Conservatives on the political right also find fault with Etzioni's proposals, but for different reasons (Pearson, 1995). To these critics, the communitarian movement amounts to little more than a rerun of the 1960s leftist agenda. That is, the communitarian vision of a good society favors liberal goals (such as social justice and protecting the environment) but says little about conservative goals (such as allowing prayer in school or restoring the strength of traditional families). Moreover, conservatives ask whether a free society should permit the kind of social engineering that Etzioni advocates (such as instituting antiprejudice programs in schools and requiring people to perform a year of national service).

Perhaps, as Etzioni himself has suggested, the fact that people on both sides of the political spectrum find fault with his views indicates that he has identified a moderate, sensible answer to a serious problem. But it may also be that, in a society as diverse as the United States, people will not readily agree about what they owe to themselves—and to each other.

Continue the debate . . .

1. *Have you ever chosen not to come to the aid of someone in need or danger? Why?*

2. *In his inaugural address, President John F. Kennedy admonished us to "Ask not what your country can do for you; ask what you can do for your country." Do you think people today support this idea? What makes you think so?*

3. *Do you agree or disagree that our society needs to balance rights with more responsibility? Explain your position.*

twentieth century, a majority of people in even the richest nations lived in relatively small settlements with limited awareness of the larger world. Now, early in the twenty-first century, the entire world has become one human village because the lives of all people are increasingly linked.

The last century witnessed unprecedented human achievement. Yet solutions to many problems of human existence—including finding meaning in life, resolving conflicts among societies, and eradicating poverty—have eluded us. The final box examines one dilemma—balancing individual freedom and personal responsibility. To the list of pressing matters new concerns have been added, such as controlling population growth and establishing a sustainable natural environment. In the new century, we must be prepared to tackle such problems with imagination, compassion, and determination. Our unprecedented understanding of human society gives us reason to look to the task with optimism.

SUMMARY

1. Every society changes continuously, although at varying speeds. Social change often generates controversy.

2. Social change is the result of invention, discovery, and cultural diffusion as well as social conflict.

3. Social movements are deliberate efforts to promote or resist change. Analysts link social movements to relative deprivation, the rootlessness of mass society, an organization's ability to muster resources, and cultural symbols that encourage change.

4. Modernity refers to the social consequences of industrialization, which, according to Peter Berger, include the erosion of traditional communities, expansion of personal choice, increasingly diverse beliefs, and a keen awareness of the future.

5. Ferdinand Tönnies described modernization as the transition from *Gemeinschaft* to *Gesellschaft*, which signifies the progressive loss of community amid growing individualism.

6. Emile Durkheim saw modernization as a function of society's expanding division of labor. Mechanical solidarity, based on shared activities and beliefs, gradually gives way to organic solidarity, in which specialization makes people interdependent.

7. According to Max Weber, modernity replaces traditional thinking with rationality. Weber feared the dehumanizing effects of rational organization.

8. Karl Marx saw modernity as the triumph of capitalism over feudalism. Viewing capitalist societies as fraught with conflict, Marx advocated revolutionary change to achieve a more egalitarian, socialist society.

9. According to mass-society theory, modernity increases the scale of life, enlarging the role of government and other formal organizations in carrying out tasks previously performed by family members and neighbors. Cultural diversity and rapid social change make it difficult for people in modern societies to agree on matters involving morality, develop stable identities, and find meaning in their lives.

10. Class-society theory states that capitalism is central to Western modernization. This approach charges that, by concentrating wealth in the hands of a few, capitalism generates widespread feelings of powerlessness.

11. Social change is both good and bad. It is too complex and controversial to be equated simply with progress.

12. Postmodernity refers to cultural traits typical of postindustrial societies. Postmodern criticism of society centers on the failure of modernity, and especially science, to fulfill its promise of prosperity and well-being.

13. In a global context, modernization theory links global poverty to the power of tradition. Therefore, some modernization theorists advocate intentional intervention by rich societies with the goal of stimulating the economic development of poor nations.

14. Dependency theory explains global poverty as the product of the world economic system. The operation of multinational corporations ensures that poor nations will remain economically dependent on rich nations.

KEY CONCEPTS

social change (p. 436) the transformation of culture and social institutions over time

social movement (p. 439) organized activity that encourages or discourages social change

relative deprivation (p. 439) a perceived disadvantage arising from some specific comparison

modernity (p. 440) social patterns resulting from industrialization

modernization (p. 440) the process of social change begun by industrialization

division of labor (p. 442) specialized economic activity

anomie (p. 443) Durkheim's designation of a condition in which society provides little moral guidance to individuals

mass society (p. 444) a society in which industry and bureaucracy have eroded traditional social ties

class society (p. 446) a capitalist society with pronounced social stratification

social character (p. 448) personality patterns common to members of a particular society

tradition-directedness (p. 448) rigid conformity to time-honored ways of living

other-directedness (p. 448) a receptiveness to the latest trends and fashions, often expressed by imitating others

postmodernity (p. 452) social patterns characteristic of postindustrial societies

CRITICAL-THINKING QUESTIONS

1. How well do you think Tönnies, Durkheim, Weber, and Marx predicted the character of today's modern society? How are their visions of modernity the same? How do they differ?

2. What traits lead some to call the United States a "mass society"? Why do other analysts describe the United States as a "class society"?

3. What is the difference between *anomie* (a trait of mass society) and *alienation* (a characteristic of class society)? Among which categories of the U.S. population would you expect each trait to be more pronounced?

4. Why do some analysts believe the United States has become a postmodern society? Do you agree? Why or why not?

APPLICATIONS AND EXERCISES

1. Do you have an elderly relative or friend? If asked, most older people will be happy to tell you about the social changes they have seen in their lifetimes.

2. Ask people in your class or friendship group to make five predictions about U.S. society in the year 2050, when today's twenty-year-olds will be senior citizens. Compare notes. On what issues is there agreement?

3. Has the rate of social change been increasing? Do some research about inventions over time and see for yourself. Consider, for example, modes of travel, including walking, riding animals, trains, cars, airplanes, and rockets in space. The first two characterized society for tens of thousands of years; the last four emerged in barely two centuries.

4. Install the CD-ROM packaged in the back of this new textbook to access a variety of study, review, and applications exercises that will help you better understand the material covered in this chapter. The CD includes an author's tip video, as well as interactive maps, video application exercises, Web links, and study questions.

SITES TO SEE

http://www.prenhall.com/macionis
Visit the interactive Web site that accompanies this text. Begin by clicking on the cover of your book. You will find a chapter-by-chapter study guide, practice test, chat room, and many suggested Web links.

http://www.gwu.edu/~ccps/
This Web site describes the goals of the Communitarian Network.

http://www.utoronto.ca/utopia/
Deliberate change is sometimes inspired by visions of utopia—ideal societies that exist nowhere. Read about the Society for Utopian Studies at this Web site.

http://www.thesociologypage.com or
http://www.macionis.com
Finally, on a personal note, I hope this book has helped you and will be a useful resource to keep for courses later on. Please visit my Web page, and send an e-mail message (macionis@kenyon.edu) with your thoughts and suggestions. And, yes, I *will* write back!

John J. Macionis

cyber.scope

NEW INFORMATION TECHNOLOGY AND SOCIAL CHANGE

Chapter 2 ("Culture") presented William Ogburn's (1964) concept of *cultural lag*, the pattern by which some elements of culture change faster than others. Usually, Ogburn explained, technology changes quickly; getting used to new technology, on the other hand, takes people much longer. This cultural pattern of "lagging behind" probably explains why we use old terminology to describe new developments, such as measuring the "horsepower" of gasoline engines or, more recently, exploring the "superhighway" of cyberspace.

The fact that developments in science and technology outpace our ability to comprehend them makes many people uneasy about social change. In a national survey, about 40 percent of U.S. adults agreed with the statement: "One trouble with science is that it makes our way of life change too fast" (NORC, 1999:356). But the majority of people are more optimistic, expecting that new technology will improve our lives. This final cyber.scope highlights how the age of computers is altering the shape of cities, forming new kinds of human communities, and bringing people together in new ways to form social movements.

The New Shape of Cities

The metropolis, as Chapter 15 ("Population, Urbanization, and Environment") explains, stands as the greatest monument to the industrial era. A century ago, factories full of huge machines offered jobs that drew people from across the countryside to form cities of unprecedented size. Industrial metropolises such as New York, Chicago, Philadelphia, and Detroit churned with activity, and new buildings of glass, mortar, and steel stretched skyward.

Cities became busier and denser as industrial technology centralized people. Businesses fused into a "central business district," where executives and managers could easily establish face-to-face communication. Factories, too, stood together near rivers and railroads, which brought them fuel and raw materials and took away their finished products.

The industrial cities of the United States reached their peak populations about 1950, just as scientists were building the first computers. Computer technology helped push the economy from industry to service and information work, and this shift spurred the decentralization of cities. Population began radiating farther from the central city so that, by 1970, most city dwellers were actually living in suburbs miles away. Businesses followed suit, deserting the downtowns for industrial parks and outlying shopping malls. Today's urban sprawl is the result.

Why have the old central cities lost much of their attraction? One reason is that, in the business world, having a central city address is no longer so important. That is, with new information technology, people can communicate efficiently without working in the same area. Thus, today's cities are growing "out" more than they are growing "up." The urban scene at the beginning of the twenty-first century shows steady central-city populations surrounded by swelling suburbs and rapidly growing "edge cities"—clusters of office buildings, shopping malls, hotels, and entertainment complexes miles from the old "downtowns."

Change in the shape of cities highlights the fact that physical distance no longer separates people the way it used to. Thus people who work together do not need to share an office building or even live in the same city. The other side of the same coin is that, in the cyber age, we may not pay very much attention to the people who are—physically speaking—all around us. In short, new information technology is forming new kinds of human communities and eroding older ones.

The Rise of Virtual Communities

Consider some dramatic changes taking place at Dartmouth College, in Hanover, New Hampshire, one of the country's most academically competitive schools and a college at the forefront of the Information Revolution. Since wiring all dormitories—sometimes called the "one plug per pillow" model—life on campus has not been the same. In the cyber age, students such as Arthur Desrosiers have discovered that they have fewer and fewer reasons to leave their rooms. Desrosiers, a sophomore, relies on his computer to browse the college library, write papers, ask questions of his professors, send notes to his girlfriend, keep up with old high school friends, and even order pizza while joining in 2:00 A.M. online bull sessions. Perhaps strangest of all, Desrosiers often fires messages back and forth to his two roommates, even though they are silently staring at screens of their own just a few feet away in the same room.

It may be a sign of the times that a once-popular restaurant just down the street from dorms that house 3,000 students has closed its doors. Similarly, the student union is far less busy that it was just a few years ago. There, some of the space once used for socializing now accommodates—you guessed it—computer terminals for students who want to check their e-mail between classes.

At Dartmouth, computers have never been more popular. All together, the 8,000 students, faculty, and staff send and receive some 250,000 messages each day. No one doubts that new information technology has expanded the possibilities for accessing more information than ever before and contacting people almost anywhere in the world. But some people are beginning to see that an older form of local community is being lost in the process. Some faculty worry that they see less and less of their students. Some students, too, are beginning to think that they ought to see more of each other. As senior Abigail Butler puts it, "I know people who sit home Friday and Saturday night and e-mail

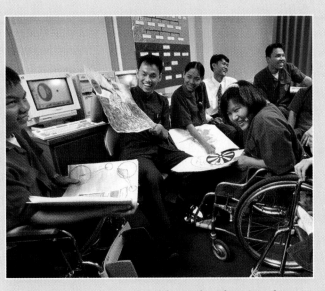

With access to the Internet, these Thai students have joined an international social movement to advance the opportunities of people with disabilities.

back and forth to people they only know by nicknames, while the rest of the world is going by. After a while it starts to be really unfulfilling. It's easier to just meet someone in person and actually talk" (Gabriel, 1996).

Social Movements: New Ways to Connect

New ways to connect with people means a rising potential for starting and expanding social movements. Today, anyone with an interest in some issue and a computer can make contact, ask questions, and spread ideas—in short, play a role in intentional social change. In addition, computers offer access to the Web pages of countless organizations and individuals with programs for change.

Perhaps most important, computer technology has made it easy to make connections on a global scale. Take the students at the Redemptorist Vocational School in Pattaya, Thailand. These young

men and women have physical disabilities, which, before the information age, might have kept them from learning at all. But using their school's computers, the students have established contact with hundreds of other people with disabilities in dozens of countries, including the United States. From these contacts, and from visiting the Web sites of national and international organizations representing people with disabilities, the students have received a rich education indeed. They have been surprised to learn that many countries have laws that protect people with disabilities from discrimination and that mandate access ramps for sidewalks and buildings; they have discovered that cities abroad feature buses that "kneel" to permit entry by people in wheelchairs, as well as public rest rooms designed to accommodate everyone. Armed with their new knowledge, the students at the Redemptorist Vocational School are now taking the lead in their own country, using the Internet to educate people about disabilities and lobbying government officials to make changes in Thailand's laws.

The Internet represents a powerful communication resource for anyone. But it is especially important for people whose ability to make contact with others is otherwise limited, including people with disabilities. As one Thai student reports, "On the 'Net, I don't feel like a handicapped person" (Smolan & Erwitt, 1996:150). Even though computer access is far from equal around the world, the Internet is providing more and more people in poor countries with the power of a "global reach."

Glossary

abortion the deliberate termination of a pregnancy

absolute poverty a deprivation of resources that is life-threatening

achieved status a social position a person assumes voluntarily and that reflects personal ability and choice

Afrocentrism the dominance of African cultural patterns

ageism prejudice and discrimination against the elderly

age-sex pyramid a graphic representation of the age and sex of a population

agriculture large-scale cultivation using plows harnessed to animals or more powerful energy sources

alienation the experience of isolation and misery resulting from powerlessness

animism the belief that elements of the natural world are conscious life forms that affect humanity

anomie Durkheim's designation of a condition in which society provides little moral guidance to individuals

anticipatory socialization learning that helps a person achieve a desired position

ascribed status a social position a person receives at birth or assumes involuntarily later in life

asexuality no sexual attraction to people of either sex

assimilation the process by which minorities gradually adopt patterns of the dominant category

authoritarianism a political system that denies popular participation in government

authority power that people perceive as legitimate rather than coercive

beliefs specific statements that people hold to be true

bisexuality sexual attraction to people of both sexes

blue-collar occupations lower-prestige work that involves mostly manual labor

bureaucracy an organizational model rationally designed to perform tasks efficiently

bureaucratic inertia the tendency of bureaucratic organizations to perpetuate themselves

bureaucratic ritualism a preoccupation with rules and regulations to the point of thwarting an organization's goals

capitalism an economic system in which natural resources and the means of producing goods and services are privately owned

capitalists people who own factories and other businesses in pursuit of profits

caste system social stratification based on ascription, or birth

cause and effect a relationship in which change in one (independent) variable causes change in another (dependent) variable

charisma extraordinary personal qualities that can turn an audience into followers

church a type of religious organization well integrated into the larger society

civil religion a quasi-religious loyalty based on citizenship

class society a capitalist society with pronounced social stratification

class system social stratification based on both birth and individual achievement

cohabitation the sharing of a household by an unmarried couple

cohort a category of people with a common characteristic, usually their age

colonialism the process by which some nations enrich themselves through political and economic control of other nations

concept a mental construct that represents some part of the world in a simplified form

concrete operational stage Piaget's term for the level of human development at which individuals first perceive causal connections in their surroundings

corporate crime the illegal actions of a corporation or people acting on its behalf

corporation an organization with a legal existence, including rights and liabilities, apart from those of its members

correlation a relationship by which two (or more) variables change together

counterculture cultural patterns that strongly oppose those widely accepted within a society

credentialism evaluating a person on the basis of educational degrees

crime the violation of a society's formally enacted criminal law

crimes against the person (violent crimes) crimes that direct violence or the threat of violence against others

crimes against property (property crimes) crimes that involve theft of property belonging to others

criminal justice system a formal response by police, courts, and prison officials to alleged violations of the law

criminal recidivism subsequent offenses committed by people previously convicted of crimes

critical sociology the study of society that focuses on the need for social change

crude birth rate the number of live births in a given year for every thousand people in a population

crude death rate the number of deaths in a given year for every thousand people in a population

cult a religious organization that is largely outside a society's cultural traditions

cultural conflict political differences, often expressed with hostility, based on disagreement over cultural values

cultural integration the close relationship among various elements of a cultural system

cultural lag the fact that some cultural elements change more quickly than others, which may disrupt a cultural system

cultural relativism the practice of evaluating a culture by its own standards

cultural transmission the process by which one generation passes culture to the next

cultural universals traits that are part of every known culture

culture the values, beliefs, behavior, and material objects that, together, form a people's way of life

culture shock personal disorientation when experiencing an unfamiliar way of life

Davis-Moore thesis the assertion that social stratification is a universal pattern because it benefits the operation of a society

democracy a type of political system which gives power to the people as a whole

demographic transition theory the thesis that population patterns reflect a society's level of technological development

demography the study of human population

denomination a church, independent of the state, that recognizes religious pluralism

dependency theory a model of economic and social development that explains global inequality in terms of the historical exploitation of poor societies by rich ones

descent the system by which members of a society trace kinship over generations

deterrence the use of punishment to discourage criminality

deviance the recognized violation of cultural norms

direct-fee system a medical care system in which patients pay directly for the services of physicians and hospitals

discrimination any action that involves treating various categories of people unequally

division of labor specialized economic activity

dramaturgical analysis Erving Goffman's term for the study of social interaction in terms of theatrical performance

dyad a social group with two members

ecologically sustainable culture a way of life that meets the needs of the present generation without threatening the environmental legacy of future generations

ecology the study of the interaction between living organisms and the natural environment

economy the social institution that organizes a society's production, distribution, and consumption of goods and services

ecosystem a system composed of the interaction of all living organisms and their natural environment

education the social institution through which society provides its members with important knowledge, including basic facts and job skills as well as cultural norms and values

ego Freud's term for a person's conscious efforts to balance innate pleasure-seeking drives with the demands of society

endogamy marriage between people of the same social category

environmental deficit profound and negative long-term harm to the natural environment caused by humanity's focus on short-term material affluence

environmental racism the pattern by which environmental hazards are greatest for poor people, especially minorities

ethnicity a shared cultural heritage

ethnocentrism the practice of judging another culture by the standards of one's own culture

ethnomethodology Harold Garfinkel's term for the study of the way people make sense of their everyday surroundings

Eurocentrism the dominance of European (especially English) cultural patterns

euthanasia (mercy killing) assisting in the death of a person suffering from an incurable disease

exogamy marriage between people of different social categories

experiment a research method for investigating cause and effect under highly controlled conditions

expressive leadership group leadership that focuses on collective well-being

extended family (consanguine family) a family unit that includes parents and children, as well as other kin

faith belief anchored in conviction rather than scientific evidence

family a social institution found in all societies that unites people in cooperative groups to oversee the bearing and raising of children

family unit a social group of two or more people, related by blood, marriage, or adoption, who usually live together

feminism the advocacy of social equality for men and women, in opposition to patriarchy and sexism

feminization of poverty the trend by which women represent an increasing proportion of the poor

fertility the incidence of childbearing in a country's population

folkways norms for routine, casual interaction

formal operational stage Piaget's term for the level of human development at which individuals think abstractly and critically

formal organization a large secondary group that is organized to achieve its goals efficiently

functional illiteracy a lack of reading and writing skills needed for everyday living

fundamentalism a conservative religious doctrine that opposes intellectualism and worldly accommodation in favor of restoring traditional, otherworldly religion

Gemeinschaft a type of social organization by which people are closely tied by kinship and tradition

gender the personal traits and social positions that members of a society attach to being female and male

gender roles (sex roles) attitudes and activities that a society links to each sex

gender stratification the unequal distribution of wealth, power, and privilege between men and women

genocide the systematic killing of one category of people by another

gerontocracy a form of social organization in which the elderly have the most wealth, power, and prestige

gerontology the study of aging and the elderly

Gesellschaft a type of social organization by which people come together only on the basis of individual self-interest

global economy expanding economic activity with little regard for national borders

global perspective the study of the larger world and our society's place in it

greenhouse effect a rise in the earth's average temperature (global warming) due to an increasing concentration of carbon dioxide in the atmosphere

groupthink the tendency of group members to conform, resulting in a narrow view of some issue

hate crime a criminal act against a person or a person's property by an offender motivated by racial or other bias

health a state of complete physical, mental, and social well-being

health maintenance organization (HMO) an organization that provides comprehensive medical care to subscribers for a fixed fee

hermaphrodite a human being with some combination of female and male genitalia

heterosexism a view stigmatizing anyone who is not heterosexual as "queer"

heterosexuality sexual attraction to someone of the other sex

high culture cultural patterns that distinguish a society's elite

high-income countries nations with very productive economic systems in which most people have relatively high incomes

holistic medicine an approach to health care that emphasizes prevention of illness and takes into account a person's entire physical and social environment

homogamy marriage between people with the same social characteristics

homophobia the dread of close personal interaction with people thought to be gay, lesbian, or bisexual

homosexuality sexual attraction to someone of the same sex

horticulture the use of hand tools to raise crops

hunting and gathering the use of simple tools to hunt animals and gather vegetation

id Freud's term for the human being's basic drives

ideology cultural beliefs that justify social stratification

incest taboo a norm forbidding sexual relations or marriage between certain relatives

income wages or salary from work and earnings from investments

industry the production of goods using advanced sources of energy to drive large machinery

infant mortality rate the number of deaths among infants under one year of age for each thousand live births in a given year

ingroup a social group commanding a member's esteem and loyalty

institutional prejudice and discrimination bias inherent in the operation of society's institutions

instrumental leadership group direction that emphasizes the completion of tasks

intergenerational social mobility upward or downward social mobility of children in relation to their parents

interpretive sociology the study of society that focuses on the meanings people attach to their social world

intragenerational social mobility a change in social position occurring during a person's lifetime

kinship a social bond based on blood, marriage, or adoption

labeling theory the assertion that deviance and conformity result, not so much from what people do, as from how others respond to those actions

language a system of symbols that allows people to communicate with one another

latent functions the unrecognized and unintended consequences of any social pattern

liberation theology a fusion of Christian principles with political activism, often Marxist in character

life expectancy the average life span of a country's population

looking-glass self Charles Horton Cooley's term referring to a self-image based on how we think others see us

low-income countries nations with less productive economic systems in which most people are poor

macro-level orientation a concern with broad patterns that shape society as a whole

manifest functions the recognized and intended consequences of any social pattern

marriage a legally sanctioned relationship, usually involving economic cooperation as well as sexual activity and childbearing, that people expect to be enduring

Marxist political-economy model an analysis that explains politics in terms of the operation of a society's economic system

mass media impersonal communications aimed at a vast audience

mass society a society in which industry and bureaucracy have eroded traditional social ties

master status a status that has special importance for social identity, often shaping a person's entire life

matriarchy a form of social organization in which females dominate males

measurement a procedure for determining the value of a variable in a specific case

medicalization of deviance the transformation of moral and legal deviance into a medical condition

medicine the social institution that focuses on combating disease and improving health

megalopolis a vast urban region containing a number of cities and their surrounding suburbs

meritocracy social stratification based on personal merit

metropolis a large city that socially and economically dominates an urban area

micro-level orientation a close-up focus on social interaction in specific situations

middle-income countries nations with moderately productive economic systems in which people's incomes are about the global average

migration the movement of people into and out of a specified territory

military-industrial complex the close association of the federal government, the military, and defense industries

minority any category of people, characterized by physical or cultural difference, that a society sets apart and subordinates

miscegenation biological reproduction by partners of different racial categories

modernity social patterns resulting from industrialization

modernization the process of social change begun by industrialization

modernization theory a model of economic and social development that explains global inequality in terms of technological and cultural differences among societies

monarchy a type of political system in which a single family rules from generation to generation

monogamy marriage uniting two partners

monopoly domination of a market by a single producer

mores norms that are widely observed and have great moral significance

mortality the incidence of death in a country's population

multiculturalism an educational program recognizing the cultural diversity of the United States and promoting the equality of all cultural traditions

multinational corporation a large business that operates in many countries

natural environment the earth's surface and atmosphere, including living organisms, air, water, soil, and other resources necessary to sustain life

neocolonialism a new form of global power relationships that involves not direct political control but economic exploitation by multinational corporations

network a web of weak social ties

nonverbal communication communication using body movements, gestures, and facial expressions rather than speech

norms rules and expectations by which a society guides the behavior of its members

nuclear family (conjugal family) a family unit composed of one or two parents and their children

oligarchy the rule of the many by the few

oligopoly domination of a market by a few producers

organizational environment a range of factors outside the organization that affects its operation

organized crime a business supplying illegal goods or services

other-directedness a receptiveness to the latest trends and fashions, often expressed by imitating others

outgroup a social group toward which one feels competition or opposition

participant observation a research method by which investigators systematically observe people while joining in their routine activities

pastoralism the domestication of animals

patriarchy a form of social organization in which males dominate females

peer group a social group whose members have interests, social position, and age in common

personality a person's fairly consistent patterns of acting, thinking, and feeling

personal space the surrounding area over which a person makes some claim to privacy

plea bargaining a legal negotiation in which the prosecutor reduces a charge in exchange for a defendant's guilty plea

pluralism a state in which racial and ethnic minorities are distinct but have social parity

pluralist model an analysis of politics that sees power as dispersed among many competing interest groups

political revolution the overthrow of one political system in order to establish another

politics the social institution that distributes power, sets a society's agenda, and makes decisions

polygamy marriage that unites three or more people

popular culture cultural patterns that are widespread among a society's population

pornography sexually explicit material that causes sexual arousal

positivism a way of understanding based on science

postindustrial economy a productive system based on service work and high technology

postmodernity social patterns characteristic of postindustrial societies

power the ability to achieve desired ends despite resistance from others

power-elite model an analysis of politics that sees power as concentrated among the rich

prejudice a rigid and irrational generalization about an entire category of people

preoperational stage Piaget's term for the level of human development at which individuals first use language and other symbols

presentation of self Erving Goffman's term for an individual's efforts to create specific impressions in the minds of others

primary group a small social group whose members share personal and enduring relationships

primary sector the part of the economy that draws raw materials from the natural environment

primary sex characteristics the genitals, organs used for reproduction

profane that which people define as an ordinary element of everyday life

profession a prestigious, white-collar occupation that requires extensive formal education

proletarians people who sell their productive labor for wages

prostitution the selling of sexual services

queer theory a growing body of knowledge that challenges the heterosexual bias in U.S. society

race a socially constructed category composed of people who share biologically transmitted traits that members of a society consider important

racism the belief that one racial category is innately superior or inferior to another

rain forests regions of dense forestation, most of which circle the globe close to the equator

rationality deliberate, matter-of-fact calculation of the most efficient means to accomplish a particular task

rationalization Max Weber's term for the change from tradition to rationality as the dominant mode of human thought

reference group a social group that serves as a point of reference in making evaluations and decisions

rehabilitation a program for reforming the offender to prevent subsequent offenses

relative deprivation a perceived disadvantage arising from some specific comparison

relative poverty the deprivation of some people in relation to those who have more

reliability consistency in measurement

religion a social institution involving beliefs and practices based on a conception of the sacred

religiosity the importance of religion in a person's life

research method a systematic plan for conducting research

resocialization radically changing an inmate's personality through carefully controlling the environment

retribution an act of moral vengeance by which society inflicts on the offender suffering comparable to that caused by the offense

role behavior expected of someone who holds a particular status

role conflict conflict among roles corresponding to two or more statuses

role set a number of roles attached to a single status

role strain tension among roles connected to a single status

routinization of charisma the transformation of charismatic authority into some combination of traditional and bureaucratic authority

sacred that which people set apart as extraordinary, inspiring a sense of awe and reverence

Sapir-Whorf thesis the assertion that people perceive the world through the cultural lens of language

scapegoat a person or category of people, typically with little power, whom people unfairly blame for their own troubles

schooling formal instruction under the direction of specially trained teachers

science a logical system that bases knowledge on direct, systematic observation

scientific management Frederick Taylor's term for the application of scientific principles to the operation of a business or other large organization

secondary group a large and impersonal social group whose members pursue a specific goal or activity

secondary sector the part of the economy that transforms raw materials into manufactured goods

secondary sex characteristics bodily development, apart from the genitals, that distinguishes biologically mature females and males

sect a type of religious organization that stands apart from the larger society

secularization the historical decline in the importance of the supernatural and the sacred

segregation the physical and social separation of categories of people

self George Herbert Mead's term for that part of an individual's personality composed of self-awareness and self-image

sensorimotor stage Piaget's term for the level of human development at which individuals experience the world only through their senses

sex the biological distinction between females and males

sexism the belief that one sex is innately superior to the other

sex ratio the number of males for every hundred females in a nation's population

sexual harassment comments, gestures, or physical contact of a sexual nature that are deliberate, repeated, and unwelcome

sexual orientation a person's romantic and emotional attraction to another person

sick role patterns of behavior defined as appropriate for those who are ill

social change the transformation of culture and social institutions over time

social character personality patterns common to members of a particular society

social-conflict paradigm a framework for building theory that sees society as an arena of inequality that generates conflict and change

social construction of reality the process by which people creatively shape reality through social interaction

social control attempts by society to regulate people's thought and behavior

social dysfunctions a social pattern's undesirable consequences for the operation of society

social epidemiology the study of how health and disease are distributed throughout a society's population

social functions the consequences of any social pattern for the operation of society as a whole

social group two or more people who identify and interact with one another

social institution an organized sphere of social life, or societal subsystem—such as the economy—designed to meet human needs

social interaction the process by which people act and react in relation to others

socialism an economic system in which natural resources and the means of producing goods and services are collectively owned

socialization the lifelong social experience by which individuals develop their human potential and learn culture

socialized medicine a medical care system in which the government owns and operates most medical facilities and employs most physicians

social mobility change in one's position in the social hierarchy

social movement organized activity that encourages or discourages social change

social stratification a system by which a society ranks categories of people in a hierarchy

social structure any relatively stable pattern of social behavior

societal protection a means by which society renders an offender incapable of further offenses, either temporarily through incarceration or permanently by execution

society people who interact in a defined territory and share culture

sociobiology a theoretical paradigm that explores ways in which human biology affects how we create culture

socioeconomic status (SES) a composite ranking based on various dimensions of social inequality

sociology the systematic study of human society

state capitalism an economic and political system in which companies are privately owned but cooperate closely with the government

state church a church formally allied with the state

status a social position that an individual occupies

status consistency the degree of consistency in a person's standing across various dimensions of social inequality

status set all the statuses a person holds at a given time

stereotype an exaggerated description that is applied to every person in some category

stigma a powerfully negative label that greatly changes a person's self-concept and social identity

structural-functional paradigm a framework for building theory that sees society as a complex system whose parts work together to promote solidarity and stability

structural social mobility a shift in the social position of large numbers of people due more to changes in society itself than to individual efforts

subculture cultural patterns that set apart some segment of a society's population

suburbs urban areas beyond the political boundaries of a city

superego Freud's term for the operation of culture within the individual in the form of internalized values and norms

survey a research method in which subjects respond to a series of statements or questions in a questionnaire or an interview

symbol anything that carries a particular meaning recognized by people who share culture

symbolic-interaction paradigm a framework for building theory that sees society as the product of the everyday interactions of individuals

technology the knowledge that people apply to the task of living in their surroundings

terrorism acts of violence or the threat of such violence used by an individual or a group as a political strategy

tertiary sector the part of the economy that involves services rather than goods

theoretical paradigm a basic image of society that guides thinking and research

theory a statement of how and why specific facts are related

Thomas theorem W. I. Thomas's assertion that situations defined as real become real in their consequences

total institution a setting in which people are isolated from the rest of society and manipulated by an administrative staff

totalitarianism a highly centralized political system that extensively regulates people's lives

totem an object in the natural world collectively defined as sacred

tracking the assignment of students to different types of educational programs

tradition sentiments and beliefs about the world passed from generation to generation

tradition-directedness rigid conformity to time-honored ways of living

transsexuals people who feel they are one sex even though biologically they are the other

triad a social group with three members

urban ecology the study of the link between the physical and social dimensions of cities

urbanization the concentration of humanity into cities

validity precision in measuring exactly what one intends to measure

values culturally defined standards by which people assess desirability, goodness, and beauty, and which serve as broad guidelines for social living

variable a concept whose value changes from case to case

victimless crimes violations of law in which there are no readily apparent victims

war organized, armed conflict among the people of various societies, directed by their governments

wealth the total value of money and other assets, minus outstanding debts

welfare capitalism an economic and political system that combines a mostly market-based economy with extensive social welfare programs

welfare state a range of government agencies and programs that provides benefits to the population

white-collar crime crime committed by people of high social position in the course of their occupations

white-collar occupations higher-prestige work that involves mostly mental activity

zero population growth the level of reproduction that maintains population at a steady state

REFERENCES

ABBOTT, ANDREW. *The System of Professions: An Essay on the Division of Expert Labor*. Chicago: University of Chicago Press, 1988.

ABERLE, DAVID F. *The Peyote Religion among the Navaho*. Chicago: Aldine, 1966.

ABRAHAMSON, PAUL R. "Postmaterialism and Environmentalism: A Comment on an Analysis and a Reappraisal." *Social Science Quarterly*. Vol. 78, No. 1 (March 1997):21–23.

ADLER, JERRY. "When Harry Called Sally . . ." *Newsweek* (October 1, 1990):74.

ADORNO, T. W., et al. *The Authoritarian Personality*. New York: Harper & Brothers, 1950.

AKERS, RONALD L., MARVIN D. KROHN, LONN LANZA-KADUCE, and MARCIA RADOSEVICH. "Social Learning and Deviant Behavior." *American Sociological Review*. Vol. 44, No. 4 (August 1979):636–55.

ALAM, SULTANA. "Women and Poverty in Bangladesh." *Women's Studies International Forum*. Vol. 8, No. 4 (1985):361–71.

THE ALAN GUTTMACHER INSTITUTE. *Teenage Pregnancy: Overall Trends and State-by-State Information*. New York: The Institute, 1999.

———. *Into a New World: Young Women's Sexual and Reproductive Lives—Executive Summary*. [Online] Available http://www.agi-usa.org/pubs/new_world_engl.html, January 24, 2000.

ALBON, JOAN. "Retention of Cultural Values and Differential Urban Adaptation: Samoans and American Indians in a West Coast City." *Social Forces*. Vol. 49, No. 3 (March 1971):385–93.

ALFORD, RICHARD. "The Structure of Human Experience: Expectancy and Affect; The Case of Humor." Unpublished paper, Department of Sociology, University of Wyoming, 1979.

ALLAN, EMILIE ANDERSEN, and DARRELL J. STEFFENSMEIER. "Youth, Underemployment, and Property Crime: Differential Effects of Job Availability and Job Quality on Juvenile and Young Adult Arrest Rates." *American Sociological Review*. Vol. 54, No. 1 (February 1989):107–23.

ALLEN, MICHAEL PATRICK, and PHILIP BROYLES. "Campaign Finance Reforms and the Presidential Campaign Contributions of Wealthy Capitalist Families." *Social Science Quarterly*. Vol. 72, No. 4 (December 1991):738–50.

ALLEN, WALTER R. "African American Family Life in Social Context: Crisis and Hope." *Sociological Forum*. Vol. 10, No. 4 (December 1995):569–92.

ALTER, JONATHAN. "Down to Business." *Newsweek* (May 12, 1997):58–60.

ALTMAN, DREW, et al. "Health Care for the Homeless." *Society*. Vol. 26, No. 4 (May–June 1989):4–5.

ALVERSON, HOYT. *Mind in the Heart of Darkness*. New Haven, Conn.: Yale University Press, 1978.

American Demographics. Zandi Group survey. Vol. 20 (March 3, 1998):38.

AMERICAN MEDICAL ASSOCIATION (AMA). Executive Summary of Media Violence Survey Analysis. [Online] Available http://www.ama-assn.org/ad-com/releases/1996/mvan1909.htm, 1997.

AMERICAN SOCIOLOGICAL ASSOCIATION. "Code of Ethics." Washington, D.C.: 1997.

AMNESTY INTERNATIONAL. "The Death Penalty: List of Abolitionist and Retentionist Countries." [Online] Available http://www.amnesty.org/ailib/intcam/dp/abrelist.htm, November 15, 2000.

ANDERSON, ELIJAH. "The Code of the Streets." *Atlantic Monthly*. Vol. 273 (May 1994):81–94.

ANDERSON, JOHN WARD. "Early to Wed: The Child Brides of India." *Washington Post* (May 24, 1995):A27, A30.

ANDO, FAITH H. "Women in Business." In Sara E. Rix, ed., *The American Woman: A Status Report 1990–91*. New York: Norton, 1990:222–30.

ANG, IEN. *Watching Dallas: Soap Opera and the Melodramatic Imagination*. London: Methuen, 1985.

ANGIER, NATALIE. "Scientists, Finding Second Idiosyncrasy in Homosexuals' Brains, Suggest Orientation Is Physiological." *New York Times* (August 1, 1992):A7.

ANNAN, KOFI. "Astonishing Facts." *New York Times* (September 27, 1998):16.

ARCHER, DANE, and ROSEMARY GARTNER. *Violence and Crime in Cross-National Perspective*. New Haven, Conn.: Yale University Press, 1987.

ARIÈS, PHILIPPE. *Centuries of Childhood: A Social History of Family Life*. New York: Vintage Books, 1965.

ARNETTE, JUNE L., and MARJORIE C. WALSLEBEN. "Combating Fear and Restoring Safety in Schools." *Juvenile Justice Bulletin* (April 1998). Washington, DC: U.S. Department of Justice.

ARONOWITZ, STANLEY. *The Politics of Identity: Class, Culture, and Social Movements*. New York: Routledge, 1992.

ASANTE, MOLEFI KETE. *Afrocentricity*. Trenton, N.J.: Africa World Press, 1988.

ASCH, SOLOMON. *Social Psychology*. Englewood Cliffs, N.J.: Prentice Hall, 1952.

ASHFORD, LORI S. "New Perspectives on Population: Lessons from Cairo." *Population Bulletin*. Vol. 50, No. 1 (March 1995).

ASTONE, NAN MARIE, and SARA S. MCLANAHAN. "Family Structure, Parental Practices and High School Completion." *American Sociological Review*. Vol. 56, No. 3 (June 1991):309–20.

BACHRACH, PETER, and MORTON S. BARATZ. *Power and Poverty*. New York: Oxford University Press, 1970.

BACKMAN, CARL B., and MURRAY C. ADAMS. "Self-Perceived Physical Attractiveness, Self-Esteem, Race, and Gender." *Sociological Focus*. Vol. 24, No. 4 (October 1991):283–90.

BAILEY, WILLIAM C. "Murder, Capital Punishment, and Television: Execution Publicity and Homicide Rates." *American Sociological Review*. Vol. 55, No. 5 (October 1990):628–33.

BAILEY, WILLIAM C., and RUTH D. PETERSON. "Murder and Capital Punishment: A Monthly Time-Series Analysis of Execution Publicity." *American Sociological Review*. Vol. 54, No. 5 (October 1989):722–43.

BAKER, MARY ANNE, CATHERINE WHITE BERHEIDE, FAY ROSS GRECKEL, LINDA CARSTARPHEN GUGIN, MARCIA J. LIPETZ, and MARCIA TEXLER SEGAL. *Women Today: A Multidisciplinary Approach to Women's Studies*. Monterey, Calif.: Brooks/Cole, 1980.

BAKER, PATRICIA S., WILLIAM C. YOELS, JEFFREY M. CLAIR, and RICHARD M. ALLMAN. "Laughter in the Triadic Geriatric Encounters: A Transcript-Based Analysis." In Rebecca J. Erikson and Beverly Cuthbertson-Johnson, eds., *Social Perspectives on Emotion*. Vol. 4. Greenwich, Conn.: JAI Press, 1997:179–207.

BAKER, ROSS. "Business as Usual." *American Demographics*. Vol. 19, No. 4 (April 1997):28.

BALTZELL, E. DIGBY. *The Protestant Establishment: Aristocracy and Caste in America*. New York: Vintage Books, 1964.

———. "Introduction to the 1967 Edition." In W. E. B. Du Bois, *The Philadelphia Negro: A Social Study*. New York: Schocken Books, 1967; orig. 1899.

———, ed. *The Search for Community in Modern America*. New York: Harper & Row, 1968.

———. "The Protestant Establishment Revisited." *The American Scholar*. Vol. 45, No. 4 (Autumn 1976):499–518.

———. *Philadelphia Gentlemen: The Making of a National Upper Class*. Philadelphia: University of Pennsylvania Press, 1979a; orig. 1958.

———. *Puritan Boston and Quaker Philadelphia*. New York: Free Press, 1979b.

———. "The WASP's Last Gasp." *Philadelphia Magazine*. Vol. 79 (September 1988):104–7, 184, 186, 188.

———. *Sporting Gentlemen: From the Age of Honor to the Cult of the Superstar*. New York: Free Press, 1995.

BARASH, DAVID. *The Whispering Within*. New York: Penguin Books, 1981.

BARKER, EILEEN. "Who'd Be a Moonie? A Comparative Study of Those Who Join the Unification Church in Britain." In Bryan Wilson, ed., *The Social Impact of New Religious Movements*. New York: Rose of Sharon Press, 1981:59–96.

BARON, JAMES N., BRIAN S. MITTMAN, and ANDREW E. NEWMAN. "Targets of Opportunity: Organizational and Environmental Determinants of Gender Integration within the California Civil Service, 1979–1985." *American Journal of Sociology*. Vol. 96, No. 6 (May 1991): 1362–401.

BARONE, MICHAEL. "How Hispanics Are Americanizing." *Wall Street Journal* (February 6, 1998a):A22.

BARRY, KATHLEEN. "Feminist Theory: The Meaning of Women's Liberation." In Barbara Haber, ed., *The Women's Annual 1982–1983*. Boston: G. K. Hall, 1983:35–78.

BARTLETT, DONALD L., and JAMES B. STEELE. "Corporate Welfare." *Time*. Vol. 152, No. 19 (November 9, 1998):36–54.

BASSUK, ELLEN J. "The Homelessness Problem." *Scientific American*. Vol. 251, No. 1 (July 1984):40–45.

BAUER, P. T. *Equality, the Third World, and Economic Delusion*. Cambridge, Mass.: Harvard University Press, 1981.

BAUMGARTNER, M. P. "Introduction: The Moral Voice of the Community." *Sociological Focus*. Vol. 31, No. 2 (May 1998):105–17.

BAYDAR, NAZLI, and JEANNE BROOKS-GUNN. "Effect of Maternal Employment and Child-Care Arrangements on Preschoolers' Cognitive and Behavioral Outcomes: Evidence from Children from the National Longitudinal Survey of Youth." *Developmental Psychology*. Vol. 27 (1991):932–35.

BECKER, HOWARD S. *Outside: Studies in the Sociology of Deviance*. New York: Free Press, 1966.

BEEGHLEY, LEONARD. *The Structure of Social Stratification in the United States*. Needham Heights, Mass.: Allyn & Bacon, 1989.

BEGLEY, SHARON. "Gray Matters." *Newsweek* (March 7, 1995):48–54.

———. "How to Beat the Heat." *Newsweek* (December 8, 1997):34–38.

BEINS, BARNEY, cited in "Examples of Spuriousness." *Teaching Methods*. No. 2 (Fall 1993):3.

BELL, ALAN P., MARTIN S. WEINBERG, and SUE KIEFER-HAMMERSMITH. *Sexual Preference: Its Development in Men and Women*. Bloomington: Indiana University Press, 1981.

BELLAH, ROBERT N. *The Broken Covenant*. New York: Seabury Press, 1975.

BELLAH, ROBERT N., RICHARD MADSEN, WILLIAM M. SULLIVAN, ANN SWIDLER, and STEVEN M. TIPTON. *Habits of the Heart: Individualism and Commitment in American Life*. New York: Harper & Row, 1985.

BELLAS, MARCIA L. "Comparable Worth in Academia: The Effects on Faculty Salaries of the Sex Composition and Labor-Market Conditions of Academic Disciplines." *American Sociological Review*. Vol. 59, No. 6 (December 1994):807–21.

BEM, SANDRA LIPSITZ. *The Lenses of Gender: Transforming the Debate on Sexual Inequality*. New Haven, Conn.: Yale University Press, 1993.

BENEDICT, RUTH. "Continuities and Discontinuities in Cultural Conditioning." *Psychiatry*. Vol. 1 (May 1938):161–67.

———. *The Chrysanthemum and the Sword: Patterns of Japanese Culture*. New York: New American Library, 1974; orig. 1946.

BENJAMIN, LOIS. *The Black Elite: Facing the Color Line in the Twilight of the Twentieth Century*. Chicago: Nelson-Hall, 1991.

BENNETT, NEIL G., DAVID E. BLOOM, and PATRICIA H. CRAIG. "The Divergence of Black and White Marriage Patterns." *American Journal of Sociology*. Vol. 95, No. 3 (November 1989):692–722.

BENNETT, STEPHEN EARL. "Left Behind: Exploring Declining Turnout among Noncollege Young Whites, 1964–1988." *Social Science Quarterly*. Vol. 72, No. 2 (June 1991):314–33.

BENNETT, WILLIAM J. "School Reform: What Remains to Be Done." *Wall Street Journal* (September 2, 1997):A18.

BENOKRAITIS, NIJOLE, and JOE FEAGIN. *Modern Sexism: Blatant, Subtle, and Overt Discrimination*. 2d ed. Englewood Cliffs, N.J.: Prentice Hall, 1995.

BENSON, MICHAEL L., and FRANCIS T. CULLEN. *Combating Corporate Crime*. Boston: Northeastern University Press, 1998.

BERGAMO, MONICA, and GERSON CAMAROTTI. "Brazil's Landless Millions." *World Press Review*. Vol. 43, No. 7 (July 1996):46–47.

BERGER, PETER L. *Invitation to Sociology*. New York: Anchor Books, 1963.

———. *The Sacred Canopy: Elements of a Sociological Theory of Religion*. Garden City, N.Y.: Doubleday, 1967.

———. *Facing Up to Modernity: Excursions in Society, Politics, and Religion*. New York: Basic Books, 1977.

———. *The Capitalist Revolution: Fifty Propositions about Prosperity, Equality, and Liberty*. New York: Basic Books, 1986.

———. "Sociology: A Disinvitation?" *Society*. Vol. 30, No. 1 (November–December 1992):12–18.

BERGER, PETER, BRIGITTE BERGER, and HANSFRIED KELLNER. *The Homeless Mind: Modernization and Consciousness*. New York: Vintage Books, 1974.

BERGER, PETER L., and HANSFRIED KELLNER. *Sociology Reinterpreted: An Essay on Method and Vocation*. Garden City, N.Y.: Anchor Books, 1981.

BERGESEN, ALBERT, ed. *Crises in the World-System*. Beverly Hills, Calif.: Sage, 1983.

BERNARD, JESSIE. *The Female World*. New York: Free Press, 1981.

———. *The Future of Marriage*. New Haven, Conn.: Yale University Press, 1982; orig. 1973.

BERNARD, LARRY CRAIG. "Multivariate Analysis of New Sex Role Formulations and Personality." *Journal of Personality and Social Psychology*. Vol. 38, No. 2 (February 1980):323–36.

BERNSTEIN, NINA. "On Frontier of Cyberspace, Data Is Money, and a Threat." *New York Times* (June 12, 1997):A1, B14–15.

BERNSTEIN, RICHARD J. *The New Constellation: The Ethical-Political Horizons of Modernity/Postmodernity*. Cambridge, Mass.: MIT Press, 1992.

BERRILL, KEVIN T. "Anti-Gay Violence and Victimization in the United States: An Overview." In Gregory M. Herek and Kevin T. Berrill, *Hate Crimes: Confronting Violence against Lesbians and Gay Men*. Newbury Park, Calif.: Sage, 1992:19–45.

BERRY, BRIAN L., and PHILIP H. REES. "The Factorial Ecology of Calcutta." *American Journal of Sociology*. Vol. 74, No. 5 (March 1969):445–91.

BERSCHEID, ELLEN, and ELAINE HATFIELD. *Interpersonal Attraction*. 2d ed. Reading, Mass.: Addison-Wesley, 1983.

BESHAROV, DOUGLAS J., and LISA A. LAUMANN. "Child Abuse Reporting." *Society*. Vol. 34, No. 4 (May/June 1996):40–46.

BEST, RAPHAELA. *We've All Got Scars: What Boys and Girls Learn in Elementary School*. Bloomington: Indiana University Press, 1983.

BEUTEL, ANN M., and MARGARET MOONEY MARINI. "Gender and Values." *American Sociological Review*. Vol. 60 (June 1995):436–48.

BIANCHI, SUZANNE M., and DAPHNE SPAIN. "Women, Work, and Family in America." *Population Bulletin*. Vol. 51, No. 3 (December 1996).

BIBLARZ, TIMOTHY J., and ADRIAN E. RAFTERY. "The Effects of Family Disruption on Social Mobility." *American Sociological Review*. Vol. 58, No. 1 (February 1993):97–109.

BILLSON, JANET MANCINI, and BETTINA J. HUBER. *Embarking upon a Career with an Undergraduate Degree in Sociology*. 2d ed. Washington, D.C.: American Sociological Association, 1993.

BLANK, JONAH. "The Muslim Mainstream." *U.S. News & World Report*. Vol. 125, No. 3 (July 20, 1998):22–25.

BLANKENHORN, DAVID. *Fatherless America: Confronting Our Most Urgent Social Problem*. New York: HarperCollins, 1995.

BLAU, JUDITH R., and PETER M. BLAU. "The Cost of Inequality: Metropolitan Structure and Violent Crime." *American Sociological Review*. Vol. 47, No. 1 (February 1982):114–29.

BLAU, PETER M. *Exchange and Power in Social Life*. New York: Wiley, 1964.

———. *Inequality and Heterogeneity: A Primitive Theory of Social Structure*. New York: Free Press, 1977.

BLAU, PETER M., TERRY C. BLUM, and JOSEPH E. SCHWARTZ. "Heterogeneity and Intermarriage." *American Sociological Review*. Vol. 47, No. 1 (February 1982):45–62.

BLAU, PETER M., and OTIS DUDLEY DUNCAN. *The American Occupational Structure*. New York: Wiley, 1967.

BLAUSTEIN, ALBERT P., and ROBERT L. ZANGRANDO. *Civil Rights and the Black American*. New York: Washington Square Press, 1968.

BLOOM, LEONARD. "Familial Adjustments of Japanese-Americans to Relocation: First Phase." In Thomas F. Pettigrew, ed., *The Sociology of Race Relations*. New York: Free Press, 1980:163–67.

BLUM, LINDA M. *Between Feminism and Labor: The Significance of the Comparable Worth Movement*. Berkeley: University of California Press, 1991.

BLUMBERG, PAUL. *Inequality in an Age of Decline*. New York: Oxford University Press, 1981.

BLUMER, HERBERT G. "Collective Behavior." In Alfred McClung Lee, ed., *Principles of Sociology*. 3d ed. New York: Barnes & Noble Books, 1969:65–121.

BLUMSTEIN, ALFRED, and RICHARD ROSENFELD. "Assessing the Recent Ups and Downs in U.S. Homicide Rates." *National Institute of Justice Journal*. Vol. 237 (October 1998):9–11.

BLUMSTEIN, PHILIP, and PEPPER SCHWARTZ. *American Couples*. New York: William Morrow, 1983.

BOBO, LAWRENCE, and VINCENT L. HUTCHINGS. "Perceptions of Racial Group Competition: Extending Blumer's Theory of Group Position to a Multiracial Social Context." *American Sociological Review*. Vol. 61, No. 6 (December 1996):951–72.

BOERNER, CHRISTOPHER, and THOMAS LAMBERT. "Environmental Injustice." *The Public Interest*. Vol. 118 (Winter 1995):61–82.

BOFF, LEONARD and CLODOVIS. *Salvation and Liberation: In Search of a Balance between Faith and Politics*. Maryknoll, N.Y.: Orbis Books, 1984.

BOGARDUS, EMORY S. "Comparing Racial Distance in Ethiopia, South Africa, and the United States." *Sociology and Social Research*. Vol. 52, No. 2 (January 1968):149–56.

BOGGESS, SCOTT, and JOHN BOUND. "Did Criminal Activity Increase during the 1980s? Comparisons across Data Sources." *Social Science Quarterly*. Vol. 78, No. 3 (September 1997):725–39.

BOHANNAN, CECIL. "The Economic Correlates of Homelessness in Sixty Cities." *Social Science Quarterly*. Vol. 72, No. 4 (December 1991):817–25.

BOHLEN, CELESTINE. "Facing Oblivion, Rust-Belt Giants Top Russian List of Vexing Crises." *New York Times* (November 8, 1998):1, 6.

BOHM, ROBERT M. "American Death Penalty Opinion, 1936–1986: A Critical Examination of the Gallup Polls." In Robert M. Bohm, ed., *The Death*

Penalty in America: Current Research. Cincinnati: Anderson Publishing Co., 1991:113–45.

BOLI, JOHN, and GEORGE M. THOMAS. "World Culture in the World Polity: A Century of International Non-Governmental Organization." *American Sociological Review.* Vol. 62, No. 2 (April 1997):171–90.

BONCZAR, THOMAS P., and ALLAN J. BECK. *Lifetime Likelihood of Going to State or Federal Prison.* Washington, D.C.: U.S. Bureau of Justice Statistics, 1997.

BONILLA-SANTIAGO, GLORIA. "A Portrait of Hispanic Women in the United States." In Sara E. Rix, ed., *The American Woman 1990–91: A Status Report.* New York: Norton, 1990:249–57.

BONNER, JANE. Research presented in "The Two Brains." Public Broadcasting System telecast, 1984.

BOOTH, ALAN, and JAMES DABBS. "Male Hormone Is Linked to Marital Problems." *Wall Street Journal* (August 19, 1992):B1.

BOOTH, ALAN, and LYNN WHITE. "Thinking about Divorce." *Journal of Marriage and the Family.* Vol. 42, No. 3 (August 1980):605–16.

BOOTH, WILLIAM. "By the Sweat of Their Brows: A New Economy." *The Washington Post* (July 13, 1998):A1, A10–A11.

BORGMANN, ALBERT. *Crossing the Postmodern Divide.* Chicago: University of Chicago Press, 1992.

BORMANN, F. HERBERT. "The Global Environmental Deficit." *BioScience.* Vol. 40 (1990):74.

BORMANN, F. HERBERT, and STEPHEN R. KELLERT. "The Global Environmental Deficit." In Herbert F. Bormann and Stephen R. Kellert, eds., *Ecology, Economics, and Ethics: The Broken Circle.* New Haven, Conn.: Yale University Press, 1991:ix–xviii.

BOSWELL, TERRY E. "A Split Labor Market Analysis of Discrimination against Chinese Immigrants, 1850–1882." *American Sociological Review.* Vol. 51, No. 3 (June 1986):352–71.

BOTT, ELIZABETH. *Family and Social Network.* New York: Free Press, 1971; orig. 1957.

BOWEN, WILLIAM G., and DEREK K. BOK. *The Shape of the River: Long-Term Consequences of Considering Race in College and University Admissions.* Princeton: Princeton University Press, 1999.

BOWLES, SAMUEL, and HERBERT GINTIS. *Schooling in Capitalist America: Educational Reform and the Contradictions of Economic Life.* New York: Basic Books, 1976.

BOYER, DEBRA. "Male Prostitution and Homosexual Identity." *Journal of Homosexuality.* Vol. 17, Nos. 1-2 (1989):151–84.

BRAITHWAITE, JOHN. "The Myth of Social Class and Criminality Reconsidered." *American Sociological Review.* Vol. 46, No. 1 (February 1981):36–57.

BRECHIN, STEVEN R., and WILLETT KEMPTON. "Global Environmentalism: A Challenge to the Postmaterialism Thesis." *Social Science Quarterly.* Vol. 75, No. 2 (June 1994):245–69.

BRIGGS, JOHN C. "The Promise of Virtual Reality." *The Futurist.* Vol. 30, No. 5 (September–October 1996):13–18.

BRIGHTMAN, JOAN. "Why Hillary Chooses Rodham Clinton." *American Demographics.* Vol. 16, No. 3 (March 1994):9–11.

BRINES, JULIE, and KARA JOYNER. "The Ties that Bind: Principles of Cohesion in Cohabitation and Marriage." *American Sociological Review.* Vol. 64, No. 3 (June 1999):333–55.

BRINTON, CRANE. *The Anatomy of Revolution.* New York: Vintage Books, 1965.

BRINTON, MARY C. "The Social-Institutional Bases of Gender Stratification: Japan as an Illustrative Case." *American Journal of Sociology.* Vol. 94, No. 2 (September 1988):300–34.

BRODER, JOHN M. "Big Social Changes Revive False God of Numbers." *New York Times* (August 17, 1997): section 4, pp. 1, 4.

BROWN, LESTER R. "Reassessing the Earth's Population." *Society.* Vol. 32, No. 4 (May–June 1995):7–10.

BROWN, LESTER R., et al., eds. *State of the World 1993: A Worldwatch Institute Report on Progress toward a Sustainable Society.* New York: Norton, 1993.

BROWN, MARY ELLEN, ed. *Television and Women's Culture: The Politics of the Popular.* Newbury Park, Calif.: Sage, 1990.

BROWNING, CHRISTOPHER R., and EDWARD O. LAUMANN. "Sexual Contact between Children and Adults: A Life Course Perspective." *American Sociological Review.* Vo. 62, No. 5 (August 1997):540–60.

Bulletin of the Atomic Scientists. Data on the "doomsday clock." [Online] Available http://www.bullatomsci.org/clock/pressrelease9.html, February 12, 2000.

BUMPASS, LARRY, and JAMES A. SWEET. *1992–1994 National Survey of Families and Households.* Reported in "Report from PPA." *Population Today.* Vol. 23, No. 6 (June 1995):3.

BURAWAY, MICHAEL. "Review Essay: The Soviet Descent into Capitalism." *American Journal of Sociology.* Vol. 102, No. 5 (March 1997):1430–44.

BURCH, ROBERT. Testimony to House of Representatives Hearing in "Review: The World Hunger Problem." October 25, 1983, Serial 98–38.

BURKE, TOM. "The Future." In Sir Edmund Hillary, ed., *Ecology 2000: The Changing Face of the Earth.* New York: Beaufort Books, 1984:227–41.

BURKETT, ELINOR. "God Created Me to Be a Slave." *New York Times* Sunday Magazine (October 12, 1997):56–60.

BURSTEIN, PAUL. "Legal Mobilization as a Social Movement Tactic: The Struggle for Equal Employment Opportunity." *American Journal of Sociology.* Vol. 96, No. 5 (March 1991):1201–25.

BUTLER, ROBERT N. *Why Survive? Being Old in America.* New York: Harper & Row, 1975.

CAMERON, WILLIAM BRUCE. *Modern Social Movements: A Sociological Outline.* New York: Random House, 1966.

CANTOR, MURIAL G., and SUZANNE PINGREE. *The Soap Opera.* Beverly Hills, Calif.: Sage, 1983.

CAPEK, STELLA A. "The 'Environmental Justice' Frame: A Conceptual Discussion and an Application." *Social Problems.* Vol. 40, No. 1 (February 1993):5–24.

CAPIZANO, JEFFREY, GINA ADAMS, and FREYA SONENSTEIN. *Child Care Arrangements for Children under Five: Variation across States.* Report of the Urban Institute. [Online] Available http://www.newfederalism.urban.org/html/series_b/b7.html, February 14, 2001.

CAPIZANO, JEFFREY, KATHRYN TOUT, and GINA ADAMS. *Child Care Patterns of School-Age Children with Employed Mothers.* Report of the Urban Institute. [Online] Available http://www.newfederalism.urban.org/html/op41/occa41.html#childcare, February 14, 2001.

CAPLOW, THEODORE, et al. *Middletown Families.* Minneapolis: University of Minnesota Press, 1982.

CAPLOW, THEODORE, HOWARD M. BAHR, JOHN MODELL, and BRUCE A. CHADWICK. *Recent Social Trends in the United States, 1960–1990.* Montreal: McGill-Queen's University Press, 1991.

CARLEY, KATHLEEN. "A Theory of Group Stability." *American Sociological Review.* Vol. 56, No. 3 (June 1991):331–54.

CARLSON, NORMAN A. "Corrections in the United States Today: A Balance Has Been Struck." *The American Criminal Law Review.* Vol. 13, No. 4 (Spring 1976):615–47.

CARMICHAEL, STOKELY, and CHARLES V. HAMILTON. *Black Power: The Politics of Liberation in America.* New York: Vintage Books, 1967.

CARR, LESLIE G. "Colorblindness and the New Racism." Paper presented at the annual meeting, American Sociological Association, Washington, D.C., 1995.

CARROLL, GINNY. "Who Foots the Bill?" *Newsweek.* Special Issue (Fall–Winter 1990):81–85.

CARROLL, JAMES R. "Congress Is Told of Coal-Dust Fraud UMW; Senator from Minnesota Rebukes Industry." *Louisville Courier Journal* (Thursday, May 27, 1999):1A.

CARSON, RACHEL. *Silent Spring.* Boston: Houghton Mifflin, 1962.

CASTELLS, MANUEL. *The Urban Question.* Cambridge, Mass.: MIT Press, 1977.

———. *The City and the Grass Roots.* Berkeley: University of California Press, 1983.

CATALYST. "Women CEOs." [Online] Available http://www.catalystwomen.org/press/infobriefs/infobrief2.html, February 2, 2001.

———. "Women Corporate Officers and Top Earners." [Online] Available http://www.catalystwomen.org/press/infobriefs/infocote.html, February 2, 2001.

CENTER FOR RESPONSIVE POLITICS. The Big Picture. [Online] Available http://www.crp.org/crpdocs/bigpicture/default.htm, February 12, 1998.

———. [Online] Available http://www.opensecrets.org/2000elect/storysofar/sectors.asp, March 15, 2001.

CENTER FOR THE STUDY OF SPORT IN SOCIETY. *1998 Racial and Gender Report Card.* [Online] Available http://www.sportinsociety.org, February 19, 2000.

CHAGNON, NAPOLEON A. *Yąnomamö: The Fierce People.* 4th ed. New York: Holt, Rinehart & Winston, 1992.

CHANDLER, TERTIUS, and GERALD FOX. *3000 Years of Urban History.* New York: Academic Press, 1974.

CHANDLER, TIMOTHY D., YOSHINORI KAMO, and JAMES D. WERBEL. "Do Delays in Marriage and Childbirth Affect Earnings?" *Social Science Quarterly.* Vol. 75, No. 4 (December 1994):838–53.

CHANGE, KWANG-CHIH. *The Archaeology of Ancient China.* New Haven, Conn.: Yale University Press, 1977.

CHARLES, MARIA. "Cross-National Variation in Occupational Segregation." *American Sociological Review.* Vol. 57, No. 4 (August 1992):483–502.

CHAUNCEY, GEORGE. *Gay New York: Gender, Urban Culture, and the Making of the Gay Male World 1890-1940.* New York: Basic Books, 1994.

CHAVES, MARK. "Ordaining Women: The Diffusion of an Organizational Innovation." *American Journal of Sociology.* Vol. 101, No. 4 (January 1996):840–73.

CHERLIN, ANDREW, and FRANK F. FURSTENBERG, JR. *The New American Grandparent: A Place in the Family, A Life Apart.* New York: Basic Books, 1986.

CHESNAIS, JEAN-CLAUDE. "The Demographic Sunset of the West?" *Population Today.* Vol. 25, No. 1 (January 1997):4–5.

CHOLDIN, HARVEY M. "How Sampling Will Help Defeat the Undercount." *Society.* Vol. 34, No. 3 (March/April 1997):27–30.

The Christian Science Monitor. "Women and Power." (September 6, 1995):1, 9, 10, 11.

CHURCH, GEORGE J. "Unions Arise—with New Tricks." *Time.* Vol. 143, No. 24 (June 13, 1994):56–58.

———. "Ripping Up Welfare." *Time.* Vol. 148, No. 8 (August 12, 1996):18–22.

CLARK, MARGARET S., ed. *Prosocial Behavior.* Newbury Park, Calif.: Sage, 1991.

CLARKE, ROBIN. "Atmospheric Pollution." In Sir Edmund Hillary, ed., *Ecology 2000: The Changing Face of the Earth.* New York: Beaufort Books, 1984a:130–48.

———. "What's Happening to Our Water?" In Sir Edmund Hillary, ed., *Ecology 2000: The Changing Face of the Earth.* New York: Beaufort Books, 1984b:108–29.

CLINARD, MARSHALL, and DANIEL ABBOTT. *Crime in Developing Countries.* New York: Wiley, 1973.

CLOUD, JOHN. "What Can the Schools Do?" *Time.* Vol. 153, No. 17 (May 3, 1999):38–40.

CLOWARD, RICHARD A., and LLOYD E. OHLIN. *Delinquency and Opportunity: A Theory of Delinquent Gangs.* New York: Free Press, 1966.

cnnsi.com. Update on men's and women's athletic performance. [Online] Available September 16, 1998.

COAKLEY, JAY J. *Sport in Society: Issues and Controversies.* 4th ed. St. Louis, Mo.: Mosby, 1990.

COE, MICHAEL D., and RICHARD A. DIEHL. *In the Land of the Olmec.* Austin: University of Texas Press, 1980.

COHEN, ADAM. "A New Push for Blind Justice." *Time.* Vol. 145, No. 7 (February 20, 1995):39–40.

———. "Test-Tube Tug-of-War." *Time.* Vol. 151, No. 13 (April 6, 1998):65.

———. "A First Report Card on Vouchers." *Time.* Vol. 153, No. 16 (April 26, 1999):36–38.

COHEN, ALBERT K. *Delinquent Boys: The Culture of the Gang.* New York: Free Press, 1971; orig. 1955.

COHEN, LLOYD R. "Sexual Harassment and the Law." *Society.* Vol. 28, No. 4 (May–June 1991):8–13.

COLEMAN, JAMES S. "The Design of Organizations and the Right to Act." *Sociological Forum.* Vol. 8, No. 4 (December 1993):527–46.

COLEMAN, JAMES S., and THOMAS HOFFER. *Public and Private High Schools: The Impact of Communities.* New York: Basic Books, 1987.

COLEMAN, JAMES, THOMAS HOFFER, and SALLY KILGORE. *Public and Private Schools: An Analysis of Public Schools and Beyond.* Washington, D.C.: National Center for Education Statistics, 1981.

COLEMAN, RICHARD P., and BERNICE L. NEUGARTEN. *Social Status in the City.* San Francisco: Jossey-Bass, 1971.

COLEMAN, RICHARD P., and LEE RAINWATER. *Social Standing in America.* New York: Basic Books, 1978.

COLLINS, RANDALL. "A Conflict Theory of Sexual Stratification." *Social Problems.* Vol. 19, No. 1 (Summer 1971):3–21.

———. *The Credential Society: An Historical Sociology of Education and Stratification.* New York: Academic Press, 1979.

———. *Sociological Insight: An Introduction to Nonobvious Sociology.* New York: Oxford University Press, 1982.

COLLOWAY, N. O., and PAULA L. DOLLEVOET. "Selected Tabular Material on Aging." In Caleb Finch and Leonard Hayflick, eds., *Handbook of the Biology of Aging.* New York: Van Nostrand Reinhold, 1977:666–708.

COLTON, HELEN. *The Gift of Touch: How Physical Contact Improves Communication, Pleasure, and Health.* New York: Seaview/Putnam, 1983.

COMMISSION FOR RACIAL JUSTICE, UNITED CHURCH OF CHRIST. *CRJ Reporter.* New York: Commission for Racial Justice, the United Church of Christ, 1994.

COMTE, AUGUSTE. *Auguste Comte and Positivism: The Essential Writings.* Gertrud Lenzer, ed. New York: Harper Torchbooks, 1975.

CONNETT, PAUL H. "The Disposable Society." In F. Herbert Bormann and Stephen R. Kellert, eds., *Ecology, Economics, and Ethics: The Broken Circle.* New Haven, Conn.: Yale University Press, 1991:99–122.

COOK, RHODES. "House Republicans Scored a Quiet Victory in '92." *Congressional Quarterly Weekly Report.* Vol. 51, No. 16 (April 17, 1993):965–68.

COOLEY, CHARLES HORTON. *Human Nature and the Social Order.* New York: Schocken Books, 1964; orig. 1902.

COONEY, MARK. "From Warfare to Tyranny: Lethal Conflict and the State." *American Sociological Review.* Vol. 62, No. 2 (April 1997):316–38.

CORLEY, ROBERT N., O. LEE REED, PETER J. SHEDD, and JERE W. MOREHEAD. *The Legal and Regulatory Environment of Business.* 9th ed. New York: McGraw-Hill, 1993.

COSE, ELLIS. "The Good News about Black America." *Newsweek* (June 7, 1999):28–40.

COSER, LEWIS. *The Functions of Social Conflict.* New York: Free Press, 1956.

———. *Masters of Sociological Thought: Ideas in Historical and Social Context.* New York: Harcourt Brace Jovanovich, 1971.

COTTLE, THOMAS J. "What Tracking Did to Ollie Taylor." *Social Policy.* Vol. 5, No. 2 (July–August 1974):22–24.

COUNCIL ON FAMILIES IN AMERICA. *Marriage in America: A Report to the Nation.* New York: Institute for American Values, 1995.

COUNTS, G. S. "The Social Status of Occupations: A Problem in Vocational Guidance." *School Review.* Vol. 33 (January 1925):16–27.

COURTNEY, ALICE E., and THOMAS W. WHIPPLE. *Sex Stereotyping in Advertising.* Lexington, Mass.: D. C. Heath, 1983.

COURTWRIGHT, DAVID T. *Violent Land: Single Men and Social Disorder from the Frontier to the Inner City.* Cambridge, Mass.: Harvard University Press, 1996.

COVINGTON, JEANETTE. "Racial Classification in Criminology: The Reproduction of Racialized Crime." *Sociological Forum.* Vol. 10, No. 4 (December 1995):547–68.

COWAN, CAROLYN POPE. *When Partners Become Parents.* New York: Basic Books, 1992.

COWGILL, DONALD, and LOWELL HOLMES. *Aging and Modernization.* New York: Appleton-Century-Crofts, 1972.

COWLEY, GEOFFREY. "The Prescription That Kills." *Newsweek* (July 17, 1995):54.

COX, HARVEY. *The Secular City.* Rev. ed. New York: Macmillan, 1971; orig. 1965.

———. "Church and Believers: Always Strangers?" In Thomas Robbins and Dick Anthony, *In Gods We Trust: New Patterns of Religious Pluralism in America.* 2d ed. New Brunswick, N.J.: Transaction, 1990:449–62.

COYOTE (Call Off Your Old Tired Ethics). [Online] Available http://www.freedomusa.org/coyotela/what_is.html, April 2, 2000.

CRISPELL, DIANE. "Grandparents Galore." *American Demographics.* Vol. 15, No. 10 (October 1993):63.

CROOK, STEPHAN, JAN PAKULSKI, and MALCOLM WATERS. *Postmodernity: Change in Advanced Society.* Newbury Park, Calif.: Sage, 1992.

CROSSEN, CYNTHIA, and ELLEN GRAHAM. "Good News—and Bad—about America's Health." *Wall Street Journal* (June 28, 1996):R1.

CROUSE, JAMES, and DALE TRUSHEIM. *The Case against the SAT.* Chicago: University of Chicago Press, 1988.

CUMMINGS, SCOTT, and THOMAS LAMBERT. "Anti-Hispanic and Anti-Asian Sentiments among African Americans." *Social Science Quarterly.* Vol. 78, No. 2 (June 1997):338–53.

CURRIE, ELLIOTT. *Confronting Crime: An American Challenge.* New York: Pantheon Books, 1985.

CURRY, GEORGE E., ed. *The Affirmative Action Debate.* Reading, Mass.: Addison-Wesley, 1996.

Curtis, James E., Edward G. Grabb, and Douglas Baer. "Voluntary Association Membership in Fifteen Countries: A Comparative Analysis." *American Sociological Review*. Vol. 57, No. 2 (April 1992):139–52.

Curtiss, Susan. *Genie: A Psycholinguistic Study of a Modern-Day "Wild Child."* New York: Academic Press, 1977.

Dahl, Robert A. *Who Governs?* New Haven, Conn.: Yale University Press, 1961.

———. *Dilemmas of Pluralist Democracy: Autonomy vs. Control.* New Haven, Conn.: Yale University Press, 1982.

Dahrendorf, Ralf. *Class and Class Conflict in Industrial Society.* Stanford, Calif.: Stanford University Press, 1959.

Daly, Martin, and Margo Wilson. *Homicide.* New York: Aldine, 1988.

Daniels, Roger. "The Issei Generation." In Amy Tachiki et al., eds., *Roots: An Asian American Reader.* Los Angeles: UCLA Asian American Studies Center, 1971:138–49.

Davidson, James D., Ralph E. Pyle, and David V. Reyes. "Persistence and Change in the Protestant Establishment, 1930–1992." *Social Forces.* Vol. 74, No. 1 (September 1995):157–75.

Davies, Christie. *Ethnic Humor around the World: A Comparative Analysis.* Bloomington: Indiana University Press, 1990.

Davies, James C. "Toward a Theory of Revolution." *American Sociological Review.* Vol. 27, No. 1 (February 1962):5–19.

Davies, Mark, and Denise B. Kandel. "Parental and Peer Influences on Adolescents' Educational Plans: Some Further Evidence." *American Journal of Sociology.* Vol. 87, No. 2 (September 1981):363–87.

Davis, Donald M., cited in "T.V. Is a Blonde, Blonde World." *American Demographics*, special issue: *Women Change Places.* Ithaca, N.Y.: 1993.

Davis, Kingsley. "Extreme Social Isolation of a Child." *American Journal of Sociology.* Vol. 45, No. 4 (January 1940):554–65.

———. "Final Note on a Case of Extreme Isolation." *American Journal of Sociology.* Vol. 52, No. 5 (March 1947):432–37.

———. "Sexual Behavior." In Robert K. Merton and Robert Nisbet, eds., *Contemporary Social Problems.* 3d ed. New York: Harcourt Brace Jovanovich, 1971:313–60.

Davis, Kingsley, and Wilbert Moore. "Some Principles of Stratification." *American Sociological Review.* Vol. 10, No. 2 (April 1945):242–49.

Davis, Nancy, and Robert V. Robinson. "Are the Rumors of War Exaggerated? Religious Orthodoxy and Moral Progressivism in America." *American Journal of Sociology.* Vol. 102, No. 3 (November 1996):756–87.

Davis, Sharon A., and Emil J. Haller. "Tracking, Ability, and SES: Further Evidence on the 'Revisionist-Meritocratic Debate.'" *American Journal of Education.* Vol. 89 (May 1981):283–304.

Deckard, Barbara Sinclair. *The Women's Movement: Political, Socioeconomic, and Psychological Issues.* 2d ed. New York: Harper & Row, 1979.

Delacroix, Jacques, and Charles C. Ragin. "Structural Blockage: A Crossnational Study of Economic Dependency, State Efficacy, and Underdevelopment." *American Journal of Sociology.* Vol. 86, No. 6 (May 1981):1311–47.

DeLuca, Tom. "Joe the Bookie and the Class Voting Gap." *American Demographics.* Vol. 20, No. 11 (November 1998):26–29.

Demerath, N. J., III. "Who Now Debates Functionalism? From *System, Change, and Conflict* to 'Culture, Choice, and Praxis'." *Sociological Forum.* Vol. 11, No. 2 (June 1996):333–45.

Dent, David J. "African-Americans Turning to Christian Academies." *New York Times*, Education Life supplement (August 4, 1996):26–29.

Dershowitz, Alan. *The Vanishing American Jew.* Boston: Little, Brown, 1997.

Der Spiegel. "Third World Metropolises Are Becoming Monsters; Rural Poverty Drives Millions to the Slums." In *World Press Review* (October 1989).

Dervarics, Charles. "Is Welfare Reform Reforming Welfare?" *Population Today.* Vol. 26, No. 10 (October 1998):1–2.

———. "The Coming Age of Older Women." *Population Today.* Vol. 27, No. 2 (February 1999):2–3.

Devine, Joel A. "State and State Expenditure: Determinants of Social Investment and Social Consumption Spending in the Postwar United States." *American Sociological Review.* Vol. 50, No. 2 (April 1985):150–65.

DiMaggio, Paul, John Evans, and Bethany Bryson. "Have Americans' Social Attitudes Become More Polarized?" *American Journal of Sociology.* Vol. 102, No. 3 (November 1996):690–755.

Dixon, William J., and Terry Boswell. "Dependency, Disarticulation, and Denominator Effects: Another Look at Foreign Capital Penetration." *American Journal of Sociology.* Vol. 102, No. 2 (September 1996):543–62.

Dizard, Jan E., and Howard Gadlin. *The Minimal Family.* Amherst: The University of Massachusetts Press, 1990.

Dobyns, Henry F. "An Appraisal of Techniques with a New Hemispheric Estimate." *Current Anthropology.* Vol. 7, No. 4 (October 1966):395–446.

Dollard, John, et al. *Frustration and Aggression.* New Haven, Conn.: Yale University Press, 1939.

Domhoff, G. William. *Who Rules America Now? A View of the '80s.* Englewood Cliffs, N.J.: Prentice Hall, 1983.

Donovan, Virginia K., and Ronnie Littenberg. "Psychology of Women: Feminist Therapy." In Barbara Haber, ed., *The Women's Annual 1981: The Year in Review.* Boston: G. K. Hall, 1982:211–35.

Doyle, James A. *The Male Experience.* Dubuque, Iowa: Wm. C. Brown, 1983.

Doyle, Richard F. *A Manifesto of Men's Liberation.* 2d ed. Forest Lake, Minn.: Men's Rights Association, 1980.

D'Souza, Dinesh. "The Billionaire Next Door." *Forbes.* Vol. 164, No. 9 (October 11, 1999):50–62.

Du Bois, W. E. B. *The Philadelphia Negro: A Social Study.* New York: Schocken Books, 1967; orig. 1899.

Dubos, René. *Man Adapting.* New Haven, Conn.: Yale University Press, 1980; orig. 1965.

Duhl, Leonard J. "The Social Context of Health." In Arthur C. Hastings et al., eds., *Health for the Whole Person: The Complete Guide to Holistic Medicine.* Boulder, Colo.: Westview Press, 1980:39–48.

Duncan, Greg J., W. Jean Yeung, Jeanne Brooks-Gunn, and Judith R. Smith. "How Much Does Childhood Poverty Affect the Life Chances of Children?" *American Sociological Review.* Vol. 63, No. 3 (June 1998):406–23.

Dunlap, David W. "Fearing a Toehold for Gay Marriages, Conservatives Rush to Bar the Door." *New York Times* (March 3, 1996):A13.

Dunn, Ashley. "Ancient Chinese Craft Shifts Building Designs in the U.S." *New York Times* (September 22, 1994):A1, B4.

Dunn, John. "Peddling Big Brother." *Time.* Vol. 137, No. 25 (June 24, 1991):62.

Durkheim, Emile. *Moral Education.* New York: Free Press, 1961; orig. 1902–3.

———. *The Division of Labor in Society.* New York: Free Press, 1964a; orig. 1895.

———. *The Rules of Sociological Method.* New York: Free Press, 1964b; orig. 1893.

———. *The Elementary Forms of Religious Life.* New York: Free Press, 1965; orig. 1915.

Dworkin, Andrea. *Intercourse.* New York: Free Press, 1987.

Ebaugh, Helen Rose Fuchs. *Becoming an EX: The Process of Role Exit.* Chicago: University of Chicago Press, 1988.

Eberstadt, Nicholas. "What Is Population Policy?" *Society.* Vol. 32, No. 4 (May–June 1995):26–29.

The Economist. "Cockfighting: 'Til Death Us Do Part." Vol. 330, No. 7851 (February 19, 1994):30.

Edin, Kathryn, and Laura Lein. "Work, Welfare, and Single Mothers' Economic Survival Strategies." *American Sociological Review.* Vol. 62, No. 2 (April 1996):253–66.

Edmondson, Brad. "The Great Money Grab." *American Demographics.* Vol. 17, No. 2 (February 1995):2.

———. "The Facts of Death." *American Demographics.* Vol. 49, No. 4 (April 1997):47–53.

Edwards, David V. *The American Political Experience.* 3d ed. Englewood Cliffs, N.J.: Prentice Hall, 1985.

Edwards, Richard. *Contested Terrain: The Transformation of the Workplace in the Twentieth Century.* New York: Basic Books, 1979.

Edwards, Tamala M. "Revolt of the Gentry." *Time.* Vol. 151, No. 23 (June 15, 1998):34–35.

———. "Harvard vs. the School of Hard Knocks." *Time.* Vol. 153, No. 24 (June 21, 1999):8.

Ehrenreich, Barbara. *The Hearts of Men: American Dreams and the Flight from Commitment.* Garden City, N.Y.: Anchor Books, 1983.

———. "The Real Truth about the Female Body." *Time.* Vol. 153, No. 9 (March 15, 1999):56–65.

Ehrenreich, John. "Introduction." In John Ehrenreich, ed., *The Cultural Crisis of Modern Medicine.* New York: Monthly Review Press, 1978:1–35.

Eichler, Margrit. *Nonsexist Research Methods: A Practical Guide.* Winchester, Mass.: Unwin Hyman, 1988.

Eisenberg, Daniel. "Rise of the Permatemp." *Time.* Vol. 154, No. 2 (July 12, 1999):48.

EISENSTEIN, ZILLAH R., ed. *Capitalist Patriarchy and the Case for Socialist Feminism.* New York: Monthly Review Press, 1979.

EKMAN, PAUL. "Biological and Cultural Contributions to Body and Facial Movements in the Expression of Emotions." In A. Rorty, ed., *Explaining Emotions.* Berkeley: University of California Press, 1980a:73–101.

———. *Face of Man: Universal Expression in a New Guinea Village.* New York: Garland Press, 1980b.

———. *Telling Lies: Clues to Deceit in the Marketplace, Politics, and Marriage.* New York: Norton, 1985.

ELIAS, ROBERT. *The Politics of Victimization: Victims, Victimology and Human Rights.* New York: Oxford University Press, 1986.

ELLIOT, DELBERT S., and SUZANNE S. AGETON. "Reconciling Race and Class Differences in Self-Reported and Official Estimates of Delinquency." *American Sociological Review.* Vol. 45, No. 1 (February 1980):95–110.

ELLISON, CHRISTOPHER G., JOHN P. BARTKOWSKI, and MICHELLE L. SEGAL. "Do Conservative Protestant Parents Spank More Often? Further Evidence from the National Survey of Families and Households." *Social Science Quarterly.* Vol. 77, No. 3 (September 1996):663–73.

ELLISON, CHRISTOPHER G., and DARREN E. SHERKAT. "Conservative Protestantism and Support for Corporal Punishment." *American Sociological Review.* Vol. 58, No. 1 (February 1993):131–44.

ELMER-DEWITT, PHILIP. "First Nation in Cyberspace." *Time.* Vol. 142, No. 24 (December 6, 1993):62–64.

———. "The Genetic Revolution." *Time.* Vol. 143, No. 3 (January 17, 1994a):46–53.

———. "Battle for the Internet." *Time.* Vol. 144, No. 4 (July 25, 1994b):50–56.

———. "Now for the Truth about Americans and Sex." *Time.* Vol. 144, No. 16 (October 17, 1994c):62–70.

EMBER, MELVIN, and CAROL R. EMBER. "The Conditions Favoring Matrilocal versus Patrilocal Residence." *American Anthropologist.* Vol. 73, No. 3 (June 1971):571–94.

———. *Anthropology.* 6th ed. Englewood Cliffs, N.J.: Prentice Hall, 1991.

EMERSON, JOAN P. "Behavior in Private Places: Sustaining Definitions of Reality in Gynecological Examinations." In H. P. Dreitzel, ed., *Recent Sociology.* Vol. 2. New York: Collier, 1970:74–97.

ENGELS, FRIEDRICH. *The Origin of the Family.* Chicago: Charles H. Kerr & Company, 1902; orig. 1884.

ENGLAND, PAULA. *Comparable Worth: Theories and Evidence.* Hawthorne, N.Y.: Aldine, 1992.

EPPS, EDGAR G. "Race, Class, and Educational Opportunity: Trends in the Sociology of Education." *Sociological Forum.* Vol. 10, No. 4 (December 1995):593–608.

ERIKSON, ERIK H. *Childhood and Society.* New York: Norton, 1963; orig. 1950.

ERIKSON, ROBERT S., NORMAN R. LUTTBEG, and KENT L. TEDIN. *American Public Opinion: Its Origins, Content, and Impact.* 2d ed. New York: Wiley, 1980.

ETZIONI, AMITAI. *A Comparative Analysis of Complex Organization: On Power, Involvement, and Their Correlates.* Rev. and enlarged ed. New York: Free Press, 1975.

———. "How to Make Marriage Matter." *Time.* Vol. 142, No. 10 (September 6, 1993):76.

ETZIONI-HALEVY, EVA. *Bureaucracy and Democracy: A Political Dilemma.* Rev. ed. Boston: Routledge & Kegan Paul, 1985.

EVANS, JOHN H. "Worldviews or Social Groups as the Source of Moral Value Attitudes: Implications for the Culture Wars Thesis." *Sociological Forum,* Vol. 12, No. 3 (September 1997):371–404.

FAGAN, JEFFREY, FRANKLIN E. ZIMRING, and JUNE KIM. "Declining Homicide in New York City: A Tale of Two Trends." *National Institute of Justice Journal.* Vol. 237 (October 1998):12–13.

FALK, GERHARD. Personal communication, 1987.

FALKENMARK, MALIN, and CARL WIDSTRAND. "Population and Water Resources: A Delicate Balance." *Population Bulletin.* Vol. 47, No. 3 (November 1992). Washington, D.C.: Population Reference Bureau.

FALLON, A. E., and P. ROZIN. "Sex Differences in Perception of Desirable Body Shape." *Journal of Abnormal Psychology.* Vol. 94, No. 1 (1985):100–5.

FALLOWS, JAMES. "Immigration: How It's Affecting Us." *The Atlantic Monthly.* Vol. 252 (November 1983):45–52, 55–62, 66–68, 85–90, 94, 96, 99–106.

FARLEY, CHRISTOPHER JOHN. "Winning the Right to Fly." *Time.* Vol. 146, No. 9 (August 28, 1995):62–64.

———. "Hip-Hop Nation." *Time.* Vol. 153, No. 5 (February 8, 1999):54–64.

FARLEY, CHRISTOPHER JOHN, and JAMES WILLWERTH. "Dead Teen Walking." *Time.* Vol. 151, No. 2 (January 19, 1998).

FARRELL, MICHAEL P., and STANLEY D. ROSENBERG. *Men at Midlife.* Boston: Auburn House, 1981.

FEAGIN, JOE. *The Urban Real Estate Game.* Englewood Cliffs, N.J.: Prentice Hall, 1983.

FEATHERMAN, DAVID L., and ROBERT M. HAUSER. *Opportunity and Change.* New York: Academic Press, 1978.

FEATHERSTONE, MIKE, ed. *Global Culture: Nationalism, Globalization, and Modernity.* London: Sage, 1990.

FEDARKO, KEVIN. "Land Mines: Cheap, Deadly, and Cruel." *Time.* Vol. 147, No. 20 (May 13, 1996):54–55.

FELLMAN, BRUCE. "Taking the Measure of Children's T.V." *Yale Alumni Magazine* (April 1995):46–51.

FERGUSON, TOM. "Medical Self-Care: Self Responsibility for Health." In Arthur C. Hastings et al., eds., *Health for the Whole Person: The Complete Guide to Holistic Medicine.* Boulder, Colo.: Westview Press, 1980:87–109.

FERNANDEZ, ROBERTO M., and NANCY WEINBERG. "Sifting and Sorting: Personal Contacts and Hiring in a Retail Bank." *American Sociological Review.* Vol. 62, No. 6 (December 1997):883–902.

FERREE, MYRA MARX, and ELAINE J. HALL. "Rethinking Stratification from a Feminist Perspective: Gender, Race, and Class in Mainstream Textbooks." *American Sociological Review.* Vol. 61, No. 6 (December 1996):929–50.

FETTO, JOHN. "Down for the Count." *American Demographics.* Vol. 21, No. 11 (November 1999):46–47.

FINE, GARY ALAN. "Nature and the Taming of the Wild: The Problem of 'Overpick' in the Culture of Mushroomers." *Social Problems.* Vol. 44, No. 1 (February 1997):68–88.

FINKELSTEIN, NEAL W., and RON HASKINS. "Kindergarten Children Prefer Same-Color Peers." *Child Development.* Vol. 54, No. 2 (April 1983):502–8.

FINN, CHESTER E., JR., and REBECCA L. GAU. "New Ways of Education." *The Public Interest.* Vol. 130 (Winter 1998):79–92.

FINN, CHESTER E., JR., and HERBERT J. WALBERG. "The World's Least Efficient Schools." *Wall Street Journal* (June 22, 1998):A22.

FIORENTINE, ROBERT. "Men, Women, and the Premed Persistence Gap: A Normative Alternatives Approach." *American Journal of Sociology.* Vol. 92, No. 5 (March 1987):1118–39.

FIORENTINE, ROBERT, and STEPHEN COLE. "Why Fewer Women Become Physicians: Explaining the Premed Persistence Gap." *Sociological Forum.* Vol. 7, No. 3 (September 1992):469–96.

FIREBAUGH, GLENN. "Growth Effects of Foreign and Domestic Investment." *American Journal of Sociology.* Vol. 98, No. 1 (July 1992):105–30.

———. "Does Foreign Capital Harm Poor Nations? New Estimates Based on Dixon and Boswell's Measures of Capital Penetration." *American Journal of Sociology.* Vol. 102, No. 2 (September 1996):563–75.

———. "Empirics of World Income Inequality." *American Journal of Sociology.* Vol. 104, No. 6 (May 1999):1597–1630.

FIREBAUGH, GLENN, and FRANK D. BECK. "Does Economic Growth Benefit the Masses? Growth, Dependence, and Welfare in the Third World." *American Sociological Review.* Vol. 59, No. 5 (October 1994):631–53.

FIREBAUGH, GLENN, and KENNETH E. DAVIS. "Trends in Antiblack Prejudice, 1972–1984: Region and Cohort Effects." *American Journal of Sociology.* Vol. 94, No. 2 (September 1988):251–72.

FIREBAUGH, GLENN, and DUMITRU SANDU. "Who Supports Marketization and Democratization in Post-Communist Romania?" *Sociological Forum.* Vol. 13, No. 3 (September 1998):521–41.

FISHER, ELIZABETH. *Woman's Creation: Sexual Evolution and the Shaping of Society.* Garden City, N.Y.: Anchor/Doubleday, 1979.

FISHER, ROGER, and WILLIAM URY. "Getting to YES." In William M. Evan and Stephen Hilgartner, eds., *The Arms Race and Nuclear War.* Englewood Cliffs, N.J.: Prentice Hall, 1988:261–68.

FISKE, ALAN PAIGE. "The Cultural Relativity of Selfish Individualism: Anthropological Evidence that Humans Are Inherently Sociable." In Margaret S. Clark, ed., *Prosocial Behavior.* Newbury Park, Calif.: Sage, 1991:176–214.

FISKE, EDWARD B. "Adults: The Forgotten Illiterates." *Christian Science Monitor* (May 30, 1997):18.

FLAHERTY, MICHAEL G. "A Formal Approach to the Study of Amusement in Social Interaction." *Studies in Symbolic Interaction.* Vol. 5. New York: JAI Press, 1984:71–82.

———. "Two Conceptions of the Social Situation: Some Implications of Humor." *The Sociological Quarterly*. Vol. 31, No. 1 (Spring 1990).

FLORIDA, RICHARD, and MARTIN KENNEY. "Transplanted Organizations: The Transfer of Japanese Industrial Organization to the U.S." *American Sociological Review*. Vol. 56, No. 3 (June 1991):381–98.

FOBES, RICHARD. "Creative Problem Solving." *The Futurist*. Vol. 30, No. 1 (January–February 1996):19–22.

Forbes. "The Forbes 400: The Ranking." Vol. 165, No. 9 (October 9, 2000). [Online] Available http://www.forbes.com/400richest/, December 6, 2000.

FORD, CLELLAN S., and FRANK A. BEACH. *Patterns of Sexual Behavior*. New York: Harper & Row, 1951.

FORNOS, WERNER. "Our Struggle Continues." *Popline*. Vol. 19 (November-December) 1997:1.

FORSTMANN, THEODORE J. "A Competitive Vision for American Education." *Imprimis*. Vol. 28, No. 9 (September 1999):1–4.

FOST, DAN. "American Indians in the 1990s." *American Demographics*. Vol. 13, No. 12 (December 1991):26–34.

FOUCAULT, MICHEL. *The History of Sexuality: An Introduction*. Vol. 1, trans. Robert Hurley. New York: Vintage, 1990; orig. 1978.

FRANK, ANDRÉ GUNDER. *On Capitalist Underdevelopment*. Bombay: Oxford University Press, 1975.

———. *Crisis: In the World Economy*. New York: Holmes & Meier, 1980.

FRANKLIN, JOHN HOPE. *From Slavery to Freedom: A History of Negro Americans*. 3d ed. New York: Vintage Books, 1967.

FRANKLIN ASSOCIATES. *Characterization of Municipal Solid Waste in the United States, 1960–2000*. Prairie Village, Kans.: Franklin Associates, 1986.

FRAZIER, E. FRANKLIN. *Black Bourgeoisie: The Rise of a New Middle Class*. New York: Free Press, 1965.

FREDRICKSON, GEORGE M. *White Supremacy: A Comparative Study in American and South African History*. New York: Oxford University Press, 1981.

FREE, MARVIN D. "Religious Affiliation, Religiosity, and Impulsive and Intentional Deviance." *Sociological Focus*. Vol. 25, No. 1 (February 1992):77–91.

FREEDOM HOUSE. *Freedom in the World 1999–2000*. New York: Freedom House, 2000.

FRENCH, MARILYN. *Beyond Power: On Women, Men, and Morals*. New York: Summit Books, 1985.

FRIEDAN, BETTY. *The Fountain of Age*. New York: Simon and Schuster, 1993.

FRIEDMAN, MEYER, and RAY H. ROSENMAN. *Type A Behavior and Your Heart*. New York: Fawcett Crest, 1974.

FRUM, DAVID, and FRANK WOLFE. "If You Gotta Get Sued, Get Sued in Utah." *Forbes*. Vol. 153, No. 2 (January 1994):70–73.

FUCHS, VICTOR R. "Sex Differences in Economic Well-Being." *Science*. Vol. 232 (April 25, 1986):459–64.

FUGITA, STEPHEN S., and DAVID J. O'BRIEN. "Structural Assimilation, Ethnic Group Membership, and Political Participation among Japanese Americans: A Research Note." *Social Forces*. Vol. 63, No. 4 (June 1985):986–95.

FUJIMOTO, ISAO. "The Failure of Democracy in a Time of Crisis." In Amy Tachiki et al., eds., *Roots: An Asian American Reader*. Los Angeles: UCLA Asian American Studies Center, 1971:207–14.

FULKERSON, JENNIFER. "When Lawyers Advertise." *American Demographics*. Vol. 17, No. 6 (June 1995):54–55.

FULLER, REX, and RICHARD SCHOENBERGER. "The Gender Salary Gap: Do Academic Achievement, Intern Experience, and College Major Make a Difference?" *Social Science Quarterly*. Vol. 72, No. 4 (December 1991):715–26.

FURSTENBERG, FRANK F., JR., and ANDREW CHERLIN. *Divided Families: What Happens to Children When Parents Part*. Cambridge, Mass.: Harvard University Press, 1991.

GAGLIANI, GIORGIO. "How Many Working Classes?" *American Journal of Sociology*. Vol. 87, No. 2 (September 1981):259–85.

GAGNÉ, PATRICIA, RICHARD TEWKSBURY, and DEANNA MCGAUGHEY. "Coming Out and Crossing Over: Identity Formation and Proclamation in a Transgender Community." *Gender and Society*. Vol. 11, No. 4 (August 1997):478–508.

GALLUP POLL. *The Gallup Poll Monthly*. December, 1993.

GALSTER, GEORGE. "Black Suburbanization: Has It Changed the Relative Location of Races?" *Urban Affairs Quarterly*. Vol. 26, No. 4 (June 1991):621–28.

GAMORAN, ADAM. "The Variable Effects of High-School Tracking." *American Sociological Review*. Vol. 57, No. 6 (December 1992):812–28.

GAMSON, WILLIAM A. "Beyond the Science-versus-Advocacy Distinction." *Contemporary Sociology*. Vol. 28, No. 1 (January 1999):23–26.

GANS, HERBERT J. *People and Plans: Essays on Urban Problems and Solutions*. New York: Basic Books, 1968.

———. *Deciding What's News: A Study of CBS Evening News, NBC Nightly News, Newsweek and Time*. New York: Vintage Books, 1980.

GARFINKEL, HAROLD. "Conditions of Successful Degradation Ceremonies." *American Journal of Sociology*. Vol. 61, No. 2 (March 1956):420–24.

———. *Studies in Ethnomethodology*. Cambridge: Polity Press, 1967.

GARREAU, JOEL. *Edge City*. New York: Doubleday, 1991.

GEERTZ, CLIFFORD. "Common Sense as a Cultural System." *The Antioch Review*. Vol. 33, No. 1 (Spring 1975):5–26.

GEIST, WILLIAM. *Toward a Safe and Sane Halloween and Other Tales of Suburbia*. New York: Times Books, 1985.

GELLES, RICHARD J., and CLAIRE PEDRICK CORNELL. *Intimate Violence in Families*. 2d ed. Newbury Park, Calif.: Sage, 1990.

GELMAN, DAVID. "Born or Bred?" *Newsweek* (February 24, 1992):46–53.

GERBER, THEODORE P., and MICHAEL HOUT. "More Shock than Therapy: Market Transition, Employment, and Income in Russia, 1991–1995." *American Journal of Sociology*. Vol. 104, No. 1 (July 1998):1–50.

GERLACH, MICHAEL L. *The Social Organization of Japanese Business*. Berkeley and Los Angeles: University of California Press, 1992.

GERSTEL, NAOMI. "Divorce and Stigma." *Social Problems*. Vol. 43, No. 2 (April 1987):172–86.

GESCHWENDER, JAMES A. *Racial Stratification in America*. Dubuque, Iowa: Wm. C. Brown, 1978.

GEWERTZ, DEBORAH. "A Historical Reconsideration of Female Dominance among the Chambri of Papua New Guinea." *American Ethnologist*. Vol. 8, No. 1 (1981):94–106.

GIBBONS, DON C., and MARVIN D. KROHN. *Delinquent Behavior*. 4th ed. Englewood Cliffs, N.J.: Prentice Hall, 1986.

GIBBS, NANCY. "When Is It Rape?" *Time*. Vol. 137, No. 22 (June 3, 1991a):48–54.

———. "The Clamor on Campus." *Time*. Vol. 137, No. 22 (June 3, 1991b):54–55.

———. "How Much Should We Teach Our Children about Sex?" *Time*. Vol. 141, No. 21 (May 24, 1993):60–66.

———. "Cause Celeb." *Time*. Vol. 147, No. 25 (June 17, 1996):28–30.

GIDDENS, ANTHONY. *Sociology: A Brief but Critical Introduction*. New York: Harcourt Brace Jovanovich, 1982.

———. *The Transformation of Intimacy*. Cambridge, UK: Polity Press, 1992.

GIELE, JANET Z. "Gender and Sex Roles." In Neil J. Smelser, ed., *Handbook of Sociology*. Newbury Park, Calif.: Sage, 1988:291–323.

GIGLIOTTI, RICHARD J., and HEATHER K. HUFF. "Role Related Conflicts, Strains, and Stresses of Older-Adult College Students." *Sociological Focus*. Vol. 28, No. 3 (August 1995):329–42.

GILBERT, NEIL. "Realities and Mythologies of Rape." *Society*. Vol. 29, No. 4 (May–June 1992):4–10.

GILBERTSON, GRETA A., and DOUGLAS T. GURAK. "Broadening the Enclave Debate: The Dual Labor Market Experiences of Dominican and Colombian Men in New York City." *Sociological Forum*. Vol. 8, No. 2 (June 1993):205–20.

GILLIARD, DARRELL K., and ALLEN J. BECK. *Prisoners in 1997*. Washington, D.C.: U.S. Bureau of Justice Statistics, 1998.

GILLIGAN, CAROL. *In a Different Voice: Psychological Theory and Women's Development*. Cambridge, Mass.: Harvard University Press, 1982.

GILLON, RAANAN. "Euthanasia in the Netherlands—Down the Slippery Slope?" *Journal of Medical Ethics*. Vol. 25, No. 1 (February 1999):3–4.

GIMENEZ, MARTHA E. "Silence in the Classroom: Some Thoughts about Teaching in the 1980s." *Teaching Sociology*. Vol. 17, No. 2 (April 1989):184–91.

GINSBURG, FAYE, and ANNA LOWENHAUPT TSING, eds. *Uncertain Terms: Negotiating Gender in American Culture*. Boston: Beacon Press, 1990.

GIOVANNINI, MAUREEN. "Female Anthropologist and Male Informant: Gender Conflict in a Sicilian Town." In John J. Macionis and Nijole V. Benokraitis, eds., *Seeing Ourselves: Classic, Contemporary, and Cross-Cultural Readings in Sociology*. 2d ed. Englewood Cliffs, N.J.: Prentice Hall, 1992:27–32.

GIUGNI, MARCO G. "Structure and Culture in Social Movements Theory." *Sociological Forum*. Vol. 13, No. 2 (June 1998):365–75.

GLADUE, BRIAN A., RICHARD GREEN, and RONALD E. HELLMAN. "Neuroendocrine Response to Estrogen and Sexual Orientation." *Science*. Vol. 225, No. 4669 (September 28, 1984):1496–99.

GLEICK, ELIZABETH. "The Marker We've Been Waiting For." *Time*. Vol. 149, No. 14 (April 7, 1997):28–42.

GLENN, NORVAL D., and BETH ANN SHELTON. "Regional Differences in Divorce in the United States." *Journal of Marriage and the Family*. Vol. 47, No. 3 (August 1985):641–52.

GLUECK, SHELDON, and ELEANOR GLUECK. *Unraveling Juvenile Delinquency*. New York: Commonwealth Fund, 1950.

GNIDA, JOHN J. "Teaching 'Nature versus Nurture': The Case of African American Athletic Success." *Teaching Sociology*. Vol. 23, No. 4 (October 1995):389–95.

GODWIN, KENNETH, FRANK KEMERER, VALERIE MARTINEZ, and RICHARD RUDERMAN. "Liberal Equity in Education: A Comparison of Choice Options." *Social Science Quarterly*. Vol. 79, No. 3 (September 1998):502–22.

GOETTING, ANN. *Getting Out: Life Stories of Women Who Left Abusive Men*. New York: Columbia University Press, 1999.

GOFFMAN, ERVING. *The Presentation of Self in Everyday Life*. Garden City, N.Y.: Anchor Books, 1959.

———. *Asylums: Essays on the Social Situation of Mental Patients and Other Inmates*. Garden City, N.Y.: Anchor Books, 1961.

———. *Stigma: Notes on the Management of Spoiled Identity*. Englewood Cliffs, N.J.: Prentice Hall, 1963.

———. *Interactional Ritual: Essays on Face to Face Behavior*. Garden City, N.Y.: Anchor Books, 1967.

GOLDBERG, STEVEN. *The Inevitability of Patriarchy*. New York: William Morrow, 1974.

———. Personal communication, 1987.

GOLDEN, FREDERIC. "Good Eggs, Bad Eggs." *Time*. Vol. 153, No. 1 (January 11, 1999a):56–59.

GOLDFARB, WILLIAM. "Groundwater: The Buried Life." In F. Herbert Bormann and Stephen R. Kellert, eds., *Ecology, Economics, and Ethics: The Broken Circle*. New Haven, Conn.: Yale University Press, 1991:123–35.

GOLDSMITH, H. H. "Genetic Influences on Personality from Infancy." *Child Development*. Vol. 54, No. 2 (April 1983):331–35.

GOODE, WILLIAM J. "The Theoretical Importance of Love." *American Sociological Review*. Vol. 24, No. 1 (February 1959):38–47.

———. "Encroachment, Charlatanism, and the Emerging Profession: Psychology, Sociology and Medicine." *American Sociological Review*. Vol. 25, No. 6 (December 1960):902–14.

GORDON, JAMES S. "The Paradigm of Holistic Medicine." In Arthur C. Hastings et al., eds., *Health for the Whole Person: The Complete Guide to Holistic Medicine*. Boulder, Colo.: Westview Press, 1980:3–27.

GORDON, SOL, and CRAIG W. SNYDER. *Personal Issues in Human Sexuality: A Guidebook for Better Sexual Health*. 2d ed. Boston: Allyn & Bacon, 1989.

GORING, CHARLES BUCKMAN. *The English Convict: A Statistical Study*. Montclair, N.J.: Patterson Smith, 1972; orig. 1913.

GOTHAM, KEVIN FOX. "Race, Mortgage Lending, and Loan Rejections in a U.S. City." *Sociological Focus*. Vol. 31, No. 4 (October 1998):391–405.

GOTTFREDSON, MICHAEL R., and TRAVIS HIRSCHI. "National Crime Control Policies." *Society*. Vol. 32, No. 2 (January–February 1995):30–36.

GOTTMANN, JEAN. *Megalopolis*. New York: Twentieth Century Fund, 1961.

GOUGH, KATHLEEN. "The Origin of the Family." *Journal of Marriage and the Family*. Vol. 33, No. 4 (November 1971):760–71.

———. "The Origin of the Family." In John J. Macionis and Nijole V. Benokraitis, eds., *Seeing Ourselves: Classic, Contemporary, and Cross-Cultural Readings in Sociology*. Englewood Cliffs, N.J.: Prentice Hall, 1998.

GRAHAM, JOHN W., and ANDREA H. BELLER. "Child Support in Black and White: Racial Differentials in the Award and Receipt of Child Support during the 1980s." *Social Science Quarterly*. Vol. 77, No. 3 (September 1996):528–42.

GRANT, KAREN R. "The Inverse Care Law in the Context of Universal Free Health Insurance in Canada: Toward Meeting Health Needs through Public Policy." *Sociological Focus*. Vol. 17, No. 2 (April 1984):137–55.

GREEN, JOHN C. "Pat Robertson and the Latest Crusade: Resources and the 1988 Presidential Campaign." *Social Sciences Quarterly*. Vol. 74, No. 1 (March 1993):156–68.

GREENBERG, DAVID F. *The Construction of Homosexuality*. Chicago: University of Chicago Press, 1988.

GREENFIELD, LAWRENCE A. *Child Victimizers: Violent Offenders and their Victims*. Washington, D.C.: U.S. Bureau of Justice Statistics, 1996.

GREENHOUSE, LINDA. "Justices Uphold Stiffer Sentences for Hate Crimes." *New York Times* (June 12, 1993):1, 8.

GREGORY, PAUL R., and ROBERT C. STUART. *Comparative Economic Systems*. 2d ed. Boston: Houghton Mifflin, 1985.

GROSS, JANE. "New Challenge of Youth: Growing Up in a Gay Home." *New York Times* (February 11, 1991):A1, B7.

GROTH, NICHOLAS A., and H. JEAN BIRNBAUM. *Men Who Rape: The Psychology of the Offender*. New York: Plenum, 1979.

GUP, TED. "What Makes This School Work?" *Time*. Vol. 140, No. 25 (December 21, 1992):63–65.

GURAK, DOUGLAS T., and JOSEPH P. FITZPATRICK. "Intermarriage among Hispanic Ethnic Groups in New York City." *American Journal of Sociology*. Vol. 87, No. 4 (January 1982):921–34.

GURNETT, KATE. "On the Forefront of Feminism." *Albany Times Union* (July 5, 1998):G-1, G-6.

GWARTNEY-GIBBS, PATRICIA A., JEAN STOCKARD, and SUSANNE BOHMER. "Learning Courtship Agression: The Influence of Parents, Peers, and Personal Experiences." *Family Relations*. Vol. 36, No. 3 (July 1987):276–82.

GWYNNE, S. C., and JOHN F. DICKERSON. "Lost in the E-Mail." *Time*. Vol. 149, No. 15 (April 21, 1997):88–90.

HABERMAS, JÜRGEN. *Toward a Rational Society: Student Protest, Science, and Politics*. Jeremy J. Shapiro, trans. Boston: Beacon Press, 1970.

HACKER, HELEN MAYER. "Women as a Minority Group." *Social Forces*. Vol. 30 (October 1951):60–69.

———. "Women as a Minority Group: 20 Years Later." In Florence Denmark, ed., *Who Discriminates Against Women?* Beverly Hills, Calif.: Sage, 1974:124–34.

HACKEY, ROBERT B. "Competing Explanations of Voter Turnout among American Blacks." *Social Science Quarterly*. Vol. 73, No. 1 (March 1992):71–89.

HADAWAY, C. KIRK, PENNY LONG MARLER, and MARK CHAVES. "What the Polls Don't Show: A Closer Look at U.S. Church Attendance." *American Sociological Review*. Vol. 58, No. 6 (December 1993):741–52.

HADDEN, JEFFREY K., and CHARLES E. SWAIN. *Prime Time Preachers: The Rising Power of Televangelism*. Reading, Mass.: Addison-Wesley, 1981.

HAFNER, KATIE. "Making Sense of the Internet." *Newsweek* (October 24, 1994):46–48.

HAGAN, JACQUELINE MARIA. "Social Networks, Gender, and Immigrant Incorporation: Resources and Restraints." *American Sociological Review*. Vol. 63, No. 1 (February 1998):55–67.

HAGAN, JOHN, and PATRICIA PARKER. "White-Collar Crime and Punishment: The Class Structure and Legal Sanctioning of Securities Violations." *American Sociological Review*. Vol. 50, No. 3 (June 1985):302–16.

HAIG, ROBIN ANDREW. *The Anatomy of Humor: Biopsychosocial and Therapeutic Perspectives*. Springfield, Ill.: Charles C. Thomas, 1988.

HALBERSTAM, DAVID. *The Reckoning*. New York: Avon Books, 1986.

HALL, JOHN R., and MARY JO NEITZ. *Culture: Sociological Perspectives*. Englewood Cliffs, N.J.: Prentice Hall, 1993.

HALL, KELLEY J., and BETSY LUCAL. "Tapping in Parallel Universes: Using Superhero Comic Books in Sociology Courses." *Teaching Sociology*. Vol. 27, No. 1 (January 1999):60–66.

HALLINAN, MAUREEN T. "The Sociological Study of Social Change." *American Sociological Review*. Vol. 62, No. 1 (February 1997):1–11.

HALLINAN, MAUREEN T., and RICHARD A. WILLIAMS. "Interracial Friendship Choices in Secondary Schools." *American Sociological Review*. Vol. 54, No. 1 (February 1989):67–78.

HAMER, DEAN, and PETER COPELAND. *The Science of Desire: The Search for the Gay Gene and the Biology of Behavior*. New York: Simon & Schuster, 1994.

HAMMOND, PHILIP E. "Introduction." In Philip E. Hammond, ed., *The Sacred in a Secular Age: Toward Revision in the Scientific Study of Religion*. Berkeley: University of California Press, 1985:1–6.

HAMRICK, MICHAEL H., DAVID J. ANSPAUGH, and GENE EZELL. *Health*. Columbus, Ohio: Merrill, 1986.

HANDGUN CONTROL, INC. Personal communication, 2001.

HANDLIN, OSCAR. *Boston's Immigrants 1790–1865: A Study in Acculturation*. Cambridge, Mass.: Harvard University Press, 1941.

HAREVEN, TAMARA K. "The Life Course and Aging in Historical Perspective." In Tamara K. Hareven and Kathleen J. Adams, eds., *Aging and Life*

Course Transitions: An Interdisciplinary Perspective. New York: Guilford Press, 1982:1–26.

HARLOW, HARRY F., and MARGARET KUENNE HARLOW. "Social Deprivation in Monkeys." *Scientific American.* Vol. 207 (November 1962):137–46.

HARPSTER, PAULA, and ELIZABETH MONK-TURNER. "Why Men Do Housework: A Test of Gender Production and the Relative Resources Model." *Sociological Focus.* Vol. 31, No. 1 (February 1998):45–59.

HARRIES, KEITH D. *Serious Violence: Patterns of Homicide and Assault in America.* Springfield, Ill.: Charles C. Thomas, 1990.

HARRINGTON, MICHAEL. *The New American Poverty.* New York: Penguin Books, 1984.

HARRIS, CHAUNCEY D., and EDWARD L. ULLMAN. "The Nature of Cities." *The Annals.* Vol. 242 (November 1945):7–17.

HARRIS, JACK DASH. Lecture on cockfighting in the Philippines. Semester at Sea (October 27, 1994).

HARRIS, MARVIN. "Why Men Dominate Women." *New York Times Magazine* (November 13, 1977):46, 115–23.

———. *Cultural Anthropology.* 1st ed., 1983; 2d ed. New York: Harper & Row, 1987.

HARVEY, DAVID. "Labor, Capital, and Class Struggle around the Built Environment." *Politics and Society.* Vol. 6 (1976):265–95.

HAWTHORNE, PETER. "South Africa's Makeover." *Time.* Vol. 154, No. 2 (July 12, 1999).

HAYNEMAN, STEPHEN P., and WILLIAM A. LOXLEY. "The Effect of Primary-School Quality on Academic Achievement across Twenty-nine High- and Low-Income Countries." *American Journal of Sociology.* Vol. 88, No. 6 (May 1983):1162–94.

HEATH, JULIA A., and W. DAVID BOURNE. "Husbands and Housework: Parity or Parody?" *Social Science Quarterly.* Vol. 76, No. 1 (March 1995):195–202.

HELGESEN, SALLY. *The Female Advantage: Women's Ways of Leadership.* New York: Doubleday, 1990.

HELIN, DAVID W. "When Slogans Go Wrong." *American Demographics.* Vol. 14, No. 2 (February 1992):14.

HENLEY, NANCY, MYKOL HAMILTON, and BARRIE THORNE. "Womanspeak and Manspeak: Sex Differences in Communication, Verbal and Nonverbal." In John J. Macionis and Nijole V. Benokraitis, eds., *Seeing Ourselves: Classic, Contemporary, and Cross-Cultural Readings in Sociology.* 2d ed. Englewood Cliffs, N.J.: Prentice Hall, 1992:10–15.

HENRY, WILLIAM A., III. "Gay Parents: Under Fire and On the Rise." *Time.* Vol. 142, No. 12 (September 20, 1993):66–71.

HERDT, GILBERT H. "Semen Transactions in Sambian Culture." In David N. Suggs and Andrew W. Miracle, eds., *Culture and Human Sexuality.* Pacific Grove, Calif.: Brooks Cole, 1993:298–327.

HEREK, GREGORY M. "Myths about Sexual Orientation: A Lawyer's Guide to Social Science Research." *Law and Sexuality.* No. 1 (1991):133–72.

HERMAN, DIANNE. "The Rape Culture." In John J. Macionis and Nijole V. Benokraitis, eds., *Seeing Ourselves: Classic, Contemporary, and Cross-Cultural Readings in Sociology.* 5th ed. Upper Saddle River, N.J.: Prentice Hall, 2001.

HERMAN, EDWARD S. *Corporate Control, Corporate Power: A Twentieth Century Fund Study.* New York: Cambridge University Press, 1981.

HERRNSTEIN, RICHARD J., and CHARLES MURRAY. *The Bell Curve: Intelligence and Class Structure in American Life.* New York: Free Press, 1994.

HERSCH, JONI, and SHELLY WHITE-MEANS. "Employer-Sponsored Health and Pension Benefits and the Gender/Race Wage Gap." *Social Science Quarterly.* Vol. 74, No. 4 (December 1993):850–66.

HESS, BETH B. "Breaking and Entering the Establishment: Committing Social Change and Confronting the Backlash." *Social Problems.* Vol. 46, No. 1 (February 1999):1–12.

HESS, STEPHEN. "Reporters Who Cover Congress." *Society.* Vol. 28, No. 2 (January-February 1991):60–65.

HIRSCHI, TRAVIS. *Causes of Delinquency.* Berkeley: University of California Press, 1969.

HOBERMAN, JOHN. *Darwin's Athletes: How Sport Has Damaged Black America and Preserved the Myth of Race.* Boston: Houghton Mifflin, 1997.

———. "Response to Three Reviews of Darwin's Athletes." *Social Science Quarterly.* Vol. 79, No. 4 (December 1998):898–903.

HOCHSCHILD, ARLIE, with ANNE MACHUNG. *The Second Shift: Working Parents and the Revolution at Home.* New York: Viking Books, 1989.

HODGE, ROBERT W., DONALD J. TREIMAN, and PETER H. ROSSI. "A Comparative Study of Occupational Prestige." In Reinhard Bendix and Seymour Martin Lipset, eds., *Class, Status, and Power: Social Stratification in Comparative Perspective.* 2d ed. New York: Free Press, 1966:309–21.

HOERR, JOHN. "The Payoff from Teamwork." *Business Week.* No. 3114 (July 10, 1989):56–62.

HOGAN, DENNIS P., and EVELYN M. KITAGAWA. "The Impact of Social Status and Neighborhood on the Fertility of Black Adolescents." *American Journal of Sociology.* Vol. 90, No. 4 (January 1985):825–55.

HOGAN, RICHARD, and CAROLYN C. PERRUCCI. "Producing and Reproducing the Class and Status Differences: Racial and Gender Gaps in U.S. Employment and Retirement Income." *Social Problems.* Vol. 45, No. 4 (November 1998):528–49.

HOGGART, RICHARD. "The Abuses of Literacy." *Society.* Vol. 55, No. 3 (March–April 1995):55–62.

HOLMES, MALCOLM D., HARMON M. HOSCH, HOWARD C. DAUDISTEL, DOLORES PEREZ, and JOSEPH B. GRAVES. "Judges, Ethnicity and Minority Sentencing: Evidence among Hispanics." *Social Science Quarterly.* Vol. 74, No. 3 (September 1993):496–506.

HOLMES, STEVEN A. "U.S. Reports Drop in Rate of Births to Unwed Women." *New York Times* (October 5, 1996a):1, 9.

———. "For Hispanic Poor, No Silver Lining." *New York Times* (October 13, 1996b): section 4, p. 5.

HOLMES, THOMAS H., and RICHARD H. RAHE. "The Social Readjustment Rating Scale." *Journal of Psychosomatic Research.* Vol. 11 (1967):213–18.

HONEYWELL, ROY J. *The Educational Work of Thomas Jefferson.* Cambridge, Mass.: Harvard University Press, 1931.

HOSTETLER, JOHN A. *Amish Society.* 3d ed. Baltimore: Johns Hopkins University Press, 1980.

HOUT, MICHAEL. "More Universalism, Less Structural Mobility: The American Occupational Structure in the 1980s." *American Journal of Sociology.* Vol. 95, No. 6 (May 1998):1358–1400.

HOUT, MICHAEL, and ANDREW M. GREELEY. "The Center Doesn't Hold: Church Attendance in the United States, 1940–1984." *American Sociological Review.* Vol. 52, No. 3 (June 1987):325–45.

HOUT, MIKE, CLEM BROOKS, and JEFF MANZA. "The Persistence of Classes in Post-Industrial Societies." *International Sociology.* Vol. 8, No. 3 (September 1993):259–77.

HOYT, HOMER. *The Structure and Growth of Residential Neighborhoods in American Cities.* Washington, D.C.: Federal Housing Administration, 1939.

HSU, FRANCIS L. K. *The Challenge of the American Dream: The Chinese in the United States.* Belmont, Calif.: Wadsworth, 1971.

HUBER, JOAN, and BETH E. SCHNEIDER, eds. *The Social Context of AIDS.* Newbury Park, Calif.: Sage, 1992.

HUET-COX, ROCIO. "Medical Education: New Wine in Old Wine Skins." In Victor W. Sidel and Ruth Sidel, eds., *Reforming Medicine: Lessons of the Last Quarter Century.* New York: Pantheon Books, 1984:129–49.

HUFFMAN, MATT L., STEVEN C. VELASCO, and WILLIAM T. BIELBY. "Where Sex Composition Matters Most: Comparing the Effects of Job versus Occupational Sex Composition of Earnings." *Sociological Focus.* Vol. 29, No. 3 (August 1996):189–207.

HULS, GLENNA. Personal communication, 1987.

HUMMER, ROBERT A., CHARLES G. ROGERS, CHARLES B. NAM, and FELICIA B. LECLERE. "Race/Ethnicity, Nativity, and U.S. Adult Mortality." *Social Science Quarterly.* Vol. 80, No. 1 (March 1999):136–53.

HUMPHREY, CRAIG R., and FREDERICK R. BUTTEL. *Environment, Energy, and Society.* Belmont, Calif.: Wadsworth, 1982.

HUNTER, JAMES DAVISON. *American Evangelicalism: Conservative Religion and the Quandary of Modernity.* New Brunswick, N.J.: Rutgers University Press, 1983.

———. "Conservative Protestantism." In Philip E. Hammond, ed., *The Sacred in a Secular Age.* Berkeley: University of California Press, 1985:50–66.

———. *Evangelicalism: The Coming Generation.* Chicago: University of Chicago Press, 1987.

———. *Culture Wars: The Struggle to Define America.* New York: Basic Books, 1991.

HYMOWITZ, CAROL. "World's Poorest Women Advance by Entrepreneurship." *Wall Street Journal* (September 9, 1995):B1.

IANNACCONE, LAURENCE R. "Why Strict Churches Are Strong." *American Journal of Sociology.* Vol. 99, No. 5 (March 1994):1180–1211.

IDE, THOMAS R., and ARTHUR J. CORDELL. "Automating Work." *Society*. Vol. 31, No. 6 (September–October 1994):65–71.

ILLICH, IVAN. *Medical Nemesis: The Expropriation of Health*. New York: Pantheon Books, 1976.

INGLEHART, RONALD. *Modernization and Postmodernization: Cultural, Economic, and Political Change in 43 Societies*. Princeton, N.J.: Princeton University Press, 1997.

INGLEHART, RONALD, et al. *World Values Surveys and European Values Surveys, 1981–1984, 1990– 1993, and 1995–1997*. [Computer file] ICPSR version. Ann Arbor, Mich.: Inter-university Consortium for Political and Social Research, 2000.

INTER-PARLIAMENTARY UNION. *Men and Women in Politics: Democracy in the Making*. Geneva: 1997.

ISAACSON, WALTER. "Our Century . . . and the Next One." *Time 100*. Special Issue. Vol. 151, No. 14 (1998).

ISAY, RICHARD A. *Being Homosexual: Gay Men and Their Development*. New York: Farrar, Straus, & Giroux, 1989.

JACOB, JOHN E. "An Overview of Black America in 1985." In James D. Williams, ed., *The State of Black America 1986*. New York: National Urban League, 1986:i–xi.

JACOBS, DAVID, and RONALD E. HELMS. "Toward a Political Model of Incarceration: A Time-Series Examination of Multiple Explanations for Prison Admission Rates." *American Journal of Sociology*. Vol. 102, No. 2 (September 1996):323–57.

JACOBS, JANE. *The Economy of Cities*. New York: Vintage Books, 1970.

JACQUET, CONSTANT H., and ALICE M. JONES. *Yearbook of American and Canadian Churches 1991*. Nashville, Tenn.: Abingdon Press, 1991.

JAGAROWSKY, PAUL A., and MARY JO BANE. *Neighborhood Poverty: Basic Questions*. Discussion paper series H-90-3. John F. Kennedy School of Government. Cambridge, Mass.: Harvard University Press, 1990.

JAGGER, ALISON. "Political Philosophies of Women's Liberation." In Laurel Richardson and Verta Taylor, eds., *Feminist Frontiers: Rethinking Sex, Gender, and Society*. Reading, Mass.: Addison-Wesley, 1983.

JAMES, DAVID R. "City Limits on Racial Equality: The Effects of City-Suburb Boundaries on Public-School Desegregation, 1968–1976." *American Sociological Review*. Vol. 54, No. 6 (December 1989):963–85.

JANIS, IRVING. *Victims of Groupthink*. Boston: Houghton Mifflin, 1972.

———. *Crucial Decisions: Leadership in Policymaking and Crisis Management*. New York: Free Press, 1989.

JANUS, CHRISTOPHER G. "Slavery Abolished? Only Officially." *Christian Science Monitor* (May 17, 1996):18.

JARRETT, ROBIN L. "Living Poor: Family Life among Single Parent, African-American Women." *Social Problems*. Vol. 41, No. 1 (February 1994):30–49.

JENCKS, CHRISTOPHER. "Genes and Crime." *The New York Review* (February 12, 1987):33–41.

JENKINS, J. CRAIG, and MICHAEL WALLACE. "The Generalized Action Potential of Protest Movements: The New Class, Social Trends, and Political Exclusion Explanations." *Sociological Forum*. Vol. 11, No. 2 (June 1996):183–207.

JENSEN, LIEF, DAVID J. EGGEBEEN, and DANIEL T. LICHTER. "Child Policy and the Ameliorative Effects of Public Assistance." *Social Science Quarterly*. Vol. 74, No. 3 (September 1993):542–59.

JOHNSON, DIRK. "Census Finds Many Claiming New Identity: Indian." *New York Times* (March 5, 1991):A1, A16.

JOHNSON, JEAN. "Americans' Views on Crime and Law Enforcement." *National Institute of Justice Journal*. Issue 233 (September 1997):9–14.

JOHNSON, PAUL. "The Seven Deadly Sins of Terrorism." In Benjamin Netanyahu, ed., *International Terrorism*. New Brunswick, N.J.: Transaction Books, 1981:12–22.

JOHNSON, ROLAND. [Online] Available http://www.personalwebs.myriad.net/ Roland, 1996.

JOHNSTON, DAVID CAY. "Voting, America's Not Keen On. Coffee Is Another Matter." *New York Times* (November 10, 1996): section 4, p. 2.

JONES, ARTHUR. "Welfare Reform Makes Children Prime Victims." *National Catholic Reporter* (April 30, 1999a):14–16.

JONES, JUDY. "More Miners Will Be Offered Free X-Rays; Federal Agency Wants to Monitor Black-Lung Cases." *Louisville Courier Journal* (Thursday, May 13, 1999b):1A.

JONES, ROBERT EMMET, and LEWIS F. CARTER. "Concern for the Environment among Black Americans: An Assessment of Common Assumptions." *Social Science Quarterly*. Vol. 75, No. 3 (September 1994):560–79.

JOSEPHY, ALVIN M., JR. *Now That the Buffalo's Gone: A Study of Today's American Indians*. New York: Alfred A. Knopf, 1982.

JOYNSON, ROBERT B. "Fallible Judgments." *Society*. Vol. 31, No. 3 (March–April 1994):45–52.

KADUSHIN, CHARLES. "Friendship among the French Financial Elite." *American Sociological Review*. Vol. 60, No. 2 (April 1995):202–21.

KAIN, EDWARD L. "A Note on the Integration of AIDS into the Sociology of Human Sexuality." *Teaching Sociology*. Vol. 15, No. 4 (July 1987):320–23.

———. *The Myth of Family Decline: Understanding Families in a World of Rapid Social Change*. Lexington, Mass.: Lexington Books, 1990.

KAIN, EDWARD L., and SHANNON HART. "AIDS and the Family: A Content Analysis of Media Coverage." Presented to National Council on Family Relations, Atlanta, 1987.

KAMINER, WENDY. "Volunteers: Who Knows What's in It for Them." *Ms.* (December 1984):93–94, 96, 126–28.

———. "Demasculinizing the Army." *New York Times Review of Books* (June 15, 1997):7.

KANAMINE, LINDA. "School Operation Fails For-Profit Test." *USA Today* (November 24, 1995):6A.

KANN, LAURA, et al. "Youth Risk Behavior Surveillance—United States, 1993." *Morbidity and Mortality Weekly Report*. Vol. 44 (S-1), March 24, 1995.

KANTER, ROSABETH MOSS. *Men and Women of the Corporation*. New York: Basic Books, 1977.

KANTER, ROSABETH MOSS, and BARRY A. STEIN. "The Gender Pioneers: Women in an Industrial Sales Force." In R. M. Kanter and B. A. Stein, eds., *Life in Organizations*. New York: Basic Books, 1979:134–60.

KAPLAN, ELAINE BELL. "Black Teenage Mothers and Their Mothers: The Impact of Adolescent Childbearing on Daughters' Relations with Mothers." *Social Problems*. Vol. 43, No. 4 (November 1996):427–43.

KAPLAN, ERIC B., et al. "The Usefulness of Preoperative Laboratory Screening." *Journal of the American Medical Association*. Vol. 253, No. 24 (June 28, 1985):3576–81.

KAPTCHUK, TED. "The Holistic Logic of Chinese Medicine." In Shepard Bliss et al., eds., *The New Holistic Health Handbook*. Lexington, Mass.: The Steven Greene Press/Penguin Books, 1985:41.

KARP, DAVID A., and WILLIAM C. YOELS. "The College Classroom: Some Observations on the Meaning of Student Participation." *Sociology and Social Research*. Vol. 60, No. 4 (July 1976):421–39.

KATES, ROBERT W. "Ending Hunger: Current Status and Future Prospects." *Consequences*. Vol. 2, No. 2 (1996):3–11.

KATZ, MICHAEL B. *In the Shadow of the Poorhouse*. New York: Basic Books, 1986.

KAUFMAN, WALTER. *Religions in Four Dimensions: Existential, Aesthetic, Historical and Comparative*. New York: Reader's Digest Press, 1976.

KEISTER, LISA. *Wealth in America: Trends in Wealth Inequality*. Cambridge, UK: Cambridge University Press, 2000.

KEITH, PAT M., and ROBERT B. SCHAFER. "They Hate to Cook: Patterns of Distress in an Ordinary Role." *Sociological Focus*. Vol. 27, No. 4 (October 1994):289–301.

KELLERT, STEPHEN R., and F. HERBERT BORMANN. "Closing the Circle: Weaving Strands among Ecology, Economics, and Ethics." In F. Herbert Bormann and Stephen R. Kellert, eds., *Ecology, Economics, and Ethics: The Broken Circle*. New Haven, Conn.: Yale University Press, 1991:205–10.

KEMP, DOMINIC. "Deaths, Diseases Traced to Environment" *Popline*. Vol. 20 (May/June 1998):3.

KENNICKELL, ARTHUR, and JANICE SHACK-MARQUEZ. "Changes in Family Finances from 1983 to 1989: Evidence From the Survey of Consumer Finances." *Federal Reserve Bulletin* (January 1992):1–18.

KENNICKELL, ARTHUR B., MARTHA STARR-MCCLUER, and BRIAN J. SURETTE. "Recent Changes in U.S. Family Finances: Results from the 1998 Survey of Consumer Finances." [Online] Available http://www.federalreserve.gov/pubs/bulletin/2000/0100lead.pdf, April 7, 2000.

KENTOR, JEFFREY. "The Long-Term Effects of Foreign Investment Dependence on Economic Growth, 1940–1990." *American Journal of Sociology*. Vol. 103, No. 4 (January 1998):1024–46.

KERCKHOFF, ALAN C., RICHARD T. CAMPBELL, and IDEE WINFIELD-LAIRD. "Social Mobility in Great Britain and the United States." *American Journal of Sociology*. Vol. 91, No. 2 (September 1985):281–308.

KIDD, QUENTIN, and AIE-RIE LEE. "Postmaterialist Values and the Environment: A Critique and Reappraisal." *Social Science Quarterly*. Vol. 78, No. 1 (March 1997):1–15.

KIDRON, MICHAEL, and RONALD SEGAL. *The New State of the World Atlas*. New York: Simon & Schuster, 1991.

KILBOURNE, BROCK K. "The Conway and Siegelman Claims against Religious Cults: An Assessment of Their Data." *Journal for the Scientific Study of Religion*. Vol. 22, No. 4 (December 1983):380–85.

KILGORE, SALLY B. "The Organizational Context of Tracking in Schools." *American Sociological Review*. Vol. 56, No. 2 (April 1991):189–203.

KILLIAN, LEWIS M. "Organization, Rationality and Spontaneity in the Civil Rights Movement." *American Sociological Review*. Vol. 49, No. 6 (December 1984):770–83.

KING, KATHLEEN PIKER, and DENNIS E. CLAYSON. "The Differential Perceptions of Male and Female Deviants." *Sociological Focus*. Vol. 21, No. 2 (April 1988):153–64.

KING, MARTIN LUTHER, JR. "The Montgomery Bus Boycott." In Walt Anderson, ed., *The Age of Protest*. Pacific Palisades, Calif.: Goodyear, 1969:81–91.

KINKEAD, GWEN. *Chinatown: A Portrait of a Closed Society*. New York: HarperCollins, 1992.

KINSEY, ALFRED, et al. *Sexual Behavior in the Human Male*. Philadelphia: Saunders, 1948.

———. *Sexual Behavior in the Human Female*. Philadelphia: Saunders, 1953.

KITTRIE, NICHOLAS N. *The Right To Be Different: Deviance and Enforced Therapy*. Baltimore: Johns Hopkins University Press, 1971.

KLEIN, J. D. "The National Longitudinal Study on Adolescent Health: Preliminary Results: Great Expectations." *JAMA: The Journal of the American Medical Association*. Vol. 278, No. 10 (1997):864.

KLEINFELD, JUDITH. "Student Performance: Males versus Females." *The Public Interest*. No. 134 (Winter, 1999):3–20.

KLUCKHOHN, CLYDE. "As an Anthropologist Views It." In Albert Deuth, ed., *Sex Habits of American Men*. New York: Prentice Hall, 1948.

KOHLBERG, LAWRENCE. *The Psychology of Moral Development: The Nature and Validity of Moral Stages*. New York: Harper & Row, 1981.

KOHLBERG, LAWRENCE, and CAROL GILLIGAN. "The Adolescent as Philosopher: The Discovery of Self in a Postconventional World." *Daedalus*. Vol. 100 (Fall 1971):1051–86.

KOHN, MELVIN L. *Class and Conformity: A Study in Values*. 2d ed. Homewood, Ill.: Dorsey Press, 1977.

KOMAROVSKY, MIRRA. *Blue Collar Marriage*. New York: Vintage Books, 1967.

———. "Cultural Contradictions and Sex Roles: The Masculine Case." *American Journal of Sociology*. Vol. 78, No. 4 (January 1973):873–84.

KONO, CLIFFORD, DONALD PALMER, ROGER FRIEDLAND, and MATTHEW ZAFONTE. "Lost in Space: The Geography of Corporate Interlocking Directorates." *American Journal of Sociology*. Vol. 103, No. 4 (January 1998):863–911.

KORNHAUSER, WILLIAM. *The Politics of Mass Society*. New York: Free Press, 1959.

KORPI, WALTER, and JOAKIM PALME. "The Paradox of Redistribution and Strategies of Equality: Welfare State Institutions, Inequality, and Poverty in the Western Countries." *American Sociological Review*. Vol. 65, No. 5 (October 1998):661–87.

KORZENIEWICZ, ROBERTO P., and KIMBERLY AWBREY. "Democratic Transitions and the Semiperiphery of the World Economy." *Sociological Forum*. Vol. 7, No. 4 (December 1992):609–40.

KOUSHA, MAHNAZ. Review of *Modernizing Women* by Valentine M. Moghadam. In *Gender and Society*. Vol. 8 (December 1994):624–26.

KOZOL, JONATHAN. *Rachel and Her Children: Homeless Families in America*. New York: Crown Publishers, 1988.

———. *Savage Inequalities: Children in America's Schools*. New York: Harper Perennial, 1992.

KRAFFT, SUSAN. "¿Quién es Numero Uno?" *American Demographics*. Vol. 15, No. 7 (July 1993):16–17.

KRANTZ, MICHAEL. "Say It with a :-)." *Time*. Vol. 149, No. 15 (1997):29.

KRASKA, PETER B., and VICTOR E. KAPPELER. "Militarizing American Police: The Rise and Normalization of Paramilitary Units." *Social Problems*. Vol. 44, No. 1 (February 1997):1–18.

KRAYBILL, DONALD B. *The Riddle of Amish Culture*. Baltimore: Johns Hopkins University Press, 1989.

———. "The Amish Encounter with Modernity." In Donald B. Kraybill and Marc A. Olshan, eds., *The Amish Struggle with Modernity*. Hanover, N.H.: University Press of New England, 1994:21–33.

KRAYBILL, DONALD B., and MARC A. OLSHAN, eds. *The Amish Struggle with Modernity*. Hanover, N.H.: University Press of New England, 1994.

KRIESI, HANSPETER. "New Social Movements and the New Class in the Netherlands." *American Journal of Sociology*. Vol. 94, No. 5 (March 1989):1078–116.

KRISTOL, IRVING. "Life without Father." *Wall Street Journal* (November 3, 1994):A18.

KRIVO, LAUREN J., RUTH D. PETERSON, HELEN RIZZO, and JOHN R. REYNOLDS. "Race, Segregation, and the Concentration of Disadvantage: 1980–1990." *Social Problems*. Vol. 45, No. 1 (February 1998):61–80.

KRUKS, GABRIEL N. "Gay and Lesbian Homeless/Street Youth: Special Issues and Concerns." *Journal of Adolescent Health*. Special Issue. No. 12 (1991): 515–18.

KÜBLER-ROSS, ELISABETH. *On Death and Dying*. New York: Macmillan, 1969.

KUHN, THOMAS. *The Structure of Scientific Revolutions*. 2d ed. Chicago: University of Chicago Press, 1970.

KUZNETS, SIMON. "Economic Growth and Income Inequality." *The American Economic Review*. Vol. XLV, No. 1 (March 1955):1–28.

———. *Modern Economic Growth: Rate, Structure, and Spread*. New Haven, Conn.: Yale University Press, 1966.

LABOVITZ, PRICISSA. "Immigration—Just the Facts." *New York Times* (March 25, 1996).

LACAYO, RICHARD. "The Brawl over Sprawl." *Time*. Vol. 153, No. 11 (March 22, 1999):44–48.

LACH, JENNIFER. "The Color of Money." *American Demographics*. Vol. 21, No 2 (February 1999):59–60.

LADD, JOHN. "The Definition of Death and the Right to Die." In John Ladd, ed., *Ethical Issues Relating to Life and Death*. New York: Oxford University Press, 1979:118–45.

LAI, H. M. "Chinese." In *Harvard Encyclopedia of American Ethnic Groups*. Cambridge, Mass.: Harvard University Press, 1980:217–33.

LAMBERG-KARLOVSKY, C. C., and MARTHA LAMBERG-KARLOVSKY. "An Early City in Iran." In *Cities: Their Origin, Growth, and Human Impact*. San Francisco: Freeman, 1973:28–37.

LANDERS, ANN. Syndicated column: *Dallas Morning News* (July 8, 1984):4F.

LANDERS, RENE M. "Gender, Race, and the State Courts." *Radcliffe Quarterly*. Vol. 76, No. 4 (December 1990):6–9.

LANDSBERG, MITCHELL. "Health Disaster Brings Early Death in Russia." *Washington Times* (March 15, 1998):A8.

LAPPÉ, FRANCES MOORE, and JOSEPH COLLINS. *World Hunger: Twelve Myths*. New York: Grove Press/Food First Books, 1986.

LAPPÉ, FRANCES MOORE, JOSEPH COLLINS, and DAVID KINLEY. *Aid as Obstacle: Twenty Questions about Our Foreign Policy and the Hungry*. San Francisco: Institute for Food and Development Policy, 1981.

LARMER, BROOK. "Dead End Kids." *Newsweek* (May 25, 1992):38–40.

LASLETT, BARBARA. "Family Membership, Past and Present." *Social Problems*. Vol. 25, No. 5 (June 1978):476–90.

LASLETT, PETER. *The World We Have Lost: England before the Industrial Age*. 3d ed. New York: Charles Scribner's Sons, 1984.

LASSWELL, MARK. "A Tribe at War: Not the Yanomami: The Anthropologists." *Wall Street Journal* (November 17, 2000):A17.

LAUMANN, EDWARD O., JOHN H. GAGNON, ROBERT T. MICHAEL, and STUART MICHAELS. *The Social Organization of Sexuality: Sexual Practices in the United States*. Chicago: University of Chicago Press, 1994.

LEACOCK, ELEANOR. "Women's Status in Egalitarian Societies: Implications for Social Evolution." *Current Anthropology*. Vol. 19, No. 2 (June 1978):247–75.

LEAVITT, JUDITH WALZER. "Women and Health in America: An Overview." In Judith Walzer Leavitt, ed., *Women and Health in America*. Madison: University of Wisconsin Press, 1984:3–7.

LEE, SHARON M. "Poverty and the U.S. Asian Population." *Social Science Quarterly*. Vol. 75, No. 3 (September 1994):541–59.

LEERHSEN, CHARLES. "Unite and Conquer." *Newsweek* (February 5, 1990):50–55.

LEFEBVRE, HENRI. *The Production of Space*. Oxford: Blackwell, 1991.

LELAND, JOHN. "Bisexuality." *Newsweek* (July 17, 1995):44–49.

LEMERT, EDWIN M. *Social Pathology*. New York: McGraw-Hill, 1951.

———. *Human Deviance, Social Problems, and Social Control*. 2d ed. Englewood Cliffs, N.J.: Prentice Hall, 1972.

LENGERMANN, PATRICIA MADOO, and RUTH A. WALLACE. *Gender in America: Social Control and Social Change*. Englewood Cliffs, N.J.: Prentice Hall, 1985.

LENSKI, GERHARD E. *Power and Privilege: A Theory of Social Stratification.* New York: McGraw- Hill, 1966.

LENNON, MARY CLARE, and SARAH ROSENFELD. "Relative Fairness and the Doctrine of Housework: The Importance of Options." *American Journal of Sociology.* Vol. 100, No. 2 (September 1994):506–31.

LENSKI, GERHARD E. *Power and Privilege: A Theory of Social Stratification.* New York: McGraw-Hill, 1966.

LENSKI, GERHARD, PATRICK NOLAN, and JEAN LENSKI. *Human Societies: An Introduction to Macrosociology.* 7th ed. New York: McGraw-Hill, 1995.

LEONARD, EILEEN B. *Women, Crime, and Society: A Critique of Theoretical Criminology.* New York: Longman, 1982.

LESLIE, GERALD R., and SHEILA K. KORMAN. *The Family in Social Context.* 7th ed. New York: Oxford University Press, 1989.

LESTER, DAVID. *The Death Penalty: Issues and Answers.* Springfield, Ill.: Charles C. Thomas, 1987.

LEVAY, SIMON. *The Sexual Brain.* Cambridge, Mass.: MIT Press, 1993.

LEVER, JANET. "Sex Differences in the Complexity of Children's Play and Games." *American Sociological Review.* Vol. 43, No. 4 (August 1978):471–83.

LEVINE, MICHAEL. "Reducing Hostility Can Prevent Heart Disease." *Mount Vernon News* (August 7, 1990):4A.

LEVINE, MICHAEL P. *Student Eating Disorders: Anorexia Nervosa and Bulimia.* Washington, D.C.: National Educational Association, 1987.

LEVINE, ROBERT V. "Is Love a Luxury?" *American Demographics.* Vol. 15, No. 2 (February 1993):27–28.

LEVINSON, DANIEL J., with CHARLOTTE N. DARROW, EDWARD B. KLEIN, MARIA H. LEVINSON, and BRAXTON MCKEE. *The Seasons of a Man's Life.* New York: Alfred A. Knopf, 1978.

LEWIS, FLORA. "The Roots of Revolution." *New York Times Magazine* (November 11, 1984):70–71, 74, 77–78, 82, 84, 86.

LEWIS, OSCAR. *The Children of Sanchez.* New York: Random House, 1961.

LEWIS, PEIRCE, CASEY MCCRACKEN, and ROGER HUNT. "Politics: Who Cares?" *American Demographics.* Vol. 16, No. 10 (October 1994):20–26.

LI, JIANG HONG, and ROGER A. WOJTKIEWICZ. "A New Look at the Effects of Family Structure on Status Attainment." *Social Science Quarterly.* Vol. 73, No. 3 (September 1992):581–95.

LIAZOS, ALEXANDER. "The Poverty of the Sociology of Deviance: Nuts, Sluts and Preverts." *Social Problems.* Vol. 20, No. 1 (Summer 1972):103–20.

———. *People First: An Introduction to Social Problems.* Boston: Allyn and Bacon, 1982.

LICHTER, DANIEL T., DIANE K. MCLAUGHLIN, and DAVID C. RIBAR. "Welfare and the Rise in Female-Headed Families." *American Journal of Sociology.* Vol. 103, No. 1 (July 1997):112–43.

LICHTER, S. ROBERT, STANLEY ROTHMAN, and LINDA S. LICHTER. *The Media Elite: America's New Powerbrokers.* New York: Hastings House, 1990.

LIN, NAN, and WEN XIE. "Occupational Prestige in Urban China." *American Journal of Sociology.* Vol. 93, No. 4 (January 1988):793–832.

LINDEN, EUGENE. "More Power to Women, Fewer Mouths to Feed." *Time.* Vol. 144, No. 13 (September 26, 1994):64–65.

LINDSTROM, BONNIE. "Chicago's Post-Industrial Suburbs." *Sociological Focus.* Vol. 28, No. 4 (October 1995):399–412.

LING, PYAU. "Causes of Chinese Emigration." In Amy Tachiki et al., eds., *Roots: An Asian American Reader.* Los Angeles: UCLA Asian American Studies Center, 1971:134–38.

LINN, MICHAEL. Noted in *Cornell Alumni News.* Vol. 99, No. 2 (September 1996):25.

LINO, MARK. "Expenditures on Children by Families: 1997." *Annual Report.* Washington, D.C.: U.S. Department of Agriculture, Center for Nutrition Policy and Promotion, 1998.

———. *Expenditures on Children by Families, 1999 Annual Report.* Washington, D.C.: U.S. Department of Agriculture, Center for Nutrition Policy and Promotion, 2000.

LINTON, RALPH. "One Hundred Percent American." *The American Mercury.* Vol. 40, No. 160 (April 1937a):427–29.

———. *The Study of Man.* New York: D. Appleton-Century, 1937b.

LIPS, HILARY. *Sex and Gender: An Introduction.* 2d ed. Mountain View, Calif.: Mayfield Publishing Co., 1993.

LISKA, ALLEN E. *Perspectives on Deviance.* 3d ed. Englewood Cliffs, N.J.: Prentice Hall, 1991.

LISKA, ALLEN E., and MARK TAUSIG. "Theoretical Interpretations of Social Class and Racial Differentials in Legal Decision Making for Juveniles." *Sociological Quarterly.* Vol. 20, No. 2 (Spring 1979):197–207.

LISKA, ALLEN E., and BARBARA D. WARNER. "Functions of Crime: A Paradoxical Process." *American Journal of Sociology.* Vol. 96, No. 6 (May 1991):1441–63.

LITTMAN, DAVID L. "2001: A Farm Odyssey." *Wall Street Journal* (September 14, 1992):A10.

LIVERNASH, ROBERT, and ERIC RODENBURG. "Population Change, Resources, and the Environment." *Population Bulletin.* Vol. 53, No. 1 (March 1998).

LOGAN, JOHN R., and MARK SCHNEIDER. "Racial Segregation and Racial Change in American Suburbs, 1970–1980." *American Journal of Sociology.* Vol. 89, No. 4 (January 1984):874–88.

LOHR, STEVE. "British Health Service Faces a Crisis in Funds and Delays." *New York Times* (August 7, 1988):1, 12.

LORENZ, KONRAD. *On Aggression.* New York: Harcourt, Brace & World, 1966.

LOY, PAMELA HEWITT, and LEA P. STEWART. "The Extent and Effects of Sexual Harassment of Working Women." *Sociological Focus.* Vol. 17, No. 1 (January 1984):31–43.

LUKER, KRISTEN. *Abortion and the Politics of Motherhood.* Berkeley: University of California Press, 1984.

LUND, DALE A. "Caregiving." *Encyclopedia of Adult Development.* Phoenix, Ariz.: Oryx Press, 1993:57–63.

LUND, DALE A., MICHAEL S. CASERTA, and MARGARET F. DIMOND. "Gender Differences through Two Years of Bereavement among the Elderly." *The Gerontologist.* Vol. 26, No. 3 (1986):314–20.

LUNDMAN, RICHARD L. Correspondence to author (1999).

LUNSFORD, JACK. Remarks at a meeting of the Arizona Task Force on the Western Virtual University. [Online] Available http://www.acpe.asu.edu/VirtualU/, May 6, 1996. LUO, JAR-DER. "The Significance of Networks in the Initiation of Small Businesses in Taiwan." *Sociological Focus.* Vol. 12, No. 2 (June 1997):297–317.

LUTZ, CATHERINE A. *Unnatural Emotions: Everyday Sentiments on a Micronesia Atoll and Their Challenge to Western Theory.* Chicago: University of Chicago Press, 1988.

LUTZ, CATHERINE A., and GEOFFREY M. WHITE. "The Anthropology of Emotions." In Bernard J. Siegel, Alan R. Beals, and Stephen A. Tyler, eds., *Annual Review of Anthropology.* Palo Alto, Calif.: Annual Reviews, Vol. 15 (1986):405–36.

LYNCH, MICHAEL, and DAVID BOGEN. "Sociology's Asociological 'Core': An Examination of Textbook Sociology in Light of the Sociology of Scientific Knowledge." *American Sociological Review.* Vol. 62, No. 3 (June 1997):481–93.

LYND, ROBERT S. *Knowledge For What? The Place of Social Science in American Culture.* Princeton, N.J.: Princeton University Press, 1967.

LYND, ROBERT S., and HELEN MERRELL LYND. *Middletown in Transition.* New York: Harcourt, Brace & World, 1937.

LYNOTT, PATRICIA PASSUTH, and BARBARA J. LOGUE. "The 'Hurried Child': The Myth of Lost Childhood on Contemporary American Society." *Sociological Forum.* Vol. 8, No. 3 (September 1993):471–91.

MA, LI-CHEN. Personal communication, 1987.

MABRY, MARCUS. "New Hope for Old Unions?" *Newsweek* (February 24, 1992):39.

MABRY, MARCUS, and TOM MASLAND. "The Man after Mandela." *Newsweek* (June 7, 1999):54–55.

MCADAM, DOUG, JOHN D. MCCARTHY, and MAYER N. ZALD. "Social Movements." In Neil J. Smelser, ed., *Handbook of Sociology.* Newbury Park, Calif.: Sage, 1988:695–737.

MCBROOM, WILLIAM H., and FRED W. REED. "Recent Trends in Conservatism: Evidence of Non-Unitary Patterns." *Sociological Focus.* Vol. 23, No. 4 (October 1990):355–65.

MCCARTHY, TERRY. "Give Me Your Tired, Your Poor . . ." *Time.* Vol. 151, No. 4 (February 2, 1998):4.

MACCOBY, ELEANOR EMMONS, and CAROL NAGY JACKLIN. *The Psychology of Sex Differences.* Palo Alto, Calif.: Stanford University Press, 1974.

MCCOLM, R. BRUCE, JAMES FINN, DOUGLAS W. PAYNE, JOSEPH E. RYAN, LEONARD R. SUSSMAN, and GEORGE ZARYCKY. *Freedom in the World: Political Rights & Civil Liberties, 1990–1991.* New York: Freedom House, 1991.

MCCORMICK, NAOMI. B. *Sexual Salvation.* Westport, Conn.: Praeger, 1994.

MacDonald, J. Fred. *Blacks and White TV: African Americans in Television since 1948*. Chicago: Nelson-Hall, 1992.

McDonald, Kim A. "Debate over How to Gauge Global Warming Heats Up Meeting of Climatologists." *Chronicle of Higher Education*. Vol. XLV, No. 22 (February 5, 1999):A17.

Mace, David, and Vera Mace. *Marriage East and West*. Garden City, N.Y.: Doubleday (Dolphin), 1960.

McGuire, Meredith B. *Religion: The Social Context*. 2d ed. Belmont, Calif.: Wadsworth, 1987.

Macionis, John J. "Intimacy: Structure and Process in Interpersonal Relationships." *Alternative Lifestyles*. Vol. 1, No. 1 (February 1978a):113–30.

———. "The Search for Community in Modern Society: An Interpretation." *Qualitative Sociology*. Vol. 1, No. 2 (September 1978b):130–43.

———. "A Sociological Analysis of Humor." Presentation to the Texas Junior College Teachers Association, Houston, 1987.

———. "Making Society (and, Increasingly, the World) Visible." In Earl Babbie, ed., *The Spirit of Sociology*. Belmont, Calif.: Wadsworth, 1993:221–24.

Macionis, John J., and Vincent R. Parrillo. *Cities and Urban Life*. 2d ed. Upper Saddle River, N.J.: Prentice Hall, 2001.

MacKay, Donald G. "Prescriptive Grammar and the Pronoun Problem." In Barrie Thorne, Cheris Kramarae, and Nancy Henley, eds., *Language, Gender and Society*. Rowley, Mass.: Newbury House, 1983:38–53.

McKee, Victoria. "Blue Blood and the Color of Money." *New York Times* (June 9, 1996):49–50.

Macklin, Eleanor D. "Nonmarital Heterosexual Cohabitation: An Overview." In Eleanor D. Macklin and Roger H. Rubin, eds., *Contemporary Families and Alternative Lifestyles: Handbook on Research and Theory*. Beverly Hills, Calif.: Sage, 1983:49–74.

McLeod, Jane D., and Michael J. Shanahan. "Poverty, Parenting, and Children's Mental Health." *American Sociological Review*. Vol. 58, No. 3 (June 1993):351–66.

McLeod, Jay. *Ain't No Makin' It: Aspirations and Attainment in a Low-Income Neighborhood*. Boulder, Colo.: Westview Press, 1995.

McLuhan, Marshall. *The Gutenberg Galaxy*. New York: New American Library, 1969.

McNeil, Donald G., Jr. "Should Women Be Sent Into Combat?" *New York Times* (July 21, 1991):E3.

McNulty, Paul J. "Who's in Jail and Why They Belong There." *Wall Street Journal* (November 9, 1994):A23.

McRae, Susan. *Cross-Class Families: A Study of Wives' Occupational Superiority*. New York: Oxford University Press, 1986.

Maddox, Setma. "Organizational Culture and Leadership Style: Factors Affecting Self-Managed Work Team Performance." Paper presented at the annual meeting of the Southwest Social Science Association, Dallas, February 1994.

Madsen, Axel. *Private Power: Multinational Corporations for the Survival of Our Planet*. New York: William Morrow, 1980.

Malthus, Thomas Robert. *First Essay on Population 1798*. London: Macmillan, 1926; orig. 1798.

Manza, Jeff, and Clem Brooks. "The Religious Factor in U.S. Presidential Elections, 1960-1992." *American Journal of Sociology*. Vol. 103, No. 1 (July 1997):38–81.

Marcuse, Herbert. *One-Dimensional Man*. Boston: Beacon Press, 1964.

Mare, Robert D. "Five Decades of Educational Assortative Mating." *American Sociological Review*. Vol. 56, No. 1 (February 1991):15–32.

Marín, Gerardo, and Barbara VanOss Marín. *Research with Hispanic Populations*. Newbury Park, Calif.: Sage, 1991.

Marini, Margaret Mooney, and Pi-Ling Fan. "The Gender Gap in Earnings at Career Entry." *American Sociological Review*. Vol. 62, No. 4 (August 1997):588–604.

Markoff, John. "Remember Big Brother? Now He's a Company Man." *New York Times* (March 31, 1991):7.

Markovsky, Barry, John Skvoretz, David Willer, Michael J. Lovaglia, and Jeffrey Erger. "The Seeds of Weak Power: An Extension of Network Exchange Theory." *American Sociological Review*. Vol. 58, No. 2 (April 1993):197–209.

Marquand, Robert. "Worship Shift: Americans Seek Feeling of 'Awe'." *Christian Science Monitor* (May 28, 1997):1, 8.

Marquand, Robert, and Daniel B. Wood. "Rise in Cults as Millennium Approaches." *Christian Science Monitor* (March 28, 1997):1, 18.

Marshall, Susan E. "Ladies against Women: Mobilization Dilemmas of Antifeminist Movements." *Social Problems*. Vol. 32, No. 4 (April 1985):348–62.

Martin, John M., and Anne T. Romano. *Multinational Crime: Terrorism, Espionage, Drug and Arms Trafficking*. Newbury Park, Calif.: Sage, 1992.

Martinez, Valerie J., R. Kenneth Godwin, Frank R. Kemerer, and Laura Perna. "The Consequences of School Choice: Who Leaves and Who Stays in the Inner City." *Social Science Quarterly*. Vol. 76, No. 1 (September 1995):485–501.

Marullo, Sam. "The Functions and Dysfunctions of Preparations for Fighting Nuclear War." *Sociological Focus*. Vol. 20, No. 2 (April 1987):135–53.

Marx, Karl. *Karl Marx: Selected Writings in Sociology and Social Philosophy*. T. B. Bottomore, trans. New York: McGraw-Hill, 1964b.

———. *Capital*. Friedrich Engels, ed. New York: International Publishers, 1967; orig. 1867

———. "Critique of the Gotha Program." In Robert C. Tucker, ed., *The Marx-Engels Reader*. New York: Norton, 1972:388.

———. "Theses on Feuer." In Robert C. Tucker, ed., *The Marx-Engels Reader*. New York: Norton, 1972:107–9; orig. 1845.

Marx, Karl, and Friedrich Engels. "Manifesto of the Communist Party." In Robert C. Tucker, ed., *The Marx-Engels Reader*. New York: Norton, 1972:331–62; orig. 1848.

———. *The Marx-Engels Reader*. 2d ed. Robert C. Tucker, ed. New York: Norton, 1978.

Marx, Leo. "The Environment and the 'Two Cultures' Divide." In James Rodger Fleming and Henry A. Gemery, eds., *Science, Technology, and the Environment: Multidisciplinary Perspectives*. Akron, Ohio: University of Akron Press, 1994:3–21.

Massey, Douglas S., and Nancy A. Denton. "Hypersegregation in U.S. Metropolitan Areas: Black and Hispanic Segregation along Five Dimensions." *Demography*. Vol. 26, No. 3 (August 1989):373–91.

Masters, William H., Virginia E. Johnson, and Robert C. Kolodny. *Human Sexuality*. 3d ed. Glenview, Ill.: Scott, Foresman/Little, Brown, 1988.

Matthiessen, Peter. *Indian Country*. New York: Viking Press, 1984.

Mauer, Marc. "Americans behind Bars: U.S. and International Use of Incarceration 1995." [Online] Available http://www.sentencingproject.org/pubs/tsppubs/9030data.html, April 1, 2000.

May, Elaine Tyler. "Women in the Wild Blue Yonder." *New York Times* (August 7, 1991):21.

Mayo, Katherine. *Mother India*. New York: Harcourt, Brace, 1927.

Mead, George Herbert. *Mind, Self, and Society*. Charles W. Morris, ed. Chicago: University of Chicago Press, 1962; orig. 1934.

Mead, Margaret. *Sex and Temperament in Three Primitive Societies*. New York: William Morrow, 1963; orig. 1935.

Meadows, Donella H., Dennis L. Meadows, Jorgan Randers, and William W. Behrens, III. *The Limits to Growth: A Report on the Club of Rome's Project on the Predicament of Mankind*. New York: Universe, 1972.

Meltzer, Bernard N. "Mead's Social Psychology." In Jerome G. Manis and Bernard N. Meltzer, eds., *Symbolic Interaction: A Reader in Social Psychology*. 3d ed. Needham Heights, Mass.: Allyn & Bacon, 1978.

Melucci, Alberto. "The New Social Movements: A Theoretical Approach." *Social Science Information*. Vol. 19, No. 2 (May 1980):199–226.

———. *Nomads of the Present: Social Movements and Individual Needs in Contemporary Society*. Philadelphia: Temple University Press, 1989.

Menjivar, Cecilia. "Immigrant Kinship Networks and the Impact of the Receiving Context: Salvadorans in San Francisco in the Early 1990s." *Social Problems*. Vol. 44, No. 1 (February 1997):104–23.

Mergenhagen, Paula. "Black-Owned Businesses." *American Demographics*. Vol. 18, No. 6 (June 1996a):24–27, 30–33.

———. "Her Own Boss." *American Demographics*. Vol. 18, No. 12 (December 1996b):37–41.

Merton, Robert K. "Social Structure and Anomie." *American Sociological Review*. Vol. 3, No. 6 (October 1938):672–82.

———. *Social Theory and Social Structure*. New York: Free Press, 1968.

———. "Discrimination and the American Creed." In *Sociological Ambivalence and Other Essays*. New York: Free Press, 1976:189–216.

Meyer, Davis S., and Nancy Whittier. "Social Movement Spillover." *Social Problems*. Vol. 41, No. 2 (May 1994):277–98.

Michels, Robert. *Political Parties*. Glencoe, Ill.: Free Press, 1949; orig. 1911.

MILBRATH, LESTER W. *Envisioning A Sustainable Society: Learning Our Way Out*. Albany: State University of New York Press, 1989.

MILGRAM, STANLEY. "Behavioral Study of Obedience." *Journal of Abnormal and Social Psychology*. Vol. 67, No. 4 (1963):371–78.

———. "Group Pressure and Action against a Person." *Journal of Abnormal and Social Psychology*. Vol. 69, No. 2 (August 1964):137–43.

———. "Some Conditions of Obedience and Disobedience to Authority." *Human Relations*. Vol. 18 (February 1965):57–76.

MILIBAND, RALPH. *The State in Capitalist Society*. London: Weidenfield and Nicolson, 1969.

MILLER, ARTHUR G. *The Obedience Experiments: A Case of Controversy in Social Science*. New York: Praeger, 1986.

MILLER, BERNA. "The Quest for Lifelong Learning." *American Demographics*. Vol. 19, No. 3 (March 1997a):20, 22.

———. "Population Update for April." *American Demographics*. Vol. 19, No. 4 (April 1997b):18.

MILLER, FREDERICK D. "The End of SDS and the Emergence of Weatherman: Demise through Success." In Jo Freeman, ed., *Social Movements of the Sixties and Seventies*. New York: Longman, 1983:279–97.

MILLER, G. TYLER, JR. *Living in the Environment: An Introduction to Environmental Science*. Belmont, Calif.: Wadsworth, 1992.

MILLER, MICHAEL. "Lawmakers Begin to Heed Calls to Protect Privacy." *Wall Street Journal* (April 11, 1991):A16.

MILLER, WALTER B. "Lower Class Culture as a Generating Milieu of Gang Delinquency." In Marvin E. Wolfgang, Leonard Savitz, and Norman Johnston, eds., *The Sociology of Crime and Delinquency*. 2d ed. New York: Wiley, 1970:351–63; orig. 1958.

MILLET, KATE. *Sexual Politics*. Garden City, N.Y.: Doubleday, 1970.

MILLS, C. WRIGHT. *The Power Elite*. New York: Oxford University Press, 1956.

———. *The Sociological Imagination*. New York: Oxford University Press, 1959.

MINK, BARBARA. "How Modernization Affects Women." *Cornell Alumni News*. Vol. III, No. 3 (April 1989):10–11.

MINTZ, BETH, and MICHAEL SCHWARTZ. "Interlocking Directorates and Interest Group Formation." *American Sociological Review*. Vol. 46, No. 6 (December 1981):851–69.

MIRINGOFF, MARC, and MARQUE-LUISA MIRINGOFF. *The Social Health of the Nation: How America Is Really Doing*. New York: Oxford University Press, 1999.

MIROWSKY, JOHN. "The Psycho-Economics of Feeling Underpaid: Distributive Justice and the Earnings of Husbands and Wives." *American Journal of Sociology*. Vol. 92, No. 6 (May 1987):1404–34.

MIROWSKY, JOHN, and CATHERINE ROSS. "Working Wives and Mental Health." Presentation to the American Association for the Advancement of Science, New York, 1984.

MOGELONSKY, MARCIA. "Reconfiguring the American Dream (House)." *American Demographics*. Vol. 19, No. 1 (January 1997):31–35.

MOLM, LINDA D. "Risk and Power Use: Constraints on the Use of Coercion in Exchange." *American Sociological Review*. Vol. 62, No. 1 (February 1997):113–33.

MOLOTCH, HARVEY. "The City as a Growth Machine." *American Journal of Sociology*. Vol. 82, No. 2 (September 1976):309–33.

MONTAGU, ASHLEY. *The Nature of Human Aggression*. New York: Oxford University Press, 1976.

MOORE, GWEN. "Structural Determinants of Men's and Women's Personal Networks." *American Sociological Review*. Vol. 55, No. 5 (October 1991):726–35.

———. "Gender and Informal Networks in State Government." *Social Science Quarterly*. Vol. 73, No. 1 (March 1992):46–61.

MOORE, JOAN, and HARRY PACHON. *Hispanics in the United States*. Englewood Cliffs, N.J.: Prentice Hall, 1985.

MOORE, WILBERT E. "Modernization as Rationalization: Processes and Restraints." In Manning Nash, ed., *Essays on Economic Development and Cultural Change in Honor of Bert F. Hoselitz*. Chicago: University of Chicago Press, 1977:29–42.

———. *World Modernization: The Limits of Convergence*. New York: Elsevier, 1979.

MORAN, JOHN S., S. O. ARAL, W. C. JENKINS, T. A. PETERMAN, and E. R. ALEXANDER. "The Impact of Sexually Transmitted Diseases on Minority Populations." *Public Health Reports*. Vol. 104, No. 6 (November-December 1989):560–65.

MORGAN, LAURIE A. "Glass Ceiling or Cohort Effect? A Longitudinal Study of the Gender Earnings Gap for Engineers, 1982 to 1989." *American Sociological Review*. Vol. 63, No. 4 (August 1998):479–93.

MOSLEY, W. HENRY, and PETER COWLEY. "The Challenge of World Health." *Population Bulletin*. Vol. 46, No. 4 (December 1991). Washington, D.C.: Population Reference Bureau.

MUFSON, STEVEN. "China's Growing Inequality." *Washington Post* (January 1, 1997):A1, A26– A27.

MULFORD, MATTHEW, JOHN ORBELL, CATHERINE SHATTO, and JEAN STOCKARD. "Physical Attractiveness, Opportunity, and Success in Everyday Exchange." *American Journal of Sociology*. Vol. 106, No. 6 (May 1998):1565–92.

MUMFORD, LEWIS. *The City in History: Its Origins, Its Transformations, and Its Prospects*. New York: Harcourt, Brace & World, 1961.

MURDOCK, GEORGE PETER. "Comparative Data on the Division of Labor by Sex." *Social Forces*. Vol. 15, No. 4 (May 1937):551–53.

———. "The Common Denominator of Cultures." In Ralph Linton, ed., *The Science of Man in World Crisis*. New York: Columbia University Press, 1945:123–42.

———. *Social Structure*. New York: Free Press, 1965; orig. 1949.

MURRAY, CHARLES. *Losing Ground: American Social Policy 1950–1980*. New York: Basic Books, 1984.

———. "Keeping Priorities Straight on Welfare Reform." *Society*. Vol. 33, No. 5 (July/August 1996):10–12.

MYERS, NORMAN. "Humanity's Growth." In Sir Edmund Hillary, ed., *Ecology 2000: The Changing Face of the Earth*. New York: Beaufort Books, 1984a:16–35.

———. "The Mega-Extinction of Animals and Plants." In Sir Edmund Hillary, ed., *Ecology 2000: The Changing Face of the Earth*. New York: Beaufort Books, 1984b:82–107.

———. "Disappearing Cultures." In Sir Edmund Hillary, ed., *Ecology 2000: The Changing Face of the Earth*. New York: Beaufort Books, 1984c:162–69.

———. "Biological Diversity and Global Security." In F. Herbert Bormann and Stephen R. Kellert, eds., *Ecology, Economics, and Ethics: The Broken Circle*. New Haven, Conn.: Yale University Press, 1991:11–25.

MYERS, SHEILA, and HAROLD G. GRASMICK. "The Social Rights and Responsibilities of Pregnant Women: An Application of Parsons' Sick Role Model." Paper presented to the Southwestern Sociological Association, Little Rock, Arkansas, March 1989.

MYERSON, ALLEN R. "This Man Wants to Bury You." *New York Times* (August 1, 1993):section 3, pp. 1, 6.

MYRDAL, GUNNAR. *An American Dilemma: The Negro Problem and Modern Democracy*. New York: Harper & Brothers, 1944.

NAGEL, JOANE. "Constructing Ethnicity: Creating and Recreating Ethnic Identity and Culture." *Social Problems*. Vol. 41, No. 1 (February 1994):152–76.

———. *American Indian Ethnic Renewal: Red Power and the Resurgence of Identity and Culture*. New York: Oxford University Press, 1996.

NAJAFIZADEH, MEHRANGIZ, and LEWIS A. MENNERICK. "Sociology of Education or Sociology of Ethnocentrism: The Portrayal of Education in Introductory Sociology Textbooks." *Teaching Sociology*. Vol. 20, No. 3 (July 1992):215–21.

NASH, J. MADELEINE. "To Know Your Own Fate." *Time*. Vol. 145, No. 14 (April 3, 1995):62.

NATIONAL COMMISSION ON EXCELLENCE IN EDUCATION. *A Nation at Risk*. Washington, D.C.: U.S. Government Printing Office, 1983.

NEERGAARD, LAUREN. "Cigarette Smoking Jumps 28% on Campus." *Bowling Green Sentinel Tribune* (November 18, 1998):9.

NELSON, AMY L. "The Effect of Economic Restructuring on Family Poverty in the Industrial Heartland, 1970-1990." *Sociological Focus*. Vol. 31 No. 2 (May 1998):201–16.

NEUHOUSER, KEVIN. "The Radicalization of the Brazilian Catholic Church in Comparative Perspective." *American Sociological Review*. Vol. 54, No. 2 (April 1989):233–44.

NEUMAN, W. LAURENCE. *Social Research Methods: Qualitative and Quantitative Approaches*. 3d ed. Boston: Allyn and Bacon, 1997.

NEWMAN, KATHERINE S. *Declining Fortunes: The Withering of the American Dream*. New York: Basic Books, 1993.

NEWMAN, WILLIAM M. *American Pluralism: A Study of Minority Groups and Social Theory*. New York: Harper & Row, 1973.

NIELSEN, A. C. Survey data cited in *Information Please Almanac 1997*. Boston: Houghton Mifflin, 1997.

NIELSEN, FRANCOIS, and ARTHUR S. ALDERSON. "The Kuznets Curve: The Great U-Turn: Income Inequality in U.S. Counties, 1970 to 1990." *American Sociological Review*. Vol. 62, No. 1 (February 1997):12–33.

NIELSEN, JOYCE MCCARL, ed. *Feminist Research Methods: Exemplary Readings in the Social Sciences*. Boulder, Colo.: Westview Press, 1990.

1991 Green Book. U.S. House of Representatives. Washington, D.C.: U.S. Government Printing Office, 1991.

NISBET, ROBERT A. *The Sociological Tradition*. New York: Basic Books, 1966.

———. *The Quest for Community*. New York: Oxford University Press, 1969.

NOCK, STEVEN L., JAMES D. WRIGHT, and LAURA SANCHEZ. "America's Divorce Problem." *Society*. Vol. 36, No. 4 (May/June 1999):43–52.

NOLAN, JAMES L., JR., ed. *The American Culture Wars: Current Contests and Future Prospects*. Charlottesville, Va.: University Press of Virginia, 1996.

NORC. *General Social Surveys, 1972–1998: Cumulative Codebook*. Chicago: National Opinion Research Center, 1999.

NOVAK, VIVECA. "The Cost of Poor Advice." *Time*. Vol. 154, No. 1 (July 5, 1999):38.

NUNN, CLYDE Z., HARRY J. CROCKETT, JR., and J. ALLEN WILLIAMS, JR. *Tolerance for Nonconformity*. San Francisco: Jossey-Bass, 1978.

OAKES, JEANNIE. "Classroom Social Relationships: Exploring the Bowles and Gintis Hypothesis." *Sociology of Education*. Vol. 55, No. 4 (October 1982):197–212.

———. *Keeping Track: How High Schools Structure Inequality*. New Haven, Conn.: Yale University Press, 1985.

O'BRIEN, DAVID J., EDWARD W. HASSINGER, and LARRY DERSHEM. "Size of Place, Residential Stability, and Personal Social Networks." *Sociological Focus*. Vol. 29, No. 1 (February 1996):61–72.

O'CONNOR, RORY J. "Internet Declared Protected Speech." *Post-Star* (Glens Fall, N.Y.: June 27, 1997):A1–A2.

OFFIR, CAROLE WADE. *Human Sexuality*. New York: Harcourt Brace Jovanovich, 1982.

OGBURN, WILLIAM F. *On Culture and Social Change*. Chicago: University of Chicago Press, 1964.

O'HARE, WILLIAM P. "The Rise of Hispanic Affluence." *American Demographics*. Vol. 12, No. 8 (August 1990):40–43.

O'HARE, WILLIAM P., WILLIAM H. FREY, and DAN FOST. "Asians in the Suburbs." *American Demographics*. Vol. 16, No. 9 (May 1994):32–38.

O'HARE, WILLIAM P., and JAN LARSON. "Women in Business: Where, What, and Why." *American Demographics*. Vol. 13, No. 7 (July 1991):34–38.

OKRENT, DANIEL. "Raising Kids Online: What Can Parents Do?" *Time*. Vol. 154, No. 18 (May 10, 1999):38–43.

OLSEN, GREGG M. "Re-Modeling Sweden: The Rise and Demise of the Compromise in a Global Economy." *Social Problems*. Vol. 43, No. 1 (February 1996):1–20.

OLZAK, SUSAN. "Labor Unrest, Immigration, and Ethnic Conflict in Urban America, 1880–1914." *American Journal of Sociology*. Vol. 94, No. 6 (May 1989):1303–33.

ONE WORLD. Data from Web site. [Online] Available http://www.oneworld.org, November 15, 1998.

ORWIN, CLIFFORD. "All Quiet on the Western Front?" *The Public Interest*. Vol. 123 (Spring 1996): 3–9.

OSGOOD, D. WAYNE, JANET K. WILSON, PATRICK M. O'MALLEY, JERALD G. BACHMAN, and LLOYD D. JOHNSTON. "Routine Activities and Individual Deviant Behavior." *American Sociological Review*. Vol. 61, No. 4 (August 1996):635–55.

OSTRANDER, SUSAN A. "Upper Class Women: The Feminine Side of Privilege." *Qualitative Sociology*. Vol. 3, No. 1 (Spring 1980):23–44.

———. *Women of the Upper Class*. Philadelphia: Temple University Press, 1984.

OUCHI, WILLIAM. *Theory Z: How American Business Can Meet the Japanese Challenge*. Reading, Mass.: Addison-Wesley, 1981.

OWEN, DAVID. *None of the Above: Behind the Myth of Scholastic Aptitude*. Boston: Houghton Mifflin, 1985.

PAKULSKI, JAN. "Mass Social Movements and Social Class." *International Sociology*. Vol. 8, No. 2 (June 1993):131–58.

PARCEL, TOBY L., CHARLES W. MUELLER, and STEVEN CUVELIER. "Comparable Worth and Occupational Labor Market: Explanations of Occupational Earnings Differentials." Paper presented to the American Sociological Association, New York, 1986.

PARENTI, MICHAEL. *Inventing Reality: The Politics of the Mass Media*. New York: St. Martin's Press, 1986.

PARK, ROBERT E. *Race and Culture*. Glencoe, Ill.: Free Press, 1950.

PARRILLO, VINCENT N. "Diversity in America: A Sociohistorical Analysis." *Sociological Forum*. Vol. 9, No. 4 (December 1994):42–45.

PARSONS, TALCOTT. "Age and Sex in the Social Structure of the United States." *American Sociological Review*. Vol. 7, No. 4 (August 1942):604–16.

———. *Essays in Sociological Theory*. New York: Free Press, 1954.

———. *The Social System*. New York: Free Press, 1964; orig. 1951.

———. *Societies: Evolutionary and Comparative Perspectives*. Englewood Cliffs, N.J.: Prentice Hall, 1966.

PARSONS, TALCOTT, and ROBERT F. BALES, eds. *Family, Socialization and Interaction Process*. New York: Free Press, 1955.

PATTILLO-MCCOY, MARY. "Church Culture as a Strategy of Action in the Black Community." *American Sociological Review*. Vol. 63, No. 6 (December 1998):767–84.

PAUL, ELLEN FRANKEL. "Bared Buttocks and Federal Cases." *Society*. Vol. 28, No. 4 (May-June, 1991):4–7.

PEAR, ROBERT. "Women Reduce Lag in Earnings, But Disparities with Men Remain." *New York Times* (September 4, 1987):1, 7.

PEAR, ROBERT, with ERIK ECKHOLM. "When Healers Are Entrepreneurs: A Debate over Costs and Ethics." *New York Times* (June 2, 1991):1, 17.

PEARSON, DAVID E. "Post-Mass Culture." *Society*. Vol. 30, No. 5 (July-August 1993):17–22.

———. "Community and Sociology." *Society*. Vol. 32, No. 5 (July-August 1995):44–50.

PEASE, JOHN, and LEE MARTIN. "Want Ads and Jobs for the Poor: A Glaring Mismatch." *Sociological Forum*. Vol. 12. No. 4 (December 1997):545–64.

PERROLLE, JUDITH A. "Comments from the Special Issue Editor: The Emerging Dialogue on Environmental Justice." *Social Problems*. Vol. 40, No. 1 (February 1993):1–4.

PERSELL, CAROLINE HODGES. *Education and Inequality: A Theoretical and Empirical Synthesis*. New York: Free Press, 1977.

PESSEN, EDWARD. *Riches, Class, and Power: America before the Civil War*. New Brunswick, N.J.: Transaction Books, 1990.

Peters Atlas of the World. New York: Harper & Row, 1990.

PETERSILIA, JOAN. "Probation in the United States: Practices and Challenges." *National Institute of Justice Journal*. No. 233 (September 1997):4.

PHELAN, JO, BRUCE G. LINK, ANN STUEVE, and ROBERT E. MOORE. "Education, Social Liberalism, and Economic Conservatism: Attitudes toward Homeless People." *American Sociological Review*. Vol. 60, No. 1 (February 1995):126–40.

PHI DELTA KAPPA INTERNATIONAL. Phi Delta Kappa International/Gallup Poll. [Online] Available http://www.pdkintl.org/kappan/kpol9909.htm#1a, February 14, 2000.

PINES, MAYA. "The Civilization of Genie." *Psychology Today*. Vol. 15 (September 1981):28–34.

PINHEY, THOMAS K., DONALD H. RUBINSTEIN, and RICHARD S. COLFAX. "Overweight and Happiness: The Reflected Self-Appraisal Hypothesis Reconsidered." *Social Science Quarterly*. Vol. 78, No. 3 (September 1997):747–55.

PIRANDELLO, LUIGI. "The Pleasure of Honesty." In *To Clothe the Naked and Two Other Plays*. New York: Dutton, 1962:143–98.

PIROG, MAUREEN A., and CHRIS MAGEE. "High School Completion: The Influence of Schools, Families, and Adolescent Parenting." *Social Science Quarterly*. Vol. 78, No. 3 (September 1997):710–24.

PITNEY, JOHN J., JR. "What Scholars Don't Know about Term Limits." *The Chronicle of Higher Education*. Vol. XLI, No. 33 (April 28, 1995):A76.

PIVEN, FRANCES FOX, and RICHARD A. CLOWARD. *Poor People's Movements: Why They Succeed, How They Fail*. New York: Pantheon Books, 1977.

PLOMIN, ROBERT, and TERRYL T. FOCH. "A Twin Study of Objectively Assessed Personality in Childhood." *Journal of Personality and Social Psychology*. Vol. 39, No. 4 (October 1980):680–88.

PODOLNY, JOEL M., and JAMES N. BARON. "Resources and Relationships: Social Networks and Mobility in the Workplace." *American Sociological Review*. Vol. 62, No. 5 (October 1997):673–93.

POHL, RUDIGER. "The Transition from Communism to Capitalism in East Germany." *Society*. Vol. 33, No. 4 (June 1996):62–65.

POLENBERG, RICHARD. *One Nation Divisible: Class, Race, and Ethnicity in the United States since 1938*. New York: Pelican Books, 1980.

POLLACK, ANDREW. "Happy in the East (^-^) or Smiling :-) in the West." *New York Times* (August 12, 1996).
———. "Overseas, Smoking Is One of Life's Small Pleasures." *New York Times* (August 17, 1997):E5.
POLLARD, KELVIN. "Play Ball! Demographics and Major League Baseball." *Population Today*. Vol. 24, No. 4 (April 1996):3.
POLLOCK, PHILIP H., III, and M. ELLIOT VITTAS. "Who Bears the Burdens of Environmental Pollution: Race, Ethnicity, and Environmental Equity in Florida." *Social Science Quarterly*. Vol. 76, No. 2 (June 1995):294–310.
POLSBY, NELSON W. "Three Problems in the Analysis of Community Power." *American Sociological Review*. Vol. 24, No. 6 (December 1959):796–803.
POMER, MARSHALL I. "Labor Market Structure, Intragenerational Mobility, and Discrimination: Black Male Advancement Out of Low-Paying Occupations, 1962–1973." *American Sociological Review*. Vol. 51, No. 5 (October 1986):650–59.
POPENOE, DAVID. *Disturbing the Nest: Family Change and Decline in Modern Societies*. New York: Aldine, 1988.
———. "Family Decline in the Swedish Welfare State." *The Public Interest*. No. 102 (Winter 1991):65–77.
———. "The Controversial Truth: Two-Parent Families Are Better." *New York Times* (December 26, 1992):21.
———. "American Family Decline, 1960–1990: A Review and Appraisal." *Journal of Marriage and the Family*. Vol. 55, No. 3 (August 1993a):527–55.
———. "Parental Androgyny." *Society*. Vol. 30, No. 6 (September-October 1993b):5–11.
POPENOE, DAVID, and BARBARA DAFOE WHITEHEAD. *Should We Live Together? What Young Adults Need to Know about Cohabitation before Marriage*. New Brunswick, N.J.: The National Marriage Project, 1999.
POPKIN, SUSAN J. "Welfare: Views from the Bottom." *Social Problems*. Vol. 17, No. 1 (February 1990):64–79.
POPULATION REFERENCE BUREAU. *2000 World Population Data Sheet*. Washington, D.C.: Population Reference Bureau, 2000.
Population Today. "Chronic Disability Declines Dramatically among U.S. Elderly." Vol. 25, No. 9 (September 1997):3.
PORTES, ALEJANDRO, and LEIF JENSEN. "The Enclave and the Entrants: Patterns of Ethnic Enterprise in Miami before and after Mariel." *American Sociological Review*. Vol. 54, No. 6 (December 1989):929–49.
POSTEL, SANDRA. "Facing Water Scarcity." In Lester R. Brown et al., eds., *State of the World 1993: A Worldwatch Institute Report on Progress toward a Sustainable Society*. New York: Norton, 1993:22–41.
POWELL, CHRIS, and GEORGE E. C. PATON, eds. *Humour in Society: Resistance and Control*. New York: St. Martin's Press, 1988.
PRESS, ANDREA L. Review of *Enlightened Racism: "The Cosby Show," Audiences, and the Myth of the American Dream*, by Sut Jhally and Justin Lewis. *American Journal of Sociology*. Vol. 99, No. 1 (July 1993):219–21.
PRESSER, HARRIET B. "The Housework Gender Gap." *Population Today*. Vol. 21, No. 7/8 (July-August 1993):5.
PRESSLEY, SUE ANNE, and NANCY ANDREWS. "For Gay Couples, the Nursery Becomes the New Frontier." *Washington Post* (December 20, 1992):A1, A22–23.
PRIMEGGIA, SALVATORE, and JOSEPH A. VARACALLI. "Southern Italian Comedy: Old to New World." In Joseph V. Scelsa, Salvatore J. LaGumina, and Lydio Tomasi, eds., *Italian Americans in Transition*. New York: The American Italian Historical Association, 1990:241–52.
PRINDLE, DAVID F. *Risky Business: The Political Economy of Hollywood*. Boulder, Colo.: Westview Press, 1993.
PRINDLE, DAVID F., and JAMES W. ENDERSBY. "Hollywood Liberalism." *Social Science Quarterly*. Vol. 74, No. 1 (March 1993):136–49.
PUTERBAUGH, GEOFF, ed. *Twins and Homosexuality: A Casebook*. New York: Garland, 1990.
PUTKA, GARY. "SAT to Become a Better Gauge." *Wall Street Journal* (November 1, 1990):B1.
PUTKA, GARY, and STEVE STECKLOW. "Do For-Profit Schools Work? These Seem To for One Entrepreneur." *Wall Street Journal* (June 8, 1994):A1, A4.
QUEENAN, JOE. "The Many Paths to Riches." *Forbes*. Vol. 144, No. 9 (October 23, 1989):149.
QUINNEY, RICHARD. *Class, State and Crime: On the Theory and Practice of Criminal Justice*. New York: David McKay, 1977.
RABKIN, JEREMY. "The Supreme Court in the Culture Wars." *The Public Interest*. Vol. 125 (Fall 1996):3–26.

RALEY, R. KELLY. "A Shortage of Marriageable Men? A Note on the Role of Cohabitation in Black-White Differences in Marriage Rates." *American Journal of Sociology*. Vol. 61, No. 6 (December 1996):973–83.
RAMO, JOSHUA COOPER. "Finding God on the Web." *Time* (December 16, 1996):60–67.
RAPHAEL, RAY. *The Men from the Boys: Rites of Passage in Male America*. Lincoln and London: University of Nebraska Press, 1988.
RATAN, SUNEEL. "A New Divide between Haves and Have-Nots?" *Time*. Special Issue. Vol. 145, No. 12 (Spring 1995):25–26.
RATNESAR, ROMESH. "Lost in the Middle." *Time*. Vol. 152, No. 17 (September 14, 1998):60–62.
———. "Not Gone, but Forgotten?" *Time*. Vol. 153, No. 15 (February 8, 1999):30–31.
RAVITCH, DIANE, and JOSEPH VITERITTI. "A New Vision for City Schools." *The Public Interest*. Vol. 122 (Winter 1996):3–16.
RECKLESS, WALTER C., and SIMON DINITZ. "Pioneering with Self-Concept as a Vulnerability Factor in Delinquency." *Journal of Criminal Law, Criminology, and Police Science*. Vol. 58, No. 4 (December 1967):515–23.
RECTOR, ROBERT. "America Has the World's Richest Poor People." *Wall Street Journal* (September 24, 1998):A18.
REICH, ROBERT B. "As the World Turns." *The New Republic* (May 1, 1989):23, 26–28.
———. *The Work of Nations: Preparing Ourselves for 21st-Century Capitalism*. New York: Alfred A. Knopf, 1991.
REINHARZ, SHULAMIT. *Feminist Methods in Social Research*. New York: Oxford University Press, 1992.
REMOFF, HEATHER TREXLER. *Sexual Choice: A Woman's Decision*. New York: Dutton/Lewis, 1984.
REMY, JACQUELINE. "Interview with Agnes Fournier de Saint-Maur, Interpol Police Lieutenant." For *L'Express*. Reprinted in *World Press Review* (November 1996):7.
RHODES, STEVE. "The Luck of the Draw." *Newsweek* (April 26, 1999):41.
RICHARDSON, JAMES T. "Definitions of Cult: From Sociological-Technical to Popular Negative." Paper presented to the American Psychological Association, Boston, August 1990.
RIDDLE, JOHN M., J. WORTH ESTES, and JOSIAH C. RUSSELL. "Ever since Eve . . . Birth Control in the Ancient World." *Archaeology*. Vol. 47, No. 2 (March/April, 1994):29–35.
RIDGEWAY, CECILIA L. *The Dynamics of Small Groups*. New York: St. Martin's Press, 1983.
RIESMAN, DAVID. *The Lonely Crowd: A Study of the Changing American Character*. New Haven, Conn.: Yale University Press, 1970; orig. 1950.
RILEY, MATILDA WHITE, ANNE FONER, and JOAN WARING. "Sociology of Age." In Neil J. Smelser, ed., *Handbook of Sociology*. Newbury Park, Calif.: Sage, 1988:243–90.
RILEY, NANCY E. "Gender, Power, and Population Change." *Population Bulletin*. Vol. 52, No. 1 (May 1997).
RITZER, GEORGE. *The McDonaldization of Society: An Investigation into the Changing Character of Contemporary Social Life*. Thousand Oaks, Calif.: Pine Forge Press, 1993.
———. *The McDonaldization of Society*. Revised edition. Thousand Oaks, Calif.: Sage, 1996.
———. *The McDonaldization Thesis: Explorations and Extensions*. Thousand Oaks, Calif.: Sage, 1998.
RITZER, GEORGE, and DAVID WALCZAK. *Working: Conflict and Change*. 4th ed. Englewood Cliffs, N.J.: Prentice Hall, 1990.
RIVERA-BATIZ, FRANCISCO L., and CARLOS SANTIAGO, cited in Sam Roberts, "Puerto Ricans on Mainland Making Gains, Study Finds." *New York Times* (October 19, 1994):A20.
ROBERTS, J. DEOTIS. *Roots of a Black Future: Family and Church*. Philadelphia: Westminster Press, 1980.
ROBINSON, JOYCE, and GLENNA SPITZE. "Whistle While You Work? The Effect of Household Task Performance on Women's and Men's Well-Being." *Social Science Quarterly*. Vol. 73, No. 4 (December 1992):844–61.
ROBINSON, VERA M. "Humor and Health." In Paul E. McGhee and Jeffrey H. Goldstein, eds., *Handbook of Humor Research, Vol. II, Applied Studies*. New York: Springer-Verlag, 1983:109–28.
ROCKETT, IAN R. H. "Population and Health: An Introduction to Epidemiology." *Population Bulletin*. Vol. 49, No. 3 (November 1994). Washington, D.C.: Population Reference Bureau.

RODGERS, JOAN R. "An Empirical Study of Intergenerational Transmission of Poverty in the United States." *Social Science Quarterly*. Vol. 76, No. 1 (March 1995):178–94.

ROESCH, ROBERTA. "Violent Families." *Parents*. Vol. 59, No. 9 (September 1984):74–76, 150–52.

ROHLEN, THOMAS P. *Japan's High Schools*. Berkeley: University of California Press, 1983.

RÓNA-TAS, ÁKOS. "The First Shall Be Last? Entrepreneurship and Communist Cadres in the Transition from Socialism." *American Journal of Sociology*. Vol. 100, No. 1 (July 1994):40–69.

ROOF, WADE CLARK. "Socioeconomic Differentials among White Socioreligious Groups in the United States." *Social Forces*. Vol. 58, No. 1 (September 1979):280–89.

ROOF, WADE CLARK, and WILLIAM McKINNEY. *American Mainline Religion: Its Changing Shape and Future*. New Brunswick, N.J.: Rutgers University Press, 1987.

ROSENBAUM, DAVID E. "Americans Want a Right to Die. Or So They Think." *New York Times* (June 8, 1997):E3.

ROSENDAHL, MONA. *Inside the Revolution: Everyday Life in Socialist Cuba*. Ithaca, N.Y.: Cornell University Press, 1997.

ROSENFELD, MEGAN. "Little Boys Blue: Reexamining the Plight of Young Males." *Washington Post* (March 26, 1998):A1, A17–A18.

ROSENFELD, MICHAEL J. "Celebration, Politics, and Selective Looting and Riots: A Micro-Level Study of the Bulls Riot of 1992 in Chicago." *Social Problems*. Vol. 44, No. 4 (November 1997):483–502.

ROSENTHAL, ELIZABETH. "Canada's National Health Plan Gives Care to All, with Limits." *New York Times* (April 30, 1991):A1, A16.

ROSS, CATHERINE E., JOHN MIROWSKY, and JOAN HUBER. "Dividing Work, Sharing Work, and In-Between: Marriage Patterns and Depression." *American Sociological Review*. Vol. 48, No. 6 (December 1983):809–23.

ROSS, JOHN. "To Die in the Street: Mexico City's Homeless Population Boom as Economic Crisis Shakes Social Protections." *SSSP Newsletter*. Vol. 27, No. 2 (Summer 1996):14–15.

ROSSI, ALICE S. "Gender and Parenthood." In Alice S. Rossi, ed., *Gender and the Life Course*. New York: Aldine, 1985:161–91.

ROSTOW, WALT W. *The Stages of Economic Growth: A Non-Communist Manifesto*. Cambridge: Cambridge University Press, 1960.

———. *The World Economy: History and Prospect*. Austin: University of Texas Press, 1978.

ROSZAK, THEODORE. *The Cult of Information: The Folklore of Computers and the True Art of Thinking*. New York: Pantheon Books, 1986.

ROTHMAN, BARBARA KATZ. "Of Maps and Imaginations: Sociology Confronts the Genome." *Social Problems*. Vol. 42, No. 1 (February 1995):1–10.

ROTHMAN, STANLEY, and AMY E. BLACK. "Who Rules Now? American Elites in the 1990s." *Society*. Vol. 35, No. 6 (September-October 1998):17–20.

ROTHMAN, STANLEY, and S. ROBERT LICHTER. "Social Science and Ideology: A Reply to Prindle, Endersby, and Gans." *Social Science Quarterly*. Vol. 75 (June 1994):455–57.

ROTHMAN, STANLEY, STEPHEN POWERS, and DAVID ROTHMAN. "Feminism in Films." *Society*. Vol. 30, No. 3 (March-April 1993):66–72.

ROWE, DAVID C. "Biometrical Genetic Models of Self-Reported Delinquent Behavior: A Twin Study." *Behavior Genetics*. Vol. 13, No. 5 (1983):473–89.

ROWE, DAVID C., and D. WAYNE OSGOOD. "Heredity and Sociological Theories of Delinquency: A Reconsideration." *American Sociological Review*. Vol. 49, No. 4 (August 1984):526–40.

ROZELL, MARK J., CLYDE WILCOX, and JOHN C. GREEN. "Religious Constituencies and Support for the Christian Right in the 1990s." *Social Science Quarterly*. Vol. 79, No. 4 (December 1998):815–27.

RUBIN, LILLIAN BRESLOW. *Worlds of Pain: Life in the Working-Class Family*. New York: Basic Books, 1976.

RUDEL, THOMAS K., and JUDITH M. GERSON. "Postmodernism, Institutional Change, and Academic Workers: A Sociology of Knowledge." *Social Science Quarterly*. Vol. 80, No. 2 (June 1999):213–28.

RUDOLPH, ELLEN. "Women's Talk: Japanese Women." *New York Times Magazine* (September 1, 1991).

RULE, JAMES, and PETER BRANTLEY. "Computerized Surveillance in the Workplace: Forms and Delusions." *Sociological Forum*. Vol. 7, No. 3 (September 1992):405–23.

RUSSELL, CHERYL. "Are We in the Dumps?" *American Demographics*. Vol. 17, No. 1 (January 1995a):6.

———. "True Crime." *American Demographics*. Vol. 17, No. 8 (August 1995b):22–31.

RUSSELL, CHERYL, and MARCIA MOGELONSKY. "Riding High on the Market." *American Demographics*. Vol. 22, No. 4 (April 2000):44–54.

RUTHERFORD, MEGAN. "Women Run the World." *Time*. Vol. 153, No. 25 (June 28, 1999):72

RYAN, WILLIAM. *Blaming the Victim*. Rev. ed. New York: Vintage Books, 1976.

RYMER, RUSS. *Genie*. New York: HarperPerennial, 1994.

SACHS, JEFFREY. "The Real Causes of Famine." *Time*. Vol. 152, No. 17 (October 26, 1998):69.

SADIK, NAFIS, ed. *Population Policies and Programmes: Lessons Learned from Two Decades of Experience*. New York: New York University Press, 1991.

ST. JEAN, YANICK, and JOE R. FEAGIN. *Double Burden: Black Women and Everyday Racism*. Armonk, N.Y.: M. E. Sharpe, 1998.

SALE, KIRKPATRICK. *The Conquest of Paradise: Christopher Columbus and the Columbian Legacy*. New York: Alfred A. Knopf, 1990.

SAMPSON, ROBERT J. "Urban Black Violence: The Effects of Male Joblessness and Family Disruption." *American Journal of Sociology*. Vol. 93, No. 2 (September 1987):348–82.

SAMPSON, ROBERT J., and JOHN H. LAUB. "Crime and Deviance over the Life Course: The Salience of Adult Social Bonds." *American Sociological Review*. Vol. 55, No. 5 (October 1990):609–27.

SANCHEZ, RENE. "Urban Students Not Making the Mark." *Washington Post* (January 8, 1998):A18.

SANTOLI, AL. "Fighting Child Prostitution." *Freedom Review*. Vol. 25, No. 5 (September-October 1994):5–8.

SAPIR, EDWARD. "The Status of Linguistics as a Science." *Language*. Vol. 5 (1929):207–14.

———. *Selected Writings of Edward Sapir in Language, Culture, and Personality*. David G. Mandelbaum, ed. Berkeley: University of California Press, 1949.

SAX, LINDA J., ALEXANDER W. ASTIN, WILLIAM S. KORN, and KATHRYN M. MAHONEY. *The American Freshman: National Norms for Fall 1999*. Los Angeles: UCLA Higher Education Research Institute, 1999.

SCAFF, LAWRENCE A. "Max Weber and Robert Michels." *American Journal of Sociology*. Vol. 86, No. 6 (May 1981):1269–86.

SCANLON, JAMES P. "The Curious Case of Affirmative Action for Women." *Society*. Vol. 29, No. 2 (January-February 1992):36–42.

SCHAUB, DIANA. "From Boys to Men." *The Public Interest*. No. 127 (Spring 1997):108–14.

SCHEFF, THOMAS J. *Being Mentally Ill: A Sociological Theory*. 2d ed. New York: Aldine, 1984.

SCHERER, RON. "Worldwide Trend: Tobacco Use Grows." *Christian Science Monitor* (July 17, 1996):4, 8.

SCHILLER, BRADLEY. "Who Are the Working Poor?" *The Public Interest*. Vol. 155 (Spring 1994):61–71.

SCHLESINGER, ARTHUR. "The City in American Civilization." In A. B. Callow, Jr., ed., *American Urban History*. New York: Oxford University Press, 1969:25–41.

SCHLESINGER, ARTHUR, JR. "The Cult of Ethnicity: Good and Bad." *Time*. Vol. 137, No. 27 (July 8, 1991):21.

SCHLESINGER, JACOB M. "Finally, U.S. Median Income Approaches Old Heights." *Wall Street Journal* (September 25, 1998):B1.

SCHNAIBERG, ALLAN, and KENNETH ALAN GOULD. *Environment and Society: The Enduring Conflict*. New York: St. Martin's Press, 1994.

SCHNEIDER, MARK, MELISSA MARSCHALL, PAUL TESKE, and CHRISTINE ROCH. "School Choice and Culture Wars in the Classroom: What Different Parents Seek from Education." *Social Science Quarterly*. Vol. 79, No. 3 (September 1998):489–501.

SCHOR, JUDITH B. Cited in Cheryl Russell, "Overworked? Overwhelmed?" *American Demographics*. Vol. 17, No. 3 (March 1995):8.

SCHUTT, RUSSELL K. "Objectivity versus Outrage." *Society*. Vol. 26, No. 4 (May-June 1989):14–16.

SCHWARTZ, FELICE N. "Management, Women, and the New Facts of Life." *Harvard Business Review*. Vol. 89, No. 1 (January-February 1989):65–76.

SCHWARTZ, MARTIN D. "Gender and Injury in Spousal Assault." *Sociological Focus*. Vol. 20, No. 1 (January 1987):61–75.

SCOMMEGNA, PAOLA. "Teens' Risk of AIDS, Unintended Pregnancies Examined." *Population Today*. Vol. 24, No. 8 (August 1996):1–2.

SCOTT, JOHN, and CATHERINE GRIFF. *Directors of Industry: The British Corporate Network, 1904–1976.* New York: Blackwell, 1985.

SCOTT, JOSEPH E., and J. CUVELIER. "Violence in *Playboy* Magazine: A Longitudinal Analysis." *Archives of Sexual Behavior.* Vol. 16 (1987):279–88.

SCOTT, W. RICHARD. *Organizations: Rational, Natural, and Open Systems.* Englewood Cliffs, N.J.: Prentice Hall, 1981.

SEGAL, MADY WECHSLER, and AMANDA FAITH HANSEN. "Value Rationales in Policy Debates on Women in the Military: A Content Analysis of Congressional Testimony, 1941–1985." *Social Science Quarterly.* Vol. 73, No. 2 (June 1992):296–309.

SEIDMAN, STEVEN. *Queer Theory/Sociology.* Oxford: Blackwell, 1996.

SEKULIC, DUSKO, GARTH MASSEY, and RANDY HODSON. "Who Were the Yugoslavs? Failed Sources of Common Identity in the Former Yugoslavia." *American Sociological Review.* Vol. 59, No. 1 (February 1994):83–97.

SELLIN, THORSTEN. *The Penalty of Death.* Beverly Hills, Calif.: Sage, 1980.

SENNETT, RICHARD. *The Corrosion of Character: The Personal Consequences of Work in the New Capitalism.* New York: Norton, 1998.

SENNETT, RICHARD, and JONATHAN COBB. *The Hidden Injuries of Class.* New York: Vintage Books, 1973.

The Sentencing Project. [Online] Available http://www.sentencingproject.org/brief/facts-pp.pdf, October 18, 2000.

SEPLOW, STEPHEN, and JONATHAN STORM. "How TV Defined Our Lives." *Philadelphia Inquirer* (November 30, 1997):A1, A16–17.

SHAPIRO, JOSEPH P. "Welfare: The Myth of Reform." *U.S. News & World Report.* Vol. 188, No. 2 (January 16, 1995):30–40.

SHAPIRO, JOSEPH P., and JOANNIE M. SCHROF. "Honor Thy Children." *U.S. News & World Report.* Vol. 118, No. 8 (February 27, 1995):39–49.

SHAREEF-COUSIN.COM. [Online] Available August, 1999.

SHARPE, ANITA. "The Rich Aren't So Different After All." *Wall Street Journal* (November 12, 1996):B1, B10.

SHAWCROSS, WILLIAM. *Sideshow: Kissinger, Nixon and the Destruction of Cambodia.* New York: Pocket Books, 1979.

SHEEHAN, TOM. "Senior Esteem as a Factor in Socioeconomic Complexity." *The Gerontologist.* Vol. 16, No. 5 (October 1976):433–40.

SHELDON, WILLIAM H., EMIL M. HARTL, and EUGENE MCDERMOTT. *Varieties of Delinquent Youth.* New York: Harper, 1949.

SHELEY, JAMES F., JOSHUA ZHANG, CHARLES J. BRODY, and JAMES D. WRIGHT. "Gang Organization, Gang Criminal Activity, and Individual Gang Members' Criminal Behavior." *Social Science Quarterly.* Vol. 76, No. 1 (March 1995):53–68.

SHELLENBARGER, SUE. "Deciding How Soon to Prepare Your Child to Stay at Home." *Wall Street Journal* (March 20, 1996):B1.

SHERMAN, LAWRENCE W., and DOUGLAS A. SMITH. "Crime, Punishment, and Stake in Conformity: Legal and Informal Control of Domestic Violence." *American Sociological Review.* Vol. 57, No. 5 (October 1992):680–90.

SHEVKY, ESHREF, and WENDELL BELL. *Social Area Analysis.* Stanford, Calif.: Stanford University Press, 1955.

SHIPLEY, JOSEPH T. *Dictionary of Word Origins.* Totowa, N.J.: Roman & Allanheld, 1985.

SHIVELY, JOELLEN. "Cowboys and Indians: Perceptions of Western Films among American Indians and Anglos." *American Sociological Review.* Vol. 57, No. 6 (December 1992):725–34.

SHLAES, AMITY. "Vermont Levels Its Schools." *Wall Street Journal* (April 22, 1998):A22.

SHUPE, ANSON. *In the Name of All That's Holy: A Theory of Clergy Malfeasance.* Westport, Conn.: Praeger, 1995.

SHUPE, ANSON, WILLIAM A. STACEY, and LONNIE R. HAZLEWOOD. *Violent Men, Violent Couples: The Dynamics of Domestic Violence.* Lexington, Mass.: Lexington Books, 1987.

SIDEL, RUTH, and VICTOR W. SIDEL. *A Healthy State: An International Perspective on the Crisis in United States Medical Care.* Rev. ed. New York: Pantheon Books, 1982a.

———. *The Health Care of China.* Boston: Beacon Press, 1982b.

SILVERBERG, ROBERT. "The Greenhouse Effect: Apocalypse Now or Chicken Little?" *Omni* (July 1991):50–54.

SIMMEL, GEORG. *The Sociology of Georg Simmel.* Kurt Wolff, ed. New York: Free Press, 1950:118–69; orig. 1902.

SIMON, JULIAN. *The Ultimate Resource.* Princeton, N.J.: Princeton University Press, 1981.

———. "More People, Greater Wealth, More Resources, Healthier Environment." In Theodore D. Goldfarb, ed., *Taking Sides: Clashing Views on Controversial Environmental Issues.* 6th ed. Guilford, Conn.: The Dushkin Publishing Group, 1995.

SIMONS, CAROL. "Japan's *Kyoiku* Mamas." In John J. Macionis and Nijole V. Benokraitis, eds., *Seeing Ourselves: Classic, Contemporary, and Cross-Cultural Readings in Sociology.* Englewood Cliffs, N.J.: Prentice Hall, 1989:281–86.

SIMONS, MARLISE. "The Price of Modernization: The Case of Brazil's Kaiapo Indians." In John J. Macionis and Nijole V. Benokraitis, eds., *Seeing Ourselves: Classic, Contemporary, and Cross-Cultural Readings in Sociology.* 5th ed. Upper Saddle River, N.J.: Prentice Hall, 2001:496–502.

SIMPSON, GEORGE EATON, and J. MILTON YINGER. *Racial and Cultural Minorities: An Analysis of Prejudice and Discrimination.* 4th ed. New York: Harper & Row, 1972.

SINGER, JEROME L., and DOROTHY G. SINGER. "Psychologists Look at Television: Cognitive, Developmental, Personality, and Social Policy Implications." *American Psychologist.* Vol. 38, No. 7 (July 1983):826–34.

SIPES, RICHARD G. "War, Sports and Aggression: An Empirical Test of Two Rival Theories." *American Anthropologist.* Vol. 75, No. 1 (January 1973):64–86.

SIVARD, RUTH LEGER. *World Military and Social Expenditures, 1987–88.* 12th ed. Washington, D.C.: World Priorities, 1988.

SIZER, THEODORE R. *Horace's Compromise: The Dilemma of the American High School.* Boston: Houghton Mifflin, 1984.

SKOCPOL, THEDA. *States and Social Revolutions: A Comparative Analysis of France, Russia, and China.* Cambridge: Cambridge University Press, 1979.

SMAIL, J. KENNETH. "Beyond Population Stabilization: The Case for Dramatically Reducing Global Human Numbers." Roundtable: World Population Policy commentary and responses. *Politics and the Life Sciences.* Vol. 16, No. 2 (September 1997):183–236.

SMALL BUSINESS ADMINISTRATION. News release on census data for women-owned businesses. January 1996.

———. *The Facts about Small Business 1999.* U.S. Small Business Administration, Office of Advocacy. [Online] Available http://www.sba.gov/ADVO/stats/facts99.pdf, February 13, 2001.

SMITH, ADAM. *An Inquiry Into the Nature and Causes of the Wealth of Nations.* New York: The Modern Library, 1937; orig. 1776.

SMITH, DOUGLAS A. "Police Response to Interpersonal Violence: Defining the Parameters of Legal Control." *Social Forces.* Vol. 65, No. 3 (March 1987):767–82.

SMITH, DOUGLAS A., and PATRICK R. GARTIN. "Specifying Specific Deterrence: The Influence of Arrest on Future Criminal Activity." *American Sociological Review.* Vol. 54, No. 1 (February 1989):94–105.

SMITH, DOUGLAS A., and CHRISTY A. VISHER. "Street-Level Justice: Situational Determinants of Police Arrest Decisions." *Social Problems.* Vol. 29, No. 2 (December 1981):167–77.

SMITH, EARL, and WILBERT M. LEONARD II. "Twenty-Five Years of Stacking Research in Major League Baseball: An Attempt at Explaining this Re-Occurring Phenomenon." *Sociological Focus.* Vol. 30, No. 4 (October 1997):321–31.

SMITH, ROBERT B. "Health Care Reform Now." *Society.* Vol. 30, No. 3 (March-April 1993):56–65.

SMITH, TOM W. Research results reported in "Anti-Semitism Decreases But Persists." *Society.* Vol. 33, No. 3 (March/April 1996):2.

SMITH-LOVIN, LYNN, and CHARLES BRODY. "Interruptions in Group Discussions: The Effects of Gender and Group Composition." *American Journal of Sociology.* Vol. 54, No. 3 (June 1989):424–35.

SMOLOWE, JILL. "When Violence Hits Home." *Time.* Vol. 144, No. 1 (July 4, 1994):18–25.

SNELL, MARILYN BERLIN. "The Purge of Nurture." *New Perspectives Quarterly.* Vol. 7, No. 1 (Winter 1990):1–2.

SNOW, DAVID A., E. BURKE ROCHFORD, JR., STEVEN K. WORDEN, and ROBERT D. BENFORD. "Frame Alignment Processes, Micromobilization, and Movement Participation." *American Sociological Review.* Vol. 51, No. 4 (August 1986):464–81.

SOUTH, SCOTT J., and KIM L. LLOYD. "Spousal Alternatives and Marital Dissolution." *American Sociological Review.* Vol. 60, No. 1 (February 1995):21–35.

SOUTH, SCOTT J., and STEVEN F. MESSNER. "Structural Determinants of Intergroup Association: Interracial Marriage and Crime." *American Journal of Sociology.* Vol. 91, No. 6 (May 1986):1409–30.

SOWELL, THOMAS. *Ethnic America*. New York: Basic Books, 1981.
———. *Race and Culture*. New York: Basic Books, 1994.
———. "Ethnicity and IQ." In Steven Fraser, ed., *The Bell Curve Wars: Race, Intelligence and the Future of America*. New York: Basic Books, 1995:70–79.

SPATES, JAMES L. "Counterculture and Dominant Culture Values: A Cross-National Analysis of the Underground Press and Dominant Culture Magazines." *American Sociological Review*. Vol. 41, No. 5 (October 1976):868–83.
———. "The Sociology of Values." In Ralph Turner, ed., *Annual Review of Sociology*. Vol. 9. Palo Alto, Calif.: Annual Reviews, 1983:27–49.

SPATES, JAMES L., and H. WESLEY PERKINS. "American and English Student Values." *Comparative Social Research*. Vol. 5. Greenwich, Conn.: JAI Press, 1982:245–68.

SPECTER, MICHAEL. "Plunging Life Expectancy Puzzles Russia." *New York Times* (August 2, 1995):A1, A2.
———. "Deep in the Russian Soul, a Lethal Darkness." *New York Times* (June 8, 1997a): section 4, pp. 1, 5.
———. "Moscow on the Make." *New York Times Magazine* (June 1, 1997b):48–55, 72, 75, 80, 84.

SPEER, JAMES A. "The New Christian Right and Its Parent Company: A Study in Political Contrasts." In David G. Bromley and Anson Shupe, eds., *New Christian Politics*. Macon, Ga.: Mercer University Press, 1984:19–40.

SPEER, TIBBETT L. "Are College Costs Cutting Enrollment?" *American Demographics*. Vol. 16, No. 11 (November 1994):9–10.
———. "A Nation of Students." *American Demographics*. Vol. 48, No. 8 (August 1996):32–39.

SPEIER, HANS. "Wit and Politics: An Essay on Laughter and Power." Ed. and trans. by Robert Jackall. *American Journal of Sociology*. Vol. 103, No. 5 (March 1998):1352–1401.

SPENCER, MARTIN E. "Multiculturalism, 'Political Correctness,' and the Politics of Identity." *Sociological Forum*. Vol. 9, No. 4 (December 1994):547–67.

SPITZER, STEVEN. "Toward a Marxian Theory of Deviance." In Delos H. Kelly, ed., *Criminal Behavior: Readings in Criminology*. New York: St. Martin's Press, 1980:175–91.

STACEY, JUDITH. *Patriarchy and Socialist Revolution in China*. Berkeley: University of California Press, 1983.
———. *Brave New Families: Stories of Domestic Upheaval in Late Twentieth-Century America*. New York: Basic Books, 1990.
———. "Good Riddance to 'The Family': A Response to David Popenoe." *Journal of Marriage and the Family*. Vol. 55, No. 3 (August 1993):545–47.

STACK, CAROL B. *All Our Kin: Strategies for Survival in a Black Community*. New York: Harper & Row, 1975.

STAGGENBORG, SUZANNE. "Social Movement Communities and Cycles of Protest: The Emergence and Maintenance of a Local Women's Movement." *Social Problems*. Vol. 45, No. 2 (May 1998):180–204.

STAHURA, JOHN M. "Suburban Development, Black Suburbanization and the Black Civil Rights Movement since World War II." *American Sociological Review*. Vol. 51, No. 1 (February 1986):131–44.

STANLEY, LIZ, ed. *Feminist Praxis: Research, Theory, and Epistemology in Feminist Sociology*. London: Routledge & Kegan Paul, 1990.

STAPINSKI, HELENE. "Let's Talk Dirty." *American Demographics*. Vol. 20, No. 11 (November 1998):50–56.

STARK, RODNEY. *Sociology*. Belmont, Calif.: Wadsworth, 1985.

STARK, RODNEY, and WILLIAM SIMS BAINBRIDGE. "Of Churches, Sects, and Cults: Preliminary Concepts for a Theory of Religious Movements." *Journal for the Scientific Study of Religion*. Vol. 18, No. 2 (June 1979):117–31.
———. "Secularization and Cult Formation in the Jazz Age." *Journal for the Scientific Study of Religion*. Vol. 20, No. 4 (December 1981):360–73.

STARK, RODNEY, and CHARLES Y. GLOCK. *American Piety: The Nature of Religious Commitment*. Berkeley: University of California Press, 1968.

STARR, PAUL. *The Social Transformation of American Medicine*. New York: Basic Books, 1982.

STEELE, SHELBY. *The Content of Our Character: A New Vision of Race in America*. New York: St. Martin's Press, 1990.

STEIN, MAURICE R. *The Eclipse of Community: An Interpretation of American Studies*. Princeton, N.J.: Princeton University Press, 1972.

STEINBERG, LAURENCE. "Failure outside the Classroom." *Wall Street Journal* (July 11, 1996):A14.

STEPHENS, JOHN D. *The Transition from Capitalism to Socialism*. Urbana: University of Illinois Press, 1986.

STERN, LARRY. Personal communication, 1998.

STERNLIEB, GEORGE, and JAMES W. HUGHES. "The Uncertain Future of the Central City." *Urban Affairs Quarterly*. Vol. 18, No. 4 (June 1983):455–72.

STIER, HAYA. "Continuity and Change in Women's Occupations following First Childbirth." *Social Science Quarterly*. Vol. 77, No. 1 (March 1996):60–75.

STODGHILL, RON, II. "Where'd You Learn That?" *Time*. Vol. 151, No. 23 (1998).

STOHL, MICHAEL, and GEORGE A. LOPEZ. *The State as Terrorist: The Dynamics of Government Violence and Repression*. Westport, Conn.: Greenwood Press, 1984.

STONE, PAMELA. "Ghettoized and Marginalized: The Coverage of Racial and Ethnic Groups in Introductory Sociology Texts." *Teaching Sociology*. Vol. 24, No. 4 (October 1996):356–63.

STOUFFER, SAMUEL A., et al. *The American Soldier: Adjustment during Army Life*. Princeton, N.J.: Princeton University Press, 1949.

STRAUS, MURRAY A., and RICHARD J. GELLES. "Societal Change and Change in Family Violence from 1975 to 1985 as Revealed by Two National Surveys." *Journal of Marriage and the Family*. Vol. 48, No. 4 (August 1986):465–79.

SUMNER, WILLIAM GRAHAM. *Folkways*. New York: Dover, 1959; orig. 1906.

SUN, LENA H. "WWII's Forgotten Internees Await Apology." *The Washington Post* (March 9, 1998):A1, A5, A6.

SUNG, BETTY LEE. *Mountains of Gold: The Story of the Chinese in America*. New York: Macmillan, 1967.

SUTHERLAND, EDWIN H. "White Collar Criminality." *American Sociological Review*. Vol. 5, No. 1 (February 1940):1–12.

SUTHERLAND, EDWIN H., and DONALD R. CRESSEY. *Criminology*. 10th ed. Philadelphia: J.B. Lippincott, 1978.

SWARTZ, STEVE. "Why Michael Milken Stands to Qualify for Guinness Book." *Wall Street Journal*. Vol. LXX, No. 117 (March 31, 1989):1, 4.

SZASZ, THOMAS S. *The Manufacturer of Madness: A Comparative Study of the Inquisition and the Mental Health Movement*. New York: Dell, 1961.
———. *The Myth of Mental Illness: Foundations of a Theory of Personal Conduct*. New York: Harper & Row, 1970; orig. 1961.
———. "Mental Illness Is Still a Myth." *Society*. Vol. 31, No. 4 (May-June 1994):34–39.
———. "Idleness and Lawlessness in the Therapeutic State." *Society*. Vol. 32, No. 4 (May-June 1995):30–35.

TAJFEL, HENRI. "Social Psychology of Intergroup Relations." *Annual Review of Psychology*. Palo Alto, Calif.: Annual Reviews, 1982:1–39.

TANBER, GEORGE J. "Freed from Death Row." *Toledo Blade* (November 22, 1998):B1, B2.

TANNAHILL, REAY. *Sex in History*. Scarborough House Publishers, 1992.

TANNEN, DEBORAH. *You Just Don't Understand: Women and Men in Conversation*. New York: Wm. Morrow, 1990.
———. *Talking from 9 to 5: How Women's and Men's Conversational Styles Affect Who Gets Heard, Who Gets Credit, and What Gets Done at Work*. New York: Wm. Morrow, 1994.

TANNENBAUM, FRANK. *Slave and Citizen: The Negro in the Americas*. New York: Vintage Books, 1946.

TAVRIS, CAROL, and SUSAN SADD. *The Redbook Report on Female Sexuality*. New York: Delacorte Press, 1977.

TAX FOUNDATION. [Online] Available http://www.taxfoundation.org, March 15, 2001.

TAYLOR, FREDERICK WINSLOW. *The Principles of Scientific Management*. New York: Harper & Brothers, 1911.

THIRUNARAYANAPURAM, DESIKAN. "Population Explosion Is Far from Over." *Popline*. Vol. 20 (January-February, 1998):1, 4.

THOMAS, EVAN, JOHN BARRY, and MELINDA LIU. "Ground Zero." *Newsweek* (May 25, 1998):28–32A.

THOMAS, PAULETTE. "Success at a Huge Personal Cost." *Wall Street Journal* (July 26, 1995):B1, B6.

THOMAS, PIRI. *Down These Mean Streets*. New York: Signet, 1967.

THOMAS, W. I. "The Relation of Research to the Social Process." In Morris Janowitz, ed., *W. I. Thomas on Social Organization and Social Personality*. Chicago: University of Chicago Press, 1966:289–305; orig. 1931.

———. *The Unadjusted Girl.* New York: Harper & Row, 1967:42; orig. 1923.

THOMMA, STEVEN. "Christian Coalition Demands Action from GOP." *Philadelphia Inquirer* (September 14, 1997):A2.

THOMPSON, DICK. "Gene Maverick." *Time.* Vol. 153, No. 1 (January 11, 1999):54–55.

THOMPSON, LARRY. "Fertility with Less Fuss." *Time.* Vol. 144, No. 20 (November 14, 1994):79.

THORLINDSSON, THOROLFUR, and THORODDUR BJARNASON. "Modeling Durkheim on the Micro Level: A Study of Youth Suicidality." *American Sociological Review.* Vol. 63, No. 1 (February 1998):94–110.

THORNBERRY, TERRANCE, and MARGARET FARNSWORTH. "Social Correlates of Criminal Involvement: Further Evidence on the Relationship between Social Status and Criminal Behavior." *American Sociological Review.* Vol. 47, No. 4 (August 1982):505–18.

THORNE, BARRIE, CHERIS KRAMARAE, and NANCY HENLEY, eds. *Language, Gender and Society.* Rowley, Mass.: Newbury House, 1983.

THORNTON, ARLAND. "Changing Attitudes toward Separation and Divorce: Causes and Consequences." *American Journal of Sociology.* Vol. 90, No. 4 (January 1985):856–72.

THORNTON, ARLAND, WILLIAM G. AXINN, and DANIEL H. HILL. "Reciprocal Effects of Religiosity, Cohabitation, and Marriage." *American Journal of Sociology.* Vol. 98, No. 3 (November 1992):628–51.

THUROW, LESTER C. "A Surge in Inequality." *Scientific American.* Vol. 256, No. 5 (May 1987):30–37.

TILLY, CHARLES. "Does Modernization Breed Revolution?" In Jack A. Goldstone, ed., *Revolutions: Theoretical, Comparative, and Historical Studies.* New York: Harcourt Brace Jovanovich, 1986:47–57.

Time Almanac 2001. Boston: Information Please, 2000.

TITTLE, CHARLES R., and WAYNE J. VILLEMEZ. "Social Class and Criminality." *Social Forces.* Vol. 56, No. 22 (December 1977):474–502.

TITTLE, CHARLES R., WAYNE J. VILLEMEZ, and DOUGLAS A. SMITH. "The Myth of Social Class and Criminality: An Empirical Assessment of the Empirical Evidence." *American Sociological Review.* Vol. 43, No. 5 (October 1978):643–56.

TOCH, THOMAS. "The New Educational Bazaar." *U.S. News & World Report* (April 27, 1998):35–45.

TOCQUEVILLE, ALEXIS DE. *The Old Regime and the French Revolution.* Stuart Gilbert, trans. Garden City, N.Y.: Anchor/Doubleday Books, 1955; orig. 1856.

TOLSON, JAY. "The Trouble with Elites." *The Wilson Quarterly.* Vol. XIX, No. 1 (Winter 1995):6–8.

TÖNNIES, FERDINAND. *Community and Society (Gemeinschaft und Gesellschaft).* New York: Harper & Row, 1963; orig. 1887.

TOWNSEND, BICKLEY. "Room at the Top for Women." *American Demographics.* Vol. 18, No. 7 (July 1996):28–37.

TREAS, JUDITH. "Older Americans in the 1990s and Beyond." *Population Bulletin.* Vol. 50, No. 2 (May 1995). Washington, D.C.: Population Reference Bureau.

TRENT, KATHERINE. "Family Context and Adolescents' Expectations about Marriage, Fertility, and Nonmarital Childbearing." *Social Science Quarterly.* Vol. 75, No 2 (June 1994):319–39.

TRISCHITTA, LINDA. "New Day of Civil Unions Dawns." *Albany Times Union* (July 2, 2000):A1, A12.

TROELTSCH, ERNST. *The Social Teaching of the Christian Churches.* New York: Macmillan, 1931.

TROIDEN, RICHARD R. *Gay and Lesbian Identity: A Sociological Analysis.* Dix Hills, N.Y.: General Hall, 1988.

TUMIN, MELVIN M. "Some Principles of Stratification: A Critical Analysis." *American Sociological Review.* Vol. 18, No. 4 (August 1953):387–94.

———. *Social Stratification: The Forms and Functions of Inequality.* 2d ed. Englewood Cliffs, N.J.: Prentice Hall, 1985.

TYLER, S. LYMAN. *A History of Indian Policy.* Washington, D.C.: United States Department of the Interior, Bureau of Indian Affairs, 1973.

UNITED NATIONS DEVELOPMENT PROGRAMME. *Human Development Report 1990.* New York: Oxford University Press, 1990.

———. *Human Development Report 1994.* New York: Oxford University Press, 1994.

———. *Human Development Report 1995.* New York: Oxford University Press, 1995.

———. *Human Development Report 1996.* New York: Oxford University Press, 1996.

———. *Human Development Report 1997.* New York: Oxford University Press, 1997.

———. *Human Development Report 1998.* New York: Oxford University Press, 1998.

———. *Human Development Report 1999.* New York: Oxford University Press, 1999.

———. *Human Development Report 1999.* New York: Oxford University Press, 2000.

UNNEVER, JAMES D., CHARLES E. FRAZIER, and JOHN C. HENRETTA. "Race Differences in Criminal Sentencing." *The Sociological Quarterly.* Vol. 21, No. 2 (Spring 1980):197–205.

UNRUH, JOHN D., JR. *The Plains Across.* Urbana: University of Illinois Press, 1979.

U.S. BUREAU OF ECONOMIC ANALYSIS. *Foreign Direct Investment in the United States. Country Detail for Selected Items.* Washington, D.C.: The Bureau, 1999.

U.S. BUREAU OF JUSTICE STATISTICS. *Violence against Women.* Washington, D.C.: U.S. Government Printing Office, 1994.

———. *Violence by Intimates.* Washington, D.C.: The Bureau, 1998.

———. *Capital Punishment 1999.* Washington, D.C.: The Bureau, 2000.

———. *Criminal Victimization 1999: Changes 1998–99 with Trends 1993–99.* Washington, D.C.: The Bureau, 2000.

———. *Sourcebook of Criminal Justice Statistics 1999.* Washington, D.C.: The Bureau, 2000.

U.S. CENSUS BUREAU. *Asset Ownership of Households: 1993.* Current Population Reports, Series P-70, No. 47. Washington, D.C.: U.S. Government Printing Office, 1995.

———. *Household and Family Characteristics: March 1994.* Current Population Reports, Series P-20, No. 483, Washington, D.C.: U.S. Government Printing Office, 1995.

———. *Income, Poverty, and Valuation of Noncash Benefits: 1993.* Current Population Reports, Series P-60, No. 188. Washington, D.C.: U.S. Government Printing Office, 1995.

———. *Marital Status and Living Arrangements:* March 1995. PPL-52. Washington, D.C.: U.C. Government Printing Office, 1996.

———. *School Enrollment—Social and Economic Characteristics of Students: October 1995 (Update).* PPL-55: The Bureau, 1997.

———. *Household and Family Characteristics: March 1998 (Update).* Current Population Reports, P20-515. Washington, D.C.: U.S. Government Printing Office, 1998.

———. *Statistical Abstract of the United States 1998.* Washington, D.C.: U.S. Government Printing Office, 1998.

———. *Household and Family Characteristics: March 1998 (Update).* Washington, D.C.: The Bureau, 1999.

———. *Money Income in the United States 1998.* P60-206. Washington, D.C.: U.S. Government Printing Office, 1999.

———. *School Enrollment—Social and Economic Characteristics of Students: October 1998 (Update).* Current Population Report, P20-521. Washington, D.C.: The Bureau, 1999.

———. *Statistical Abstract of the United States 1999.* Washington, D.C.: U.S. Government Printing Office, 1999.

———. *Educational Attainment in the United States—March 2000 (Update).* Current Population Reports, P20-536. Washington, D.C.: U.S. Government Printing Office, 2000.

———. *Health Insurance Coverage 1999.* (P60–211). Washington, D.C.: The Bureau, 2000.

———. Historical Income Tables—Families. Table F-3. Mean Income Received by Each Fifth and Top 5 Percent of Families (All Races): 1966 to 1999. [Online] Available http://www.census.gov/hhes/income/histinc/f03.html, December 6, 2000.

———. *Housing Vacancies and Home Ownership: Annual Statistics: 1999.* Table 20. [Online] Available http://www.census.gov/hhes/www/housing/hvs/annual99/ann99t20.html, October 30, 2000.

———. *International Data Base.* [Online] Available http://www.census.gov/ipc/www/idbprint.html, February 24, 2000.

———. Metropolitan Area Population Estimates for July 1, 1999, and Population Change for April 1, 1990, to July 1, 1999. Washington, D.C.: The Bureau, 2000.

———. *Money Income in the United States 1999.* Current Population Reports P60–209. Washington, D.C.: U.S. Government Printing Office, 2000.

——. *Poverty in the United States 1999*. Current Population Reports P60–210. Washington, D.C.: U.S. Government Printing Office, 2000.

——. Projections of the Total Resident Population by 5-Year Age Groups and Sex with Special Age Categories: Middle Series. [Online] Available http://www.census.gov/population/projections/nation/summary/np-t3-?.pdf, February 24, 2000.

——. *Statistical Abstract of the United States 2000*. Washington, D.C.: U.S. Government Printing Office, 2000.

——. Table F-1. Income Limits for Each Fifth and Top 5 Percent of Families (All Races): 1947 to 1999. [Online] Available http://www.census.gov/hhes/income/histinc/f01.html, December 6, 2000.

——. Table F-2. Share of Aggregate Income Received by Each Fifth and Top 5 Percent of Families (All Races): 1947 to 1999. [Online] Available http://www.census.gov/hhes/income/histinc/f02.html, December 6, 2000.

——. Table F-7. Type of Family (All Races) by Median and Mean Income: 1947 to 1999. [Online] Available http://www.census.gov/hhes/income/histinc/f07.html, December 6, 2000.

——. Table P-31. Years of School Completed: Workers 18 Years Old and Over by Mean Earnings, Age, and Sex: 1974 to 1979. [Online] Available http://www.census.gov/hhes/income/histinc/p31.html, December 6, 2000.

——. Table P-28. Years of School Completed: Workers 18 Years Old and Over by Mean Earnings, Age, and Sex: 1991 to 1998. [Online] Available http://www.census.gov/hhes/income/histinc/p28.html, December 6, 2000.

——. Historical Income Tables—People, Table P-10. [Online] Available http://www.census.gov/hhes/income/histinc/p10.html, March 1, 2001.

——. Resident Population Estimates of the United States by Sex, Race, and Hispanic Origin: April 1, 1990, to July 1, 1999, with Short-term Projections to November 1, 2000. [Online] Available http://www.census.gov/population/estimates/nation/intfile3-1.txt, January 2, 2001.

U.S. CENSUS OFFICE. *Census of the United States (1900)*. Vol. II: Population. Washington, D.C.: The Office, 1902.

U.S. CENTERS FOR DISEASE CONTROL AND PREVENTION. *HIV/AIDS Surveillance Report*. Vol. 12, No. 1 (Midyear 2000).

——. *Morbidity and Mortality Weekly Report*. Vol. 49, No. 43 (November 3, 2000):978–82. [Online] Available http://www.cdc.gov/mmwr/preview/mmwrhtml/mm4943a2.htm

——. *Sexually Transmitted Disease Surveillance 1999*. Atlanta, Ga.: The Centers, 2000.

U.S. DEPARTMENT OF HEALTH AND HUMAN SERVICES. Administration for Children and Families. Temporary Assistance for Needy Families (TANF) Program; Third Annual Report to Congress, August 2000. Washington, D.C.: The Administration, 2000.

U.S. DEPARTMENT OF LABOR. Bureau of Labor Statistics. *Employment Projections*. Table 5. Civilian Labor Force by Sex, Age, Race, and Hispanic Origin, 1978, 1988, 1998, and Projected 2008. Washington, D.C.: The Bureau, 1999.

——. *International Comparisons of Hourly Compensation Costs for Production Workers in Manufacturing, 1975–1999*. Supplementary tables for BLS News Release USDL 00-254, September 7, 2000. Washington, D.C.: The Bureau, 2000.

——. *Employment and Earnings*. Vol. 48, No. 1 (January 2001).

U.S. DEPARTMENT OF STATE. Bureau of Arms Control. *World Military Expenditures and Arms Transfers 1998*. Washington, D.C.: The Bureau, 1999.

——. *Patterns of Global Terrorism 1999*. Washington, D.C.: The Department, 2000.

USEEM, BERT. "Disorganization and the New Mexico Prison Riot of 1980." *American Sociological Review*. Vol. 50, No. 5 (October 1985):677–88.

U.S. EQUAL EMPLOYMENT OPPORTUNITY COMMISSION. *Job Patterns for Minorities and Women in Private Industry, 1996*. Washington, D.C.: The Commission, 1997.

——. *Job Patterns for Minorities and Women in Private Industry 1997*. Washington, D.C.: The Commission, 1998.

——. *Job Patterns for Minorities and Women in Private Industry, 1998*. Washington, D.C.: The Commission, 2000.

——. Table 1—Occupational Employment in Private Industry by Race/Ethnic Group/Sex, United States, 1998. [Online] Available http://www.eeoc.gov/stats/jobpat/tables-1.html, October 18, 2000.

U.S. FEDERAL BUREAU OF INVESTIGATION. *Crime in the United States 1999*. Washington, D.C.: The Bureau, 2000.

U.S. FEDERAL ELECTION COMMISSION. "18-Month Summary on Political Action Committees." News release, September 27, 2000. [Online] Available http://www.fec.gov

U.S. HOUSE OF REPRESENTATIVES. "Street Children: A Global Disgrace." Hearing on November 7, 1991. Washington, D.C.: U.S. Government Printing Office, 1992.

U.S. IMMIGRATION AND NATURALIZATION SERVICE. Table 3: Immigrants Admitted by Region and Selected Country of Birth, Fiscal Years 1984–94. Fax received from INS January 1996.

——. *Legal Immigration, Fiscal Year 1998*. Washington, D.C.: The Service, 1999.

U.S. INTERNAL REVENUE SERVICE. *Statistics of Income Bulletin* (Spring 1993).

U.S. NATIONAL CENTER FOR EDUCATION STATISTICS. *Dropout Rates in the United States: 1997*. Washington, D.C.: The Center, 1999.

——. *Digest of Education Statistics 2000*. Washington, D.C.: U.S. Government Printing Office, 2001.

U.S. NATIONAL CENTER FOR HEALTH STATISTICS. *National Vital Statistics Report*. Vol. 47, No. 4 (October 7, 1998).

——. *Current Estimates from the National Health Interview Survey 1996*. Series 10, No. 200. Hyattsville, Md.: The Center, 1999.

——. *National Vital Statistics Report*. Vol. 47, No. 25 (October 5, 1999).

——. *National Vital Statistics Report*. Vol. 48, No. 11 (July 24, 2000). [Online] Available http://www.cdc.gov/nchs/data/nvs48_11.pdf

——. "Nonmarital Childbearing in the United States, 1940–99." *National Vital Statistics Report*. Vol. 48, No. 16 (revised) (October 18, 2000). [Online] Available http://www.cdc.gov/nchs/data/nvs48_16.pdf

——. "Births, Marriages, Divorces, and Deaths: Provisional Data for November 1999." *National Vital Statistics Report*. Vol. 48, No. 17 (October 31, 2000).

——. *National Vital Statistics Report*. Vol. 48, No. 18 (February 7, 2001). [Online] Available http://www.cdc.gov/nchs/data/nvsr/nvsr48/nvs48_18.pdf, February 6, 2001.

U.S. National Clearinghouse on Child Abuse and Neglect. Child abuse and neglect national statistics (April 2000). Washington, D.C.: The Clearinghouse, 2000.

VALDEZ, A. "In the Hood: Street Gangs Discover White-Collar Crime." *Police*. Vol. 21, No. 5 (May 1997):49–50, 56.

VALLAS, STEPHEN P., and JOHN P. BECK. "The Transformation of Work Revisited: The Limits of Flexibility in American Manufacturing." *Social Problems*. Vol. 43, No. 3 (August 1996):339–61.

VAN BIEMA, DAVID. "Parents Who Kill." *Time*. Vol. 144, No. 20 (November 14, 1994):50–51.

——. "Spiriting Prayer into School." *Time*. Vol. 152, No. 20 (April 27, 1998):38–41.

——. "A Surge of Teen Spirit." *Time*. Vol. 153, No. 20 (May 31, 1999):58–59.

VAN DEN HAAG, ERNEST, and JOHN P. CONRAD. *The Death Penalty: A Debate*. New York: Plenum Press, 1983.

VAUGHAN, MARY KAY. "Multinational Corporations: The World as a Company Town." In Ahamed Idris-Soven et al., eds., *The World as a Company Town: Multinational Corporations and Social Change*. The Hague: Mouton Publishers, 1978:15–35.

VAYDA, EUGENE, and RAISA B. DEBER. "The Canadian Health Care System: An Overview." *Social Science and Medicine*. Vol. 18, No. 3 (1984):191–97.

VINOVSKIS, MARIS A. "Have Social Historians Lost the Civil War? Some Preliminary Demographic Speculations." *Journal of American History*. Vol. 76, No. 1 (June 1989):34–58.

VOGEL, EZRA F. *The Four Little Dragons: The Spread of Industrialization in East Asia*. Cambridge, Mass.: Harvard University Press, 1991.

VOGEL, LISE. *Marxism and the Oppression of Women: Toward a Unitary Theory*. New Brunswick, N.J.: Rutgers University Press, 1983.

VOLD, GEORGE B., and THOMAS J. BERNARD. *Theoretical Criminology*. 3d ed. New York: Oxford University Press, 1986.

VON HIRSH, ANDREW. *Past or Future Crimes: Deservedness and Dangerousness in the Sentencing of Criminals*. New Brunswick, N.J.: Rutgers University Press, 1986.

VOYDANOFF, PATRICIA., and BRENDA W. DONNELLY. *Adolescent Sexuality and Pregnancy*. Newbury Park, Calif.: Sage, 1990.

WAITE, LINDA J., GUS W. HAGGSTROM, and DAVID I. KANOUSE. "The Consequences of Parenthood for the Marital Stability of Young Adults." *American Sociological Review*. Vol. 50, No. 6 (December 1985):850–57.

WALDER, ANDREW G. "Career Mobility and the Communist Political Order." *American Sociological Review*. Vol. 60, No. 3 (June 1995):309–28.

WALDFOGEL, JANE. "The Effect of Children on Women's Wages." *American Sociological Review*. Vol. 62, No. 2 (April 1997):209–17.

WALDMAN, STEVEN. "Deadbeat Dads." *Newsweek* (May 4, 1992):46–52.

WALKER, BOB. "Bob Walker's Official New Orleans Area Wedding Guide: Louisiana's Covenant Marriage Law." [Online] Available http://www.acadiacom.net/walker/covenant_marriage.htm, accessed August 13, 1998.

WALKER, KAREN. "'Always There For Me': Friendship Patterns and Expectations among Middle- and Working-Class Men and Women." *Sociological Forum*. Vol. 10, No. 2 (June 1995):273–96.

WALL, THOMAS F. *Medical Ethics: Basic Moral Issues*. Washington, D.C.: University Press of America, 1980.

WALLER, DOUGLAS. "Onward Cyber Soldiers." *Time*. Vol. 146, No. 8 (August 21, 1995):38–44.

WALLERSTEIN, IMMANUEL. *The Modern World-System: Capitalist Agriculture and the Origins of the European World-Economy in the Sixteenth Century*. New York: Academic Press, 1974.

———. *The Capitalist World-Economy*. New York: Cambridge University Press, 1979.

———. "Crises: The World Economy, the Movements, and the Ideologies." In Albert Bergesen, ed., *Crises in the World-System*. Beverly Hills, Calif.: Sage, 1983:21–36.

———. *The Politics of the World Economy: The States, the Movements, and the Civilizations*. Cambridge: Cambridge University Press, 1984.

WALLERSTEIN, JUDITH S., and SANDRA BLAKESLEE. *Second Chances: Men, Women, and Children a Decade after Divorce*. New York: Ticknor & Fields, 1989.

WALLIS, DAVID. "After Cyberoverkill Comes Cyberburnout." *New York Times* (August 4, 1996):43, 46.

WALMSLEY, ROY. *World Prison Population*. 2d ed. United Kingdom Home Office Research, Development, and Statistics Directorate (July 2000).

WALTON, JOHN, and CHARLES RAGIN. "Global and National Sources of Political Protest: Third World Responses to the Debt Crisis." *American Sociological Review*. Vol. 55, No. 6 (December 1990):876–90.

WARNER, R. STEPHEN. "Work in Progress toward a New Paradigm for the Sociological Study of Religion in the United States." *American Journal of Sociology*. Vol. 98, No. 5 (March 1993):1044–93.

WARNER, W. LLOYD, and PAUL S. LUNT. *The Social Life of a Modern Community*. New Haven, Conn.: Yale University Press, 1941.

WARREN, JOHN ROBERT, and ROBERT M. HAUSER. "Social Stratification across Three Generations: New Evidence from the Wisconsin Longitudinal Study." *American Sociological Review*. Vol. 62 (August 1997):561–72.

WASKUL, DENNIS. "Selfhood in the Age of Computer Mediated Symbolic Interaction." Paper presented to the annual meeting of the Southwest Social Science Association, New Orleans, La., March, 1997.

WATERS, MELISSA S., WILL CARRINGTON HEATH, and JOHN KEITH WATSON. "A Positive Model of the Determination of Religious Affiliation." *Social Science Quarterly*. Vol. 76, No. 1 (March 1995):105–23.

WATTENBERG, BEN J. "The Population Explosion Is Over." *New York Times Magazine* (November 23, 1997):60–63.

WEBER, ADNA FERRIN. *The Growth of Cities*. New York: Columbia University Press, 1963; orig. 1899.

WEBER, MAX. *The Protestant Ethic and the Spirit of Capitalism*. New York: Charles Scribner's Sons, 1958; orig. 1904–5.

———. *Economy and Society*. G. Roth and C. Wittich, eds. Berkeley: University of California Press, 1978.

WEBSTER, ANDREW. *Introduction to the Sociology of Development*. London: Macmillan, 1984.

WEBSTER, MURRAY, JR., and STUART J. HYSOM. "Creating Status Characteristics." *American Sociological Review*. Vol. 63, No. 3 (June 1998):351–78.

WEBSTER, PAMELA S., TERRI ORBUCH, and JAMES S. HOUSE. "Effects of Childhood Family Background on Adult Marital Quality and Perceived Stability." *American Journal of Sociology*. Vol. 101, No. 2 (September 1995):404–32.

WEIDENBAUM, MURRAY. "Beyond Handouts." *Across the Board* (April 1991). In Kurt Finsterbusch and George McKenna, eds., *Taking Sides: Clashing Views on Controversial Social Issues*. 8th ed. Guilford, Conn.: Dushkin Publishing Group, 1994.

———. "The Evolving Corporate Board." *Society*. Vol. 32, No. 3 (March/April 1995):9–20.

WEINBERG, GEORGE. *Society and the Healthy Homosexual*. Garden City, N.Y.: Anchor Books, 1973.

WEINER, TIM. "Head of C.I.A. Plans Center to Protect U.S. Cyberspace." *New York Times* (June 26, 1996):B7.

WEINRICH, JAMES D. *Sexual Landscapes: Why We Are What We Are, Why We Love Whom We Love*. New York: Charles Scribner's Sons, 1987.

WEISBERG, D. KELLY. *Children of the Night: A Study of Adolescent Prostitution*. Lexington, Mass.: D.C. Heath, 1985.

WEISBURD, DAVID, STANTON WHEELER, ELIN WARING, and NANCY BODE. *Crimes of the Middle Class: White Collar Defenders in the Courts*. New Haven, Conn.: Yale University Press, 1991.

WEISNER, THOMAS S., and BERNICE T. EIDUSON. "The Children of the '60s as Parents." *Psychology Today* (January 1986):60–66.

WEITZMAN, LENORE J. *The Divorce Revolution: The Unexpected Social and Economic Consequences for Women and Children in America*. New York: Free Press, 1985.

———. "The Economic Consequences of Divorce Are Still Unequal: Comment on Peterson." *American Sociological Review*. Vol. 61, No. 3 (June 1996):537–38.

WELLFORD, CHARLES. "Labeling Theory and Criminology: An Assessment." In Delos H. Kelly, ed., *Criminal Behavior: Readings in Criminology*. New York: St. Martin's Press, 1980:234–47.

WESTERN, BRUCE. "Postwar Unionization in Eighteen Advanced Capitalist Countries." *American Sociological Review*. Vol. 58, No. 2 (April 1993):266–82.

———. "A Comparative Study of Working-Class Disorganization: Union Decline in Eighteen Advanced Capitalist Countries." *American Sociological Review*. Vol. 60, No. 2 (April 1995):179–201.

WHEELIS, ALLEN. *The Quest for Identity*. New York: Norton, 1958.

WHELAN, CHRISTINE B. "No Honeymoon for Covenant Marriage." *Wall Street Journal* (August 17, 1998):A14.

WHITE, JACK E. "I'm Just Who I Am." *Time*. Vol. 149, No. 18 (May 5, 1997):32–36.

WHITE, RALPH, and RONALD LIPPITT. "Leader Behavior and Member Reaction in Three 'Social Climates.'" In Dorwin Cartwright and Alvin Zander, eds., *Group Dynamics*. Evanston, Ill.: Row, Peterson, 1953:586–611.

WHITMAN, DAVID. "Shattering Myths about the Homeless." *U.S. News & World Report* (March 20, 1989):26, 28.

WHORF, BENJAMIN LEE. "The Relation of Habitual Thought and Behavior to Language." In *Language, Thought, and Reality*. Cambridge, Mass.: The Technology Press of MIT/New York: Wiley, 1956:134–59; orig. 1941.

WIARDA, HOWARD J. "Ethnocentrism and Third World Development." *Society*. Vol. 24, No. 6 (September-October 1987):55–64.

WIATROWSKI, MICHAEL A., DAVID B. GRISWOLD, and MARY K. ROBERTS. "Social Control Theory and Delinquency." *American Sociological Review*. Vol. 46, No. 5 (October 1981):525–41.

WIDOM, CATHY SPATZ. "Childhood Sexual Abuse and Its Criminal Consequences." *Society*. Vol. 33, No. 4 (May/June 1996):47–53.

WILCOX, CLYDE. "Race, Gender, and Support for Women in the Military." *Social Science Quarterly*. Vol. 73, No. 2 (June 1992):310–23.

WILES, P. J. D. *Economic Institutions Compared*. New York: Halsted Press, 1977.

WILKINSON, DORIS. "Transforming the Social Order: The Role of the University in Social Change." *Sociological Forum*. Vol. 9, No. 3 (September 1994):325–41.

WILLIAMS, RHYS H., and N. J. DEMERATH, III. "Religion and Political Process in an American City." *American Sociological Review*. Vol. 56, No. 4 (August 1991):417–31.

WILLIAMS, ROBIN M., JR. *American Society: A Sociological Interpretation*. 3d ed. New York: Alfred A. Knopf, 1970.

WILLIAMSON, JEFFREY G., and PETER H. LINDERT. *American Inequality: A Macroeconomic History*. New York: Academic Press, 1980.

WILSON, BARBARA. "National Television Violence Study." Reported by Julia Duin, "Study Finds Cartoon Heroes Initiate Too Much Violence." *Washington Times* (April 17, 1998):A4.

WILSON, EDWARD O. "Biodiversity, Prosperity, and Value." In F. Herbert Bormann and Stephen R. Kellert, eds., *Ecology, Economics, and Ethics: The Broken Circle*. New Haven, Conn.: Yale University Press, 1991:3–10.

WILSON, JAMES Q. "Crime, Race, and Values." *Society*. Vol. 30, No. 1 (November-December 1992):90–93.

WILSON, JAMES Q., and RICHARD J. HERRNSTEIN. *Crime and Human Nature.* New York: Simon and Schuster, 1985.

WILSON, LOGAN. *American Academics Then and Now.* New York: Oxford University Press, 1979.

WILSON, THOMAS C. "Urbanism and Tolerance: A Test of Some Hypotheses Drawn from Wirth and Stouffer." *American Sociological Review.* Vol. 50, No. 1 (February 1985):117–23.

———. "Urbanism and Unconventionality: The Case of Sexual Behavior." *Social Science Quarterly.* Vol. 76, No. 2 (June 1995):346–63.

WILSON, WILLIAM JULIUS. *When Work Disappears: The World of the New Urban Poor.* New York: Alfred A. Knopf, 1996a.

———. "Work." *New York Times Magazine* (August 18, 1996b):26–31, 40, 48, 52, 54.

WINNICK, LOUIS. "America's 'Model Minority'." *Commentary.* Vol. 90, No. 2 (August 1990):22–29.

WINTERS, REBECCA. "Who Needs an M.B.A.?" *Time Select: Business.* Vol. 153, No. 19 (May 17, 1999).

WIRTH, LOUIS. "Urbanism as a Way of Life." *American Journal of Sociology.* Vol. 44, No. 1 (July 1938):1–24.

WITKIN, GORDON. "The Crime Bust." *U.S. News & World Report.* Vol. 124, No. 20 (May 25, 1998):28–40.

WITKIN-LANOIL, GEORGIA. *The Female Stress Syndrome: How to Recognize and Live with It.* New York: Newmarket Press, 1984.

WOLF, DIANE L., ed. *Feminist Dilemma of Fieldwork.* Boulder, Colo.: Westview Press, 1996.

WOLF, NAOMI. *The Beauty Myth: How Images of Beauty Are Used against Women.* New York: William Morrow, 1990.

WOLFGANG, MARVIN E., ROBERT M. FIGLIO, and THORSTEN SELLIN. *Delinquency in a Birth Cohort.* Chicago: University of Chicago Press, 1972.

WOLFGANG, MARVIN E., TERRENCE P. THORNBERRY, and ROBERT M. FIGLIO. *From Boy to Man, From Delinquency to Crime.* Chicago: University of Chicago Press, 1987.

WOLKOMIR, MICHELLE, MICHAEL FUTREAL, ERIC WOODRUM, and THOMAS HOBAN. "Substantive Religious Belief and Environmentalism." *Social Science Quarterly.* Vol. 78, No. 1 (March 1997):96–108.

WONG, BUCK. "Need for Awareness: An Essay on Chinatown, San Francisco." In Amy Tachiki et al., eds., *Roots: An Asian American Reader.* Los Angeles: UCLA Asian American Studies Center, 1971:265–73.

WOOD, PETER B., and MICHELE CHESSER. "Black Stereotyping in a University Population." *Sociological Focus.* Vol. 27, No. 1 (February 1994):17–34.

WOODWARD, KENNETH L. "Feminism and the Churches." *Newsweek.* Vol. 13, No. 7 (February 13, 1989):58–61.

———. "Talking to God." *Newsweek.* Vol. 119, No. 1 (January 6, 1992a):38–44.

THE WORLD BANK. *World Development Report 1993.* New York: Oxford University Press, 1993.

———. *1999 World Development Indicators.* Washington, D.C.: The World Bank, 1999.

———. *World Bank Atlas 2000.* Washington, D.C.: The World Bank, 2000.

———. *World Development Indicators 2000.* Washington, D.C.: The World Bank, 2000.

———. *World Development Report 2000/2001.* Washington, D.C.: The World Bank, 2001.

WORLD HEALTH ORGANIZATION. *Constitution of the World Health Organization.* New York: World Health Organization Interim Commission, 1946.

WORSLEY, PETER. "Models of the World System." In Mike Featherstone, ed., *Global Culture: Nationalism, Globalization, and Modernity.* Newbury Park, Calif.: Sage, 1990:83–95.

WREN, CHRISTOPHER S. "In Soweto-by-the-Sea, Misery Lives on as Apartheid Fades." *New York Times* (June 9, 1991):1, 7.

WRIGHT, ERIK OLIN. "Typologies, Scales, and Class Analysis: A Comment on Halaby and Weakliem." *American Sociological Review.* Vol. 58, No. 1 (February 1993):31–34.

WRIGHT, ERIK OLIN, and BILL MARTIN. "The Transformation of the American Class Structure, 1960–1980." *American Journal of Sociology.* Vol. 93, No. 1 (July 1987):1–29.

WRIGHT, QUINCY. "Causes of War in the Atomic Age." In William M. Evan and Stephen Hilgartner, eds., *The Arms Race and Nuclear War.* Englewood Cliffs, N.J.: Prentice Hall, 1987:7–10.

WRIGHT, RICHARD A. "Curing Doonesbury's Disease—A Prescription for Dialogue in the Classroom." *Quarterly Journal of Ideology.* Vol. 9, No. 4 (1985):3–8.

———. *In Defense of Prisons.* Westport, Conn.: Greenwood Press, 1994.

WRIGHT, ROBERT. "Hyperdemocracy." *Time.* Vol. 145, No. 3 (January 23, 1995):15–21.

———. "Sin in the Global Village." *Time.* Vol. 152, No. 16 (October 19, 1998):130.

WU, LAWRENCE L. "Effects of Family Instability, Income, and Income Instability on the Risk of a Premarital Birth." *American Sociological Review.* Vol. 61, No. 3 (June 1996):386–406.

YANKELOVICH, DANIEL. "How Changes in the Economy Are Reshaping American Values." In Henry J. Aaron, Thomas E. Mann, and Timothy Taylor, eds., *Values and Public Policy.* Washington, D.C.: The Brookings Institution, 1994:20.

YEATTS, DALE E. "Self-Managed Work Teams: Innovation in Progress." *Business and Economic Quarterly* (Fall-Winter 1991):2–6.

———. "Creating the High Performance Self-Managed Work Team: A Review of Theoretical Perspectives." Paper presented at the annual meeting of the Southwest Social Science Association, Dallas, February 1994.

YODER, JAN D., and ROBERT C. NICHOLS. "A Life Perspective: Comparison of Married and Divorced Persons." *Journal of Marriage and the Family.* Vol. 42, No. 2 (May 1980):413–19.

YOELS, WILLIAM C., and JEFFREY MICHAEL CLAIR. "Laughter in the Clinic: Humor in Social Organization." *Symbolic Interaction.* Vol. 18, No. 1 (1995):39–58.

ZACHARY, G. PASCAL. "Not So Fast: Neo-Luddites Say an Unexamined Cyberlife Is a Dangerous One." *Wall Street Journal* (June 16, 1997):R18.

ZHAO, DINGXIN. "Ecologies of Social Movements: Student Mobilization during the 1989 Prodemocracy Movement in Beijing." *American Journal of Sociology.* Vol. 103, No. 6 (May 1998):1493–1529.

ZHAO, DINGXIN. "Ecologies of Social Movements: Student Mobilization during the 1989 Prodemocracy Movement in Beijing." *American Journal of Sociology.* Vol. 103, No. 6 (May 1998):1493–1529.

ZHOU, MIN, and JOHN R. LOGAN. "Returns of Human Capital in Ethnic Enclaves: New York City's Chinatown." *American Sociological Review.* Vol. 54, No. 5 (October 1989):809–20.

ZHOU, XUEGUANG, and LIREN HOU. "Children of the Cultural Revolution: The State and the Life Course in the People's Republic of China." *American Sociological Review.* Vol. 64, No. 1 (February 1999):12–36.

ZICKLIN, G. "Re-Biologizing Sexual Orientation: A Critique." Paper presented at the Annual Meeting of the Society for the Study of Social Problems, Pittsburgh, Penn., 1992.

ZUBOFF, SHOSHANA. "New Worlds of Computer-Mediated Work." *Harvard Business Review.* Vol. 60, No. 5 (September-October 1982):142–52.

PHOTO CREDITS

Dilip Mehta/Contact Press Images Inc., ii.

CHAPTER 1: The Image Bank, xxviii; Caroline Penn/Corbis, 2 (top left); Paul Liebhardt, 2 (top center, bottom left, bottom center, bottom right); Minh-Thu Pham, (top right); Paul W. Liebhardt, 5; Louise Gubb/SABA Press Photos, Inc., 6; The Stapleton Collection/The Bridgeman Art Library International Ltd., 9; Corbis, 10 (left); Brown Brothers, 10 (center, right); © Paul Marcus, *Furnishings*, oil painting on canvas, 64 in. x 48 in. Studio SPM Inc., 12; Emil Bisttram, American (1895-1976), *Domingo Chorus*, 1936, gouache and pencil on paper, 57.8 x 43.5 cm. Christie's Images/The Bridgeman Art Library, 13; Jacob Lawrence, American, b. 1917, *Munich Olympic Games*, Poster, 1972. Courtesy of the artist and Francine Seders Gallery, Seattle. Photo: Spike Mafford, 16; Diego Rivera, Mexican (1886-1957), *The Creation of the Earth*, page from *Popol Vuh*, watercolor on paper. Museo Casa Diego Rivera (INBA), Guanajuato, Mexico. Index/The Bridgeman Art Library. © 2001 Banco de Mexico Diego Rivera Museum Trust, 18; Tony Freeman/PhotoEdit, 21;

CYBER.SCOPE I: Eugene Fisher/Eugene Fisher Photography Worldwide, 28; General Electric Company, 29.

CHAPTER 2: Still Pictures/Peter Arnold, Inc., 32; Paul W. Liebhardt, 34 (top left, middle left); Carlos Humberto/TDC/Contact/Corbis/Stock Market, 34 (top center); Doranne Jacobson/International Images, 34 (top right, bottom left); David Austen/Stock Boston, 34 (middle center); J. Du Boisberran/The Image Bank, 34 (middle right); Jack Fields/Photo Researchers, Inc., 34 (bottom right); Dimitri Lovetsky/AP/Wide World Photos, 35; G. Humer/Liaison Agency, Inc., 36; Jeff Greenberg/Index Stock Imagery, Inc., 37 (left); Pedrick/The Image Works, 37 (center); CLEO Photo/Jeroboam, Inc., 37 (right); *Mrs. Picasso Dusts the Mantelpiece*, from *Great Housewives of Art* by Sally Swain, copyright ©1988, 1989 by Sally Swain. Used by permission of Viking Penguin, a division of Penguin Putnam Inc., 40; Patrick Bordes/Photo Researchers, Inc., 43 (top left); James R. Holland/Stock Boston, 43 (top right); Paul W. Liebhardt, 43 (middle left); Rosenfeld Images Ltd./Science Photo Library/Photo Researchers, Inc., 43 (middle right); Cameramann/The Image Works, 43 (bottom right); John Marshall Mantel/Corbis, 45; J.P. Laffont/Corbis/Sygma, 50; Jesse Levine, Laguna Sales, Palo Alto, 51; Photographer Bill Coleman, www.amishphoto.com (814) 238-8495 #174, *One Day's Work*, 53; Copyright 1952, 1980 Ruth Orkin, 55.

CHAPTER 3: Telegraph Colour Library/FPG International LLC, 60; Ted Horowitz/Corbis/Stock Market, 62 (left); Henley & Savage/Corbis/Stock Market, 62 (center); Tom Pollak/Monkmeyer Press, 62 (right); London International Gallery of Children's Art, 63; Salvador Dali (Spanish, 1904-1989), *Soft Construction with Boiled Beans (Premonition of Civil War)*, 1936, oil on canvas, 39 5/16 x 39 3/8 in. 50-134-41. Philadelphia Museum of Art: The Louise and Walter Arensberg Collection. © 2002 Kingdom of Spain, Gala-Salvador Dali Foundation/Artists Rights Society (ARS), New York, 64; Laura Dwight/PhotoEdit, 65; Rimma Gerlovina and Valeriy Gerlovin, *Manyness*, 1990, © the artists, New City, NY, 67; Henry Ossawa Tanner, *The Banjo Lesson*, 1893, oil on canvas. Hampton University Museum, Hampton, Virginia, 69; Everett Collection, Inc., 73; Mary Ellen Mark, 74; Laima Druskis/Pearson Education/PH College, 77; Elliott Erwitt/Magnum Photos, Inc., 78 (left); AP/Wide World Photos, 78 (right); Chris Rainier/Corbis, 79; Eastcott/Momatiuk/Woodfin Camp & Associates, 80.

CHAPTER 4: Stone, 84; Jim Anderson/Woodfin Camp & Associates, 86; AP/Wide World Photos, 87; Dimaggio/Kalish/Corbis/Stock Market, 91; Alexander Nemenov/Agence France-Presse, 92; David Cooper/Liaison Agency, Inc., 95 (top left); Alan Weiner/Liaison Agency, Inc., 95 (top center); Lynn McLaren/Index Stock Imagery, Inc., 95 (top right); Guido Rossi/The Image Bank, 95 (bottom left); Richard Pan, 95 (bottom center); Costa Manos/Magnum Photos, Inc., 95 (bottom right); Paul W. Liebhardt, 96; Duke University Hartman Center for Sales Advertising and Marketing History with permission of Pepsi-Cola Company, 97; Paul W. Liebhardt, 98; Angela Maynard/PhotoDisc, Inc., 99; Michael Newman/PhotoEdit, 100; Jason Plotkin/The York Dispatch/AP/Wide World Photos, 103.

CHAPTER 5: Peter Christopher/Masterfile Corporation, 106; Christopher Brown/Stock Boston, 108; Angela Fisher/Carol Beckwith/Robert Estall Photo Agency, 112; Jonathan Green, *Friends*, 1992, oil on masonite, 14 in. x 11 in. © Jonathan Green—Naples, FL, collection of Patric McCoy, 114; Cliché Bibliothéque Nationale de France, Paris. From *The Horizon History of China* by the editors of *Horizon* Magazine, The Horizon Publishing Co., Inc., 551 5th Avenue, New York, NY 10017, ©1969, 118; Paul W. Liebhardt, 120; George Tooker, *Government Bureau*, 1956, egg tempera on gesso panel, 19 5/8 x 29 5/8 inches, The Metropolitan Museum of Art, George A. Hearn Fund, 1956 (56.78). Photograph ©1984 The Metropolitan Museum of Art, 121; Gerhard Steiner/Corbis/Stock Market, 123; Ed Lallo/Liaison Agency, Inc., 125.

CHAPTER 6: Rich Pedroncelli/AP/Wide World Photos, 132; SIPA Press, 134; North Wind Picture Archives, 136; Paul W. Liebhardt, 138; Bushnell/Soifer/Stone, 140; Stan Honda/Agence France-Presse, 141; Frank Romero, *Freeway Wars*, 1990, serigraph, 31 1/2 x 38 inches, © Frank Romero. Nicolas and Cristina Hernandez Trust Collection, Pasadena, California, 143; Mark Wilson/Liaison Agency, Inc., 145; © Paul Marcus, *Cracked-up*, oil on panel, 24 in. x 30 in. Studio SPM Inc., 150; Washoe County, Nevada Police Department, 153; Bob Daemmrich Photography, Inc., 157.

CHAPTER 7: Andy Warhol, *Marilyn*, 1967, © 2001 Andy Warhol Foundation for the Visual Arts/Artists Rights Society (ARS), New York. Tate Gallery, London/Art Resource, NY, 160; Andre Gallant/The Image Bank, 162 (top left); Pete Turner/The Image Bank, 162 (top center); Brun/Photo Researchers, Inc., 162 (top right); Bruno Hadjih/Liaison Agency, Inc., 162 (bottom left); Elliot Erwitt/Magnum Photos, Inc., 162 (bottom middle); George Holton/Photo Researchers, Inc., 162 (bottom right); Kim D. Johnson/*The Sacramento Bee*, 163 (left); Bryan Patrick/*The Sacramento Bee*, 163 (right); Reproduced by special permission of *Playboy* magazine. Copyright ©1953, ©1981 by *Playboy*. All rights reserved, 164; Dan McCoy/Rainbow, 165; Biophoto Associates/Science Source/Photo Researchers, Inc., 167a; Robert Noonan/Photo Researchers, Inc., 167b; Ray Ellis/Science Source/Photo Researchers, Inc., 167c; SIU/Photo Researchers, Inc., 167 d,e; Scott Camazine/Sue Trainor/Photo Researchers, Inc., 167f; Mark Richards/PhotoEdit, 167g; John Marshall Mantel/Corbis, 169; Charlesworth/SABA Press Photos, Inc., 175; Mark Peterson/SABA Press Photos, Inc., 177; Jean-Baptiste Greuze (1725-1805), *The Broken Jug*, 1772-1773 (le cruche cassee), rococo painting, canvas, 85 x 86.5 cm. Louvre, Dpt. des Peintures, Paris, France. © Photograph by Erich Lessing/Art Resource, NY, 178; Corbis Digital Stock, 179.

CYBER.SCOPE II: T. Crosby/Liaison Agency, Inc., 184; © *The New Yorker* Collection 1993 Peter Steiner from cartoonbank.com. All rights reserved, 185.

CHAPTER 8: © Paul Marcus, *The New Nanny*, oil painting on wood, 48 x 72 in., Studio SPM, Inc., 186; Sebastiao Salgado/Contact Press Images Inc., 188; Doranne Jacobson/International Images, 189; Per-Anders Pettersson/Black Star, 190; Alexander Zemlianichenko/AP/

Wide World Photos, 192; September: Harvesting Grapes by the Limbourg Brothers. *Tres Riches Heures du Duc de Berry* (early 15th century). Victoria & Albert Museum, London, UK. The Bridgeman Art Library, 194; Ford Madox Brown (1821-93), *Work*, SuperStock, Inc., 198; Camilo Jose Vergara, 206; Russell Lee/Corbis, 207; Bob Krist/Corbis, 208; George Tooker (b. 1920), *Laundress*, 1952, oil on gesso panel, 23 1/2 x 24 in. (59.7 x 61 cm.) Christies Images, NY, © George Tooker, 212; Phil Schermeister/Corbis, 214; Brooks Kraft/Corbis/Sygma, 216.

CHAPTER 9: D. Aubert/Corbis/Sygma, 220; Martin Benjamin/The Image Works, 223 (top left); Peter Turnley/Corbis, 223 (top right); Pablo Bartholomew/Liaison Agency, Inc., 223 (bottom right); Tony Arruza/Corbis, 224 (left); Reuters/Juan Carlos Ulate/Archive Photos, 224 (right); David Stewart-Smith/SABA Press Photos, Inc., 225; Malcolm Linton/Liaison Agency, Inc., 230; Claus Meyer/Black Star, 231; Steve Maines/Stock Boston, 232; Joe McDonald/Corbis, 233 (left); Robert van der Hilst/Corbis, 233 (center); Wolfgang Kaehler/Corbis, 233 (right); Sean Sprague/Impact Visuals Photo & Graphics, Inc., 235; Diego Rivera, *Colonial Domination*, The Granger Collection, © Banco de Mexico Diego Rivera Museums Trust, 237; Brian Brake/Photo Researchers, Inc., 239; Steve McCurry/Magnum Photos, Inc., 243.

CHAPTER 10: The Image Bank, 246; Jon Feingersh/Corbis/Stock Market, 248; Angela Fisher/Carol Beckwith/Robert Estall Photo Agency, 250; Ed Malitsky/Index Stock Imagery, Inc., 253; R.W. Jones/Corbis, 261; Willinger/FPG International LLC, 262; Bettmann/Corbis, 264 (left); APA/Archive Photos, 264 (center); Hulton-Deutsch Collection/Corbis, 264 (right); UNICEF/HQ96-1041/Tapas Barua, 266.

CHAPTER 11: Adam Nadel/AP/Wide World Photos, 270; Joel Gordon/Joel Gordon Photography, 272 (top left); Leong Ka Tài/Material World, 272 (top center); Owen Franken/Corbis, 272 (top right); Charles O'Rear/Corbis, 272 (bottom left); Paul W. Liebhardt, 272 (bottom center); Lisi Dennis/The Image Bank, 272 (bottom right); Bob Daemmrich Photography, Inc., 275; Peter Turnley/Corbis, 276; Archive Photos, 277 (left); Photo by Robbie Robinson. ©1995 Paramount Pictures, all rights reserved, courtesy Foto Fantasies, 277 (right); National Baseball Hall of Fame Library, Cooperstown, NY, 281; Photo by Sheldon Preston. From *The Native Americans* by Turner Publishing, Inc. Atlanta, 282; Corbis, 286 (far left); Culver Pictures, Inc., 286 (left center); Photographs and Prints Division, Schomburg Center for Research in Black Culture/The New York Public Library/Astor, Lenox and Tilden Foundations, 286 (center right); UPI/Corbis, 286 (far right); UPI/Corbis, 289; A. Ramey/Woodfin Camp & Associates, 290; © Nick Quijano 1997, *La Vida en Broma, 1988: Streetlife in Old San Juan*, 292; Bob Daemmrich Photography, Inc., 294.

CYBER.SCOPE III: Beth Kreiser/AP/Wide World Photos, 298.

CHAPTER 12: Stephane/Liaison Agency, Inc., 300; Bob Daemmrich Photography, Inc., 303; Bellavia/REA/SABA Press Photos, Inc., 307 (left); John Bryson/Corbis/Sygma, 307 (right); Scott Cunningham/Merrill Education, 309 (left); Jeff Maloney/PhotoDisc, Inc., 309 (right); Jose Clemente Orozco, *The Unemployed*, © Licensed by Orozco Valladares Family. Reproduction authorized by the Instituto Nacional de Bellas Artes and Literature, 310; Chris Brown/SABA Press Photos, Inc., 313; Durand/SIPA Press, 317; Philip Evergood "American Tragedy" 1936, oil on canvas, 29 1/2 x 39 1/2 in. Terry Dintenfass Gallery, New York, 319; Joel Gordon/Joel Gordon Photography, 321 (left); A. Ramey/Woodfin Camp & Associates, 321 (right); *A Versailles, A Versailles (March of the Women on Versailles)*, Paris, October 5, 1789, engraving by French School (18th century). Musee Carnavalet, Paris,

France. Bulloz/The Bridgeman Art Library, 325; Bulloz/The Bridgeman Art Library International Ltd., 326; Bob Daemmrich Photography, Inc., 331.

CHAPTER 13: Steve Liss/Liaison Agency, Inc., 334; Cameron Davidson/Liaison Agency, Inc., 336; Barbara Walton/AP/Wide World Photos, 340; Christian Pierre, B. 1962, *I Do*, American Private Collection. Superstock, Inc., 342; D. Young-Wolfe/PhotoEdit, 345; © Susan Pyzow, *Bridal Bouquet*, watercolor on paper, 10 x 13.5 in. Studio SPM Inc., 346; Donna Binder/Impact Visuals Photo & Graphics, Inc., 351; Michael Freeman/Corbis, 354; Owen Franken/Corbis, 355; Mathieu Polak/Corbis/Sygma, 357; Doranne Jacobson/International Images, 359; James L. Amos/Corbis, 363; Anna Belle Lee Washington/SuperStock, Inc., 364.

CHAPTER 14: Marty Katz/*New York Times* Pictures, 368; Stephen Ferry/Liaison Agency, Inc., 373 (left); James D. Wilson/Liaison Agency, Inc., 373 (right); Tom & Dee Ann McCarthy/Corbis/Stock Market, 377; Mugshots/Corbis/Stock Market, 380; Tony Freeman/PhotoEdit, 384; Tom Prettyman/PhotoEdit, 387; A.F. Seligmann, *Allgemeines Krankenhaus (General Hospital)* 19th Century Painting, canvas. *Professor Theodor Billroth lectures at the General Hospital, Vienna. 1880.* Erich Lessing/Art Resource, NY, 390; Galen Rowell/Mountain Light Photography, Inc., 391; John Cancalosi/Stock Boston, 392; ABC Television/Globe Photos, Inc., 395 (left); NBC/Everett Collection, Inc., 395 (right); Al Diaz, 397; Steve Murez/Black Star, 399.

CYBER.SCOPE IV: Courtesy of L. L. Bean. Reprinted by permission, 402; ©Tara Sosrowardovo/Indo-pix, 403.

CHAPTER 15: Millard Sheets, *Tenement Flats (Family Flats)*. ca. 1934. National Museum of American Art, Washington D.C./Art Resource, NY, 404; Lauren Goodsmith/The Image Works, 412; Cotton Coulson/Woodfin Camp & Associates, 414; Ernest Fiene (1894-1965), *Nocturne*, photograph © Christie's Images, 417; John Wang/PhotoDisc, Inc., 419; Tony Freeman/PhotoEdit, 421 (left); Gregory G. Dimijian/Photo Researchers, Inc., 421 (right); Culver Pictures, Inc., 424; Paul W. Liebhardt, 426; Eric Pasquier/Corbis/Sygma, 428; Rick Gerharter/Impact Visuals Photo & Graphics, Inc., 429.

CHAPTER 16: James Willis/Stone, 434; Tom Kelley/FPG International LLC, 436 (top left); Inge Morath/Magnum Photos, Inc., 436 (top center); Owen Franken/Stock Boston, 436 (top right); Willie L. Hill, Jr./Stock Boston, 436 (bottom left); Michael Grecco/Stock Boston, 436 (bottom right); Mark Peters, 437; Hans Edinger/AP/Wide World Photos, 440; George Tooker, *The Subway*, 1950, egg tempera on gesso panel, 18 1/8 x 36 1/8", Whitney Museum of American Art, New York, purchased with funds from the Juliana Force Purchase Award, 50.23. Photograph ©2000 Whitney Museum of American Art, 441; Pearson Education/PH College, 443; Mirta Cerra (1904-1986), *Trabajadores*, oil on canvas laid down on panel, 46 x 62 in. (107.3 x 157.5 cm). © Christie's Images, 447; Edvard Munch, *The Scream*, Oslo, National Gallery. Scala/Art Resource, NY, © 1998 Artists Rights Society (ARS), New York/ADAGP, Paris, 449 (left); © Paul Marcus, *Crossing the Rio Grande*, 1999, oil painting on canvas, 63 x 72 in. Studio SPM Inc., 449 (right); Mauri Rautkari/WWF UK (World Wide Fund For Nature), 450; Archive Photos, 452 (left); John Launois/Black Star, 452 (right); Universal Studios and Amblin/Foto Fantasies, 453; R. Crandall/The Image Works, 456.

CYBER.SCOPE V: Peter Charlesworth/SABA Press Photos, Inc., 461

Dan Laskin, 513.

Name Index

Fujimoto, Isao, 289
Fuller, Rex, 257
Furstenberg, Frank F., Jr., 343, 347

Gabriel, Trip, 461
Gadlin, Howard, 354
Gagliani, Giorgio, 197
Gagné, Patricia, 163
Gagnon, John H., 41, 166–68, 170–71, 178, 342
Galileo, 9
Gallup, George H., Jr., 151
Galster, George, 415
Gamoran, Adam, 374
Gamson, William A., 19
Gandhi, Mahatma, 316
Gans, Herbert J., 72, 418
Garfinkel, Harold, 14, 91, 139
Garreau, Joel, 416
Gartin, Patrick R., 143
Gartner, Rosemary, 156
Gates, Bill, 120, 298
Gau, Rebecca L., 381
Geertz, Clifford, 6, 163
Geist, William, 415
Gelles, Richard J., 260–61, 349–50
Gelman, David, 170
Genovese, Kitty, 456
Gerber, Theodore P., 193
Gerbner, George, 70
Gerlach, Michael L., 307
Gerlovin, Valeriy, 67
Gerlovina, Rimma, 67
Gerschwender, James A., 278
Gerson, Judith M., 452
Gerstel, Naomi, 347
Gewertz, Deborah, 249
Gibbons, Don C., 135
Gibbs, Nancy, 74, 173, 175, 177
Gibson, William, 29
Giddens, Anthony, 177, 197
Giele, Janet Z., 263
Gigliotti, Richard J., 88
Gilbert, Neil, 177
Gilbertson, Greta A., 288
Gilligan, Carol, 66, 82, 135, 252
Gillon, Raanan, 390
Gimenez, Martha E., 378
Ginsburg, Faye, 260
Gintis, Herbert, 13, 373–74
Giovannini, Maureen, 20
Giugni, Marco G., 440
Gladue, Brian A., 170
Gleick, Elizabeth, 359
Glenn, Norvall D., 349
Glock, Charles Y., 360
Glueck, Eleanor, 135
Glueck, Sheldon, 135

Gnida, John J., 17
Godwin, Kenneth, 380
Goetting, Ann, 260
Goffman, Erving, 14, 67, 80, 92–93, 95, 97, 100, 105, 109, 117, 139, 141, 185, 449
Goldberg, Steven, 251
Golden, Frederic, 399
Goldfarb, William, 426
Golding, William, 83
Goldsmith, H. H., 62
Goode, William J., 310, 342
Goodwin, R. Kenneth, 380
Gorbachev, Mikhail, 193
Gordon, James S., 391, 397
Gordon, Sol, 173
Goring, Charles Buckman, 134
Gotham, Kevin Fox, 279
Gottfredson, Michael R., 142
Gough, Kathleen, 249
Grabb, Edward G., 117
Graham, John W., 349
Grant, Karen R., 393
Grasmick, Harold G., 395
Graves, Joseph B., 150
Greckel, Fay Ross, 248
Greeley, Andrew M., 360, 362
Green, John C., 364
Green, Jonathan, 114
Green, Richard, 170
Greenberg, David F., 169
Greenfield, Lawrence A., 177
Greenhouse, Linda, 147, 310
Greer, Joe, 397
Gregory, Paul R., 307
Greuze, Jean-Baptiste, 178
Griff, Catherine, 313
Griffin, John Howard, 13
Griswold, David B., 143
Gross, Jane, 352
Groth, Nicholas A., 175
Gugin, Linda Carstarphen, 248
Gup, Ted, 377
Gurak, Douglas T., 114, 288
Gurnett, Kate, 247
Gwartney-Gibbs, Patricia A., 350
Gwynne, S. C., 120

Habermas, Jürgen, 446
Hacker, Helen Mayer, 260, 263
Hackey, Robert B., 323
Hadaway, C. Kirk, 360
Hadden, Jeffrey K., 365
Hafner, Katie, 115
Hagan, Jaqueline Maria, 115
Hagan, John, 145
Haggstrom, Gus W., 347
Haig, Alexander, 323
Haig, Robin Andrew, 103

Halberstram, David, 119
Hall, Elaine J., 247
Hall, John R., 46, 53, 66, 452
Hall, Kelley J., 82
Haller, Emil J., 374
Hallinan, Maureen T., 374
Hamer, Dean, 170
Hamilton, Charles, 279
Hamilton, Mykol, 94, 96, 99
Hammond, Philip E., 362
Hamrick, Michael H., 395
Handlin, Oscar, 293
Hansen, Amanda Faith, 259
Hareven, Tamara K., 78
Harlow, Harry F., 63
Harlow, Margaret Kuenne, 63
Harpster, Paula, 256
Harries, Keith D., 150
Harrington, Michael, 446
Harris, Chauncy D., 418
Harris, Jack Dash, 140
Harris, Marvin, 35, 44, 249
Hart, Shannon, 386
Hartl, Emil M., 135
Harvey, David, 419
Haskins, Ron, 70
Hassinger, Edward W., 115
Hatfield, Elaine, 342
Hauser, Robert M., 209–10
Hawthorne, Peter, 190
Hayneman, Stephen P., 372
Hazelwood, Lonnie R., 261, 350
Heath, D. Terri, 75
Heath, Julia A., 256
Heath, Will Carrington, 361
Helgesen, Sally, 123
Helin, David W., 52
Hellman, Ronald E., 170
Helms, Ronald E., 150
Henley, Nancy, 94, 96, 99
Henretta, John C., 150
Herdt, Gilbert H., 169
Herek, Gregory M., 170
Herman, Dianne, 54, 261
Herman, Edward S., 313
Hernstein, Richard J., 135, 278–79
Hersch, Joni, 394
Hess, Beth B., 19, 72
Hirschi, Travis, 142–43, 156
Hitler, Adolf, 316
Hobbes, Thomas, 8–9, 325
Hoberman, John, 16
Hochschild, Arlie, 76, 339
Hodge, Robert W., 202
Hodson, Randy, 47
Hoerr, John, 125
Hoffer, Thomas, 374, 377
Hogan, Dennis P., 345
Holmes, Malcolm D., 150

Holmes, Steven A., 172, 293
Holmes, Thomas H., 69
Homans, George C., 14
Honeywell, Roy J., 372
Hosch, Harmon M., 150
Hostetler, John A., 47, 54, 448
House, James S., 351
Hout, Michael, 193, 209, 362
Hoyt, Homer, 418
Hsu, Francis L. K., 288
Huber, Bettina J., 5
Huber, Joan, 346, 389
Huet-Cox, Rocio, 391
Huff, Heather K., 88
Huffman, Matt L., 257
Hughes, James W., 415
Huls, Glenna, 134
Hume, David, 15
Humphrey, Craig R., 429
Hunt, Roger, 323
Hunter, James Davison, 56–57, 364
Hussein, Saddam, 240, 326–27
Hutchings, Vincent L., 113
Hymowitz, Carol, 229
Hysom, Stuart J., 87

Iannaccone, Laurence R., 363
Idle, Thomas R., 127
Illich, Ivan, 396
Inglehart, Ronald, 117, 452
Isaacson, Walter, 435
Isay, Richard A., 170

Jacklin, Carol Nagy, 248
Jackson, Jesse, 362
Jacob, John E., 287
Jacobs, David, 150
Jacobs, Jane, 302
Jacquet, Constant H., 363
Jagarowsky, Paul A., 282
Jagger, Alison, 263, 265
James, David R., 374
Janis, Irving L., 111–12
Janus, Christopher G., 229
Jarrett, Robin L., 343
Jefferson, Thomas, 372
Jenckins, W. C., 386
Jencks, Christopher, 135
Jenkins, J. Craig, 440
Jensen, Lief, 217, 288
Jesus of Nazereth, 316
John Paul II (Pope), 358
Johnson, Dirk, 284
Johnson, Paul, 326
Johnson, Roland, 45
Johnson, Virginia E., 387
Johnston, Lloyd D., 143
Johnston, R. J., 418
Jones, Alice M., 363

SUBJECT INDEX

Abortion issue, 180–81
Absolute poverty, 211, 225, 227
Academic standards, 378–79
Achieved status, 86
Achievement as value, 40
Acid rain, 426
Acquaintance rape, 176–77
Acquired immune deficiency syndrome (AIDS), 384, 387–89, 395
  HIV infection, global map of, 388
Act 60, 369
Activity, value of, 40
Adolescence, 74–76
Adoption, by gay couples, 351
Adult education, 380–81
Adulthood, 76–77
Advertising, 253
Affirmative action, 267, 294–95
Affluence (see Income; Wealth)
Africa, 6, 228, 231, 236, 237, 238, 239, 299, 305, 337, 370, 371, 387, 424 (see also global maps, specific countries)
  housework in, 89
African Americans, 274–75, 285–87 (see also Race)
  and affirmative action, 294–95
  and AIDS, 389
  and art, 69, 364
  and civil rights movement, 286–87
  and crime, 150
  demographics, map of, 291
  and education, 271, 279–80, 287, 375
  and family, 345, 350
  great women, 286
  and health, 385, 386, 389
  and income, 204, 205, 209, 260, 286–87, 345
  and intelligence debate, 278–79
  and mass media, 73
  in medical profession, 391
  and politics, 287, 321
  population growth, 311
  and poverty, 212
  and religion, 362
  and segregation, 271, 279–80, 281–82
  and slavery, 281, 285–86
  and social mobility, 209
  social standing of (1999), 287

in sports, 16–17
and stereotyping, 24
and stratification, 204
and suicide, 3
and unemployment, 287, 311
and wealth, 205
and the workplace, 309, 311, 312
Afrocentrism, 48–49
Age
  and criminal activity, 148
  and voting frequency, 322
Age, old
  and biology, 77
  and culture, 77–79
  and family life, 343–44
  graying of U.S., 76, 77
  and health, 77
  in industrial society, 78
  in postindustrial society, 299
  and poverty, 78, 212
  in preindustrial society, 78
  socialization in old age, 77–79
Ageism, 78
Age-sex pyramid, 409
Agrarian society, 371 (see also Agriculture)
  and aging, 78
  agricultural employment, global map of, 305
  economy of, 302
  and education, 371
  and family, 337–39, 342–43
  and gender, 249
  and health, 382
  and marriage, 337–39, 341
  compared to modern, 445
  and patriarchy, 250
  patterns of descent, 338
  and population growth, 411
  and religion, 360
  and social revolution, 199
Agricultural revolution, 302
Agriculture, 42–44, 235, 238, 242, 410
  global employment in, 305
Aid for Dependent Children (AFDC), 216–17
AIDS (see Acquired immune deficiency syndrome [AIDS])
Air pollution, 225, 426–27
Alcoholism, 141
Algeria, 224
Alienation, 196
  bureaucratic, 120
  voter, 322–23
Alternative social movements, 439

AMA (see American Medical Association)
American dilemma, 286
American Dream, 210
American Medical Association (AMA), 391
American Psychiatric Association, on homosexuality, 171
American Revolution, 325
American Sociological Association (ASA), 20
Amish, 53–54, 234, 281, 358, 448
Anal sex, 388
Androcentricity, 20
Animism, 359–60
Anomie, 443
Anorexia nervosa, 386
Anticipatory socialization, 71, 112
Anti-Malthusians, 431
Apartheid, 189, 190, 194
Apathy, voter, 322–23
Applied sociology, 5
Arapesh of New Guinea, 248
Argentina, 223, 224, 328
Arms race, 327
Arranged marriage, 340, 341
Art, 9, 12, 13, 18, 32, 40, 51, 63, 64, 67, 69, 84, 114, 118, 121, 143, 160, 186, 194, 198, 212, 237, 292, 310, 319, 342, 346, 364, 390, 417, 441, 447, 449
Artifacts, 41
Ascribed status, 86
Asexuality, 168, 179
Asia, 45, 224, 228, 236, 240, 299, 305, 337, 371, 408 (see also global maps, specific countries)
  housework in, 89
  slavery, 230
Asian Americans, 287–90, 350, 386
  and AIDS, 389
  and crime, 150
  demographics, map of, 291
  and education, 287, 290
  and family, 345–46
  and income, 288, 290
  and intelligence debate, 278–79
  population growth, 311
  and poverty, 212
  social standing of (1990), 288
Asian Indian Americans, 287

Assimilation, 281, 283–84, 293, 345
Athletic performance, and gender, 248, 249
Attention and language, 99–100
Australia, 6, 222, 226, 305, 341
Authoritarian leaders, 110, 119
Authoritarian personality theory, 277–78
Authoritarianism, 317
Authority, 316
  patterns of, 339
Automation, 127, 129
Automobiles
  and environment, 426
  ownership of, 41
  and social change, 437
Average-middle class, 205

Baby boom, 409, 415
Baby boomers, 166, 344
Baby bust, 409
Bangladesh, 223, 224, 234, 266, 371
Baseball fans, national map of, 93
Beauty myth, 253, 386
Behaviorism, 62
  social, 67–68
Belgium, 316
Beliefs, cultural, 38
Bell curve concept, 278–79
Bible, 355, 356, 364
Bilateral descent, 338
Bill of Rights, 320
Biodiversity, declining, 427–28
Biology (see also Sociobiology)
  and aging, 77
  and deviance, 134–35
  and gender, 161–63
  and race, 271–72
  and sexual orientation, 169–70
  and sexuality, 161–62
Birth control, 166, 229, 342, 410, 412
  methods, 167
Birth rate, 343, 406, 410
Bisexuality, 168, 179
Black Americans (see African Americans)
Black church, 362
Black power movement, 286
Blaming the victim, 236
Blasé urban attitude, 417
Blended family, 349

Blue-collar occupation, 197, 202, 206, 309
Body language, 95–96
Bosnia, 327
Botswana, 224, 226, 387
Bourgeoisie, 414
Brazil, 224, 226, 229, 328, 429, 450, 455
Brown v. The Board of Education of Topeka (1954), 271, 279–80
Bulgaria, 308
Bureaucracy, 117–21
  and democracy, 317
  and education, 377–78
  in mass society, 445
  and privacy, 128–29
  and rationality, 117
  and social movements, 440
  and student passivity, 377–78
Bureaucratic inertia, 121
Bureaucratic ritualism, 120–21
Bushmen, 42
Busing, 375

Calvinism, 357
Cambodia, 282
Canada, 226, 305, 309
  medical system in, 393
Capital punishment
  global map of, 152
  in U.S., map of, 156
Capitalism, 305–6
  and alienation, 196
  characteristics of, 306
  and class conflict, 196–98
  and deviance, 144
  and gender stratification, 265
  Marxist analysis of, 54, 196–97
  and medicine, 396
  and modernity, 446–47
  and patriarchy, 263
  and Protestantism, 357
  and socialism compared, 307–8
  state, 307, 329
  welfare, 307, 329
  world economy, 237–38
Capitalist revolution, 444
Capitalist world economy, 237–38
Capitalists, 196
Carbon dioxide, 427
Caste system, 188–92
Category, 2
Catholic Church (*see* Religion)
Caucasoid (Caucasian), 272–73

Cause and effect, 15, 18
Central Intelligence Agency (CIA), 328
Chad, 224
Charisma, 316, 359
Charter schools, 380
Chattel slavery, 229–30
Chechnya, 327
Chicanos, 292
Child abuse, 61, 63–64, 350
Child care, 312, 373
Child custody, 267, 349
Child labor, 50, 74, 371
Child support, 349
Childbirth, 229
Children
  Aid for Dependent Children (AFDC), 216–17
  and AIDS, 389
  and child weddings, 340
  and divorce, 352
  and family form, 350–54
  latchkey kids, 343
  and poverty, 212, 229, 336
  and slavery, 229–30
  and socialization, 69–74
  violence against, 61, 63–64, 350
  and virtual culture, 184–85
Chile, 223, 319
China, 33, 299, 424 (*see also* People's Republic of China)
Chinese Americans, 274, 279, 287–88, 294
Chinese language, 39
Christianity, 356, 360, 362
Chukchee Eskimo, 169
Church
  black, 362
  defined, 358
  electronic, 365
Cigarette smoking, 385–86
Cities (*see also* Urbanization)
  evolution of, 8, 413–16
  and poverty, 213
  regional, 416
  Snowbelt, 415
  suburbs, 415
  Sunbelt, 415–16
  U.S., 414–15
Civil law, 145
Civil religion, 362
Civil Rights Act (of 1964), 295
Civil rights movement, 54, 286–87, 357
Civil unions, 335
Civil War, 415
Class (*see* Social class)

Class conflict, 196–98, 438 (*see also* Social conflict; Social-conflict paradigm)
Class-society theory of modernity, 446–47
Class system, 189–92
CMSA (*see* Consolidated metropolitan statistical area)
Coercive organization, 117
Cognitive development (Piaget), 65–66
Cohabitation, 351
Cohort, 79
Collective behavior (*see* Social movements)
College
  attendance, national map of, 374
  degrees, 258
  student passivity, 378
Colonial settlement, 414
Colonialism, 231–32, 236–37, 238, 455–56
Common sense, and sociology, 14
Commonwealth of Independent States (*see* Soviet Union, former)
Communications, 6, 28, 45 (*see also* Internet)
Communism, 192
Communitarian movement, 456–57
Community, loss of, 441–42
Comparable worth policy, 257
Competition, 306, 314
Competitive work teams, 124–25
Complementarity, theory of, 262–63
Computers, 381 (*see also* Information Revolution)
  and education, 185
  and income, 30
  invention of, 28–29
  and workplace changes, 312–13
Concentric zone urban model, 418
Concept, defined, 15
Concrete operational stage (Piaget), 65–66
Conflict (*see also* Social conflict)
  and humor, 103
  role, 87–88
Conflict theory of prejudice, 278

Conformity
  and deviance, 142
  group, 110–12
Confucianism, 358
Conglomerate, 313
Conjugal family, 337
Consanguine family, 337
Conservative politics, 364
Consolidated metropolitan statistical area (CMSA), 416
Constitution of the United States, 286, 320
Constitutional monarchy, 316
Containment theory deviance, 135
Control theory (Hirschi), 142–43
Conventional level (Kohlberg), 66
Conversion, religious, 359
Corporate crime, 145–46
Corporate welfare, 330–31
Corporations, 313–15
  defined, 313
  downsizing, 301–2
  and global economy, 314
  multinational, 232, 314
  women in, 257, 312
Correlation
  spurious, 18
  of variables, 15, 18
Counterculture, 49, 444
Coup d'état, 325
Courts, 154
Courtship, 341
Covenant marriage, 348
Creationism, 364
Credentialism, 376
Crime, 134 (*see also* Violence against women)
  corporate crime, 145–46
  criminal statistics, 148
  decline in rate, 157
  deterrence of, 155
  and deviance, 147–53
  deviant subcultures, 137–38
  and gender, 148
  in global perspective, 151–53
  hate-crimes, 146–47
  incarceration rates, global, 154
  organized crime, 146
  and race, 150
  rates in U.S., 149
  and social class, 148–50
  types of, 147–48
  victimless, 148
  white-collar, 144–45

and inequality, 247–51
inequality in sexuality,
   179–80
and Information
   Revolution, 299
and intelligence, 248
and language, 99–100
and leadership, 109–10
and life expectancy, 248,
   267, 344, 383, 384
and marriage, 346
masculine traits, 252
and mass media, 253
and military, 259
and modernization, 235
and moral development,
   66–67, 252
and networking, 115
and occupations, 202, 204,
   254–55
and patriarchy, 249–51, 266
and peer groups, 252
and personal performances,
   96–97
and play, 252
and politics, 258–59, 260
and pornography, 172
and poverty, 212–13,
   216–17, 229, 260
and power, 72, 179, 249–51,
   261
premarital sex, 167
and religion, 356–57
and research, 20, 248–49
and sexual revolution, 166
and slavery, 230
and social class, 263
social-conflict analysis of,
   263
and social mobility, 210
and socialization, 66–67,
   252–53
and sports, 16
and stratification, 203–4,
   254–62
structural-functional
   analysis of, 262–63
and suicide rates, 3
in the twenty-first century,
   266–67
and violence against
   women, 147, 260–61,
   349–50
and voting, 322
women's power, global map,
   251
and work, 252–56, 309
and workplace, 66
Gender blindness, 20
Gender discrimination, 180

Gender identity, masculine
   and feminine traits, 252
Gender roles, 252
Gender stratification, 247–51,
   254–62
Generalized other (G. H.
   Mead), 68
Genetic (DNA) research,
   398–99
Genital herpes, 387
Genocide, 282–83
German Americans, 289, 293
Germany, 282, 308, 319
Gerontocracy, 78
Gerontology, 77
Gesellschaft, 441–42, 447
Gestures, 37, 95–96, 98
Glass ceiling, 257, 312
Global culture, 52–53
Global economy, 210–11,
   303–4, 314
Global issues (*see also* global
   maps list in table of
   contents)
   authority, 316
   comparative economic
      systems, 304–8
   comparative political
      systems, 304–8
   and crime, 151–53
   demography, 405–9
   emotions, 94–95
   and environment, 410–11,
      420–31
   family life, 337–39
   formal organization,
      123–24
   gender roles, 251
   geography of race, 272–73
   global economy, 52, 210–11
   global patterns of health,
      382–83
   global perspective,
      importance of, 5–8
   incarceration rates (2000),
      154
   inequality, future of,
      240–42
   liberty, 318
   medicine and economics in
      global perspective,
      392–94
   patriarchy, 249–51, 339,
      346, 353, 356–57
   prosperity and stagnation,
      map of, 241
   revolution, 325
   schooling, 370–72
   sexual behavior, 178

social construction of
   reality, 88–92
stages of family life, 341–44
stratification, 188–89,
   199–201, 299
technological change, 302
terrorism, 326
urbanization, 413–16
war and peace, 326–29
water consumption, map of,
   425
world religion, 356–57
Gonorrhea, 386–87
Government (*see also* Politics)
   and economic regulation,
      304–8
   growth of welfare state, 320
Graying of America, 77, 78
Great Britain, 226, 234, 305,
   316, 328, 341
   medical system in, 393
   religion in, 356
   social class in, 191–92
Great Depression, 3, 165
Greece, 413
Greek Americans, 279, 293
Green Revolution, 235,
   242–43
Greenhouse effect, 427
Gross domestic product
   (GDP), 226, 307
   economic development,
      global map of, 7
Group (*see* Social Group)
Group conformity, 110–12
Group leadership, 109–10
Group size, 113–14
Group superiority, 40
Groupthink, 111–12
Guam, 237, 290
Guinea, 226
Gun control, 151
Gynecological examination,
   396
Gynocentricity, 20
Gypsies, 276

Haiti, 222, 226, 237
Hate crimes, 146–47
Health, 382–99 (*see also*
   Medicine)
   access to health care, 396
   and aging, 77
   cigarette smoking, 385–86
   defined, 381
   distribution of, 384–85
   eating disorders, 386
   ethical issues, 389–90
   and gender, 384

genetic (DNA) research,
   398–99
global survey of, 382–83
and income, 384–85
and industrialization, 382
and Information
   Revolution, 403
and poverty, 382
and race, 386
sexually transmitted diseases
   (STD), 386–89
and social class, 207,
   384–85
social-conflict analysis of,
   396–97
and society, 381
structural-functional
   analysis of, 394–95
symbolic-interaction
   analysis of, 395–96
and technology, 381,
   389–90
in twenty-first century, 397
in U.S., 383–89
Health care (*see* Health;
   Medicine)
Health insurance, 394
Health maintenance
   organization (HMO), 394
Heaven's Gate cult, 358
Hermaphrodite, 163
Herpes, 387
Heterosexism, 179–80
Heterosexuality, 168–69, 171
   and AIDS, 388, 389
Hidden curriculum, 70
High culture, 46, 47
High-income countries,
   222–23 (*see also* individual
   topics; specific countries)
   defined, 6
   and dependency theory,
      238–39
   division of population and
      global income, 227
   economic development of,
      7, 222–23
   gross domestic product in,
      7, 226
   median age at death, global
      map of, 228
   and modernization theory,
      233–36
   schooling in, 371–72
Higher education (*see also*
   College)
   access to, 375–76
   college attendance, national
      map of, 374
Hinduism, 38, 362

Intergenerational social
    mobility, 208
Internet
    access to, 299
    global network of, 115–116
    national map of, 30
    privacy issues, 128–29
Internment, Japanese-
    Americans, 289
Interpretation, 19
Intragenerational social
    mobility, 208
Intravenous drug use, 388–89
Invention, 50, 437
Investigation, methods of
    sociological, 22–25
Iran, Islamic Republic of,
    224, 226, 239
Iraq, 240, 326, 328
Irish Americans, 293
Iroquois Indians, 337
Irrigation, 235, 410, 426
Islam, 337, 358
Israel, 248, 328
Issei, 289
Italian Americans, 279, 289,
    293
Italy, 307, 351

Japan, 222, 223, 226, 239,
    307, 309, 329, 451–52
    and formal organization,
    123–24, 125
    medicine in, 393–94
    recycling in, 423
    schooling in, 372
Japanese Americans, 273,
    279, 289–90, 294
Jehovah's Witnesses, 359
Jericho, 413
Jews, 271, 273, 274, 293, 321,
    355 (*see also* Judaism)
    and genocide, 282
    in preindustrial cities, 414
    and social class, 361
Jim Crow laws, 286
Judaism, 358, 362 (*see also*
    Jews)
    and patriarchy, 357
Juvenile delinquency, 138

Kaiapo of Brazil, 450, 451,
    455
Kaska Indians, 42
Kibbutzim, 248
Kinsey studies, 166–67
Kinship, 308, 311 (*see also*
    Family)
Koran, 355, 356
Korean Americans, 287, 290

Ku Klux Klan, 49
Kuwait, 317
Kuznets curve, 199

Labeling theory, 139–40, 146
Labor, division of, 442–43
Labor force (*see also* Work)
    child labor, 50, 74, 371
    global map of, 75
    job projections (to 2010) in
        U.S., 315
    participation across U.S.,
        254, 308–9
    and social diversity, 254,
        309, 311, 312
    in the twenty-first century,
        312
    women in, 49, 252–56, 309,
        312
Labor unions, 302, 309
Laissez-faire capitalism, 306
Laissez-faire leadership, 110,
    119
Landfills, 423
Language
    cyber-symbols, 31
    defined, 38
    diversity, national map of,
        48
    and gender, 99–100
    global map of, 39
    and Internet, 299
    and multiculturalism, 48
    "spinning" words, 90
Latent function, 11
Latin America, 7, 45, 228,
    231, 238, 255, 357, 358,
    370, 371 (*see also* global
    maps, specific countries)
    housework in, 89
    slavery in, 230
Latinos (*see* Hispanics
    (Latinos))
Lawsuits, national map of,
    110
Leadership, group, 109–10
Lesbians, 171, 351 (*see also*
    Gay people; Gay rights
    movement;
    Homosexuality)
Liberal feminism, 265
Liberal politics, 321
Liberation theology, 357–58
Liberty, 8, 317
    in global perspective, 318
Libya, 328, 425
Life course
    and family, 341–44
    and socialization, 74–79
Life expectancy, 397, 407

and gender, 248, 267, 344,
    384
global map of, 228
and race, 384–85
and social class, 207
U.S., map of, 383
Limits to growth thesis, 422
Literacy, 199
Lithuania, 226, 279
Lobbyists, 321–22
Logic of growth, 421–22
Looking-glass self, 67
Love, 341
Low-income countries,
    224–25 (*see also* individual
    topics; specific countries)
    debt of, 238
    defined, 6
    division of population and
        global income, 227
    economic development of,
        7, 224–25
    gross domestic product in,
        7, 226
    median age at death, global
        map of, 228
    and modernization theory,
        233–36
    multinational corporations
        in, 232, 314
    and poverty, 224–25
    schooling in, 371
    urbanization in, 419–20
Lower class, 206
Lower-upper class, 205
Luddites, 185

McDonaldization of society,
    126–27
Machismo, 345
Macro-level orientation, 13
Mainstreaming in schools,
    380
Malaysia, 35, 42, 223, 238,
    327
Malthusian theory, 410–11,
    431
Mandatory education law, 371
Manifest functions, 11
Manufacturing, 8, 210, 302,
    314
Marginality (*see* Social
    marginality)
Marital rape, 350
Marriage (*see also* Family)
    arranged, 340, 341
    child weddings, 340
    covenant, 348
    Defense of Marriage Act
        (1996), 335

defined, 336
divorce, 336, 342, 347–49,
    352
endogamous, 189
endogamous and
    exogamous, 337
global map of, 338
ideal and real, 342
interracial, 281, 345–46
patterns of, 337
religion and social
    construction of, 356
remarriage, 349
same sex, 335–36
servile forms of, 230
types, global map of, 349
Marxist political-economy
    model, 323–24
Marxist theory, 54, 144, 192,
    193, 198, 438, 444
Masculinity, and health, 384
Mass consumption, 234
Mass media
    advertising, 253
    and cultural conflict, 57
    and gender, 253
    and minorities, 73
    national map, of, 72
    and religion, 365
    and socialization, 71–74
    television, 71–73
Mass production, 302
Mass-society theory of
    modernity, 439, 444–46
    defined, 444
Master status, 86–87, 275
    stigma as, 139
Materialism, 40, 54
Matriarchy, 249
Matrilineal descent, 338
Matrilocality, 337
Matrimony (*see* Marriage)
"Me" (G. H. Mead), 67
Mean, 15
Measurement, 17–18
Mechanical solidarity,
    416–17, 442
Media (*see* Mass media)
Median, 15
Medicaid, 394
Medicalization of deviance,
    141–42
Medicare, 394
Medicine, 390–99 (*see also*
    Health)
    in capitalist societies, 394
    cost of care, 392–94
    defined, 354
    in global perspective,
        392–94

holistic, 391
as politics, 396–97
rise of scientific, 390–91
in Russian Federation, 392, 393
social-conflict analysis of, 396–97
in socialist societies, 392–93
structural-functional analysis of, 394–95
symbolic-interaction analysis of, 395–96
in U.S., 394–95
Megalopolis, 416
Melanesians, 178
Melting pot, 47, 48, 280–81
Men (*see also* Family; Gender; Marriage)
and athletic performance, 248
extramarital sex, 168
and gender distinctions, 248–51
gender-related traits, 252
and homosexuality, 168, 170–71
and intelligence, 248
and life expectancy, 248, 383
masculine traits, 252
masculinity and health, 384
and parenting, 354
patriarchy, 249–51
premarital sex, 167
rights of, 267
sex characteristics of, 161–62
and social mobility, 210
Men's rights movement, 267
Mental illness, and labeling, 141
Mercy killing, 390
Meritocracy, 190–91, 199
Metaphysical stage (Comte), 9
Metropolis, 415
Metropolitan statistical area (MSA), 416
Mexican Americans, 292, 295
Mexico, 226, 341, 409, 419, 429
Micro-level orientation, 14
Middle Ages (*see also* Agrarian society)
cities in, 414
Middle class, 205
Middle East, 255, 271, 362, 424, 425

Middle-income countries, 223–24 (*see also* individual topics; specific countries)
defined, 6
division of population and global income, 227
economic development of, 7
gross domestic product in, 7, 226
median age at death, global map of, 228
Migration, 438–39
defined, 377
national map of, 407
Militarism, 327–28
Military
and gender, 259
and language, 90
Military-industrial complex, 327
Minority
characteristics, 274–76
defined, 259, 274
majority interaction patterns, 280–82
national map of, 274
women as, 259–60
Miscegenation, 281
Mobility (*see* Social mobility)
Mode, 15
"Model minority" image, 287
Modernity, 435, 440–44
class society, 446–47
and individual, 448–49
mass society, 439, 444–46
and progress, 451
Modernization, characteristics of, 440–41
Modernization theory, 238, 240, 440
and future, 453–57
and global inequality, 233–36
Monarchy, 316
Mongoloid, 272–73
Monoculture, 44–45
Monogamy, 337
Monopoly, 314
Moral development
Gilligan, 66–67, 252
Kohlberg, 66
Mores, 41
Morocco, 5, 50
Mortality, 406–7
MSA (*see* Metropolitan statistical area (MSA))
Multiculturalism, 47–49
Multinational corporation, 232, 237, 314
Mundugumor culture, 248

Mutually assured destruction (MAD), 329

Names, changes in, 4
Namibia, 387
Native Americans, 41, 273, 274, 283–84, 386–87, 413
and AIDS, 389
citizenship of, 284, 294
and income, 284
religion of, 360
social standing of (1990), 284
Nativist movements, 284, 293
Natural environment, 410–11, 420–31
acid rain, 426
air pollution, 426–27
declining biodiversity, 427–28
defined, 420
desertification, 427
in global perspective, 420
and global warming, 427
limits of growth, 422
logic of growth, 421–22
rain forests, 242, 420, 421, 427
and recycling, 423
and role of sociology, 420
and sociocultural evolution, 420–21
solid waste, 423
sustainable ecosystem, 429
and technology, 420–21
water, 424–26
Natural selection, 54
Nature vs. nurture, 61–62
Navajo Indians, 163, 164
Nazi Germany, 282, 316, 319
Negroid, 272–73
Neo-Malthusians, 422, 431
Neocolonialism, 232
Neolocality, 337
Netherlands, 316
Networks, 114–15
New information technology, 28–31, 184–85 (*see also* Information Revolution)
and social change, 460–61
social-conflict analysis of, 30
and social institutions, 402–3
and social stratification, 298–99
structural-functional analysis of, 30
symbolic-interaction analysis of, 30

New reproductive technology, 352–53, 354
New Zealand, 33, 35, 222
Newspaper reading, national map of, 72
Nicaragua, 199, 371
Niger, 234
Nigeria, 238
Nisei, 298
Non-governmental organization (NGO), 319
Nonmaterial culture, 35
Nonverbal communication, 94–96
Normative organization, 117
Norms
and authority, 316
and deviance, 135–36
and sexual behavior, 178
North Korea, 317, 328, 329
Northern Mariana Islands, 221
Norway, 250, 316
Nuclear family, 337
Nuclear proliferation, 328
Nuclear weapons, 328–29
Nurture vs. nature, 61–62

Objectivity in scientific research, 18
Occupations
and gender, 254–55
and prestige, 202–3, 204, 205
Old age (*see* Age, old)
Oligarchy, 121
Oligopoly, 314
Oman, 224
One-parent family, 350–51
Operationalizing a variable, 15
Oral contraceptives, 166
Oral tradition, 370
Organic solidarity, 442
Organizational environment, 119
Organized crime, 146
Osteopathy, 391
Other-directedness, 448–49
Outgroup, 112–13
Overgeneralizing, 20

PAC (*see* Political action committee)
Pacific Rim, 307
Pakistan, 328, 341
Panama, 240
Paradigm (*see* Theoretical paradigm)
Paraprofessionals, 310

Parenting, 342–43
  aging parents, 343–44
  alternative family forms, 350–54
  and men, 354
  single parents, 345
Parochial schools, 374
Participant observation, 22–23
Pastoralism, 42, 43, 199, 420
Patriarchy, 339, 346
  defined, 249
  and feminism, 264–65, 353
  and religion, 356–57
  and sexism, 249–51, 266
Patrilineal descent, 338
Patrilocality, 337
Peace, 329
Pearl Harbor, 289
Peer group, 70–71, 449
  and gender socialization, 252
People's Republic of China, 38, 226, 328, 329
  medicine in, 392–93
Perestroika, 192
Performance, 93–94, 98
  and gender, 96–97
Persian Gulf War (1991), 327
Personal freedom, and social responsibility, 456–57
Personal space, 96–97
Personality, 61
  authoritarian, 277–78
  and charisma, 316
  and deviant behavior, 135
  Erikson's model of, 68–69
  Freud's model of, 64–65
Philippines, 225–26, 240, 341, 419, 428, 429
Physical disability (see Disability[ies])
Physicians
  and idealization, 97
  role of, 395
  social interaction of, 93–94
Pink-collar jobs, 254–55
Plant biodiversity, 427
Play, and gender, 252
"Play" stage (G. H. Mead), 68
Plea bargaining, 154
Pluralist model, 280–81, 323, 324
Pokot, 163
Poland, 226
Police, 153–54, 157
Polish Americans, 273, 279, 293
Political action committee (PAC), 322

Political change, 8
Political party, 321
Political revolution, 325
Political spectrum, 320–21
Politics, 315–24
  and African Americans, 287, 321
  apathy, 322–23
  and authority, 316
  defined, 315
  and economics, 320, 322
  and gender, 258–59, 260
  global system, 318
  and Hispanics, 322
  history of, 315–16
  and Information Revolution, 319, 402–3
  medicine as, 396–97
  and organizational environment, 119
  party identification, 321
  and peace, 329
  political freedom, global map of, 318
  and religion, 356
  and revolution, 325
  and social class, 207
  and special-interest groups, 321–22
  systems of, 316–19
  terrorism, 326
  theoretical analysis of, 323–24
  in twenty-first century, 329
  U.S., 320–23
  and war, 327
Pollution
  air, 426–27
  water, 426
Polyandry, 337
Polygamy, 337
Popular culture, 46, 47
Population, 405–9
  composition, 409
  demography, 405–9
  global map of, 408
  in global perspective, 411–13
  and global poverty, 231
  growth in, 242, 407–9, 411–13, 419
  history of, 410–13
  and income distribution, 227
  and natural environment, 428–29
  neo- vs. anti-Malthusians, 431
  and social change, 438–39
  in survey research, 22

in twenty-first century, 419
Population control, 235
Pornography, 172, 179, 261–62
Portugal, 237
Positivism (Comte), 9
Postconventional level (Kohlberg), 66
Postindustrial economy, 128–29, 303
  and information, 45
  work in, 308–13
Postindustrial society, 303
Postmodernity, 435, 452–53
Poverty, 211–16
  and African Americans, 212
  and aging, 78, 212
  and Asian Americans, 212
  causes of, 213–14
  and children, 212, 229, 233, 336
  culture of, 213
  and environmental racism, 428
  extent of, 227–28
  and families, 212–13, 345, 350
  feminization of, 212
  and gender, 212–13, 216–17, 229
  in global perspective, 6, 221–42
  and health, 382
  and Hispanics, 212, 292, 293
  homelessness, 214–15
  and Native Americans, 284
  negative stigma with, 217
  relative vs. absolute, 211, 227
  and society, 213–14
  in U.S., 211–16
  and women, 212–13, 216–17, 345, 350
  working poor, 206, 214
Power (see also Politics)
  defined, 315
  and deviance, 144
  and gender, 72, 179, 249–51, 261
  global power relationships, 231–32
  in interaction, 96, 99
  and language, 99
  and wealth, 204
Power-elite model, 323, 324
Powerlessness, and modernity, 449–51
Practicality, value of, 40
Prayer in school, 363

Preconventional level (Kohlberg), 66
Predestination, 357
Preindustrial society (see Agrarian society; Horticultural society; Hunting and gathering society; Pastoralism)
Prejudice, 276, 279–80, 288
Premarital sex, 167–68
Preoperational stage (Piaget), 65
Presentation of self, 92–98, 185
Presidential election (2000), 322
Prestige, 202–3, 204, 205, 323
Primary deviance, 139
Primary economic sector, 303
Primary group, 108–9
Primary sex characteristics, 162
Primates, 35, 63
Primogeniture, 191
Prison, 80, 155, 156, 157
Privacy, 128–29
  national map of, 129
Private school, 374–75
Pro-choice position, 180–81
Productivity, 307
Profane, 354
Professions, 310
Profit motive, 306, 396
Progress
  and social change, 450–51
  as value, 40
Projective labeling, 140
Proletariat, 196
Pro-life position, 180–81
Promotion practices, 312
Property, 306, 339
Property crime, 148
Prostitution, 148, 173–75, 175, 177, 179
  global map of, 174
Protestant work ethic, 284, 357
Protestantism, 357, 360
Psychiatry across the U.S., national map of, 142
Psychoanalysis, 64
Psychosomatic disorders, 395
Puberty, sexual maturity, 162–63
Public-private partnerships, 330–31
Public school, 374–75

medicine, 392–93
  vs. capitalism, 307–8
  welfare capitalism, 307
Socialist feminism, 265
Socialization, 61–81
  anticipatory, 71, 112
  and cognitive development,
    65–66
  and deviant behavior, 134
  and education, 372
  Erikson's stages of
    development, 68–69
  and family, 70
  and freedom, 81
  Freudian model of
    personality, 64–65
  and gender, 66–67, 252–53
  and information technology,
    184–85
  and isolation, 63–64
  and life course, 74–79
  and mass media, 71–74
  and moral development,
    66–67
  and peer groups, 70–71
  resocialization, 80
  and schooling, 70
  social behaviorism, 67–68
  and social class, 70
  in total institutions, 80
  in totalitarian societies, 319
Socialized medicine, 393
Societal protection, 155
Society
  defined, 35
  rationality (Weber), 117,
    443–44
  and sexual orientation, 169
  social conflict (Marx),
    196–97, 444
  technological development
    (Lenski), 41–44
Sociobiology, 54–56
  deviant behavior, 134–35
Sociocultural evolution,
  41–44, 199
Socioeconomic status (SES),
  198
Sociological investigation,
  15–24
Sociological perspective, 2–8
Sociology (see also individual
    topics)
  applied, 5
  critical, 19
  defined, 1
  in global perspective, 5–8
  interpretive, 19
  origins of, 8–10
  research methods, 22–25

and science, 8–9
  scientific, 14–18
  and social change, 8
  theory in, 10–14
Solid waste, 423
Somalia, 234, 240, 327
South Africa, 223, 224
  apartheid in, 189, 190, 194
South Korea, 226, 236, 239,
    307, 328, 329, 454
South Koreans, 294
Soviet Union (see also
    Commonwealth of
    Independent States;
    Russian Federation)
  classless society in, 192–93
  former, 198, 224, 240, 271,
    319, 329, 444
  move from socialism, 308
Space, personal, 96–97
Spanish language, 39, 48
Special-interest groups,
  321–22
Specialization, 118, 302, 378
Species extinction, 427–28
Sports, theoretical analysis of,
  16–17
Spurious correlation, 18
Sri Lanka, 341, 413
Stalking laws, 350
Staring, 97
Starvation, 242–43
State capitalism, 307, 329
State church, 358
State terrorism, 326
Status, 86–87
  ascribed and achieved
    forms, 86
  master status, 86–87, 139
Status consistency, 191,
  204–5
Status set, 86
Status symbol, 207
STD (see Sexually transmitted
    disease)
Steam engine, 302
Stereotypes, 24, 73, 276, 280
Stigma, 139–40, 144, 156,
  217
Strain, role, 88
Strain theory of deviance,
  137, 147
Strategic Defense Initiative
  (SDI), 329
Stratification (see Social
    stratification; individual
    topics)
"Street smarts," 89–90
Streetwalkers, 173

Structural-functional
    paradigm, 11–12, 30 (see
    also individual topics)
Structural social mobility,
  192–93, 208
Student passivity, 377–78
Subculture, 46–47, 444
  deviant forms of, 137–38
Sublimation, 65
Suburbs, 415
Sudan, 221, 240
Suicide, 443
  national map of, 11
  and race, 3
Sunbelt cities, 415–16
Superego, 65, 68, 135
Surrogate motherhood,
  352–53
Survey research, 22, 23
"Survival of the fittest," 195
Survivalists, 137
Sustainable ecosystem, 429
Sweden, 226, 307, 329, 351
  medical system in, 393
Symbol, 37–38
Symbolic institution, 336
Symbolic interaction, 67
Symbolic-interaction
    paradigm, 13–14 (see also
    individual topics)
Syphilis, 386–87

Tact, 98
Taiwan, 236, 454
Tan't Batu people, 428
Tchambuli, 249
Technology, 6 (see also Cyber
    issues; Information
    Revolution)
  and cities, 414, 460
  and culture, 41–44, 184
  and defense, 328, 329
  and ethical issues over
    death, 389–90
  and gender, 263
  and global poverty, 231
  and health, 381, 389–90
  and Information
    Revolution, 45
  and modernity, 444
  and natural environment,
    420–21, 426
  and networking, 115, 116
  and organizations, 119
  and population, 411
  and presentation of self, 185
  and religion, 365
  and reproductive issues,
    352–53, 354
  and research, 30–31

and social change, 460–61
  and social institutions,
    402–3
  and social movements, 461
  and socialization, 184–85
  and sociocultural evolution,
    41–44
  and stratification, 199,
    298–99
  and urbanization, 415
  and war, 327–28, 328, 329
  and work, 312–13
Teenage pregnancy, 171–72,
  350
  national map of, 172
Television (see also Mass
    media)
  education, 377
  national map of, 72
  ownership, in global
    perspective, 71
  religion, 365
  viewing habits, 71–73
Temporary Assistance for
    Needy Families (TANF),
    217
Terminal illness, 389–90
Terrorism, 326
Tertiary economic sector, 303
Test-tube babies, 352–53
Testing, 373
Thailand, 175, 226, 234, 341
Thanatos, 64
Theological stage (Comte), 9
Theoretical paradigm, 11–14
Theory, sociological, 10–11
  (see also individual topics)
Theory game, 16–17
Thomas theorem, 91
"Three Worlds" model, 222
Tibet, 327, 337
Time, awareness of, 441
Titanic, 187, 196
Tobacco industry, 385–86
Torah, 355
Total institution, 80
Totalitarianism, 317, 319, 326
Totem, 355
Touching, 97
Tracking in schools, 12,
  373–74
Tradition, 117, 234
Tradition-directedness, 448,
  454
Traditional authority, 316
Traditional family, 352–53
Transnational corporation (see
    Multinational
    corporation)
Transportation, 415, 442

Transsexuals, 163, 179
Triad, 113–14
Turkey, 35
Type A personality, 250, 384

Unemployment, 3, 311
United Kingdom (*see* Great
  Britain))
United Nations, 319
United States (*see also* national
  maps list in table of
  contents; individual
  topics)
  age-sex ratio, 409
  aging in, 76
  core values, 38, 40
  crime in, 147–50
  cultural diversity of, 255–67
  divorce rate in, 347
  education in, 371, 372–76
  fertility and mortality rates,
    406
  gender in, 161–81
  growth of cities in, 414–15
  health in, 383–89
  impact of new information
    technology in, 28–31,
    184–85, 298–99, 460–61
  inequality in, 174–204
  McDonaldization of,
    126–27
  medicine in, 394–95
  minority-majority in, 274
  occupational prestige in,
    204
  politics in, 320–23
  poverty in, 211–16
  quality of life in, 454–55
  quality of life index, 226
  race and ethnicity in,
    271–80
  religion in, 360–65
  social classes in, 204–8
  suicide rates in, 3, 4, 11
  work in postindustrial
    period, 308–13
Upper class, 204–5
Upper-middle class, 205
Upper-upper class, 205
Upward social mobility, 208
Urban cleansing, 229
Urban decentralization, 415
Urban ecology, 418
Urban political economy, 418
Urban revolution, 413–14,
  419
Urban sprawl, 405
Urbanism, as way of life,
  416–19
Urbanization, 413–16

growth of cities, 414–15
and Information
  Revolution, 460
in poor societies, 419–20
theories of, 416–19
in twenty-first century, 419
USSR (*see* Commonwealth of
  Independent States;
  Soviet Union, former)
Utilitarian organizations, 117

Validity of measurement, 15
Values, 38–41
  defined, 38
  deviance, 136
  education, 372
  and language, 99
  science, 18
  social class, 207
Variable, 15
Venereal disease, 386–89
Verstehen, 19
Veto group, 323
Victimization survey, 148
Victimless crime, 148,
  174–75
Vietnam, 304, 317, 327
Vietnam War, 357
Vietnamese Americans, 290
Violence
  in families, 349–50
  and mass media, 74
  in schools, 376–77
  in war, 327
Violence against women, 147,
  175–76, 250, 264, 350
  date rape, 175–77
  and social stratification,
    260–61
Virginity, 178
Virtual community, 460–61
Virtual culture, 45
Voluntary organization, 117
Voter apathy, 322–23

Wage labor, 302
War, 326–29
  deterrence of, 329
  global issues, 326–29
  peace, 329
  technology, 327–28, 328,
    329
  violence in, 327
WASP (*see* White Anglo
  Saxon Protestant
  [WASP])
Water pollution, 426
Water supply, 424–26
Wealth (*see also* Income;
  Power)

defined, 202
distribution in U.S., 201,
  205
gender, 257
as value, 40
Web sites, 31, 461
Weddings (*see* Marriage)
Wedge-shaped sectors, 418
Welfare, 216–17
  corporate, 330–31
Welfare capitalism, 307, 329
Welfare state, 320
White Anglo Saxon
  Protestant (WASP), 205,
  284–85 (*see also* Race)
White-collar crime, 144–45
White-collar occupation, 197,
  203, 205, 309
White Ethnic Americans, 293
  (*see also* Race)
Women (*see also* Family;
  Feminism; Gender;
  Marriage; individual
  topics)
  and abortion issue, 180–81
  and aging, 76–77
  and athletic performance,
    248
  and beauty myth, 253, 386
  and child rearing, 342–43
  and development of
    sociology, 10
  and eating disorders, 386
  economic disadvantages of,
    260
  education, 258, 375
  extramarital sex, 168
  gender distinctions, 248–51
  gender-related traits, 252
  housework, 256, 257
  intelligence, 248
  labor force participation,
    254–56, 309, 311, 312
  life expectancy, 248
  marriage, 346
  in medicine, 391
  the military, 259
  as minority, 259–60
  modernization, 235
  networking, 115
  and occupation, 202,
    254–55
  politics, 258–59, 260
  population control, 412
  and pornography, 172,
    261–62
  poverty, 212–13, 216–17,
    229
  power of, global map, 251
  premarital sex, 167

prostitution, 173–75, 177
religion, 356–57
sexual slavery, 175
singlehood, 352
violence against, 147,
  175–76, 250, 260–61,
  264, 350
Women's movement, 54, 247
  (*see also* Feminism)
Women's networks, 115
Work (*see also* Capitalism;
  Housework)
  agricultural employment,
    global map of, 305
  alienation, 120, 196
  changing nature of, 124–26
  changing pattern of, 308
  child labor, global map of,
    75
  and corporate welfare,
    330–31
  earnings of workers by sex,
    258
  gender, 254–56, 309
  and immigrants, 275
  job projections to 2010 in
    U.S., 315
  labor force, U.S., 254,
    308–9
  occupational prestige,
    202–3, 204
  in postindustrial economy,
    308–13
  professions, 310
  self-employment, 310–11
  service-sector employment,
    global map of, 305
  technology, 312–13
  temporary workers, 301–2
  unemployment, 4, 311
  as value, 40
  and women, 254–56, 309,
    311, 312
Work ethic, 284, 357
Working class, 206
Working poor, 206, 214

Yanomamö, 35, 36, 41, 44,
  327
Yonsei, 290
Yugoslavia, 46

Zaire, 240
Zambia, 327, 387
Zero population growth, 412
Zimbabwe, 371, 387

ABOUT THE AUTHOR

John J. Macionis (pronounced ma-SHOW-nis) was born and raised in Philadelphia, Pennsylvania. He received his bachelor's degree from Cornell University and his doctorate in sociology from the University of Pennsylvania. His publications are wide-ranging, focusing on community life in the United States, interpersonal intimacy in families, effective teaching, humor, new information technology, and the importance of global education. He and Nijole V. Benokraitis have edited the companion volume to this text, *Seeing Ourselves: Classic, Contemporary, and Cross-Cultural Readings in Sociology*. Macionis has also authored *Sociology*, the leading hardback text in the field, and he collaborates on international editions of the texts: *Sociology: Canadian Edition* (with Linda M. Gerber, from Prentice Hall Canada), *Society: The Basics, Canadian Edition* (with Cecelia Benoit and Mikael Jansson, also from Prentice Hall Canada), and *Sociology: A Global Introduction* (with Ken Plummer, published by Prentice Hall Europe). *Sociology* is also available in various international and foreign language editions. In addition, Macionis and Vincent Parrillo have written the urban studies text, *Cities and Urban Life* (Prentice Hall). Macionis's newest text is *Social Problems* (Prentice Hall). The latest on all the Macionis textbooks, as well as news, information, and dozens of Internet links of interest to students and faculty in sociology, can be found at the author's personal Web site, http://www.macionis.com or http://thesociologypage.com Additional information, as well as online study guides for the texts, is available at the Prentice Hall site, http://www.prenhall.com/macionis

John Macionis is Professor of Sociology and Prentice Hall Distinguished Scholar at Kenyon College in Gambier, Ohio. During a career of almost twenty-five years at Kenyon, he has chaired the Sociology Department, directed the college's multidisciplinary program in humane studies, and presided over the campus senate and also the college's faculty.

In 1998, the North Central Sociological Association named Macionis recipient of the Award for Distinguished Contribution to Teaching, citing his work with textbooks and his pioneering use of new technology in sociology.

Professor Macionis has been active in academic programs in other countries, having traveled to some fifty nations. In the fall of 1994, he directed the global education course for the University of Pittsburgh's Semester at Sea program, teaching 400 students on a floating campus that visited twelve countries as it circled the globe.

Macionis writes, "I am an ambitious traveler, eager to learn and, through the texts, to share much of what I discover with students, many of whom know so little about the rest of the world. For me, traveling and writing are all dimensions of teaching. First and foremost, I am a teacher—a passion for teaching animates everything I do." At Kenyon, Macionis offers a wide range of upper-level courses, but his favorite course is Introduction to Sociology, which he schedules every semester. He enjoys extensive contact with students and each term invites his students to enjoy a home-cooked meal.

The Macionis family—John, Amy, and children McLean and Whitney—live on a farm in rural Ohio. Their home serves as a popular bed and breakfast where they enjoy visiting with old friends and making new ones. In his free time, John enjoys bicycling through the Ohio countryside, swimming, sailing, and playing oldies rock and roll on his guitar. He is currently learning to play the Scottish bagpipes.

Professor Macionis welcomes (and responds to) comments and suggestions about this book from faculty and students. Write to the Sociology Department, Palme House, Kenyon College, Gambier, Ohio 43022, or direct e-mail to MACIONIS@ KENYON.EDU

USE TECHNOLOGY
to enhance your learning experience . . .
www.prenhall.com/macionis

Chapter Overview: Focuses your learning on the most important sociological points made in that chapter.

Study Guide: Offers multiple-choice, true-false, essay questions, and line art essays that can be graded immediately and e-mailed to your instructor.

Applications & Exercises: Brings to life the exercises from the end of each chapter by linking you directly to Internet sites.

Boxed Material: Links to relevant Internet sites so you can delve more deeply into topics covered in the text's boxed features.

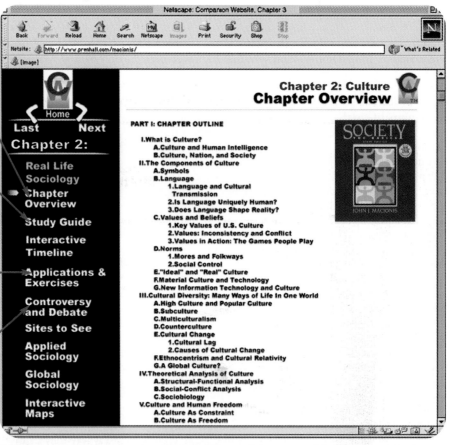

The Macionis *Companion Website*™ provides you with review and assessment tools for each chapter of the text while offering a direct gateway to the wealth of resources available on the World Wide Web. Through quizzes and links to related sites on the Internet, this site will reinforce what you are learning in the classroom and in the textbook. So, if you are looking for the easiest way to improve your grade in this course, your solution is to make use of this innovative tool in your studies throughout the semester.

CONTENTSELECT
from EBSCO and Prentice Hall

As part of the *Society: The Basics, Sixth Edition*, **Companion Website**™, you have one full year of free and unlimited access to a customized sociological database of over 100 of the world's leading peer-reviewed journals from EBSCO's **ContentSelect** service. Whether you are researching for a paper or pursuing a personal interest in a particular topic, you will be off to a great start with this powerful search engine by **ContentSelect**. In an age of questionable sources, it's nice to know that you have this unquestioned resource in your corner. Just access the *Society: The Basics, Sixth Edition*, **Companion Website**™, and click on the **ContentSelect** icon on your navigation bar.

and improve your grade in the process!!

SOCIETY: INTERACTIVE EDITION

This exciting new **CD-ROM** serves as a true resource to help you master the material in this course with or without an Internet connection. It provides multiple tools for review and reinforcement of the chapter material while offering multimedia-rich content and a substantial portion of the textbook to enrich, engage, and enlighten your study of sociology. The features include chapter-opening author tip videos, multimedia chapter introductions, real-life sociology application videos, interactive maps, learning objectives, interactive study quizzes and essays, Web links, Internet activities, and an interactive glossary and time line.

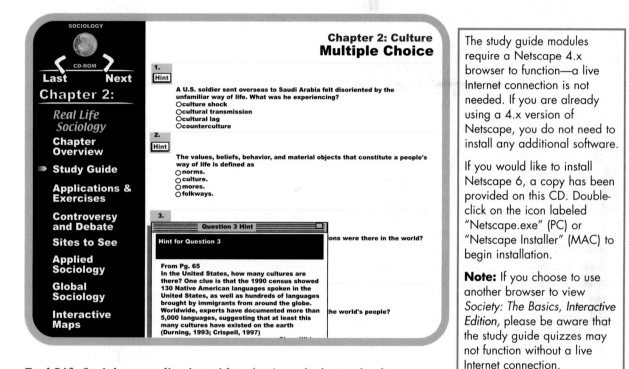

The study guide modules require a Netscape 4.x browser to function—a live Internet connection is not needed. If you are already using a 4.x version of Netscape, you do not need to install any additional software.

If you would like to install Netscape 6, a copy has been provided on this CD. Double-click on the icon labeled "Netscape.exe" (PC) or "Netscape Installer" (MAC) to begin installation.

Note: If you choose to use another browser to view *Society: The Basics, Interactive Edition,* please be aware that the study guide quizzes may not function without a live Internet connection.

Real Life Sociology application videos begin each chapter by demonstrating how the material to be covered helps you to look at everyday life in a sociological way.

Chapter Overviews include:
- an Author Tip videoclip featuring John J. Macionis.
- a multimedia chapter-opening vignette.
- a chapter outline and chapter learning objectives.
- a chapter summary for easy student review, with each point linked to the actual page in the text for deeper review.

The **Study Guide** offers multiple-choice, true-false, essay questions, and line art essays that can be graded immediately and e-mailed to your instructor.

Boxed material is brought to life through sections that include the full box contents as well as relevant links to the Internet.

The **Seeing Ourselves national maps** and **Window on the World global maps** become interactive on the CD as you roll your cursor over the key for each map.

And much, much more!

How to Install:

Windows 95/98/00/NT

Insert CD
Double-click "My Computer"
Double-click CD-ROM icon for "Society: The Basics"
Double-click "Macionis.html" (or open this file from within your Internet browser)

Macintosh:

Insert CD
Double-click CD-ROM icon for "Macionis"
Double-click "Macionis.html" (or open this file from within your Internet browser)

SINGLE PC LICENSE AGREEMENT AND LIMITED WARRANTY

READ THIS LICENSE CAREFULLY BEFORE OPENING THIS PACKAGE. BY OPENING THIS PACKAGE, YOU ARE AGREEING TO THE TERMS AND CONDITIONS OF THIS LICENSE. IF YOU DO NOT AGREE, DO NOT OPEN THE PACKAGE. PROMPTLY RETURN THE UNOPENED PACKAGE AND ALL ACCOMPANYING ITEMS TO THE PLACE YOU OBTAINED THEM.

1.   GRANT OF LICENSE and OWNERSHIP: The enclosed computer programs ("Software") are licensed, not sold, to you by Prentice-Hall, Inc. ("We" or the "Company") and in consideration of your purchase or adoption of the accompanying Company textbooks and/or other materials, and your agreement to these terms. We reserve any rights not granted to you. You own only the disk(s) but we and/or our licensors own the Software itself. This license allows you to use and display your copy of the Software on a single computer (i.e., with a single CPU) at a single location for <u>academic</u> use only, so long as you comply with the terms of this Agreement. You may make one copy for backup, or transfer your copy to another CPU, provided that the Software is usable on only one computer.

2.   RESTRICTIONS: You may <u>not</u> transfer or distribute the Software or documentation to anyone else. Except for backup, you may not copy the documentation or the Software. You may <u>not</u> network the Software or otherwise use it on more than one computer or computer terminal at the same time. You may <u>not</u> reverse engineer, disassemble, decompile, modify, adapt, translate, or create derivative works based on the Software or the Documentation. You may be held legally responsible for any copying or copyright infringement which is caused by your failure to abide by the terms of these restrictions.

3.   TERMINATION: This license is effective until terminated. This license will terminate automatically without notice from the Company if you fail to comply with any provisions or limitations of this license. Upon termination, you shall destroy the Documentation and all copies of the Software. All provisions of this Agreement as to limitation and disclaimer of warranties, limitation of liability, remedies or damages, and our ownership rights shall survive termination.

4.   LIMITED WARRANTY AND DISCLAIMER OF WARRANTY: Company warrants that for a period of 60 days from the date you purchase this SOFTWARE (or purchase or adopt the accompanying textbook), the Software, when properly installed and used in accordance with the Documentation, will operate in substantial conformity with the description of the Software set forth in the Documentation, and that for a period of 30 days the disk(s) on which the Software is delivered shall be free from defects in materials and workmanship under normal use. The Company does <u>not</u> warrant that the Software will meet your requirements or that the operation of the Software will be uninterrupted or error-free. Your only remedy and the Company's only obligation under these limited warranties is, at the Company's option, return of the disk for a refund of any amounts paid for it by you or replacement of the disk. THIS LIMITED WARRANTY IS THE ONLY WARRANTY PROVIDED BY THE COMPANY AND ITS LICENSORS, AND THE COMPANY AND ITS LICENSORS DISCLAIM ALL OTHER WARRANTIES, EXPRESSED OR IMPLIED, INCLUDING WITHOUT LIMITATION, THE IMPLIED WARRANTIES OF MERCHANTABILITY AND FITNESS FOR A PARTICULAR PURPOSE. THE COMPANY DOES NOT WARRANT, GUARANTEE, OR MAKE ANY REPRESENTATION REGARDING THE ACCURACY, RELIABILITY, CURRENTNESS, USE, OR RESULTS OF USE, OF THE SOFTWARE.

5.   LIMITATION OF REMEDIES AND DAMAGES: IN NO EVENT, SHALL THE COMPANY OR ITS EMPLOYEES, AGENTS, LICENSORS, OR CONTRACTORS BE LIABLE FOR ANY INCIDENTAL, INDIRECT, SPECIAL, OR CONSEQUENTIAL DAMAGES ARISING OUT OF OR IN CONNECTION WITH THIS LICENSE OR THE SOFTWARE, INCLUDING LOSS OF USE, LOSS OF DATA, LOSS OF INCOME OR PROFIT, OR OTHER LOSSES, SUSTAINED AS A RESULT OF INJURY TO ANY PERSON, OR LOSS OF OR DAMAGE TO PROPERTY, OR CLAIMS OF THIRD PARTIES, EVEN IF THE COMPANY OR AN AUTHORIZED REPRESENTATIVE OF THE COMPANY HAS BEEN ADVISED OF THE POSSIBILITY OF SUCH DAMAGES. IN NO EVENT SHALL THE LIABILITY OF THE COMPANY FOR DAMAGES WITH RESPECT TO THE SOFTWARE EXCEED THE AMOUNTS ACTUALLY PAID BY YOU, IF ANY, FOR THE SOFTWARE OR THE ACCOMPANYING TEXTBOOK. BECAUSE SOME JURISDICTIONS DO NOT ALLOW THE LIMITATION OF LIABILITY IN CERTAIN CIRCUMSTANCES, THE ABOVE LIMITATIONS MAY NOT ALWAYS APPLY TO YOU.

6.   GENERAL: THIS AGREEMENT SHALL BE CONSTRUED IN ACCORDANCE WITH THE LAWS OF THE UNITED STATES OF AMERICA AND THE STATE OF NEW YORK, APPLICABLE TO CONTRACTS MADE IN NEW YORK, AND SHALL BENEFIT THE COMPANY, ITS AFFILIATES AND ASSIGNEES. THIS AGREEMENT IS THE COMPLETE AND EXCLUSIVE STATEMENT OF THE AGREEMENT BETWEEN YOU AND THE COMPANY AND SUPERSEDES ALL PROPOSALS OR PRIOR AGREEMENTS, ORAL, OR WRITTEN, AND ANY OTHER COMMUNICATIONS BETWEEN YOU AND THE COMPANY OR ANY REPRESENTATIVE OF THE COMPANY RELATING TO THE SUBJECT MATTER OF THIS AGREEMENT. If you are a U.S. Government user, this Software is licensed with "restricted rights" as set forth in subparagraphs (a)-(d) of the Commercial Computer-Restricted Rights clause at FAR 52.227-19 or in subparagraphs (c)(1)(ii) of the Rights in Technical Data and Computer Software clause at DFARS 252.227-7013, and similar clauses, as applicable.

Should you have any questions concerning this agreement or if you wish to contact the Company for any reason, please contact in writing: Senior Media Editor, Social Sciences, HSS, Prentice Hall, One Lake Street, Upper Saddle River, NJ 07458.

SYSTEM REQUIREMENTS
MACINTOSH: minimum 68040/33MHz, System 7.5 or above, 12mb RAM (16mb recommended), 1mb free HD space, 2x CD-ROM, 640X480 screen resolution, color monitor (thousands of colors required). QuickTime 4.0 installed from CD.

PC: minimum 486/DX25, Windows 95/98 (minimum 16mb RAM), 1mb free HD space, 2X CD-ROM, SVGA monitor, thousands of colors, sound and video cards required. QuickTime 4.0 installed from CD.